AF333676

Mᵈᵉ Vallayer-Coster

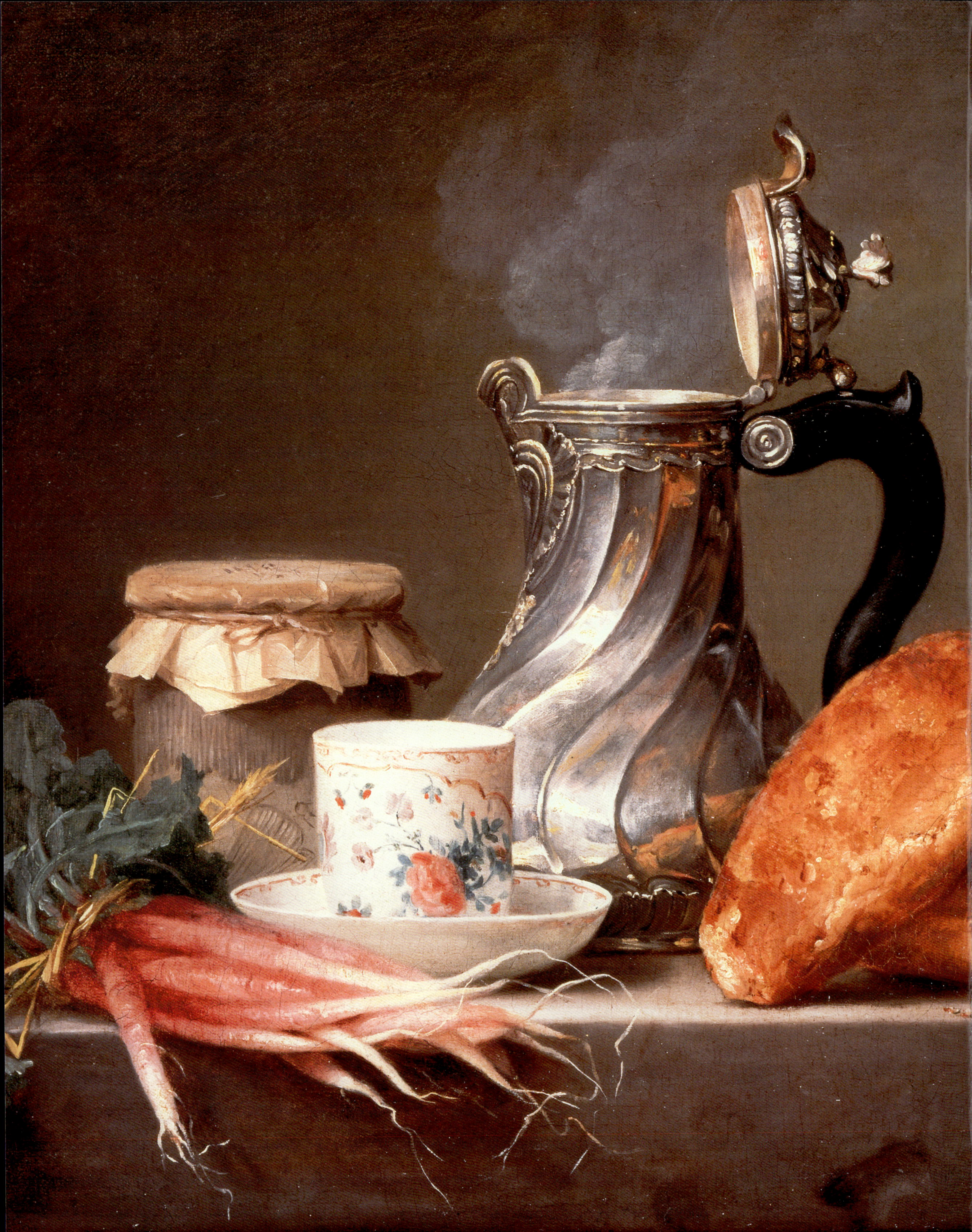

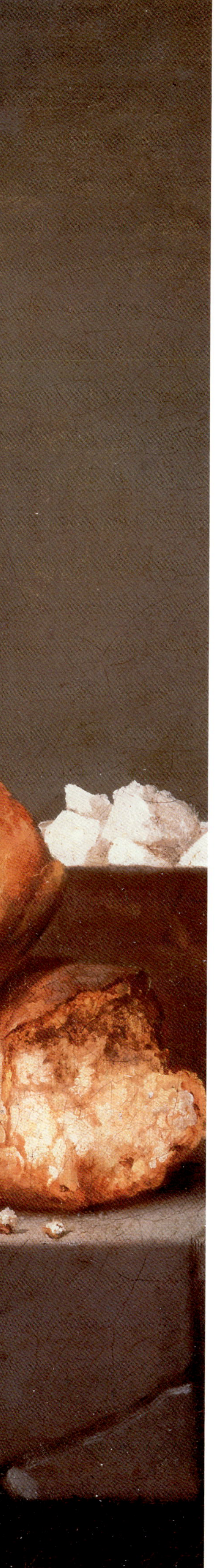

ANNE VALLAYER-COSTER

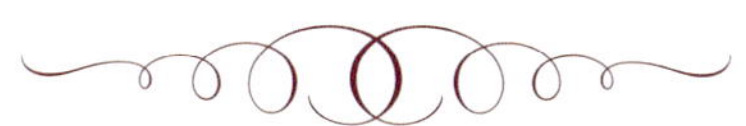

Painter to the

Court of

Marie-Antoinette

Eik Kahng

Marianne Roland Michel

WITH CONTRIBUTIONS BY

Colin B. Bailey

Claire Barry

Laurent Hugues

Melissa Hyde

DALLAS MUSEUM OF ART

YALE UNIVERSITY PRESS
New Haven and London

Anne Vallayer-Coster: Painter to the Court of Marie-Antoinette was organized by the Dallas Museum of Art.

Exhibition support in Dallas was provided by the Dallas Museum of Art League, the Samuel H. Kress Foundation, and Charlene C. and Tom F. Marsh. Additional support was provided by Mrs. John Tolleson/The Tolleson Family Foundation. The exhibition catalogue was generously underwritten by Mr. Michael L. Rosenberg. This exhibition was supported by an indemnity from the Federal Council on the Arts and the Humanities.

Exhibition Itinerary:

National Gallery of Art
6th Street and Constitution Avenue, N.W.
Washington, D.C. 20565
June 30–September 22, 2002

Dallas Museum of Art
1717 North Harwood Street
Dallas, Texas 75201
October 13, 2002–January 5, 2003

The Frick Collection
1 East 70th Street
New York, New York 10021
January 21–March 23, 2003

Published by Yale University Press in association with the Dallas Museum of Art

Library of Congress Cataloging-in-Publication Data
Kahng, Eik
    Anne Vallayer-Coster, painter to the court of Marie-Antoinette / Eik Kahng, Marianne Roland Michel ; with contributions by Colin B. Bailey . . . [et al.].
      p. cm.
    Catalog of an itinerant exhibition.
    Includes bibliographical references and index.
    ISBN: 0-300-09329-2 (cloth : alk. paper)
    1. Vallayer-Coster, Anne, 1744–1818—Exhibitions.
2. Still-life painting, French—Exhibitions. 3. Women artists—France—History—Exhibitions. I. Title: Anne Vallayer-Coster. II. Vallayer-Coster, Anne, 1744–1818. III. Roland Michel, Marianne. IV. Bailey, Colin B. V. Title.
    ND553.V327 A4 2002
    759.4—dc21   2001059860

Frontispiece: Anne Vallayer-Coster, *Still Life with Silver Pitcher* (detail), 1767 (cat. 5)
Pages 114–115: Anne Vallayer-Coster, *Still Life with Glasses and Mackerels* (detail), 1787 (cat. 83)
Pages 194–195: Anne Vallayer-Coster, *Flowers in a Crystal Vase* (detail), 1789 (cat. 86)

Curator: Eik Kahng
Head of Exhibitions and Curatorial Publications:
    Tamara Wootton-Bonner
Curatorial Administrative Assistant: Leslie Ureña

Edited by Fronia W. Simpson
Indexed by Frances Bowles
Proofread by Sharon Vonasch
Designed by Susan E. Kelly
Typeset by Jennifer Sugden in Emigre Filosofia
Produced by Marquand Books, Inc., Seattle
    www.marquand.com
Color separations by iocolor, Seattle
Printed and bound by CS Graphics Pte., Ltd., Singapore

The preparation and publication of this volume were underwritten
by a generous gift from Michael L. Rosenberg,
patron of the Dallas Museum of Art.

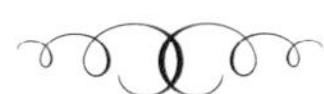

Lenders to the Exhibition

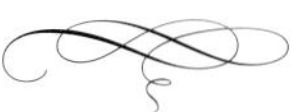

Bibliothèque nationale de France
Florence Bouchy-Picon
The Bowes Museum, Barnard Castle, Co. Durham, England
The Cleveland Museum of Art
Cooper-Hewitt, National Design Museum, Smithsonian Institution
Dallas Museum of Art
Fine Arts Museums of San Francisco
Galerie Gismondi, Paris
Wallace and Wilhelmina Holladay
Jeffrey E. Horvitz, Boston
Anne Lévy-Freitag and Pierre Lévy-Freitag
The Metropolitan Museum of Art, New York
Musée des Arts décoratifs, Paris
Musée des Beaux-Arts, Bordeaux
Musée des Beaux-Arts, Nancy
Musée Carnavalet, Paris
Musée du Louvre, Paris
Musée municipal de Châlons-en-Champagne
Musée national des Châteaux de Versailles et de Trianon
Musée de Tessé, Le Mans
Musées d'art et d'histoire, Ville de Genève
Napoleonmuseum Arenenberg, Salenstein, Switzerland
National Gallery of Art, Washington
National Gallery of Canada, Ottawa
National Gallery of Scotland, Edinburgh
Nationalmuseum, Stockholm
Mr. and Mrs. Saam Nystad
Abigail Owen-Pontez, Houston
Michael L. Rosenberg, Dallas
Marina Rust
Staatliche Kunsthalle Karlsruhe
Staatliche Museen zu Berlin, Gemäldegalerie
Toledo Museum of Art
Rafael Valls, Ltd, London
Villa Ephrussi de Rothschild—Institut de France, Saint-Jean Cap Ferrat
Private collectors and lenders who wish to remain anonymous

Contents

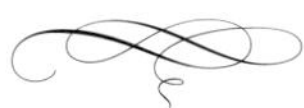

Director's Foreword and Acknowledgments

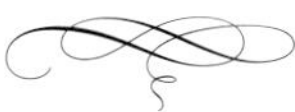

ANNE VALLAYER-COSTER was considered the foremost French still-life painter of her generation. One of only four women elected to the Académie royale de peinture et de sculpture in the years preceding the French Revolution, Vallayer-Coster won the acclaim of critics and the patronage of the queen, Marie-Antoinette. Yet her achievements have in ensuing years gone largely unheralded and underappreciated and, remarkably, this is the first major exhibition dedicated to her art. In it, and in this accompanying publication, we explore her importance to the genre of still-life painting, her relationship to other still-life painters of the period, the cultural and political worlds of late-eighteenth- and early-nineteenth-century France in which she was involved, and the position of herself and other women as artists and patrons in the decades surrounding the French Revolution.

The idea for this exhibition arose from the purchase for the Dallas Museum of Art in 1996 of a splendid pair of floral still-life paintings by this gifted artist. Our then assistant curator of European art, Eik Kahng (now associate curator of eighteenth- and nineteenth-century art at the Walters Art Museum, Baltimore), seized on the acquisition as an incentive to initiate the project, which she did with the support of my predecessor, Jay Gates, and the informed encouragement of Dorothy Kosinski, the Museum's Barbara Thomas Lemmon Curator of European Art. Much to our delight, the interest of the Dallas Museum of Art in the exhibition was reciprocated by The Frick Collection, New York, and the National Gallery of Art, Washington. We thank our colleagues at The Frick Collection, Samuel Sachs II, Director, Edgar Munhall, former Chief Curator, and Colin B. Bailey, Chief Curator;

at the National Gallery of Art, Earl A. Powell III, Director, Philip Conisbee, Senior Curator of European Paintings, and D. Dodge Thompson, Chief of Exhibitions, for their supportive engagement with this cultural enterprise and the presentation of the exhibition at their institutions.

Building on the benevolence of the Foundation for the Arts through its Mrs. John B. O'Hara Fund, which was instrumental in bringing the Vallayer-Coster paintings into the collection of the Dallas Museum of Art, key individuals in the Dallas community rallied around the idea of enriching the Museum's diverse special exhibitions program by mounting an old master painting show. In particular, Michael L. Rosenberg, a distinguished collector of eighteenth-century French art who has served as a trustee of the Museum and who had himself contributed generously to the acquisition of our Vallayer-Coster paintings, immediately expressed his support for the project, and we appreciate enormously his commitment, which underwrote this ambitious scholarly publication. We are indebted, too, to Charlene C. and Tom F. Marsh and to Debbie and John Tolleson for their early support. We gratefully acknowledge the Samuel H. Kress Foundation for its significant grant in aid of the research phase of the project. Lead sponsorship of this exhibition has been graciously afforded by the Dallas Museum of Art League, and we extend special thanks to the League membership, its past-year president, Cynthia Mitchell, and its current president, Susan Fisk, who designated substantial funding to help the Museum realize this undertaking. We are very much obliged to the many institutional and individual lenders who so generously agreed to share their works of art for the duration of this exhibition. And, we give our heartfelt thanks and compliments to Eik Kahng for her dedicated and erudite endeavors as organizing curator of *Anne Vallayer-Coster: Painter to the Court of Marie-Antoinette* and scholarly contributor to this book.

The Dallas Museum of Art and Eik Kahng join to recognize with appreciation the many individuals who have contributed to the realization of this project. Marianne Roland Michel could not have been kinder or more helpful to its development, for which we warmly thank her and add our gratitude for her catalogue essay and contributions as co-editor, as well. We offer a similar expression of appreciation to our other authors, Colin B. Bailey, Claire Barry, Melissa Hyde, and Laurent Hugues. For their invaluable advice we thank Claire Barry, Philip Conisbee, Melissa Hyde, and John Goodman, who also acted as our translator from the French. We appreciate the efforts on behalf of the making of this book of Laura Hulscher, Susan Kelly, Matt Lechner, Ed Marquand, Jennifer Sugden, Marta Vinnedge, and Marie Weiler at Marquand Books, of its copy editor, Fronia W. Simpson, of its proofreader and indexer, Frances Bowles, of its proofreader, Sharon Vonasch, and of Patricia Fidler representing our copublishers at Yale University Press. We thank the many individuals who have so generously shared their scholarship, connoisseurship, institutional resources, and passion for our artist and this project: Jean-Pierre Angremy, Pierre Arizzoli-Clementel, Katherine Baetjer, Joseph Baillio, Roger M. Berkowitz, Delphine Bishop, Thomas and Brenda Brod, Thomas Campbell, Toby Campbell, Dominique Cante, Görel Cavalli-Björkman, Françoise Chaserant, Blandine Chavanne, Alvin L. Clark Jr., Michael Clarke, James Clifton, Elizabeth Conran, Jean-Pierre Cuzin, Gail Davidson, Bruno Desmarest, Fabrice Faré, Hélène Fauré, Jacques Foucart, Clara Gelly-Saldias, Jean Gismondi, Diane De Grazia, Dominik Gügel, Torsten Gunnarsson, Rosann Gutman, Wilhelmina Holladay, Laurent Hugues, Adrian Jenkins, Isabelle Julia, William Johnston, Jan Kelch, Jim Landman, Paul Lang, Patrick Le Chanu, Jean-Marc Léri, Christophe Leribault, David Liot, Stéphane Loire, Henri Loyrette, Dietmar Lüdke, Patrick Matthiesen, Cäsar Menz, Philippe de Montebello, Brigitte Monti, Edgar Munhall, Steven A. Nash, Lawrence W. Nichols, Lynn Federle Orr, Harry S. Parker, Joachim Pissarro, Jean-Pierre Ravaux, Katherine Lee Reid, Francis Ribemont, Pierre Rosenberg, Marie-Catherine Sahut, Nicolas Sainte-Fare Garnot, Béatrice Salmon, Xavier Salmon, Alan Salz, Klaus Schrenk, Marion C. Stewart, Charles Stuckey, Marilyn Symmes, Joakim Tan, Burton Tansky, Pierre Théberge, Paul Warwick Thompson, Eric Turquin, Gary Vikan, Jeffrey Weiss, Alan Wintermute, and Andrea Zanella.

At the Dallas Museum of Art, Leslie Ureña, curatorial administrative assistant, Beverly Gibbons, volunteer intern, and their French counterpart, Mélanie Leboucher, were devoted in their efforts on behalf of the project, and Dr. Kosinski and Deputy Director Bonnie Pitman provided wise leadership at important junctures. Other members of the Museum's staff who are due particular acknowledgment include Kim Beachum, Carolyn Bess, Giselle Castro-Brightenburg, Judy Conner, Gail Davitt, Diana Duke Duncan, Brad Flowers, Robert Goodman, Andrea Guidry, Tom Jenkins, Rita Lasater, Mary Leonard, Michael Mazurek, Debra Phares, Dan Rockwell, Gabriela Truly, Charles Venable, and Tamara Wootton-Bonner.

John R. Lane
The Eugene McDermott Director

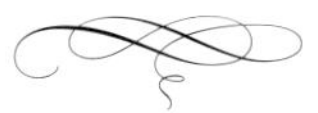

Introduction

Anne Vallayer-Coster (1744–1818) is not a name that springs to mind when considering the canonical history of eighteenth-century French art. Even though Vallayer-Coster's fame was considerable in her lifetime, her art celebrated by the critics, and her prestige ensured by royal patronage, Vallayer-Coster has long been an artist familiar only to specialists of the period. Indeed, many of her most beautiful paintings have remained in private collections in France, where the aura of her legendary association with Marie-Antoinette probably helped to maintain her reputation through successive generations—at least in select circles. In the past several decades, revisionist art history, with its crusade to reinstate artists unfairly neglected or little published, has helped to spark interest in Vallayer-Coster, primarily from a feminist point of view. Like Elisabeth-Louise Vigée-Le Brun (1755–1842) and Adélaïde Labille-Guiard (1749–1803), her better-known female contemporaries, Vallayer-Coster presents the rare case of a woman artist accepted into the male-dominated institution of the French Académie royale de peinture et de sculpture. More recently, Vallayer-Coster has begun to attract the attention of major museums. In 1992 the Musée du Louvre acquired *Still Life with Seashells and Coral* (pl. 4), a large-scale work of astounding originality that once belonged to the prince de Conti. Just a few years later, the Dallas Museum of Art acquired a pendant pair of floral still-life paintings (pls. 19, 20), exhibited in the Salon of 1777, and listed as belonging to the distinguished *associé-libre de l'Académie*, Jean-Baptiste-François de Montullé.

As was the case with many eighteenth-century artists whose reputations fell following the French Revolution in 1789 because of their association with the ancien régime, the art of Vallayer-Coster has been something of a well-kept secret, revered by cognoscenti but conspicuously underacknowledged in most accounts of the period. Unlike the older still-life painter Jean-Siméon Chardin, whose reputation has skyrocketed since his critical exhumation in the mid–nineteenth century, Vallayer-Coster has been the subject of only one monograph, published in 1970 by the well-known expert on eighteenth-century art Marianne Roland Michel. Indeed, it is largely because of Dr. Roland Michel's efforts that the artist's oeuvre can be reconstructed. The 1970 monograph, now out of print and available only as a rare book, was based on Roland Michel's master's thesis, to which she refers with typical humility as her "oeuvre de jeunesse." With the author's characteristic rigor and insight, the monograph lays out her careful research of the artist's life and career, as well as supplying an indispensable catalogue raisonné of the artist's works, including paintings, tapestries, drawings, and miniatures. As any collector or scholar of the eighteenth century will attest, it is an invaluable tool for connoisseurship of the artist and has been the sole resource to which one might turn.

I was lucky enough to be employed at the Dallas Museum of Art when it made the bold acquisition of a pendant pair of floral still-lifes by Vallayer-Coster, one of which graces the cover of this book. Long an admirer of Chardin, I was immediately impressed with the technical virtuosity of these paintings by this little-known woman painter. I realized that not only had Vallayer-Coster's oeuvre never enjoyed the attention of a full-scale retrospective but also that the 1970 monograph, illustrated in black-and-white only, was sorely in need of an update. I was delighted, then, that when

I approached Marianne Roland Michel with the idea
of an exhibition, she consented to act as curatorial con-
sultant to the project and co-editor of the catalogue.
Roland Michel had been collecting information on our
painter for the past thirty years and was eager to revise
her youthful text with new archival information and
rediscovered paintings (the Dallas pictures, for instance,
were not known in 1970). With the graciousness that
distinguishes the greatest art historians, she generously
agreed to share her files and led me through her vast
knowledge of the artist, taking me to visit private collectors in France. The selection of paintings included
in the exhibition represents our choice of the finest
extant works by the artist.

Each of the contributing authors to this catalogue
offers expertise on a different dimension of Vallayer-
Coster's art and career. Roland Michel's overview includes new information on the artist's professional
affiliations, helping us to understand her rapid technical advancement early in her career. She also provides
much-needed insight into the longevity of Vallayer-
Coster's example in the first decades of the nineteenth
century, especially as propagated through tapestry repro-
ductions and the print medium. My essay deals with the
thorny problem of Vallayer-Coster's discursive and pictorial relationship with Chardin. The insistent privileging
of his art has unintentionally led to the neglect of other
still-life painters of the period, including Vallayer-Coster,
a phenomenon for which I attempt an historical explanation. Colin B. Bailey's essay gives a detailed account of the
prestigious eighteenth-century collections that included
works by our artist, while Melissa Hyde draws a fascinating portrait of the different artistic milieus available to

women artists during the second half of the eighteenth
century. Claire Barry provides new information based
on original technical research on Vallayer-Coster's
method of painting. She compares it with the technique
of the painter's contemporaries, as well as with the Dutch
and Flemish "little masters," so avidly collected by
eighteenth-century *amateurs*. In an appendix, Laurent
Hugues chronicles his exciting detective work, leading
to the attribution to Vallayer-Coster of the portraits
of Mesdames, the daughters of Louis XV, preserved at
Versailles, which we publish for the first time as such.
Together, these essays provide both a general introduction and a wealth of scholarly material that we hope will
encourage further study of Vallayer-Coster. The catalogue of extant paintings will provide a much-needed
visual guide to the artist's oeuvre that should prove useful to the student and collector of our artist.

I am fully aware that some might object to what might
seem to be an old-fashioned, connoisseurship-driven,
largely monographic species of exhibition. I have inten-
tionally chosen not to dwell on the feminist aspect of
Vallayer-Coster's career, despite the cultural currency
it represents. Instead, I have focused on her painterly
achievements, the sheer beauty of which deserves to
be made abundantly visible. This is not to say that feminist discourse is not a legitimate arena for the study
of Vallayer-Coster's life and work. However, it was my
objective to provide an overview of her paintings, their
unique virtues and shortcomings, so that scholars
and nonspecialists alike would have renewed access
to her art.

Eik Kahng

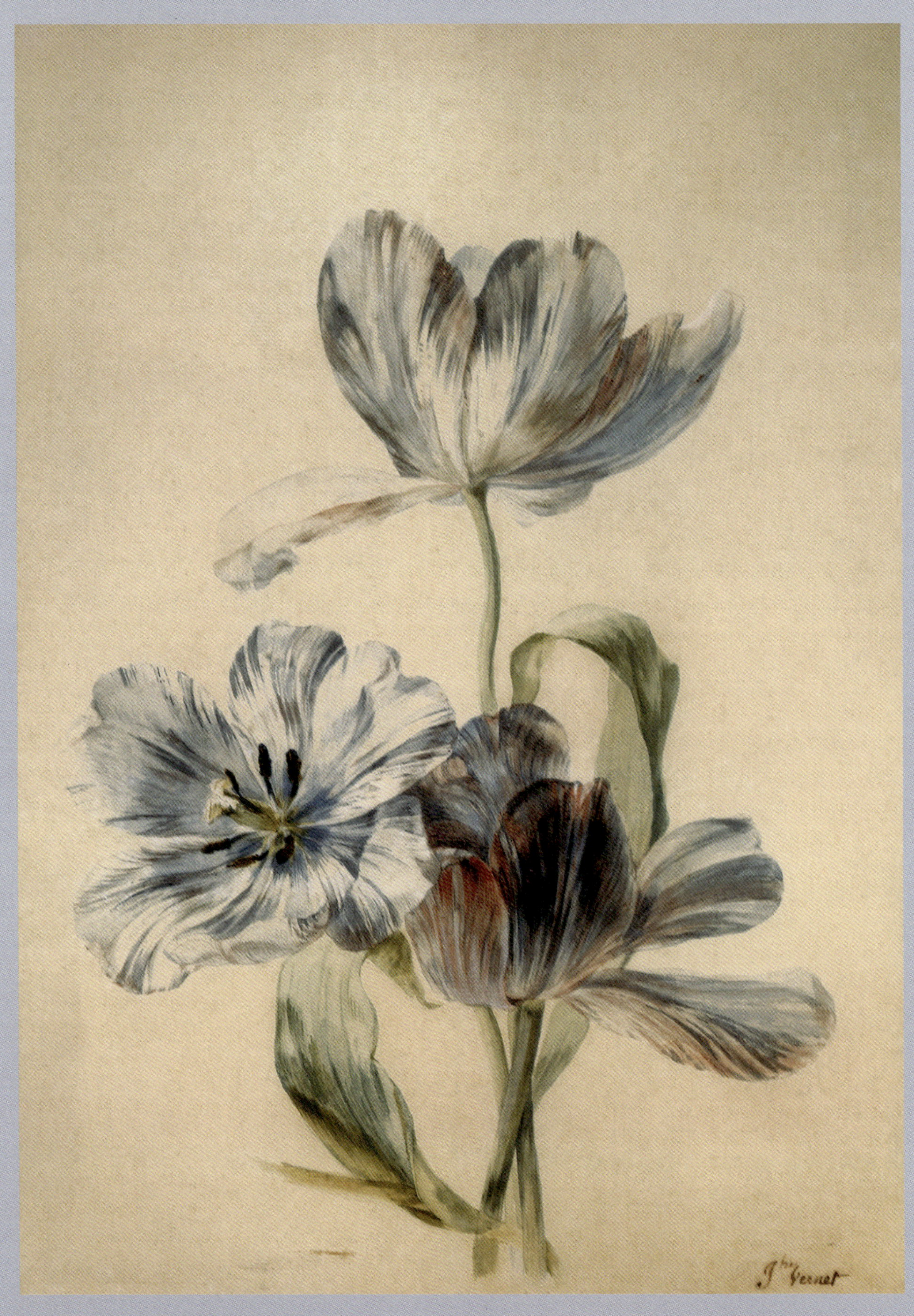

Joseph Vernet, *Tulip*, c. 1768–1770
Watercolor, 11½ × 8¼ in. (29 × 21 cm). Galerie Jean-François Baroni, Paris (fig. 2).

— Marianne Roland Michel —

Vallayer in Her Time

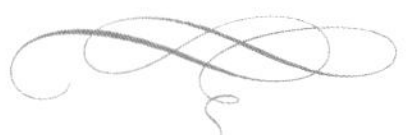

Artistic perfection places any genre above distinctions of rank.
—*Mercure de France*, October 1765[1]

I am well aware that Chardin's models, the inanimate natures that he imitates,
change neither place nor color nor form, and that, all things being equal, a portrait by La Tour
has more merit than a genre piece by Chardin. . . . But La Tour will be talked about,
whereas Chardin will be looked at.
—Denis Diderot, *Salon of 1767*[2]

[Mlle Vallayer is exhibiting eleven works] that, for the most part, have the merit of painting
a nature that is mute yet sensible, even to the coarsest viewers. . . . Her depiction of
Still Life with Military Musical Instruments is handled more amply,
and would not be unworthy as a study by a history painter.
—*Mémoires secrets*, regarding the Salon of 1771[3]

In this essay, I propose to establish a basic framework for assessing the life and career of Anne Vallayer-Coster, working only from the facts and from a few documents that cast an especially revealing light on them. Along the way, I will study her art and define the qualities specific to her large oeuvre, which is more varied than has often been thought. I will also situate her work in relation to the art of her time, by way of clarifying her position within it, her artistic models, and the nature and extent of her influence. Finally, I will extend the little game of resemblances and comparisons so dear to her contemporaries by arguing that she is, in some respects, superior to some of her more famous contemporaries and will suggest how we might best characterize her undeniable originality.

FORMATIVE YEARS

Born on 21 December 1744, Anne Vallayer was the daughter of the goldsmith Joseph Vallayer (1704–1770), then an apprentice at the Gobelins Manufactory, where he became a full master in 1750. Earlier, however, his name appears in the register of gifts from the king to the Ministry of Foreign Affairs, as well as in the account books of the Menus-Plaisirs, where he figures as an executant of decoration for gold enamel boxes.[4] He and his wife lived in the Gobelins complex, where their four daughters were born: Madeleine (b. 1743), whose godmother was Madeleine Basseporte (discussed below); Anne; Elisabeth (b. 1747), who in 1772 married Josué de Bouhébent;[5] and, finally, Simone.

The goldsmith left the Gobelins in 1754 for the rue du Doyenné (in the quarter between the Louvre and the Tuileries, since demolished), whence he moved about 1755 to the rue du Roule, at the sign of the Soleil d'Or.

A trade card, designed and engraved by Pierre-Philippe Choffard (1730–1809), mentions him as a "marchand orfèvre bijoutier joaillier," one who buys, sells, and exchanges all kinds of jewelry.[6] There he died, but his wife, who assisted him in his work, was authorized to continue stamping crosses of Saint Louis and military merit crosses, the workshop's specialty.[7] It was probably to her that Diderot turned in 1762, when he had a miniature portrait of Sophie Volland enameled and set into the binding of a volume of Horace.[8]

Even if Anne Vallayer spent only the first ten years of her life at the Gobelins, I must insist on the formative importance of this experience, and on the special nature of the milieu of artists and craftsmen who lived and worked at the manufactory.

Tradition has it that Vallayer studied drawing with Madeleine Basseporte (1701–1780)[9]—like Marie-Thérèse Reboul (1735–1805), who was received by the Académie royale de peinture et de sculpture (the Académie) in 1757, the year of her marriage to Joseph-Marie Vien (1716–1809), as a "painter of miniatures and gouaches specializing in flowers, butterflies, and birds."[10] Although there is no incontrovertible proof of this tutelage, it gains credibility from the stylistic similarity of certain watercolors by Anne Vallayer-Coster to those of Basseporte, who instructed Mesdames, the daughters of Louis XV, in the art of painting. We should recall here that Basseporte's main claim to fame is her having been draftswoman *(dessinatrice)* of the Jardin des Plantes. Trained in the tradition of Nicolas Robert (1614–1685), in 1742 she succeeded Claude Aubriet (1651–1742) in the post of Painter of the *velins du roi.* In 1749 she was awarded an annual pension of 1,100 livres to be drawn from the royal treasury, a figure supplemented in 1774 by an additional 400 livres "à titre de subsistance" (for living expenses). In addition to her regular work for the Jardin des Plantes (for which she produced twelve drawings on vellum per year), the comte d'Argenson asked her in 1750 to go to Compiègne to paint a species of pineapple,[11] and she was often asked to visit other royal châteaux to paint rare plants and animals: for example in 1774, when she was summoned to Versailles to render some birds and monkeys recently presented to the king. She signed a gouache representing the *Echium fastuosum,*[12] a plant introduced into France in 1779, further evidence of her having continued such activity into her maturity. We know of several mediocre prints by her after portraits by P.-P. Robert de Séri (1686–1733), who had founded a small drawing

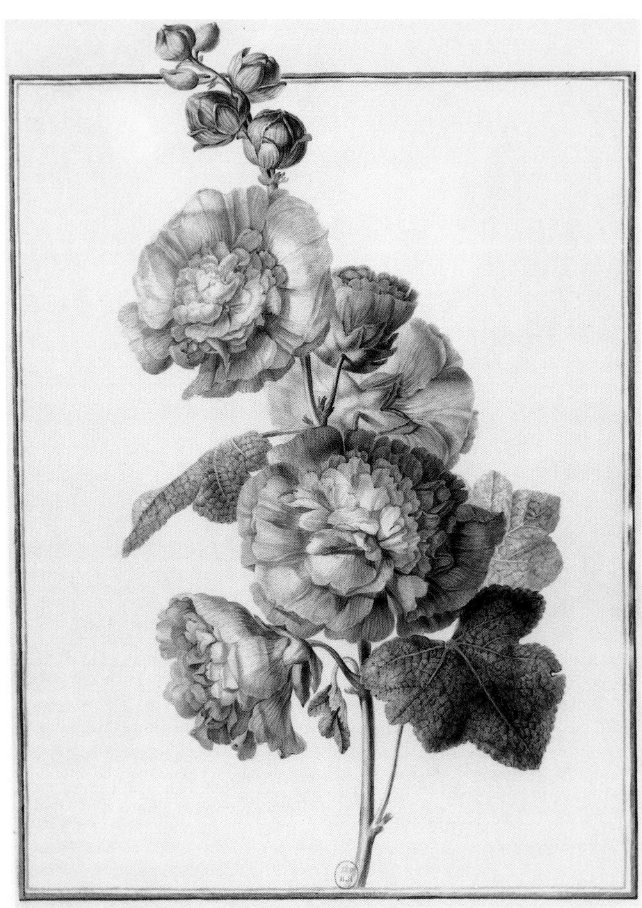

Fig. 1. Madeleine Basseporte, *Roses trémières*, n.d. Watercolor on vellum, 12⅝ × 9⅛ in. (32 × 23 cm). Bibliothèque nationale de France.

school at which she taught. When he died in 1733, he left her the portfolios of drawings he had made of the Duomo in Parma, which she sold to the marquis de Vandières in 1745.[13] One of her compositions, *Young Girl Caressing a Rabbit,* was engraved by Dubos, but most prints after her work are depictions of flowers. To these minor works we must add the five hundred or so admirable watercolors on vellum preserved in the library of the Museum d'Histoire naturelle of the Jardin des Plantes, and some twenty in the Cabinet des Estampes of the Bibliothèque nationale (fig. 1).[14]

Doubtless our artist also studied with Joseph Vernet. There is proof of ties between the great landscape painter and Joseph Vallayer;[15] furthermore, Anne Vallayer owned three paintings by Vernet, one of which he gave her, as well as twenty-seven landscape and marine drawings.[16] Vernet also owned works by Anne Vallayer. To this evidence we can now add a watercolor study of a tulip signed *J^{ph} Vernet* that recently surfaced on the market and that conveys further information (fig. 2).[17] The verso is inscribed in ink: *Joseph Vernet peintre de Marine / fit cette étude à la campagne pour / Donner une leçon à Mde vallaÿer*

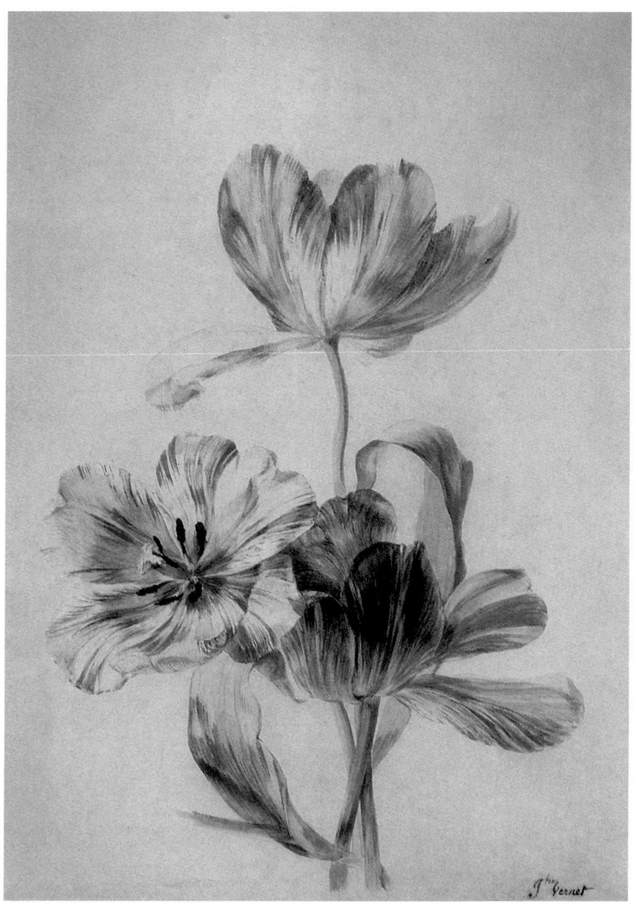

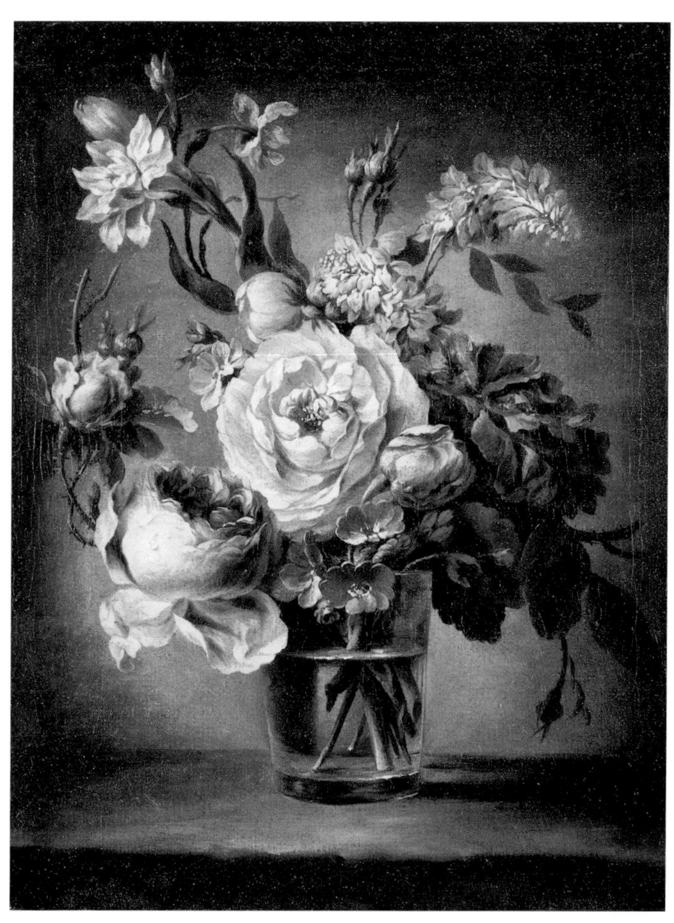

Fig. 2. Joseph Vernet, *Tulip*, c. 1768–1770. Watercolor, 11½ × 8¼ in. (29 × 21 cm). Galerie Jean-François Baroni, Paris.

Fig. 3. Antoine Vernet, *Flowers in a Glass*, 1770. Oil on canvas, 12⅝ × 9½ in. (32 × 24 cm). Formerly Galerie Coatalem, Paris.

coster / qui était son élève et qui s'était adonné [sic] *a ce genre // Mr Vernet fit présent de cette etude / a Mde Biche en 1789* (Joseph Vernet marine painter / made this study in the country to / Give a lesson to Madame Vallayer-Coster / who was his student and who devoted herself to this genre // Monsieur Vernet made a present of this study / to Madame Biche in 1789). It is the year of Vernet's death, and there is no reason to doubt the authenticity of this old inscription; it is consistent with the painter's ideas about teaching, and it confirms that this artist, so fond of working directly after nature,[18] did not limit himself to studies of landscapes and trees but also represented individual plants.[19]

This watercolor can also help us to sort out the sometimes confusing relations among the various members of the Vernet family. Antoine Vernet (1689–1753), Joseph's father, was a decorative painter; we have from his hand, notably, some sedan-chair panels painted with birds and stylized bouquets.[20] He had three sons, all painters, of whom Claude-Joseph was the oldest (1714–1789). The other two are often confused, probably because of the similarity of their first names, Antoine-Ignace (1716–before 1780) and Antoine-François (1730–1779). It is generally accepted that the latter, usually called François, settled in Paris, where he worked for the Bâtiments du roi and was entrusted with decorating the dining room at Choisy.[21] However, he is best known as a landscape painter; he copied a few compositions by Joseph, and in 1775 he gave others to be engraved by Jean-Baptiste de Lorraine (b. 1737) and Jacques-Nicolas Tardieu (1716–1791). The Musée Calvet owns a marine by him that is indebted stylistically both to his famous brother and to Jean-Baptiste Pillement (1728–1804).[22] It is also generally accepted that the second brother, who was called Antoine, followed Joseph to Italy and died in Naples. But the more likely landscape painter is François, and Antoine, a decorative painter like his father, would have worked as such for the Bâtiments du roi. This hypothesis is supported by the existence of a lovely painting signed *A. Vernet* and dated 1770, a bouquet of flowers in a glass whose composition is very close to that of some of Anne Vallayer's paintings from these years (fig. 3).[23] It seems likely, then, that Joseph Vernet, on returning from Italy, gave lessons to his brother at the same time as to Joseph Vallayer's young daughter, whose gifts he may have discerned.

THE ACADÉMIE

Was she following the advice of Vernet, or perhaps that of Alexandre Roslin (1718–1793)—who urged his wife, Suzanne Giroust (1734–1772), to stand for membership—when, in 1770, Vallayer sought membership in the Académie? Little is known about the works she produced prior to this date, but most of them were apparently still lifes of ordinary domestic objects, a genre for which Jean-Siméon Chardin (1699–1779) clearly would have been the most significant model.[24] A composition whose date is difficult to read (1765 or, more likely, 1763) brings together two peaches, a stemmed glass, some plums in a basket, a ham, a dish, and a glazed earthenware jug, all placed close together on a table draped with a white tablecloth (see Kahng, fig. 5). All these elements reappear in her later work, but here one senses the young painter's struggle to master perspective and to render the surfaces of the various objects. From 1766 we have *The Dessert* and *The Lunch*, two pendants that would later serve as models for tapestries (see Kahng, figs. 9, 10).[25] From 1767, we have a mention of a study of *A Loin of Mutton*[26] and above all the superb *Still Life with Silver Pitcher* (cat. 5),[27] and *Still Life with Ham, Bottles, and Radishes* in Berlin (pl. 1), both of which indicate that henceforth, Chardin notwithstanding, Anne Vallayer knew how to use space, how to paint reflections on silver, and how to differentiate various surfaces. In passing, it is worth mentioning that the pitcher is quite close to one in the Musée des Arts Décoratifs, Paris, made by the goldsmith Jean-Guillaume Véalle in 1755–1756.[28] From 1769 we have *Peaches and Cherries* (cat. 9), a painting of such manifest quality that it was once sold at auction as a Chardin, as well as a pastel that probably was a preparatory study for it and that, with its pendant, *Basket of Plums and Grapes*, figured in the 1824 sale of the artist's effects.[29] The same year, we find the same level of inspiration in a different genre, for the young woman painted still lifes of dead animals that do not mitigate their brutal aspect: *Still Life with Dead Hare* in the Horvitz collection (pl. 3) and *Hare, Partridge, and Ham* in the Musée des Beaux-Arts in Reims (cat. 8).[30] Finally, there can be little doubt that when she painted *The Attributes of Painting, Sculpture, and Architecture* (cat. 6) and *The Attributes of Music* (pl. 5), she was thinking about the overdoors that

Chardin painted for Choisy in 1765 (see Kahng, figs. 3, 4). The first of these paintings dates from 1769, its pendant from 1770. Here we can only admire the complete mastery achieved by this young artist of twenty-five who had neither frequented an academician's atelier nor studied at the Académie. In *The Attributes of Painting, Sculpture, and Architecture,* she plays with perspective: the parallel obliques of the brushes and right angle; the rulers and the volumes that lie flat; the books placed at a right angle against the boxes of drawings. The center is dominated by a plaster cast of the Belvedere Torso, up against a turntable on which is placed a terracotta female head draped with a damp cloth, perhaps a deliberate reference to the opposition of ancient and modern sculpture. This might be an ideal head, a kind of allegory of timeless beauty (as was suggested to me by Guilhem Scherf), but the facial features are not unlike those of Anne Vallayer, and we should not dismiss the possibility that she meant to represent herself in this guise. In *The Attributes of Music,* the rendering of materials and the compositional architecture are perhaps still more dazzling: the amply brushed velvet of the carpet, the impasto of the gold embroidery on the bagpipe, the reflections in the wood of the violin and the mandolin, in the silver of the candlestick. The most magical passage is the bell of the horn; it is rendered by juxtaposed touches of various colors that when examined close-up resemble a kind of colored jigsaw puzzle, whereas from a distance the desired effect is fully achieved, evoking slightly hammered copper over which daylight plays. One cannot resist quoting Diderot on Chardin's handling: "you can't make things out from close up, but as you move back the object coalesces and ends up being the one in nature."[31]

Aware of the quality of these canvases, perhaps encouraged by well-known painters,[32] Anne Vallayer thought she was ready to present herself to the Académie. The proceedings of the meeting of 28 July 1770 inform us that

The Demoiselle *Anne Vallayer,* Painter, born in Paris, presented, in view of obtaining provisional membership, several pictures painted in oil, representing scientific and artistic instruments. The Académie, after having taken the usual voice vote and acknowledging her abilities, accepted her presentation, and, there having been among the pictures that she presented and that belonged to her, two paintings, one of a group of musical instruments, and the other those of the Arts of Painting and Sculpture, in which the Company took particular satisfaction, the Académie accepted them for her reception. In consequence, the Académie received and receives the Demoiselle *Vallayer* as Académicienne qualified to sit in its assemblies and enjoy the privileges, prerogatives, and honors accruing to this status, on the understanding that she is to observe the Statutes and Regulations of the Académie, and she sat in the assembly in this capacity.[33]

Notable on the list of witnesses to the proceedings are the names of Jean-Baptiste-Marie Pierre (1713–1789), First Painter to the King, and recently named director of the Académie; of Joseph-Marie Vien and his wife, an *académicienne* since 1757; of the still-life painters Chardin, Jean-Jacques Bachelier (1724–1806), and Claude-François Desportes (1695–1774); of Joseph Vernet; of the portraitist Alexandre Roslin; and of Hubert Robert (1733–1808), some of whose works Anne Vallayer owned.

Two things about this reception should be emphasized. The first is that the "Demoiselle Vallayer" who presented her candidacy for provisional membership as was customary was granted full membership at the same time, which was "by no means in accordance with the statutes," as the comte d'Angiviller reminded Pierre in 1787.[34] This procedure was not unique, Chardin and Robert, among others, having benefited from it. Furthermore, John Goodman has pointed out to me that some 90 percent of the women inscribed in the rolls of the Académie since its inception were accorded provisional and full membership in a single sitting. Might this imply a desire to preclude subsequent entreaties from these ladies? In addition, Anne Vallayer was the only woman to be accepted during these years without having been the wife or daughter of an academician, and without official support from the royal family.[35]

The status of women painters in France and the position of the Académie with regard to this question have been addressed in several recent publications,[36] and I will not dwell on the subject here. It is worth recalling, however, that women could not enroll in the courses at the Académie, its having been thought indecent for them to draw after the nude model.[37] For this reason, history painting, the most prestigious of all genres, was closed to them; they had to make do with lesser genres such as portraiture, still life, or perhaps landscape painting, which meant that they could not become professors at the Académie. Apparently, no *académicienne* was ever even considered for the administrative post of *conseiller*

(adviser), the only one open to genre painters. Furthermore, although the statutes did not exclude female members, the Académie consisted mostly of men, and their attitude toward the acceptance of women varied greatly over the years between 1648 and the French Revolution. In the period that interests us here, the number of *académiciennes* was limited to four, and in 1770 Madame Vien was the only woman who could attend meetings. So the current regulations did not stand in the way of Anne Vallayer's admission. It is amusing to note that one month later it was the turn of Suzanne Giroust, Roslin's wife, "painter in the genre of pastel portraiture," to be granted provisional and full membership at a single sitting, on the evidence of her portrait of Jean-Baptiste Pigalle (1714–1785).

To return to Anne Vallayer: the *Mercure de France* of September 1770 informed its readers that she had been received as a full member of the Académie on the basis of "paintings in the genre of flowers, fruit, bas-reliefs, animals [that] were the best recommendation of her talent"; and in a poem addressed to the new *académicienne* by Guichard, we find more information about the pictures presented to the Académie, for after having exclaimed, "You paint two arts that you cherish / Music and painting," he added, "Bas-relief, vase, fruit, legumes, and rabbit / Under your magic fingers have their very features."[38]

It seems reasonable to deduce from this that the works presented by Vallayer included, aside from the two *Attributes* in the Musée du Louvre, one of the two paintings of a dead rabbit (see above), the trompe-l'oeil painting of a relief entitled *Children Playing (Jeux d'enfants)* that she exhibited at the Salon of 1771,[39] some still lifes like those she painted in 1767, and *Still Life with Seashells and Coral* (pl. 4; doubtless invoked by the phrase "scientific instruments" in the passage from the Académie proceedings, and by "her shells, her fruit, her animals under glass" in the anonymous pamphlet *La Muse errante au Sallon*).[40]

The canvases exhibited in 1771 were universally admired by the critics, beginning with Diderot, who emphasized their "imitative magic" and their illusionism, pronouncing: "It is certain that if all new members made a showing like Mademoiselle Vallayer's, and sustained the same high level of quality there, the Salon would look very different!"[41]

Imitation is especially prominent in the feigned bas-relief, and one admires the young artist for not having feared comparison with the two grisailles after Gérard

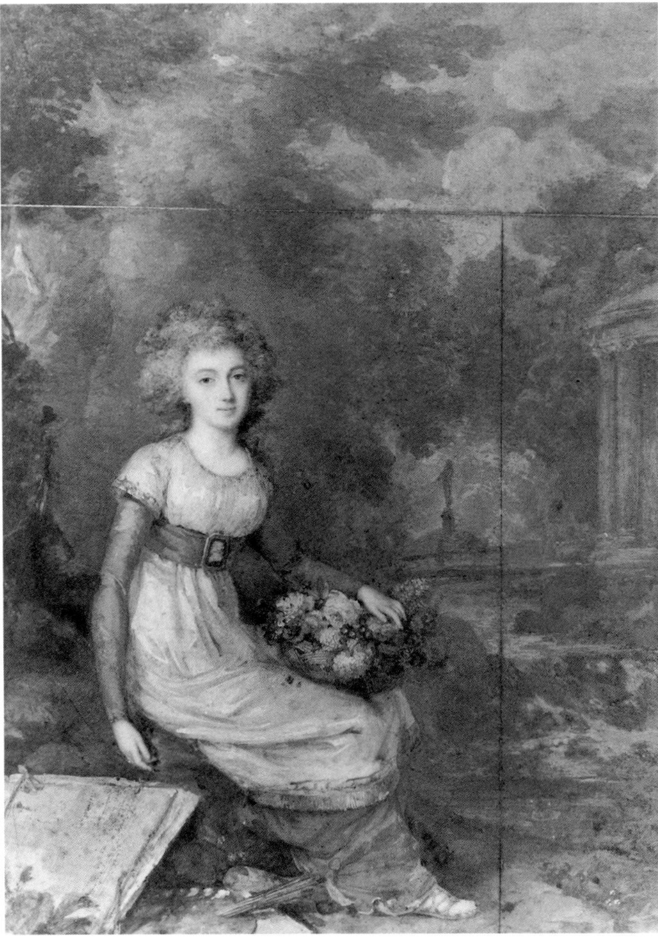

Fig. 4. François Dumont, *Portrait of Anne Vallayer*, 1769. Watercolor on ivory. Present whereabouts unknown.

van Opstal (1605–1668) that Chardin had exhibited in 1769, the memory of which was still fresh. The warm reception of this work explains her having multiplied such imitations of sculpture in the years that followed: the *Trompe l'Oeil of a Terracotta Bas-Relief (after La Rue) Pinned to a Wooden Panel,* which was acquired by Vernet (pl. 7); and the Clodion-inspired *Female Faun and Putti* (pls. 8, 11). She also painted François Duquesnoy's (1597–1643) famous bas-relief *Children with a Goat* (cat. 102), bronze and plaster copies of which were numerous in Paris, and which had previously been painted by the young Chardin and by Desportes.[42] In the catalogue of the sale of the jeweler Aubert in 1786, we find a description of "this piece imitated from a plaster cast [that] is of a striking truth; the skillful and accurate touch admirably produces the effect and illusion of sculpture."[43]

An Established Artist

Before proceeding further, it should be noted that all the praise bestowed on Vallayer took into account not only her talent, about which all the critics agreed, but also the fact that she was a woman, and an attractive one at that, modest and personable in her relations with others. Ambiguity stemming from this consistently inflects the texts: she is a woman, but she paints like a "skilled man" *(habile homme)*; she is condemned to an inferior genre— still life—but practices it with superior ability, and her paintings of martial musical instruments, of curious natural objects, and of dead animals are worthy of a history painter. Her femininity and her charm are insisted on from the moment of her reception and her first showing at the Salon. In 1775 Gabriel Bouquier lauded the talent of "this Demoiselle who combines in her person all the graces of her sex."[44] In 1777 anonymous verses dedicated "to Mademoiselle Vallayer painter to the king" praise her work and conclude: "Ah! I admire her character / Even more than her talent. / She knows how decently / To combine agreeable pleasure / Candor and prudence / Intelligence and feeling. / The common-place art of seduction / Has ever been foreign to her heart; / She pleases as she breathes / Without effort or reflection."[45] All of these qualities are consistent with the known portraits of the artist: a large miniature by François Dumont (1751–1831), made in 1769 (fig. 4); a self-portrait drawn in 1774 (pl. 60); an engraving by Charles-François Letellier (1743–1800) after a drawing clearly to be dated slightly later (pl. 86); and, finally, the superb portrait that Roslin exhibited at the Salon of 1783 (pl. 87). Even in the late miniature by Dumont (pl. 85), produced long after the sitter's fiftieth birthday, her features remain pleasing.

Nonetheless, her celebrity was based neither on her beauty nor on her moral qualities but on her talent and on the work that she exhibited, whether still lifes of various kinds, flower paintings, trompe-l'oeil paintings, or portraits, even genre scenes.[46] We find proof of this reputation in the quality of her clientele, which included several great collectors, notably Louis-Gabriel, marquis de Véri-Raionard,[47] the abbé Terray, the prince de Conti, the financier Beaujon, and the comte de Merle, a portrait of whom she exhibited at the Salon of 1779 along with *Flowers in a Blue Porcelain Vase,* which he owned; and Jean-Baptiste-François de Montullé, the second cousin of Jean de Jullienne, *associé-libre* of the Académie and *secrétaire des commandements de la reine*, to whom belonged *Urn with Fruit and Lobster*, exhibited in 1775, as did two paintings of flowers and fruit exhibited in 1777. Jean Girardot de Marigny, another discerning collector as well as a friend and patron of Vernet, with whom he traveled to Switzerland, acquired from Anne Vallayer two small still lifes that were exhibited in 1779,[48] as well as a painting of dead game exhibited in 1783 (pl. 34).[49] Another *Trophies of the Hunt* dated 1774 belonged to the marquis de Marigny and figured in his 1782 estate sale (pl. 14). As for the *Trophies of the Hunt* that belonged to Roslin and appeared in the Salon of 1785, it might be supposed that Vallayer-Coster gave it to him in exchange for his portrait. But it is interesting to see that other artists, for example Vernet and Piat-Joseph Sauvage (1744–1818), owned works by her. One is less surprised to see listed in the 1831 estate inventory of the miniaturist François Dumont three paintings and a watercolor by Vallayer-Coster.[50] Other, less famous collectors also acquired paintings by our artist, if we can believe the Salon booklets and guidebooks like that of Thierry.[51] Furthermore, there is a good chance that the ravishing portrait of a child dated about 1779 (cat. 58), which belonged, according to family tradition, to the marquise, then duchesse, de Tourzel, represents one of the latter's own children and not one of the dauphins, as has been thought. Madame de Tourzel was not appointed governess of the *enfants de France* until 26 July 1789, after which she was scarcely ever apart from the royal family, whose imprisonment in the Temple she shared. Even if we misread the date of this painting, commissioning a portrait of the dauphin at this time would have been unthinkable. Before taking up princely and royal commissions, I will consider briefly various documents pertaining to the artist's career between 1779 and 1824, when her collection was sold.

The first of these concerns the lodgings allocated to Anne Vallayer in the galleries of the Louvre, below the Grande Galerie. This decided financial advantage was granted certain artists who did everything within their power to obtain support for their suit. I have published several letters relating to this campaign from which we learn that attention must be paid "to the recommendation of the Queen in favor of Mlle Vallayer" (17 March 1779); and, furthermore, that "the Queen, who honors Mlle Vallayer with particular protection, desires that the lodgings be accorded her without delay" (23 June

1779).[52] In fact, Vallayer did not take possession of them until early in 1780, despite the fact that the letter announcing their having been awarded her, under certain conditions, is dated 9 April 1779. In all likelihood, the *Bust of a Young Vestal* exhibited at the Salon of 1779 as belonging to the queen (pl. 25) may have been a gift from the artist, an expression of gratitude to the sovereign who had intervened in her favor.

In any event, she was awarded the fourteenth lodging under the Grande Galerie, previously occupied by the inspectors of the *Gazette de France*, where her close neighbors included Vernet, Jean-Baptiste Greuze (1725–1805), and Joseph-Charles Roettiers (1691–1779). Also housed below the Grande Galerie were the painters Jean-Bernard Restout (1732–1796), Hubert Robert, Joseph-Siffred Duplessis (1725–1802), Gabriel-François Doyen (1726–1806), Louis Lagrenée, known as Lagrenée the elder (1725–1805), Charles-Nicolas Cochin (1715–1790), and, from 1780, Gérard van Spaendonck (1746–1822).[53] Until the arrival of Marguerite Gérard (1761–1837) in 1790, Anne Vallayer was the only woman artist with lodgings of her own in the Louvre, the sole exception being Madame Vien, who lived there with her husband. Adélaïde Labille-Guiard had requested such lodgings, which were refused her "because of her sex" *(en raison de son sexe)*; but the real reason was that she had many female students, and no one wanted the Galeries du Louvre to be overrun by young girls. By way of compensation, the portraitist received a pension of 1,000 livres in 1785 that was renewed in 1789.

It was a year after she moved into the Louvre, on 21 April 1781, that Anne Vallayer married Jean-Pierre-Silvestre Coster, a lawyer in the Parlement and *receveur général du tabac* (collector of taxes levied on tobacco) in Domfront. Born in Nancy in 1745, he was the son of a former first consul in that city, a banker to the Polish king Stanisław.[54] Doubtless his origins partly explain the importance of Anne Vallayer-Coster's ties to Nancy.[55]

I have published the essential portions of the marriage contract elsewhere,[56] so here I will simply mention its most notable features, first, its having been executed at Versailles in the presence of Queen Marie-Antoinette, who signed it. In addition to relatives of the two parties, the list of other signatories includes several noteworthy personalities: the comte d'Angiviller, Marigny's successor as director of the Bâtiments du roi; the First Painter Pierre, described as a friend; the marquis de Véri; and the comte de La Ferté. At the very least, we might say that this "modest" artist had a real sense of her own interests, and that she knew how to cultivate powerful protectors. Her future husband brought to the alliance 15,000 livres, exclusive of revenue from his tax levies; the future wife promised a dowry of 34,000 livres: 20,000 from her father's estate, the balance in furnishings and income "from the art of painting."[57] This is a very respectable sum, evidence of a steady clientele.

For the moment, I will pass over the commissions for portraits of Mesdames and of the queen (to be discussed below) and proceed directly to the Revolutionary period. First, an eyewitness account: that of Madame Campan, first lady-in-waiting to the queen, former reader to Mesdames, and sister of Madame Auguié, whose portrait Anne Vallayer-Coster had painted in 1781. In her memoirs, she relates that during preparations for the flight to Varennes (June 1791),

> The queen told me that she had something precious to entrust to me and that I would have to find some respectable people, financially independent and wholly devoted to their sovereigns, to whom I was to consign a portfolio that she gave me. I had the idea of choosing Madame Vallayer-Coster, painter of the Académie, residing in the galleries in the Louvre, and in whom I found, as in her husband, all of the qualities required by the queen of the persons to be charged with this article. They were as loyal as I had declared them to be. Only in September 1791, after the constitution had been accepted, did they return this portfolio to me.[58]

Next comes a document from the Ministry of the Interior, dated 30 pluviôse an VII (18 February 1799), an "extract from the report of citizens Naigeon and Bréa on available art objects that might be given *citoyenne* Vallayer-Coster as a compensation of 2,400 francs for a painting of her composition . . . included among objects given in payment by the government for essentials."[59] Unfortunately, we do not know what painting is meant. But the list of proposed objects, seized from émigrés and from those condemned to death, is interesting. It includes a marble group of Aria and Poetus from the collection of the comte d'Orsay (assessed at 800 francs); a marble by Charles Ricourt, *La Douleur (Pain* or *Sorrow)*, owned by the condemned Du Châtelet (200 francs), like-wise the source of four Chinese porcelain potpourris and a teapot made of old Japanese lacquer. Also listed are a cameo mounted on a ring and a tortoiseshell snuffbox

decorated with a miniature of the convicted and con-demned Noailles-Mouchy, two small pieces of case fur-niture by André-Charles Boulle (1642–1732) from the collection of the condemned Gilbert-Voisin (300 francs each), and a gilt lacquer box from the Brissac household (100 francs). The total comes to 1,724 francs, and the list is signed by Madame Vallayer-Coster, who acknowledges on 8 ventôse (26 February) having received all of these objects in the galleries of the "Palais National des Arts," as the Louvre was then called. This document certainly provides valuable information about the use of works of art during the revolutionary period, when cash was scarce. But it is also noteworthy that the artist kept some of the objects she had received in 1799 until her death. Among the items listed in the catalogue of her 1824 estate sale we find the two marble sculptures, two Boulle cabinets or medal cases, and two lacquer boxes, one of them probably from the group of objects allocated to her in 1799.

Only in 1804 does the name of Anne Vallayer-Coster appear in the official correspondence of Dominique Vivant Denon.[60] A letter from the director of the Musée du Louvre to Duvivier, director of the Savonnerie manu-factory, dated 10 January, requests the return to Paris, to the Musée Napoléon (the Louvre), of two hunting paintings by Bachelier,[61] two hunting paintings by Desportes, two paintings of flowers and fruit by Jean-Marc Ladey (1710–1749), and "a painting represent-ing a hen, a rooster, by Madame Valayer-Coster [*sic*]"[62] (pl. 39). On 27 March Denon informed Goulard, direc-tor of the domain of Versailles, that he was to send to Paris Vernet's *La Pêche du thon (View of the Gulf of Bandol: Tuna Fishing)*, destined for the Musée du Sénat, and that he would receive by way of compensation a painting by Pierre-Narcisse Guérin (1774–1833), the two Bacheliers, and the Vallayer-Coster, which were to be exhibited in the museum in the château.[63]

At the end of the same year, the name of our painter appears in another connection. This time, Denon wrote the minister of the interior to tell him that, Napoleon having added the Gobelins, Beauvais, Sèvres, and Savon-nerie manufactories to his own administrative purview, he had to find a venue where the artists employed by them could work. Because the locale occupied by Denon in the galleries of the Louvre was too small, he thought he might enlarge it by offering Madame Vallayer-Coster, "who occupies an arcade of the galleries close to myself, the lodgings in the Quatre-Nations vacant since the death of

Monsieur Julien, sculptor." He added that it would of course be necessary to accord the artist "a compensatory fee proportionate to her likely moving expenses."[64] In the end, for reasons unknown, this proposal came to naught; instead, Anne Vallayer-Coster moved into the rue Neuve des Bons Enfants, then into the rue du Coq Héron, where she died on 28 February 1818. Her husband, who then moved to the boulevard du Temple, survived her by six years; after his death on 29 April 1824, their collection was sold on 21 and 22 June.[65]

The catalogue includes a list of seventy-nine lots, preceded by an enthusiastic two-page text by Charles Paillet, the dealer entrusted with the sale, such as would be expected in the circumstances, and in which he says that the most striking works left by the artist are "a painting representing flowers arranged in a vase, and of very large dimensions, some medallions painted *au fixé* [i.e., painted on taffeta and then placed under glass], genre paintings and paintings of bas-reliefs whose illusionism remains convincing when they are seen up close."[66] The first thirty-seven lots are works by Vallayer-Coster: twenty-five paintings of various genres, six *fixés* of flowers, two watercolors, fourteen framed studies of flowers to be sold by the pair, eight others that were unframed, and under a single lot sixty-five studies of flowers, which sold at about fifteen francs each. There follow some forty wash drawings by the artist, including fourteen said to have been engraved by Louis-Jean Allais (1762–1833). Thereafter come the paintings by other artists, which, judging from their character, were probably acquired during the 1770s, when Parisian auctions were especially rich in Northern painting: a small panel by Nicolaes Berchem (1620–1683) that went for 1,550 francs and a landscape by Teniers, acquired by the dealer Pérignon for 410 francs (Paillet noted the latter work's prestigious provenance: it had figured in the Choiseul sale [580 livres] and the Conti sale [600 livres], where the artist probably acquired it). She also owned a landscape by Jan Asselijn (c. 1615–1652) and a still life, the only one in her collection (her own excepted), by Jan Davidsz de Heem (1606–1683/84). The French school was represented by a portrait of a man by Pierre Mignard (1612–1695) and by several contemporary works: two Roman views by Hubert Robert, drawings by Jean-Honoré Fragonard (1732–1806) and Philippe-Jacques de Loutherbourg (1740–1813), and, above all, three paintings by Vernet,[67] as well as twenty-seven marine and landscape drawings that he had given her. She also owned many studies of heads, several *académies*

(male nudes), and a few prints, as well as the copperplates of the ten prints engraved by Allais. We already saw that some of the furnishings, objects, and marble sculptures in the estate had been allocated to her in 1799; in addition to these, I will mention only number 75, a terracotta bas-relief by Clodion (1738–1814) representing a female faun surrounded by children, which doubtless served as the model for her trompe-l'oeil paintings (pls. 8, 11); and number 73, a small water jug and its saucer made of turquoise Sèvres porcelain, a "gift from the queen to Madame Coster's mother."[68]

The Court Painter

This mention apart, it is surprising that Paillet, six years after the artist's death, did not remember—had he ever known?—that she had been the painter of royal princesses, of a queen, of an empress, and of a king.

I will review schematically the honorific benchmarks of this career, which began on 3 July 1779 with a commission from the comte d'Angiviller for a full-length portrait of Madame Sophie, a project studied in depth by Laurent Hugues elsewhere in the present volume. Here I will simply note that in April 1781 the artist listed among her assets the 6,000 livres due her for the portrait of Madame Sophie, doubtless executed in 1779. Her invoice for a bust portrait painted from life (pl. 26) and for a full-length portrait after this bust portrait was signed by Pierre, Jardin, and Hazon in November 1781; an initial payment of 1,500 livres was remitted in February 1782, the final payment, 2,500 livres, followed in June 1782.[69]

It is worth mentioning that the Walters Art Museum in Baltimore owns a mediocre miniature portrait of the queen, bearing a "signature" and the date 1778. Even if it is a nineteenth-century copy after a lost original, it would attest to relations between Anne Vallayer and Marie-Antoinette at that date, which would be consistent with the sovereign's having intervened in 1779 to support the artist's being allocated lodgings in the Louvre.[70]

In 1780 Vallayer executed a pastel portrait of Marie-Antoinette; until recently, we knew of it only through a letter from Anne Vallayer to d'Angiviller and dated June 1780,[71] but it has now been located in a private collection (pl. 63). Laurent Hugues has provided me with excerpts from unpublished letters from Marie-Antoinette to Princess Louise von Hesse-Darmstadt, who sojourned in Paris in 1780 with her sister Charlotte, referring to a portrait said to be "a very poor likeness" and thus unworthy of being sent to her.[72] This might be a reference to the pastel portrait by Anne Vallayer.

As for the bust portraits of Madame Victoire and Madame Adélaïde, identified and discussed by Laurent Hugues (pls. 27, 28), they were commissioned and painted after those of Madame Sophie.

One might think that after the Revolution there would be no further mention of Anne Vallayer-Coster in official documents. In 1804, however, Josephine acquired two works from her (perhaps specially commissioned: according to Denon, the artist "made them for Her Majesty the Empress"[73]), and, given the empress's tastes, we are not surprised to learn that they were representations of flowers. Two watercolors, a bouquet of roses and a bouquet of dahlias (pl. 56),[74] were hung at Saint-Cloud. On 14 September 1804 Denon wrote the château's concierge instructing him to turn them over to the artist, who wished to exhibit them at the Salon; and she indeed showed two gouaches at the exhibition that year (nos. 481 and 482). Both were later sent to Malmaison; on Josephine's death, one of them went to her son, Prince Eugene, who sold it in 1829, and the other to her daughter, Queen Hortense (pl. 56).

The last "royal painting" by Anne Vallayer-Coster is the large *Still Life with Lobster* (pl. 45), which she exhibited at the Salon of 1817 as belonging to the king.[75] Marie-Claude Chaudonneret has noted the importance of this Salon, the first under the Restoration,[76] but she does not indicate that Louis XVIII acquired this painting. Very likely the artist conceived it as an homage to the sovereign, the large fleur-de-lys branch resting in the bottle carrier being an intentional allusion to the restored monarchy.

"Madame Vallayer-Coster, célèbre peintre de fleurs"

Such is the title of the notice that precedes the catalogue of the sale of "FLOWER PAINTINGS and diverse objects from the collection of the late M. and Mme Coster." In this preliminary text (which contains several wrong dates), Paillet writes that "she consistently sustained in her chosen genre, that of flowers, the high reputation that she had won for herself and for which she vied with the most famous professors." He concludes by noting the richness of form and color of her flowers, "so beautiful, so perfect, and so true."[77]

One can only subscribe to this assessment, so brilliantly confirmed by the present exhibition, but it should also be acknowledged that, apparently, it was not as a flower painter that Anne Vallayer-Coster first made herself known. To be sure, in 1770, she presented in support of her candidacy for membership in the Académie several "paintings in the genre of flowers, fruit, bas-reliefs, animals";[78] but she exhibited no such works at her first two Salons, those of 1771 and 1773, preferring to show what I would not hesitate to call more ambitious productions: depictions of minerals, musical instruments, illusionistic bas-reliefs, animals, still lifes of fruit in which she clearly courted comparison with Chardin, as well as portraits. It is true, in any case, that in the two portraits of her by the miniaturist Dumont, one dating from the threshold of her career in 1769, the other from 1804 (pl. 85), she is represented holding a basket of roses and fruit or presenting a vase of flowers. It is likewise true that when Paillet wrote his catalogue, he would have had foremost in his mind the many paintings, oil studies, watercolors, and miniatures of flowers that constituted the bulk of what she had kept for herself or had not been able to sell.

At present, we know of no flower paintings before 1772, whereas the earliest dated work represents a ham and some vegetables (cat. 1). In 1775 she finally exhibited "several paintings of flowers and fruit" under a single number, seeking at the same time to make a stronger impression with her *Vase of Flowers with a Bust of Flora*, a large painting that displays, to striking effect, her mastery not only in the rendering of flowers and fruit but also in that of such materials as porcelain, bronze, marble, and velvet (cat. 30). Furthermore, this work was conceived as an allegory, for she showed as its pendant *The Attributes of Hunting and Gardening* (cat. 24). Was she inspired here by Jean-Louis Prévost (c. 1740– c. 1810), who devised many allegories in which flowers figure prominently: tomb designs, altars, decorative compositions, female busts crowned with roses or laurel and placed on marble tablets close to baskets of flowers, books, and other objects?[79]

Thereafter, she exhibited flower paintings regularly, but they still did not predominate in her production. At every Salon she also showed still lifes of fruit, trophies of the hunt, genre scenes, and portraits, which sometimes collectively outnumbered her flower paintings. This prompted the critics to praise "This admirable girl [who] has a unique truth and skill; all of nature's productions seem to hatch under her brush";[80] and to assert that she was "incomparably the first for inanimate things, grapes,

peaches, plums."[81] In her flowers, Anne Vallayer worked
within the great Northern tradition of Rachel Ruysch
(1664–1750) and, especially, Jan van Huysum (1682–
1749), whose reputation in France was immense,[82] and
who was the inescapable point of reference whenever
anyone wanted to praise a painter's work in this genre,
whether the Prévost brothers, Anne Vallayer-Coster,
or, above all, Gérard van Spaendonck, "incontrovertibly
the Van Huysum of our century."[83] We should not over-
look the influence of the French tradition, notably the
two Monnoyers, despite the fact that late-eighteenth-
century bouquets have little in common with their grand
compositions. But certain bouquets and flowers in a
vase or a basket painted by Jean-Baptiste (1636–1699) or
Antoine (1677–1745) Monnoyer and engraved by Jacques
Vauquer (1621–1686) might well have served as models
for Anne Vallayer-Coster, as for her contemporaries.[84]

From our knowledge of her production and of the contents of the 1824 estate sale, we can reconstruct something of Vallayer's working methods. This student of
Basseporte began by making painted or drawn studies
that combine precision with a very free touch. The vivid
or pale colors of these roses, hollyhocks, and gillyflowers,
painted in oil on mounted paper, stand out delicately
against backgrounds of gray or light brown (pls. 51, 52,
53); the watercolors are rendered more precisely, in a
style reminiscent of botanical engravings (pls. 56, 58, 59),
but in both cases we are dealing with more or less finished
studies that she could use for her various bouquets.

Her contemporaries apparently proceeded likewise,
and it is worth mentioning a few of them who were often
associated with our artist by the critics. Michel-Bruno
Bellengé (1726–1793), received as a full academician in
1764 with a vase of flowers and nearby fruit, produced
easel paintings with compositions that are close to hers.
He exhibited at the same Salons, which made comparison of the two artists inevitable.[85] In the *Almanach des
Artistes* of 1776, both are listed as "painters of flowers
and fruit."

But her great rival was her contemporary, Gérard van
Spaendonck, successor of Basseporte and predecessor
of Pierre-Joseph Redouté (1759–1840) as painter of the
Jardin des Plantes. Curiously, we find little in common
today between the two artists (save for their oil, gouache,
and watercolor studies), for the sumptuous bouquets of
Van Spaendonck, a true heir of Van Huysum, are very
different from Vallayer-Coster's floral compositions.
But the critics were in agreement that she "sustains her

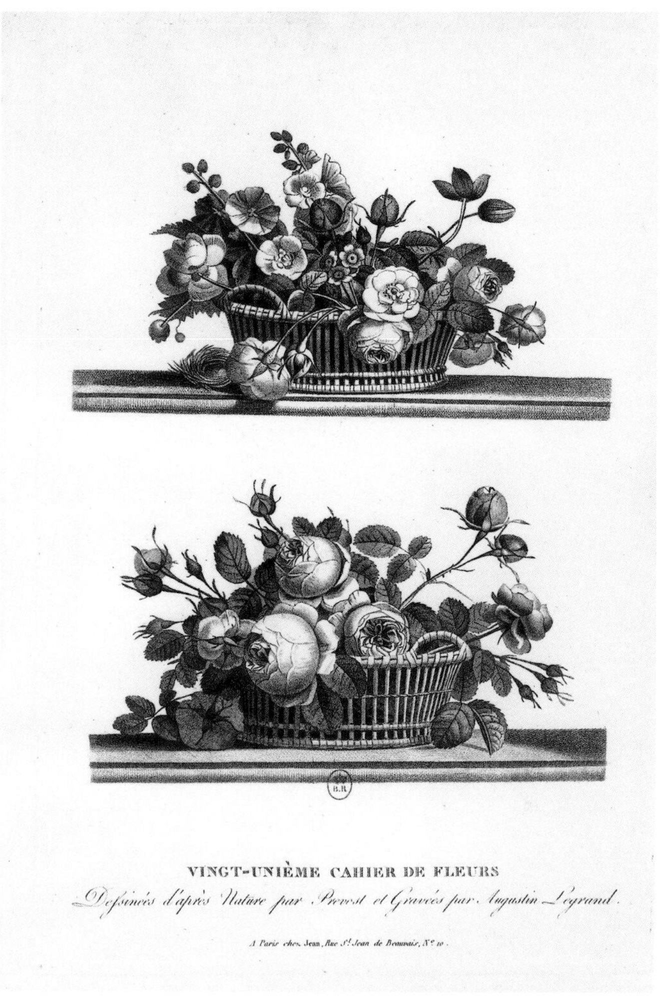

Fig. 5. Augustin Legrand after Jean-Louis Prévost, *Vingt-unième
cahier de fleurs*, c. 1810. Color engraving. Bibliothèque nationale
de France.

reputation admirably, and even survives proximity to
M. van Spaendonck, the most famous of her rivals in the
genre [of flowers and fruit],"[86] noting further that hers
was "the more precious touch, [his] the more virile."[87]

We will return to the Prévost brothers, and especially
to the younger one, Jean-Louis, the author of countless
floral compositions, many destined to be engraved, whose
compositions resemble those of Anne Vallayer-Coster
(fig. 5), and which occasioned the standard invocations of
Van Huysum. We note in passing that contemporary collections reveal a pervasive taste for floral representations,
whether more "botanical" or more aesthetic in tenor,
whether destined "for the Sciences or for the Fine Arts."[88]
As examples, we might cite La Live de Jully, who owned
flowers by Alexis-Nicolas Pérignon (1726–1782) and
Prévost as well as butterflies by Madame Vien; the prince
de Conti, who owned two paintings by Vallayer-Coster
as well as paintings on vellum by Nicolas Robert and by
Basseporte; and so on.

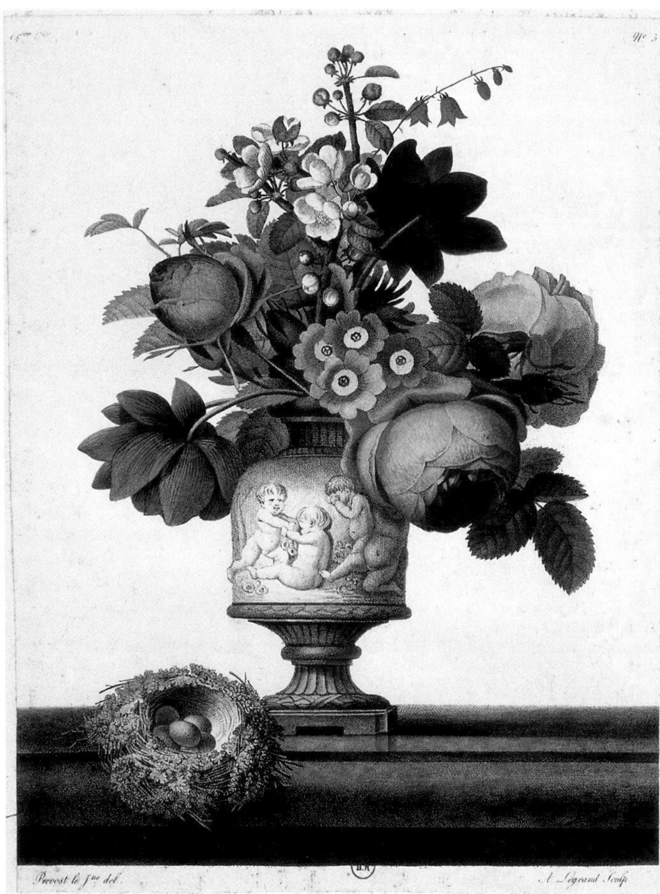

Fig. 6. Augustin Legrand after Jean-Louis Prévost, *Flowers in a Vase with Bas-Relief*, c. 1810. Color engraving. Bibliothèque nationale de France.

Fig. 7. Charles-Germain de Saint-Aubin, 2 plates from *Mes Petits bouquets*, n.d. Etching. Bibliothèque nationale de France.

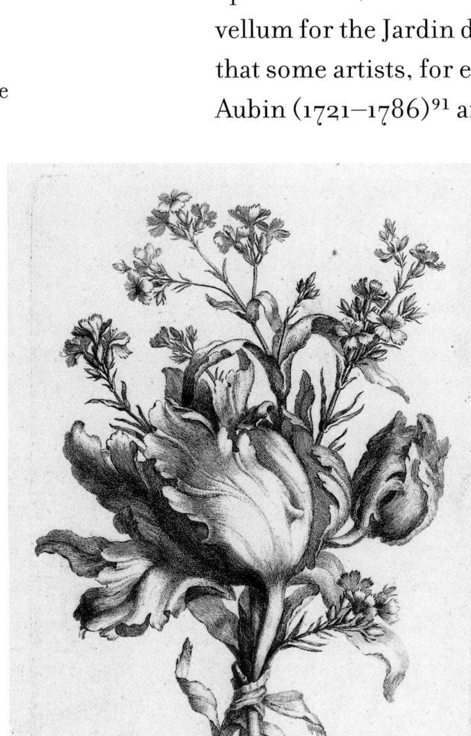

I will permit myself another brief digression, again concerning bas-reliefs. Like Van Huysum, both Prévost (fig. 6) and, especially, Van Spaendonck painted magnificent vases decorated with bas-reliefs in the antique style or representing children at play. Anne Vallayer did likewise, as can be seen in one of the vases of flowers in the Dallas Museum of Art, where the terracotta answers nicely to the blue vase of its pendant (pls. 19, 20).[89] Better yet, if she copied bas-reliefs by Clodion, she was not alone in doing so, for Sauvage, admittedly a specialist in such images, did so, too, along with her "floral emulators" Van Spaendonck and Prévost.[90]

We will see shortly that this taste may have manifested itself to an even greater extent in the more widely disseminated medium of prints.

Sets of Prints

By making drawings of flowers destined to be engraved, Anne Vallayer-Coster was again working within a tradition that dated back at least to the seventeenth century. The titles of the various published sets allow room for doubt as to whether these renderings of plants were executed directly from nature or from other botanical images, even from prints. There is no clear answer to this question, for among the plates offered for public sale were engravings after drawings by Basseporte, Van Spaendonck, and Redouté, painters of "miniatures" on vellum for the Jardin des Plantes. By contrast, we know that some artists, for example Charles-Germain de Saint-Aubin (1721–1786)[91] and Jean-Baptiste Pillement, used

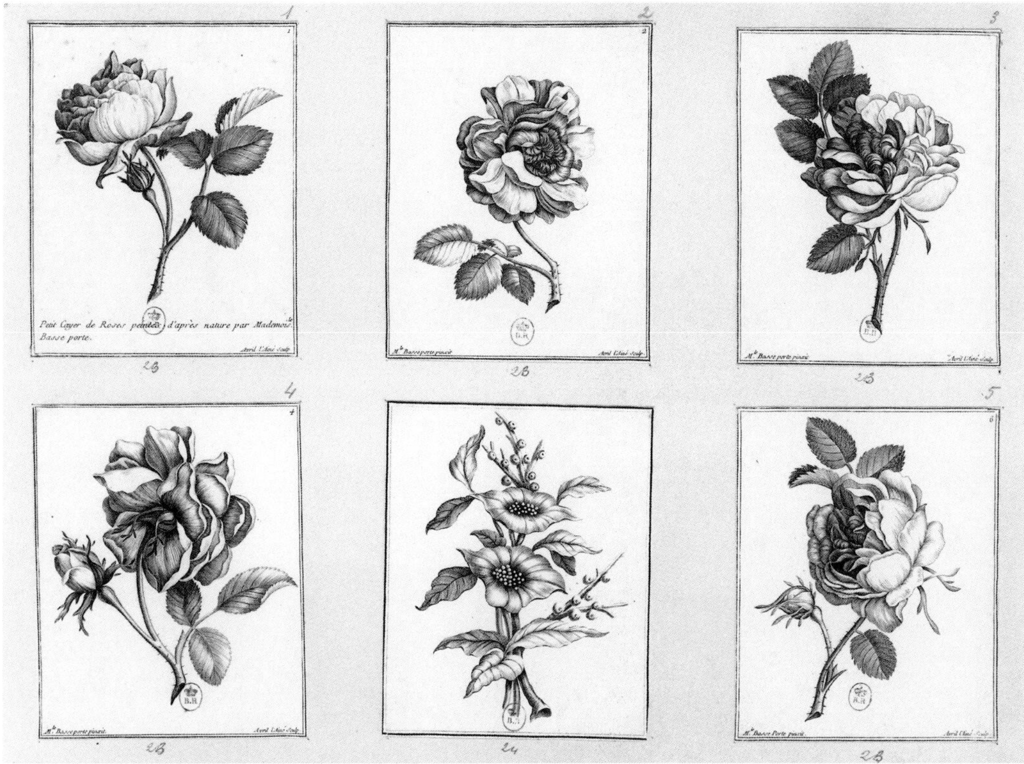

flowers merely as elements in ornamental prints intended for use by the silk and porcelain manufactories. Note, however, that two of the six plates of Saint-Aubin's *Petits bouquets* (a carnation; some roses) are presented as naturalistic bouquets (fig. 7). As for Bachelier, who from 1751 devised floral models for the Sèvres manufactory, he engraved floral *fleurons* and tailpieces between 1755 and 1760 for the celebrated edition of La Fontaine's *Fables* with illustrations after drawings by Jean-Baptiste Oudry (1686–1755).

We can be certain, however, about the specialization of certain editors and/or engravers. Thus we find the *excudit* of Nicolas de Poilly (1626–1696) on plates engraved by Vauquer after Monnoyer.[92] The same holds for a *Livre de vases propre pour Peintres, Brodeurs et Dessinateurs* (Book of vases suitable for painters, embroiderers, and designers), another set of *Vases de fleurs* (Vases of flowers) meant for the same audience, a *Livre de fleurs* (Book of flowers), and numerous studies of flowers, including some with several flowers grouped on a single plate. Vauquer also published with Langlois twenty plates of flowers, either isolated or in bunches tied with ribbon, that Anne Vallayer-Coster might well have used as models.[93] He also engraved after "Baptiste" (Jean-Baptiste Monnoyer, called Baptiste, the greatest French flower painter in his time), a *Livre de toutes sortes de fleurs d'après nature* (Book of all sorts of flowers after nature), as well as a *Livre de plusieurs paniers de fleurs* (Book of various baskets of flowers). Many of

Vauquer's plates in the Sèvres archives were apparently used as models by painters at the manufactory. These books would be retouched in the second half of the eighteenth century by Jean-Jacques Avril, known as Avril the elder (1744–1831), who seems to have specialized in floral prints from the outset of his career.[94] He began his reworking of Vauquer with six plates of *Bouquets de fleurs dessinés d'après nature par Baptiste* (Bouquets of flowers drawn after nature by Baptiste), two *Cahier[s] de bouquets* (Gathering of bouquets), and *Douze fleurs différentes dessinées d'après nature par Baptiste* (Twelve different flowers drawn after nature by Baptiste). Then he engraved after Madeleine Basseporte two *Cahier[s] de fleurs dessinées d'après nature* (Gathering of flowers drawn after nature), as well as a *Petit Cayer* [sic] *de Roses peintes d'après nature* (Small gathering of roses painted after nature), all six of whose plates are signed "Mle Basseporte pinxit" (fig. 8).

Louis Tessier (c. 1719–1781), flower painter at the Gobelins manufactory, had Juste Chevillet (1729–1790) engrave his *Livre de principes de fleurs dédiés aux Dames* (Book of examples of flowers dedicated to the ladies), and Gilles Demarteau (1729–1776), in the *manière de crayon*, a *Livre de fleurs* (Book of flowers) dedicated to Buffon (fig. 9), but it was Avril who signed two *Cahier[s] de bouquets* (Gathering[s] of bouquets), a *Livre de fleurs* (Book of flowers), a *Livre de six bouquets* (Book of six bouquets; fig. 10), another "book" of *corbeilles et vases de fleurs dessinés d'après nature* (baskets and vases of flowers

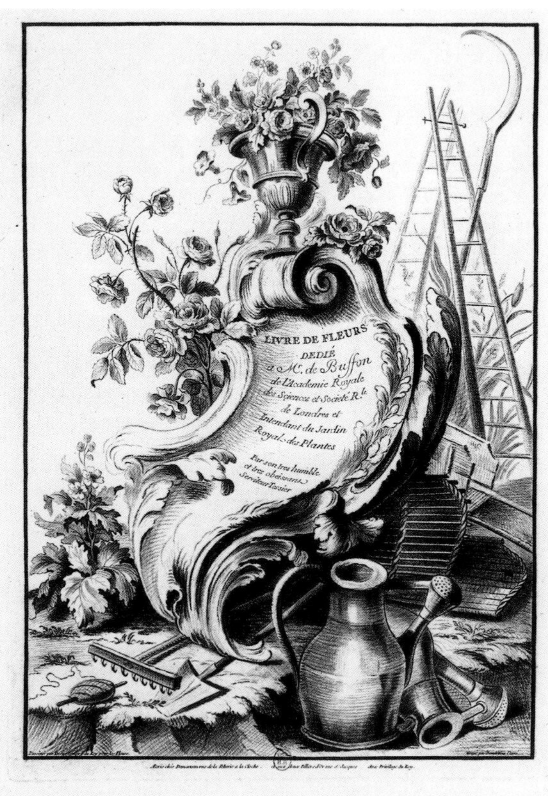

Fig. 9. Gilles Demarteau after Louis Tessier, *Livre de fleurs*, c. 1770. Black chalk–manner engraving. Bibliothèque nationale de France.

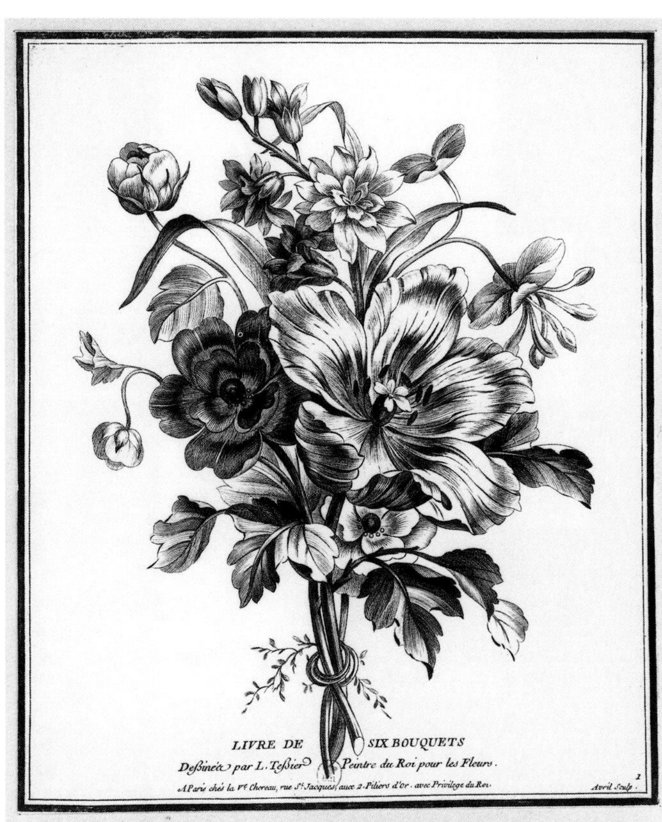

Fig. 10. Avril the elder after Louis Tessier, *Livre de six bouquets*, c. 1770. Engraving. Bibliothèque nationale de France.

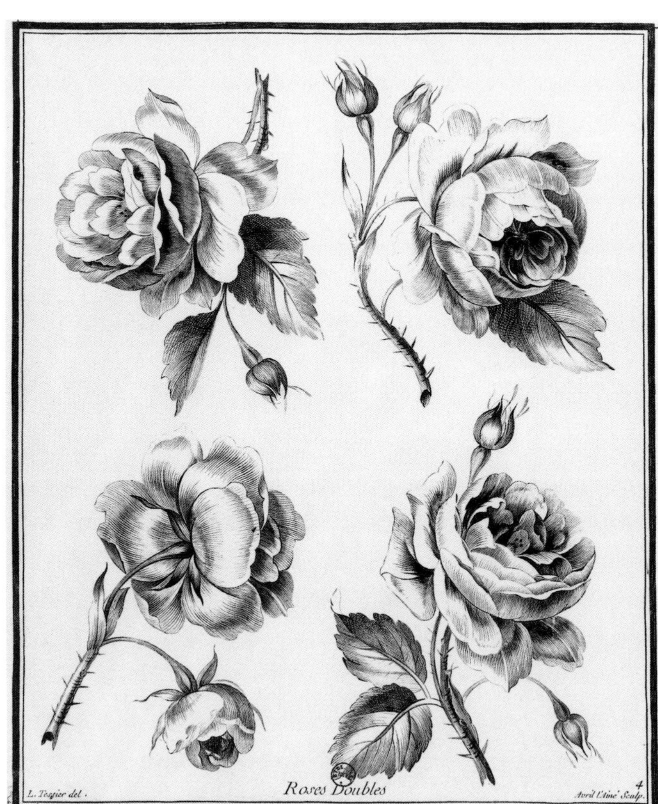

Fig. 11. Avril the elder after Louis Tessier, *Roses doubles*, c. 1770. Engraving. Bibliothèque nationale de France.

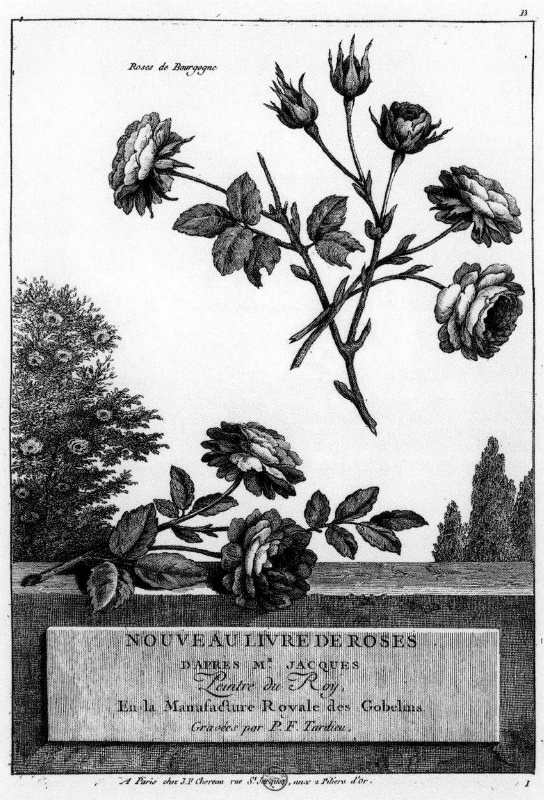

Fig. 12. Pierre-François Tardieu after Maurice Jacques, *Nouveau livre de roses d'après M. Jacques*, c. 1770. Engraving. Bibliothèque nationale de France.

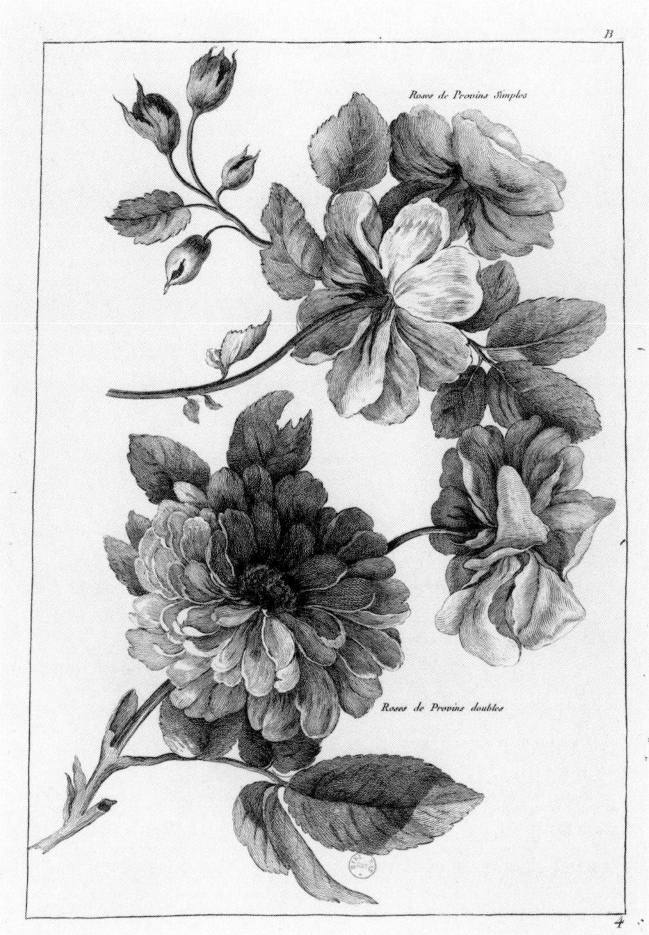

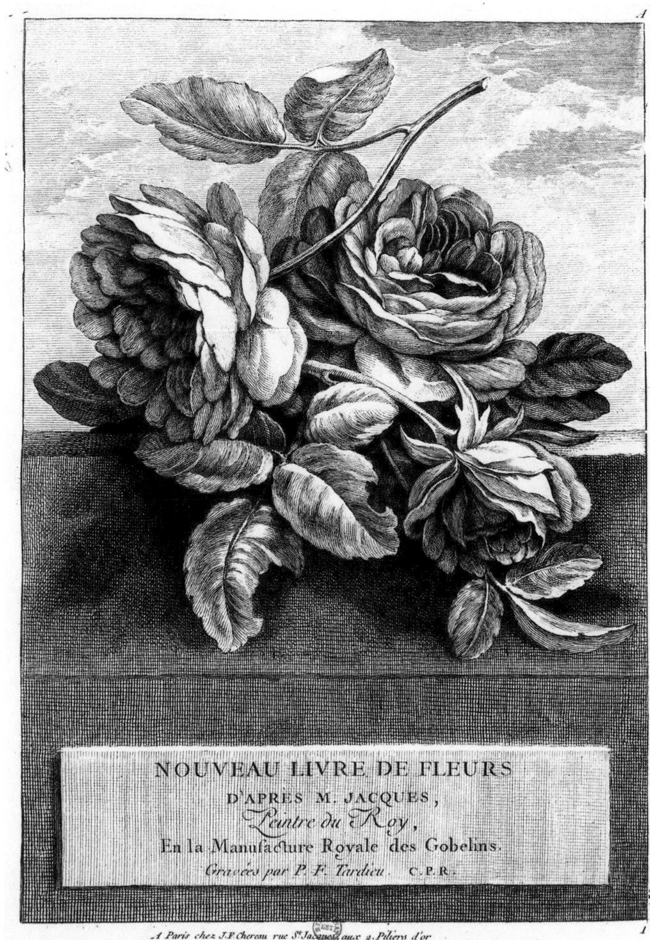

Fig. 13. Pierre-François Tardieu after Maurice Jacques, *Roses de Provins* from *Nouveau livre de roses d'après M. Jacques.* Engraving, c. 1770. Bibliothèque nationale de France.

Fig. 14. Pierre-François Tardieu after Maurice Jacques, *Nouveau livre de fleurs*, n.d. Engraving. Bibliothèque nationale de France.

drawn after nature), as well as other collections of this kind (fig. 11), not to mention the *Livre de fleurs dessinées d'après nature pour servir de Principes dans ce genre, par Tessier, peintre du roi* (Book of flowers drawn after nature to serve as examples in this genre, by Tessier, painter of the king), published by Chéreau, as were almost all of these print sets. Another painter at the Gobelins, Maurice Jacques (1712–1784), also had some of his flower images engraved: a *Nouveau livre de roses d'après Mr. Jacques, "peintre du roy en la Manufacture des Gobelins"* (New book of roses after M. Jacques, "painter of the king in the Gobelins manufactory"; fig. 12), which included renderings of Burgundian, nutmeg, white, four seasons, simple and double Provins roses (fig. 13), shown in bunches or on stems, was engraved by Pierre-François Tardieu (1711–1771) and published by Chéreau, as was a *Nouveau livre de fleurs* (New book of flowers; fig. 14).

Gilles Demarteau, who made a specialty of sets of didactic prints, notably for students of landscape,

anatomy, or botany, also engraved, in addition to the above-mentioned drawings by Tessier, a *Livre de principes et leçons de fleurs* (Book of floral examples and lessons) after Jean-Baptiste Hüet (1745–1811). He likewise produced four more "books" bearing this title engraved in the *manière de crayon*, the first two dedicated to Mademoiselle de Rochemore, and several individual plates of flowers. To these must be added four *Cahier[s] de principes et leçons de fleurs* (Gathering[s] of floral examples and lessons) after Prévost the younger. According to Claudia Salvi, Redouté, who arrived in Paris in 1782, met Chéreau, who acquired a few of his studies after nature in view of their being engraved by Demarteau, "to serve as drawing examples for young people devoting themselves to this genre of painting."[95] Redouté apparently seized this occasion to enter Demarteau's atelier.[96]

The same holds for Augustin Legrand (1765/66–after 1843?), most of whose prints are colored; he became professor to the Société royale d'Horticulture,[97] and about

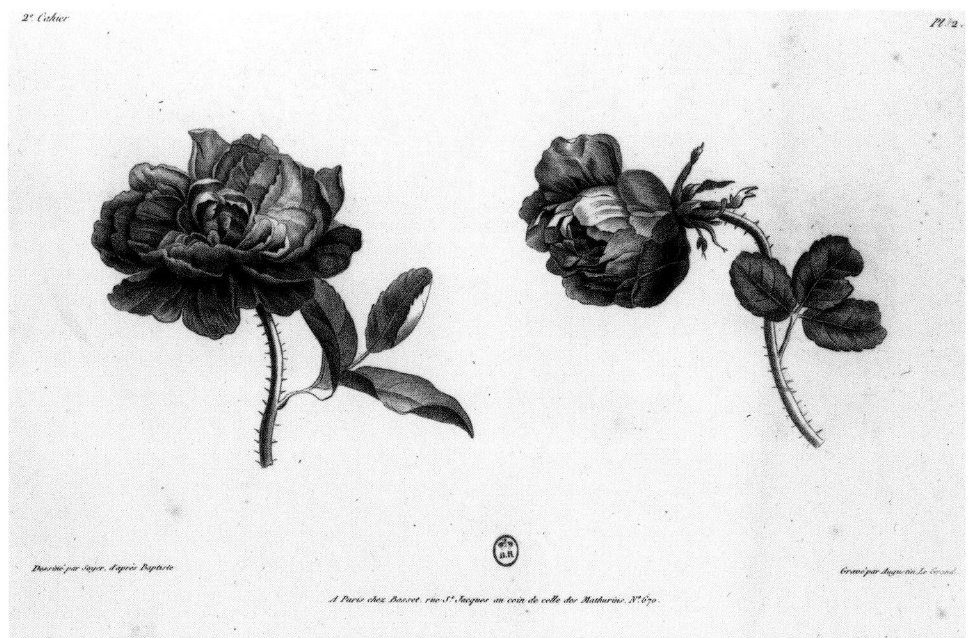

Fig. 15. Augustin Legrand after Soyer after Jean-Baptiste Monnoyer, *Two Studies of Roses*, n.d. Engraving. Bibliothèque nationale de France.

1816 he engraved, after his own drawings, a *Parterre ou Recueil de fleurs* (Parterre or collection of flowers) and an *Alphabet de fleurs* (Alphabet of flowers). But earlier, in 1805, he had engraved sixteen plates of flowers drawn by Soyer after Monnoyer (fig. 15), then between 1808 and 1813 some one hundred plates of flowers and fruit after Prévost. There are colored examples of all of these prints. Augustin Legrand's brother, Pierre-François Legrand (1743–after 1824), engraved about 1800 the *Fleurs dessinées d'après nature* (Flowers drawn after nature) by Van Spaendonck.

A place apart should be reserved here for Pierre-Joseph Buchoz (1731–1807), medical doctor, botanist, and typical Enlightenment man of science from Lorraine, who undertook to publish the *Tournefortius lotharingiae ou Cabinet des Plantes qui croissent dans la Lorraine* (Tournefortius lotharingiae or cabinet of plants native to Lorraine), which he followed with a *Traité des plantes de la Lorraine* (Treatise on the plants of Lorraine).[98] Their most beautiful plates are dedicated to various prominent individuals, and the dedications underscore the connections between Parisian and provincial academies. But Buchoz did not limit himself to plants from his native region; he also oversaw the publication in Paris of *Bouquets de Flore ou Recueil de bouquets et d'autres objets d'histoire naturelle* (Bouquets of Flora or collection of bouquets and other objects of natural history), which are presented more or less like botanical plates. The first six, engraved in colors and with titles on vellum, are surrounded by gilt filets like the king's vellum paintings and are devoted to bouquets of various kinds and to

flowers "that bloom during the month[s]" of May, August, and October. Like the plants of Lorraine, they are dedicated to the memory of the king of Denmark, Stanisłas I, and Louis XV. Two of them are dedicated to the comte d'Artois, who named Buchoz doctor-botanist and *quartier surnuméraire* of his household. These bouquets are of interest here in that they show what flowers bloomed in the same season, making it possible to verify whether Anne Vallayer-Coster's composite bouquets derive from pre-existing images or from firsthand observation. In the bouquet for May we find roses, ranunculus, poppies, irises, syringa flowers, narcissi, yellow jasmine, peonies, carnations, pansies, and buttercups. In the one for August, hollyhocks, nasturtiums, honeysuckle, larkspur, sweet peas, and white jasmine. September brings asters, balsam, bellflowers, geraniums, snapdragons, pomegranate flowers, and African marigolds (fig. 16); and October, flowering blackberry, tomato flowers, African marigolds, convulvulus, jasmine. We can trust the veracity of Buchoz's groupings, for he called on Madeleine Basseporte to illustrate his *Histoire universelle du règne végétal ou nouveau dictionnaire physique & économique de toutes les plantes* (Universal history of the vegetal domain or new physical and economic dictionary of all plants; Paris, 1775–1780).[99] Yet again, we see how closely intertwined were naturalism and ornament, botany and diversions for the eye. As Daniel Roche has noted with regard to botanical gardens and their place in provincial academies, they "offered health to all, made it possible to combat boredom and idleness, and to break away from the agitation of a life spoiled by luxury. . . . The botanical

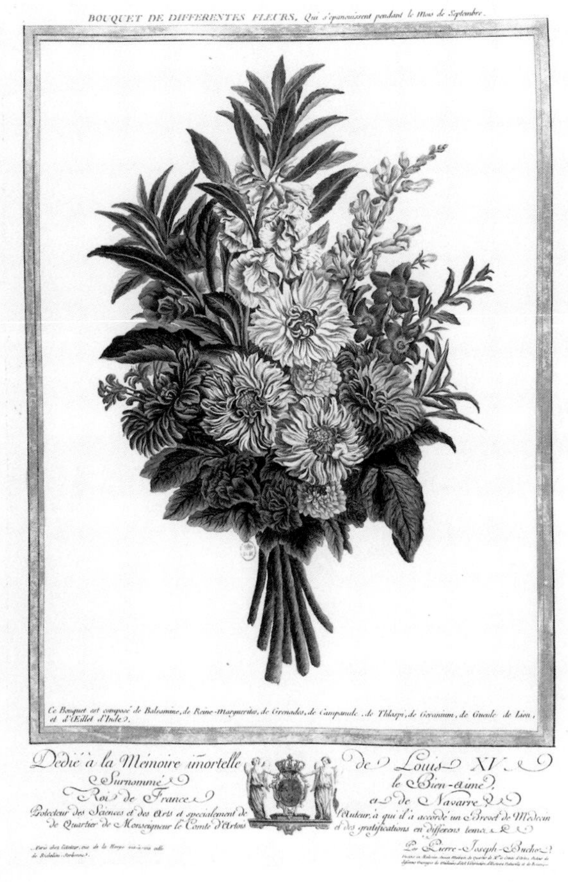

Fig. 16. Pierre-Joseph Buchoz, *Bouquet of Different Flowers That Bloom during the Month of September*, c. 1765–1770. Color engraving. Bibliothèque nationale de France.

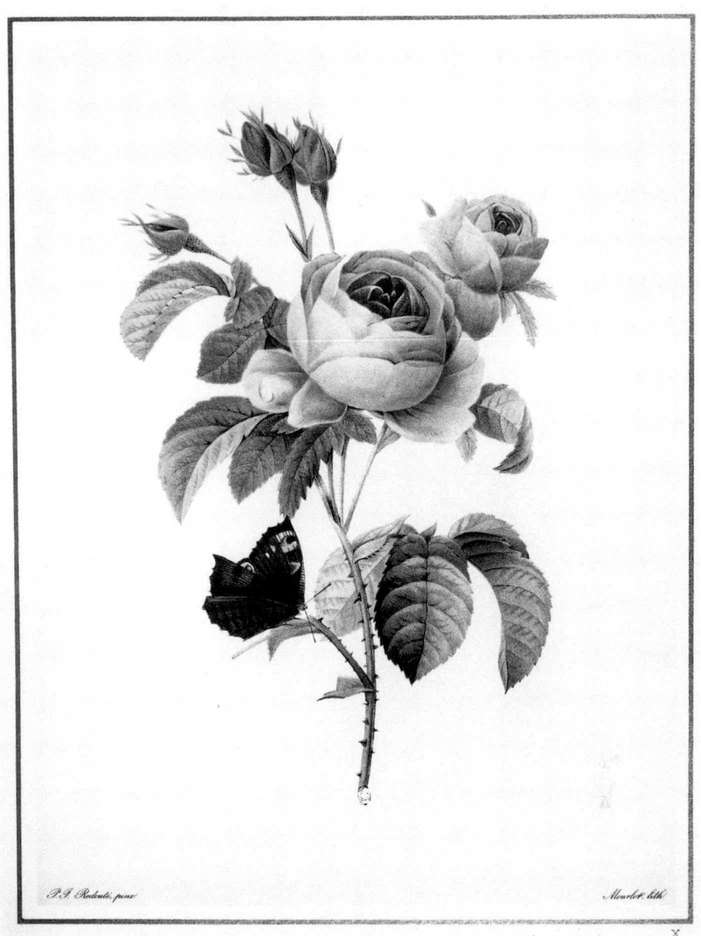

Fig. 17. Fernand Mourlot after Pierre-Joseph Redouté, *The Redouté Rose*, 20th-century lithograph after an 1820 engraving. Bibliothèque nationale de France.

garden of academicians was at the end of the century of Enlightenment a cherished solitary retreat."[100] Contemporaries said much the same thing. For example, one wrote of Prévost's work that "henceforth [it] will be for society an estimable monument, in which fortune will find a resource against boredom and laziness. . . . In the country, it will occasion recreation and discussion among sensitive beings who love to study nature when they delight in its spectacle."[101]

It is in this context that we should examine the ten plates engraved about 1810 by Allais after drawings by Anne Vallayer-Coster. The set in the Bibliothèque nationale is dated in pencil 12 January 1811,[102] doubtless the date of its deposit at the Bibliothèque impériale. It consists of four large prints of roses numbered 1–4 and six smaller ones numbered 1–vi, all of them bearing the indication "Dessiné par Mme Vallayer-Coster—Gravé par L. J. Allais" (Drawn by Mme Vallayer-Coster—Engraved by L. J. Allais). The fourth plate of roses is captioned "Rosa Gallica"; the captions on the others

are the Latin names of the flowers represented, as in botanical prints (pls. 71–80).[103]

Of the four plates of roses, the only model presently known to us is the one for the third (pl. 71), a delicate watercolor in shades of white, engraved by Allais in the same direction as the watercolor, which shows royal white roses (pl. 57). The disposition on the sheet of this double study of roses brings to mind the watercolors made by Redouté for Josephine in the gardens of Malmaison, although the Vallayer-Coster study is more precise, clearly having been made in view of its being engraved. Furthermore, the drawings by Redouté intended for his *Roses*, published between 1817 and 1824, have this same character of botanical accuracy (fig. 17). We encounter it again in a plate of *Roses doubles* engraved by Avril after Tessier (fig. 11), where the four studies of these roses bring to mind the plates by Vallayer-Coster. The same holds for the *Rose unique* and the *Rose à cent feuilles* engraved early in the nineteenth century by Antoine Chazal (1793–1854), a student of Van Spaendonck, for his *Flore pittoresque dédiée aux Dames* (Picturesque flora dedicated to the ladies), a kind of treatise on floral watercolor painting. Of the "hundred-petal rose," the author writes, "this flower is the most difficult of all to imitate. . . . It is usually placed in the center foreground of a composition. No other flower has so exercised the brushes of artists; it can be seen in almost all flower paintings" (fig. 18).[104]

In this context, it is not surprising that Anne Vallayer-Coster, at a moment in her career when she was less occupied, and in which, despite having lost none of her sureness of touch (she was producing mostly miniatures and watercolor drawings), should have wanted to orient her work toward the fashion for engravings of flowers. The catalogue of the 1824 Coster sale mentions fourteen "original drawings engraved by Allais" (whereas we know of only ten), and furthermore states that only a small number of impressions were pulled from the ten copperplates. Perhaps the artist envisaged their publication in several different sets. One can easily imagine that

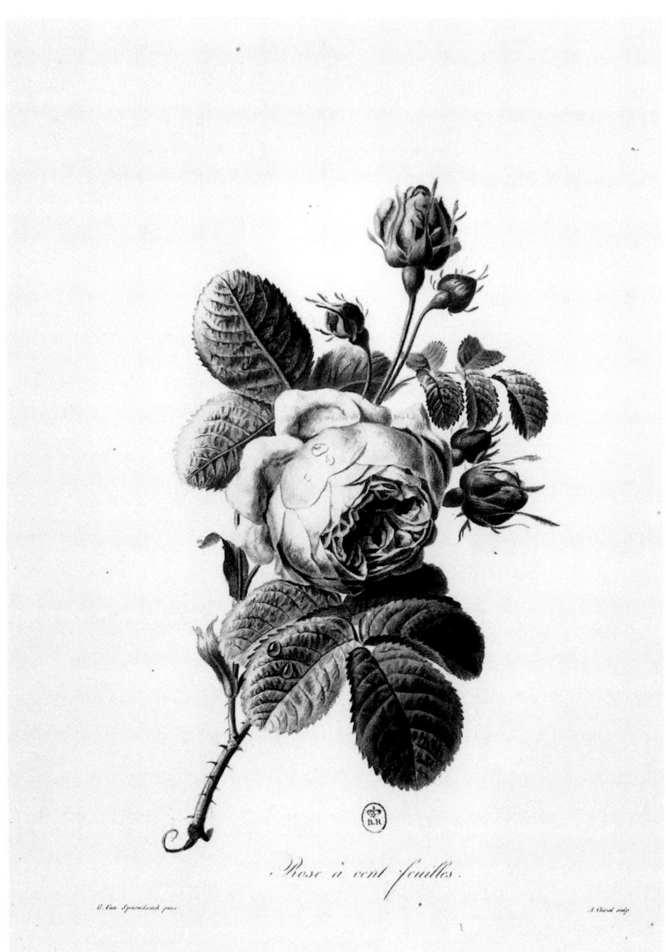

Fig. 18. Antoine Chazal after Gérard van Spaendonck, *Rose à cent feuilles* from the *Flore pittoresque*, 1818. Lithograph. Bibliothèque nationale de France.

certain very finished watercolors, for example a bouquet dated 1812,[105] were meant to be engraved, but that no engraver or publisher was willing to risk introducing still more sets of flowers into an already saturated market. There is also reason to ask why Vallayer-Coster settled on Allais, who specialized in portraits and allegories of the revolutionary and imperial years, for no other botanical engravings by him are known. The same holds for his wife, Angélique Briceau. As it happens, these two engravers had a daughter, Jenny-Augustine, born in 1796, who studied with her mother, with Van Spaendonck, and, in all likelihood, with the aging Vallayer-Coster, for she signed copies of still lifes by the latter artist "Reys-Allais" (the composite name she used after her marriage to one Monsieur Reys). Thus we can easily imagine that Allais and our painter were on friendly terms, which would explain her choice of this engraver.

Flower Painters and the Manufactories

In addition to delighting a public interested in such things, these print sets had a practical aim, sometimes made explicit in their titles. They served as *principes* (examples or models) and *leçons* (lessons) for use by amateurs of the female sex, but intended primarily, like all sets of ornamental prints from the first half of the eighteenth century, for painters, designers, embroiderers, fan makers, and, finally, the craft manufactories. The *Collection de fleurs et de fruits* (Collection of flowers and fruit) by Jean-Louis Prévost is preceded by an "introduction on the use of this collection in the arts and the manufactories, followed by an historical overview of the art of embroidery," in which we read further that the collection "will offer riches to the amiable sex to embellish those moments of the day that it will devote to drawing and to embroidery; *and precious models for the manufactories of porcelain, hangings, and textiles used for furnishings and clothing.*"[106] Here again there is a wealth of examples; I will simply mention the Lyonnais flower painters who devised models for the silk factories, the most prestigious of them doubtless being Antoine Berjon (1754–1843), whose indebtedness to Anne Vallayer-Coster is discussed elsewhere in the present volume by Eik Kahng.

Tamara Préaud has elucidated the origins of the painted floral designs on Vincennes and Sèvres porcelain, notably the use of engraved models.[107] The first botanical flowers were taken from seventeenth-century

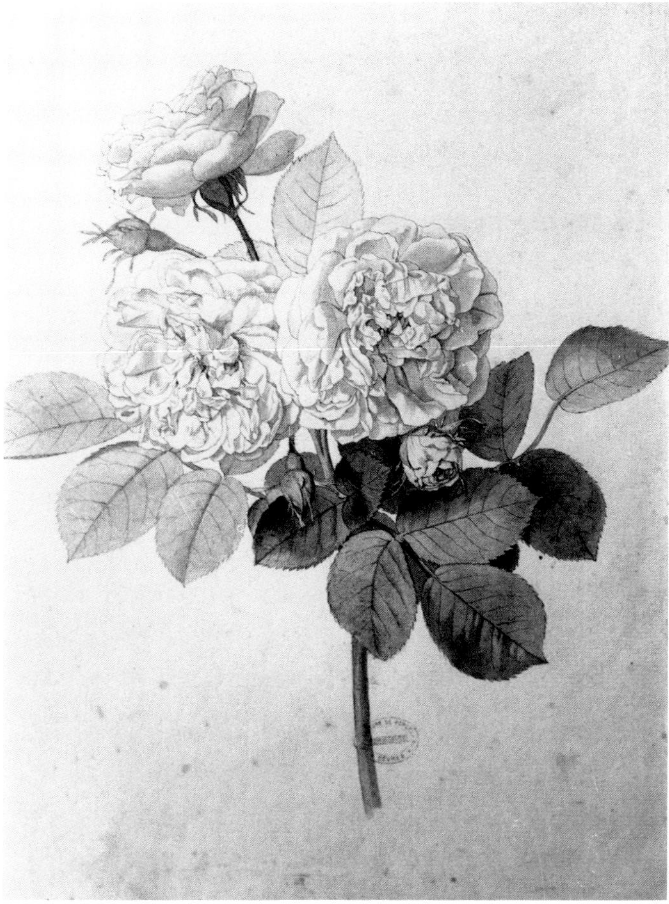

Fig. 19. Nicolas-Pierre Pithou, *Study of a Rose*, c. 1769–1795. Watercolor. Archives of the Manufacture de Sèvres.

prints (Monnoyer, Vauquer, Jacques Bailly [1700–1768], Nicolas Robert). The arrival at Sèvres in 1751 of Bachelier as *artiste en chef* responsible for all decoration there was a new beginning, for this painter provided models and trained the workers to copy them. He himself exhibited at the Salon of 1753 a bouquet painted on a porcelain plaque that was greatly admired. Thereafter, the manufactory's painters provided models, either of their own invention or inspired by those of Bachelier. A case in point is Philippe Parpette (1738–after 1793), who worked at Sèvres as a flower painter in 1755, 1757, and again in 1773, after a stint at the Chantilly porcelain factory.[108] The Sèvres manufactory also retains in its archives watercolors by Nicolas-Pierre Pithou (1750–1818), a painter there from 1760 to 1767, and again from 1769 to 1795, whose studies of roses bring to mind, although on a lower level of quality, those of Anne Vallayer-Coster (fig. 19).[109] In 1795 Corneille van Spaendonck (1756–1840), Gérard's talented brother, was named *artiste en chef-adjoint* responsible for decoration at Sèvres; his bouquets became favored models, and under his tenure references proliferated to "flowers after nature" and

"portraits of flowers." One painter at the manufactory, Jacques-François Micaud (1757–1810), executed in 1800 some gouaches of "natural flowers in the Jardin des Plantes," doubtless after the drawings on vellum. Furthermore, Van Spaendonck offered his own paintings as models for plaques and large vases. His best disciple, and friend, Jan Frans van Daël (1764–1840), did likewise for the Parisian factory of Dihl and Guerhard. There is from his hand a beautiful bouquet of roses, hortensia, irises, and auricula (fig. 20) that is signed and dated "Vandael an 8" (Vandael year 8). This canvas was translated into porcelain in identical dimensions, and with only slight changes of detail; this time it is signed "Coste d'après Van Daël / maf^e de Dihl" (Coste after Van Daël / Dihl manufactory; fig. 21).

The example of Van Daël is illuminating insofar as this artist, who was twenty years younger than Anne Vallayer-Coster, was influenced by her floral compositions at least as much as by those of Van Spaendonck. He produced variations on the latter's large vases overflowing with flowers in the tradition of Van Huysum.[110] The works by Vallayer-Coster that he imitated, however, were her compositions of modest glasses containing two or three roses, buds or blossoms, which he rendered with greater precision and less impasto.

Let us return to ceramics with floral decoration, found throughout Europe in this period, with two examples. The first corresponds to the apogee of Paul Hannong (1700–1760) in Strasbourg (from 1748), and to the creation of patterns based on prints by Bailly, Nicolas Robert, Georg Hoefnagel (1542–1600), and Maria Sibylla Merian (1647–1717), which made possible floral decoration of great verisimilitude, especially roses. About 1755 new designs were created after prints by Monnoyer and Vauquer. Under the direction of Joseph Hannong (dir. 1760–1782; 1738–c. 1800), the bouquets increasingly came to resemble models drawn and engraved in Paris.

The second example concerns the so-called botanical services, the most famous of which is doubtless the Flora Danica service,[111] roughly contemporary with the botanical service elaborated at Sèvres, and with the botanical dessert service, on which the plants are named, designed for Josephine between 1802 and 1805.

If models by Anne Vallayer-Coster do not seem to have been used at Sèvres, other manufactories did use them. Beginning in 1779 her still lifes with fruit were woven at the Savonnerie manufactory; the downy aspect

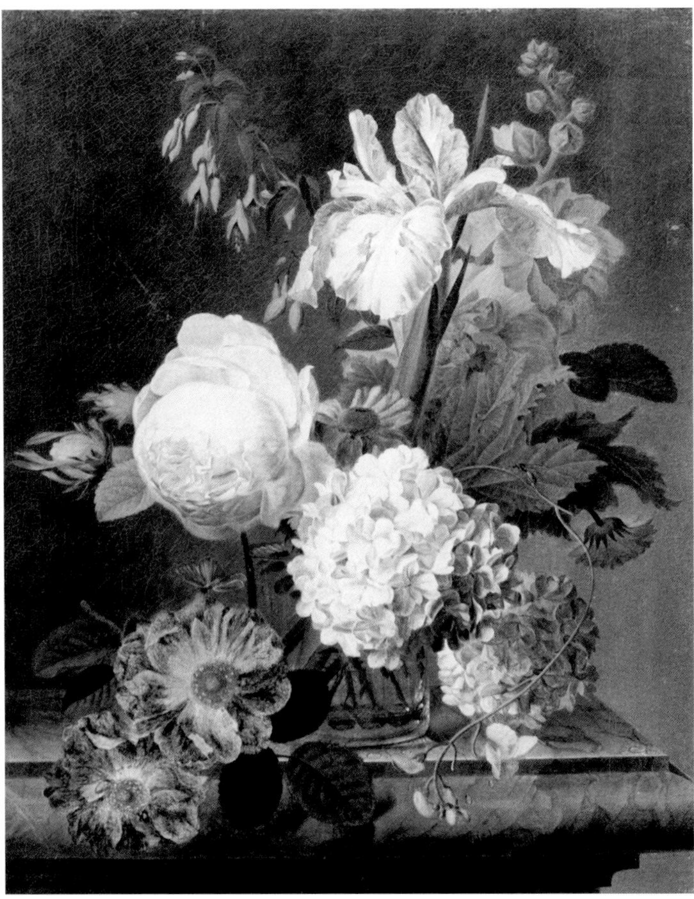 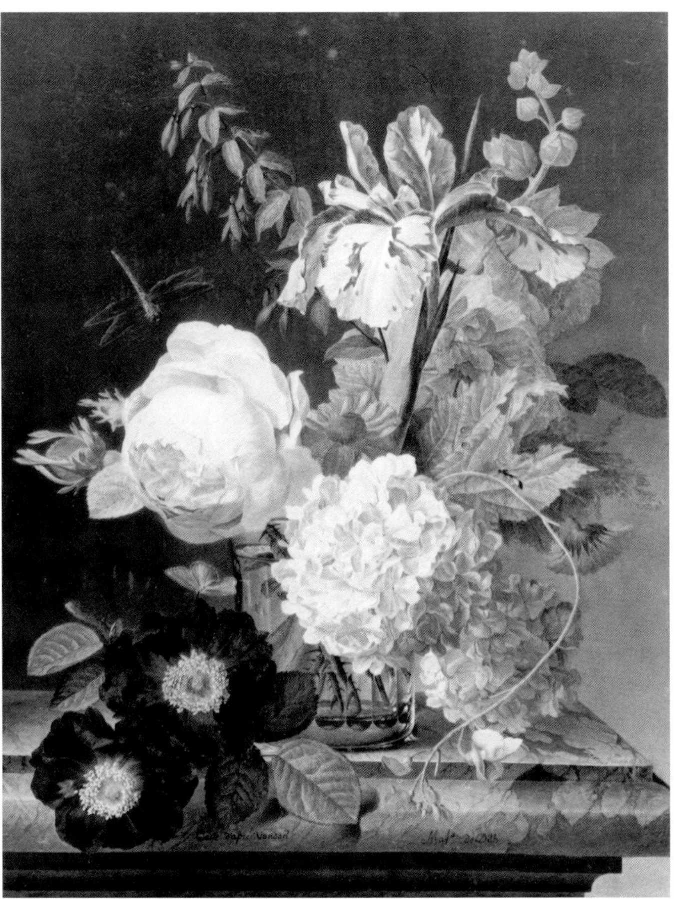

Fig. 20. Jan Frans van Daël, *Flowers in a Vase*, 1800. Oil on canvas. Private collection.

Fig. 21. L. Coste after Jan Frans van Daël, *Flowers in a Vase*, c. 1800. Painted on porcelain. Private collection.

of these little textile compositions is wonderfully apt for the velvet surfaces of peaches and almonds, which explains their success with informed collectors like the marquis de Marigny.[112] Her floral bouquets were woven in low warp by Deyrolle at the Gobelins beginning in 1781, and again early in the next century, and the weaver took pride in having rendered "the spiritual touch, tonal finesse, and nuanced color harmonies of the original."[113] Admittedly, Deyrolle's success was complete, and we can only admire his *Flowers in a Vase and Two Plums* and *Flowers in a Blue Vase with Dead Canary* (pls. 69, 70), seductive transpositions that are effectively new works. Finally, in 1809, two early works by Anne Vallayer-Coster were woven at the Savonnerie and presented to Empress Marie-Louise, then to the duchesse d'Angoulême,[114] which attests to the perenniality of the taste for refined, intelligently composed still lifes.

The translation of flower paintings into tapestries was not a privilege enjoyed solely by Vallayer-Coster: Michel-Bruno Bellengé drew models for carpets decorated with flowers and garlands for the Savonnerie, while Tessier and Jacques, flower painters at the Gobelins, participated between 1758 and 1763 in the design of the *Elements* tapestry suite under the supervision of François Boucher (1703–1770). Nonetheless, Vallayer-Coster was apparently the only artist to provide models for small tapestry "pictures" during the century's final two decades.

Even if these woven "pictures" could not translate the form and color of the originals, lacking the impasto characteristic of her paintings, or even of her masterpieces in miniature, they unequivocally evoke refined easel paintings. Carefully framed (several paintings by Anne Vallayer-Coster retain their original frames, bearing the stamp of Pépin, Leverd, or E.-L. Infroit, indications of the value ascribed to them), they were meant to be hung against either light wood paneling or delicate silk for the delectation of sophisticated viewers. The seeming simplicity of their compositions, and of their assembled objects, dissimulates the great care and skill that went into them. The choice of a vase, of its shape and color, of the flowers that it contains, of the objects placed nearby (fruit, shells, a bird's nest) was no more random than that of a piece of silver (hot chocolate pitcher, glass cooler) or ceramic (celadon vase, creamer, tureen, even an earthenware jug). Even the decision to opt for an oval or square format was carefully considered in view of the final effect.

We are seduced today by this gathering of exceptional works. The contemporaries of Anne Vallayer-Coster were as well, when they visited the successive Salons at which she exhibited her finest work, recognizing and admiring the quality of an oeuvre that far transcended the minor genre within which she was officially contained, something that was acknowledged by a critic writing that "she has, so to speak, treated them [flowers] like history painting."[115]

translated by John Goodman

I would like to express my warm gratitude to Joseph Baillio, Jean-François Baroni, Sylvain Boyer, Susanna Caviglia-Brunel, Eric Coatalem, Fabrice Faré, Guillaume Faroult, Alden R. Gordon, Florence Grassignoux, Bodo Hofstetter, Laurent Hugues, Isabelle Julia, Gisèle Lambert, Mélanie Leboucher, Gérard Mabille, Stéfanie Maison, Christian Michel, Olivier Michel, Roland Michel, Emmanuel Moatti, Stéphane Pinta, Alain Pougetoux, Tamara Préaud, Pierre Provoyeur, François Pupil, Marie-Catherine Sahut, Xavier Salmon, Guilhem Scherf, David Scrase, Eric Turquin, Leslie Ureña, Udo Van de Sandt, and Andrea Zanella, who were generous with their assistance, as well as to the many collectors who generously welcomed me into their homes and allowed me to see again or discover various works by Anne Vallayer-Coster.

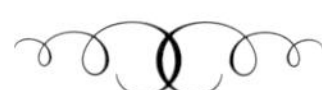

NOTES

1. "La perfection de l'art met tout genre au dessus de la distinction des rangs." *Mercure de France*, October 1765, 193.

2. "Je n'ignore pas que les modèles de Chardin, les natures inanimées qu'il imite ne changent ni de place, ni de couleur, ni de formes; et qu'à perfection égale, un portrait de La Tour a plus de mérite qu'un morceau de genre de Chardin. . . . On parlera de La Tour, mais on verra Chardin." Goodman 1995, 2:96 (translation altered) (original in Versini 1994–1997, vol. 4, *Esthétique—Théâtre*, 593).

3. "[Mlle Vallayer expose onze morceaux] qui, la plupart, ont le mérite de peindre une nature muette, mais sensible, aux spectateurs les plus grossiers. . . . Sa représentation des *Instruments de musique militaire* est d'un faire plus grand, et ne serait point indigne d'un peintre d'histoire." *Mémoires secrets*, vol. 13 (1780), 100 ("Lettre sur le Salon de 1771").

4. See Grandjean 1981, cat. 95. A snuffbox from 1747 with inset decoration against a white tortoiseshell ground is signed *Vallayer aux Gobelins*.

5. In 1773 Anne Vallayer painted a portrait of her sister Elisabeth, which she exhibited at the Salon of this year as "Portrait of Mme B . . ." Until recently this work was in the possession of the artist's descendants, but its present whereabouts are unknown.

6. Bibliothèque nationale de France, Cabinet des Estampes (hereafter BNF, Cab. des Est.), Ef 18a réserve, Choffard. See Michel 1987, cat. 214.

7. Cf. Nocq 1926–1931, 4:79.

8. In 1970 I thought that this was Anne (see Roland Michel 1970, 17–18).

9. A fanciful, error-strewn article in *Harper's New Monthly Magazine* (42, no. 251 [April 1871]: 719–724) maintains that Anne Vallayer also studied with Joseph-Marie Vien, who supported her with his friendship and advice throughout her career.

10. "Peintre en miniature et à la gouache pour les fleurs, les papillons et les oiseaux." Montaiglon 1875–1892, 30 July 1757.

11. "Nécrologe des artistes et des curieux," xxxii.

12. Formerly in the Peñard y Fernandez collection; sold Paris, Galliera, 7 December 1960, lot 26.

13. See Paris 1964. See also Aulanier 1958, 76.

14. BNF, Cab. des Est., Jd 33, réserve, *Fleurs peintes par Mle Basseporte*.

15. Roland Michel 1970, 16.

16. Coster sale 1824, lots 48, 52–56.

17. Paris, Galerie Jean-François Baroni.

18. He advised Elisabeth-Louise Vigée-Le Brun to "do as much as you can after nature . . . the first of all teachers." Quoted in London 1976, [11].

19. That Vernet did not regard the direct study of landscape, and more generally of nature, as the artist's only pedagogic resource is confirmed by a letter to Jean-Baptiste Descamps (1715–1791) in 1784, where he notes that "Mdle Harisson travaille d'après Madᵉ Vallayer-Coster, je lui procureray quelques Chardin pour que après cela elle puisse mieux travailler d'après nature" (Mademoiselle Harrison is working after Madame Vallayer-Coster; I will obtain some Chardins for her to help her work better after nature). Quoted in Lagrange 1864, 457. The notion that nature is the best of all teachers was a veritable topos and was endorsed by many artists of the day.

20. Avignon, Musée Calvet, inv. no. 376.

21. M. and F. Faré 1976, 268. The Musée Calvet in Avignon owns a small canvas representing some flowers tied with gold ribbon, probably part of a decor in which several such paintings were set into paneling. Antoine-François Vernet may have done work like this for the Bâtiments du roi.

22. Avignon, Musée Calvet, inv. no. 836-4.

23. Paris, Galerie Coatalem, as of 2000.

24. See the essay by Eik Kahng in the present volume.

25. Roland Michel 1970, nos. 218–219, 435–436.

26. Roland Michel 1970, no. 387.

27. Roland Michel 1970, no. 220.

28. Mabille 1984, no. 211.

29. Roland Michel 1970, nos. 217, 388–389. The pastels figured in a sale in Paris, Galerie Charpentier, 19 June 1934 (lots 4, 5; pl. 2), as works by Chardin, although it was stated on a label on the verso that they had been in the collection of the late M. and Mme Coster.

30. Roland Michel 1970, no. 281.

31. "De près, on ne sait ce que c'est, et à mesure qu'on s'éloigne, l'objet se crée et finit par être celui de la nature." Goodman 1995, 1:64 (translation altered) (original in Versini 1994–1997, vol. 4, *Salon de 1765*, 349).

32. In a letter to the marquis de Marigny and apparently dating from July 1770 (Paris, Archives nationales [hereafter AN], O^1 1925–10^B—the *cote* indicated to me by Alden Gordon, although I was unable to find it there), Charles-Nicolas Cochin supports the candidacy of Anne Vallayer and praises her work, saying that it makes a worthy contribution to the genre favored by Chardin.

33. "La demoiselle *Anne Vallayer*, Peintre, née à Paris, a présenté, pour être agréée, plusieurs tableaux peints à l'huile, représentant des instruments des sciences et des arts. L'Académie, après avoir pris les voix à l'ordinaire et reconnu sa capacité, a agréé sa présentation, et, s'étant trouvés, dans les tableaux qu'elle a présentés et qui lui appartenaient, deux tableaux, l'un d'un groupe des instruments de Musique, et l'autre ceux des Arts de Peinture et de Sculpture, dont la Compagnie a été particulièrement satisfaite, l'Académie les a acceptés pour sa réception. En conséquence, l'Académie a reçu et reçoit la Demoiselle *Vallayer* Académicienne pour avoir séance dans ses assemblées et jouir des privilèges, prérogatives et honneurs attribués à cette qualité, à charge d'observer les Statuts et Règlements de l'Académie, et elle a pris séance en cette qualité." Montaiglon 1875–1892, 8:48.

34. "Nullement conforme aux statuts." Quoted by McAllister Johnson in Tours 2000, 33.

35. Labille-Guiard's candidacy was sponsored by Roslin; as for Vigée-Le Brun, she was received at the insistence of Marie-Antoinette. See "Repertoire" in Tours 2000.

36. See esp. Los Angeles 1976, esp. 37–43; Caviglia 1997 (I would like to thank the author for having kindly given to me a copy of her typescript).

37. In the anonymous pamphlet *Plaintes de M. Badigeon, marchand de couleurs, sur les critiques du Sallon de 1771*, we read, with regard, precisely, to the works exhibited by Anne Vallayer, that "on doit savoir gré aux dames de s'adonner à ces sortes de genre; elles n'ont pas décemment la ressource de la nature nue, comme les hommes, pour lesquels le modèle vivant est toujours prêt à poser" (we should forgive the ladies for devoting themselves to such genres; they cannot decently refer to nude nature as can the men, who always have ready access to live models).

38. "Tu peins deux arts que tu chéris / Et la musique et la peinture / Bas-Relief, vase, fruits, légumes et lapin / Sous tes magiques doigts tout a son trait certain."

39. This trompe-l'oeil painting of a bas-relief of *Children Playing* (Roland Michel 1970, no. 240) measures roughly 19¾ × 27⅝ in. (50 × 70 cm), which makes it larger than most paintings of this kind.

40. "Ses coquilles, ses fruits, ses animaux sous verre."

41. "Il est certain que si tous les récipiendaires se présentaient comme Mademoiselle Vallayer et s'y soutenaient avec autant d'égalité, le Sallon serait autrement meublé." Seznec and Adhémar 1957–1967, 4:202.

42. See Cailleux 1969b.

43. "Ce morceau imité d'un plâtre moulé est d'une vérité frappante; la touche savante et juste produit admirablement l'effet et l'illusion de la sculpture."

44. "Cette Demoiselle qui réunit dans sa personne toutes les grâces de son sexe." Soubeyran and Vilain 1975, 101.

45. "Ah! J'admire son caractère / Encore plus que ses talens. / Elle sait avec la décence / Allier l'aimable enjouement / La candeur avec la prudence / L'esprit avec le sentiment. / Dans l'art si commun de séduire, / Son coeur fut toujours étranger; / Elle plait comme elle respire / Sans effort et sans y songer." Collection Deloynes, vol. 10, no. 193, p. 119 (re: Salon of 1777).

46. Unfortunately, the few documented genre paintings by our artist, exhibited for the most part in 1777 and 1779, have disappeared; but note that Dupont de Nemours went so far as to compare them with genre scenes by Greuze. See Dupont de Nemours 1908, on the Salon of 1777.

47. It seems likely, at any rate, that this collector of contemporary painting owned works by Anne Vallayer-Coster, for otherwise it would be difficult to explain his having witnessed her marriage contract in 1781. Among the paintings known to have been owned by him are Fragonard's *The Bolt* and *The Adoration of the Shepherds* (both in the Musée du Louvre), both of which he commissioned from the artist. [See Paris 1988, cats. 234, 236—trans.]

48. Roland Michel 1970, nos. 140–141.

49. On this subject, see the essay by Colin B. Bailey in the present volume.

50. Estate inventory of François Dumont, 2 September 1831 (AN, Minutier Central, Et. XLVI, 842), 16: "Bouquet de roses par Mme Vallayer-Coster," assessed at 10 francs; "1 bouquet, aquarelle," assessed at 10 francs; "2 petits tableaux de nature morte."

51. Thierry 1787–1788. Notably, he mentions paintings by Mme Vallayer-Coster in the hôtel de Noailles (where there was a fine collection of contemporary painting), in the residences of M. de Courmont, of the widowed Mme Sorin, etc.

52. "Par égard à la recommandation de la Reine en faveur de Mlle Vallayer" (17 March 1779); "la Reine, qui honore

Mlle Vallayer d'une protection particulière, désire que le logement lui soit accordé sans distraction" (23 June 1779). Roland Michel 1970, 260–264. See also "État des logements employés pour le service du Roi dans le Louvre et ses Galleries et dans les maisons appartenant au Roi," 1790, AN, O¹ 1914 ff.; and Guiffrey 1873.

53. In 1780 Van Spaendonck was residing provisionally in lodgings allocated to Duplessis on Vien's departure for Rome. Van Spaendonck was still living in the Louvre in 1790, having been accorded, on the death of Joseph Vernet, one half of the latter's lodgings, the other half having been allocated to his son, Carle Vernet (1758–1836). This example gives some idea of how these lodgings were passed from artist to artist.

54. In Michaud's biographical dictionary (Michaud 1854–1865, 9:317–318), there are entries on three members of the Coster family from Nancy who might be older brothers or cousins of Jean-Pierre-Silvestre. Two of them, Jean-Louis and Sigisbert-Etienne, were priests. Both gave funeral orations on the death of Stanisław Leszczyńszki, and then on the death of his daughter Marie Leszczyńska; the second of them was a delegate to the Assemblée Nationale allied with the defenders of religion and the monarchy. Their brother, Joseph-François, a man of letters, worked in their father's banking firm and later, in 1770, became *secrétaire des États de Languedoc.* He was *secrétaire perpétuel* of the Académie de Nancy.

55. We recall that the miniaturists François Dumont and Jean-Baptiste Augustin (1759–1832) lived in Nancy. The first made at least two portraits of Anne Vallayer-Coster. As for the second, he married the artist's niece, the daughter of Elisabeth de Bouhébent, and produced "cameo" group portraits of members of his family. One of these belongs to the Saint Louis Art Museum (Rosenberg 1972, no. 3); another is in the Musée du Louvre (Jean-Richard 1994, no. 27). A portrait of a woman executed in black and white crayon, recently sold in London (Christie's, South Kensington, 9 July 2001, lot 138), also came from the Bouhébent collection. Comparison of this work with the painting exhibited at the Salon of 1773 (Roland Michel 1970, no. 309, illus.) suggests that it might well be a likeness of the sister of Anne Vallayer-Coster.

56. Roland Michel 1970, 264–267.

57. "Dans l'art de peindre." Also included are two outstanding payments: 6,000 livres due for the portrait of Mme Sophie; and 2,400 livres due for portraits of the marquis and marquise de Créqui.

58. "La reine me dit qu'elle avait un dépôt bien précieux à me confier et qu'il fallait que je trouvasse des gens honnêtes, d'une existence indépendante et entièrement dévoués à leurs souverains, auxquels je confierais un portefeuille qu'elle me remettait. J'eus l'idée de choisir Mme Vallayer Coster, peintre de l'Académie, logée aux galeries du Louvre, et à laquelle je trouvai, ainsi qu'à son mari, toutes les qualités que la reine exigeait dans les personnes qui se chargeraient de ce dépôt. Ils furent aussi fidèles que je l'avais annoncé. Ce ne fut qu'en

septembre 1791, aprés l'acceptation de la constitution, qu'ils remirent ce portefeuille." Campan 1988, 342.

59. "Extrait du rapport des citoyens Naigeon et Bréa sur les objets d'art [dont] l'on peut disposer pour être donnés à la citoyenne Vallayer Coster en indemnité de 2,400 francs pour un tableau de sa composition . . . compris parmi les objets donnés en payement par le Gouvernement pour des subsistances." 5ᵉ division, bureau des Beaux-Arts et des Fêtes nationales: AN, F¹⁷ 1192ᴮ, dr. 45 and dr. 52. Letter from the Minister of the Interior to the Conseil de Conservation, signed by François de Neufchâteau.

60. Denon 1999.

61. The works in question are *La Chasse au lion (Lion Hunt)* and *La Chasse à l'ours (Bear Hunt).* For citation, see note 62.

62. "Un tableau représentant une poule, un coq, par madame Valayer-Coster [*sic*]." Denon 1999, 1:154, letter 327. We may note that Ladey was a painter of flowers and fruits who worked in the Gobelins.

63. Denon 1999, 1:165, letter 358.

64. "Qui occupe une arcade des galeries près de chez moi, le logement vacant aux Quatre-Nations par la mort de M. Julien, statuaire"; "une indemnité proportionnée aux frais que pourrait coûter son déménagement." Denon 1999, 1:165, letter 550, dated 3 nivôse an XIII (24 December 1804). See also AN, F¹⁷ 1095, dossier 14, "projet de concéder à Mme Vallayer-Coster un logement au Collège des 4 Nations."

65. *Notice des tableaux de fleurs peints par Mme Vallayer Coster, Ancien membre de l'Académie royale de Peinture.* The extended title continues: "Tableaux anciens, Estampes, Groupes en marbre, Bas reliefs en terre cuite, Vases en porcelaine de Chine et de Sèvres, Meubles de boule, Coffrets en laque, Tabatières précieuses, Plaques en émail, Bagues en pierres gravées et differens Objets de curiosité, provenant du Cabinet de feu M. et Mad. Coster—par Ch. Paillet. La vente aura lieu en la maison des défunts, boulevard du Temple, no. 47, le lundi 21 juin et jours suivans" (Old paintings, prints, marble groups, terracotta bas-reliefs, vases of Chinese and Sèvres porcelain, Boulle furniture, lacquer boxes, precious snuffboxes, enamel plaques, rings with engraved stones, and various objects of curiosity, from the collection of the late M. and Mme Coster—by Ch. Paillet. The sale will take place in the house of the deceased, boulevard du Temple, no. 47, on Monday, 21 June and the following days).

66. Coster sale 1824. "Un tableau représentant des fleurs groupées dans un vase, et d'une dimension très capitale, des médaillons peints au fixé, des tableaux de genre et des bas-reliefs, dont l'illusion n'est pas encore dissipée quand on les voit de près."

67. Coster sale 1824, lot 48: "un paysage de bord de mer, daté de 1775, offert à cette date par Vernet à la jeune académicienne" (A seaside landscape dated 1775, given that year by Vernet to the young académicienne).

68. Coster sale 1824, "cadeau fait par la reine à la mère de madame Coster."

69. Bibliothèque du musée du Louvre, Ms 33, Registre des paiements des Bâtiments du roi, 1762–1785, pp. 327 and 331. Nicolas-Henri Jardin (1720–1799) and Barthélemy-Michel Hazon (1722–1822), both architects, were functionaries in the Bâtiments du roi, the latter *intendant des Bâtiments du roi*.

70. This miniature might be the one that Marie-Antoinette gave to Louise von Hesse-Darmstadt after 1780 (see note 72).

71. AN, O^1 1211, fol. 146, 21 July 1780 (Roland Michel 1970, no. 329). The artist here informs d'Angiviller that she has been in communication with the princesse de Chimay, *dame d'atours* to the queen, regarding this subject. In a second letter, dated 31 July, she says that the portrait is almost finished. She was probably able to complete it so quickly because it was a pastel.

72. Letters dated 12 August 1780 (in which she writes that the portrait was almost finished but that she had judged it unworthy of being sent) and 28 September 1781, figuring in the manuscript text by Vuaflart and Bourin on the iconography of Marie-Antoinette (Bibliothèque d'Art et d'Archéologie Jacques Doucet, Paris, Bibliothèque nationale de France, Ms 380, Vuaflart and Bourin papers, vol. 4, *L'apogée*, 1779–1786). These authors assume that a first portrait, given to Charlotte, was a miniature, and that a second, sent to Louise, was the one by Anne Vallayer. They also refer to an article by M. A. Leesenberg-Hartotte, published in 1894 in the *Bulletin du Bibliophile*, that mentions, as then being in the grand-ducal collection of the castle of Darmstadt (Louise), two oil portraits of Marie-Antoinette as well as a miniature, and in the collection of Neu Strelitz (Charlotte), a pastel and a canvas. In the absence of further information, we might ask whether the pastel is not the one exhibited here as pl. 63, and the miniature has a copy now in the Walters Art Museum in Baltimore. Assuming this is correct, it must now be determined when these works left Germany.

73. "[Elle] les a faites pour Sa Majesté l'Impératrice": Denon 1999, 1:195, letter 1450, dated 27 fructidor an XII (14 September 1804), to M. Charvel, "concierge du palais de Saint-Cloud."

74. Alain Pougetoux, who is preparing a study of Josephine's collections based on an inventory of them, not only made it possible for me to locate one of these works (bearing the unusual signature: *Mme Coster-Vallayer: an XII*), but he also communicated to me their histories and a bibliography of related publications.

75. At the same Salon, she also exhibited a fire screen that figured in the Coster sale of 1824.

76. Chaudonneret 1999, 110 ff.

77. Coster sale 1824: "Elle soutint constamment dans le genre qu'elle avait adopté, celui des fleurs, la haute réputation qu'elle s'était acquise et qu'elle disputait aux professeur les plus renommés"; "si belles, si parfaites et si vraies."

78. "Tableaux dans le genre des fleurs, de fruits, de bas-reliefs, d'animaux." *Mercure de France*, September 1770.

79. The works in question are undated gouaches, preserved in BNF, Cab. des Est., Dc 28. The dynamic of influence between these two artists was probably reciprocal.

80. "Cette fille admirable a une vérité, un savoir unique; & toutes les productions de la nature semblant éclore sous son pinceau." *Mémoires secrets*, vol. 13 (1780), 153 (re: Salon of 1773).

81. "Elle est de plus incomparablement la première pour les choses inanimées, les raisins, les pêches, les prunes." Dupont de Nemours 1908, 27.

82. In auctions in eighteenth-century Paris, paintings by Jan van Huysum often attained prices higher than those of history paintings. Antoine-Nicolas Dézallier d'Argenville, in a rather long entry on him in his *Abrégé de la vie des plus fameux peintres* (Dézallier d'Argenville 1762, 3:228–233), compares him to such great still-life painters as Andrea Belvedere (1642–1732), Samuel Seghers (1590–1661), de Heem, and Jean-Baptiste Monnoyer, noting that "par la supériorité de sa touche, la délicatesse de son pinceau, ses détails étonnants, son précieux fini, & par un je ne sçais quoi de difficile à exprimer, [il] a deviné toutes les ressources de la nature" (228; with his superior touch, his delicate brush, his astonishing detail, his precious finish, and I know not what qualities that elude description, [he] has figured out all of nature's resources).

83. "Sans contredit le Van Huysum de notre siècle." *Mercure de France*, 24 October 1789.

84. See Salvi 2000, esp. the chapter devoted to Antoine Monnoyer. On the use of seventeenth-century models, see my discussion below of sets of engraved prints and how these were used by porcelain factories.

85. According to the author of the anonymous pamphlet *Lettres pittoresques à l'occasion des tableaux exposés au Sallon, en 1777*, the "manner" of Bellengé "est plus claire que celle de Mlle Vallayer" (is clearer than that of Mlle Vallayer).

86. "[Elle] soutient admirablement sa réputation, et même le voisinage de M. Van Spaendonck, le plus illustre des rivaux qu'elle ait à combattre dans le genre [des fleurs et des fruits]." *Panard au Salon*, 1781, 13–14.

87. "[Elle a] des touches plus précieuses, l'autre des touches plus mâles." [Moufle d'Angerville?], "Deuxième Lettre sur le Salon de 1779," *Mémoires secrets*, vol. 13, London, 1780, 259–260.

88. A distinction proposed by Gault de Saint-Germain in the preface to *Collection de fleurs et de fruits peints d'après nature par Jean Louis Prévost*, 1805.

89. Roland Michel 1993, 353–371.

90. Scherf 1991, 47–59.

91. In his print series *Mes petits bouquets* (dedicated to the duchesse de Chevreuse) and *Les Fleurettes*.

92. According to Salvi 2000, the artist in question is Antoine Monnoyer, son of Jean-Baptiste, sometimes called Baptiste le jeune (Baptiste the younger).

93. BNF, Cab. des Est., Ee 6 fol.

94. BNF, Cab. des Est., Ef 83 fol. See BNF, Cab. des Est., *Inventaire du Fonds français, graveurs du XVIIIe siècle*, vol. 1 (1931), entry "Avril," nos. 19–24.

95. Salvi 1999. The author cites manuscript notes by Redouté published by Léger 1945.

96. At this date, the artist in question would seem to be Gilles-Antoine Demarteau (1750–1802), nephew of and collaborator with the famous engraver who specialized in *manière de crayon* engravings, for the latter died in 1776. On the other hand, prudence may be in order here, for there is no mention of Redouté's having collaborated with Gilles-Antoine in the above-cited entries devoted to him in the *Inventaire du Fonds français*, vol. 6 (1946).

97. *Inventaire du Fonds français après 1800*, vol. 13 (1965).

98. 5 vols. (Nancy, 1761–1767). This publication contains roughly a hundred prints, some of them engraved by Fessard, others, among the last ones (and of mediocre quality), by Mme Pinard, for the most part after Mlle François.

99. Madeleine Basseporte also produced the many drawings of plants "executed after nature" and engraved by Madeleine Hortemels (1686–1767) and Jean-Baptiste Guélard (act. 1733–1755) to serve as illustrations for *Le Spectacle de la nature* by the abbé Pluche, published in Paris between 1732 and 1752 (8 vols.).

100. Roche 1978, 1:130–131.

101. "Il sera désormais pour la société un monument estimable, dans lequel la fortune trouvera des ressources contre les ennuis de l'oisiveté. . . . A la campagne, il sera un objet de récréation et de conférence pour les êtres sensibles qui aiment à étudier la nature lorsqu'ils jouissent de son spectacle": Gault de Saint-Germain 1805 (as in n. 88).

102. BNF, Cab. des Est., Ef 150 fol., engravings by Louis-Jean Allais and Angélique Briceau, Allais's wife.

103. Pl. I: "No. 1. Zinnia Hybrida"; pl. II: "No. 1. Solanum Pyracantum," "No. 2. Cineraria Amelloides"; pl. III: "No. 1. Alyssum Incanum," "No. 2. Coronilla Emerus," "No. 3. Cerastium Fomentosum"; pl. IV: "No. 1. Convolvulus Purpureus"; pl. V: "No. 1. Senecio Elegans fl. Simplex," "No. 2. Senecio Elegans fl. Yslena"; pl. VI: "No. 1. Primula Auricula," "No. 2. Viola Grandiflora."

104. "Cette fleur est de toutes la plus difficile à imiter. . . . On la met ordinairement au milieu et en premier plan dans une composition. Jamais aucune fleur n'a exercé le pinceau des artistes comme celle-ci; on la remarque dans presque tous les tableaux de fleurs." Antoine Chazal, *Flore pittoresque dédiée aux Dames*. Chazal, who exhibited paintings of flowers, fruit, and animals at the Salon from 1822 to 1853, worked in watercolor

and in 1841 published a treatise entitled *Enseignement du dessin*; he was one of several "professeurs d'iconographie" at the Jardin des Plantes. Note that since the mid-eighteenth century and the introduction of Linnaeus's classification system, there had been many publications on the various species of roses, including the very successful one by Miss Lawrence (London, 1796) and Roessig (Leipzig, 1801).

105. Roland Michel 1970, repr. on 233.

106. "Introduction sur l'usage de cette collection dans les Arts et les Manufactures, suivi d'un précis historique sur l'art de la broderie"; "[ce recueil] offrira des richesses au sexe aimable pour embellir l'instant du jour qu'il consacrera au dessin et à la broderie; *et des modèles précieux pour les manufactures de porcelaine, de tentures et d'étoffes d'ameublement et de parure*" (my emphasis). Gault de Saint-Germain 1805 (as in n. 88).

107. Préaud 1990, 105–115. In addition, Tamara Préaud (to whom I would like to express my gratitude for her gracious and generous assistance) gave me the text of an unpublished article (undated) containing valuable information about the vegetal elements in painted decoration on Vincennes and Sèvres porcelain until the beginning of the nineteenth century.

108. Parpette also painted miniatures of flowers and signed an oval snuffbox dating from 1763–1764 decorated with a painting of bouquets lying on a stone table (see Grandjean 1981, no. 182).

109. Archives de la manufacture de Sèvres, inv. of 1814, nos. 224, 225.

110. There is a beautiful example, dated 1810, in the Musée du Louvre, Paris, inv. no. 1196.

111. Regarding these "botanical services," the earliest of which was produced at Meissen in 1745, followed by a Chelsea service in 1755, see the fine article by Baer 1999.

112. Roland Michel 1970, nos. 426–428.

113. Roland Michel 1970, nos. 429–433 (la touche spirituelle, la finesse du ton et ces accords de nuances de l'original).

114. Roland Michel 1970, nos. 435–436. As noted previously, Denon recalled from the Savonnerie the painting that is now in the museum in Le Mans. It seems likely that he was already thinking about having it woven.

115. The full quotation is "[Ses fleurs] sont si fraîches, si vives, si brillantes qu'on serait tenté de les prendre pour l'en couronner. Elle les a traitées pour ainsi dire historiquement" ([Her flowers] are so fresh, so vibrant, so brilliant that one is tempted to pick them and make them into a crown for her. She has, so to speak, treated them like history painting [that is, the most prestigious genre of painting]). *Lettres pittoresques* 1777, 56.

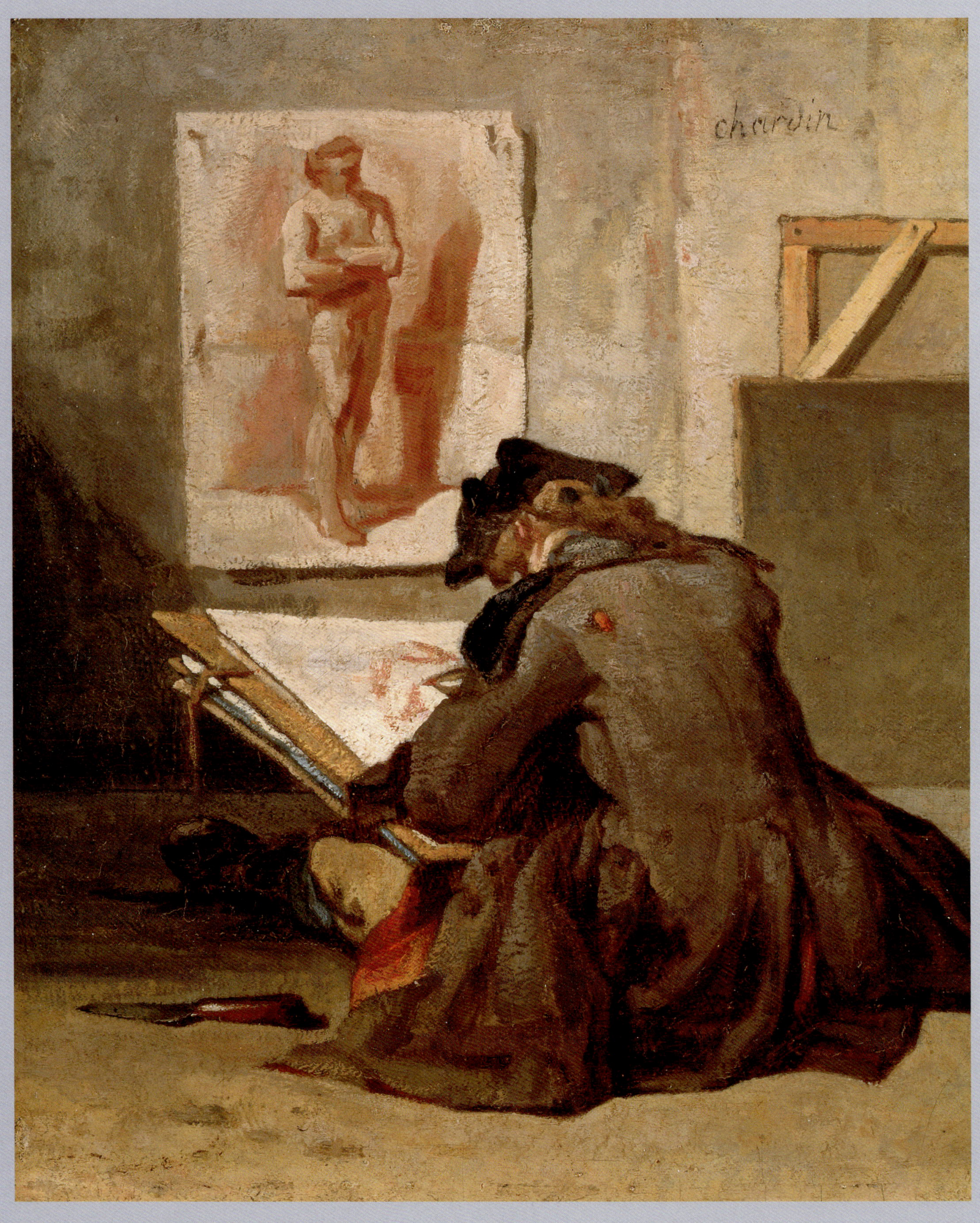

Jean-Siméon Chardin, *Young Student Drawing*, c. 1738
Oil on panel, 8¼ × 6¾ in. (21 × 17.1 cm). Kimbell Art Museum, Fort Worth, Texas (fig. 27).

— Eik Kahng —

Vallayer-Coster / Chardin

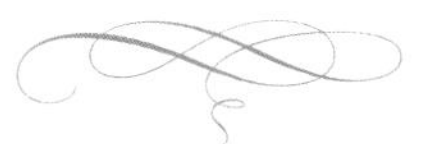

The Shadow of Chardin

Offering a critical perspective on Anne Vallayer-Coster poses the opposite problem to that embodied by the case of Jean-Siméon Chardin. Indeed, the case file on Chardin (its density, scope, and philosophical tenor) is daunting for any art historian attempting to add his or her thoughts to the brief.[1] Since Chardin's "rediscovery" in the middle of the nineteenth century, he, like Paul Cézanne, has attracted the attention of the best scholars.[2] The most silent of Chardin's unassuming kitchen still-life paintings has provoked an endless stream of critical interpretation. Ever since the Goncourt brothers' somewhat misleading, if impassioned, defense of Chardin as the humble painter of the bourgeoisie,[3] his still-life paintings and genre scenes have never ceased to enjoy a wide range of interpretive response. By contrast, very little has been written about the art of Vallayer-Coster. Aside from the work of Marianne Roland Michel, who published the only monograph on the artist in 1970 as well as a string of articles, no in-depth analysis of her art exists.[4] As one of the few women artists accepted into the prestigious Académie royale de peinture et de sculpture (the Académie), Vallayer-Coster is always cited in the art-historical literature on the period, yet the fact of her gender has tended to supersede any serious consideration of her oeuvre.[5] Indeed, this exhibition catalogue is the first publication since 1970 to offer an array of essays devoted to her art.

This is not, in some ways, simply a matter of the swings in attention that always define the changing story of the history of art. During his lifetime, Chardin's art was one of the cornerstones of Denis Diderot's Salon criticism,

and the *philosophe* had much to do with the habit of reading-in to Chardin's paintings. The difficulty we now associate with the art of Chardin, not only in its technical evolution but also in its interpretive complexity, has ensconced this painter's painter in the collective cultural memory as one of the greatest artists of the French tradition. Chardin's canonical status thus makes him necessary to a consideration of any other eighteenth-century still-life painter, including Vallayer-Coster.

But Chardin's critical shadow is not just an art-historical construction. If we try to imagine what it must have been like for a young painter with aspirations in the still-life genre during the 1760s, Chardin's example must have loomed very large indeed. When Anne Vallayer applied to the Académie in 1770, Chardin was internationally renowned as one of the most beloved painters of the French school. His appeal, long established through regular Salon exhibitions, extended to the elite of European royalty, as well as to his more general Parisian audience. A dedicated officer (most notably, treasurer and then, *tapissier,* responsible for the installation of the Salon, beginning in 1755) of the august Académie, Chardin was well liked and respected by his fellow academicians. He was recognized by critics, artists, and connoisseurs as the one who had reinvented French still-life painting, imbuing it with a depth of feeling that distinguished the lowly genre and elevated it above its seventeenth-century Dutch and Flemish precedents.

And so it must have been with more than a little trepidation that the young Vallayer, the daughter of a goldsmith and apparently with no academician sponsoring

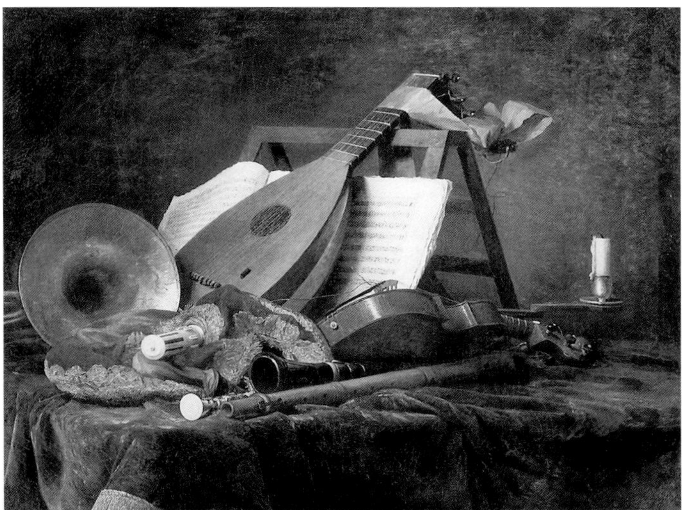

Fig. 1. Anne Vallayer-Coster, *The Attributes of Music*, 1770. Oil on canvas, 35⅝ × 45⅝ in. (88 × 116 cm). Musée du Louvre, Paris (cat. 12).

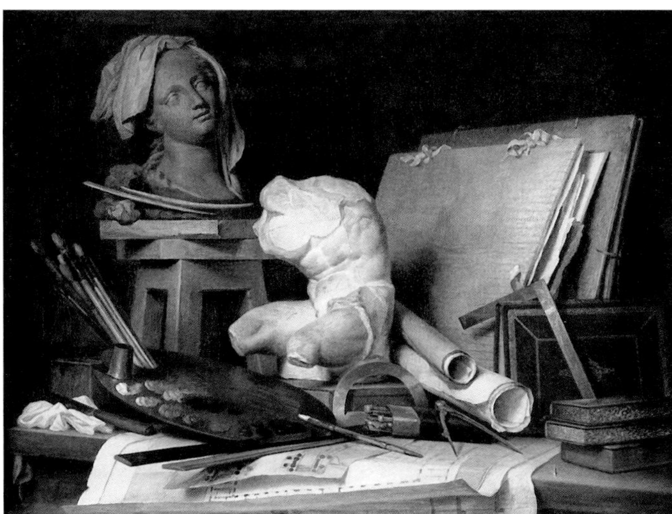

Fig. 2. Anne Vallayer-Coster, *The Attributes of Painting, Sculpture, and Architecture*, 1769. Oil on canvas, 35⅜ × 47⅝ in. (90 × 121 cm). Musée du Louvre, Paris (cat. 6).

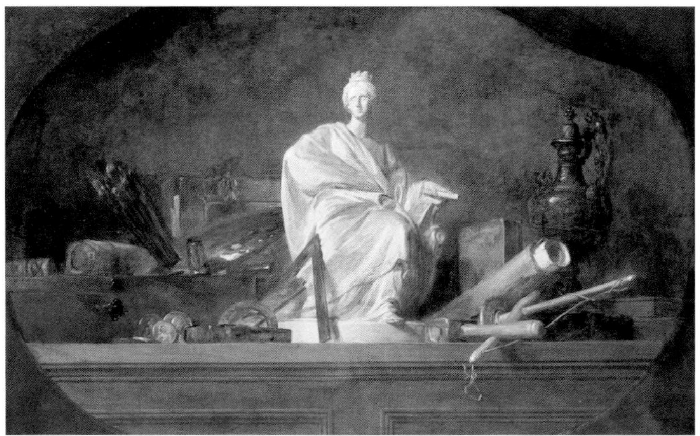

Fig. 3. Jean-Siméon Chardin, *The Attributes of the Arts*, 1765. Oil on canvas, 35⅞ × 57⅛ in. (91 × 145 cm). Musée du Louvre, Paris.

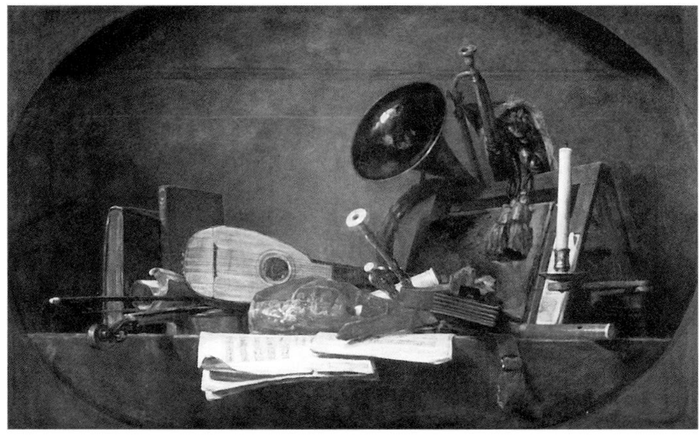

Fig. 4. Jean-Siméon Chardin, *The Attributes of Music*, 1765. Oil on canvas, 35⅞ × 57⅛ in. (91 × 145 cm). Musée du Louvre, Paris.

her application, exposed herself to the trial of being judged by that body of accomplished artists. Her submissions, as Marianne Roland Michel has recounted,[6] included a variety of still-life subjects, from smaller kitchen still-lifes and flower paintings to the more ambitious pendant pair of allegorical compositions that were ultimately accepted as her reception pieces (figs. 1, 2). The members of the Académie must have realized that Vallayer had chosen to treat precisely the same kind of grand allegorical themes for which Chardin had won so much praise just a few years before (figs. 3, 4). If anything, Vallayer seems to have been provoking the comparison with the great master. We can only wonder what Chardin must have thought of this young woman's audacity.

Unfortunately, we do not know any particulars of what must have been the lively discussion that took place behind the closed doors of the Académie on the day of Vallayer's evaluation. We do know, however, through Jean-Georges Wille (1715–1808), an artist who witnessed the consideration of her application on 28 July 1770, that the academicians were unanimous in their enthusiasm for the young woman's talents.[7] Aside from this brief mention and the smattering of critical praise in the press when her reception pieces were exhibited the following year,[8] all we have is the precious document confirming her *agrément* (acceptance) and reception to the institution, signed by those academicians attending, including Chardin.[9] Vallayer must have been especially elated, since the rules usually required the aggregated artist (*agréé*) to undergo another evaluation through reception pieces (*morceaux de réception*) submitted several months (or even years) after the initial acceptance. She thus joined an elite few, including the great Chardin, whose

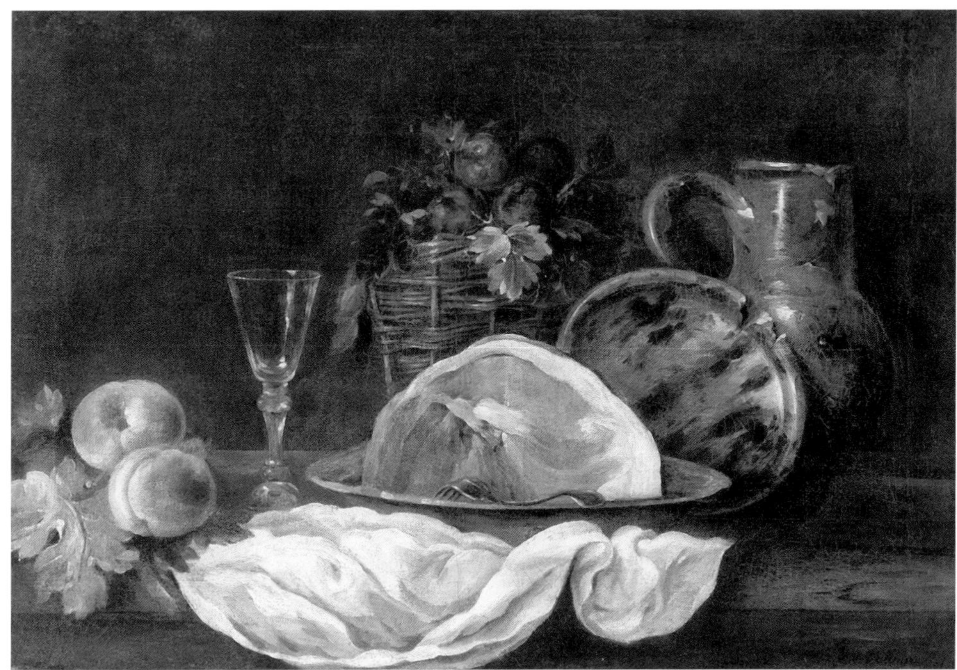

Fig. 5. Anne Vallayer-Coster, *Still Life with Ham*, 1763 or 1765. Oil on canvas, 21½ × 30⅜ in. (54.5 × 77 cm). Private collection, Basel (cat. 1).

talents were so undeniable that the academicians decided to bend the rules by formally granting her the rights and privileges of academic membership on the spot.

The achievement represented by Vallayer's triumphant reception into the Académie is, without exaggeration, astounding. Here was a young woman artist who seemed to come from nowhere. Like Chardin and Jean-Baptiste Greuze (1725–1805),[10] her sudden appearance on the scene fits the model of what Thomas Crow has called the "surprise invader."[11] Usually, an aspiring artist was apprenticed to one of the senior members of the Académie and relied on him to recommend his application. So far as we know, Vallayer had no such sponsor. If she was the student of the established landscape painter Joseph Vernet,[12] she does not seem to have needed his authorial endorsement to make her case, or at least, we have no record of Vernet's official involvement. Even more impressive is the level of sophistication of her art, which attracted the prince de Conti,[13] one of the most prestigious collectors of the second half of the century. He bought Vallayer's glorious rendition of shells and coral (cat. 11), which was executed in 1769, the same year as *The Attributes of Painting, Sculpture, and Architecture* (fig. 2). A comparison of these monumental compositions with the early kitchen still-life from 1763 or 1765 (fig. 5) shows her progress to have been phenomenal.

Here we begin to sense a major difference between the fast start of the precocious Vallayer and the comparatively slow development of the youthful Chardin. At least some of our penchant to feel the difficulty of

Chardin's art is directly tied to eighteenth-century hagiographic assertions about his early development. Chardin's lack of technical facility is made part and parcel of a notion of his art as inextricably bound with direct observation of the model. There are three famous anecdotes—two told by Cochin and one by Pierre-Jean Mariette—that have been continually recycled in the Chardin literature, at times somewhat uncritically, given their suspiciously apocryphal character. It is worth repeating them here, if only to introduce the larger question of the status of still-life painting in the second half of the eighteenth century.

The story, as told by Chardin's close friend and colleague Charles-Nicolas Cochin (1715–1790) in his obituary of the artist,[14] describes Chardin's inadequate early training under the little-known history painter Pierre-Jacques Cazes (1676–1754). Rather than work from the live model (a luxury, according to Cochin, Cazes could not afford), his students spent their time copying their master's drawings and paintings. It was only in the course of his own practical experience that Chardin began to realize the difficulty of capturing the truth of nature, a lesson he supposedly first learned when assigned the humble task of painting a musket. As Cochin tells it, Chardin was taken aback when the established painter Noël-Nicolas Coypel (1690–1734) carefully arranged an actual musket, lit as it would appear in the painting, and asked Chardin to paint it. Like most young painters in the early part of the century, Chardin had been taught that only artists lacking in genius should

need to rely on copying nature. It was something of an
epiphany, then, for the as yet unexceptional painter to
understand at last the difficulty of painting even the
simplest objects as they actually appear to the senses.
A second anecdote relates much the same information.
Chardin's first attempt to paint a rabbit made him sensitive to the necessity of seeing the object from a sufficient
distance, so as to grasp the masses of light and dark,
rather than become distracted by the details. Cochin
even assumes Chardin's voice in the course of his nar-
ration, having him proclaim, "In order to paint only the
truth, I must forget everything I have seen, and even the
way in which these subjects have been treated by others.
I must put myself at such a distance that I can no longer
see the details. I must apply myself above all to imitating
well and with the greatest truth the general masses, the
tonal color, the volume, and the effects of light and shade."

Of course, the great esteem in which Cochin held his
old friend meant that Chardin's eventually doctrinaire
reliance on direct observation is not held against him
too much. Instead, Chardin's deep study of nature is
championed as the antidote to the kind of mannered
affectations that marred the output of so many of his
contemporaries. In this, Cochin seems to be echoing
the sentiments of Diderot, who also mouthed the still-
life painter's words of wisdom as a means of grounding
his art criticism in studio practice. Indeed, from Cochin's
point of view, Chardin's dependence on the model is in
some ways the inevitable consequence of an insufficient
initiation in the tradition of academic history painting,
a fact that he insists Chardin himself recognized and
deeply regretted. Cochin is quick to point to Chardin's
late pastels as evidence of the master's unrealized potential as a history painter of great psychological penetra-
tion. It is also a fact that Chardin encouraged his only
son to pursue a career as a history painter, which Cochin
is also quick to underscore.

Hand in hand with this emphasis on Chardin's reliance on the model is his reputation as an incredibly slow
painter, agonizing over every stroke of paint. As Cochin
tells it, Chardin's fidelity to nature meant that he had
to return continually to the canvas, always searching
for the most nuanced effects in his representation of the
play of light and shadow. Chardin had none of the facility,
or in the comte de Caylus's (1692–1765) sense, *légèreté
de l'outil* (literally, the lightness of the tool),[15] that was
traditionally associated in the classed terminology of
the eighteenth-century Académie with inventive genius,

in which the handling of the brush was likened to the
graceful comportment of the courtier. Instead, Chardin's
canvases are worked and reworked, laborious accumula-
tions of distinct perceptions that result in the kind of
magical illusion that, to Cochin, was Chardin's alone.

If Cochin painted a portrait of Chardin as an artist
humbled by the true complexity of nature, whose art was
born of a dedication to the phenomenon of visual perception, Pierre-Jean Mariette (1694–1774)[16] was much less
sympathetic in his account of the artist's limitations:

> One must concede, the paintings of M. Chardin retain too
> much of a feeling of fatigue and pain. His touch is heavy
> and not at all varied. There is nothing easy in his brush-
> work, and he expresses everything in the same manner,
> and with a sort of indecision that makes his works too
> cold. Even his color is not truthful enough, although it
> is in general harmonious. Because his draftsmanship is
> forced and he is incapable of making his studies and prep-
> arations on paper, M. Chardin is obliged to have the model
> continually in sight, which he then sets out to imitate from
> the first stroke of the brush to the last; a thing that takes a
> very long time and would defeat anybody else but him.[17]

How different, then, is the case of Vallayer, whose precocious technical facility developed rapidly throughout
her twenties. If her identification with Marie-Antoinette
led to her critical neglect in the years following the Revolution, her apparent difference from Chardin in this
respect has done little to alleviate the assumption that
she was just another "victim," as Diderot liked to put it,
of the older master. We must remember that Chardin's
resurrection in the nineteenth century coincided with
the rise of realism in the arts. The eighteenth-century
master's legendary fidelity to nature was all too easily wed
to an avant-garde agenda that set the stage for Cézanne's
apples. In many art-historical accounts, Cézanne's
notion of the motif leads us effortlessly back to the story
of Chardin and his rabbit, as if the eighteenth-century
painter had anticipated his countryman's obsessiveness
in all but its crankiness. Compounding the confusion
between the aesthetic framework of Cézanne in the nineteenth century and that of Chardin in the eighteenth
is the shared vocabulary of difficulty both in critical
reception and technical execution that is habitually used
to characterize the two artistic personae. In this version
of the history of modern art, Vallayer's reported and
ostensible technical facility has no place, and her art
has therefore been trivialized as a shallow imitation of

Chardin's achievements. Whereas Chardin's still-life paintings are revered as precious records of the artist's struggle to capture the visual world *à la* Cézanne, Vallayer-Coster's art has been all too easily ignored as facile and decorative, the perfect visual backdrop to the essential frivolity of the age of Marie-Antoinette.

The nineteenth century's view of Chardin, however anachronistic, has inured us to the eighteenth-century sense of the anecdotes so affectionately related by Cochin and so bluntly pronounced by the less sympathetic Mariette. If one can speak of a nascent trend toward a protorealist agenda in the eighteenth century as exemplified by the working habits of a Chardin, this view must be tempered by the constancy of an academic tradition that was rooted in the positive ideal of emulation. Just as the aspiring history painter was encouraged actively to call on the rich repertoire of earlier masters, so too was the young still-life painter by necessity dependent on the examples of her predecessors for the development of her own, distinct style. Emulation, in the case of still-life painting, is perhaps even more obvious than it is with history painting. The extreme conventionalism of the subject matter in itself belies the literal understanding of still-life painting as the record of things seen. But why, then, would Cochin and Mariette insist on this aspect of Chardin's art?

The Status of Still-Life Painting in the Eighteenth Century, Truth to Nature, and the Crusade against "la Manière"

To answer this question, it is necessary to retrieve some of the larger institutional context in which both Mariette and Cochin were active participants. The story of the revival of history painting, culminating in the emergence of Jacques-Louis David (1748–1825) and his followers in the 1780s, has been thoroughly narrated in the literature.[18] In 1747 La Font de Saint-Yenne published his tirade against the excesses of the rococo, calling for a return to the *grand goût* (grand taste) of seventeenth-century history painting, as it was practiced at the time of Jean-Baptiste Colbert and Charles Le Brun (1619–1690) in the service of Louis XIV.[19] The establishment of regular Salon exhibitions allowed such unsanctioned critiques of the academicians' output to multiply, and La Font's rallying cry found widespread support. Over the next decade, the Académie responded to the growing perception of the French school's decline with an array

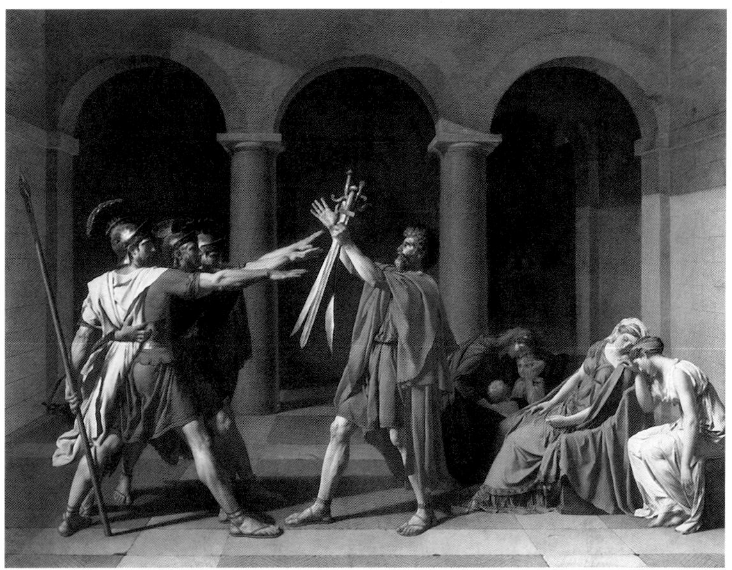

Fig. 6. Jacques-Louis David, *Oath of the Horatii*, 1784. Oil on canvas, 132 × 170 in. (330 × 425 cm). Musée du Louvre, Paris.

of reforms, meant to reignite the flames of French genius. The Ecole des élèves protégés was founded to instill in the most talented students the classical fluency now deemed necessary to achieve a return to the golden age of Nicolas Poussin (1594–1665). Formal lectures in anatomy, perspective, costume, and classical literature—areas that had been allowed to lapse—were resurrected. The French Academy in Rome, where winners of the Grand Prix were sent to immerse themselves in the great tradition, became more doctrinaire in its guidance of the best and brightest toward an art that would both please and instruct, in accordance with the noble aims of seventeenth-century history painting.

As Roland Michel has pointed out, it is instructive to remember that Vallayer's most prosperous period in the 1770s and 1780s coincided with a trend toward an increasingly austere classicism.[20] Indeed, Vallayer-Coster participated in the Salon of 1785 in which David's *Oath of the Horatii* (fig. 6) was the sensation of the year.[21] The art of Vallayer-Coster could almost be mistaken for a *retardataire* vestige of a type of decorative painting that has little to do with Davidian ideals, with their emphasis on didactic themes taken from antiquity, a moralizing emphasis on civic virtue, resonantly transmitted through a classicizing figural treatment, set against a shallow, architecturally defined space *à la* Poussin. However, it is also the case that the elevated status of still-life painting by midcentury was itself helped by the same calls for reform that prepared the way for David's eventual triumph. The antidote to *la manière*[22] was a return to nature. In other words, there was widespread belief that the copying of other works of art (which had always been a standard part of academic training, but now untempered by the study of nature in all its particularity) had led to the moral vacuity of rococo artifice (fig. 7). This critical stance is nowhere more apparent than in the vitriolic ire we find in Diderot's tirades against the fantastical art of François Boucher (1703–1770):

> I'd say this man has no conception of true grace; I'd say he's never encountered truth; I'd say the ideas of delicacy, forthrightness, innocence, and simplicity have become almost foreign to him; I'd say he's never for a single instant seen nature, at least not the one made to interest my soul, yours, that of a well-born child, that of a sensitive woman; I'd say he's without taste. Of the infinite number of proofs I could provide to support this, a single one will suffice: in all the multitude of male and female figures he's painted, I defy anyone to find four that would be suitable for treatment in relief, much less as free-standing sculpture. There are too many little pinched faces, too much mannerism and affectation for an austere art. He can show me all the clouds he likes, I'll always see in them the rouge, the beauty spots, the powder puffs, and all the little vials of the make-up table.[23]

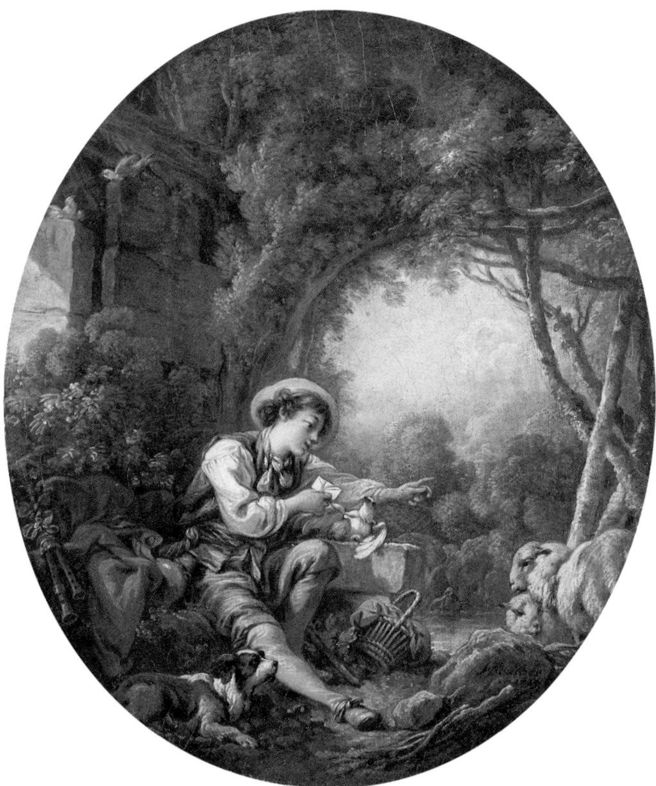

Fig. 7. François Boucher, *The Dispatch of the Messenger*, 1765. Oil on canvas, oval, 12⅝ × 10½ in. (32.1 × 26.7 cm). The Metropolitan Museum of Art, Gift of Mrs. Joseph Heine, in memory of her husband, I. D. Levy, 1944 (44.141).

By 1765 the reaction against the rococo was in full force. The gender-encoded terms of Diderot's critique of Boucher are conventional: rococo artifice is described through the implements of the vanity table. Like the comte de Caylus[24] and Cochin, Diderot blames the descent into mannerism of French artists such as Boucher on an insufficient study of nature. A few pages later, he comments acidly, "Having reached fifty, my friend, scarcely any painter works from the model, they work by rote, and this goes for Boucher."[25] The austere art of David would soon gratify Diderot's vision of a revivified history painting, based on truth to nature. But the call for a return to the *grand goût* did not allude only to a revival of worthy subjects drawn from the classical tradition. It was also an overt recognition of the necessity of studying nature, since nature was the ultimate basis for the perfected bodies that should people the artist's canvases. This renewed emphasis on the artistic value of studying nature, which had always been a staple of the classical tradition,[26] was another corrective supplied by the reaction to the rococo.

Thus, the terms of praise applied to Chardin, the lowly still-life painter, as the "great magician," whose "truth" to nature was unmatched, were not just the means by which critics registered their admiration for his powers of illusion. They were also an implicit critique of those painters who suffered from *la manière*. Mariette's emphasis on Chardin's supposed dependence on the model as a sign of his weak imagination was the writer's way of defending the supremacy of history painting. After all, Mariette's commentary on Chardin was written two years after La Font de Saint-Yenne's salvo, and it was likely motivated in part by a disdain for self-proclaimed experts who dared criticize established history painters while praising the artless naivete of a lowly still-life painter like Chardin.[27] By contrast, Cochin's more affectionate recollection of his old friend's development is written with the advantage of hindsight. As Christian Michel has so persuasively documented, Cochin's pivotal role as *chargé du détail des arts* of the Académie was not curtailed until the assumption of Jean-Baptiste-Marie Pierre (1714–1789)[28] to the directorship in 1770. During his years of service, Cochin had tirelessly promoted the most talented artists, without regard to the hierarchy of genres. In 1780, when Cochin wrote Chardin's obituary, he had one more chance to reassert his philosophy of academic reform, which, unlike Pierre's, was not solely invested in the institutionalized privileging of history painting that would increasingly dominate the Académie under Charles-Claude de la Billarderie, comte d'Angiviller (1730–1809).[29] Cochin presented the return to nature, the step needed to rejuvenate and restore the credibility of the French school, including history painting, as embodied in Chardin, the simple still-life painter. For Cochin and Diderot, Chardin's most articulate supporters, the return to nature would benefit all painters, no matter what genre they chose to pursue.

This is not to say, however, that the story of Chardin's fidelity to the model is entirely unfounded. It seems entirely credible that Chardin did teach himself through direct observation, consciously rejecting the representational tricks (*effets pittoresques*) he might have picked up through the likes of Cazes.[30] The relative breadth of technical options open to the still-life painter who, unlike the aspiring history painter, was trained in the studio setting more than in the institutionalized setting of the Académie, must have allowed for more opportunity to experiment. However, Chardin's struggle to represent things as they appear does not mean that he was not looking very actively at other paintings to achieve this end. His inventive genius, as Diderot recognized, derived from his technical originality in the extremely conventional genre of still-life painting. It has always been recognized that Chardin's compositions were inspired by seventeenth-century Dutch and Flemish precedents.[31] The ordinary objects he chose to represent (a copper cauldron, an earthenware bowl, a pile of peaches, etc.) may have been easily procured models. But they are also the same objects that are repeated so often in seventeenth-century Northern painting. From this point of view, Chardin's invitation to the viewer is quite plain. His paintings ask for comparison with other paintings as much as they ask for comparison to the experience of everyday life. Indeed, our awareness of the representational tradition that so evidently influenced the painter heightens our sensitivity to the way in which Chardin's canvases seem, by contrast, to breathe with life.

It is necessary to dwell on the import of the fragmented biographical anecdotes reported by Cochin and Mariette because an uncritical acceptance of them automatically condemns all subsequent practitioners of the genre. As recycled by the literature on the basis of these few anecdotes, Chardin's "originality" is guaranteed, since he supposedly acquired it through the sheer activity of looking, untutored by other means. If this were true, then no artist could replicate the effects Chardin rendered through the purity of his subjectivity without being accused of plagiarism,[32] a kind of facile copying of representational tricks that were rooted in the "truth" of direct observation only on the part of the master. It is no accident that this notion of originality resides at the heart of a modernist and distinctly nineteenth-century ideology of individual genius. Chardin and Cézanne, both practitioners of still life as the necessary vehicle for perceptual honesty, are in this scenario nearly interchangeable.

But what, in the end, do we really know of how eighteenth-century still-life paintings were made? Did the painter learn by copying other paintings? Was there a set list of objects belonging to the still-life repertoire that the student mastered, one after the other, by imitating as closely as he could the objects set before him by his master? Which was prioritized, direct perception of nature or the study of the most accomplished examples of the tradition of still-life painting?

A historical consideration of eighteenth-century still-life painting is hampered by the very practical problem of an absence of textual documentation. The greatly expanded discourse on art that grew up in the Enlightenment has very little to say on this topic. As a kind of literature that was more often directed at the aspiring connoisseur than at the art student, it concerned itself with how to exercise correct judgment in the appreciation of works of art. Technical matters (how to paint) were the purview of the studio, a kind of shoptalk that was presumed not to be of interest to the art lover. Instead, "reflections" or "encyclopedias" on the fine arts posed such philosophical topics as the relation between the arts or the nature of beauty. The selection of subject matter, with its obvious relation to literature, was a frequently discussed topic. By contrast, such questions as how to learn the complexities of color were addressed simply with the recommendation that the student go to the Luxembourg Palace and study the great Medici cycle of Peter Paul Rubens (1577–1640) that was housed there. The Académie's efforts to shore up the skills of the history painter resulted in more attention given to the problem of representing the figure. The insistence on drawing after the nude and such newly implemented academic competitions as the *tête d'expression*[33] reflect this attitude. Cochin's suggestion that a similar competition be implemented to focus attention on the problems posed by color was never realized.[34]

The only extended discussion of the technical training of the still-life painter in the eighteenth century occurs in the lectures delivered by Jean-Baptiste Oudry for the regular sessions of the Académie's *conférences* (lectures). The most frequently cited of these has an appropriately utilitarian title, "How to study color by comparing objects to each other," and was delivered on 7 June 1749. Oudry, who had studied with the Flemish-born Nicolas de Largillierre (1656–1746), spent the majority of his lecture outlining the ways in which direct study of nature can benefit the painter's understanding of color. As opposed to Roger de Piles (1635–1709), Oudry reported that Largillierre insisted on imitating nature in all its imperfections, rather than correcting nature's faults through idealization. For Oudry, the student will benefit more by studying the object *au naturel* than he would by copying a painting of the same subject by even as great a colorist as Titian (c. 1485/90–1576). As Oudry pronounced with great conviction, "The truth of color cannot be learned except by painting everything from nature. Those painters who have not troubled to do so have often fallen into falseness, because these effects that are so compelling and interesting do not derive at all from the imagination: they must be seen, and with a well-trained eye, in order to render them in all their truthfulness."[35]

Diderot tells us that no one had ever witnessed Chardin painting.[36] Despite the wealth of attention the artist has received in the form of monographs, exhibition catalogues, and even conservation-driven analysis,[37] we still do not know much about the master's studio practice.

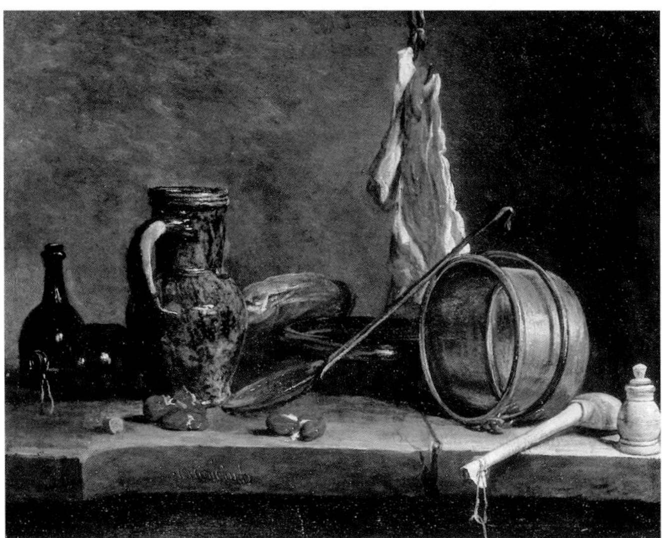

Fig. 8. Jean-Siméon Chardin, *Fast Day Meal*, 1731. Oil on canvas, 13 × 16⅛ in. (33 × 41 cm). Musée du Louvre, Paris.

However, it must be pointed out, as Katie Scott has done most recently,[38] that even if we believe Mariette's assertion that Chardin could not paint except after the model, it is a fact that his compositions, whether pure still-lifes or figural subjects, frequently exist in multiple versions. Even in his own production, then, it is clear that Chardin, like all eighteenth-century French artists, often painted after other paintings, if in this case, his own.

We may never know precisely how Vallayer could have matured so rapidly (see Roland Michel's discussion of her possible teachers, including Vernet, in this volume). But by looking with care at Vallayer's technical achievements, it is clear that she benefited from Chardin's example. It is equally clear that in so obviously imitating her supposed nemesis, she was not afraid of the inevitable comparisons that must have been drawn. We have even less anecdotal information on Vallayer's early training and technical approach than we do in the case of Chardin. However, if we are able to see past the literal view of still-life painting as the simple imitation of things seen and reinsert the practice of still-life painting in an aesthetic context where imitation in its classical sense was the primary mode of artistic expression, then Vallayer-Coster can be seen as the legitimate heir to Chardin's artistic achievements.

Challenging the Master

In a letter written to Jean-Baptiste Descamps in 1784, Joseph Vernet gives us a glimpse of the influence of not only Chardin but Vallayer-Coster on the aspiring student of still life: "Mademoiselle Harrison is working after Madame Vallayer-Coster; I will obtain some Chardins for her to help her work better after nature."[39] By 1784 Vallayer-Coster was the undisputed leader of French still-life painting and Chardin had been dead for five years. Again, the opposing terms of "la manière" and "la nature" are at work. Here, it seems, the young artist in question had been too closely imitating the brilliant effects of Vallayer-Coster, and Chardin's art is the antidote to such fashionable affectations. Note that Vernet links Chardin's manner of painting with the direct study of nature.

The young Vallayer, like the unknown "Mademoiselle Harrison," was most likely given the same task by her mentor, Vernet. We can see her struggling with Chardin's idiom in one of the earliest known of her canvases from 1763 or 1765 (fig. 5). An array of unremarkable objects—

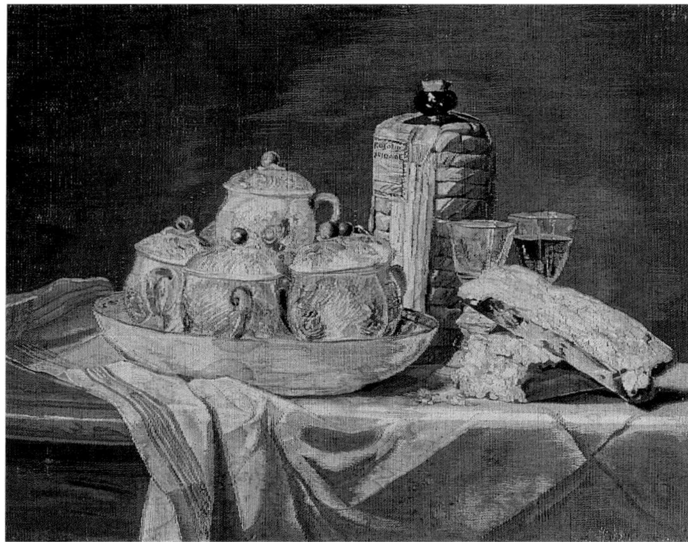

Fig. 9. Tapestry after Anne Vallayer-Coster, *The Dessert*, 1811 (painting completed 1766). Wool tapestry, 22⅞ × 26 in. (58 × 66 cm). Musée Nissim de Camondo, Paris (cat. 2).

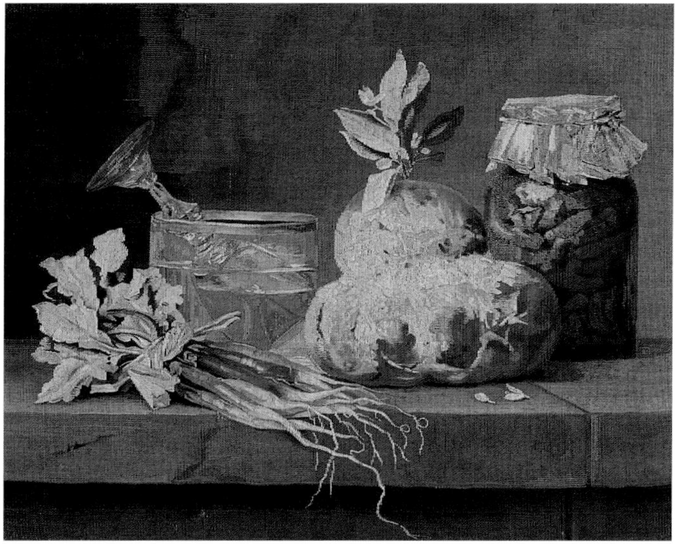

Fig. 10. Tapestry after Anne Vallayer-Coster, *The Lunch*, 1811 (painting completed 1766). Wool tapestry, 22⅞ × 26 in. (58 × 66 cm). Musée Nissim de Camondo, Paris (cat. 3).

some peaches, a basket of plums, and the predictable earthenware plate and jug—surround a ham on a simple wooden table. At the center of the composition, a rumpled white tablecloth crests improbably from the edge of the table; this is a common spatial device used to establish a shallow plane in front of the ledge of the table. The selection of such humble objects immediately calls to mind Chardin's kitchen still-lifes (fig. 8). As if to emphasize further the rustic simplicity of the objects, the earthenware plate and jug are conspicuously chipped. The muted palette, dominated by browns, is a further declaration of the artist's allegiance to Chardin and his Northern inspiration, as is the thick facture throughout. The clumsiness of the paint handling, along with the somewhat unremarkable recycling of a familiar Chardinesque theme, gives little hint of the artist's mature style. Spatially, the objects are neither convincingly nor comfortably situated. Recession is conventionally implied through an overlapping of objects that strands the earthenware jug at an elevation that is not accounted for in the rest of the composition. The ham is muddily described with broad swipes of the brush, and arbitrary dabs of white do not convincingly describe the different reflective properties of glass and ceramic. It is significant, however, that the novice painter attempted a complex composition of multiple objects, rather than simplifying her task by concentrating on a single motif. She was proud enough of the result to sign the canvas, a practice that she consistently observed throughout her career.

Most of Vallayer's paintings from the early 1760s are lost, so we lack evidence that would help us understand her continued wrestling with Chardin's example in the early 1760s, when the artist was still in her late teens. She was already well advanced by 1766, when she produced a pendant pair of kitchen still-lifes that demonstrate all of the suavity of an assured artist (figs. 9, 10), the compositions of which are preserved only in tapestry. The compositional arrangements have none of the hesitations of an unschooled student. The debt to Chardin in the choice of motifs (porcelain pots, a jug of wine, two glasses, loaves of bread, a bunch of radishes, a brioche, an overturned glass in a bowl of water, a jar of pickles) is still pronounced. Judging from the tapestries' precise record of coloristic nuance, the backgrounds were delicately scumbled. A quiet, pyramidal symmetry, again reminiscent of Chardin, characterizes both compositions. Vallayer's penchant for more refined, luxury objects is already present in this pendant pair. We can only marvel at the leaps and bounds she has somehow managed in the course of a few short years when we consider the level of technical accomplishment at her disposal by 1767. *Still Life with Silver Pitcher* (fig. 11) is light years beyond the amateurish efforts of just four years earlier.

Even more pronounced in this stunning painting is Vallayer's willingness to engage with Chardin's example. The rising steam from the silver pitcher recalls Chardin's interest in depicting such ephemeral effects (fig. 12). The choice of objects, like Chardin's, immediately places the viewer in the context of domestic comfort. We can almost smell the aroma of the hot coffee, and the sugar tongs are within easy reach. And yet, if Vallayer is still indebted to Chardin's loving depictions of the instruments of bourgeois contentment, she has already begun to develop a singular approach to their description. Whereas Chardin suggests the steam rising from his porcelain cup with a slow, dry brush, Vallayer meticulously renders her puffs of rising steam, forgoing the rough texture of Chardin's summary brushwork in favor of a smoother application. Her attentiveness to the textural difference between polished silver and delicate porcelain or crusty bread and cold stone ledge is evidenced by a scrupulous recording of detail. Compare, for example, the precision of the pattern on Vallayer's delicate coffee cup to Chardin's similarly decorated demitasse. Chardin suggested the rose motif with indistinct swirls of pink, red, and green, whereas Vallayer minutely recorded every arabesque of the decorative border circling the rims of cup and saucer and each petal of the spray of flowers gracing the surface. The sum of these details, however, does not detract from the overall unity of the composition. Like Chardin, Vallayer arranges her objects to produce a harmonious play of geometric shapes, in this case, keyed to an oval. The strong illumination that warms the composition provides an excuse to include colored reflections that conjoin the local tones of each element, a ploy that Vallayer will use again and again throughout her career and for which she is, again, indebted to Chardin.

Vallayer's individual style emerges in full force at the end of the 1760s, and most dramatically in her *morceaux de réception*. As mentioned earlier, this pendant pair of still lifes, elevated by their allegorical mode to the highest pitch possible for the lowest genre in the hierarchy, pays overt homage to Chardin, specifically to Chardin's overdoors (figs. 3, 4) that were a royal commission, secured for the artist by Cochin, as part of the decorative scheme for the château de Choisy. The audacity of Vallayer's choice to rival Chardin's masterpieces, which were exhibited at the Salon of 1765, should not be underestimated. Diderot had only unmitigated praise for the three canvases in his *Salon of 1765*: "It's all but impossible to choose between them, they're all of like perfection."[40] If Vallayer boldly invoked Chardin's canvases, she also sought to assert her own distinctive artistic voice. In *The Attributes of Painting, Sculpture, and Architecture* (fig. 2), the composition, like Chardin's, places a plaster cast at the center. However, unlike the stately personification of Paris that stabilizes Chardin's classically balanced composition (an homage to the sculptor Edme Bouchardon [1698–1762]), the familiar contours of the Belvedere Torso are situated in such a way as immediately to set the entire composition in motion. Vallayer's canvas is as charged as Chardin's and includes much the same array of objects: palette and brushes, rolled drawings, a portfolio secured with ribbon, reference books, compass, T square, and architectural plans. But whereas Chardin's composition is dominated by intersecting horizontals and verticals, Vallayer's radiates with diagonals. We see only partial aspects of the attributes peeking out from Chardin's heavily foreshortened niche; by contrast, Vallayer delights in her ability to show us as much of each compositional element as possible, all the while maintaining a credible spatial coherence. If Chardin's allegory reconciles *anciens* and *modernes* through his glowing tribute to his recently deceased colleague Bouchardon, Vallayer invents an equally elegant means of acknowledging the merits of contemporary sculpture: a clay bust (perhaps a self-portrait, as Roland Michel has suggested), still damp and obviously a work in progress, gazes sightlessly from the dark background.

The success of this allegorical invention is matched by the technical virtuosity of its pendant, *The Attributes of Music* (fig. 1). Again, oblique diagonals energize the composition. Whereas occasional warm notes of red interrupt Chardin's somber palette, Vallayer's canvas glows with jewel-like tones. The hot light shows off to dramatic effect her descriptive powers, lingering on the wood grain of the instruments and the rich texture of velvet. If, by contrast, Vallayer's attention to detail is again more pronounced throughout, her brushwork could be just as astoundingly summary as Chardin's. Close inspection of the gold-embroidered red velvet of the bagpipe reveals a myriad of unblended touches of color (fig. 13), an effect Diderot had described in looking at Chardin's canvases at the Salon of 1765, "Come close and everything becomes blurred, flattens and disappears; stand back and everything is created and takes shape again."[41]

This effect was already designated by a term in eighteenth-century art parlance: *la manière heurtée.* The adjective "heurté," which does not translate precisely into English, refers to a kind of brushwork that is immediately visible to the naked eye as literal strokes of color

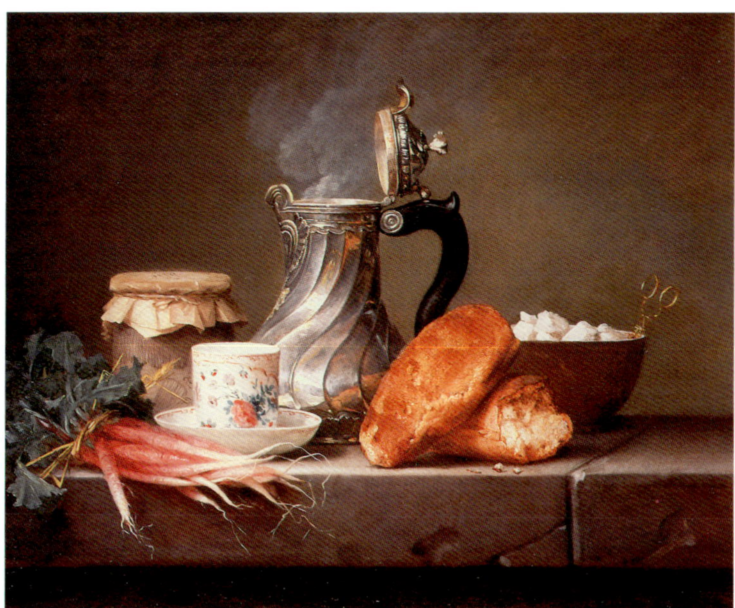

Fig. 11. Anne Vallayer-Coster, *Still Life with Silver Pitcher*, 1767. Oil on canvas, 19½ × 23⅜ in. (49.5 × 59.5 cm). Private collection, United Kingdom, courtesy of Thomas and Brenda Brod (cat. 5).

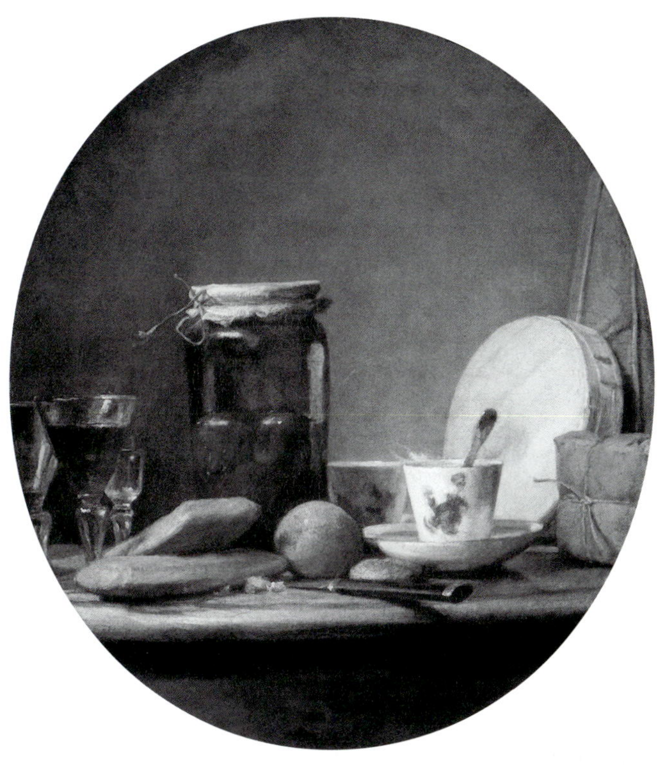

Fig. 12. Jean-Siméon Chardin, *Jar of Apricots*, 1758. Oil on canvas, 22½ × 20 in. (57.2 × 50.8 cm). Art Gallery of Ontario, Toronto.

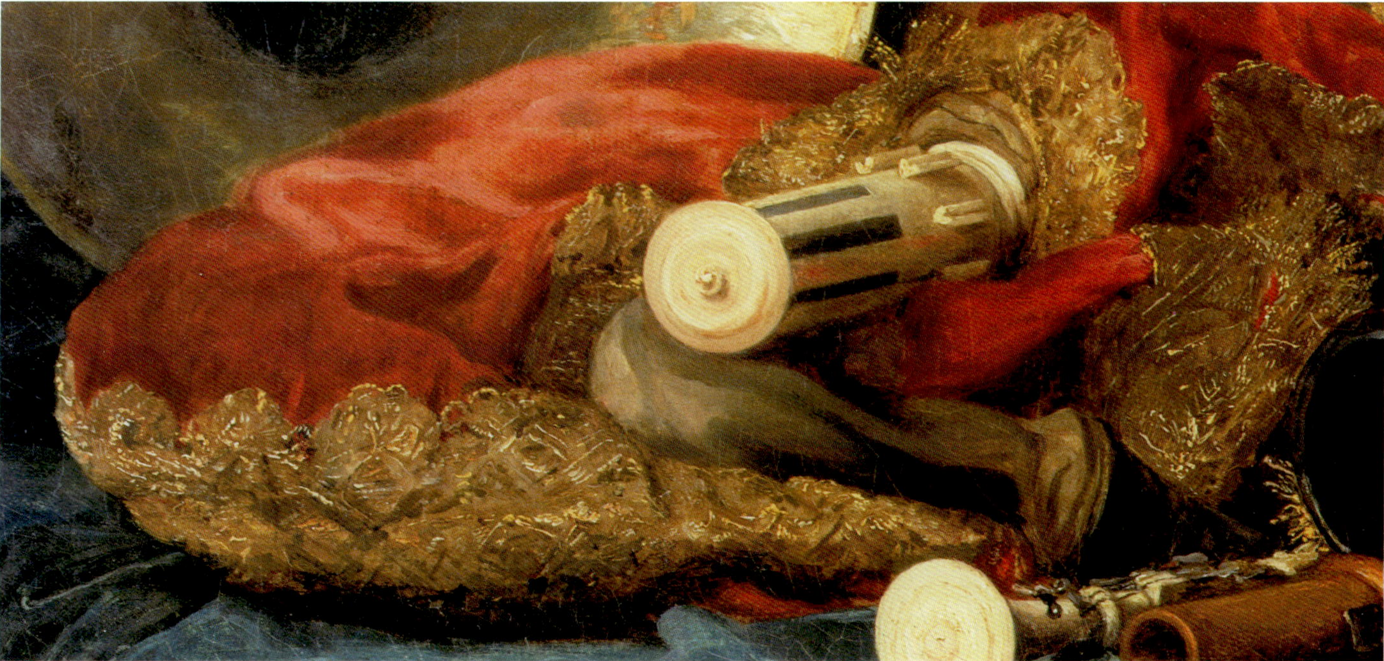

Fig. 13. Detail of fig. 1, bagpipe.

on the canvas surface, which, when viewed at the appropriate distance, magically blend to generate a persuasive illusion. In the *Dictionnaire des arts de peinture, sculpture, et gravure* (first published from 1788 to 1791), it is defined by Pierre-Charles Lévêque as the opposite of *fondu* (blended), when used positively, and as the opposite of *leché* (polished), when used to describe a fault. As explained by Lévêque:

In a blended painting *[un tableau fondu]*, the hues, by succeeding each other through undetectable nuances, lose themselves, one into another, & can only be discerned by the expert's eye. In a rough painting *[un tableau heurté]*, the hues are applied broadly, one could even say brutally, one next to the other; their brusque succession is not only very visible—when viewed from close up, it is even shocking. But, when seen from a distance, the air interposed

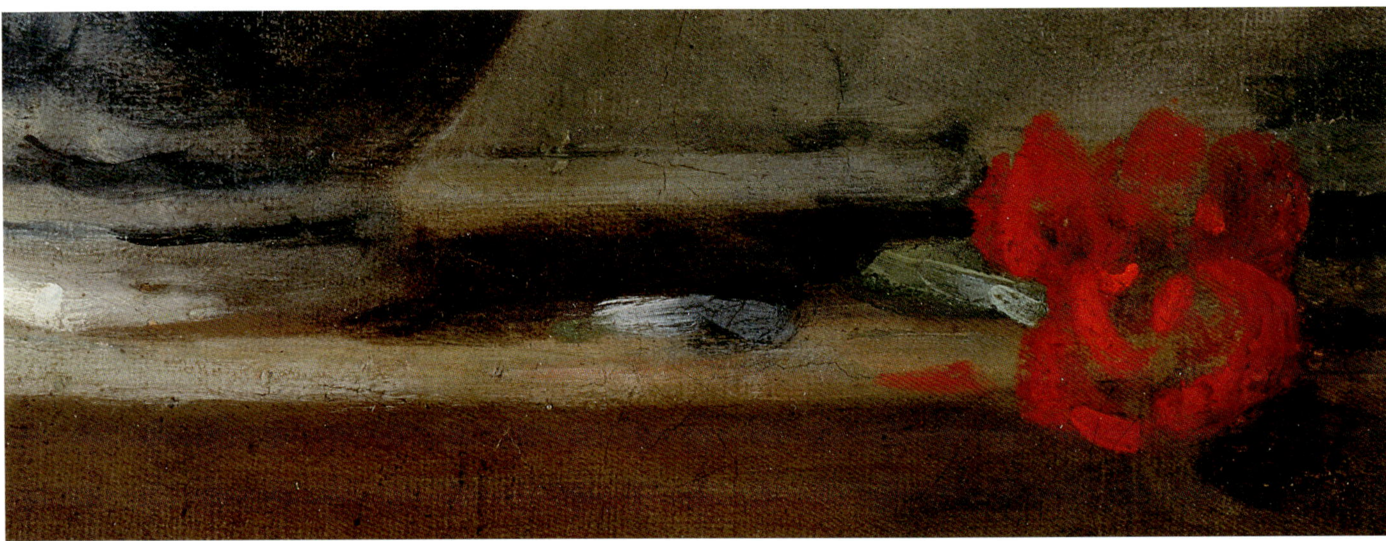

Fig. 14. Jean-Siméon Chardin, *Flowers in a White and Blue Porcelain Vase*, detail of flower, n.d. Oil on canvas, 17³⁄₈ × 14¹⁄₈ in. (44 × 36 cm). National Gallery of Scotland, Edinburgh (cat. A).

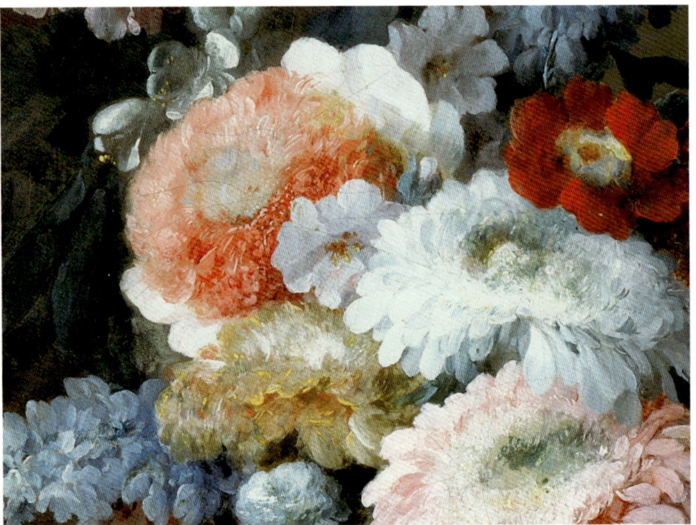

Fig. 15. Anne Vallayer-Coster, *Vase of Flowers*, detail of flowers, 1780. Oil on canvas, oval, 19³⁄₄ × 15 in. (50.2 × 38.1 cm). The Metropolitan Museum of Art; gift of J. Pierpont Morgan, 1906, 07.225.504 (cat. 61).

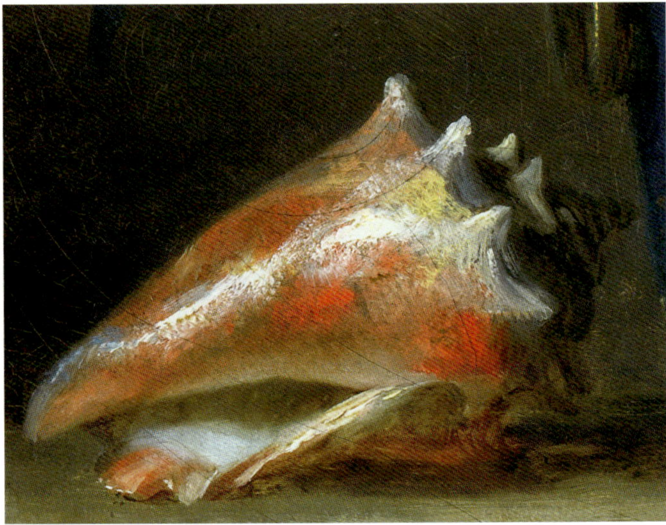

Fig. 16. Anne Vallayer-Coster, *Vase of Flowers*, detail of conch shell, 1780. Oil on canvas, oval, 19³⁄₄ × 15 in. (50.2 × 38.1 cm). The Metropolitan Museum of Art; gift of J. Pierpont Morgan, 1906, 07.225.504 (cat. 61).

between the painting and the spectator mixes and blends the hues & transforms a crude sketch into a finished painting.[42]

If one used these terms to characterize Vallayer's paintings as opposed to Chardin's, one would say that her use of *la manière heurtée* is much more selective. In a single canvas, as is true in the case of *The Attributes of Music*, one can find passages of paint that are manifestly just that, as in the gold-flecked red velvet of the bagpipe. And yet, in the same work, for example in the precisely rendered sheet music propped up behind the lute or in the smooth wood grain of the violin, the brushwork is

nearly undetectable, no matter how near to or far from the canvas one is. In Lévêque's sense, Vallayer uses both *la manière fondue* and *la manière heurtée*, whereas Chardin's highly individual facture is never concerned with the kind of meticulous description made possible through *la manière fondue*.

Nowhere is this more dramatically evident than in the comparison between any of Vallayer's numerous flower paintings and the single extant example we have of Chardin's work in this subgenre of still life (fig. 14). The blue-and-white vase in Edinburgh is a patchwork of white and blue. It is so broadly described that its pattern refuses to come into focus. The red paint used to present the single blossom resting on the ledge declares itself as a swirl of pigment. We are hard pressed to identify it as any particular species of flower (a rose? a carnation?). By contrast, Vallayer's flowers can be almost clinically precise in their description of each stem, as in *Vase of Flowers* (fig. 15). But in the same canvas she can choose to indulge in a broad, almost abstract application of unblended color. The level of detail in the abundant flowers suggests the use of a magnifying glass, whereas the conch shell is conjured out of obvious brushstrokes of unblended paint, as though merely glimpsed on the fringes of peripheral vision (fig. 16).

As has been pointed out by Roland Michel, the assumption that Vallayer-Coster's art is stylistically akin to Chardin's is appropriate only in a limited regard.[43] They are closest in simple still-life themes of fruit or dead game. For example, Vallayer-Coster's version of the typical motif of a basket of grapes exudes an elegance that is foreign to Chardin's treatment of the same theme (fig. 17). One cannot imagine Chardin adorning his basket of grapes with the tiny forget-me-nots that wave gently from the far side of the basket in Vallayer-Coster's lovely painting (pl. 12). Yet the two paintings are very close in sensibility. A gentle participation between light and color resonates with an Enlightenment awareness of the subjectivity of vision. Like Chardin, Vallayer-Coster avoids the superhuman clarity of seventeenth-century Dutch and Flemish still life, opting instead for a softly blurred effect that is not unlike the "relaxed" vision that

has been remarked on in the literature on Chardin.[44] Her treatment of dead rabbits, as in the 1787 *Trophies of the Hunt* (fig. 18), could almost be mistaken as by the hand of Chardin, were it not for the blue silk cord in the foreground that betrays Vallayer-Coster's penchant for decorative accents of vivid color.

Perhaps it was Vallayer-Coster's love of brilliant hues that led her away from Chardin's somber palette to embrace the special category of flower painting. Her preeminence in this domain was universally recognized by contemporary critics and hardly needs justification in this essay. Interestingly, although we have several examples of repetition when it comes to *bas-reliefs imités* or still life with fruit, there is not one incidence of self-copying in her many flower paintings. Even though her favorite species of flowers may recur, no two roses are exactly alike (figs. 19, 20, 21). Flower compositions gave Vallayer-Coster ample opportunity to indulge in a daring use of brilliant hues, often encompassing the gamut from fiery reds to cool blues and pearlescent grays in the same composition (fig. 22). In this area of still-life painting, Vallayer-Coster is entirely liberated from the shadow of Chardin. An overwhelming sense of the artist's intimate knowledge of each stem and every individual vase pervades these exuberant floral compositions. The handling of paint is expertly varied: imperceptible brushwork captures the delicate drops of water on drooping flower petals, and then boldly gestural strokes of white paint denote the light reflecting

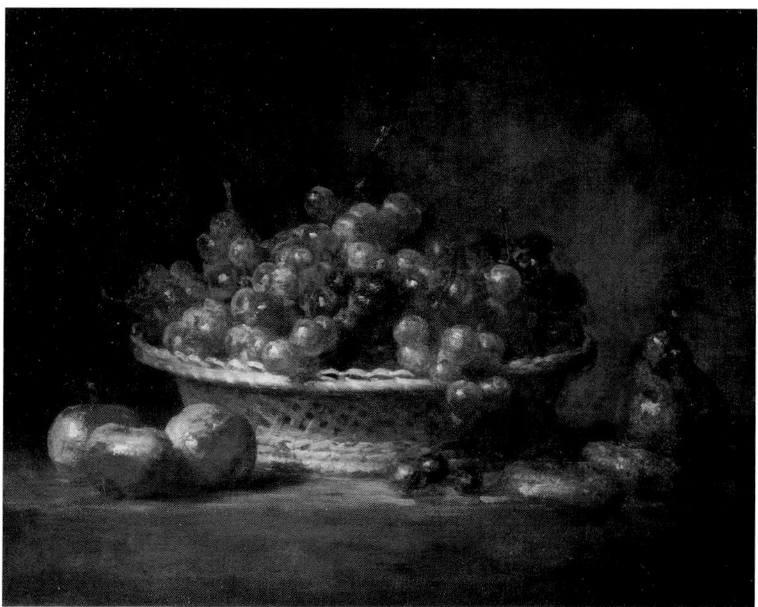

Fig. 17. Jean-Siméon Chardin, *Basket of Grapes with Three Apples, a Pear and Two Marzipan*, 1764. Oil on canvas, 12 × 15 in. (32 × 40 cm). Musées d'Angers.

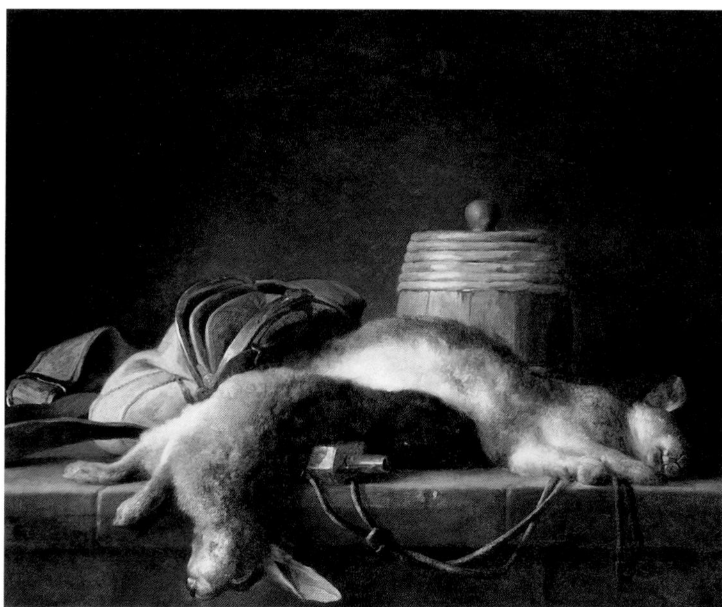

Fig. 18. Anne Vallayer-Coster, *Trophies of the Hunt*, 1787. Oil on canvas, 21¼ × 25⅜ in. (55 × 64.5 cm). Present whereabouts unknown (cat. 84).

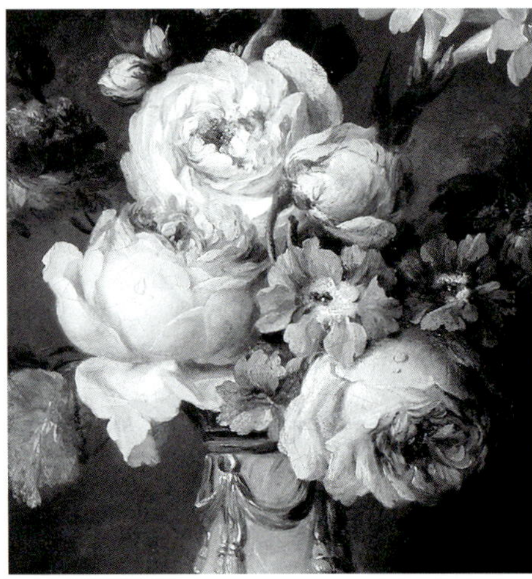

Fig. 19. Anne Vallayer-Coster, *A Vase of Flowers and Two Plums on a Marble Tabletop*, detail, 1781. Oil on canvas, 18⅞ × 15¾ in. (48 × 39.8 cm). Michael L. Rosenberg, Dallas (cat. 67).

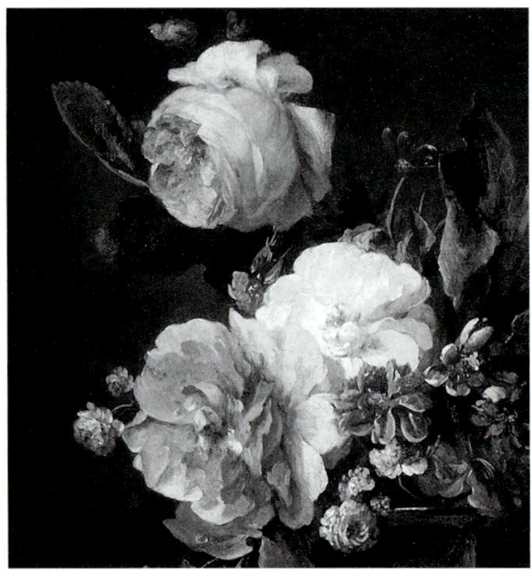

Fig. 20. Anne Vallayer-Coster, *Flowers in a Glass Vase*, detail, 1777. Oil on canvas, 16¼ × 13¼ in. (41.5 × 34 cm). Segoura Collection (cat. 45).

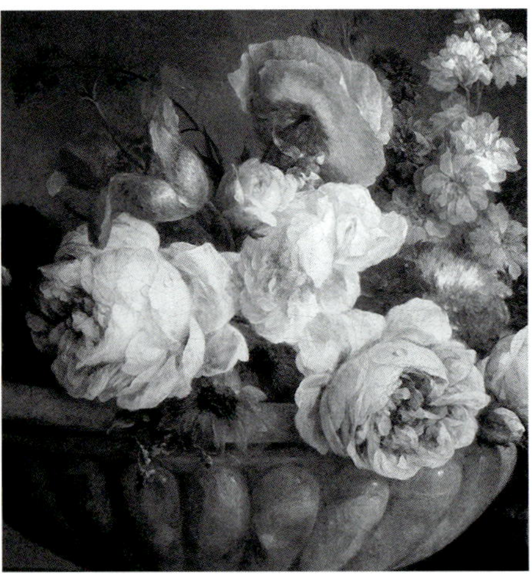

Fig. 21. Anne Vallayer-Coster, *Bouquet of Flowers in an Alabaster Vase*, detail, 1801. Oil on canvas, 14¾ × 17¾ in. (37.5 × 45 cm). Private collection, North America (cat. 93).

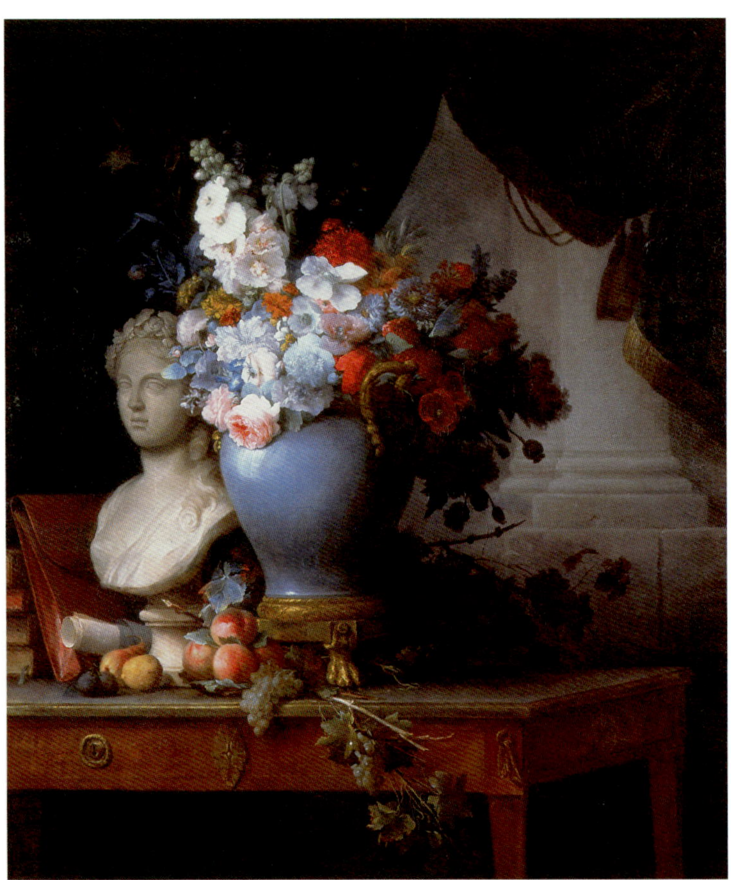

Fig. 22. Anne Vallayer-Coster, *Vase of Flowers with a Bust of Flora*, 1774. Oil on canvas, 60⅝ × 51⅛ in. (154 × 130 cm). Private collection (cat. 30).

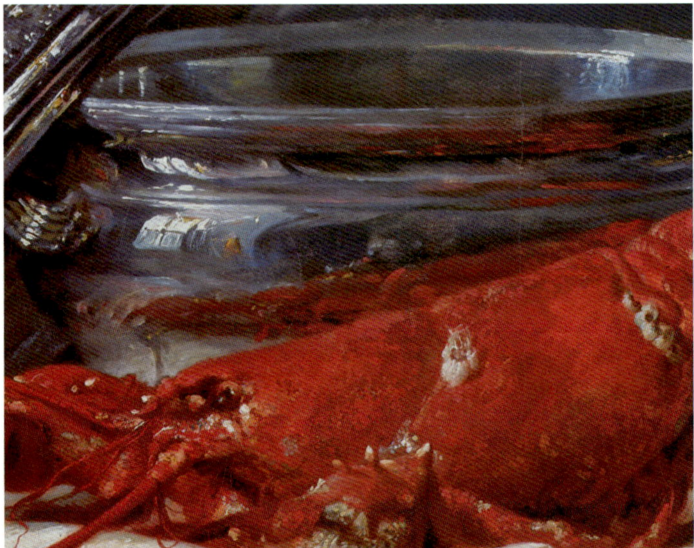

Fig. 23. Anne Vallayer-Coster, *Still Life with Lobster*, detail of reflection on silver tureen, 1781. Oil on canvas, 27¾ × 35¼ in. (70 × 88 cm). Toledo Museum of Art; Purchased with funds from the Libbey Endowment, Gift of Edward Drummond Libbey (cat. 65).

off a porcelain or glass vase. Vallayer-Coster's transcendence as a colorist is most spectacularly evident in her theatrical play with colored reflections (fig. 23). These explosions of color for the sheer sake of painterly indulgence nearly overpower their illusionistic function, acting as harmonizers of a palette that might otherwise verge on garish discord.

One more similarity between the careers of Vallayer-Coster and Chardin should be recognized: their attempts to rise through the academic ranks by conquering the human figure. It is probably in this arena that Vallayer-

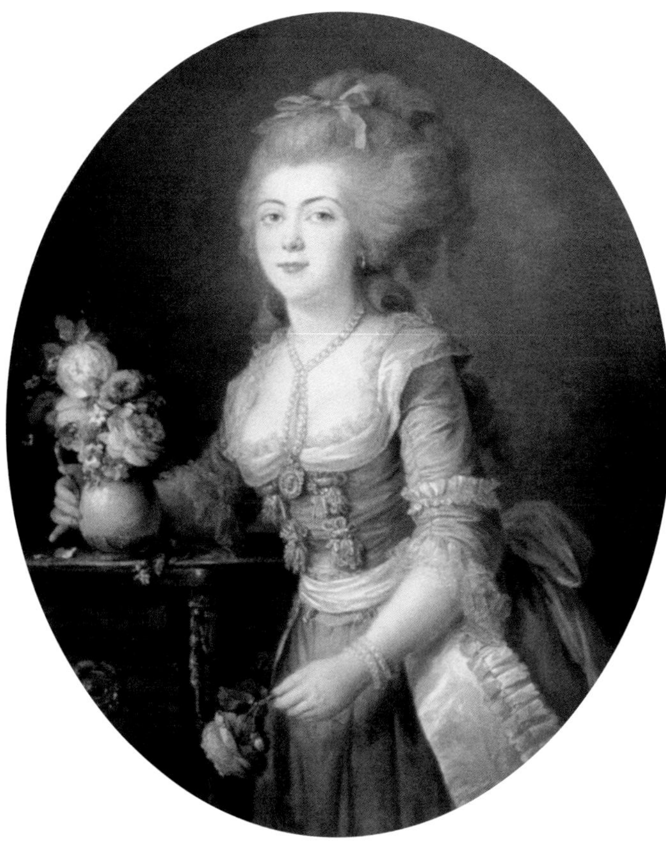

Fig. 24. Anne Vallayer-Coster, *Portrait of Madame Auguié*, n.d. Oil on canvas, oval, 38⅛ × 29⅞ in. (97 × 76 cm). Private collection, Monaco (cat. 123).

Coster departs most from Chardin, in both technical approach and degree of success. She seems to have shared Chardin's awkwardness when confronted with the task of animating the human physiognomy, but her portraits are oddly miniature-like in their execution, an accusation one would not level at even the most clumsy of Chardin's early portraits. It is as though she has simply blown up in scale a resemblance that would better suit the tiny, more forgiving proportions of a miniature. Mariette tells us that Chardin used a real child as a model when he attempted his early figural subject of a boy blowing bubbles, painting directly on the canvas without the benefit of preparatory drawings.[45] One wonders if Vallayer-Coster ever studied the living model with the same attentiveness that is so obvious in her flower studies. Strangely, her exquisite miniatures of flowers have all the painterly freedom of her larger paintings (pl. 68), whereas her few extant portraits, with the exception of the sensitively observed portrait of Joseph-Charles Roettiers (pl. 23), an old friend of her father's, seem hesitant and somewhat wooden. Vallayer-Coster's insufficient knowledge of anatomy is most evident in her treatment of the figure in three-quarters length, as in the portrait of Madame Auguié (fig. 24), or the critically disastrous portrait of Madame de Saint-Huberty (pl. 35).[46]

In her 1970 monograph Roland Michel stressed Vallayer-Coster's ultimate dependence on, not just Chardin, but a range of French artists whose examples she must have known while developing her own style.[47] In choice of subject matter she shares much with the oeuvre of Horace-Henri Roland Delaporte (c. 1724–1793) (fig. 25), who made typical kitchen still-lifes as well as more elaborate set-pieces of the allegorical type (pl. 84). However, on close inspection, there is little of Roland Delaporte's dry touch in Vallayer-Coster's flowing brushwork. Her suave use of *la manière heurtée* brings her closer in technique to Chardin, although she is capable of Roland Delaporte's self-effacing manner, as in the relatively tight handling in the loaves of bread and heavy ceramic cup of *Still Life with a Frugal Repast* (fig. 26). However, even in this tonally muted composition, the nervous scumbling of the background animates the canvas, allowing the yellow underground to create an atmospheric depth that is, again, closer to Chardin than to Roland Delaporte.

One of Chardin's most beloved paintings is a little work on panel that depicts a student seen from behind, copying a drawing of a male nude tacked up before him (fig. 27). This diminutive painting has often been taken as the visual counterpart to Chardin's reported lament over the plight of the aspiring artist, again as reported by Diderot:

> The chalk holder is placed in our hands, [he said], at the age of seven or eight years. We begin to draw eyes, mouths, noses, and ears after patterns, then feet and hands. After having crouched over our portfolios for a long time, we're placed in front of the *Hercules* or the *Torso*, and you've never seen such tears as those shed over the *Satyr*, the *Gladiator*, the *Medici Venus*, and the *Antinous*. . . . Then, after having spent entire days and even nights, by lamplight, in front of immobile, inanimate nature, we're presented with living nature, and suddenly the work of all the preceding years seem reduced to nothing; it's as though one were taking up the chalk for the first time. The eye must be taught to look at nature; and many are those who've never seen it and never will! It's the bane of our existence. After having spent five or six years in front of the model, we turn to the resources of our own genius, if we have any. Talent doesn't reveal itself in a moment; judgments about one's limitations can't be reached on the basis of first efforts.[48]

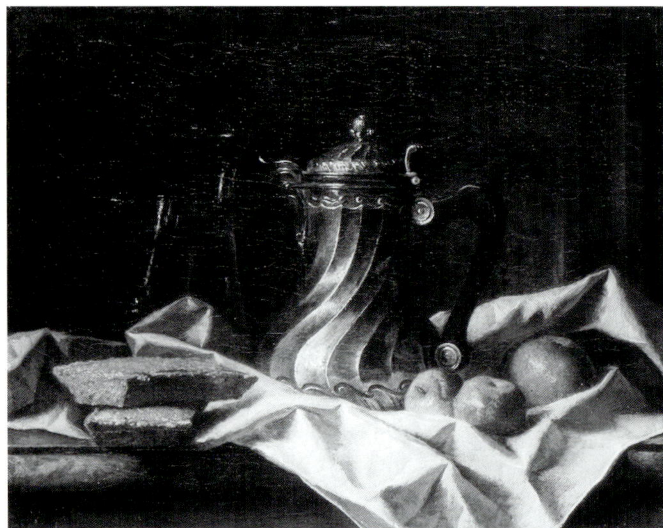

Fig. 25. Henri-Horace Roland Delaporte, *Still Life with Silver Coffeepot,* n.d. Oil on canvas, 14⅝ × 17¾ in. (37 × 45 cm). Private collection.

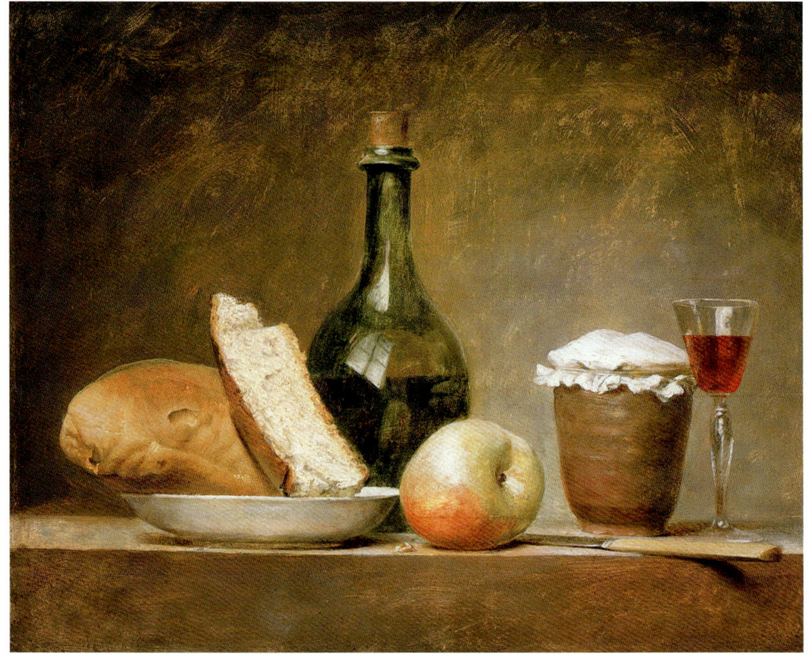

Fig. 26. Anne Vallayer-Coster, *Still Life with a Frugal Repast,* n.d. Oil on panel, 10⅞ × 12¾ in. (27.5 × 32.5 cm). Staatliche Museen zu Berlin, Gemäldegalerie (cat. 128).

Again, *la manière,* as transmitted through copying, is set in opposition to the real challenge to the painter's development, the conquering of *la nature.* However, another theme runs through Chardin's lament: the weight of tradition as represented by the fabled exemplars of antiquity. In the painting, the male nude in the drawing seems to look disapprovingly at the student's unsatisfactory efforts, mirroring the position of the stern master whom we can imagine peering over his student's shoulder. Peculiarly, the shadow seems to

fall toward the young apprentice, and a deep shadow to his left seems ready to swallow him whole. Ironically, Chardin's empathy for the struggling artist takes on another dimension when we consider the plight of those still-life painters who followed him. In the case of Vallayer-Coster, it was Chardin's shadow the young artist had to escape. After two centuries of neglect, her success in doing so can finally be acknowledged.

The revival of interest in Chardin in the nineteenth century has been well documented.[49] Legions of painters, it would seem, from the realist Gustave Courbet (1819–1877) and the self-declared Chardin imitators François Bonvin (1817–1887) and Antoine Vollon (1833–1900) to Edouard Manet (1832–1883) and Henri Fantin-Latour (1836–1904) were inspired by Chardin, especially his still lifes. But have we perhaps, been too quick to assume that these nineteenth-century practitioners of still life were exclusively interested in this single eighteenth-century precedent of the French school? Though little published, Antoine Berjon paid specific homage to Vallayer-Coster during her lifetime in his 1810 rendition of seashells and coral specimens (fig. 28). Is it possible that Fantin-Latour's floral still-lifes, in their daring use of vivid hues, were also inspired by Vallayer-Coster's example? Again, the critical shadow of Chardin may have prevented us from even posing the question.

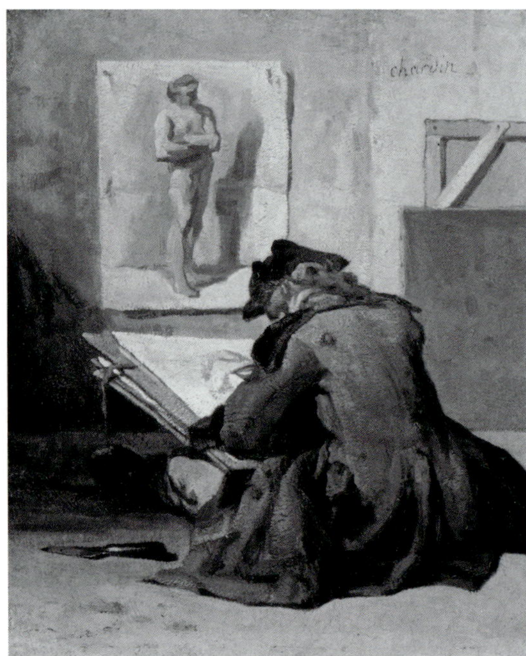

Fig. 27. Jean-Siméon Chardin, *Young Student Drawing,* c. 1738. Oil on panel, 8¼ × 6¾ in. (21 × 17.1 cm). Kimbell Art Museum, Fort Worth, Texas.

for my husband, Joakim Tan

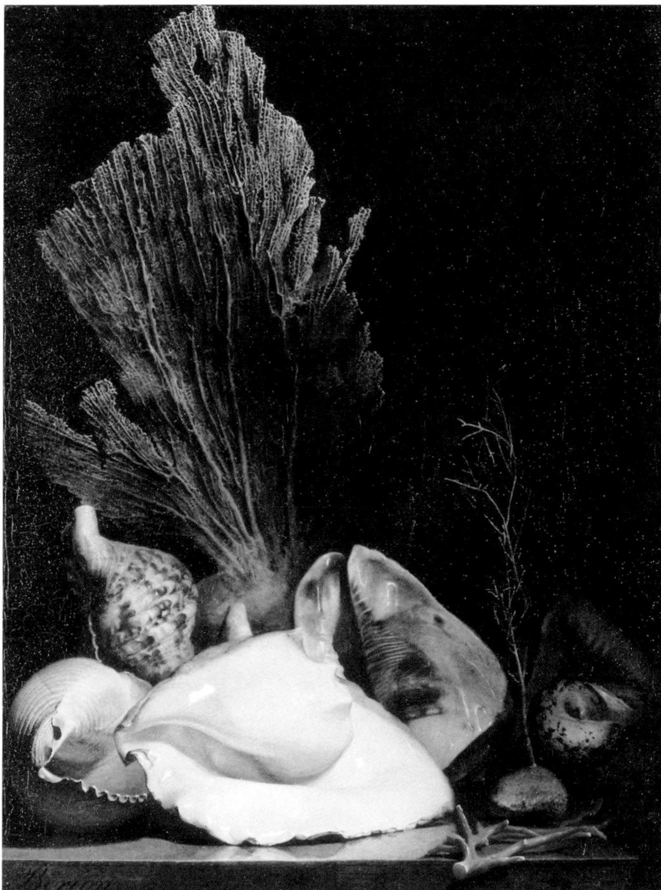

Fig. 28. Antoine Berjon, *Seashells and Coral*, 1810. Oil on canvas, 29½ × 22 in. (75 × 56 cm). Musée des Beaux-Arts de Lyon.

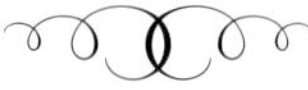

Notes

1. The literature on Chardin is vast. It is indebted to the irreplaceable catalogue raisonné of 1933 (G. Wildenstein 1933), an emended version of which was published in 1963 (G. Wildenstein 1963), and again, in 1969 (D. and G. Wildenstein 1969). The most recent exhibition, in celebration of the tercentenary of the artist's birth, was organized by Pierre Rosenberg (Paris 1999). Rosenberg has published other important accounts of the artist (Rosenberg 1983; Rosenberg and Temperini 1999), plus the groundbreaking exhibition catalogue of 1979 (Paris 1979). Two other major monographs are Conisbee 1986 and Roland Michel 1996. The most recent Rosenberg catalogue (Paris 1999) includes an exhaustive bibliography on the artist, as well as an overview of more recent Anglo-American scholarship on Chardin by Colin B. Bailey.

2. For a summary of Chardin's critical resurrection, beginning at midcentury, see Paris 1979, 85–96.

3. Edmond and Jules de Goncourt published their essays on Chardin in 1863 and 1864, which provided the basis for their chapter devoted to Chardin in Goncourt 1880/1884. The Goncourts' view of Chardin played an important role in the revival of interest in the artist.

4. Roland Michel 1970 and Roland Michel 1960, 1965, 1966, 1973, and 1993. A useful account of Vallayer-Coster's career is given in Michel and Fabrice Faré's monumental opus on eighteenth-century French still-life painting (1976). Vallayer-Coster has also been included in several exhibitions devoted to women artists. See the publication from 1926 that accompanied the exhibition *Femmes peintres du XVIIIe siècle* in Paris or the important exhibition *Women Artists, 1550–1950* (Los Angeles 1976). More recently, she was included in the exhibition *Trois femmes peintres dans le siècle de Fragonard* (Grasse 1998, 31–37). Vallayer-Coster is discussed as a follower of Chardin in F. Faré 1999.

5. In fact, the habit of dwelling on Vallayer-Coster's gender originates in the eighteenth century. Denis Diderot, for example, commented on Vallayer's reception pieces (Musée du Louvre, Paris; see figs. 1, 2), exhibited in the Salon of 1771: "Excellent, vigorous, harmonious: it is not Chardin, but while it is below the level of that artist, it is greatly above that of a woman" (quoted by Roland Michel 1996, 256). Vallayer-Coster makes a brief appearance in the chapter "Amateurs and Academics: A New Ideology of Femininity in France and England" in Chadwick 1990, 127–164.

6. Roland Michel 1970, 21.

7. "I was utterly enchanted with the talent of this amiable young woman whom I saw for the first time and whose talent is truly that of a man who is perfect in the genre of paintings representing inanimate nature. . . . The Académie chose two paintings for the reception of this young woman, who took her place after the usual thanks with a modesty equal to her skill, and not a single voice was raised against her in this scrutiny" (Je fus extrêmement enchanté du talent de cette aimable personne, que je voyais pour la première fois et dont le talent est vraiment celui d'un homme parfait dans ce genre de tableaux représentant la nature immobile. . . . L'Académie choisit deux tableaux, pour la réception de cette demoiselle, qui prit sa place après remerciements usités, avec autant de modestie qu'elle est habile, aussi n'eut-elle pas une seule voix contre elle au scrutin). Quoted in Roland Michel 1970, 42.

8. Roland Michel 1970, 54–55.

9. Roland Michel 1970, 260. The document was signed as follows: "Pierre, Coustou, J. du Mont Le Rom, Belle, van Loo, Pigalle, Demachy, Lemoyne, Jeaurat, Mariette, Soufflot, d'Azaincourt, Dandré-Bardon, Hallé, Vien, Vassé, De Lautherborg, Pajou, Allegrain, L. Lagrenée, Wille, Huet, Caffiéri, N. S. Adam, Amédée Van Loo, Bachelier, d'Huez, Taraval, Briard, Francin, Doyen, Lépicié, Chardin, C. F. Desportes, Guérin, Vernet, Roslin S, Leclerc, Voiriot, M. F. Vien, Gois, Julliar, Vallayer, E. Dumont, Drouais."

10. Greuze was a popular genre painter who, like Chardin, had no official sponsor when he was accepted by the Académie in June 1755. Unfortunately, the arrogant Greuze aspired to the

prestige of the history painter, although he had hitherto been acclaimed as a genre painter. The story of his failed *morceau de réception, Septimius Severus and Caracalla* (Musée du Louvre, Paris) of 1769 is effectively recounted in Crow 1985.

11. While it was certainly exceptional for a woman artist to be accepted into the Académie, the significance of the simultaneous acceptance and reception of women artists is more ambiguous than is often presumed. As pointed out by Thomas Crow, this honor was yet another dimension of the mythology that fed into the discursive identity of "the surprise invader"— an artist who seems to burst onto the academic scene by virtue of sheer talent, rather than academic sponsorship from within (Crow 1985, 135–138). However, as pointed out to me by Melissa Hyde and John Goodman, simultaneous acceptance and reception seem to have been the norm, rather than the exception, for female candidates. Indeed, of the thirteen women admitted into the ranks of the Académie, only one submitted a *morceau de réception* subsequent to her initial *agrégation:* Sophie Chéron (1648–1711). It is unclear if this was the consequence of male chivalry or of a reluctance on the part of the academicians to expend more time in the assessment of female candidates. See the "Répertoire chronologique des morceaux de réception," in Tours 2000, 221–283. For a general discussion of reception pieces from 1648 to 1793, see McAllister Johnson's essay, "Les morceaux de réception: protocole et documentation," in Tours 2000, 31–49.

12. See the discussion of this point in the essay by Marianne Roland Michel in this volume.

13. Louis-François de Bourbon (1717–1776), the sixth prince de Conti, amassed an impressive art collection that included, as was typical of the time, examples from the Italian, Dutch and Flemish, and French schools. Fortunately, his collection was documented by Gabriel de Saint-Aubin (1724–1780), who made thumbnail sketches of the paintings in the auction catalogues of the prince's estate sale in 1777 (see Bailey, fig. 4). In January 1776 the prince de Conti purchased Vallayer's early masterpiece *Still Life with Seashells and Coral* (1769, pl. 4) along with its pendant (now lost). See L'Isle-Adam 2000, 38–41.

14. Cochin was a famous illustrator and engraver, who served as secretary of the Académie in charge of the arts from 1755 to 1770. He was the official adviser to the marquis de Marigny, director of the Bâtiments du roi. Cochin's obituary of Chardin was written in 1780. It was preserved at the Académie de Rouen and was first published in 1875–1876 by C. de Beaurepaire. The text was also reproduced in Pascal and Gaucheron 1931, 1–15. For a useful translation, see Roland Michel 1996, 267–270.

15. The influential *amateur honoraire* the comte de Caylus played an instrumental role in the Académie during the 1740s. Among his lectures, written for the benefit of his fellow academicians, was "De la légèreté de l'outil," in which Caylus attempts to describe the correct handling of the brush as an essential part of the painter's facility. See Fontaine 1910b, 149–159.

16. Mariette, first an *associé libre* of the Académie in 1750 and then *amateur honoraire* in 1767, is best remembered for his important dictionary of artists, *Abécédario.* See Mariette 1966.

17. Quoted in Pascal and Gaucheron 1931, 30–31.

18. The classic account of the resurgence of history painting in the eighteenth century is Locquin 1978. More recently, Crow 1985 has provided an in-depth account of the politics surrounding the revival of history painting that subtended the rising star of David.

19. La Font de Saint-Yenne 1970.

20. Roland Michel 1970, 7, 58.

21. One could argue that one of Vallayer-Coster's submissions to the Salon of 1785, *Portrait of Madame de Saint-Huberty in the Rôle of Dido* (pl. 35), shares in the same revival of interest in the Greco-Roman tradition. The portrait records the famous actress's innovation of a body-baring, historically accurate costume, complemented by the architectural setting and cropped statue of the Venus Pudica. The climactic narrative moment depicted is just as sublime in its intent as that in David's *Oath of the Horatii.*

22. This term is defined by Cochin in a lecture given in 1778 to the Académie in Rouen: "What I mean by manner, or to be mannered, is everything that distances one from nature; all conventions learned or imagined, that do not have the truth as their basis, whether the result of the imitation of other masters or of our own mistakes" (J'appelle ici manière, ou être maniéré, tout ce qui s'éloigne de la nature; toute convention apprise ou imaginée, qui n'a pas le vrai pour base, soit qu'elle vienne de l'imitation des maîtres, ou de nos propres erreurs). Quoted in Michel 1993, 280.

23. Goodman 1995, 1:23.

24. See, for example, the comte de Caylus's lecture, "Sur la manière et les moyens de l'éviter" (On *la manière* and the means to avoid it), first delivered to the Académie on 2 September 1747 and re-read on 7 April 1751, 3 July 1762, and 6 August 1768 (reprinted in Fontaine 1910a, 175–182). For a cogent discussion of Cochin's critique of *la manière,* see Michel 1993, 279–281.

25. Goodman 1995, 1:24.

26. Roger de Piles was an influential *amateur,* best known for his vigorous defense of the artistic merits of *colore,* in the seventeenth-century academic debate between the proponents of Poussin and those of Peter Paul Rubens. In 1699 he was made *conseiller honoraire amateur* to the Académie. The lectures he delivered at the Académie were published under the title *Cours de peinture par principes* in 1708. The terms of de Piles's theory of art were frequently used in criticism and treatises on painting throughout the century.

27. See Fontaine 1909, 254 n. 1. Mariette claimed to have actively tried to dissuade La Font de Saint-Yenne from publishing his inflamatory *Réflexions sur quelques causes de l'état*

présent de la peinture en France. He obviously feared the consequences of an unauthorized, public critique of members of the Académie. Mariette goes on to comment that La Font must have been mortified to find that his treatise was claimed as the model for the slew of would-be, self-appointed critics who followed in his footsteps.

28. Pierre became First Painter to the King and director of the Académie in 1770. From a wealthy family, Pierre had a stellar institutional career, especially during the reign of the comte d'Angiviller as director of the Bâtiments du roi (1774–1794). Pierre was resented by some of his colleagues for his favoritism of his own students and despotic behavior. In 1777 he subjected the elderly Cochin, whom he did not like, to the indignity of being placed at the bottom of the hierarchy of official councillors to the Académie. When Chardin protested in defense of his old friend, he was rebuffed by Pierre. Pierre also opposed Chardin's request for an additional annuity, pointing out that the still-life painter already enjoyed more financial remuneration than many history painters, whose more elevated genre qualified them for greater compensation. Roland Michel 1996, 98–99.

29. Charles-Claude Flahaut de la Billarderie, comte d'Angiviller, assumed the directorship of the Bâtiments du roi in 1774. His systematic implementation of programming, meant to promote a new generation of history painters, prepared the way for David's ascent.

30. The term *effets pittoresques* is Cochin's. See Pascal and Gaucheron 1931, 10.

31. Chardin was labeled "the French Teniers" by contemporary critics. For a recent reexamination of Chardin in the context of Northern precedents, see Karlsruhe 1999. For a close examination of the role of Dutch emblematic prints in the development of Chardin's subject matter, see Snoep-Reitsma 1973, 147–243.

32. This is an issue well addressed by Roland Michel in her overview of the negative critical appraisal of Vallayer-Coster as necessarily inferior to Chardin by such art historians as Michel Florisoonne and Charles Sterling (Roland Michel 1970, 72–74).

33. In 1759, at the suggestion of the comte de Caylus, the Académie initiated a competition in facial expression, using a live model. This was intended by Caylus as a corrective to the mannered, learned conventions for signifying emotion through contortions of the face that students learned through copying set recipes in the tradition of Le Brun.

34. Cochin wanted the *Prix de torse*, which consisted of depicting the head and hands, painted from nature, from three different points of view, to be renamed the *Prix du coloris*, since it involved using color to capture the effects of light and shadow. Cited by Locquin 1978, 81 n. 4.

35. Jouin 1883, 387.

36. Goodman 1995, 2:86.

37. See, for example, the note on materials and techniques by the paintings conservator Joseph Fronek in Los Angeles 1990, 23–25.

38. See Katie Scott, "Chardin Multiplied," in Paris 1999, 68–73.

39. Quoted in Lagrange 1864, 457.

40. Goodman 1995, 1:61.

41. Diderot, *Salon of 1765*, Seznec and Adhémar, 1957–1967, 2:114.

42. "Dans un tableau fondu, les teintes, se succédant les unes aux autres par des nuances insensibles, se noyent les unes dans les autres, & ne peuvent être discernées que par un œil expert: dans un tableau heurté, les teintes sont posées largement, on pourroit dire brutalement, les unes à côté des autres; non-seulement leur succession brusque est très sensible, elle est même choquante, si l'on regarde l'ouvrage de fort près: mais quand on le voit de loin, l'air s'interpose entre le tableau et l'œil du spectateur, fond & noie ces teintes, & change l'ébauche grossière en une peinture terminée." Watelet and Lévêque 1972, 20.

43. Roland Michel 1970, 74.

44. For example, see Michael Baxandall's careful consideration of Chardin and eighteenth-century ideas on the nature of visual perception (Baxandall 1985, 74–104); see also Norman Bryson's extended meditation on the blurry quality of Chardin's still-life painting in his chapter "Still Life and 'Feminine' Space" (Bryson 1990, 92–95). Bryson uses the word "relaxed" on page 167.

45. Pascal and Gaucheron 1931, 29. As pointed out by Roland Michel, the accuracy of Mariette's account is thrown into question by the fact that *Boy Blowing Soap Bubbles* was not Chardin's first attempt at a figural subject. Roland Michel 1996, 33.

46. For the generally negative critical reception of the portrait at the Salon of 1785, see Roland Michel 1970, 222–224.

47. Roland Michel 1970, 77.

48. Goodman 1995, 1:4–5.

49. See, for example, Cleveland 1979. For a general discussion of nineteenth-century still-life painting in France, see Hardouin-Fugier 1998.

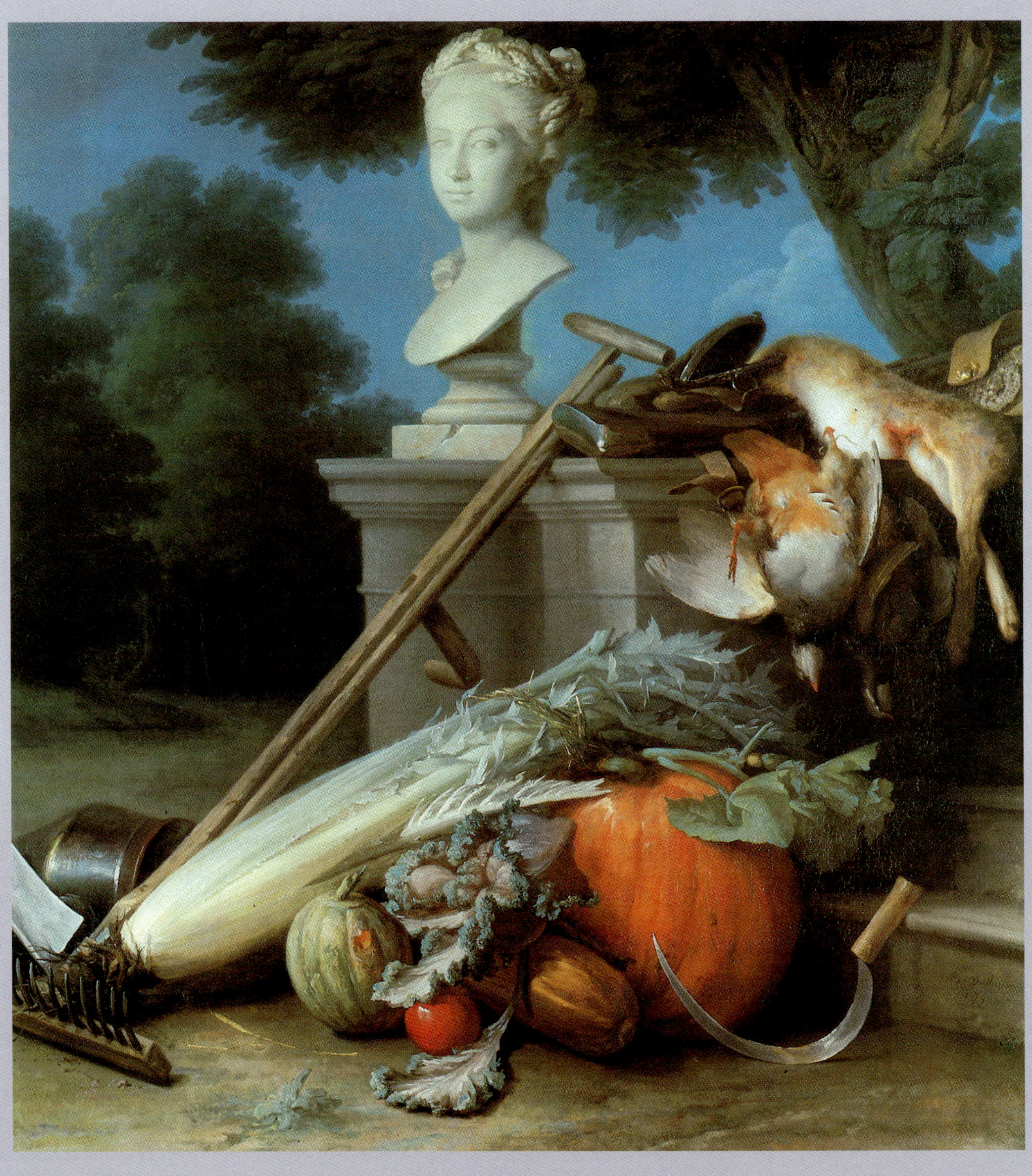

Anne Vallayer-Coster, *The Attributes of Hunting and Gardening*, 1774
Oil on canvas, 59 × 53 in. (150 × 134.5 cm). Present whereabouts unknown (fig. 7).

— Colin B. Bailey —

A Still-Life Painter and Her Patrons: Collecting Vallayer-Coster, 1770–1789

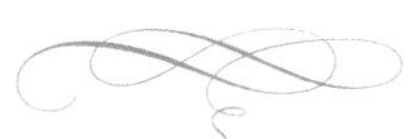

The category of painting we call genre is best suited to old men or those born old.
—Diderot, *Salon de 1765*[1]

DESPITE DIDEROT'S CAVEAT—in his criticism, the term *genre* is always associated with still-life painting—Mademoiselle Anne Vallayer was presented, accepted, and made a full member of the Académie royale de peinture et de sculpture at the tender age of twenty-six on 28 July 1770, with the seventy-six-year-old Pierre-Jean Mariette and the slightly younger Jean-Siméon Chardin (seventy-one) in attendance.[2] Her reception into the Académie was something of a media event—the *Mémoires secrets* reported on it, adulatory verses appeared in the *Mercure de France*—and her maiden appearance at the Salon just over a year later was greeted with rapture by the critics.[3] That a practitioner of the lowest and least venerable of the genres enjoyed consistent official support and enduring critical acclaim—it was only when she strayed from the representation of "la nature immobile" that Vallayer-Coster ran into difficulties with the press—is consistent with the laissez-faire ideology that informed both theory and practice at the Académie and the Salon. Even under an increasingly doctrinaire administration, with the State wedded to the regeneration of history painting and its promotion at all levels, members of the Académie who specialized in the lower genres were perfectly able to establish thriving and, it may be assumed, lucrative practices without in any sense running afoul of the authorities. Charles-Claude de la Billarderie, comte d'Angiviller, Louis XVI's imperious *surintendant des Bâtiments* who considered himself a crusader for artistic reform, insisted on the subordinate role of women painters in the Académie and limited its female membership to four, a "number sufficient to do justice to their talent": "Women can never truly contribute to the progress of the Arts, since propriety ["la décence de leur sexe"] forbids them from studying the figure from life, and from entering the school established and founded by Your Majesty."[4] Yet two years earlier d'Angiviller had been one of several well-born signatories at Vallayer's wedding to Jean-Pierre-Silvestre Coster, a lawyer and scion of a banking dynasty from Lorraine (the ceremony had taken place at Versailles, in the presence of the queen).[5] Not only had d'Angiviller campaigned vigorously for Vallayer to be given lodgings in the Louvre—whence she had finally moved in the spring of 1780—he would also acquire one of her still lifes for his choice collection devoted to the French school. The slightly crazed *Rooster and a White Chicken on a Stone Ledge* (pl. 39), shown at the Salon of 1787, was among the thirty-five French paintings that Republican commissioners considered "worthy of being preserved for the Nation" after their inspection of his abandoned mansion on the rue de l'Oratoire in April 1793, d'Angiviller, "one of the most ardent of aristocrats," having emigrated two years earlier.[6]

It has long been pointed out that during the 1770s and 1780s Anne Vallayer-Coster's Parisian clientele was an impressive one.[7] Most recently, and with only slight exaggeration, she has even been called "painter to the aristocracy."[8] Her patrons and collectors included the queen and members of her entourage, an ageing prince of the blood royal, three successive ministers of fine arts, an assiduous honorary member of the Académie, and a retired and philanthropic Protestant banker. The

phenomenon of prominent, well-born, and immensely
rich art lovers collecting modern French painting in an
encyclopedic (or at the least evenhanded) manner and
thereby presenting the French school as a whole, rather
than favoring a particular genre or style of painting, can
be related to the model established by Ange-Laurent de
La Live de Jully (1725–1779) in the 1750s and early 1760s.[9]
Ironically, it is highly unlikely that La Live de Jully, whose
collecting came to a premature end in the late 1760s
after he lost his mind, ever encountered Mademoiselle
Vallayer or knew her work. Yet "Patriotic Taste" *(le goût
patriotique)* as defined by La Live de Jully's enterprise
encouraged collectors to represent the modern and contemporary school systematically and to acquire the work
of a relatively broad range of practitioners (each of whom
showed at the Salon), from history painters to painters
of still life. It is within this framework that the collecting
of Vallayer-Coster's paintings can most fruitfully be
approached.[10]

While there are certainly collectors about whom we
would very much like to know more—in particular the
intriguingly named "Madame Vissitier" who lent two
monumental allegories of the Arts by Vallayer to the
Salon of 1777, both of which have resurfaced in recent
years[11]—many of Vallayer-Coster's clients were part of
a Parisian elite whose commitment to French art (and,
more precisely, to contemporary French art), although
in the vanguard of taste, was well established by the
1770s. It is not clear how she sold her work, but if stock
books of the sort that have survived for Joseph Vernet
(a good friend and supporter) and Louis Lagrenée are
any indication, it is likely that she sold directly to collectors, that she did not use dealers as intermediaries,
and that after 1780 her studio in the Louvre would also
have served as the meeting point for these transactions—
one reason, perhaps, for her eagerness to leave the top
floor of her mother's house on the rue de Roule.[12]

Theory and pedagogy aside, in Paris the practice of
art was rigorously monitored during the ancien régime.
Until an artist had been accepted into the Académie,
he or she could not show work, much less sell it, unless
affiliated with the despised guild, the Académie de
Saint-Luc (or unless the recipient of a royal dispensa-
tion, increasingly rare after midcentury). Because of
the legalities of production, artists might well learn
their craft through apprenticing within the family—as
Vallayer had done—but they could not function as independent makers of art without institutional protection.

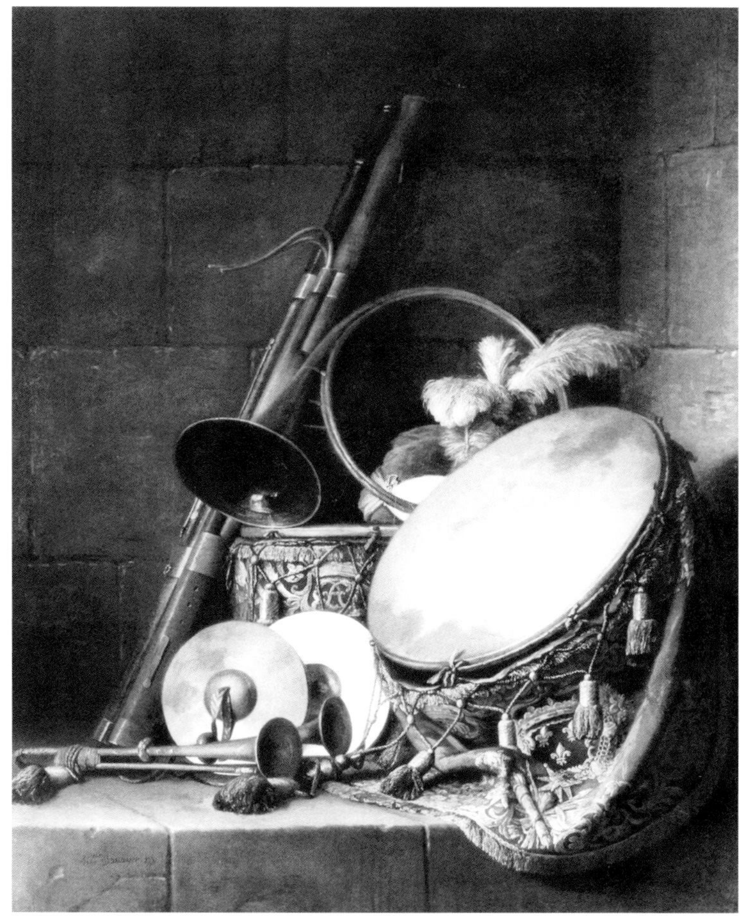

Fig. 1. Anne Vallayer-Coster, *Still Life with Military Musical
Instruments,* 1771. Oil on canvas, 63 × 51 in. (160 × 129.5 cm).
Private collection (cat. 13).

Hence not only Chardin, but both Elisabeth-Louise
Vigée-Le Brun and Adélaïde Labille-Guiard, the female
portraitists with whom Vallayer-Coster would be compared during the 1780s, had been obliged to seek membership of the Académie de Saint-Luc in the early stages
of their careers.[13]

Acceptance into the Académie royale, however, not
only conferred prestige (and protection from the guild
until its abolition in 1776) but more importantly perhaps provided access to the biennial Salon, which—in
the absence of dealers specializing in the marketing
of modern painting—functioned as a primary venue for
exposure and, more discreetly, for the sale of one's work.
The "nine or ten" canvases that Vallayer presented to
the Académie in July 1770[14]—two of which, the most
Chardinesque, were retained as *morceaux de réception*—
were, in all likelihood, back on view a year later at the
Salon of 1771. It seems likely that Vallayer, along with
practitioners of the lower genres generally, was obliged
to paint speculatively: only portraitists and history
painters had the luxury of embarking on pictures with

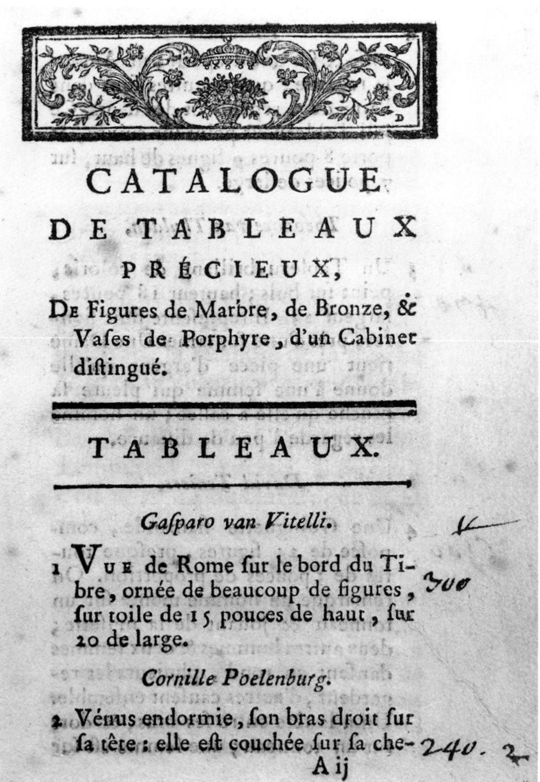

CATALOGUE DE TABLEAUX PRÉCIEUX, De Figures de Marbre, de Bronze, & Vases de Porphyre, d'un Cabinet distingué.

TABLEAUX.

Gasparo van Vitelli.

1 VUE de Rome sur le bord du Tibre, ornée de beaucoup de figures, sur toile de 15 pouces de haut, sur 20 de large. *300*

Cornille Poelenburg.

2 Vénus endormie, son bras droit sur sa tête : elle est couchée sur sa che- *240. 2*
A ij

ADDITION.
Mademoiselle Vallayer.

31 Une jeune Arabe, en pied, de grandeur naturelle, habillée selon le costume du pays, dans une espece de Sérail, ce Tableau est d'une touche large & fiere ; il porte 4 pieds 10 pouces de haut, sur 3 pieds 4 pouces de large, dans une bordure dorée, décorée d'un vase & de branches de palmier entrelassées de rangs de perles.

32 Un Trophée d'instrument militaire, composé d'une paire de timbale, basson, trompette, &c. avec le bonnet de Negre. Ce Tableau, vigoureusement touché, est connu, ayant été exposé au Sallon de l'Académie Royale de 1771. Il porte 5 pieds de haut, sur 4 de large, dans une bordure dorée de 5 pouces de large, à deux ornements.

33 Un Tableau, faisant pendant au précédent, représensentant un Bureau, dans le genre de Boule, sur lequel sont divers accessoirs de Sculpture, de Musique & d'Astronomie. Le fond est un rideau de velours vert. Ce Tableau, précieusement fait, a été exposé au Sallon de l'Académie Royale, de 1773.

34 Autre, représentant plusieurs objets d'Histoire naturelle, comme Minéraux & Animaux, dans des bocaux d'esprit de vin, grouppé avec un vase de porcelaine, garni de bronze doré, le fond est orné d'un rideau de taffetas. On remarque dans ce Tableau particuliérement la couleur séduisante, & la touche fine & hardie. Il porte 4 pieds de haut sur 3 de large, bordé d'une tringle de bois simple.

16 ADDITION.

35 Autre Tableau. Il représente divers productions d'Histoire naturelle, dans le genre maritime, comme Coquilles, Coreaux, Madrépores, &c. Etant de la même main, il y a les mêmes avantages, tant pour la couleur que pour la touche.

36 Un Tableau de *François Desportes*, représentant un Chien épagneul, attaquant des canards & des cignes dans une mare, bordée de roseaux & sureau. Ce Tableau est fait facilement & d'une couleur vigoureuse ; il porte 5 pieds & demi de long, sur 4 pieds de haut.

37 Un très beau Dessein sur toile, par *Carle Vanloo*. C'est le projet du fameux tableau d'Iphigénie, qu'il a fait pour le Roi de Prusse. Il porte 6 pieds de long, sur 4 de haut, dans une bordure dorée, de 2 pouces & demi de large.

Lu & approuvé, ce 9 Décembre 1775, COCHIN.

Vu l'approbation, permis d'imprimer, ce 13 Décembre 1775. ALBERT.

De l'Imprimerie de DIDOT, rue Pavée, 1775.

Fig. 2. Remy sale catalogue.

a clear sense of who would own them. Vallayer's splendid and imposing pair of natural history still lifes, signed and dated 1769—set pieces initially painted for submission to the Académie—were exhibited at the Salon of 1771, where, although highly praised, they failed to attract a buyer.[15] This was true of several other works as well: the full-length *Figure of a Young Arab Girl* and a large vertical pair of *Still Life with Military Musical Instruments*, one of which is illustrated here (fig. 1). All five Salon pictures were on view again just over four years later, this time as an addition to the sale of Madame Du Barry's collection, organized by Pierre Remy at the convent of the Pères Augustins in December 1775. Consigned in all likelihood by the artist herself, the appearance at public auction of so many recent Salon submissions, each meticulously catalogued and elegantly framed (fig. 2), serves to remind us how much remains to be discovered about the marketing of contemporary art at the end of the ancien régime.[16] Yet Du Barry's sale did not take place, and Vallayer's pair of natural history still lifes seem to have reverted to their owner, who promptly sold them the following month (January 1776) to the prince de Conti for 960 livres.[17]

In the more embittered environment of the 1780s, with competition from Gérard van Spaendonck in the very genre that she had made her own, Vallayer-Coster may have exhibited virtuoso flower paintings and hunt pieces that were primarily intended to "advertise" her proficiency within the public arena of the Salon. This, at least, was the argument of the compiler of her posthumous sale catalogue in June 1824, who noted of the *Vase of Flowers and Fruits* (present whereabouts unknown) exhibited at the Salon of 1783 ("one of the most capital works of this celebrated artist") that "She steadfastly refused the repeated demands of those illustrious figures and distinguished art lovers who so ardently wished to possess this picture, for she had no desire to relinquish the work that she considered her finest."[18] Dealer's hyperbole, perhaps, but it is also true that both *A Hound with Dead Game in a Landscape* (cat. 71), praised at the Salon of 1785, and the much maligned *Madame de Saint-Huberty in the Rôle of Dido* (pl. 35), also exhibited there, remained in the artist's possession at the time of her death and were doubtless among the stock to be viewed in her well-appointed studio by prospective buyers of her work.[19]

If, for the still-life painter no less than the history painter, the Académie and the Salon functioned as joint and complementary avenues of access to collectors and clients—with fellow (and more senior) academicians occasionally acting as the conduit to potential buyers—between 1770 and 1789 an interesting transformation may be said to have taken place with regard to the production and marketing of Vallayer-Coster's art. Simply put, during the 1770s she appears to have benefited from the traditional and broadly seigneurial model of patronage, depending on the good graces and tangible support of courtiers, administrators, and prominent academicians. She sold directly to collectors and seems to have been content (more or less) to paint "within her genre." While much of this would remain unchanged during the following decade, in the 1780s the experience of the Salon—the admonitions of the critics, the appearance of artists a decade younger competing in both genre and sex—emerges as a dominant force in her production. The marketplace had become her new Maecenas, and, after 1781, not only is Vallayer-Coster obliged to measure herself against Vigée-Le Brun and Labille-Guiard, portraitists much in demand and favored by various members of the royal family, but she is also under pressure from the thunderingly successful Dutch flower painter Gérard van Spaendonck, whose virtuoso performances earn him the critics' adulation as the "Van Huysum of the century."[20] To be the century's second Rosalba Carriera (1675–1757) is scant consolation, but even this sobriquet is soon dropped. With the ascendancy of her younger fellow female academicians, against whom she measures herself with generally disastrous consequences, Vallayer-Coster is urged again and again to return to her "premier genre," namely flower painting, and to stay there.[21]

In this argument, the more protected, traditional milieu of the Académie, the administration, the congeries of well-disposed collectors cohere to make the 1770s *decem anni mirabili* for an artist still in her thirties, eager to devote herself to the various categories of still-life painting. Although she had shown full-length figures from her first appearance at the Salon, Vallayer initially positioned herself as a worthy successor to Chardin, content to ennoble the genre of still life as he had done. The horizontal allegories claimed by the Académie amply displayed her potential as a painter of overdoors working in the manner of Chardin's recent commissions for Choisy and Bellevue.[22] As Madeleine Pinault Sørensen and Marie-Catherine Sahut have noted, the still lifes of shells and minerals eventually acquired by Conti were of the vertical format customarily imposed on portrait painters for their *morceaux de réception*.[23] Vallayer's lost *Still Life with Urn, Fruits, and a Lobster,* shown at the Salon of 1775 as in the possession

of Jean-Baptiste-François de Montullé, *associé-libre de l'Académie,* was of even grander scale, the size of gallery paintings made for private consumption.[24] Her ambitions for the genre of still life were noted by several sympathetic observers, Bachaumont concluding that the *Still Life with Military Musical Instruments* "would do justice to the studies made by a history painter."[25]

Critics wrote with unremitting generosity and enthusiasm about her early submissions to the Salon, even if the wording of their praise would hardly be acceptable today. Her talent was that of "a man perfectly at home in this genre of painting";[26] no other artist of the French school had achieved her "strength of coloring";[27] she was "far and away the leading artist for inanimate objects, grapes, peaches, plums, musical instruments."[28] It is noteworthy that such encomia were penned at a time when Chardin was still alive, even if his recent production was confined to portraits in pastel. Whereas Vallayer-Coster's modern historians have been at pains to distance her from Chardin and assert an originality and independence that sometimes strain the evidence at hand, contemporaries seem to have been more or less oblivious to his influence.[29] Diderot, in the portions of the *Salon of 1771* that are now securely attributed to him, was a lone dissenting voice: "Excellent, vigorous, harmonious: it's not Chardin, however, but if it's less good than this master, it's far above what is to be expected of a woman."[30]

In the following decade, Vallayer-Coster's career might be characterized as a casualty of the open market: the system of competition and exchange promoted by the Salon and its ever more trenchant critics provides an alternative context in which her art is judged and found lacking. In 1783 and 1785 her efforts in figure painting, both portraiture and genre, are savaged in the press, while even her flower paintings are now seen to lack "the precious finish" of Van Spaendonck (more than one reviewer considered them inferior to those of Piat-Joseph Sauvage as well).[31] Again and again, writers took her to task for having abandoned a genre in which she was "superior" in favor of one more elevated, certainly, but in which her performance was marred by mistakes in anatomy, faulty draftsmanship, and infelicities in drapery and accoutrements.[32] In discussing *Madame de Saint-Huberty in the Rôle of Dido* (which seems never to have been owned by its sitter), the *Mercure de France* was unsparing: "Her portraits are generally drawn in the most incorrect manner and their coloring is absolutely to be condemned. Her genre paintings, on the other hand, are true, natural in tone, and worthy of the highest praise."[33] At the Salon of 1787, Vallayer-Coster exhibited eleven works, only two of which were small (and unidentified) oval portraits; she was thanked for finally "remaining in her sphere."[34]

If the experience of the Salon—the tribunal of the critics, the appearance of younger competitors, the expectations of potential clients—played an increasing role in helping to shape Vallayer-Coster's production in the decade between 1779 and 1789, the artist's principal supporters and collectors remained attached to a different world, drawn as they were from the highest echelons of society at court and in the capital (and so less attentive to the rhetoric and polemic of the art press). In what sense might *their* expectations and requirements have influenced her production? Did collectors of still-life painting impose any constraints on an artist whose repertoire already offered an admirable range—from Chardinesque overdoors and baskets of fruits, to trophies of game and plate that evoked Jean-Baptiste Oudry and Claude-François Desportes, to grandiose displays of household objects in the manner of the Dutch and Flemish masters of the Golden Age (Balthasar van der Ast [1593/94–1657], Jan Davidsz de Heem, Pieter Claesz [1597/98–1661])? Or were they content to follow Diderot's injunction that one should never commission anything from an artist: "If one wants a fine painting by him, all that needs to be done is to say, 'Make me a painting and choose whatever subject you wish.'"[35]

Although the well-born collectors discussed here form only a small sample of her clients—of the 140 or so documented paintings listed by Marianne Roland Michel as having been made in the twenty years before the Revolution, we consider only a handful—it is instructive to note the various ways in which Vallayer-Coster's work might have entered these prestigious picture cabinets, as well as to evoke, however summarily, the different types of patrician collector to whom her precise and occasionally hard-edged representations of "la nature immobile" seem to have appealed.

The most prominent of Vallayer-Coster's early collectors was the fifty-nine-year-old Louis-François-Joseph de Bourbon (1717–1776), prince de Conti (fig. 3), the free-thinking and libertine cousin of Louis XV, who in the twenty years before his death maintained a rival court at the Palais du Temple, in the heart of Paris, which he occupied in his capacity as *grand prieur de France de l'ordre de*

Malte.[36] Conti's enormous collections—from mineralogy to optical instruments, from bronzes and porcelains to lacquer and antiquities—were rapidly assembled in the last decade of his life (purchases were made at the Saint-Aignan sale, barely a month before he died). Almost one-third of his paintings collection was devoted to the French school, offering an enviable survey of the seventeenth and eighteenth centuries, from Simon Vouet (1590–1649) to François Boucher, yet the vast majority of these had been bought on the secondary market, either at auction or through dealers. We now know that almost one hundred of Conti's French pictures were displayed together in *les Pièces françoises*, three ground-floor rooms in his state apartments that formed a gallery of sorts connecting the two north and south wings of his palace, and such a distinction was in keeping with the latest fashion for showing the French school in discrete spaces, separate from the Northern and Italian old masters (although it is clear that many of his French pictures did indeed hang with those of the other schools, as was the general custom).[37]

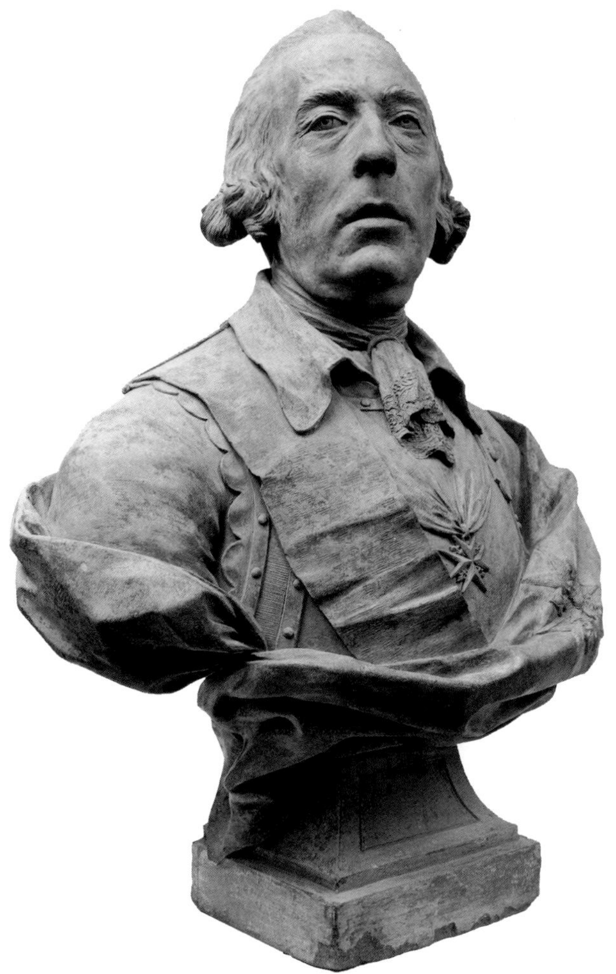

Fig. 3. Pierre Mérard, *Portrait Bust of Louis-François de Bourbon, prince de Conti*, 1776. Terracotta, 27½ in. (70 cm). Musée des Beaux-Arts, Dijon.

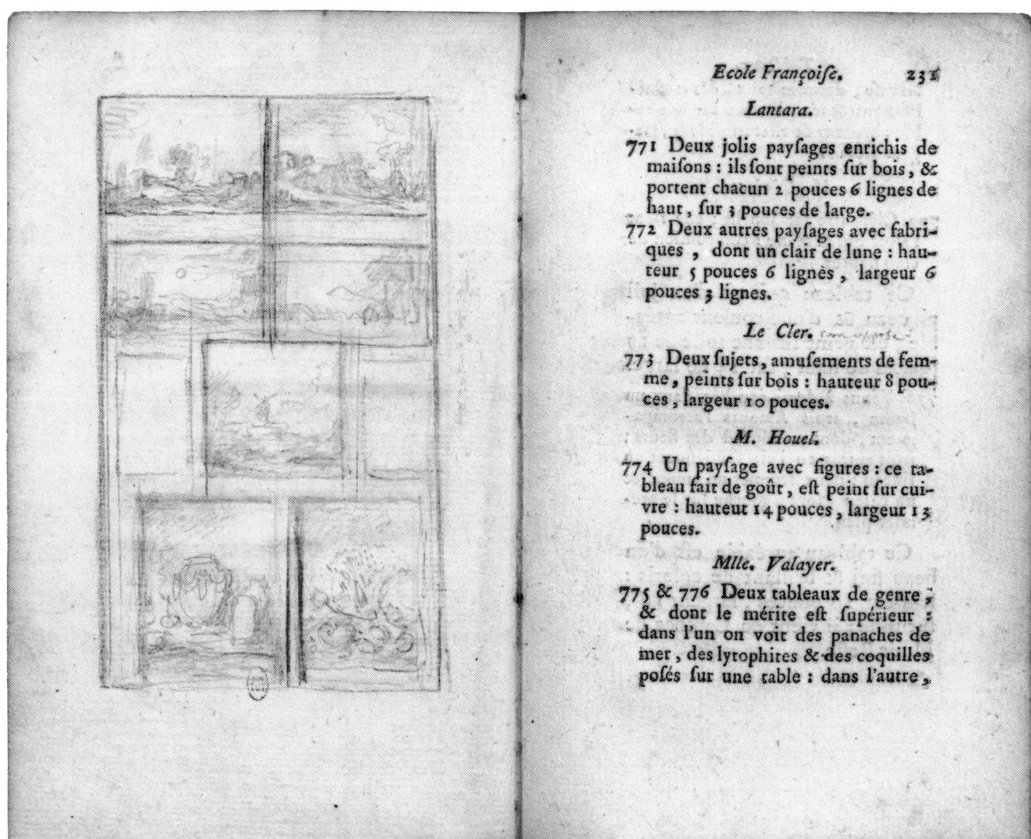

Fig. 4. *Catalogue of the Sale of the prince de Conti*, 1777. Bibliothèque nationale de France, Cabinet des Estampes.

Conti was also an avid collector of natural curiosities, and he reserved seven rooms on the first floor of his palace, named after their contents—*l'appartement dit le Coquiller, la Pièce des Papillons, le Laboratoire de l'abbé Boileau*—for his collections of shells, botanical specimens, stuffed animals, and insects.[38] It would be tempting to associate Vallayer's pendants of shells and minerals with Conti's passion for conchology, especially since her unusual pairing of exotic shells with more mundane rocks and crystals would have been understood by those interested in such things as a novel contrast of the animal and mineral worlds (the gorgonia and aquatic curiosities meticulously described in her canvas having recently been reassigned from the vegetable to the animal realm).[39] Yet we know that Conti had nothing to do with the striking subject of Vallayer's still lifes, and that it was only five years after the pendants had first been exhibited at the Salon that he chose to acquire them (fig. 4). Conti did buy new work by younger artists on occasion—Pierre-Alexandre Wille's (1748–1821) *Return to Virtue* had been shown at the Salon of 1775—but it was exceptional that he dealt directly with them.[40] In this sense, Vallayer was privileged to have been approached by the prince (or a member of his household), and to have received the generous payment of 960 livres (a year later, the pair would sell at auction for only a quarter of that sum), although it is quite possible that Conti had first been alerted to her still lifes in Remy's catalogue of the abortive Du Barry sale a month before he decided to purchase them.[41]

If Conti's pendants, while not having been painted *for* him, may be said to be reflective generally of a savant culture that appealed to him and others of his rank (had not d'Angiviller bequeathed his collection of minerals to the Museum d'Histoire naturelle in 1780?) an even closer link between artist and patron may be proposed in the pair of pendants Vallayer painted for the abbé Terray in 1774. The most hated finance minister of the ancien régime, Joseph-Marie Terray (1715–1778; fig. 5)—"the sultan in a clerical collar"—had succeeded the marquis de Marigny as *directeur-général des Bâtiments* in July 1773, and he held this post in conjunction with his other ministerial functions until his dismissal in August of the following year. While in office, he began to commission prominent sculptors and painters of the Académie to create a series of statues and gallery pictures for his private collection that reflected his commitment to French agriculture and commerce, an unpromising agenda that nevertheless inspired some of the finest genre paintings and allegorical statuary of the 1770s.[42]

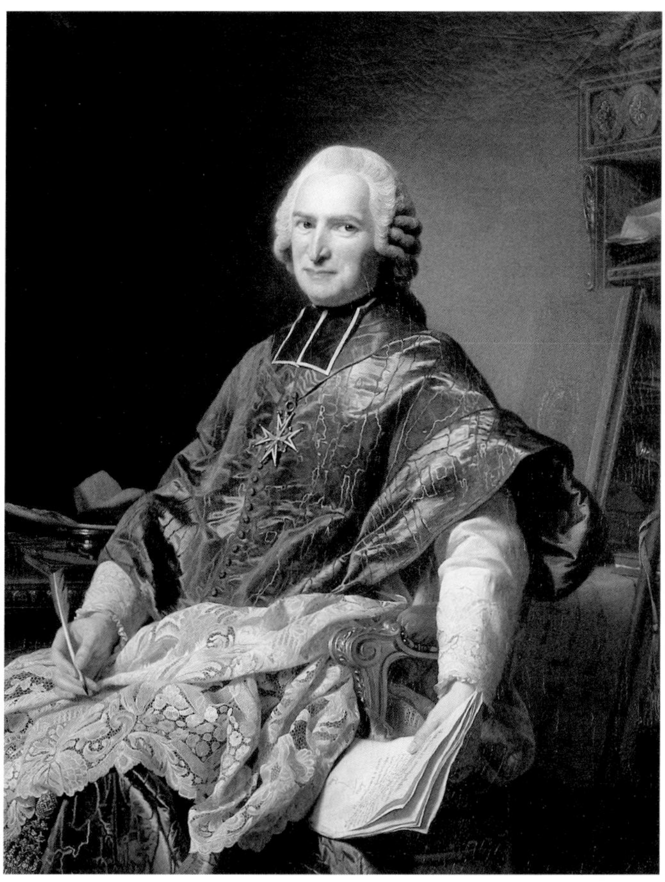

Fig. 5. Alexandre Roslin, *Portrait of Joseph-Marie Terray, abbé de Molesmes, ministre*, 1774. Oil on canvas, 50¾ × 38⅛ in. (129 × 97 cm). Musée national des Châteaux de Versailles et de Trianon.

Among his earliest commissions were two impressive still lifes by Vallayer, *Vase of Flowers with a Bust of Flora* (fig. 6) and *The Attributes of Hunting and Gardening* (fig. 7), both signed and dated 1774, one of which was noted when they were sold in April 1783 as having been executed "when he was Minister of Finance," in other words, before he left office in August 1774.[43] Vallayer's pendants were listed at the Salon of 1775 as "Un Buste de Flore, & un vase rempli de Fleurs sur un Bureau" and "Un Buste de Cerès & les attributs de la Moisson, avec différentes espèces de légumes," but in neither case was Terray's ownership mentioned.[44] Such was his unpopularity that he withheld his name from all the paintings he lent to the Salons of 1775 and 1777.

Neither of Terray's pendants received extended commentary in the Salon reviews—Vallayer was once again praised for having painted the flowers and fruits "like a talented man"[45]—and while both still lifes were catalogued in Terray's posthumous sale in January 1779, they are not recorded in his postmortem inventory.[46] Thus we cannot state with any assurance in which room of his *hôtel* on the rue Notre-Dame des Champs they would have hung. Despite Terray's passion for porcelain, there is little in *Vase of Flowers with a Bust of Flora* that can be

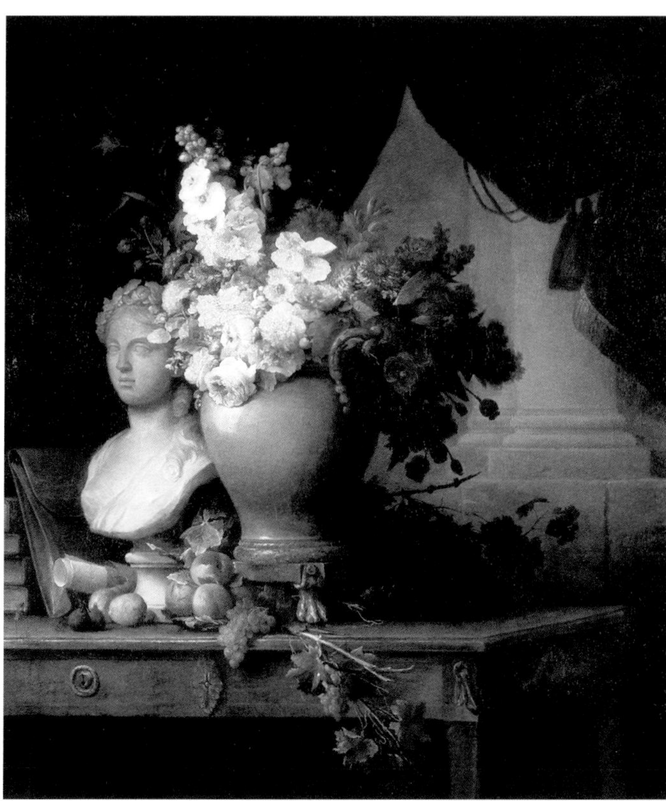

Fig. 6. Anne Vallayer-Coster, *Vase of Flowers with a Bust of Flora*, 1774. Oil on canvas, 60⅝ × 51⅛ in. (154 × 130 cm). Private collection (cat. 30).

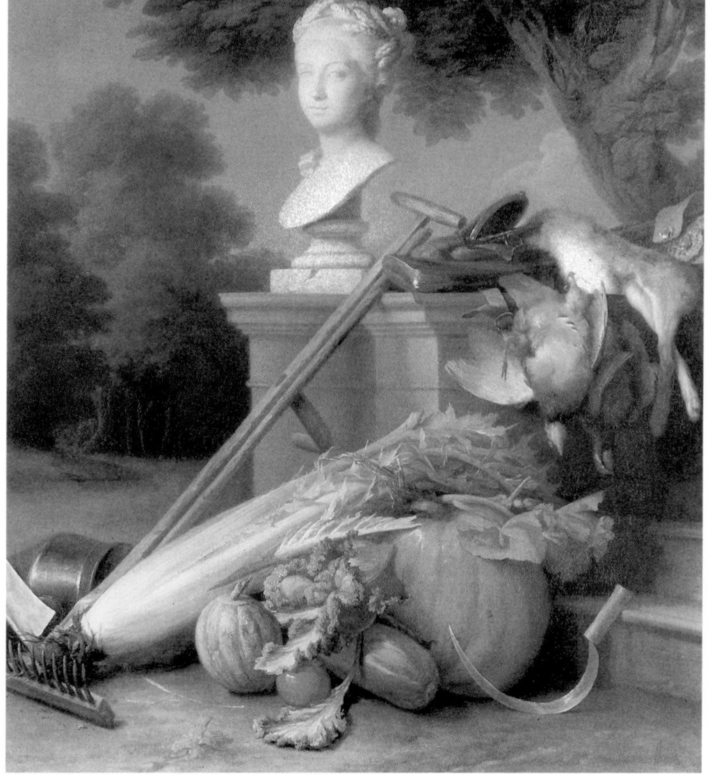

Fig. 7. Anne Vallayer-Coster, *The Attributes of Hunting and Gardening*, 1774. Oil on canvas, 59 × 53 in. (150 × 134.5 cm). Present whereabouts unknown (cat. 24).

associated more personally with him: the books and portfolio of red Moroccan leather evoke studiousness generally, and the furniture and gilt-bronze mounts (the lion's paws on the base of the vase, the drapery through rings on the corner of the table) are motifs that reappear in several of Vallayer's still lifes.

However, without burdening the somewhat meager evidence at hand, it may be possible to relate the iconography of Vallayer's pendant, described in the Salon *livret* as an allegory of the Harvest, and catalogued in 1779 as representing "The Attributes of Hunting and Gardening," to issues of more immediate concern to the minister. Here Ceres, goddess of Nature, presides in a verdant landscape over dead game and hunting equipment that are dwarfed by the assorted vegetables and gardening implements in the foreground: particularly prominent are the rake and scythe. This unlikely ensemble, the latter elements of which are repeated in no other painting by her, would appear to signal Terray's private interest in horticulture—he was a keen gardener—as well as his more public commitment to a flourishing agrarian economy. His single commission to a history painter, Nicolas-Guy Brenet's (1728–1792) *Roman Farmer (L'Agriculteur romain)*, showed Caius Furius Cressinus with his oxen, plow, and assorted farming instruments painstakingly described.[47] Terray's obsession with the fruits of the land had been mocked by Voltaire earlier that year in his *Dialogue de Pégase et du vieillard*, in which he quipped that the creations of Parnassus were of little interest to the minister: "Monsieur l'abbé Terray, pour le bien du royaume / Préfère un laboureur, un prudent économe / A tous nos vains écrits, qu'il ne lira jamais."[48] Indeed, two books on the theory and practice of gardening by the abbé Roger Schabol (1691–1768), published posthumously in 1770 by his nephew Antoine-Nicolas Dézallier d'Argenville, had been dedicated to Terray, praised as "a Minister who values agriculture and who takes pleasure in encouraging it."[49]

Although it might be straining credulity to argue that Vallayer's *Attributes of Hunting and Gardening* was intended as an illustration of the reforming ideas presented in Schabol's manuals, certain correspondences are suggestive, and it is quite possible that Terray, or a member of his household, may have indicated certain elements that were to be included. Schabol had championed the cultivation of the melon, a fruit unknown in France thirty years before that was now grown in over forty varieties; he had also provided detailed instructions

for the planting of cardoons (an artichoke-like plant). Both species appear prominently in Terray's still life.[50] His *Théorie du Jardinage* had also criticized the practice of paring leaves from cucurbitaceous fruits such as melons and pumpkins, all the more misguided since these "false flowers contain the strongest seeds and are essential to the propagation of the species."[51] Among the array of vegetables and gardening implements that surround Ceres in Vallayer's *Attributes of Hunting and Gardening,* such leaves are shown in profusion. Thus, at the very least, did one of her pair of still lifes for the abbé Terray conform to the practices of good gardening.

Whereas Terray had insisted on anonymity at the Salon of 1775, Jean-Baptiste-François de Montullé (1721–1787), the owner of Vallayer's impressive *Still Life with Urn, Fruits, and a Lobster* (present whereabouts unknown), exhibited at the same Salon, had not hesitated to present himself as *associé-libre de l'Académie.* At the following Salon of 1777, to which he lent a pair of imposing floral still lifes painted the previous year (pls. 19, 20), he was listed in the *livret* as "Secrétaire des Commandemens de la Reine," a reference to the office he had held in Queen Marie Leszczyńska's household some twenty years before. A *conseiller au Parlement* whose wife, Elisabeth Haudry, the daughter of a *fermier-général*, had brought a dowry of 400,000 livres to their marriage, Montullé was one of the most active honorary members of the Académie (during the 1780s he rarely missed a Saturday meeting). As the second cousin and heir of Jean de Jullienne, this post had been reserved for him on the express wishes of the latter, and his collection of French paintings, housed in his *hôtel* on the rue de la Cherche Midi that had once belonged to the comtesse de Verrue, included many canvases formerly owned by Jullienne, among them masterpieces by Antoine Watteau (1684–1721) and Jean-Baptiste Greuze.[52]

Montullé had taken over the Gobelins dye works and weaving establishment after Jullienne's death in 1766, but a series of financial and familial reversals in the 1770s and early 1780s would greatly diminish his fortune. In December 1783 he was obliged to sell his collection of paintings to raise funds for the ailing Gobelins. He also separated from his wife and went to live with his youngest daughter and her husband, the marquis Lancelot de Turpin de Crissé, another honorary member of the Académie.[53] Not all of Montullé's collection appeared at auction in 1783. His drawings, which included several splendid sheets by Watteau, were not sold until his death

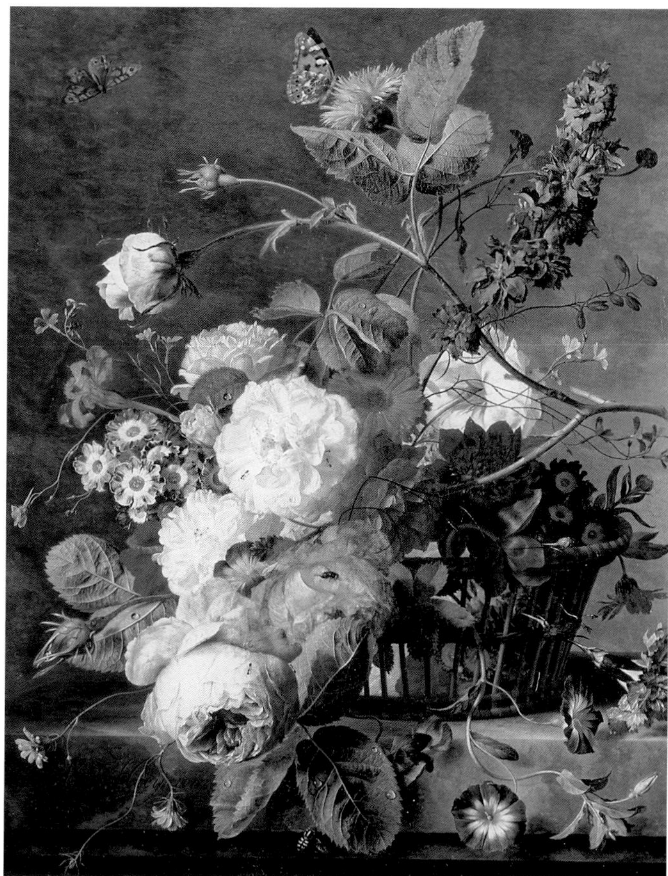

Fig. 8. Jan van Huysum, *A Basket of Flowers with Butterflies*, n.d. Oil on wood, 20⅞ × 16⅛ in. (53 × 41 cm). Musée du Louvre, Paris.

four years later, and, alone among the work of living artists, he retained Vallayer-Coster's still lifes (none of which appeared in either of his sales). Given Montullé's reduced circumstances, this may be interpreted as signaling a certain attachment. With regard to his old masters, there was less sentiment (and more money) involved. In September 1784 d'Angiviller purchased Jan van Huysum's small *A Basket of Flowers with Butterflies* (fig. 8) for the nascent museum from Madame de Montullé for the considerable sum of 8,000 livres, justifying the expenditure as both charitable and opportune: "her financial difficulties are well known."[54]

Despite his ownership of the Gobelins, Montullé was a member of the nobility of the Robe, allied through marriage to the richest officeholders in the land (the *fermiers-généraux*). Vallayer could also boast collectors from the even more exalted ranks of the *noblesse d'épée*: at the Salon of 1779 she exhibited the oval *Flowers in a Lapis Vase* (present whereabouts unknown), listed as belonging to the comte de Merle, who also owned a bust-length *Portrait of a Woman* by her (both appeared in his sale of March 1784). An *avignonnais* aristocrat, Charles-Louis

de Beauchamp, comte de Merle (1723–1793; fig. 9), was "un homme de condition" of relatively modest fortune, who in February 1750 had married the dishonored but extremely wealthy heiress Anne-Marie Peyrenc de Moras, daughter of the millionaire financier Abraham Peyrenc de Moras who had built the *hôtel* on the rue de Varenne that is now home to the Musée Rodin. This propitious union enabled Merle to purchase an office in the blue-blooded Compagnie des Mousquetaires du roi and eventually to secure the appointment of ambassador to Portugal, a post he served for only eighteen months before being recalled by Etienne-François, duc de Choiseul, in August 1760. Thereafter Merle resided in the aristocratic quarter of Paris, renting an *hôtel particulier* in the faubourg Saint-Germain, and rising in the army to become *maréchal de camp* by 1780.[55]

His collection, formed in the 1770s, was renowned for its Dutch and Flemish old masters.[56] Among his more modest group of thirty-two French paintings only Vernet's monumental early Italian pendants, *Seaport: Sunset* (Timken Art Gallery, San Diego) and *View of Naples with a Rainbow* (private collection) stand out as works of real distinction.[57] Merle's Northern cabinet pictures were coveted by the Maison du roi—as soon as the sale of March 1784 had been announced, Pierre noted, "what a fine opportunity! one will be able to see the pictures for oneself"[58]—and the crown purchased David Teniers the Younger's (1610–1690) *Denial of Saint*

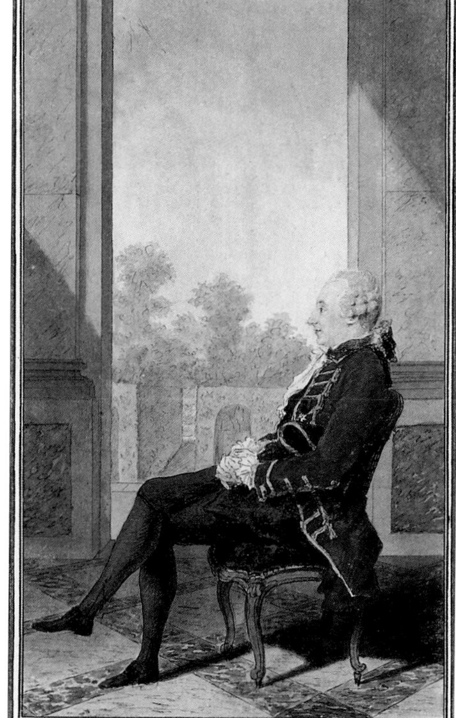

Fig. 9. Louis de Carmontelle, *Portrait of Charles-Louis de Beauchamp, comte de Merle*, 1768. Watercolor, 9⅞ × 7 in. (25 × 18 cm). Musée Condé, Chantilly.

Peter for 10,319 livres. At the same sale Vallayer-Coster's flower picture fetched a modest 128 livres.[59]

Pierre's comment, cited above, suggests that Merle's picture cabinet may not have been accessible, even to senior members of the Académie, and we do not know by what route Vallayer came to know the comte de Merle well enough not only to sell him pictures but to request their loan to the Salon of 1779. It was probably through Merle that she also secured an introduction to the most important collector of contemporary French painting of the 1770s, an aristocrat of similar age and pedigree, and an old friend who had been a witness at Merle's marriage twenty-five years before. Louis-Gabriel, marquis de Véri-Raionard (1722–1785), who owned masterpieces by Jean-Honoré Fragonard (1732–1806) and Greuze and who assembled the most rigorously modern collection of French painting of his day, seems to have had an aversion to still-life painting: Chardin was the *grand absent* in his picture cabinet.[60] Although Véri did not own a single work by Vallayer-Coster, he appeared for the bride at the signing of her wedding contract at Versailles in April 1781, a mark of distinction he is not known to have conferred on any of the artists whose work he collected.[61]

That Vallayer-Coster should be married in such grandeur at Versailles was the most conspicuous indication of the "particular protection" with which Marie-Antoinette had been honoring her since 1779. Until the ascendancy of the Polignacs and Joseph-Hyacinthe-François, comte de Vaudreuil, and their sponsorship of Vigée-Le Brun, the queen's circle provided the most important nexus of patronage outside the Salon. Unlike ministerial and aristocratic circles in Paris, however, it championed Vallayer-Coster as a portraitist and figure painter, with not altogether happy results.

As early as March 1779, in the complicated arrangements for the construction of her lodgings in the Louvre, which required the intervention of two ministers of state (d'Angiviller and Charles-Gravier, comte de Vergennes), it was noted that the twenty-four-year-old queen had sanctioned the project.[62] It may have been at about this time that Marie-Antoinette commissioned the small oval *Bust of a Young Vestal* (pl. 25), exhibited at the Salon of 1779 as "belonging to the Queen": an unusual work, looking back to Jean Raoux's (1677–1734) vestals of the Regency, and which inspired the inevitable comparisons with Rosalba Carriera.[63] In July 1779 d'Angiviller commissioned a full-length portrait of the king's aunt, Madame Sophie, in which she was to be shown holding the plan of the abbey of L'Argentière. Intended for Marie-Madeleine de Gayardon de Fenoyl, prioress of the "dames comtesses de Largentière," this rather lackluster project was encouraged by d'Angiviller since it would provide Vallayer with an opportunity "to become better acquainted with the royal family."[64] This indeed seems to have been the case, for within a year Vallayer was working at Versailles on portraits of the queen, as well, perhaps, as of one of her ladies-in-waiting, the devout Laure de Fitz-James, princesse de Chimay (1744–1817). In July 1780 Vallayer informed d'Angiviller that she would wait "until her portrait [of the latter] is completely finished" before presenting his letter of introduction to her.[65] At the same time she may also have received the commission to paint a portrait of Adélaïde Auguié, one of Marie-Antoinette's chambermaids and sister to her lady-in-waiting (and memorialist) Madame Campan, whose family attempted to regulate lay access to the queen. The portraits of Madame Sophie and Madame Auguié would both be shown at the Salon of 1781. Diderot criticized the former as trivially painted and dull in color ("The face looks nothing like her, so much the better"); the latter, which showed the sitter arranging flowers in a vase (perhaps cat. 123), fared better, but it reminded him of a picture "in need of retouching."[66]

With the admission of Vigée-Le Brun to the Académie in May 1783 and her appearance at the Salon the following August, Vallayer-Coster's standing at court rapidly diminished, although she would work for the aristocratic Coigny brothers, the eldest of whom, Marie-François-Henri de Franquetot, duc de Coigny (1737–1821), *maréchal de France* and governor of Choisy, was a favored member of the queen's inner circle.[67] His small collection, impounded after his emigration in 1792, included polished genre paintings by Marguerite Gérard and Marc-Antoine Bilcoq (1755–1838), Fragonard's bravura sketch for *The Lock (Le Verrou)* (formerly in the Ojjeh collection), as well as "A Vase filled with different flowers, on canvas, height twelve inches, width ten inches, by Vallaier [*sic*] Coster."[68] Coigny's younger brother, Gabriel-Augustin de Franquetot, comte de Coigny (1740–1817), *gentilhomme d'honneur* to Madame Elisabeth and lover of the princesse de Guéménée (the disgraced *gouvernante* of the royal children), commissioned Vallayer-Coster to paint a wedding portrait of his fifteen-year-old daughter, Anne-Françoise-Aimée (1769–1820) (present whereabouts unknown), who was married at Choisy to the fourteen-year-old marquis de Fleury in June 1785.[69] Vallayer-Coster's

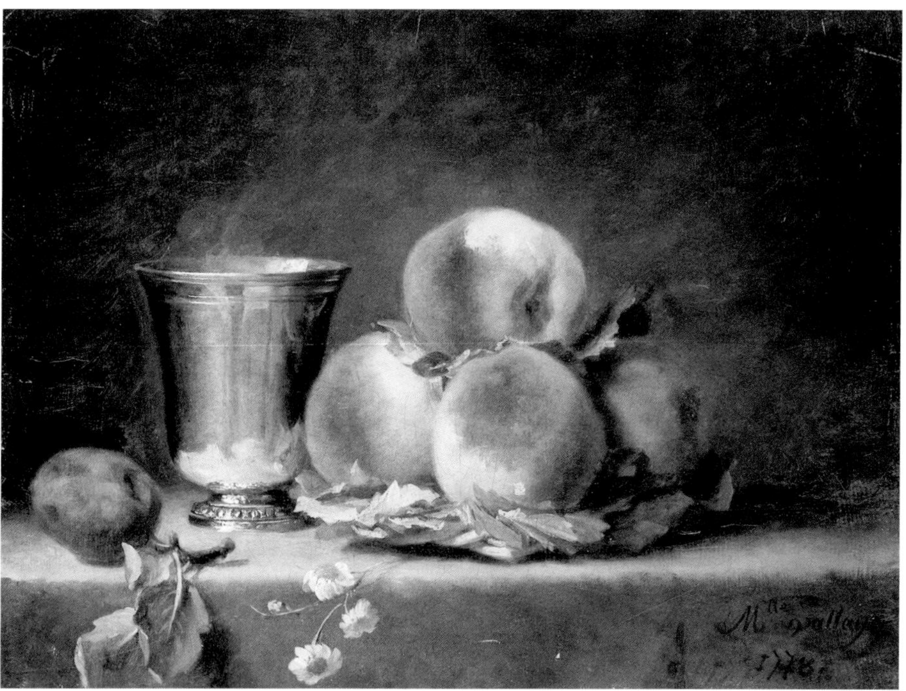

Fig. 10. Anne Vallayer-Coster, *Still Life with a Basket of Peaches and a Silver Goblet*, 1778. Oil on canvas, 12 × 16⅜ in. (30 × 38.5 cm). Present whereabouts unknown (cat. 48).

sizable portrait of Mademoiselle Coigny picking flowers in a garden was shown at the Salon that year, where it received a marginally less bitter press than her disastrous portrait of the actress Saint-Huberty: the bookseller Simon-Prosper Hardy considered it indecent.[70] It is perhaps not surprising that after 1785 Vallayer-Coster's commissions from courtiers came to an end.

Of quite different pedigree was the collector who emerges as the artist's most eager supporter of the 1780s, and whose acquisitions were of greater quality and significance than those that originated at court. Jean Girardot de Marigny (1733–1796) was the son of a wealthy Protestant timber merchant whose family fortune had been made supplying Paris with wood.[71] Connected to some of the most powerful banking houses in Paris and Geneva, in 1762 Girardot de Marigny had formed his first partnership with Louis Germany de Necker. Fifteen years later he established a second bank with another Swiss financier, Rodolphe-Emmanuel Haller, and within two years Girardot, Haller et Cie was competing with Pierre-Augustin Caron de Beaumarchais for contracts to finance France's involvement in the American War of Independence. In 1782 he took over as administrator of the Caisse d'Escompte, the institution responsible for introducing paper money into general circulation, and for the rest of the decade the services of his bank would be sought by both the crown and the city of Paris.[72]

Girardot de Marigny began to collect contemporary art in 1777, and Joseph Vernet was by far his favorite artist. Between 1777 and 1789 Vernet painted no fewer than nineteen landscapes for his *cher patron*, who regularly paid the artist's standard fee of 3,000 livres in advance and came to inspect work in progress only when bidden.[73] It was possibly Vernet who introduced Girardot de Marigny to Vallayer-Coster—the families had been friends since the 1760s and both artists owned examples of each other's work—and this connection proved crucial, for unlike many collectors of French painting, Girardot de Marigny did not feel obliged to represent the school comprehensively. He did not collect the work of previous generations of academicians and showed no interest in history painting of any sort, although he would commission Jean-Antoine Houdon's (1741–1828) monumental bronzes of Diana and Apollo.[74]

Girardot de Marigny owned two pairs of pendants by Vallayer-Coster: a pair of modest Chardinesque still lifes first shown at the Salon of 1779, one of which has recently reappeared (fig. 10), and the more ambitious *Still Life with Lobster*, dated 1781 (pl. 33), with its pair *Still Life with Game*, dated 1782 (pl. 34), the latter exhibited at the Salon the following August.[75] Although Vallayer-Coster had shown at the Salon since 1771, it was thanks to Girardot de Marigny's enthusiasm for Mammès-Claude Pahin de la Blancherie's alternative venue for contemporary art that her work was seen at the Salon de la Correspondance at the Hôtel Villayer on the rue Saint-André des Arts.[76] Her *Still Life with Lobster* made its first public appearance at one of Pahin's weekly assemblies on 19 December 1782; it appeared for a second time in

July 1783 as part of his ambitious survey of three centuries of French painting.[77] In May 1785 Girardot de Marigny lent three other still lifes by her to the Salon de la Correspondance, all of which had first been shown at the official Salon, as was proudly noted in Pahin's catalogue.[78] D'Angiviller considered Pahin de la Blancherie's enterprise a threat to the Académie royale, and he steadfastly refused to grant it the slightest official recognition. Yet for collectors such as Girardot de Marigny, who not only lent his paintings to the Salon but also offered to donate the work of living artists to the royal collection, it is not clear that these institutions were seen to be in any conflict whatsoever.[79]

Vigorously supported at the highest levels of officialdom; her work purchased by an array of well-born, wealthy, and prominent collectors; enjoying regular exposure in public exhibitions: for all this, many questions remain to be answered about the ways in which Vallayer-Coster produced and sold her work in the privileged environment to which she had access before the Revolution. Do the number of replicas and repetitions in her oeuvre indicate the existence of a thriving secondary market, and if so, how was this market organized? Did her marriage to a well-to-do lawyer reduce her need to sell? It is noteworthy that of her substantial dowry of 34,000 livres, nearly one-quarter came from outstanding fees for commissioned portraits.[80] Given the wretched resale value of her still lifes—Terray's pendants sold for 230 livres, Conti's for a little more, 240 livres—her eagerness to present herself as a portraitist may have had financial implications as well.[81] Until more is known about the investments and landholdings of the Coster household, and the marketing of genre painting in the final decades of the ancien régime, it is impossible to answer these questions adequately; but it would be timely to turn our attention to them.

for Marianne Roland Michel

I am indebted to Alicia Lubowski for her painstaking and meticulous research, as I am to Margaret Iacono for her practical support and assistance. Thanks are also due to Anel Piageat, Martin Chapman, Carol Togneri, Axel Rügger, and Alan Wintermute.

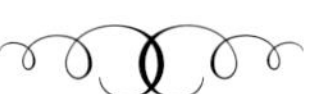

NOTES

1. "Cette peinture qu'on appelle de genre devrait être celle des vieillards ou de ceux qui sont nés vieux." Goodman 1995, 1:60 (original in Bukdahl and Lorenceau 1984, *Diderot, Salon de 1765*, 118).

2. Montaiglon 1875–1892, 8:48–49.

3. See *Mercure de France*, September 1770, 74–75: "Malgré les obstacles de son sexe, elle a porté l'art si difficile de rendre la nature, à un degré de perfection qui enchante & qui étonne" (The disadvantages of her sex notwithstanding, she has taken the difficult art of rendering nature to a degree of perfection that enchants and surprises us). See also Roland Michel 1970, 21–23, 272.

4. "Ce nombre est suffisant pour honorer le talent, les femmes ne pouvant jamais être utiles au progrès des Arts, la décence de leur sexe les empêchant de pouvoir étudier d'après nature et dans l'École publique établie et fondée par Votre Majesté." Montaiglon 1875–1892, 9:157, 14 May 1783. This comment was made in response to the royal order to confer membership of the Académie on Mme Vigée-Le Brun.

5. Roland Michel 1970, 264–267, for the publication of Vallayer's marriage contract of 21 April 1781.

6. On d'Angiviller as a collector, see Bailey 1989, 17–18. For his ownership of Vallayer-Coster's *Animaux de Basse-Cour* see Tuetey 1902, 2:334: "No. 10, Un de Madame *Vallayer*, de 20 pouces sur 2 pieds, rep une poule et un coq morts." A footnote indicates that this work was offered to a certain "citoyen Savounen."

7. Roland Michel 1970, 45–50. Her magisterial summary still stands: "Au total, une clientèle variée, mais pourtant recrutée en grande partie dans le milieu des courtisans, des hauts fonctionnaires, et des personnages influents" (In general, she was supported by a clientele of courtiers, high officers of state, and other influential figures).

8. Hardouin-Fugier and Grafe 1996, 289.

9. See introduction to Bailey 1988, vii–xliii.

10. Much of the material in the second part of this essay is taken from Bailey 2002.

11. See cats. 41, 44.

12. For the documents relating to her move to custom-built lodgings in the Louvre, see Roland Michel 1970, 260–264. Desperate to move in, even if the plaster was still wet, in January 1780 Vallayer complained to d'Angiviller that her present domestic arrangements were causing her great difficulties, being "logée très haut et manquant absolument de jour."

13. For Chardin's membership of the Académie de Saint-Luc between 1724 and 1727, see Paris 1999, 19–20. Vigée-Le Brun had been obliged to join the Académie de Saint-Luc in October 1774, after her studio had been seized by officers of the

Châtelet; see Fort Worth 1982, 12. Labille-Guiard also exhibited at the Académie de Saint-Luc's Salon of 1774; see Passez 1973, 12, where it is noted that she had been "agréée à l'Académie de Saint-Luc depuis plusieurs années."

14. The number comes from Jean-Georges Wille's diary entry for 28 July 1770: "Dans la même assemblée fut agréée et reçue mademoiselle Vallayer, fille d'un orfévre, sur neuf ou dix tableaux qu'elle avait exposés." Duplessis 1857, 1:450.

15. On these pendants, one of which has recently been acquired by the Musée du Louvre, see Foucart et al. 1996, 146–150; and Pinault Sørensen and Sahut 1998.

16. *Catalogue de Tableaux Précieux* 1775, nos. 31–35. These unusually complete entries, of interest also for their descriptions of the frames in which the pictures were presented, are reprinted in the appendix to this essay.

17. For the prince de Conti's payment to Vallayer in January 1776, see Sahut, in Foucart et al. 1996, 146.

18. "Elle a constamment résisté aux instances réitérées des personnages illustres et des amateurs distingués qui désiraient posséder ce tableau, dont elle n'a jamais voulu se désaisir, le regardant comme le meilleur des ses ouvrages," Coster sale 1824, reprinted in Roland Michel 1970, 274.

19. Roland Michel 1970, 274, nos. 2, 32.

20. See, for example, the comments in the *Journal de Paris* and the *Affiches de Paris* for September 1781.

21. For an example of the general lament, see the comments in the *Mémoires secrets* for 1785: "Quant à Madame Coster, on est fâché de lui voir abandoner presque entièrement le genre de la nature morte où elle était supérieure, pour se livrer au portrait et au portrait historié, dans lequel elle est bien inférieure à ses rivales" (As for Madame Coster, we are vexed that she has almost completely abandoned the genre of still life, in which she excelled, in order to paint portraits and historiated portraits in which she is greatly inferior to her rivals). Fort 1999, 86.

22. For Chardin's royal decorations of the 1760s, see Paris 1999, 302–305, 310–313.

23. Pinault Sørensen and Sahut 1998, 57.

24. Roland Michel 1970, 168, no. 225. The *livret* gave the dimensions as "de 6 pieds sur 4."

25. "Ne serait point indigne des études d'un peintre d'histoire." Fort 1999, 86 ("Salon de 1771").

26. "Dont le talent est vraiment celui d'un homme parfait dans ce genre de tableaux." Duplessis 1857, 450.

27. "Nul de l'École française n'a atteint la force de coloris de Mlle Valayer." Bukdahl et al. 1995, 196 ("Salon de 1771").

28. "Elle est de plus incomparablement la première pour les choses inanimées, les raisins, les pêches, les prunes, les groupes d'instruments de musique, etc.," Dupont de Nemours 1908, 27 ("Salon de 1773").

29. Roland Michel 1970, 72–74; M. and F. Faré 1976, 220–221.

30. "Excellents, vigoureux, harmonieux: ce n'est pas Chardin pourtant, mais au dessous de ce maître, cela est fort au-dessus d'une femme." Bukdahl et al. 1995, 199 ("Salon de 1771").

31. "Son tableau de fleurs ne cède qu'à la nature ou à Van Spaendonck." *Mercure de France*, September 1783, 130; "Madame Vallayer-Coster suit de près ces deux excellens artistes." *Discours sur l'origine* 1785, 34. Gérard van Spaendonck, who had first exhibited at the Salon of 1775, was deemed her equal by Dupont de Nemours as early as 1779; by 1781 he is generally considered superior to her: "Je suis persuadé que vous êtes aujourd'hui le plus grand peintre de ce genre"; see *La Verité Critique* 1781, 26.

32. Though it should be noted that such advice had been given during the 1770s as well: *La Prêtresse* (1777) had counseled her "de s'en tenir au genre" (to stay within her genre)—i.e., still-life painting—since "le beau sexe est privé de certains secours, sans lesquels, dans les genres qui exigent plus de génie, l'on ne saurait arriver à l'immortalité" (the fair sex is denied certain training, without which one can never aspire to immortality in the genres that demand greater genius). Quoted in Roland Michel 1970, 56.

33. "Ses portraits sont, du plus au moins, dessinés d'une manière très incorrecte, et d'un ton de couleur décidement condamnable; mais les tableaux de genre sont vrais, d'un ton naturel et dignes des plus grands éloges." *Mercure de France*, October 1785, 28.

34. "Madame Vallayer-Coster se tient enfin dans sa sphère et le public l'en applaudit" (Madame Vallayer-Coster is finally remaining in her sphere and the public applauds her for so doing). *Lanlaire* 1787, 21. Relief was tempered by condescension, however (an opinion widely held): "Réussir au genre mignon vaut mieux qu'écheoir dans un plus élevé" (To succeed in one of the nice little genres is better than to fail in the more elevated ones). *Lanlaire* 1787, 21.

35. "C'est qu'il ne faut rien commander à un artiste, et quand on veut avoir un beau tableau de sa façon, il faut lui dire, Faites-moi un tableau et choissisez le sujet qui vous conviendra," Diderot 1984, 230 ("Salon de 1763").

36. See, most recently, the essays in the excellent exhibition catalogue L'Isle-Adam 2000.

37. F. Fournis, "Louis-François de Bourbon Conti, amateur et collectionneur," 42–47, in L'Isle-Adam 2000.

38. Fournis, in L'Isle-Adam 2000, 43.

39. Pinault Sørenson and Sahut 1998, 65.

40. M. Roland Michel, "La collection Conti en son temps," 38–41, in L'Isle-Adam 2000.

41. See the listing of these pendants in the *Catalogue de Tableaux Précieux* 1775, nos. 34 and 35, reproduced in the appendix to this essay.

42. See, most recently, Bailey 1993.

43. *Catalogue raisonné de Tableaux de [Le Boeuf]* 1783, no. 92, "Ce tableau a été fait pour M. l'Abbé Terray, quand il étoit Ministre des Finances."

44. *Explication* 1775, nos. 99, 100.

45. "Les tableaux de fleurs et de fruits sont traités en habile homme." *Observations* 1775, 20.

46. *Catalogue d'une très-belle collection . . . de feu M. l'Abbé Terray* 1779, nos. 12, 13. There are discrepancies in the measurements given, however. *Vase of Flowers with a Bust of Flora,* which appeared most recently at Christie's, New York, 31 January 1997, lot 102, with the dimensions 60⅝ × 51⅛ in., is listed in the Terray catalogue as more or less the same size, "Hauteur 4 pieds 8 pouces [59½ in.] largeur 4 pieds [51 in.]." *The Attributes of Hunting and Gardening,* which last appeared at Sotheby's, New York, 7 December 1986, lot 76, with the dimensions 59 × 53 in., is listed in the Terray catalogue as being considerably larger, "Hauteur 4 pieds 8 pouces [59½ in.], largeur 4 pieds 11 pouces [60 in.]."

47. Brenet's canvas is lost, but is known from the version commissioned for the crown by d'Angiviller, shown at the Salon of 1777, and today in Toulouse, Musée des Augustins; see Sandoz 1979, no. 87, plate VII, 2.

48. Beuchot 1829–1834, 14:292: "For the good of the kingdom, Monsieur l'abbé Terray prefers a plowman or a wise steward to all our foolish writings, which he will never read." When Voltaire's verses were published in the *Mercure de France* in May 1774, Terray's name was omitted.

49. Schabol 1770, 1:i: "un Ministre qui connoît . . . le prix de l'agriculture et qui se plaît à l'encourager."

50. Schabol 1770, 2:573, where he notes, "il y a trente ans que nous ne connoissons que le gros melon brodé."

51. "Les fausses fleurs . . . renferment la première semence et sont par conséquent essentielle à la propagation de l'espèce." Quoted in *Mercure de France,* September 1774, 95, which published excerpts from both Schabol's *La Théorie du Jardinage* and *La Pratique du Jardinage,* noting that the latter was a best seller ("la rapidité avec laquelle la première édition a été enlevée en prouve suffisamment l'utilité").

52. For Montullé's biography, see the unsurpassed account in Dacier, Hérold, and Vuaflart 1921–1929, 1:203–204, 252–258. Watteau's *Les plaisirs du bal* is in the Dulwich Picture Gallery; Greuze's *Silence!* is in the collection of Her Majesty Queen Elizabeth II.

53. Dacier, Hérold, and Vuaflart 1921–1929, 1:256–258.

54. "Ses malheurs sont connus quant à sa fortune," Furcy-Raynaud 1905–1906, 2:66, Pierre to d'Angiviller, 9 September 1784.

55. On Merle, see Malouet 1868, 2:281–284 (Malouet had served in Merle's embassy to Portugal).

56. For a recent discussion of his collection, see Gaskell 1990, 15–17; and Edwards 1998, 245–247.

57. For the former, see *Timken Art Gallery* 1983, 80–83; Vernet's *View of Naples with a Rainbow* appeared most recently at Christie's, London, 16 December 1998, lot 71.

58. "Voilà une belle occasion: on verra les tableaux soy-même, et ce ne sera pas la dernière vente." Pierre's notes, dated October 1783, in Furcy-Raynaud 1905–1906, 2:34.

59. *Catalogue des Tableaux . . . Merle* 1784, no. 39; her oval bust portrait sold for a mere 40 livres.

60. On Véri, see Bailey 1985; a chapter is devoted to Véri in Bailey 2002.

61. "Et de la part de la future épouse . . . de très haut et très puissant Seigneur Louis Gabriel Marquis de Veri, Chevalier, Seingr. de Raionard et de Montbullon." "Contrat de mariage," 12 April 1781, published in Roland Michel 1970, 264 (with slight emendations).

62. "Vous avez bien voulu, Monsieur . . . autant ceder à votre amour pour les arts qu'avoir égard à la recommandation de la Reine en faveur de Mlle Vallayer." d'Angiviller to Vergennes, 17 March 1779, in Roland Michel 1970, 261.

63. Roland Michel 1970, 211.

64. "Vous verrez naître avec plaisir cette occasion de vous faire connaître à la famille royale." Engerand 1901, 468, d'Angiviller to Vallayer, 3 July 1779.

65. Engerand 1901, 469, Vallayer to d'Angiviller, 27 July 1780: "Je n'ai pas remis la lettre que vous avez eu la bonté de me donner pour Mme la princesse de Chimay, parce qu'elle n'étoit pas à Versailles lorsque j'y ai été pour travailler au portrait de la Reine et que l'on m'a conseillé d'attendre que son portrait soit entièrement terminé pour réclamer ses bontés."

66. "La tête ne ressemble pas et tant mieux. . . . Cela ressemble à un tableau que l'on s'est promis de retoucher." Bukdahl et al. 1995, 326 ("Salon de 1781").

67. *Dictionnaire de biographie française,* 9: col. 154.

68. Archives nationales, Paris, F 17 1190/1, no. 7B: "Inventaire des objets trouvés au dépôt national de Nesles provenant de Coigny, émigré," inventoried by J.-B.-P. Le Brun, 30 prairial an II (18 June 1794). For his ownership of Fragonard's ravishing sketch, see Paris 1988, 484.

69. *Dictionnaire de biographie française,* 9: cols. 156, 150–151; Roland Michel 1970, 221, no. 343.

70. Wrigley 1995, 312.

71. Antonetti 1963, 14–23.

72. Bouchary 1939–1942, 3:113–115.

73. The term *cher patron* comes from Vernet's letter to Girardot de Marigny of 1 June 1779; see Guiffrey 1893, 79.

74. See Réau 1960, 1–9.

75. See cat. 48. The larger pendants are catalogued in Toledo Museum of Art 1976, 161–162.

76. On Pahin de la Blancherie, see, most recently, Haskell 2000, 15–22.

77. M.-C. Pahin de la Blancherie, *Nouvelles de la République des lettres et des arts*, 19 December 1782, no. 3; Pahin de la Blancherie 1783, no. 146.

78. M.-C. Pahin de la Blancherie, *Nouvelles de la République des lettres et des arts*, 12 May 1785, nos. 1–3, "ces tableaux ont été exposés au Salon du Louvre."

79. In August 1783 Girardot de Marigny offered Pierre a painting by Pierre-Antoine de Machy (1723–1807); as the First Painter informed d'Angiviller, "l'amateur se contenta de faire simplement à l'artiste compliment sur le premier tableau de sa main qui entroit dans la collection du Roy" (the art lover wants only to be able to compliment the artist on the first work by him to have entered the king's collection). At the Salon of 1783, de Machy showed *Une Vue prise du Pont-Neuf*, with a view of the "galerie du Louvre"; it was listed as belonging to the king. See Furcy-Raynaud 1905–1906, 2:30–31.

80. Roland Michel 1970, 266.

81. The crown paid 3,600 livres for the bust and full-length portraits of Mme Sophie (which had been valued at 6,000 livres in Vallayer's marriage contract); see Engerand 1901, 469; the marquis and marquise de Créqui owed 2,400 livres for theirs.

APPENDIX

Catalogue de Tableaux Précieux, de Figures de Marbre antique, de Bronze, & Vases de Porphyre, d'un Cabinet distingué [Madame Du Barry], Paris, 22 December 1775

Addition

Mademoiselle Vallayer

31. Une jeune Arabe, en pied, de grandeur naturelle, habillée selon le costume du pays, dans une espece de Sérail, ce Tableau est d'une touche large & fiere; il porte 4 pieds 10 pouces de haut, sur 3 pieds 4 pouces de large, dans une bordure dorée, décorée d'un vase & de branches de palmier entrelassées de rangs de perles.

32. Un Trophée d'instrument militaire, composé d'une paire de timbale, basson, trompette, &c. avec le bonnet de Negre. Ce Tableau, vigoureusement touché, est connu, ayant été exposé au Sallon de l'Académie Royale de 1771. Il porte 5 pieds de haut, sur 4 de large, dans une bordure dorée de 5 pouces de large, à deux ornements.

33. Un Tableau, faisant pendant au précédent, représensentant un Bureau, dans le genre de Boule, sur lequel sont divers accessoirs de Sculpture, de Musique & d'Astronomie. Le fond est un rideau de velours vert. Ce Tableau, précieusement fait, a été exposé au Sallon de l'Académie Royale, de 1773.

34. Autre, représentant plusieurs objets d'Histoire naturelle, comme Minéraux & Animaux, dans des bocaux d'esprit de vin, grouppé avec un vase de porcelaine, garni de bronze doré, le fond est orné d'un rideau de taffetas. On remarque dans ce Tableau particuliérement la couleur séduisante, & la touche fine & hardie. Il porte 4 pieds de haut sur 3 de large, bordé d'une tringle de bois simple.

35. Autre Tableau. Il représente divers productions d'Histoire naturelle, dans le genre maritime, comme Coquilles, Coreaux, Madrépores, &c. Etant de la même main, il y a les mêmes avantages, tant pour la couleur que pour la touche.

APPENDIX TRANSLATION

Catalogue of Precious Paintings, of Antique Marble & Bronze Sculpture, and Porphyry Vases from a Distinguished Collection [Madame Du Barry], Paris, 22 December 1775

Addition

Mademoiselle Vallayer

31. A young Arab woman, standing, life-size, dressed according to the custom of the country, in a kind of harem, this painting is ample and ardent of handling; it is 4 pieds 10 pouces* high by 3 pieds 4 pouces wide, in a gilt frame decorated with a vase and with palm branches interspersed with strings of pearls.

32. A trophy of military instruments, consisting of a pair of drums, a bassoon, a trumpet, etc., with *le bonnet de Nègre*. This painting, vigorously executed, is well known, having been exhibited at the Salon of the Académie royale in 1771. It is 5 pieds high by 4 wide, in a gilt frame 5 pouces wide with two ornaments.

33. A painting, pendant to the preceding, representing a desk in the genre of Boulle on which are various attributes of Sculpture, Music, and Astronomy. The background is a curtain of green velvet. This painting, meticulously executed, was exhibited at the Salon of the Académie royale in 1773.

34. Another, representing several objects of natural history, such as minerals and animals, in vials of spirit alcohol, grouped with a porcelain vase with gilt-bronze fittings; the background is decorated with a taffeta curtain. Particularly remarkable in this painting is the seductive color, & the refined and vigorous touch. It is 4 pieds high by 3 wide, with a simple wooden border.

35. Another painting. It represents various products of natural history in the maritime genre, such as shells, corals, madrepores, etc. Being from the same hand, it has the same virtues, with regard to color as much as touch.

*A pied is equivalent to about 12¾ inches, a pouce, to about 1¹/₁₆ inches.

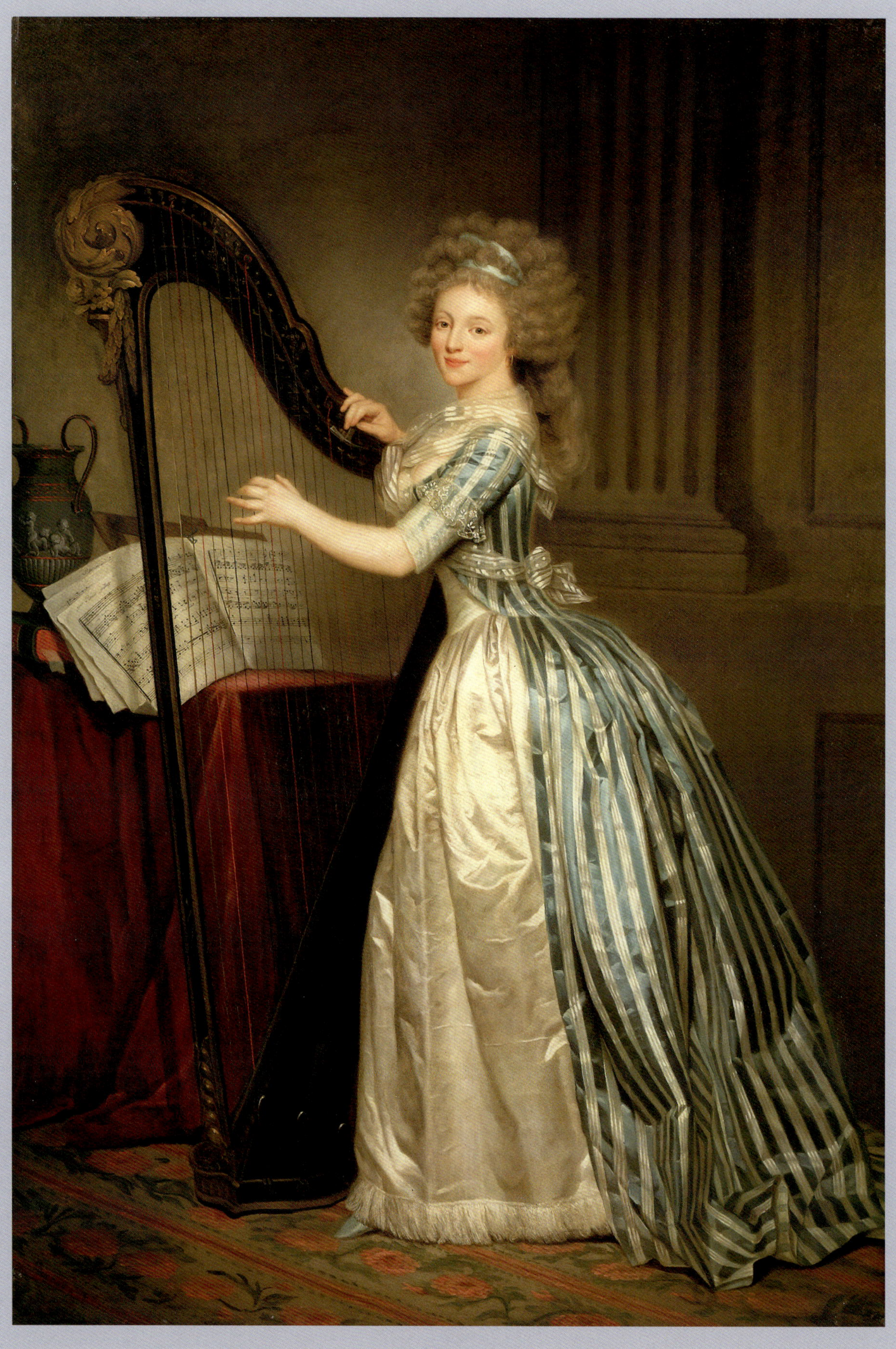

Rose-Adélaïde Ducreux, *Self-Portrait with a Harp*, c. 1791
Oil on canvas, 75⅞ × 50¾ in. (193 × 128.9 cm). The Metropolitan
Museum of Art, Bequest of Susan Dwight Bliss, 1967 (67.55.1) (fig. 13).

— MELISSA HYDE —

Women and the Visual Arts in the Age of Marie-Antoinette

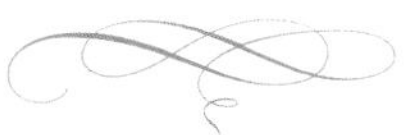

> Woman in the eighteenth century is the principle that governs, the reason that directs,
> the voice that commands. She is the universal and fatal cause, the origin of events, the source of things. . . .
> Nothing escapes her, she holds within her grasp the King, France, the will of the sovereign,
> and the authority of opinion—everything. She gives orders at court, she is mistress of the home.
> She holds the revolutions of alliances and political systems, peace and war, the literature,
> the arts and the fashions of the eighteenth century, as well as its destinies in the folds of her gown.
> —Jules and Edmond de Goncourt, *The Woman of the Eighteenth Century*, 1880

WOMAN IN THE EIGHTEENTH CENTURY: "CHERCHEZ LA FEMME"

The eighteenth century so vividly conjured up by Jules and Edmond de Goncourt in their famous books on French art and society is a dreamy, perfumed world of extravagant privilege and delightful frivolity. When reading the Goncourts one envisages pretty duchesses in dainty silk slippers tripping lightly through moonlit evenings to meet with their gallant lovers in lush, secluded gardens. One thinks of wistful strains of harpsichord, frothy ball gowns in pale pastel colors, graceful curtsies, painted fans, powdered wigs, rouge and beauty spots, rococo excess. This eighteenth century is all urbane wit and politesse, romantic dalliance and decadent pleasure. But above all it bears the indelible mark of the feminine—it is, for the Goncourts "the century of woman and her caressing domination over manners and customs."[1] It is an idyllic, golden age of a vanished past.

Whereas the inspired confabulations of the Goncourts make for pleasant reading and are true in many of their particulars (the brothers were meticulous researchers and cullers of archives), ultimately the picture they paint of France before the fall of the monarchy in 1789 belongs to the realm of fiction. Their portrayal is at once highly selective and highly embellished, especially in its figuring of Woman and the ascendancy ascribed to her. This Woman, a generalized category rather than any specific individual, was a matter of endless fascination for the Goncourts. They devoted entire tomes to her, and to many of the most famous individual women of the century, including the marquise de Pompadour, Madame Du Barry, and Queen Marie-Antoinette.

The Goncourts' idealized view of the ancien régime and the women who "dominated" it was intimately bound up with their own reactionary politics and personal eccentricities, as well as their deep aversion to the nineteenth century in which they lived and their revulsion for contemporary women.[2] Rather like the ancient sculptor Pygmalion, they fashioned for themselves an ideal woman of their own imagining and a realm for her to preside over. To some extent their interpretations of the period reflect less on the eighteenth century than on themselves. Yet the Goncourts did offer a compelling and influential corrective to the no less mythified and much uglier accounts of the ancien régime first advanced by proponents of the Revolution, whose sturdy democratic ideals of Liberty, Fraternity, and Equality were abhorrent to the brothers' effete and aristocratic sensibilities.

Much of the rhetoric of the French Revolution had laid blame for the ills of the world at the feet of society women and women of the court, with special hostility being reserved for royal mistresses and queens. The belief in women's culpability and the particular notions of femininity that attended it (femininity as profligacy, innate frivolity, the inability to reason or to wield power wisely, a taste for luxury and excess) were to have a long afterlife in the nineteenth and twentieth centuries—making the Goncourts' celebration of their own motivated, Pygmalion-like version of eighteenth-century Woman and her world one of the only counterpoints to the dominant views inherited from the Revolution.

Modern scholarship on this period has tended to set aside the questions of praise or blame in favor of a different set of concerns. Chief among them has been the critical examination of representations, textual and pictorial, of women during the second half of the century. This has proved to be an especially fruitful line of inquiry, for it has exposed the deep structural relationships between politics, culture, and the politics of gender.[3] Careful study of women's involvement in the Republic of Letters and the art world has begun to show that their roles in shaping culture—whether through sponsorship or participation in literary and philosophical salons,[4] patronage, writing, art making, or some other means—were complex, multifold, and sometimes paradoxical.

Women's involvement with the visual arts in particular is a topic about which a great deal remains to be said, for if past accounts have exaggerated their influence on the arts, more recent ones have sometimes erred in the opposite direction. Looking back to her glory days as the chosen portraitist of Marie-Antoinette, and one of the most fashionable painters in Paris, Elisabeth-Louise Vigée-Le Brun asserted in her memoirs that "women reigned then: the Revolution dethroned them."[5] This lofty claim, argued so seductively by the Goncourts, was wryly amended by Jean Starobinski in *The Invention of Liberty* (1964, French ed.), where he wrote, "Woman reigned (she was made to believe she reigned)."[6] The reality would seem to lie somewhere in between. Women's influence over politics and culture, government and art, was rarely ever so complete or straightforward as writers of the past, for better or worse, would have us believe. Neither was it negligible, as others have more lately maintained.

In the age of Marie-Antoinette, however, there *were* unquestionably three reigning women artists, and Anne Vallayer-Coster (pl. 87) was one of them (even as she was one of the most prominent still-life painters of the day). Along with Vigée-Le Brun (fig. 1) and Adélaïde Labille-Guiard (fig. 2), her female compatriots at the Académie royale de peinture et de sculpture, Vallayer-Coster has been regarded historically as the exception proving the rule that French painting was the exclusive province of men. But the "rules" of the art world were far more complex than received wisdom allows. This essay outlines some aspects of the eighteenth-century art world in France to put Vallayer-Coster's career as a woman artist in context.

An intriguing aspect of the overlapping yet strikingly divergent careers and personalities of Vallayer-Coster, Vigée-Le Brun, and Labille-Guiard is how very differently the three negotiated the problems of visibility and the "problems" presented by femininity itself. How and why Vallayer-Coster, whose modesty and goodness were praised by her contemporaries, remained almost entirely untouched by the kinds of salacious rumors, innuendo, and notoriety that peppered the careers of Vigée-Le Brun and Labille-Guiard would make for an engaging study.[7] However, in the following pages I want to address broader questions about women and the visual arts: I want to make a substantive case for women's presence in aesthetic culture before the Revolution and will trace some of the complex circumstances that conditioned women's making of art as well as their sponsorship of it.[8] I will focus on a few telling instances and exemplary aspects of both. As we shall see, even if Vallayer-Coster was anomalous in achieving admission to the Académie, as well as in her adroit negotiation of the difficult terrain of the painter's profession and the public sphere, she was not an anomaly simply because she was a woman artist. During the ancien régime there were many artists who were women.

Spectacular Women and Unbecoming Visibility

In the eighteenth century itself the matter of women's influence (the nature of that influence, its degree and kind, its merits and failings) and women's role in society more generally were as widely acknowledged as they were theorized and debated. Long before the Revolution, progressive thinkers and social reformers identified with the Enlightenment (Jean-Jacques Rousseau, most famously) had begun to argue that the influence of women—namely of wealthy and aristocratic women in the salons and at court—in the traditionally male

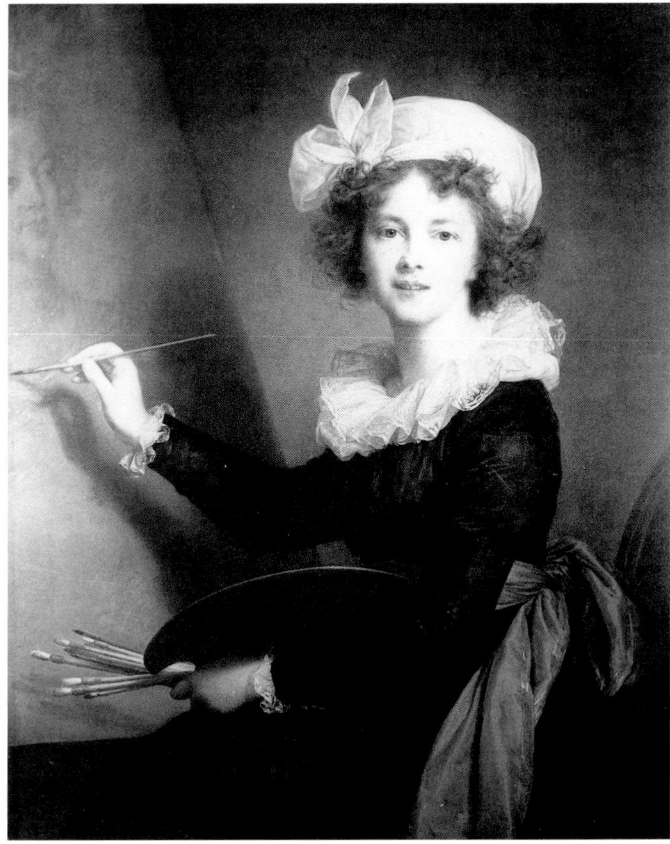

Fig. 1. Elisabeth-Louise Vigée-Le Brun, *Self-Portrait*, 1790. Oil on canvas, 39⅜ × 31⅞ in. (100 × 81 cm). Galleria degli Uffizi, Piazzale degli Uffizi, Florence.

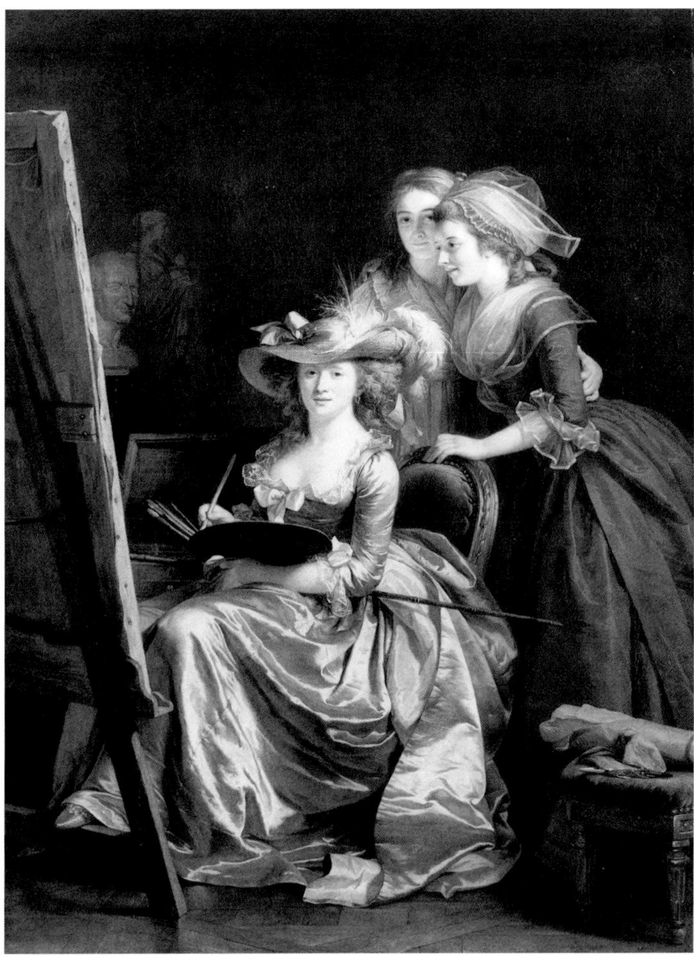

Fig. 2. Adélaïde Labille-Guiard, *Self-Portrait with Two Pupils*, 1785. Oil on canvas, 83 × 59½ in. (210.8 × 151.1 cm). The Metropolitan Museum of Art, Gift of Julia A. Berwind, 1953 (53.225.5).

domains of politics, literature, and art had degraded and effeminized French culture.[9] Though some saw women's presence and influence, which was in certain respects significant, as a salutary sign of France's civilization, the negative view came to dominate in Revolutionary ideology. Also at stake in these debates were ancient, vexed questions about the nature of women themselves and newer ones about what should be their proper role in an era that was drawing increasingly clear distinctions between private and public life, and defining these as gendered domains. This was also a period in which the concepts of the "public sphere" and "public opinion" were being articulated for the first time, as the power of the absolutist monarchy diminished and the sovereign faced ever greater challenges to his authority in the face of the desires of the people (or those who claimed to represent them).[10]

Women's relationship to the public sphere and traditionally masculine domains of culture presented a complex situation for women artists.[11] Their pursuit of painting as a profession often took them beyond the domestic sphere, and it did so in an especially conspicuous way if they exhibited their work, at the Salon as

Vallayer-Coster and her fellow academicians did, or in one of the other venues, such as the Salon de la Correspondance and the Exposition de la Jeunesse, that were more readily available to women. High visibility alone could make these artists morally suspect, like actresses, courtesans, and other such spectacular women.[12] This suggestive visibility put them at odds with ideals of feminine propriety that were being widely promoted during the Enlightenment, as did the ambition it took to vie for recognition and patrons.[13]

The Académie and the Salon: Becoming Visible

In *Les Femmes comme il convient de les voir*, a who's who of women written by Madame de Coicy in 1784, only Vallayer-Coster and Vigée-Le Brun rate as contemporary painters of note.[14] Today Vigée-Le Brun continues to be renowned: her paintings are often reproduced, her memoirs widely read. An exhibition in 1982 was devoted to her

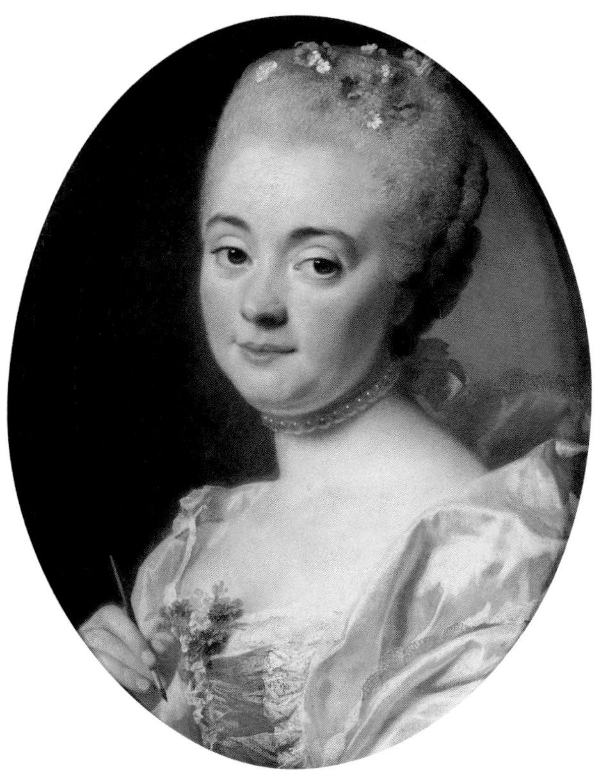

Fig. 3. Alexandre Roslin, *Portrait of Madame Joseph-Marie Vien*, n.d. Oil on canvas, 19¾ × 15⅜ in. (50 × 39 cm). Musée national des Châteaux de Versailles et de Trianon.

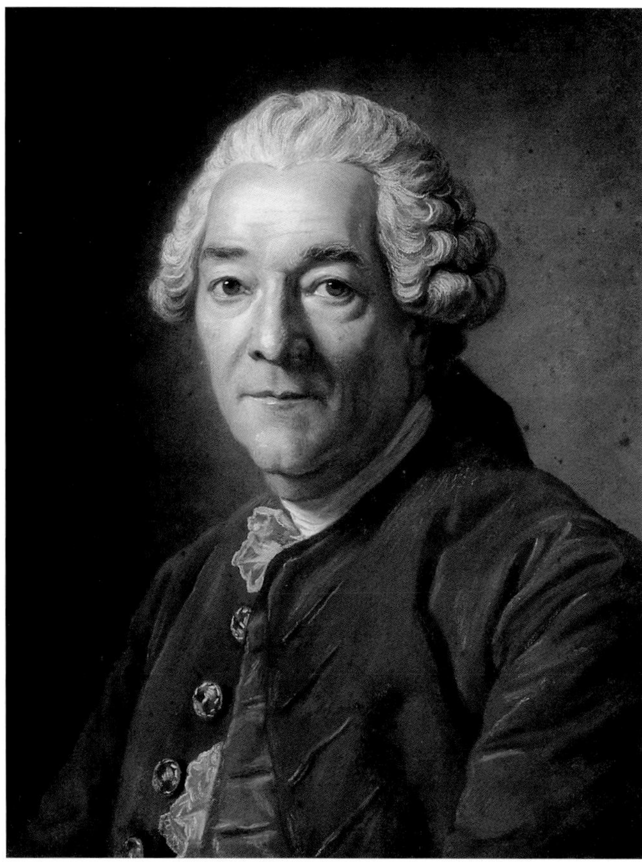

Fig. 4. Marie-Suzanne Giroust-Roslin, *Portrait of Dumont Le Romain*, c. 1770–1771. Pastel on blue paper mounted on canvas, 22 × 18¼ in. (55.9 × 46.3 cm). Musée national des Châteaux de Versailles et de Trianon.

work (as are numerous popular websites today),[15] and she has been the subject of serious scholarly attention, if intermittently, since the early twentieth century. By contrast, Vallayer-Coster's name is no longer nearly so well known, and her work has received less study.[16] The same may be said of Labille-Guiard, who is curiously absent from Madame de Coicy's list even though she too was a member of the Académie and a prominent artist of the time. Other women were admitted to the Académie during the second half of the eighteenth century—among them Marie-Thérèse Vien, née Reboul (1735–1805; fig. 3), Suzanne Roslin, née Giroust (1734–1772; fig. 4), and the Prussian painter Anna-Dorothea Liziewska-Therbouche (1721/22–1782; fig. 5)—but little has been written about them, despite their having achieved extraordinary status in the profession.[17]

Given the spareness of the scholarship on the painters with the highest profiles, it is easy to understand how one might assume that there were few women in the arts during the eighteenth century. In fact, as Mary Sheriff has been one of the few to point out, this was not at all the case, for throughout the century there were numerous women who made careers as portraitists, miniaturists, pastelists, engravers, botanical illustrators, genre painters, as copyists and even as teachers (especially of drawing).[18] Few were illustrious, it is true, but it does not follow that few were gifted. This, at least, was the position taken up by the *Almanach historique et raisonné des architectes, peintres, sculpteurs, graveurs et ciseleurs* of 1776, which included the heading "Painters of Talent though not Members of the Académie" and listed three sisters, Jeanne-Françoise (1731–1829), Marie (1743–1824), and Thérèse (1745–1835) Parrocel, among others, as belonging to that category.[19] We can never know how many of these "ordinary" artists might have been on a par with the extraordinary ones. It is certain, however, that no artist, male or female, attained real preeminence (again, not the only measure of talent) without the advantage of membership in the Académie.[20]

Membership entitled the handful of women to whom the privilege was accorded the right to show work in the prestigious state-sponsored exhibitions that after 1737 were held every two years in the famous Salon Carré of the Louvre. Unlike the men admitted to this elite institution, they could not swear allegiance to its rules, teach, hold office, or vote, nor were they held to the same requirements for admission. But the public exposure that came with exhibiting work in the Salon and the official

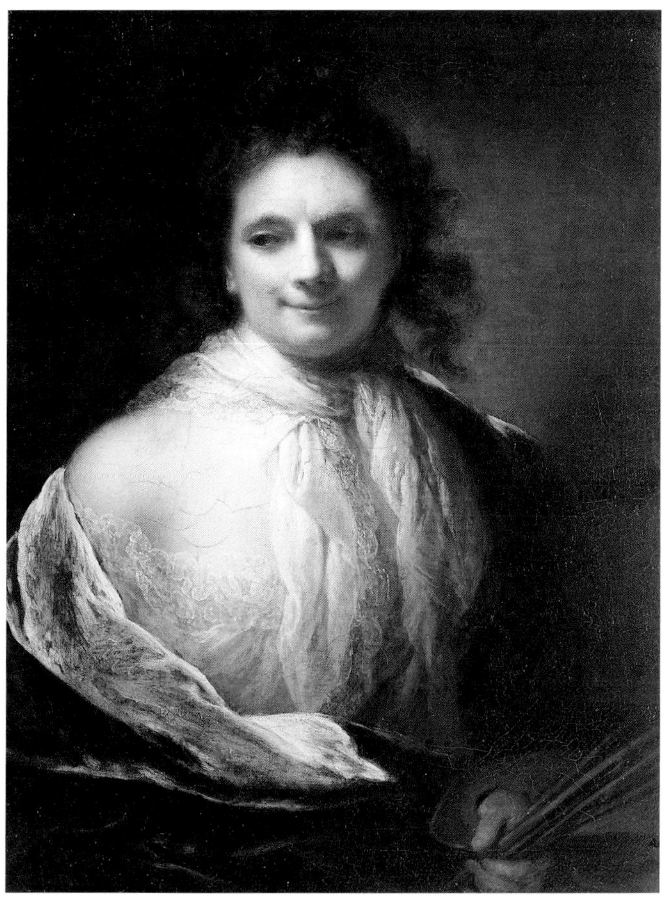

Fig. 5. Anna-Dorothea Liziewska-Therbouche, *Self-Portrait*, 1762. Oil on canvas, 26 × 19¼ in. (66 × 49 cm). Staatsgalerie Stuttgart.

by exhibiting works at the Exposition de la Jeunesse, and she sent work to the Salon de la Correspondance on several occasions (I will return to these extra-academic art venues). More unusually, she also followed the enterprising example of her teacher and held private exhibitions of her work in her studio during the 1780s. These shows were announced and received positive press in widely read gazettes like the *Journal de Paris,* the *Journal général de France,* and the *Mercure de France,* with the latter devoting several pages to her work in 1785 and 1788.[22] In a self-deprecating show of modesty (perhaps designed to preempt any disapproval of this fundamentally immodest display and "unfeminine" desire for recognition), Beaulieu at one point explained to the readers of the *Journal de Paris* that in making her works available for public view she was only ceding to the wishes of distinguished artists and art lovers who deemed her paintings worthy of such publicity.[23] The first exhibition featured her painting *Poetry Mourning the Loss of Voltaire* (fig. 6), a picture that aroused much interest. That Beaulieu's private exhibitions received as much press as they did suggests that influential artists and connoisseurs were supportive of her, a supposition strengthened by

imprimatur it bestowed gave an enormous advantage to these artists over their nonacademic counterparts in attracting the interest of patrons and critics. It gave them greater visibility, then and now.

Geneviève Brossard de Beaulieu (1755–c. 1835), an obscure name now known only to eighteenth-century specialists, was one painter who was acutely aware of the advantages of membership, labored mightily to obtain it, and failed. Beaulieu's case contrasts markedly with that of Vallayer-Coster, who was admitted to the Académie with unanimous acclaim and who enjoyed the friendship and support of its director, Jean-Baptiste-Marie Pierre, as well as that of the upper arts administration and the queen. Beaulieu's attempt to affiliate herself with the Académie reveals the options and recourse that were available to women artists with aspirations; how the system worked; and the fortunes of artists who did not make it into the Académie—artists whose numbers far exceeded those who did.

Beaulieu was the daughter of an artist from the provinces and a student of Jean-Baptiste Greuze in the early 1780s.[21] Like many young artists, she began her career

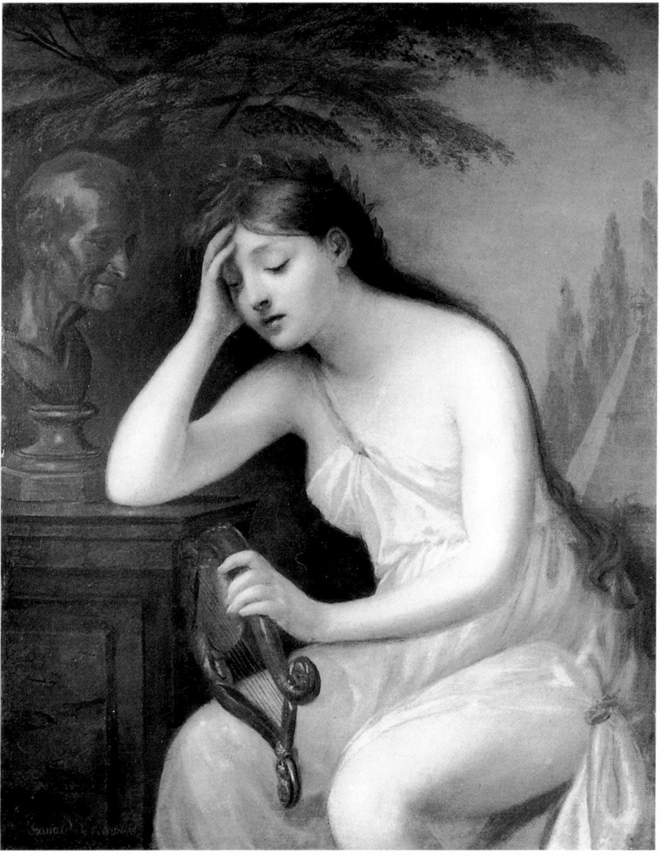

Fig. 6. Geneviève Brossard de Beaulieu, *Poetry Mourning the Loss of Voltaire,* 1785. Musée Sainte-Croix, Poitiers.

the fact that her Voltaire painting was acquired for the collection of Catherine the Great by 1788.[24] At the least, she was successful in securing the favor of members of the Académie (as Labille-Guiard had cannily done to win support for her own admission, and as Vallayer-Coster must have done before her), since Beaulieu convinced the whole body to sign letters of recommendation for her. But whatever support she may have enjoyed, it was not enough to get her what she really sought: membership in the Académie.[25]

When the Académie admitted its first female member, Catherine Duchemin (1630–1698), in 1662, it did not stipulate the number of women who could join. By 1706 six women were members. That year, prompted by the news that "several ladies who have applied themselves to painting have planned to present themselves to be received as *académiciennes*," the Académie decreed that it would admit no woman as academician.[26] The resolution, which did not have the force of law without royal consent, was not adhered to, and a few more women were elected to the Académie before the admission of Suzanne Roslin and Vallayer-Coster in 1770. But shortly thereafter women's membership was officially limited to four.[27] That was how the rules stood when Beaulieu introduced herself to the Académie in 1784. Knowing there was no place for her, she nevertheless sought some sort of official affiliation with the institution.[28] She might have felt there was reason to hope the Académie would relax its policy: it had extravagantly admitted both Vigée-Le Brun and Labille-Guiard on the same day the year before (and had grudgingly bent the rules for the former), and Madame Vien had not exhibited work since 1767.

The little we know of this incident comes from a letter written by Vallayer-Coster's friend Pierre, the First Painter to the King and director of the Académie, to Charles-Claude de la Billarderie, comte d'Angiviller, who was the director of the Bâtiments du roi, the royal arts ministry.[29] Since the record is fragmentary, it is difficult to know precisely what transpired, but here is what I believe happened: Pierre's account of Beaulieu to his superior was prompted by the woman's plaintive entreaties to d'Angiviller for lodging in the Louvre (a singular request, since this was a favor granted only to certain members of the Académie, their immediate families, and functionaries of the court, and one for which d'Angiviller evidently sought some explanation from Pierre). The request was made in a letter she wrote

to the comte in 1786, in which she states that she is sure that d'Angiviller's wife will have acquainted him with her dire circumstances. (Had Beaulieu gone to the comtesse first? Other women artists appealed to the comtesse d'Angiviller to intercede for them, but of that, more later.) Pierre explains to d'Angiviller that Beaulieu, knowing the Académie to be closed to additional female members, had taken it on herself to obtain recommendations (*certificats*, he calls them) from all the members of the Académie. Recognizing her to be "a girl of some talent" and wishing to oblige her (or rid himself of her?), Pierre proposed at an Académie meeting that she be given an "authentic" certificate signed by its secretary, Antoine Renou (1731–1806), and that the many written recommendations she had collected be disposed of.[30] Perhaps because she understood that the certificate was essentially meaningless and wanted it to have some weight, Beaulieu contrived to get this piece of paper signed by senior academicians.[31]

It is a mystery why the Académie did not formally refuse her. Was it gallantry? Perhaps Pierre (under whose directorship Vallayer-Coster, Suzanne Roslin, and Labille-Guiard had been admitted) wanted to recognize her talents in some way, since the rules would not allow the Académie to admit her (or allowed it not to admit her).[32] But if Pierre and his cohort intended to quiet her ambitions with the specious certification, they succeeded only in fueling her expectations with the ambiguity of their response. It was surely on the basis of this slim endorsement that she felt entitled to request a lodging at the Louvre. During the Restoration she claimed to have been "titled" by the defunct Académie, and as such she proved to be an importunate (and quite successful) solicitor of governmental support and favors for nearly forty years.

Beaulieu's case highlights the internecine politics of the Académie. This was literally "an old boys'" club. Talent and ambition were only partial requirements to get a foot in the door—no matter who you were; it also took the sponsorship of the right people, as attested by Joseph-Marie Vien's (1716–1809) account of his difficulties in gaining admission (to say nothing of the opposition that Vigée-Le Brun encountered).[33] Beaulieu clearly knew how the system worked, even if she was powerless to work it. That Vallayer-Coster and the other women of the Académie were able to make it work renders their achievement all the more impressive: in addition to being superb artists, they had to be savvy diplomats and lucky enough to be in the right place at the right time. Even then, having the backing of the queen could be essential, as Vigée-Le Brun's admission to the Académie by royal fiat demonstrates.[34] The uncontroversial and acclaimed Vallayer-Coster, too, only obtained the favor of lodgings in the Louvre at the queen's behest.

The privileges of membership would be rendered moot by the Revolution. The most dramatic change came in 1791 when the National Assembly decreed the Salon open to all who would exhibit. Twenty-two women immediately took advantage of this opportunity. Not long after that the Académie was abolished and replaced by the Commune Générale des Arts, which for a few months in 1793 admitted women.[35] Their participation in the Commune Générale des Arts was cut short by the National Assembly's decree of 30 October 1793, which suppressed all women's political clubs and prohibited women from engaging in public debate, only to be reinstated, at least on paper, the following year.[36] The Salon, however, remained open to them, and the number of women participating in it would increase by 1,600 percent in less than twenty years.[37] The number of female artists seems to have increased as well—though it may be that they simply became more visible, for as I suggested earlier, significant numbers of women had made their livings as professional artists throughout the century.

Re-viewing the Artists

Because they did not exhibit at the Salon or otherwise inhabit the official art world of the Académie and the Bâtiments du roi, the great majority of women artists are not to be found in the most widely known art historical sources: the Salon literature, the proceedings of the Académie, the correspondence and records of the official commissions for the king directed by the Bâtiments.[38] However, they were to be found everywhere else in the thriving art world of the eighteenth century, even if always in the minority. Women were even employed regularly by the Bâtiments in the artistic services of the Maison du roi (Household of the King) and elsewhere. For instance, the miniaturist and botanical illustrator Madeleine Basseporte (see Roland Michel, fig. 1), who may have been one of Vallayer-Coster's first teachers, was painter to the king at the Jardin des Plantes and was also the drawing instructor of Mesdames, the daughters of Louis XV.[39] Madame Godefroy and Madame Van Merlen were restorers of the king's paintings around the

middle of the century.[40] Mainly though, women were employed as copyists and miniaturists for the department in the Maison du roi known as the Menus-Plaisirs. Among its many duties, the Menus-Plaisirs had to supply a seemingly endless demand for portraits of the king, queen, and members of the royal family.[41] Relatives, friends, foreign monarchs and their representatives, members of the court and government, functionaries and favor-seekers of all kinds wanted to be gratified by a royal effigy—whether as a simple souvenir, diplomatic gift, recompense, or mark of appreciation for services rendered. These gifts were given habitually by the king and by most members of the royal family, and they might range from original full-length portraits to prints. In between there were replicas, full-size or reduced copies, half-length or bust-length copies, images that combined elements of various painted models, and miniatures (which might themselves be original images painted from life or copies).[42] The gift of a large portrait had a decidedly political connotation, while miniatures tended to be for loved ones, but they were also given as christening or wedding presents, or as tokens of gratitude and personal favor.[43]

Women who worked as painters for the Menus-Plaisirs in the 1770s and 1780s included a Madame Nivelon (act. 1780s) and Jeanne-Angélique Boquet (act. 1774) who painted copies of portraits of Marie-Antoinette after Joseph Ducreux (1735–1802) and Joseph Krantzinger (1740–d. after 1772), as well as portraits of the king and the dauphin, after Louis-Michel van Loo (1707–1771) and Joseph-Siffred Duplessis.[44] Anne-Rosalie Filleul (née Bocquet; 1752–1794), Jeanne-Angélique's cousin and Vigée-Le Brun's childhood friend, also worked for the Menus-Plaisirs, as did Vigée-Le Brun herself early in her career.[45] Between 1776 and 1778, before she was commissioned to paint her first portrait of Marie-Antoinette from life, Vigée-Le Brun had been engaged by her friend's uncle, Louis-Réné Boquet (1717–1814), an inspector-general of the Menus-Plaisirs, to make half-length copies of the queen's portrait.[46] The Ministry of Foreign Affairs also kept its own pleiad of miniaturists who produced copies of portraits that were given as gifts. These artists included one of the Mademoiselles Parrocel. During the Regency a Mademoiselle Brisson appears as miniaturist in the *Régistres des présents du Roi*.[47] There may well have been other women who worked in the king's service. It would be surprising if there were not, especially considering the close connections that painters like Marie-Cathérine François, née Frédou (1712–1773), had to the Cabinet des tableaux du roi: her husband, Jean-Charles François (1717–1769), and brother Jean-Martial Frédou (1711–1795) were both artists there.[48]

Women were not only producers of miniatures, they were also important collectors and patrons of these small-scale works. Marie-Antoinette had a special affinity for them, gave them as personal gifts, and employed favorite miniaturists, including François Dumont (1751–1831; who at the precocious age of eighteen painted the portrait of Vallayer-Coster that is in the present exhibition [pl. 85], suggesting that Vallayer-Coster herself acted as patron to Dumont), Jean-Laurent Mosnier (1743/44–1808), and Vittoriano Campana (1744–1786), giving them direct commissions.[49] Campana's wife, Marie-Christine Vagliengo (act. late 18th–early 19th cent.), was also a miniaturist in Marie-Antoinette's circle; her first royal commission was for a portrait of the queen in 1789.[50] It is certain that other miniaturists who were women also enjoyed the favor of Marie-Antoinette: Madame Cadet, née Aglaé Joly (d. 1801), was one of her painters in 1787.[51] Vallayer-Coster may have painted the queen's portrait in miniature as early as 1778. These intimate, small-scale images—especially the ones the queen personally commissioned—typically showed her in informal settings as loving mother or lady of fashion, a very different Marie-Antoinette from the stately queen consort who appears in official portraits.

The coveted objects produced by the Menus-Plaisirs artists belong to an economy of production entirely separate from that of the Académie and the Salon. Their meaning and value derived, not from the genius of the individual who made them, but from their proximity to the subject depicted (that is, a likeness painted from life was of greater value than a third-generation copy of a copy). In addition, the format of the objects, the skill of the rendering, and the intrinsic worth of the materials (often a miniature would be mounted on a precious gold box or as jewelry) would affect their value. These objects functioned as a symbolic currency that was circulated by the king and royal family and enhanced the cultural capital of the recipient. At times they functioned as actual currency, as when the recipient of a mounted miniature returned the box to the crown for cash compensation.[52] On a conceptual level, then, these artworks are of a completely different order from those that have defined the history of art in which primacy is accorded to the individual artist as the source of meaning, to traditional genres and media, and to originality as an essential criterion of value. Because miniatures and copy work stand outside the traditional concerns of art history, their practitioners, who were so often women, have remained invisible. If the history of high art has little to say about these forgotten artists, there is much to be said about the cultural meanings of their work. The fact that these objects were sometimes made by women adds an important dimension to our understanding of aesthetic culture in the eighteenth century and women's role in it.

At the same time, it should be said that working for the Menus-Plaisirs or one of the other services was not restricted to rote copying of official portraits by renowned academicians. Miniaturists could be granted a sitting with the king or queen if the work was intended for someone important.[53] Even the composite portraits that combined elements of several portraits involved a certain amount of creativity.

For most royal commissions d'Angiviller and Pierre played a crucial role in introducing artists to the court and in recommending them. (This was certainly the case, for example, in Vallayer-Coster's commission to paint Madame Sophie in 1779 [pl. 26]. D'Angiviller was involved, if unofficially, with Vallayer-Coster's painting of the queen in 1780.[54]) One of the few artists who appears to have been introduced by the court to the Bâtiments, rather than the other way around, was a woman referred to only as Demoiselle [Catherine] Read (1723–1778). This English pastelist was the protégée of the duc de Nivernois, who brought her to France. In 1764 the Bâtiments paid her for portraits of the comte d'Artois and of Madame Elisabeth, the sister of Louis XVI. Read was the only woman besides Vigée-Le Brun and Vallayer-Coster to receive a commission from the Bâtiments.[55] There were others, though—among them Vigée-Le Brun, Labille-Guiard, and Rosalie Filleul (fig. 7)—who worked for the royal family outside the orbit of the Bâtiments. Vallayer-Coster herself fell into this category when she painted Mesdames Adélaïde and Victoire.[56] Soon thereafter she painted the portrait of Madame Adélaïde Auguié (fig. 8), one of the queen's ladies-in-waiting, which suggests how important the royal family could be in connecting artists to other patrons at court. Artists introduced at Versailles through unofficial channels were often able to receive royal patronage, or at the very least were benefited by publicity when the court accepted works made on speculation. For example, the *Mercure de*

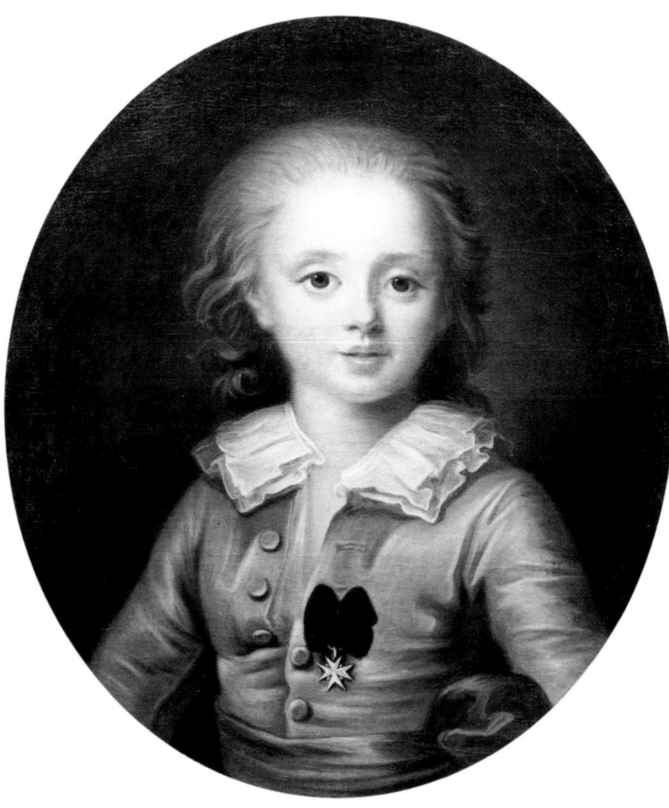

Fig. 7. Anne-Rosalie Filleul, *Louis-Antoine d'Artois, duc d'Angoulême*, c. 1781–1783. Oil on canvas, 20⅝ × 17¼ in. (52.4 × 43.8 cm). Courtesy of the Fogg Art Museum, Harvard University Art Museums, Bequest of Grenville L. Winthrop.

France reported that a pastelist named Mademoiselle de Briancourt presented two allegories to Louis XV's queen, Marie Leszczyńska, in 1757 celebrating the dauphin's recent recovery from illness, with which the queen and her daughters were "very pleased."[57]

Prominent artists who had made successful portraits of the royal family would produce their own replicas and copies for the crown in workshops that included their female relatives and students. Yet unlike the work by women whose names appear in the accounts of the Menus-Plaisirs, the work of these artists generally remains anonymous. An exception is Catherine Lusurier (1753–1781), a cousin of François-Hubert Drouais (1727–1775), who was the favorite portraitist of Madame Du Barry and one of the most sought-after portraitists of the 1760s and 1770s. Marie-Antoinette sat for Drouais several times, and Lusurier used his sketches to paint a number of half-length portraits.[58] There were other women who worked in Drouais's studio and studied with him—including his wife Anne-Françoise, née Doré (1732–1809; fig. 9), and his sister-in-law Marie-Jeanne Doré (b. 1736), and Pauline Gauffier, née Chatillon (d. 1801). It is likely that they, too, made copies after his

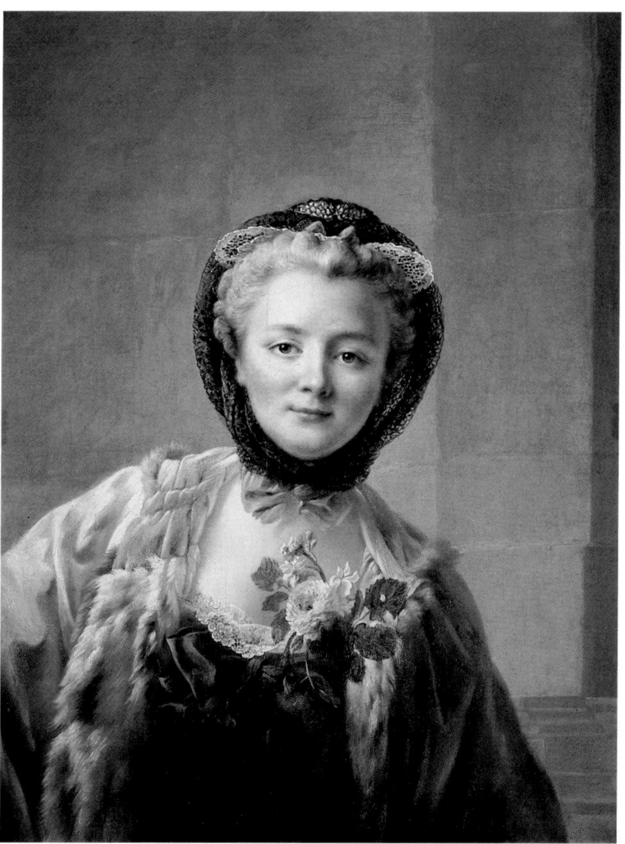

Fig. 8. Anne Vallayer-Coster, *Portrait of Madame Auguié*, n.d. Oil on canvas, oval, 38⅛ × 29⅞ in. (97 × 76 cm). Private collection, Monaco (cat. 123).

Fig. 9. François-Hubert Drouais, *Portrait of Madame Drouais*, n.d. Oil on canvas, 32½ × 24⅜ in. (82.5 × 62 cm). Musée du Louvre, Paris.

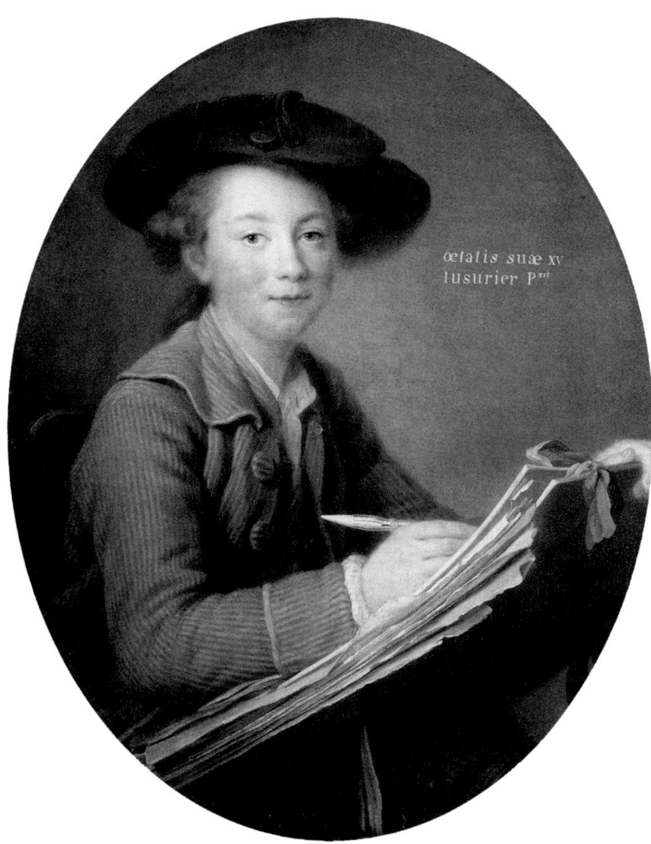

Fig. 10. Catherine Lusurier, *Portrait of Germain-Jean Drouais*, n.d. Oil on canvas, 31½ × 25¼ in. (80 × 64 cm). Musée du Louvre, Paris.

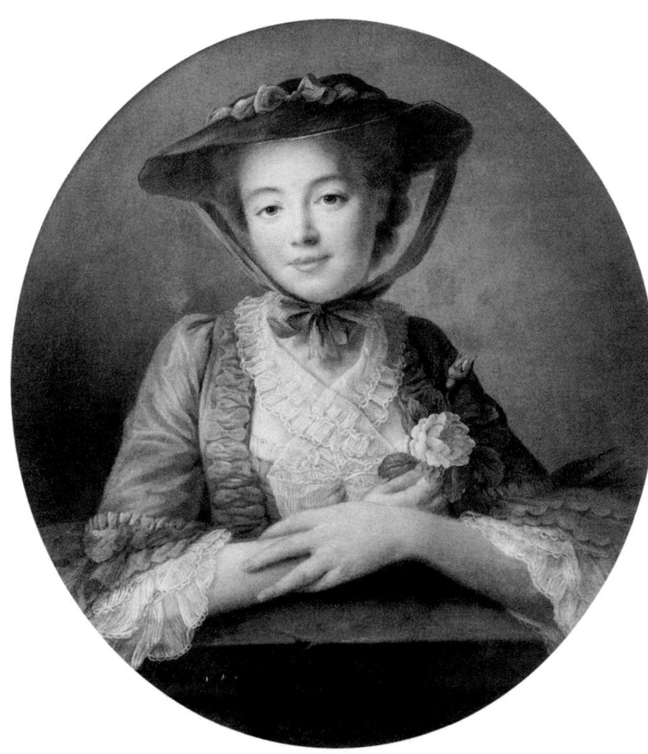

Fig. 11. Marie-Jeanne Doré, *Girl Holding a Rose*, 1765. Oil on canvas, 27 × 24 in. (68.6 × 61 cm). Victoria and Albert Museum, London.

portraits.[59] However, their work made independently is difficult to trace. Nothing by Madame Drouais has come to light, and Gauffier's career was cut short by her premature death. Because Lusurier and Doré painted in a style close to that of Drouais, identifying their work is uncertain, and few paintings have been attributed to them. The works we do have by them, including Lusurier's *Portrait of Germain-Jean Drouais* (François-Hubert's son; fig. 10) and Doré's exquisite *Girl Holding a Rose* of 1765 (possibly a portrait of her sister Anne-Françoise; fig. 11) give every reason to hope that more of their paintings will surface or be correctly attributed.[60]

Drouais was only one of the prominent artists with an important studio that included female students, though the ones that have been studied at all tend to be from the 1780s and 1790s. Maurice Quentin de La Tour (1704–1788) had a few female students (Labille-Guiard being one of them), and other women studied with Jacques-André-Joseph-Camelot Aved (1702–1766), Vien, Henri-Pierre Danloux (1753–1809), and Duplessis.[61] Joseph Vernet appears to have been one of Vallayer-Coster's teachers and at least counseled Vigée-Le Brun with some regularity and, according to her, presented her for membership in the Académie. Geneviève de Beaulieu came out of Greuze's studio, as did his closest disciple Jeanne-Philiberte Ledoux (1767–1840), along with Marie-Françoise-Constance Mayer (1775–1821), and Caroline de Valori, née d'Ette (act. early 19th cent.). Greuze's daughter Anne-Geneviève (1762–1842) also studied with him. Of the artists who came to the fore in the decades preceding the Revolution, Labille-Guiard was the only woman (whom we know about) to have significant numbers of female pupils, but several of her male contemporaries also taught women: the most famous of these is undoubtedly Jacques-Louis David, but Jean-Baptiste Regnault (1754–1829), François-Guillaumme Ménageot (1744–1816), and Joseph-Benoît Suvée (1743–1807) also taught young women, the latter with the assistance of his painter-wife, Charlotte-Louise Rameau (b. c. 1746).[62] Madame Suvée was very likely the Mademoiselle Rameau who exhibited oil and miniature portraits at the Exposition de la Jeunesse in 1768 and 1773. She later showed her work at the Salon de la Correspondance, as did the miniaturists Madame François Boucher, née Jeanne Buseau (1716–c. 1785), and Madame Honoré Fragonard, née Marie-Anne Gérard (1745–1823; fig. 12), along with many other women connected with well-known male artists.[63]

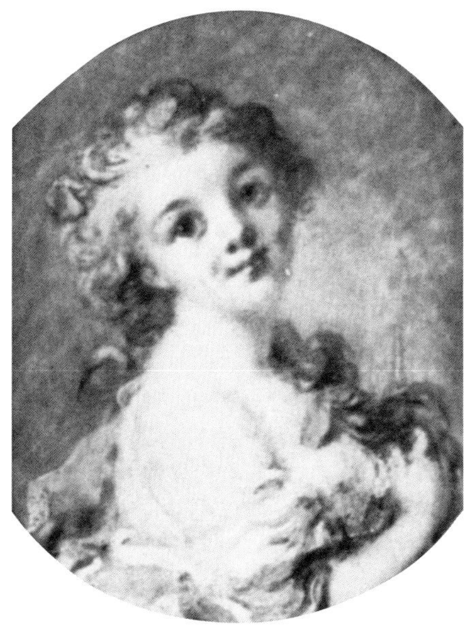

Fig. 12. Marie-Anne Fragonard, née Gérard, *An Unknown Girl*, n.d. Gouache on ivory, 2³⁄₈ × 2¹⁄₈ in. (7.1 × 5.3 cm). The Wallace Collection, London.

Looking back to the beginning of the century, we find a pronounced pattern of mothers, wives, sisters, cousins, and especially daughters of artists who were practicing, if not professional, artists.[64] For example, Charles-Nicolas Cochin's mother and two of his aunts were engravers, as were Renée-Elisabeth Lépicié, née Marlier (1714–1773), wife of Bernard Lépicié (1735–1784), and Marie-Marguerite Oudry, née Froissé (d. 1780), who had been Jean-Baptiste Oudry's student.[65] Another of Oudry's relatives, Mademoiselle de St. Martin, was a painter and a member of the Académie de Saint-Luc (see below); she began to exhibit in its Salons in 1751. Charles-Joseph Natoire's (1700–1777) sister was a pastelist patronized by Madame Jean de Jullienne, the wife of the famous collector who promoted the careers of Rosalba Carriera and Antoine Watteau.[66] Pastel was the preferred medium of the wife and daughter of Louis Silvestre (1675–1760); Marie-Maximilienne (1708–1797), the daughter, was reader and drawing teacher to the dauphine Marie-Josephe de Saxe.[67] Later in the century Elisabeth Pigalle (1751–1827), daughter of the sculptor Jean-Baptiste Pigalle, was a painter, as were Rose-Adélaïde Ducreux (1761–1802; fig. 13) and Nicole Dumont, née Vestier (1767–1846) (who married François Dumont; fig. 14).[68] Marguerite Gérard (fig. 15), sister of Madame Fragonard and the pupil of Jean-Honoré Fragonard, was an artist of renown by 1785 (on a par with Vallayer-Coster, Vigée-Le Brun, and Labille-Guiard), and the first woman to make a name for herself as a genre painter. Marie-Anne Collot (1748–1821; fig. 16) was, unusually, a sculptor who studied with Etienne-Maurice Falconet (1716–1791) and married his son.

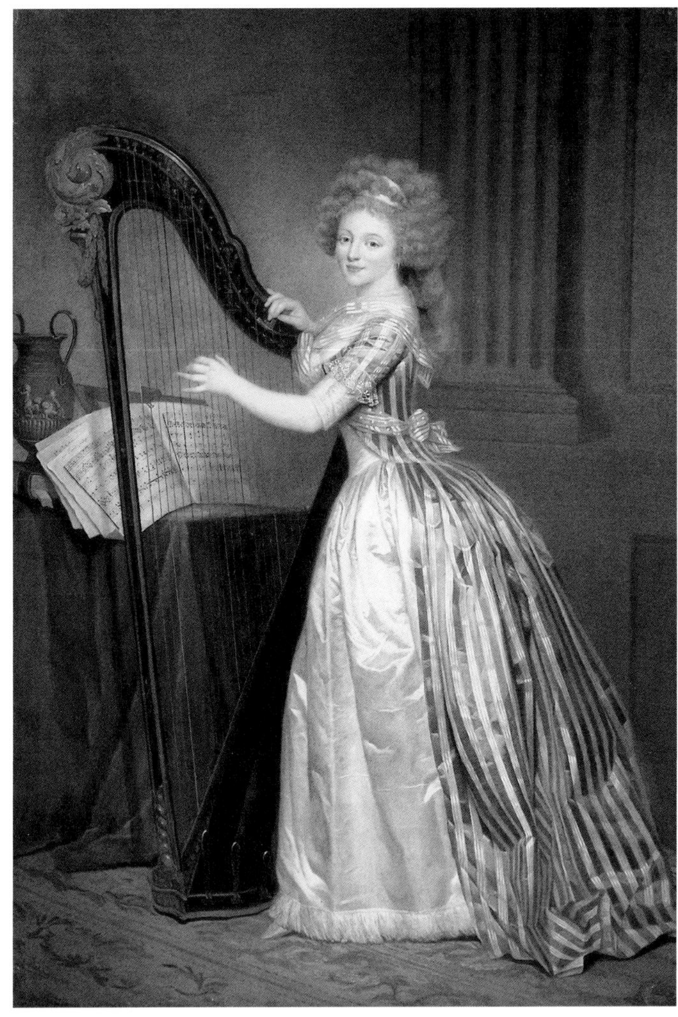

Fig. 13. Rose-Adélaïde Ducreux, *Self-Portrait with a Harp*, c. 1791. Oil on canvas, 75⁷⁄₈ × 50³⁄₄ in. (193 × 128.9 cm). The Metropolitan Museum of Art, Bequest of Susan Dwight Bliss, 1967 (67.55.1).

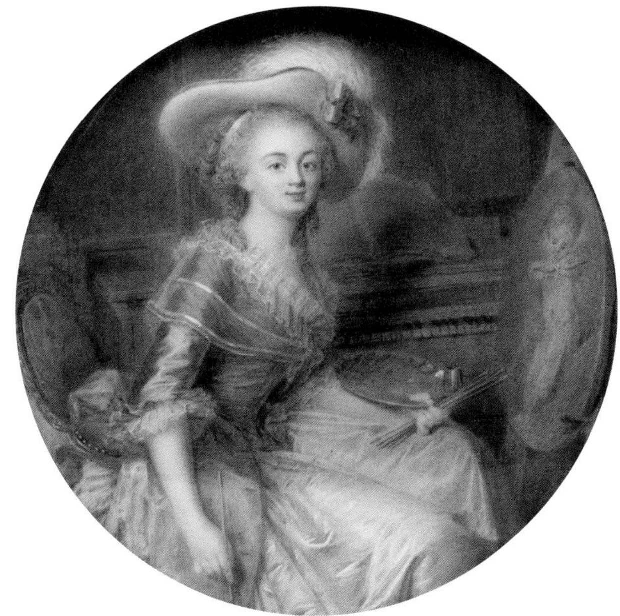

Fig. 14. Antoine Vestier, *Mademoiselle Nicole Vestier at Her Easel*, n.d. Oil on ivory, 2⁷⁄₈ in. diam. (7.5 cm). The Walters Art Museum, Baltimore.

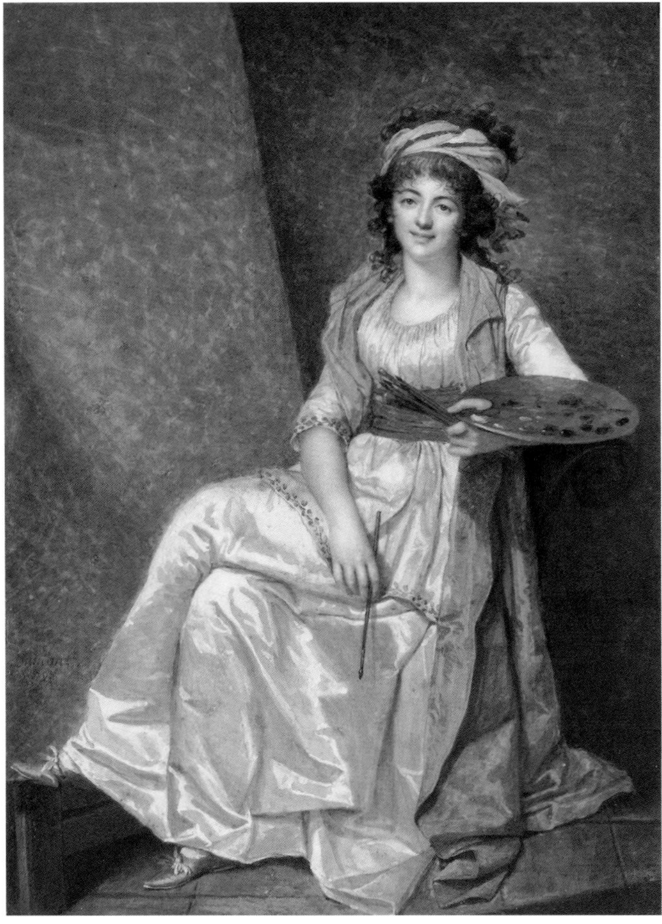

Fig. 15. François Dumont, *Portrait of Marguerite Gérard (sometimes identified as Elisabeth Vigée-Le Brun)*, n.d. Watercolor on ivory, 6³⁄₈ × 4⁵⁄₈ in. (16.2 × 11.7 cm). The Wallace Collection, London.

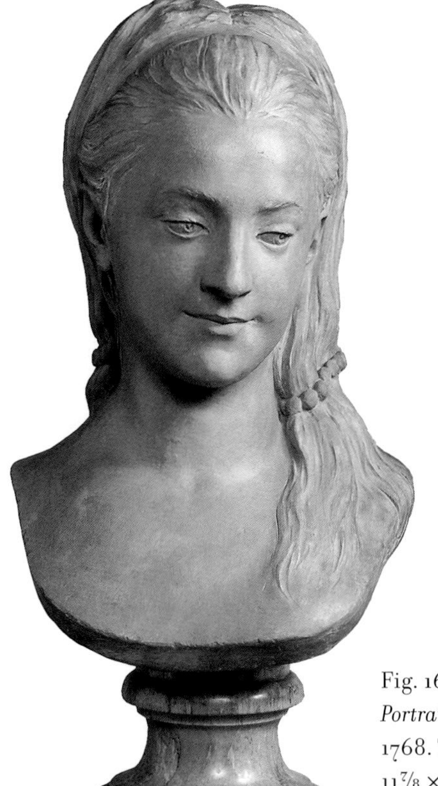

Fig. 16. Marie-Anne Collot, *Portrait of Mary Cathart*, 1768. Terracotta, 23⁵⁄₈ × 11⁷⁄₈ × 9⁷⁄₈ in. (60 × 30 × 25 cm). Musée du Louvre, Paris.

The list could go on. My point is that art history's traditionally sectarian focus on a single segment of the art world has yielded little understanding of the larger visual culture to which the official institutions of the Académie and the Salon belonged—a vibrant and diverse visual culture in which women constituted an abiding and significant presence.

The Other Académies and Beyond

The biographies and works by these eclipsed artists are slowly coming to light. Though many are lost to history, women artists are present in the historical record in gazettes, newspapers, memoirs, and archives. They worked as painters and engravers in their own right, though many more worked anonymously in family workshops. They were found not only in the capital but also in the provinces, where the regional académies admitted more female members to their ranks than in Paris and allowed female students. Two of the best-known examples of women who lived independent careers in the provinces before the Revolution are Marianne Loir (fig. 17) and Françoise Duparc (1705–1778; fig. 18), both of whom were painters and members of the Académie of Marseilles. Given that by 1755 the Académie at Toulouse counted some thirty female students who were learning to paint and draw, it seems reasonable to assume there were many more practicing women artists throughout France.[69]

The wonderful richness of the eighteenth-century art world in which most women artists lived has tended to be overshadowed by the towering art institutions of the monarchy, which privileged certain subjects (namely literary, religious, and historical subjects) and media (oil painting and sculpture). In the broader aesthetic culture, however, there were no doctrinal hierarchies of subject matter or proscriptions of media. There were only the dictates of fashion and the art market, which favored the "lower" genres: portraiture, genre painting, still life, pastel portraiture, engravings, and *objets de luxe*, like miniatures. Artists not in the Académie worked in a broad range of media, including wax, painting in enamel, painting on glass, or, most curious of all, painting "en cheveux" (fashioning images from hair). These were all genres and media that women could and readily did practice, as a look at the almanacs and biographical dictionaries will confirm: they are listed as engravers, painters of all sorts, and drawing teachers.[70]

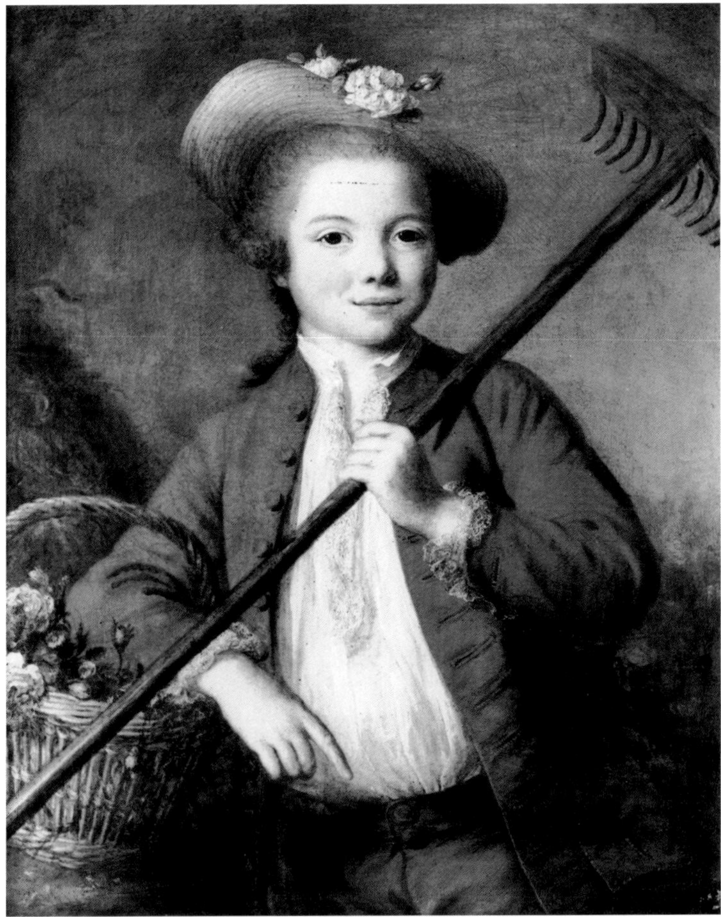

Fig. 17. Marianne Loir, *Portrait of Antoine-Vincent-Louis-Barbe Duplaa*, c. 1763. Oil on canvas, 29½ × 23¼ in. (75 × 59 cm). Palais des Archevêques, Musée des Beaux-Arts, Tours.

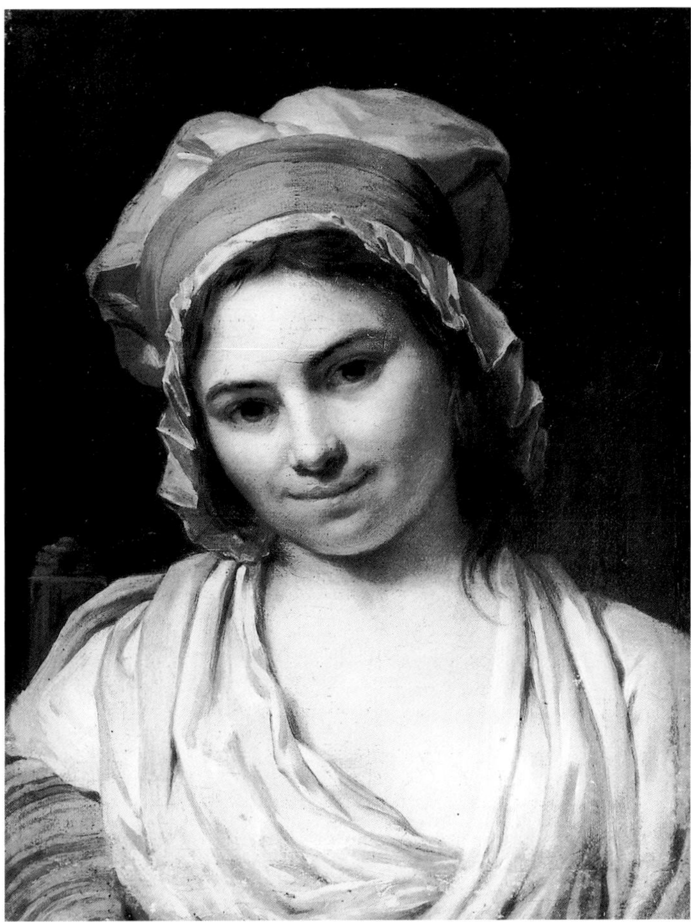

Fig. 18. Françoise Duparc, *Head of a Young Woman*, n.d. Oil on canvas, 17⅜ × 13 in. (44 × 33 cm). Musée Hyacinthe Rigaud–Ville de Perpignan.

In France women had long distinguished themselves in miniature painting, Mademoiselles Geneviève Navarre (1737–1795) and Xavery (act. 1767) being some of the most prominent miniaturists during the first half of the eighteenth century.[71] Labille-Guiard, her student Marie-Gabrielle Capet (1761–1818; fig. 19), Vallayer-Coster, and many others continued the practice successfully during the second half of the century.

One of the most important institutions for women artists before the Revolution was the Académie de Saint-Luc, an outgrowth of the centuries-old guild of master painters. Over the course of the eighteenth century 130 of its 4,500 members were women. Though it was less selective and always connected to the applied arts and trade (one of its major distinctions from the Académie), its aspirations in the fine arts went far beyond those of the traditional corporation of master painters.[72] Under the sponsorship of the marquis Paulmy d'Argenson, the Académie de Saint-Luc followed the example of its far more privileged counterpart by offering life drawing classes, competitions, and prizes for painting and

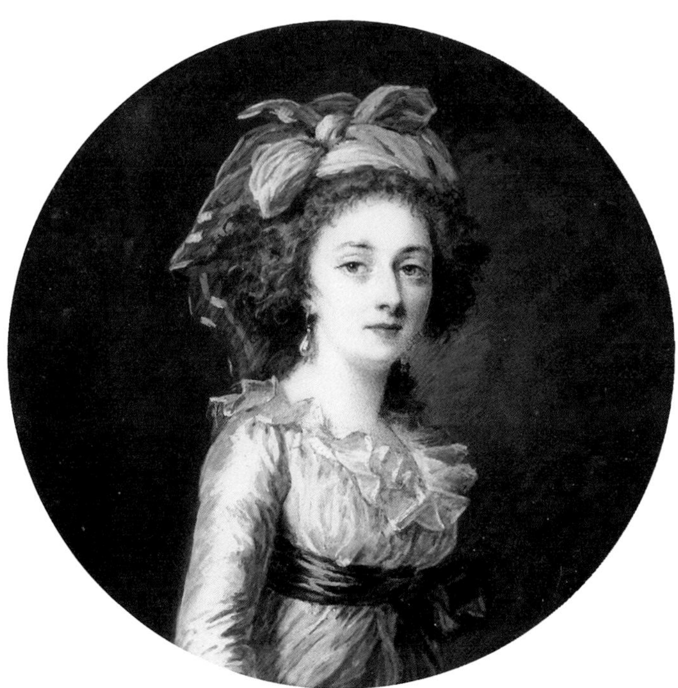

Fig. 19. Marie-Gabrielle Capet, *Presumed Portrait of Madame Elisabeth*, n.d. Gouache on ivory, 2¼ in. diam. (5.7 cm). Musée du Louvre, Paris.

drawing and by mounting seven Salons of its own between 1751 and 1774, in which its female members exhibited paintings, pastels, engravings, and miniatures.

In fact, women exhibited at all the occasional venues
that were available to extra-academic painters in Paris:
throughout the century their work appeared in the
ephemeral, but important, Exposition de la Jeunesse
(an open-air exhibition in the place Dauphine, which
took place on the Feast of Corpus Christi from six in the
morning until midday). From 1777 to 1787 the Salon de
la Correspondance was mounted by the entrepreneur
Pahin de la Blancherie, and the Exposition du Colisée
took place in 1776.

The Workings of Patronage:
Ghosts in the Machine

The role played by women as patrons and sponsors of the
fine arts is an area of inquiry that is just beginning to be
addressed seriously by art historians.[73] Hampering the
study of patronage by women of the court is the fact that
they did not often act through the official channels gov-
erned by the royal bureaucracy. The support and patronage undertaken by women like Marie-Antoinette or
the aunts of Louis XVI either were not regularized and
documented systematically or were frequently effected
indirectly, so that our knowledge of them is somewhat
fragmentary and at times speculative.

A perfect example of this can be found in the tantaliz-
ing evidence of a few lines in letters brought to light by
Marianne Roland Michel that attest to Marie-Antoinette's
personal interest in Vallayer-Coster.[74] Similarly suggestive references are to be found in connection with another
prominent woman at court and in salon society: the
comtesse d'Angiviller. Well known as a *salonnière* and
a patron of the arts, the comtesse was a particularly important resource for Labille-Guiard, not only as a collector but also as a protector or intercessor, as Laura
Auricchio has shown in her superb dissertation on the
artist.[75] Apparently, the comtesse had taken an interest
in Vallayer-Coster as well—or so Labille-Guiard thought
when in 1783 she sought the comtesse's able assistance
in taking action against the seller of a pamphlet that
insulted Vallayer-Coster and slandered Labille-Guiard
herself. (As Auricchio notes, Labille-Guiard called
on the comtesse to act on behalf of "the interest that
you take in Mme. Coster and in your sex generally."[76])
Geneviève de Beaulieu also mentions the comtesse in

the letter she wrote to the comte d'Angiviller. During
the Consulate Vallayer-Coster is supposed to have re-
sorted to a similar strategy of enlisting the help of an
influential woman. A contemporary source claims that
Vallayer-Coster applied to Josephine de Beauharnais
in an attempt to obtain a pardon for her nephew, Coster
de St. Victor, who was involved in a plot to assassinate
Napoleon. She offered "one of her best paintings" in her
unsuccessful bid for clemency, which may explain how
several of her works entered Josephine's collection, even
though she did not receive any encouragement from the
Napoleonic regime.[77]

That there were other instances of more straightforward artistic sponsorship of women by women much
earlier is attested by the poem that Jeanne Natoire published in the *Mercure de France* in 1744. Addressing herself to Madame de Jullienne, Natoire prefaces her poem
by saying: "Madame, since I owe to your advice and your
love for the Arts, the taste and small talent I have for
painting in pastel, it is right that I should take this occasion to demonstrate to you my gratitude."[78] The patronage of Mesdames enjoyed by Labille-Guiard, who was
officially named their First Painter, is very well known
(if understudied). But the financial accounts of Madame
Victoire show that her interest extended to aspiring artists as well: she paid a pension that enabled the painter
Pomponne Hubert to study with Labille-Guiard.[79]

As I noted earlier, the Bâtiments orchestrated the
official commissions carried out for the crown, and
they played a central role in selecting the artists who
would receive those commissions. This is clearly how
the system worked when in 1753 d'Angiviller's predecessor, Abel-François Poisson de Vandières, marquis de
Marigny, chose the young Joseph Vien to execute two
paintings of religious subjects to decorate the cabinet
of Queen Marie Leszczyńska. The official correspondence concerning these images shows that the queen
(herself an amateur painter) dictated much of the compositions and even the fine details of Vien's paintings.[80]
For her part, Marie-Antoinette helped select artists who
worked under the auspices of the Bâtiments on projects
that pertained to her. The choice of Vigée-Le Brun to
paint the great state portrait *Marie-Antoinette and Her
Children* (1787, Musée du Château de Versailles) was
surely made according to the queen's preferences.[81]

We do not know for certain how Marie-Antoinette
came to own Vallayer-Coster's painting of a Vestal Virgin
(pl. 25), whether through desire or gift. Yet it seems likely

that she had a voice in choosing Vallayer-Coster to paint her portrait in 1780, though d'Angiviller seems to have had a hand in that as well.[82] There were times when artists worked for the queen directly. Some of these artists, such as François Dumont and Vigée-Le Brun, were academicians.[83] But frequently her chosen painters were nonacademic artists like Joseph Krantzinger, Campana, Jean-Baptiste-André Gautier Dagoty (1740–1786), Louis-Auguste Brun (1758–1815), Perrin de Salbreux, and the famous Pierre-Joseph Redouté.[84] Campana signed his name "Painter of the Cabinet de la Reine," and though there is no evidence that he was officially granted this title, his biographers have suggested that permission to use it was granted unofficially. There is also evidence that some of the queen's painters asked for permission to be associated with her. A charming little painting by Gautier Dagoty of the queen at her toilette (now at Versailles) includes the following inscription: *To the Queen. Madame, having had the honor of painting your Majesty and of making several portraits for her, J.B.A. Dagoty, humbly begs her to grant him the permission of carrying the title of her painter.* Vallayer-Coster's descendants passed on the tradition that she was head of the queen's cabinet of painting. Although no evidence supports this claim, there can be no doubt that she too qualified as "the queen's painter" on a number of counts: Marie-Antoinette not only owned and commissioned works by Vallayer-Coster, but she also acted as her patron in helping to secure lodgings for her in the Louvre and in putting her in contact with other patrons. The scarcity of hard evidence attesting to Vallayer-Coster's relationship with the queen highlights the difficulties one often encounters in the study of women artists and women patrons.

In his famous *Persian Letters*, the philosopher Charles de Secondat, baron de Montesquieu, described the French court and society as ruled by a "republic of women." He claimed that "any man who is at Court, in Paris, in the Provinces, and sees ministers, magistrates, prelates in action without knowing the women who govern them, is like a man who perceives very well a machine that works, but has no idea what makes it run."[85] Perhaps, like most fictions, there is an element of truth in Montesquieu's assertions. While the "machine" of the art world was surely not powered solely by women, we are beginning to understand something about its invisible and intricate workings, and the important roles women played in it—both as artists and as patrons.

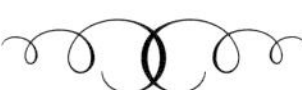

NOTES

1. Goncourt 1854, n.p.

2. For an excellent account of the Goncourts, see Silverman 1989.

3. The literature on this subject is vast. Some of the most important texts include Hunt 1992, Hunt 1984, Gutwirth 1992, Landes 1988, and Outram 1989.

4. See especially the work of Goodman 1994.

5. Vigée-Lebrun 1986, 1:122.

6. Starobinski 1987, 55.

7. Laura Auricchio has begun to address some of these very questions, particularly in connection with Labille-Guiard and Vigée-Le Brun. See Auricchio 2000. I am indebted to her for generously providing me with a copy of her illuminating study.

8. Although there is relatively little scholarship on women and the arts during the reign of Louis XV and before, that on the Revolutionary period is quite rich: Vivian Cameron's dissertation, "Woman as Image and Image-Maker in Paris during the French Revolution," Cameron 1984, was one of the first major contributions to the subject; more lately Margaret Oppenheimer has written an important dissertation on women artists, which includes an indispensable glossary, Oppenheimer 1995. Women artists and patrons during the earlier years of the ancien régime constitute still relatively uncharted terrain. One of the most important texts remains the exhibition catalogue Los Angeles 1976. See also Chadwick 1996.

Whenever possible, I have reproduced a work by the artist in question; when these were unavailable, a portrait of the artist by another painter is shown.

9. An exemplary articulation of Rousseau's views about women and their influence on society is to be found in Rousseau 1989.

10. The classic text on the formation of the public sphere is Habermas 1989. See also Landes 1988 and Goodman 1994; and Crow 1985.

11. For an excellent discussion of women artists and issues of visibility, see Sheriff 1996.

12. For discussion of woman as spectacle in this period, see Landes 1988, 71ff.

13. For a study of female ambition in the eighteenth century, with particular attention to the marquise du Châtelet, a mathematician and Voltaire's mistress, see Badinter 1983. Auricchio 2000 makes a convincing argument about the ways in which impropriety was used to advantage by women artists.

14. Cited by Sheriff 1996, 263.

15. Fort Worth 1982. See http://www.batguano.com/vigee.html for a list of websites on Vigée-Le Brun.

16. This is one reason the present exhibition of Vallayer-Coster's work is a significant event for art history. Aside from the fact that comparatively few shows are devoted to an eighteenth-century artist—much less an artist who was a woman—it affords the rare opportunity to see many works by a painter who was extremely well respected by her contemporaries and was one of the major still-life painters of her day. Seeing her exquisite paintings together for the first time greatly furthers our knowledge of her work, in a happy continuation of the project begun by Marianne Roland Michel with her essential monograph on Vallayer-Coster (Roland Michel 1970).

17. Besides Auricchio's dissertation there is only one twentieth-century monograph on Labille-Guiard, Passez 1973, and one article, Cailleux 1969a, i–iv. See also Hyde forthcoming. Rosalba Carriera, the Venetian pastelist, was also admitted to the Académie; the scholarship on her is still relatively scant. See the excellent essay on Carriera in West 1999; Christopher Johns, "An Ornament of Italy and the Premier Female Painter in Europe," in Hyde and Milam forthcoming; Sani 1985; and Sani 1988. On Therbouche, see Los Angeles 1976, 169–170 and Sheriff 1996, 115–120. Angela Rosenthal also discusses Therbouche, in Rosenthal 1997.

It should be noted that Mme Roslin, a portraitist, died prematurely, and most of Mme Vien's works are lost, which no doubt accounts partly for the dearth of scholarship on them. Interestingly, Charles-Nicolas Cochin, the secretary of the Académie, noted that Mme Vien was a talented miniaturist but that she never attempted portraiture, even though she could have made very good money at it. She was fearful of irritating the comte de Caylus (she enjoyed his protection, as did her husband), who was absolutely determined that she should practice only "natural history" (flower paintings and so forth). Chatelus 1991, 310.

18. See Sheriff 1996, 262 ff.

19. Lebrun 1776, 118. Jeanne-Françoise, Marie, and Thérèse Parrocel were the daughters of the Joseph-François Parrocel (1704–1781) who made it to the first stage of admission to the Académie (was *agréé*) in 1753 though never achieved full membership. The eldest, Jeanne-Françoise, painted flowers and animals; Marie, historical subjects and copies; while Thérèse was a miniaturist. All three died in Avignon. See Peloux 1930, 1:109.

20. Exceptions to this might be Jean-Honoré Fragonard and possibly his student/sister-in-law, Marguerite Gérard, both of whose careers developed entirely independently of the established institutions, though he was trained and his career launched by the Académie. On Gérard, see Wells-Robertson 1978.

21. Marie-Renée-Geneviève Brossard de Beaulieu was a member of the fine arts academies at Lyon and Rome, and founded a public drawing school for young women at Lille in the 1790s. See Moissy 1947; and Oppenheimer 1995, 124–127.

22. Chatelus 1991, 52 ff.

23. Chatelus 1991, 52.

24. Oppenheimer 1995, 127, speculates that the 1785 discussion of Beaulieu in the *Mercure* was written by her uncle, whom Pierre refers to as "a writer of petitions and letters at court" (un faiseur de placets, de lettres à la cour). On Beaulieu, see also "Lettre au Rédacteur du Mercure," *Mercure de France*, November 1785, 89–90; *Mémoires secrets*, 13 November 1785; and *Mercure de France*, June 1788, 128.

25. Germaine Greer claims that Catherine-Elisabeth Allais (act. 1779–1786) also attempted to gain admission to the Académie in 1769, but she does not give the source of her information. Greer 1979, 261–262.

26. Montaiglon 1875–1892, 4:34; Sheriff 1996, 78.

27. This was the number who belonged at that time. Mme Therbouche had been admitted three years earlier; and Mme Vien in 1757. See Oulmont 1928; Fidière 1885; Montaiglon 1875–1892, 8:53. The quota of four women was reiterated by d'Angiviller at the time of the admissions of Vigée-Le Brun and Labille-Guiard. Montaiglon 1875–1892, 9:153, 157.

28. She gives the date 1784 in a letter of 1806 when she paid homage to the Academy of Sciences by presenting it with her *Portrait of Lavoisier*. Moissy 1947, 183.

29. "Marie-Renée-Geneviève Brossard de Beaulieu," in "Lettres inédites" 1907, 105–106. My thanks to Laura Auricchio for providing me with a copy of this letter and for sharing her thoughts on the episode.

30. Renou had involved himself in a more public debate about women artists in 1785 and wrote an article in the *Journal de Paris* in which he defended the right of women to work as artists and to exhibit in the Exposition de la Jeunesse. See Cameron 1984, 64.

31. Perhaps it is not quite right to say the certificate was entirely meaningless: it did open the way for her admission to the Accademia di San Luca in Rome in 1785.

32. Pierre must not have been so unconditionally ill-disposed toward women artists as one might think in light of Vigée-Le Brun's memoirs and his well-publicized opposition to her admission. Sheriff has observed that Pierre seems to have backed Labille-Guiard strongly (Sheriff 1996, 78). It is worth noting, too, that the Goncourts owned a charming drawing by him of a woman painting a landscape. See Launay 1991, 415.

33. The process that led up to Vien's admission is telling. In his memoirs he recounts how one of his mentors, Charles Natoire, called for a committee of academicians to go to Vien's studio to assess his work. The committee consisted of Jean-Marc Nattier (1685–1766), Jean Restout, Hyacinthe Collin de Vermont (1693/95–1761), and Pierre. Only Pierre, who had been Natoire's student, was favorably disposed toward the young artist. It took the intervention of the influential comte

de Caylus, and above all, of François Boucher, to win the Académie's support for Vien's nomination. See Gaehtgens and Lugan 1988, 20–23, 303–304. Though Vallayer-Coster had no official sponsor, she surely had unofficial ones. Labille-Guiard's candidacy was presented by Alexandre Roslin. Vigée-Le Brun was admitted at the request of the queen. On Vigée-Le Brun's admission and Pierre's resistance, see Sheriff 1996 and Vigée-Lebrun 1986.

34. Sheriff 1996, 74–78.

35. At least twenty-two were admitted between August and October, while others had been attending its meetings since 1790. Oppenheimer 1995, 14, lists them. Cameron 1984, 89, mentions Mme Elisabeth-Claire Tardieu (1731–1773), too.

36. Cameron 1984, 89; Oppenheimer 1995, 14–15. Oppenheimer, 16, notes that by 1794 women were once again admitted to the Commune Générale des Arts, by then renamed the Société Populaire et Républicaine des Arts, but there are no records of whether this reversal was effected.

37. Oppenheimer 1995, 2, gives this figure. The number of women exhibiting at the Salon ranged between twenty and thirty up until 1798. After 1798 the number steadily increased, as did the overall number of artists exhibiting. Between 1791 and 1810 women exhibitors constituted between 7 and 15 percent of the total. Oppenheimer 1995, 13.

38. Official Bâtiments commissions almost never went to women; the notable exceptions being Vallayer-Coster's commission for the portrait of Mme Sophie in 1779 and the portraits of Mme Elisabeth and the comte d'Artois painted by Demoiselle Read in 1764. Engerand 1901, 468, 408. Finally and most famously, Vigée-Le Brun was awarded the commission in 1785 to paint the formal state portrait of Marie-Antoinette and her children. Though commissioned at the behest of the queen, this work was carried out under the auspices of the Bâtiments.

39. Peloux 1930.

40. Godefroy's granddaughter, Marie-Eléonore Godefroid (1778–1849), was a student of Jacques-Louis David, and became the long-standing studio assistant of François Gérard, another of David's students. She exhibited regularly in the Salons of the First Empire and Restoration and won a number of prizes. Oppenheimer 1995, 187–188.

41. Alden Gordon (1996, 131) has described the duties of the Maison du roi: "[It] had responsibility for the daily living arrangements of the king and his court from the smallest detail of his wardrobe to the construction of palaces and supervision of the king's properties." Gordon offers a lengthy description of the Menus-Plaisirs (137–138). See Lespinasse 1929; and Pinon 1989.

42. James-Sarazin 2001, 15–16; Lespinasse 1929, 76.

43. Jallut 1955, 24.

44. Mme Nivelon was the wife of Anne-Baptiste Nivelon (act. 1750–1764), who was employed by the Cabinet du roi,

the king's personal painting collection. Jeanne-Angélique Boquet was married to the painter Louis Charny (act. 1748–1762?), and so is distinct from the Anne-Rosalie Bocquet-Filleul who also worked for the Menus-Plaisirs (Jallut 1955, 16). However, both were related to Louis-Réné Boquet, a draftsman and costume designer. See Tessier 1926, 23–24; Vuaflart and Bourin 1909–1910, 1:33; and Peloux 1930.

45. Rosalie Bocquet's father, Blaise Boquet, a fan painter, was probably the brother of Louis-Réné. Her mother, Marie-Rosalie Hallé, came from a family of well-known painters. See Vuafluart and Bourin 1909–1910, 2:37; Tessier 1926; and Cleray 1910.

A member of the Académie de Saint-Luc, the guild academy, Mme Filleul is mentioned in the accounts of the Menus-Plaisirs in 1773, 1776, 1777, and 1782 (Vuafluart and Bourin 1909–1910, 2:32–37). She also painted a portrait of the queen—presumably from life—about the time of the birth of the dauphin (Jallut 1955, 36). Filleul was accorded the privilege of painting the royal family several times between 1781 and 1783, during their sojourns at La Muette, where she and her husband were the concierges. During the Revolution she was arrested as "the intimate friend of the Messalina Antoinette" and would be sent to the guillotine with her lifelong friend, Joseph Vernet's daughter Emilie Chalgrin, ostensibly for burning candles at the wedding of Chalgrin's daughter. Salmon 1997, 78. Vigée-Lebrun 1986, 1:32–34, 41–42.

46. In a 1777 letter to the *surintendant* of the Menus-Plaisirs, Denis-Pierre-Jean Papillon de la Ferté, requesting payment for a bill she submitted eighteen months earlier, Mme Le Brun states that it was "at the request of M. Boquet" (sur la demande de M. Boquet) that she had made two portraits of the queen. Tessier 1926, 96. See Archives nationales, Paris (hereafter AN), O¹ 3054.

47. James-Sarazin 2001, 16. Pierre mentions Mlle Parrocel in one of his letters to d'Angiviller: Furcy-Raynaud 1905–1906, 56–57. Hofstetter 1995, 15.

48. In addition, Agathe Lemoine, née Bonvallet (first mentioned 1794), was known for her miniature circular portraits of Louis XVII. See Thieme and Becker, s.v. "Lemoine, Agathe"; and Jeffares 1999, 65.

The Cabinet du roi had its own stable of painters and copyists; some twenty are recorded over the course of the century (Chatelus 1991, 185). On the Frédous, see Thieme and Becker, s.v. "Frédou, Jean-Martial." For a good description of the functions of the Cabinet du roi with instructive illustrations, see Salmon 1999, 18–19.

49. Dumont and Mosnier would both be admitted to the Académie, after having made their reputations as painters of the queen. On Dumont, see Lespinasse 1929, 155; and Hofstetter 1994. On Mosnier, see Roche 1921.

The inscription on a miniature of Marie-Antoinette by Dumont of 1777 demonstrates the queen's giving a miniature as a token of favor: *given to a femme de chambre whose daughter died* (Versailles 1955, 39); see also James-Sarazin 2001, 15–16. Vallayer-Coster was apparently the recipient of one of these coveted gifts. Roland Michel 1970, 30.

50. Campana probably received verbal permission to use the title Painter of the Cabinet of the Queen. His wife may have painted many of the works attributed to him. Jeannerat 1923. See Thieme and Becker, s.v. "Campana, Marie-Christine."

51. According to Lespinasse 1929, 129, Mme Cadet was a student of the academician and miniaturist Jean-Baptiste Weyler (1747–1791) and painted the queen in 1787. (She may have been related to the Joly who was a keeper of the Cabinet du roi in the 1770s.) Whether this was a commission directly from the queen or through the Menus-Plaisirs he does not say. See Bénézit 1999, s.v. "Cadet, Aglaé." In 1787 and 1788 Vallayer-Coster also painted the queen's portrait in miniature, though it is unknown whether these were royal commissions. Roland Michel 1970, 31.

52. Lespinasse 1929, 84.

53. Lespinasse 1929, 84.

54. Roland Michel 1970, 31.

55. A note on the royal account books in AN, O¹ 1934B, includes this somewhat cryptic comment: "It is right that M. Cochin knows that M. Darthenay is a[n] . . . idiot, because he announced this proposition and did not send it" (Il est bon que M. Cochin sache que M. Darthenay est une f . . . bête, puisqu'il a annoncé cette proposition et qu'il ne l'a pas envoyée). This might suggest the commission did not originate with the Bâtiments through the usual channels. Engerand 1901, 408. Thieme and Becker imply that Demoiselle Read was Catherine Read, a well-known pastelist who studied for a time with Quentin de La Tour and had a successful career in England.

56. See Laurent Hugues's contribution on Vallayer-Coster's portraits of Mesdames, in this volume.

57. Chatelus 1991, 26.

58. Jallut 1955, 18; Vuafluart and Bourin 1909–1910, 2: pl. XIII.

59. The Musée national du Château de Versailles has a three-quarter-length copy of a Drouais portrait of Marie-Antoinette by a Mlle Denizard. Perhaps she too was a member of Drouais's studio. On the Doré sisters, see Kauffman 1972, 184.

60. Two portraits, signed *Mlle. Doré* (like the painting reproduced here), appeared in sales of the 1930s: an unknown man, dated 1763, Drouot, Paris, 20–21 December 1937, lot 4, repr.; an unknown woman, sale Fischer, Lucerne, 21–23 August 1930, lot 288, repr. Kauffman 1972, 185.

61. Studying with Quentin de La Tour were Mlle Navarre, Belle de Zuylen (not a professional artist), and Labille-Guiard (Passez 1971, 11). Mlle Allais may have studied with Aved; Mme Roslin with Vien (Salmon 1997, 122); the Gueret sisters with Danloux (Cameron 1984, 95 ff.), and Marie-Geneviève Bouliar (1772–1819) with Duplessis (Los Angeles 1976, 202–204).

62. A letter written by Suvée to d'Angiviller suggests that Mme Suvée also taught these students. See Cameron 1984, 75; Guiffrey 1874–1875, 396–397; Chatelus 1991, 114. Los Angeles 1976, 205–206, 213–214, discusses a number of Greuze's students. Marie-Victoire Lemoine (1754–1820) studied with Ménageot; her sisters Marie-Elisabeth Gabiou and Marie-Denise Villers were also painters (the latter was a student of Anne-Louis Girodet de Roucy Trioson [1767–1824]). Lemoine's best-known work, *Interior of the Atelier of a Woman Painter* (1789), is in the Metropolitan Museum of Art, New York. Oppenheimer 1995, 222–224. Baillio 1996. For an excellent discussion of some of David's students after the Revolution, see Denton 1998. Cameron 1984 and Greer 1979 discuss a good many of the women connected with the studios of David and Regnault.

63. Miniatures by Mme Boucher were in the collections of Ange-Laurent de La Live de Jully and Berthélémy-Augustin-Blondel d'Azincourt and appeared in eighteenth-century sales. See Lespinasse 1929, 44, for discussion. For drawings attributed to her, see Bjürstrom 1987. Mme Fragonard was evidently an important miniaturist, though almost none of her works has been firmly attributed; most if not all of the miniatures ascribed to her husband may actually be her work. Her miniatures appeared in private exhibitions and in sale catalogues (thirty works in sixteen sales between 1778 and 1785). See Paris 1988, 559.

64. Jean-Marc Nattier's mother Marie Courtois (c. 1655–1703) was a miniaturist, though her career was cut short by a paralysis that struck her in her twenties. Much of the information on the relatives of male artists comes from Peloux 1930.

65. Mme Oudry gave birth to thirteen children, and one of the daughters married Antoine Boizot (c. 1702–1782), a draftsman at the Gobelins tapestry manufactory. Antoine's daughter Marie (1744–1800) was a painter and engraver and her father's student. On Lépicié, Oudry, and Boizot, see Peloux 1930.

66. Similarly, Charles-Antoine Coypel's sister Anne is thought to have been a painter (she may be the sitter in the lovely unattributed *Portrait of a Woman Artist*, c. 1730, in the Art Institute of Chicago).

67. Weigert 1959, 129–135. Marie-Maximilienne's mother, Marie-Catherine Herault (1680–1743), was the daughter of the landscape painter Charles-Antoine Herault (1644–1718), associated with the Coypels. She, like her four sisters, was a painter. She made copies of her husband's paintings and was likely the drawing teacher of the daughters of the Elector of Saxony.

68. Rose-Adélaïde Ducreux was the daughter of Joseph; Nicole Vestier, daughter of Antoine Vestier (1740–1824). Baillio 1988. There is some discussion of Ducreux in Lyon 1958. Auricchio 2000, 153–155, addresses Nicole Dumont at some length; a brief discussion can be found in Passez 1989, 134–136.

69. Locquin 1978, 36. Other members of the Marseilles Académie, founded in 1752, included a Mme M.-J. Guilbert (also a painter of the Academy of Madrid), Mlle Mille, also a painter, and Mme Hémery de Lingée (b. 1753), the engraver (Peloux 1930, 1:32, 33). I have not been able to find further information about them. There were also French women working as artists in other countries. Besides Mme Guilbert, the Real Academia de Bellas Artes de San Fernando in Madrid admitted Faronne-Marie-Madeleine Ollivier, née Lefebvre (wife of Michel-Barthélémy Ollivier [1712–1784]), in 1759 and Marie-Joseph Carron in 1761. Luxenburg 1997, 49, 61. François-Hubert Drouais's student Pauline Gauffier, née Chatillon, lived and worked in Italy with her husband M.-L. Gauffier (Oppenheimer 1995, 182–183). On Loir and Duparc, see Los Angeles 1976, 167–168 and 171–173. Xavier Salmon also discusses Marianne Loir in connection with Nattier in Versailles 1999, 30–31.

70. Women generally did not practice history painting because it required studying the nude male body. For discussion of this subject, see Linda Nochlin's classic article, "Why Have There Been No Great Women Artists?" (Nochlin 1988). For more recent discussions of women's art education, see Sheriff and Roworth 1994.

71. Catherine Perrot, Anne-Marie-Renée Stressor (1651–1713), and occasionally Sophie Chéron all painted in miniature and were members of the Académie in the seventeenth century. Rosalba Carriera, admitted in 1720, was extremely influential as a miniaturist, having introduced innovations like painting on ivory. See Chennevières 1903, 179.

72. In 1786 the Académie de Saint-Luc listed 40 *demoiselles peintres* (Oppenheimer 1995, 8). See also Grasse 1998, 9. Ever jealous of its prerogatives, the Académie, at the behest of Pierre, would eventually suppress the Académie de Saint-Luc. See Katie Scott's fascinating article on the conflicts between the Académie and the guild, Scott 1989.

73. For recent scholarship in this area, see Lawrence 1997; and Hyde and Milam forthcoming.

74. See Roland Michel 1970, 26–31.

75. Auricchio 2000. The comtesse also took a particular interest in Gabriel-François Doyen, according to Locquin 1978, 42. The comtesse de Boigne describes the comtesse d'Angiviller as the "empress" of the coterie of "true" art lovers at Versailles. Chatelus 1991, 264.

76. The text is to be found in "Suite de Marlborough au Salon 1783," Collection Deloynes, no. 302. Portions of the text are published in Passez 1971, 24–25. See Auricchio 2000, 100–101, 125. The text also defamed Vigée-Le Brun.

77. Vallayer-Coster offered "one of her best paintings, hoping that, touched by the position of a woman of talent, who was on the point of seeing the only bond that she had in life shattered, the consul would accord the grace that she so ardently solicited. The painting was presented, admired, and accepted; but the young Coster was nonetheless sent to the scaffold, where he nobly ended a life that he had devoted to the Bourbons" (un de ses meilleurs tableaux; espérant que, touché par la position d'une femme de talent, qui était au moment de voir briser le seul lien qui l'attachait à la vie, le consul accorderait cette grâce si vivement solicitée. Le tableau fut présenté, admiré, et accepté; mais le jeune Coster n'en fut pas moins conduit à l'échaufaud, où il termina noblement une vie qu'il avait dévouée aux Bourbons). [Ducrest] 1829, 3: 234–235. This interesting piece of information was discovered by Oppenheimer 1995, 273.

78. *Mercure de France*, June 1744, 1354. Jullienne's posthumous sale included eight pastels by Mlle Natoire.

79. Passez 1973, 22. AN, O^1 3766, Comptes et pensions de Madame Victoire.

80. Furcy-Raynaud 1903–1904, 32–33.

81. Marie-Antoinette appears to have been involved to some degree with the commission of Drouais in 1772, in which he painted her as Hebe for one of Louis XV's rooms at Choisy. See Garnier-Pelle 1995, 35–37.

82. On the Vestal Virgin painting, see Bailey's essay in the present volume.

83. I refer here to the queen's intervention on Vigée-Le Brun's behalf in getting her elected to the Académie. Dumont, too, is thought to have been accorded lodgings in the Louvre because of the queen's protection.

84. Redouté is said to have received the title of Dessinateur et peintre du Cabinet de la Reine in 1787, though I have not been able to find reliable confirmation of this often-repeated assertion. In her excellent new biography of the queen, Antonia Fraser (2001, 164–165) notes that Marie-Antoinette enjoyed sketching flowers at Choisy under his tutelage.

85. Montesquieu 1964, letter 107.

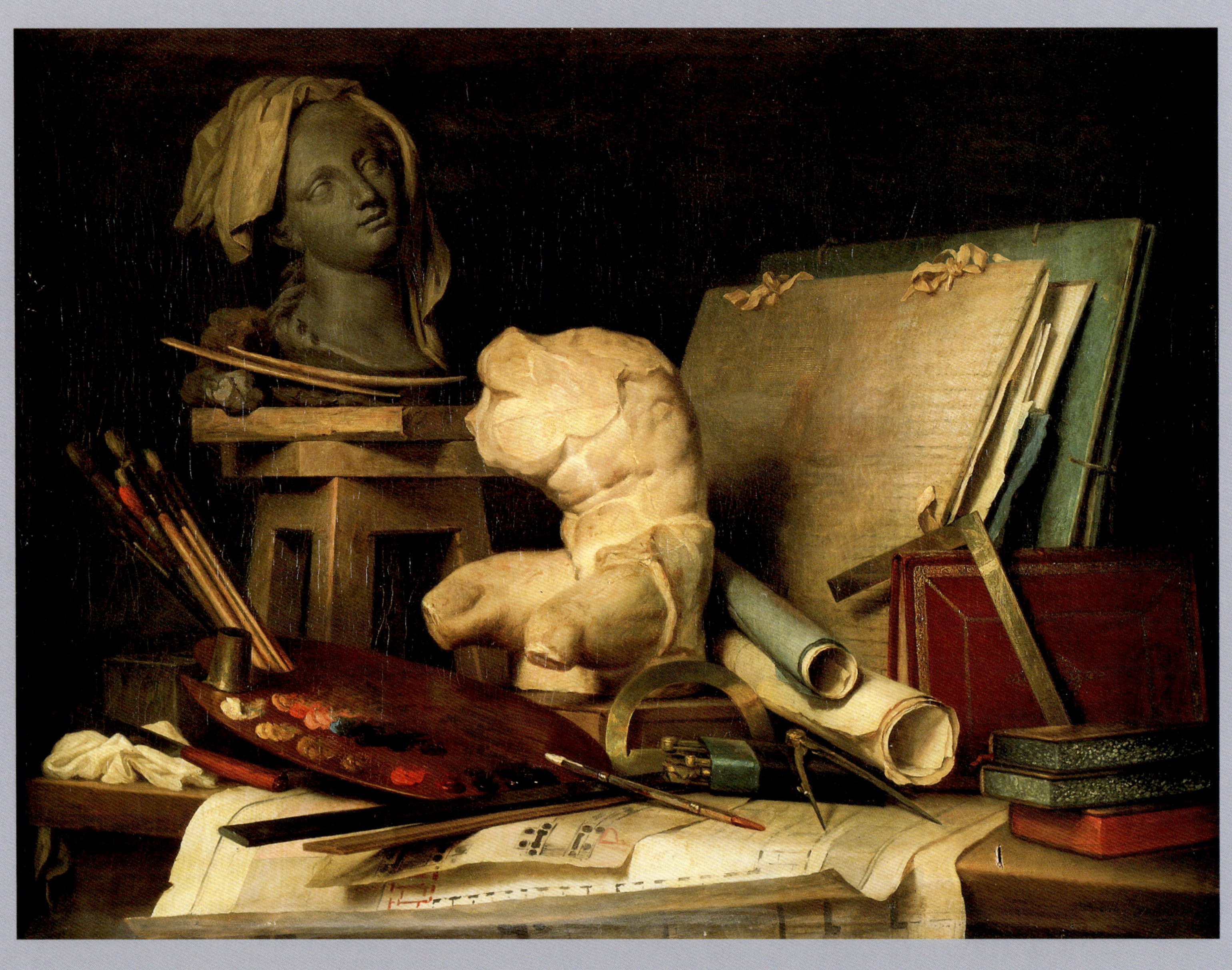

Anne Vallayer-Coster, *The Attributes of Painting, Sculpture and Architecture*, 1769.
Oil on canvas, 35⅜ × 47⅝ in. (90 × 121 cm). Musée du Louvre, Paris (fig. 1).

— CLAIRE BARRY —

The Painting Technique of Anne Vallayer-Coster: Searching for the Origins of Style

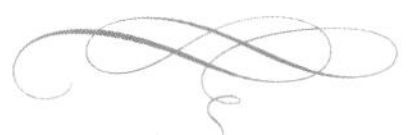

THIS INVESTIGATION HOPES to shed light on some of the origins and aspects of Anne Vallayer-Coster's painting technique. In spite of her phenomenal success in a long and prolific career that survived the French Revolution and her facility in creating a diverse group of works in oil, watercolor, and pastel, we know little about her teachers or artistic training. As Marianne Roland Michel has observed in this volume, Vallayer-Coster most likely studied drawing with Madeleine Basseport, the draftswoman of the Jardin des Plantes, and painting with the landscape artist Joseph Vernet, who instructed Vallayer-Coster in painting studies from nature. What explains the artist's rapid advances in mastering the techniques of painting by the time she reached her early twenties?

The diversity of techniques evident in Vallayer-Coster's paintings sometimes leaves the impression of a woman who is teaching herself, drawing from a wide variety of artistic sources. Jean-Siméon Chardin served as a major influence, as Eik Kahng discusses elsewhere in this volume, despite the fact that he rarely painted flowers, the genre in which Vallayer-Coster excelled. Only one flower painting by Chardin's hand survives, the simple *Flowers in a White and Blue Porcelain Vase* (pl. 81), although contemporary references point to the existence of a few other examples.[1] Although Chardin seemed to enjoy advising other artists, and as Diderot commented, "No one spoke as well as he on painting,"[2] he was reticent about his working methods, and it is unlikely that Vallayer-Coster ever observed him in the act of painting.[3] She followed Chardin's practice of painting *bas-reliefs imités* and replicas, as well as still lifes, and although her technique is sometimes indebted

to his evocative style, she stopped short of fawning imitation.[4] Vallayer-Coster's paintings also reflect an understanding of French academic teachings as well as Dutch and Flemish painting.

In the current study, Vallayer-Coster's still lifes were compared with those of Chardin as well as with the more highly polished visually descriptive works of Horace-Henri Roland Delaporte, where possible, in an attempt to understand how her technique relates to the divergent styles of these eighteenth-century French practitioners of still-life painting. In reevaluating Vallayer-Coster's artistic oeuvre in an exhibition such as this, it is also important to take into account the physical condition of her works. To what extent have her paintings withstood the test of time? It is important to acknowledge how irreversible pigment changes have sometimes altered the original appearance of Vallayer-Coster's works, in particular her flower paintings that are based on subtle color harmonies.

Several paintings presented in the exhibition were examined for the current study, either by the author or by conservators at the museums owning the works, as well as other examples not included here. In all, twenty works were examined, eighteen oil paintings and two works on paper. The following oil paintings on canvas were examined: *Still Life with Dead Hare*, 1769 (pl. 3); *Still Life with Seashells and Coral*, 1769 (pl. 4); *The Attributes of Music*, 1770 (pl. 5), and *The Attributes of Painting, Sculpture, and Architecture*, 1769 (fig. 1); *Female Faun and Putti*, 1773 (pl. 8); *Basket of Grapes*, 1774 (pl. 12); *Bouquet of Flowers in a Blue Porcelain Vase* (pl. 19) and *Bouquet of Flowers in a Terracotta Vase, with Peaches and Grapes*, 1776 (pl. 20); *Portrait of Joseph-Charles Roettiers (1692–1779)*, 1777 (pl. 23);

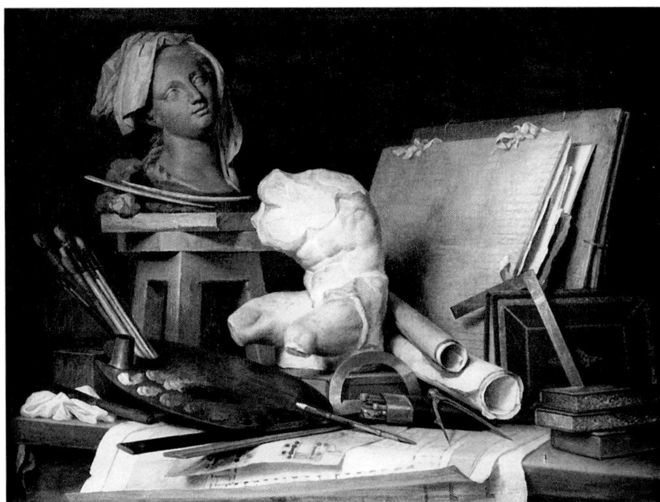

Fig. 1. Anne Vallayer-Coster, *The Attributes of Painting, Sculpture, and Architecture*, 1769. Oil on canvas, 35⅜ × 47⅝ in. (90 × 121 cm). Musée du Louvre, Paris (cat. 6). The painting, which the artist presented to the Académie in 1770, survives unlined, unlike its pendant, *The Attributes of Music* (pl. 5).

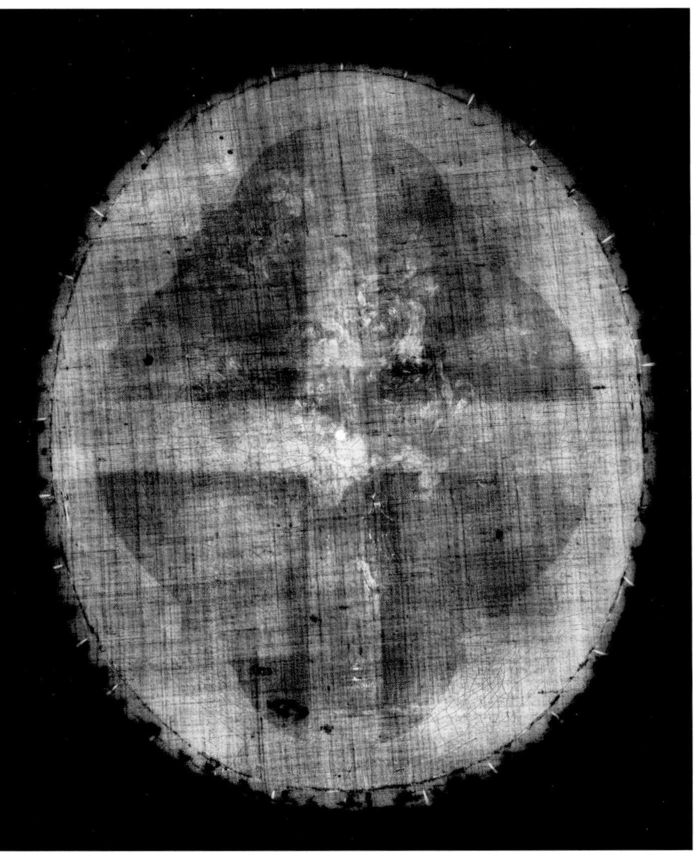

Fig. 2. Anne Vallayer-Coster, *A Vase of Flowers and Two Plums on a Marble Tabletop*, 1781. Oil on canvas, 18⅞ × 15¾ in. (48 × 39.8 cm). Michael L. Rosenberg, Dallas (cat. 67). The oval canvas preserves its original tacking edges primed with a double ground of pale gray over white.

Portrait of Sophie-Philippe-Elisabeth-Justine de France (1734–1782), called Madame Sophie, 1779 (pl. 26); *Portrait of Marie-Adélaïde-Louise de France (1732–1800), called Madame Adélaïde*, 1780 (pl. 28); *Portrait of Marie-Louise-Thérèse Victoire de France (1733–1799), called Madame Victoire*, 1780 (pl. 27); *Vase of Flowers*, 1780 (pl. 29); *Still Life with Lobster*, 1781 (pl. 33); *Still Life with Game*, 1782 (pl. 34); *Vase of Flowers* (pl. 50); *A Vase of Flowers and Two Plums on a Marble Tabletop*, 1781 (pl. 30); and *Still Life with Lobster*, 1817 (pl. 45). The two works on paper examined were *Roses* (pl. 58) and *Autumn Daisies* (pl. 59). All the paintings were examined under low magnification, and many with the additional help of X-radiography, infrared reflectography, and/or ultraviolet fluorescence. This study is particularly indebted to the Centre de Recherche et de Restauration des Musées de France, where two paintings from the Louvre, *Still Life with Seashells and Coral* and *The Attributes of Painting, Sculpture, and Architecture*, were examined with the help of several French colleagues.[5]

Supports

Vallayer-Coster used a variety of materials for her painting supports, ranging from ivory and vellum (for miniatures) to copper and canvas (for larger works). She executed the vast majority of her paintings, however, on canvas. Fortunately, a handful of the studied canvases survive unlined, including *The Attributes of Painting,*

Sculpture, and Architecture; and the portraits of Mesdames Sophie, Adélaïde, and Victoire, allowing direct examination of the original support. Other paintings, including *A Vase of Flowers and Two Plums on a Marble Tabletop* (fig. 2) and *Joseph-Charles Roettiers*, preserve their original tacking edges. Among other works studied, the fabric supports were determined from examination of the paint surfaces or with the help of X-radiographs.

If Vallayer-Coster varied the shape of her canvases to include both oval and rectangular formats for portraits, still lifes, and flower paintings, she was fairly consistent in her choice of fabrics. Like most eighteenth-century French painters, including Claude-François Desportes, Jean-Baptiste Oudry, Chardin, Jean-Honoré Fragonard, and Elisabeth-Louise Vigée-Le Brun, Vallayer-Coster typically employed hand-loomed, plain-weave canvases likely made from hemp rather than linen.[6] Some, presumably less-expensive, canvases were loosely woven, while others exhibited closer weaves and were probably more expensive. Vallayer-Coster seems to have used

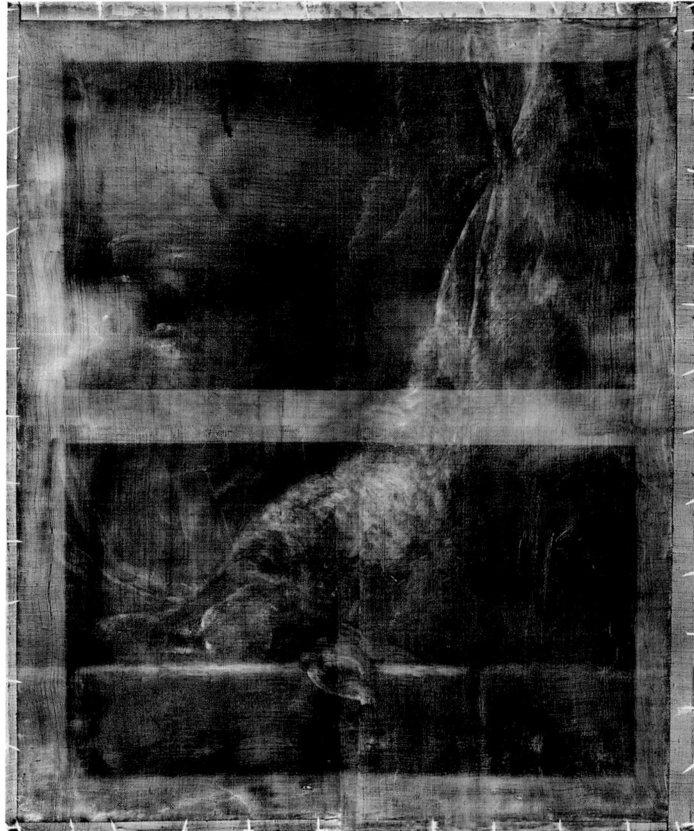

Fig. 3. Anne Vallayer-Coster, X-radiograph, *Still Life with Dead Hare*, 1769. Oil on canvas, 29⅜ × 24 in. (74.5 × 61 cm). Collection of Jeffrey E. Horvitz, Boston (cat. 10). The original support was enlarged with modern canvas strips on all four sides.

Fig. 4. Detail of fig. 1.

the finer canvas weaves for some of her more ambitious compositions. For example, *Still Life with Dead Hare* (fig. 3), *The Attributes of Music*, *The Attributes of Painting, Sculpture, and Architecture* (fig. 4), and *Basket of Grapes* have similar open canvas weaves, while *Still Life with Seashells and Coral*, *Bouquet of Flowers in a Blue Porcelain Vase* (fig. 5), and *Bouquet of Flowers in a Terracotta Vase, with Peaches and Grapes* (fig. 6) are much finer examples of her work and are executed on finely woven canvases.[7]

Several of the canvases examined, including *Still Life with Dead Hare*, *Basket of Plums* (pl. 2), *The Attributes of Painting, Sculpture, and Architecture*, *Bouquet of Flowers in a Blue Porcelain Vase* (fig. 5), and *Bouquet of Flowers in a Terracotta Vase, with Peaches and Grapes* (fig. 6), show marked cusping along the edges, a distortion of the canvas weave that results from the initial stretching and tacking of the fabric onto its stretcher; this is also referred to as "scalloping." Vallayer-Coster must not have been overly concerned about the aesthetic impact of these distortions, since they are an obvious feature of

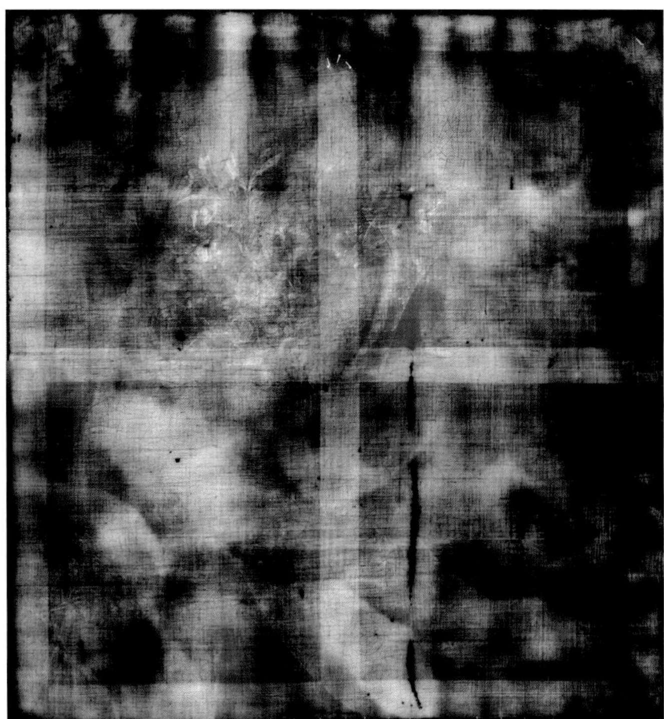

Fig. 5. Anne Vallayer-Coster, X-radiograph of *Bouquet of Flowers in a Blue Porcelain Vase*, 1776. Oil on canvas, 48¼ × 44½ in. (122.6 × 113 cm). Dallas Museum of Art, Dallas, Texas; Dallas Museum of Art Foundation for the Arts Collection, Mrs. John O'Hara Fund and gift of Michael L. Rosenberg, 1998.52 (cat. 36).

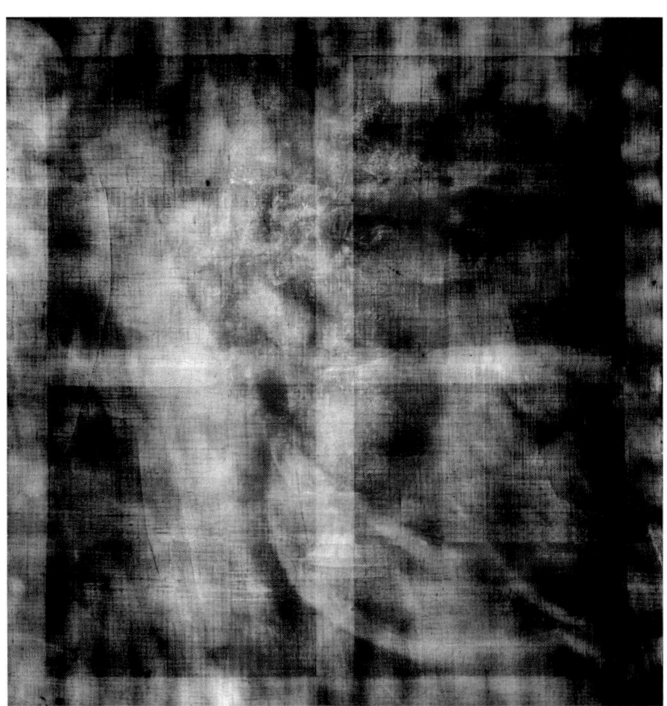

Fig. 6. Anne Vallayer-Coster, X-radiograph of *Bouquet of Flowers in a Terracotta Vase, with Peaches and Grapes*, 1776. Oil on canvas, 47⅝ × 44⅝ in. (121 × 113.3 cm). Dallas Museum of Art, Dallas, Texas; Dallas Museum of Art Foundation for the Arts Collection, Mrs. John O'Hara Fund and gift of Michael L. Rosenberg, 1998.51 (cat. 37). The two finely woven supports were primed with thick lead-white grounds, applied with a palette knife.

many of her works, in particular her still lifes. They also appear on Chardin's canvases, such as *Flowers in a White and Blue Porcelain Vase* and *The Smoker's Box*, about 1737–1740 (Musée du Louvre, Paris).

The X-radiographs of paintings in which Vallayer-Coster employed loose-weave canvases, such as *Still Life with Dead Hare*, show regularly spaced clusters of irregular threads. These threads were actually pulled out of alignment when the canvas was stretched under tension at the tack points. Sometimes these irregularities were visible in the final paint surfaces. For example, vertical irregular threads run through the sitter's eyes and nose in the portrait of Madame Victoire. The ease with which these threads could be pulled out of alignment suggests that the canvas was not of the highest quality. The differences in tension between loose and slack areas of canvas affected the condition of the final paint layers. Where the canvas was tightly stretched the paint film has few cracks, while slack areas are marked with a network of age craquelure, presumably because these areas allowed greater movement of the support.

In addition to providing information about the preparation and overall quality of the weave, cusping can also indicate that a painting retains its original dimensions. Since *The Attributes of Painting, Sculpture, and Architecture* (fig. 4) is unlined, it preserves its original format; however *The Attributes of Music* was backed with a modern plywood panel. In other cases Vallayer-Coster's paintings have been enlarged. The artist most likely enlarged *Still Life with Seashells and Coral* herself, because her signature extends over the seven-eighths-inch canvas extension along the bottom edge.[8] In *Still Life with Dead Hare* (fig. 3), however, the canvas was extended with modern canvas strips measuring one-half to one inch along all four edges. The X-radiograph shows the cusping of the original canvas within these additions.

Two of the paintings examined, *Female Faun and Putti* (cat. 20) and *A Vase of Flowers and Two Plums on a Marble Tabletop* (fig. 2), lacked stretching distortions, even though the paintings obviously retain their original dimensions. *A Vase of Flowers and Two Plums on a Marble Tabletop*, executed on an oval canvas, preserves its tacking edges, while *Female Faun and Putti* has its original trompe-l'oeil painted frame. The unlined portraits of Mesdames Victoire, Adélaïde, and Sophie as well as the portrait of Roettiers provide additional insights into the artist's use of oval canvases. These portraits are executed on moderately coarse, plain-weave canvases,

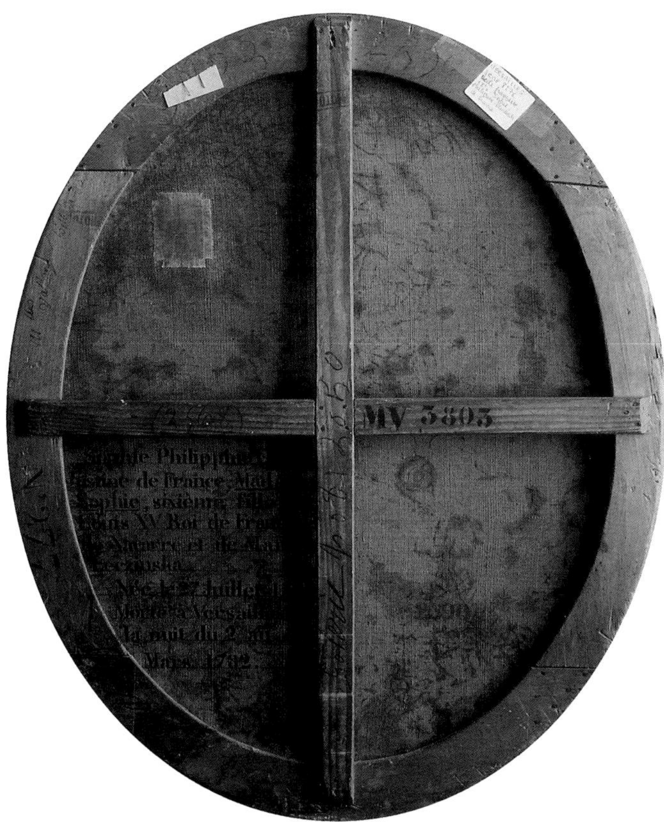

Fig. 7. Anne Vallayer-Coster, reverse of *Portrait of Sophie-Philippe-Justine-Elisabeth de France (1734–1782), called Madame Sophie*, showing original strainer and canvas inscription, 1779. Oil on canvas, oval, 28⅛ × 22⅞ in. (71.4 × 58 cm). Musée national des Châteaux de Versailles et de Trianon (cat. 55).

with tacking edges trimmed to the edges of the stretchers. The fact that these supports were preprimed suggests that Vallayer-Coster most likely cut these oval supports from larger, prestretched canvases, possibly commercially prepared, as she had for *Female Faun and Putti* and *A Vase of Flowers and Two Plums on a Marble Tabletop*.

The portraits retain their original six-member softwood strainers. These extremely lightweight, simple, and utilitarian structures were probably inexpensive. Although the strainers share similar designs, they exhibit slight differences in degrees of finish. Both the ends and sides of the narrow wooden planks used in the strainers for the portraits of Madame Sophie (fig. 7) and Madame Victoire, for example, are beveled, while those for Madame Adélaïde are not. For her larger rectangular pictures such as *The Attributes of Music*, *The Attributes of Painting, Sculpture, and Architecture*, and *Still Life with Seashells and Coral*, Vallayer-Coster used strainers with diagonal corner braces commonly used by eighteenth-century French artists.[9] This design can also be glimpsed in the background of Chardin's *Young Student Drawing* (see Kahng, fig. 27).

Grounds

Like Chardin and other eighteenth-century artists such as Oudry, François Boucher, and Noël-Nicolas Coypel, Vallayer-Coster often used a double ground that consists of a red underlayer with iron oxide pigments superimposed with a light gray or off-white upper layer containing lead white.[10] Chardin also used a double ground with a neutral tone over red for his still lifes; the stretched canvas that is primed with a neutral-toned ground depicted in the background of Chardin's *Young Student Drawing* is typical. Seventeenth-century Dutch still-life painters also used this double ground, where the purpose of the red underlayer, which contained inexpensive earth pigments, was to cover the weave of the canvas.[11] In Vallayer-Coster's paintings, the red underlayer fills the canvas without obscuring its overall texture. These primings could also have accelerated the drying of the paint layers, since they often contained manganese, a component of umber. This rapid drying would have enabled the artist to paint more quickly. Indeed, technical evidence suggests that Chardin, contrary to previous belief, was a rapid painter.[12] In this double-layer ground, the second layer, often a gray containing lead white, influenced the tonality of the painting. Together the visual impact of the two layers imparted depth and resonance to the final image.[13] Jean-Baptiste Corneille (1649–1695) also advised that novice painters use a ground with a half-tint, while he suggested that advanced painters employ light gray grounds to better preserve their colors.[14]

Vallayer-Coster used a double ground with a red underlayer in several of the paintings examined, including *Basket of Plums* (pl. 2), *The Attributes of Painting, Sculpture, and Architecture*, *The Attributes of Music*, *Basket of Grapes*, and *Female Faun and Putti*. Since all these examples have loose-weave supports, a red earth underlayer would have been a practical choice. While Vallayer-Coster seems to have always painted on light-colored grounds containing lead white, usually toned light gray, she used double grounds selectively. So far, this red-based preparation was found only in still lifes, the *bas-relief imité*, and *The Attributes of Painting, Sculpture, and Architecture* (and presumably also *The Attributes of Music*).

Still Life with Seashells and Coral has a double ground of light gray over pink, with a fine-weave support (fig. 8). Similarly, both *Bouquet of Flowers in a Blue Porcelain Vase* and *Bouquet of Flowers in a Terracotta Vase, with Peaches*

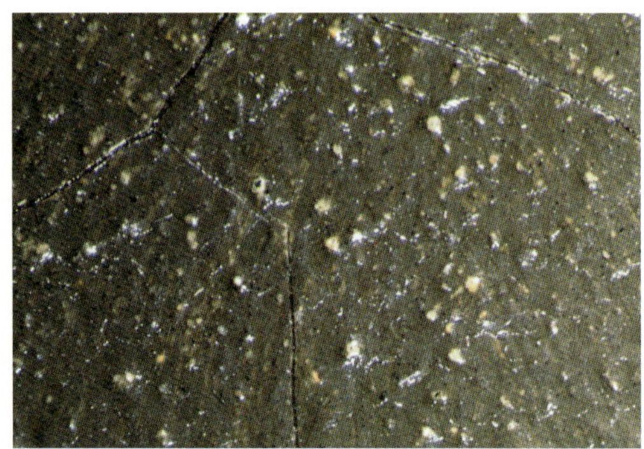

Fig. 8. Photomicrograph showing ground of Anne Vallayer-Coster, *Still Life with Seashells and Coral,* 1769. Oil on canvas, 51⅛ × 38¼ in. (129.9 × 97.2 cm). Musée du Louvre, Paris (cat. 11). The artist used a textural ground containing numerous tiny white grains, which were applied to the second layer of the ground.

and Grapes are painted on thick, light gray, lead-white grounds with fine-weave fabrics. All the oval paintings were painted on preprimed canvases. *A Vase of Flowers and Two Plums on a Marble Tabletop* exhibits a pale gray over white double ground, while the oval portraits of Roettiers, Madame Victoire, Madame Adélaïde, and Madame Sophie were also executed on light gray grounds.

The manner in which the preparations were applied to the canvases varied with the type of ground used. The X-radiographs for *The Attributes of Painting, Sculpture, and Architecture* (fig. 4) and *Basket of Grapes* reveal that the upper layer of the ground was brushed on using small diagonal strokes about one-half to one inch long. These brushstrokes appear in the X-radiograph in clusters with variable directions. By contrast, the thick lead-white ground in *Bouquet of Flowers in a Blue Porcelain Vase* and *Bouquet of Flowers in a Terracotta Vase, with Peaches and Grapes* was applied to the fine-weave support in broad, sweeping movements using a palette knife or spatula (figs. 5, 6). This thick, smooth ground layer contributed to the enamel-like surfaces of these paintings.

Vallayer-Coster not only adjusted the tone of ground according to the needs of different genre paintings, but she also varied the texture. In several of the paintings examined, the grounds exhibit a slightly rough or granular surface. These scattered lumps are seen on the surfaces of still-life paintings, portraits, and flower paintings alike.[15] The haphazard quality of these textural variations, however, suggests that they were accidental, due to coarse particles of lead white used in the upper layer.[16]

In still-life paintings where Vallayer-Coster depicted lobsters or seashells, she used a fine canvas prepared with a pebbly textured ground. The entire surface of *Still Life with Seashells and Coral* (fig. 8) has a gritty quality due to the inclusion of numerous tiny white grains similar to sand. Microscopic examination revealed that the particles appeared in the form of hollow shells, which seem to have been added to the second ground layer.[17] Perhaps Vallayer-Coster enjoyed the working properties of this textured ground, which would have provided a tooth for her paint layers; or she may have selected this surface for its compatibility with the subject matter, enhancing the trompe-l'oeil aspect of a still life with shells. She may have recalled the techniques used by some seventeenth-century Dutch still-life painters such as Pieter de Ring (1615–1660), who imitated the surface texture of objects by adding particles to his paint. In *Still Life with a Golden Goblet* (Rijksmuseum, Amsterdam), for example, de Ring added gritty white paint to the highlights of the lobster's shell.[18] Vallayer-Coster must have had knowledge of Northern still-life techniques from the numerous Dutch paintings in Paris collections, which in turn sparked her interest in collecting Dutch art, including a still life by Jan Davidsz de Heem.[19]

Chardin also added texture to his still lifes by bulking his pigments with chalk. This formula helped to create the characteristic dry and crumbly appearance of his paint layers.[20] Although Vallayer-Coster's exact reasons for selecting a textured ground remain unclear, we can only surmise that she made an intentional choice. The artist used these grounds as early as 1769, as well as in both versions of *Still Life with Lobster* (pls. 33, 45), dating from 1781 and 1817. This indicates that she remained fascinated by the aesthetic possibilities of a textured surface throughout her career. Jacques-Louis David, working in the early nineteenth century, also used a similarly granular-textured ground in *Portrait of the Sisters Zénaide and Charlotte Bonaparte,* 1821 (The J. Paul Getty Museum, Los Angeles).[21] Since it was David's usual practice to purchase commercially prepared canvases, both textured and smooth, the possibility exists that Vallayer-Coster purchased the textured canvas especially for *Still Life with Seashells and Coral,* signaling the importance she placed on this ambitious early work.[22]

Vallayer-Coster applied a warm gray *imprimatura,* or toning layer, beneath the forms of the shells in *Still Life with Seashells and Coral.* In the X-radiograph these areas appear more radiopaque due to the additional lead white—

containing layer. The use of an *imprimatura* represented
a traditional, organized approach to painting, promulgated by the French Académie, where every layer contributes to the illusion of the final image. The artist also
applied an *imprimatura* beneath the stone wall in *Bouquet
of Flowers in a Blue Porcelain Vase*, a technique she may
have found particularly useful when tackling ambitious,
complex compositions.

From these examples, perhaps some preliminary
observations can be made regarding the artist's choice
of grounds. Although Vallayer-Coster frequently adopted
the traditional double ground used by Chardin and other
eighteenth-century painters, she showed flexibility in
her choices—selecting different types of grounds for different paintings. For her flower paintings and portraits,
she seems to have used a thick, light, lead-white ground,
a preparation that provided brilliance and luminosity.
By contrast, she opted for the light-gray-over-red double
ground for her still lifes and *bas-reliefs imités*, for the
greater depth and resonance it could provide. Vallayer-
Coster used preprimed canvases for her small oval pictures, including both portraits and flower paintings,
suggesting that these supports were cut from larger
prestretched canvases. Throughout her career, she
consciously manipulated texture as well as tone in
her grounds to heighten the illusion of objects such
as lobsters and shells.

Underdrawing and Preparatory Sketches

Examination of several of Vallayer-Coster's paintings
under infrared reflectography did not reveal any evidence of underdrawing.[23] Did she work directly on
canvas, without benefit of the elaborate preliminary
sketches used, for example, by seventeenth-century
Dutch still-life painters? The lack of any visible underdrawing in Vallayer-Coster's canvases, however, could
be misleading. Like many of her contemporaries, including Vigée-Le Brun, Vallayer-Coster may have initially sketched her compositions on canvas using white
or red chalk, neither of which can be detected under infrared reflectography. The importance of underdrawing
in eighteenth-century French academic painting was
emphasized by Oudry. In 1752 when he was a teacher at
the Académie, he lectured on the importance of sound
painting practices and the techniques of "underdrawing,
underpainting, and retouching."[24] Oudry described how
to prepare the canvas and then how to draw the sketch

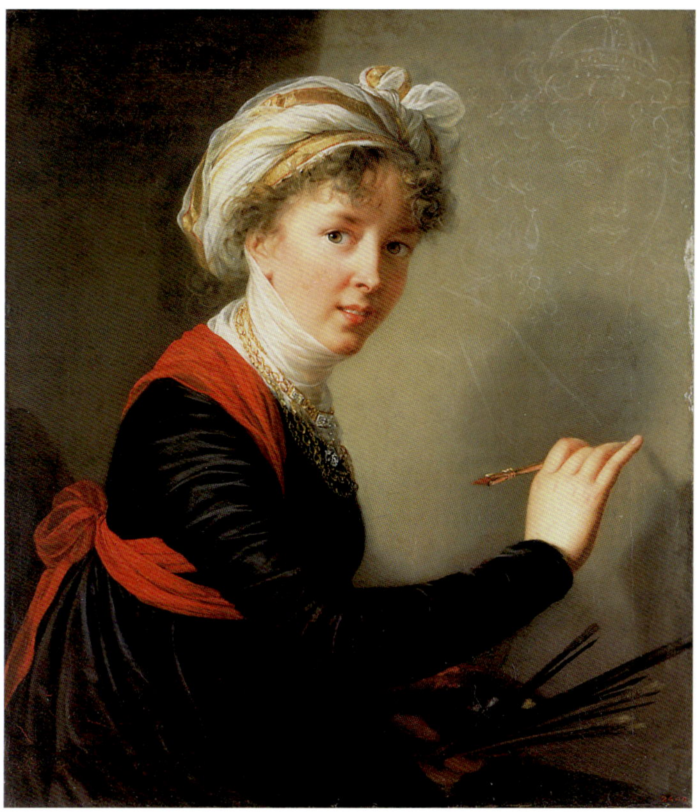

Fig. 9. Elisabeth-Louise Vigée-Le Brun, *Self-Portrait*, 1800. Oil
on canvas, 30⅞ × 26¾ in. (78.5 × 68 cm). The State Hermitage
Museum, St. Petersburg. Vallayer-Coster most likely also followed the practice, illustrated in Vigée-Le Brun's *Self-Portrait*,
of sketching in white chalk on a tinted ground to provide a
guide for painting.

that would serve as a guide for the painting on top of
the ground. His remarks provide a valuable record of
French academic technique, which emphasized good
craftsmanship.

Indeed, in *The Attributes of Painting, Sculpture, and
Architecture* the artist depicts a chalk holder containing
white and red chalk resting on the edge of a palette.
These hypothetical preliminary chalk sketches would
also have been clearly visible on the light gray grounds
she preferred. The white-chalk technique is illustrated
in numerous eighteenth-century French paintings,
including Marie-Victoire Lemoine's *Atelier of Madame
Vigée-Le Brun and Her Pupils*, 1796 (The Metropolitan
Museum of Art, New York),[25] and *Self-Portrait* by Vigée-
Le Brun (fig. 9). By contrast, Chardin's *Le Singe Peintre*
depicts a monkey painting on a canvas prepared with
red chalk.[26] If Vallayer-Coster used this method, it
would be impossible to ascertain, since chalk lines
disappear when saturated with oil during the painting process.

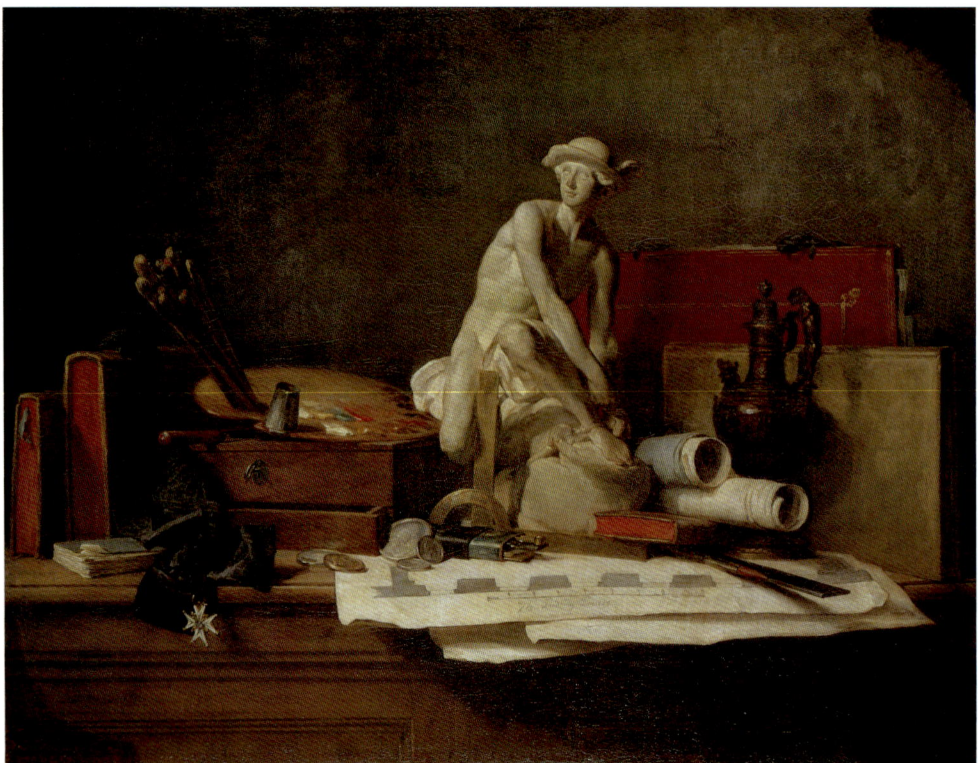

Fig. 10. Jean-Siméon Chardin, *The Attributes of the Arts and Their Rewards*, 1766. Oil on canvas, 44⅛ × 55¼ in. (112 × 140.5 cm). The State Hermitage Museum, St. Petersburg. Similar to Vallayer-Coster, Chardin depicted an oval palette, but with a different arrangement of colors and two whites.

Although few drawings are attributed to Vallayer-Coster, she used preliminary sketching in some of her works on paper. In the two watercolors examined, *Autumn Daisies* and *Roses*, the artist used graphite lines to lay out the composition and placed a faint blue horizontal line on the lower half of the paper to position the image on the page. These preparatory lines remain barely visible in the final image. A far more extensive study of watercolors is necessary, however, to provide significant information on her working methods in this medium. She also made numerous careful flower studies, probably from life, a task that required an ability to draw with precision. These studies were engraved by Louis-Jean Allais.[27] Such studies must have proved useful to the artist when inventing her flower compositions on canvas, since, like most paintings in this genre, they were fabrications pieced together from various sources. Like some of her Dutch predecessors who practiced this genre, including Ambrosius Bosschaert (1573–1621), Vallayer-Coster may have composed her flower paintings from assorted studies, watercolors, and botanical engravings from her collection.[28] Vallayer-Coster's remarkable ability to render floral specimens accurately must have also been informed by a connoisseur's knowledge of flowers, as well as a collection of botanical sources.

Paint Layers

Pigments and Use of Color

Alexandre Roslin's portrait of Vallayer-Coster (pl. 87) captures the artist in the act of painting, her pigments partially visible along the edge of her oval palette. The palette represented in *The Attributes of Painting, Sculpture, and Architecture* provides the only complete visual record by Vallayer-Coster of an artist's palette. The pigments are carefully arranged following the conventions established by the French Académie during the eighteenth century. This was appropriate since Vallayer-Coster submitted this painting for acceptance into the Académie's prestigious ranks.[29] This palette also appears similar to the one Chardin depicted in his *The Attributes of the Arts and Their Rewards*, 1766 (fig. 10). Both artists portray oval palettes with several colors arranged along the outer edge, with white at one end, followed by earth colors and ending with black. The two palettes differ, however, in the arrangement of colors along the inner row. Chardin set out four pigments, a second white next to yellow, blue, and red. These represent three of the four colors he considered necessary for the "harmony of a picture."[30] By contrast, Vallayer-Coster shows an inner row of mixed colors: yellow next to mixed flesh tones, followed by blue and black. Roger de Piles, a member of the Académie, wrote about a similar pigment arrangement in 1684, describing mixtures for light and dark tones placed at the center of the palette.[31]

The existence of the second white in Chardin's palette is significant. When the pigments from another version of Chardin's *Attributes of the Arts and Their Rewards* (The Minneapolis Institute of Arts) were analyzed, it was found that one white contained lead white, while the other contained a mixture of lead white and chalk.[32] Chardin habitually added chalk to enhance the texture and translucency of his paint, thus creating "effects of directly reflected light," which were admired by his contemporaries.[33] This method is by now well known and represents one of the most intriguing aspects of his idiosyncratic technique, and one that was apparently not adopted by Vallayer-Coster.[34]

Analysis of Chardin's pigments helped to identify the range of colors he used, providing a basis for comparison with Vallayer-Coster's colors.[35] Although the colors in her works have not yet been fully identified, examination of pigments used in *The Attributes of Painting, Sculpture, and Architecture* and *Still Life with Seashells and Coral* was carried out by Christine Benoit and Eric Laval at the Centre de Recherche et de Restauration des Musées de France using X-ray fluorescence. Their investigation included analysis of the colors depicted on the artist's palette as well as from selected points within this painting, such as colors on the tips of brushes, the chalks, books, pen case, and background. The following pigments were identified: lead white, vermilion, ocher, and Naples yellow. X-ray fluorescence could not provide a positive identification, however, for the blues. While traces of copper were found, they were in insufficient quantities to characterize the blue pigment as azurite. Prussian blue is the more likely possibility, due to the presence of iron, and the fact that the use of azurite was largely abandoned in the eighteenth century.[36] Since the preparation layers also consist of earth pigments containing iron, however, the contributions of pigments found in different layers makes it impossible to discern one from the other.

After its discovery at the beginning of the eighteenth century, the artificial pigment Prussian blue enjoyed widespread use throughout Europe, providing artists with an alternative blue pigment to the expensive ultramarine.[37] Chardin and Antoine Watteau were among the many eighteenth-century French artists who used the pigment. Vallayer-Coster could have used the blue colors ultramarine or indigo, but these consist of chemical

elements that are too light to be detected by X-ray fluorescence.[38] All the darkest colors on the palette in *The Attributes of Painting, Sculpture, and Architecture* were mixed, containing portions of vermilion and ochers. Three of the colors showed traces of copper, suggesting the presence of dark blues or greens.[39]

Pigment analysis in *Still Life with Seashells and Coral* using the method of X-ray fluorescence yielded results similar to those found in *The Attributes of Painting, Sculpture, and Architecture.* In each work, the preparation layers contained ochers and white lead, while the paint layers included white lead, vermilion, ochers, and various earth pigments and Naples yellow.[40] Once again, the blues were difficult to identify. As in *The Attributes of Painting, Sculpture, and Architecture*, these pigments contained weak traces of copper. The relative quantities of iron between the spectra for light and dark blues, however, indicated that this element participated in the intensity of the color, suggesting the likelihood of Prussian blue.[41] Vallayer-Coster used a range of earth pigments and ochers, including raw umber and green earth, which she mixed with other pigments to obtain different nuances of color.[42]

These colors are consistent with those employed by Chardin, who also used the following pigments: vegetable carbon black, chalk, realgar and orpiment (brilliant orange and yellow pigments used since ancient times), red and yellow lakes, ultramarine and Prussian blue, and organic brown earth (possibly Van Dyck brown).[43] Vallayer-Coster probably used many of these pigments as well. When reflections on the ormolu mounts on the blue porcelain vase in *Bouquet of Flowers in a Blue Porcelain Vase* were examined (fig. 11) under the microscope, pigment particles in the bright orange and yellow highlights exhibited the optical characteristics of realgar and orpiment. In particular, the yellow particles displayed the flat, shiny surfaces and glittering, sparkling appearance typical of orpiment. Vallayer-Coster's use of these pigments followed that not only of Chardin but also of Dutch and Flemish painters of the previous century, showing an archaic tendency in her pigment choices. Orpiment and realgar pigments also featured prominently in Venetian Renaissance painting, a tradition celebrated for its brilliant color.

Visual analysis of Vallayer-Coster's flower painting suggests that, similar to Chardin, she also made extensive use of red and yellow lake pigments. To produce the green foliage in *Bouquet of Flowers in a Blue Porcelain Vase,*

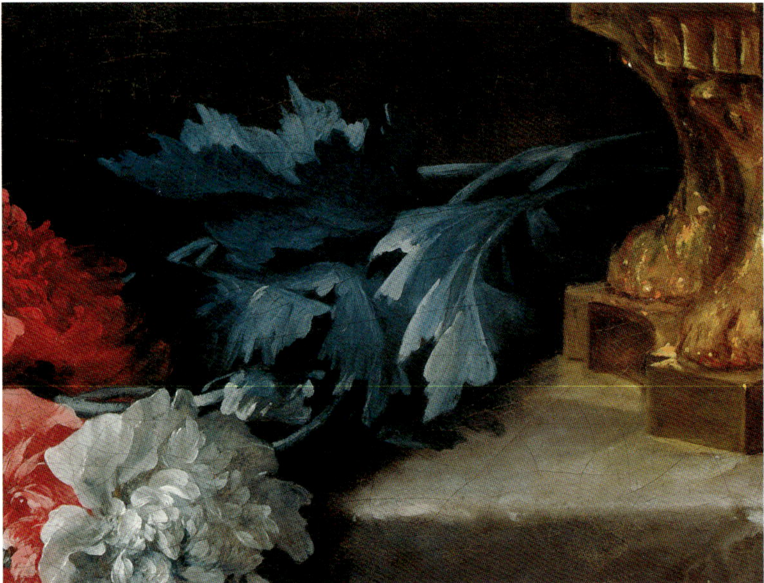

Fig. 11. Detail of pl. 19, showing ormolu mounts and carnations with blue foliage showing loss of organic yellow glaze.

Fig. 12. Detail of pl. 19, showing yellow flower showing loss of pigment and flower showing loss of organic purplish glaze, revealing dead coloring.

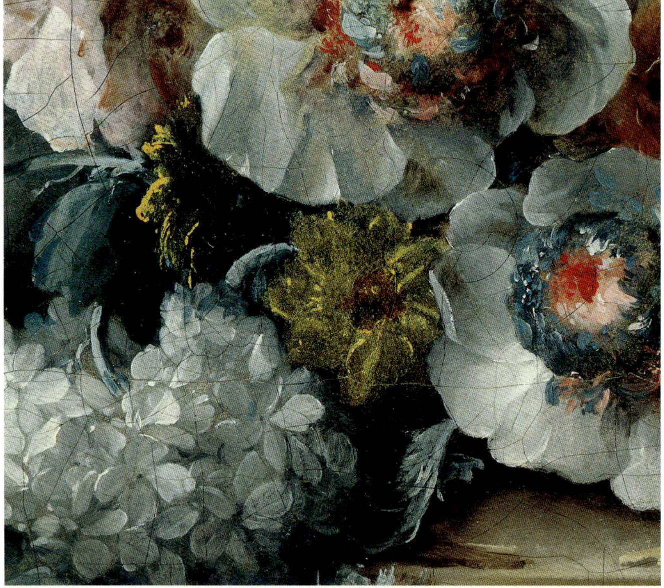

Fig. 13. Detail of pl. 20, yellow flower showing loss of pigment.

she probably applied a yellow lake glaze over an opaque blue underlayer, a technique used by seventeenth-century Dutch still-life painters. Unfortunately, due to the fading of the fugitive yellow-lake glaze, many of the leaves now appear blue because the underlayer is exposed. The blue foliage for the carnations in the lower left, for example, creates an imbalance in the color harmony the artist must have originally intended (fig. 11).

Vallayer-Coster most likely toned her flowers and leaves with orpiment in addition to yellow lake. One of the drawbacks of using this pigment, however, is its tendency to flake. The underpainting in the yellow flowers in both *Bouquet of Flowers in a Blue Porcelain Vase* and *Bouquet of Flowers in a Terracotta Vase, with Peaches and Grapes* has become more apparent due to pigment loss through flaking (figs. 12, 13).[44] Yellow highlights along the edges of leaves in *Bouquet of Flowers in a Blue Porcelain Vase* have also flaked off, resulting in some loss of clarity and detail, due to the weak bond between the orpiment and the underlayer.[45]

A comparison of this important pair of flower paintings with a watercolor, such as *Roses* (pl. 58), reveals striking differences in the appearance of the foliage. Although it is difficult to draw conclusions from this one example, the foliage in the watercolor displays gradations in shades of greens now lacking from the larger oils on canvas. In *Bouquet of Flowers in a Blue Porcelain Vase*, however, some of the leaves and stems near the top of the bouquet still preserve some of their green tonality, suggesting a treatment different from the areas where the yellow component has completely disappeared (fig. 14). The partial loss of green from her flower paintings has serious implications for Vallayer-Coster's color scheme because the blue elements are now dominant. One must try to imagine the original subtlety of her greens. The subject of mixing greens was the focus of

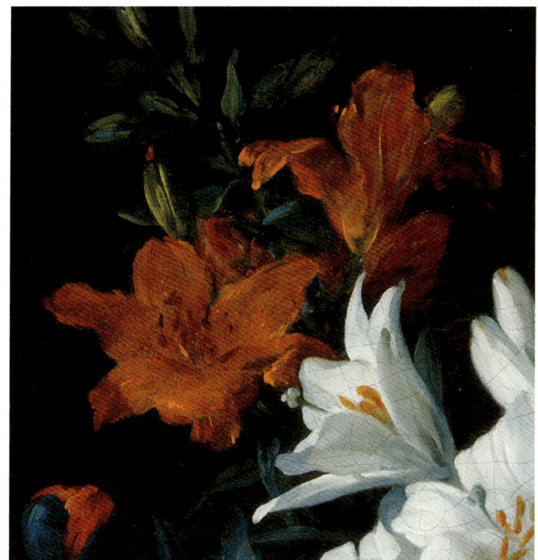 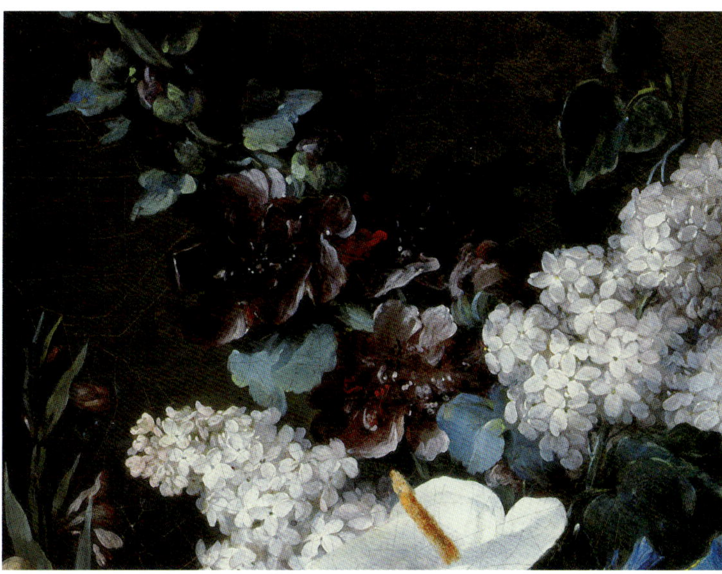

Fig. 14. Detail of pl. 19, showing green foliage and orange lilies, the edges of which were "toned down" because they were painted over dark background.

Fig. 15. Detail of pl. 20, showing loss of purple glaze from flowers as a result of fading, revealing dead coloring.

contemporary painting treatises.[46] Fortunately, these are better preserved in *A Vase of Flowers and Two Plums on a Tabletop* as well as in her watercolors.

In a similar manner, Vallayer-Coster's use of fugitive red and violet lake glazes in the modeling of flowers also resulted in irreversible fading. We may assume that the gray flowers in the lower right of both *Bouquet of Flowers in a Blue Porcelain Vase* and *Bouquet of Flowers in a Terracotta Vase, with Peaches and Grapes* would have originally appeared purplish red. The final thin, transparent red lake glazes have faded, however, leaving only the highlights and the artist's gray underpainting, or so-called dead coloring, exposed (figs. 12, 15).[47] Dead coloring is the even, flat layer of color underlying individual forms that provided the basis for the final painting in greater detail.[48] The use of dead coloring as an underlayer was a technique also used in seventeenth-century Dutch flower painting. This layer structure reflects the work of an artist familiar with the techniques of French academic training, which taught the development of a painting in three distinct stages: *esquisse, ébauche,* and *retouche.* Eighteenth-century painting treatises gave particular emphasis to building up the underpainting.[49] Vallayer-Coster's technique of modeling flowers suggests that she fully exploited the method of glazing to maximize the intensity of her pigments. This was both a traditional and economical painting technique.

The eighteenth-century art theorist Charles-Nicolas Cochin, however, cautioned about the fugitive nature of glazes. He advised that "a picture painted in full color and with impasto exceeds the transitory brilliance of paintings where glazing has been skillfully applied."[50] Cochin wrote that colors applied boldly, in layers of impasto, had the benefit of not changing, becoming more harmonious with age, whereas the paintings in which glazes were used lose some of their harmony because of the unstable brilliance of these delicate layers.[51] This would seem to endorse the painting practices of Chardin, who relied more on modeling forms with full color and impasto, as opposed to Vallayer-Coster, who used traditional glazing techniques to achieve brilliant color in her flower paintings.

As Roland Michel has observed, theories about vision and color, such as the rendering of shadows, were intensely debated during the eighteenth-century. Chardin demonstrated his ability to use color to create the illusion of forms advancing and receding in space in his simple *Flowers in a White and Blue Porcelain Vase.*[52] To the viewer the red carnation lying on the table appears to project, while the vase, reflecting blue, appears to recede. Whether consciously or not, Vallayer-Coster followed Chardin's example in *Bouquet of Flowers in a Blue Porcelain Vase.* By placing red carnations on the stone ledge, she helped to create the illusion of the flowers encroaching into the viewer's space.

The colors red and blue were extremely important to Vallayer-Coster's palette: their significance is evident in *The Attributes of Painting, Sculpture, and Architecture,* where they appear on the tips of the artist's brushes. Vallayer-

Coster frequently played with warm and cool color contrasts, using shades of red and blue, to enliven her compositions and suggest the relative position of forms in space. She used this device especially in her still lifes. The subtle color harmony in *Still Life with Seashells and Coral* is derived from the collection of blue, pink, ivory, and coral shells arranged on the stone ledge, played against the neutral background elements. Similarly, in *The Attributes of Music* the artist used blue and red color contrasts to energize the dynamic composition. The blue ribbon tied to the lute helps to create the illusion of the instrument tilting back in space, while the musical instruments, painted in shades of red, project. This technique can be seen in a number of other works, including both *Still Life with Lobster* and *Still Life with Game* (pls. 33, 34). Even in her last ambitious work, *Still Life with Lobster* (pl. 45), the central elements in the composition represent a careful study in warm and cool contrasts.

The most remarkable aspect of Vallayer-Coster's approach to color, however, may be her use of boldly colored reflections. She seemed to take particular delight in creating brilliant reflections on metal surfaces. Her adventurous technique is already evident in the early *Attributes of Music,* where a kaleidescope of yellow, orange, red, blue, and pink reflections is mirrored on the bell of the horn. Her treatment of the ormulu mounts on the vase in *Bouquet of Flowers in a Blue Porcelain Vase* (fig. 11), with their yellow, orange, and blue reflections, is equally daring. By juxtaposing orange and blue reflections, she heightened the intensity of each color. This technique was later named "simultaneous contrast" by Michel-Eugène Chevreul, a nineteenth-century color theorist,[53] and would be adopted by such French impressionist artists as Pierre-Auguste Renoir (1841–1919).

Paint Handling

Vallayer-Coster's paint handling reflects an idiosyncratic synthesis of techniques. She was influenced by the Académie, with its systematic approach to painting, as well as by Chardin's unorthodox methods. Vallayer-Coster appeared to change her technique to meet the demands of working in different genres. She used the more traditional academic method of painting in layers with underpaint and glazes in her flower paintings. It should be recalled that Oudry, when he spoke at the Académie, advised that the underpainting should be applied on top of the varnished sketch. In fact, most eighteenth-

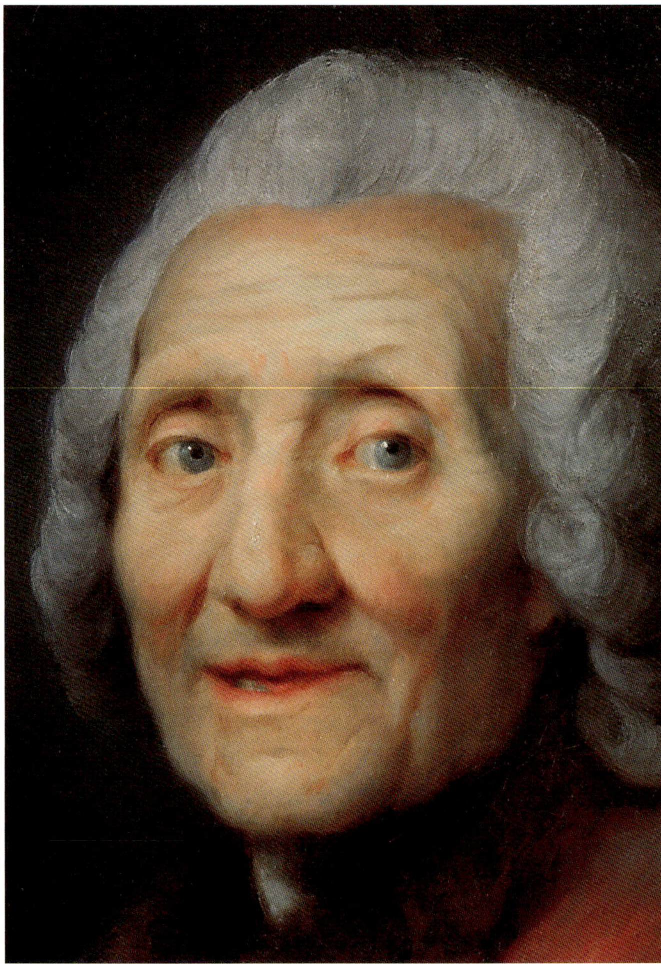

Fig. 16. Anne Vallayer-Coster, *Portrait of Joseph-Charles Roettiers (1692–1779)*, detail of face, 1777. Oil on canvas, oval, 25⅝ × 21¼ in. (65 × 54 cm). Musée national des Châteaux de Versailles et de Trianon (cat. 46). The artist modeled the face with carefully blended brushwork but treated the costume with greater freedom.

century artist's manuals recommended that one layer be painted on top of another. When Vallayer-Coster painted her still lifes and *bas-reliefs imités*, however, she worked in a more Chardinesque mode, sometimes working *alla prima.* Like Chardin, she also painted replicas of these two genres, for example, the two *bas-reliefs imités* of *Female Faun and Putti* (pls. 8, 11), although we are not sure how they were accomplished.

The two versions of *Female Faun and Putti* were painted *alla prima* using a restricted, neutral palette. First the artist roughly sketched the forms with a liquid brown paint that also served to delineate features and shadows. She used impasto for highlights to create the illusion of three-dimensionality. Vallayer-Coster revealed her wit in the Dallas version by highlighting and shading her signature as if it were carved in low relief. The artist also painted a chiaroscuro trompe-l'oeil frame on which the fauness rests her hooves. In the Grasse version she

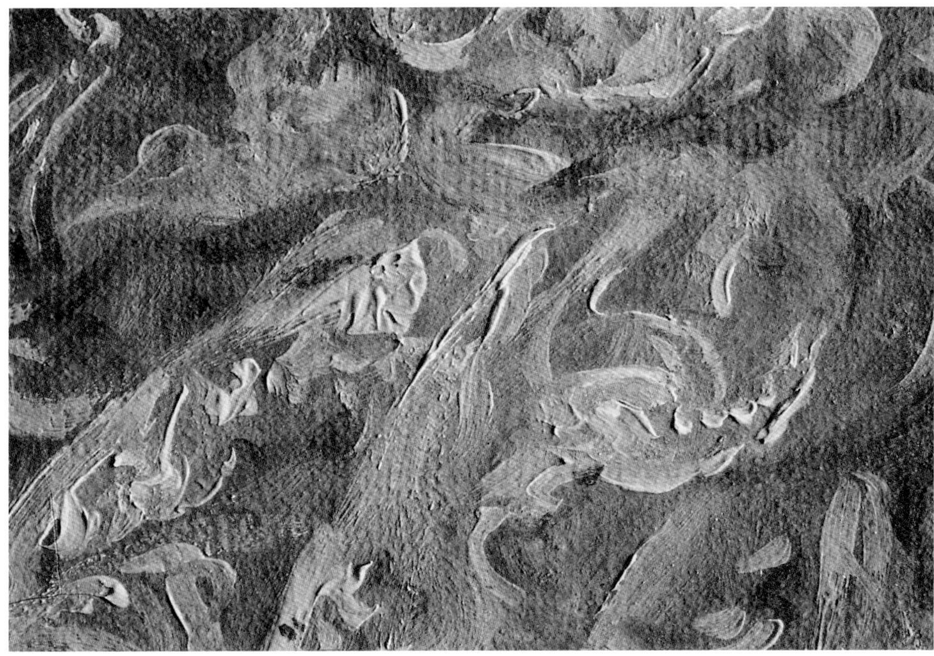

Fig. 17. Anne Vallayer-Coster, *Portrait of Sophie-Philippe-Justine de France (1734–1782), called Madame Sophie*, detail of lace, 1779. Oil on canvas, oval, 28⅛ × 22⅞ in. (71¼ × 58 cm). Musée national des Châteaux de Versailles et de Trianon (cat. 55). The artist combined dry brush and wet-in-wet techniques in her treatment of the lace.

painted trompe-l'oeil canvas tacks on the reverse of the stretcher.[54] Vallayer-Coster sometimes incorporated elements of *bas-reliefs imités* in larger works such as *Bouquet of Flowers in a Terracotta Vase, with Peaches and Grapes.* The number of surviving trompe-l'oeil pictures suggest they were in demand. She must have employed an efficient method of replicating them; Marianne Roland Michel has recently rediscovered another version of the *Female Faun and Putti.*[55] Joseph Vernet, Vallayer-Coster's friend and teacher, owned one of her *bas-reliefs imités.*[56]

Vallayer-Coster's portraits, perhaps her weakest genre, reveal a disparity in the treatment of the flesh tones and costumes. For the portrait of Roettiers (fig. 16), the artist used carefully blended brushwork and finishing glazes to model the planes of the face. By contrast, she treated the gilded chair and red jacket in a loose, impressionistic manner. Vallayer-Coster suggested the play of light on the various fabrics and chair using impasto, as she would do in her still lifes. In fact, the energetic brushwork of the decorations on Roettiers's jacket recalls the freedom with which Vallayer-Coster described the lobster shell in *Still Life with Lobster* (pl. 33). The handling of these areas gives the impression of speed, as opposed to her sensitive treatment of Roettiers's face, with his lips parted to reveal a protruding bottom tooth. She most likely painted the portrait from life, but could have completed the costumes in her studio at a later stage.

The portraits of Mesdames Sophie, Adélaïde, and Victoire, the three paintings recently rediscovered at Versailles, are remarkably similar in their conception. The three sisters wear similar hairstyles and costumes, with the exception that Madame Victoire's dress is trimmed in fur. It is almost as if their likenesses were applied, like masks, on top of similar, preexisting models. Vallayer-Coster rendered the women's faces with soft brushwork and glazes, in a tentative, almost hesitant, manner, quite unlike the portraiture of her contemporaries, Vigée-Le Brun and Adélaïde Labille-Guiard, her superiors in this genre. As in the portrait of Roettiers, Vallayer-Coster followed a more adventurous technique in her treatment of the costumes. She seemed to take special pleasure in her handling of the lace collars and satin ribbons, where impasto is combined with dry brush and wet-in-wet techniques (fig. 17).

If Vallayer-Coster's portraiture sometimes lacked finesse, her flower paintings were perhaps her greatest achievement. The artist perfected this genre by the 1780s in paintings such as *Vase of Flowers* (pl. 29) and *A Vase of Flowers and Two Plums on a Marble Tabletop* (pl. 30), where the delicacy of her palette is coupled with the verve of her handling. Her flower paintings are based on preplanned compositions. In these works, she most likely began by outlining the shapes of individual forms in chalk, then painted the dark background around the sketched design. In *Vase of Flowers*, for example, Vallayer-Coster covered the lead-white ground with a thin gray wash, reserving areas of the ground unpainted for the forms of individual flowers. Over the gray wash she then applied the background color, an opaque greenish gray.

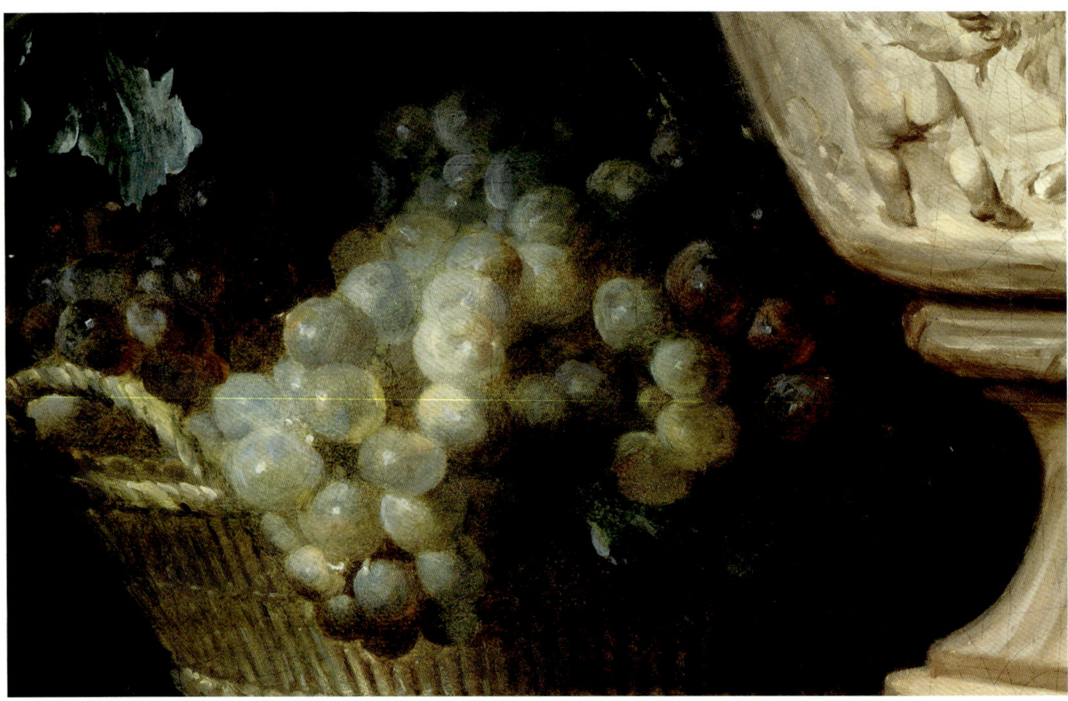

Fig. 18. Anne Vallayer-Coster, *Bouquet of Flowers in a Terracotta Vase, with Peaches and Grapes*, detail of grapes, 1776. Oil on canvas, 47⅝ × 44⅝ inches (121 × 113.3 cm). Dallas Museum of Art, Dallas, Texas; Dallas Museum of Art Foundation for the Arts Collection, Mrs. John O'Hara Fund and gift of Michael L. Rosenberg, 1998.51 (cat. 37). The artist painted the shadowed area of grapes over the dark background; the illuminated area is executed over the light ground.

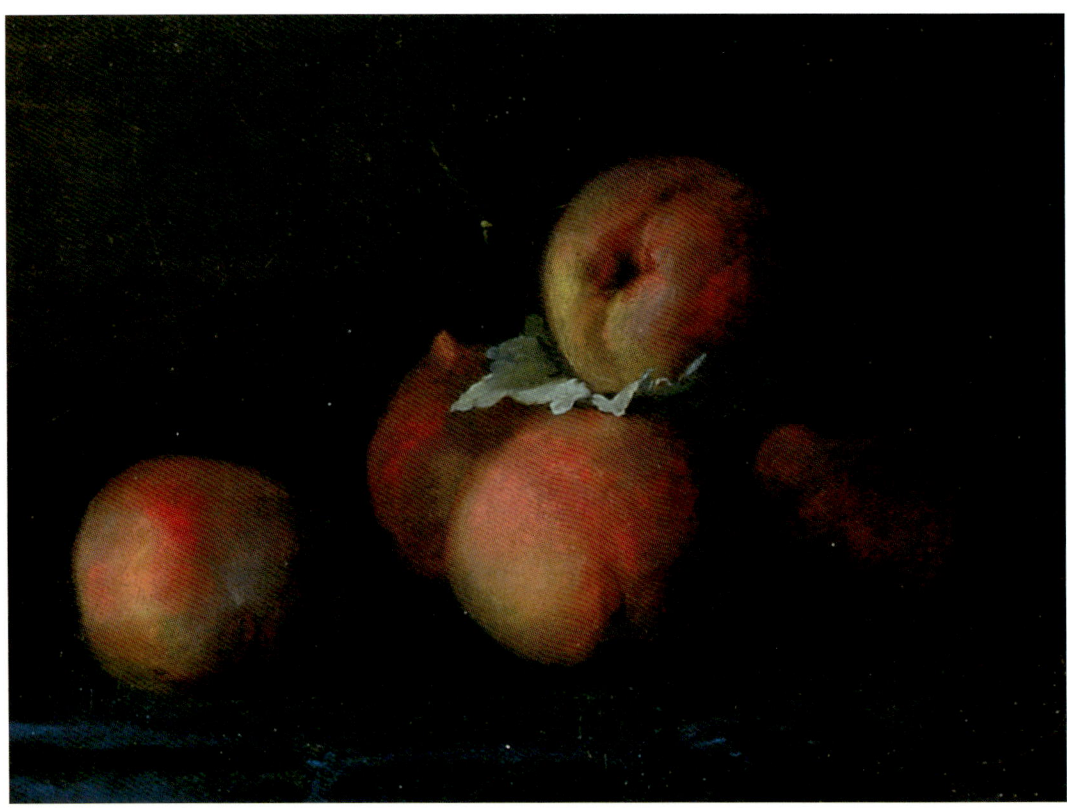

Fig. 19. Anne Vallayer-Coster, *Bouquet of Flowers in a Terracotta Vase, with Peaches and Grapes*, detail of peaches, 1776. Oil on canvas, 47⅝ × 44⅝ inches (121 × 113.3 cm). Dallas Museum of Art, Dallas, Texas; Dallas Museum of Art Foundation for the Arts Collection, Mrs. John O'Hara Fund and gift of Michael L. Rosenberg, 1998.51 (cat. 37). Vallayer-Coster adjusted the tonality of the peaches by painting them on top of the dark blue tablecloth.

She then painted several flowers directly on top of the reserved areas of white ground, their edges overlapping the dark background. The artist used the traditional technique of applying layers of color, underpaint and glazes, to model the forms, applying impasto with an assured, pointillist technique in a final stage.

The rich enamel-like surfaces of Vallayer-Coster's flower paintings, especially *Bouquet of Flowers in a Terracotta Vase, with Peaches and Grapes* and *Bouquet of Flowers in a Blue Porcelain Vase,* are due in part to her use of a thick lead-white ground. The technique of selectively painting forms directly on unpainted areas of this ground enabled the artist to achieve a range of effects using an economy of means. The light ground imparts a luminosity to the flowers and allowed the artist to paint thinly. In *A Vase of Flowers and Two Plums on a Marble Tabletop,* for example, Vallayer-Coster created the roses by covering the unpainted ground with pink glazes. In *Bouquet of Flowers in a Blue Porcelain Vase* and *Bouquet of Flowers in a Terracotta Vase, with Peaches and Grapes* the artist employed the opposite technique, "toning down" flowers at the edges by painting them on top of the dark background, to make them recede in shadow (fig. 14).[57]

Using a combination of these two methods helped the artist to enhance the illusion of three-dimensionality in her still lifes. In *Bouquet of Flowers in a Terracotta Vase, with Peaches and Grapes,* for example, she executed half of the grapes on top of the reserved light ground and painted others over the dark background (fig. 18). The fruit appears partly in light and shadow; the illuminated bunches of grapes protrude, spilling over the edge of the basket, while those in the background recede into shadow. Numerous other examples of this technique can be found, for example, in the treatment of the green leaves in *A Vase of Flowers and Two Plums on a Marble Tabletop.* By contrast, Vallayer-Coster rendered the peaches in the lower right entirely on top of the dark blue tablecloth (fig. 19). The use of this dark blue underlayer imparts a soft, atmospheric quality to the fruit that recalls Chardin's technique, and helps to place these elements in shadow.

Vase of Flowers (pl. 50) exhibits the flexibility of Vallayer-Coster's brushwork. With a freedom not observed in earlier examples she combined a soft and blended treatment of the roses with the more abstract handling of the small blue and white flowers. The mélange of colors and the brushwork in the red carnation recall the "mosaic or prism" effect that Chardin achieved and that was cited by his contemporaries.[58] This jewel-like painting has the brilliant, polished surface and enamel-like color seen in the earlier Dallas pendants. In later works, Vallayer-Coster seemed to adopt a softer, more atmospheric effect. Two works from 1780 and 1781, *Vase of Flowers* and *A Vase of Flowers and Two Plums on a Marble Tabletop,* exhibit a range of brushwork similar to that in *Vase of Flowers,* but the color contrasts are softer. The light, painterly treatment as well as the overall atmosphere recall the paintings of Fragonard.

Although Vallayer-Coster began her flower paintings with careful planning, she frequently made revisions, or *pentimenti,* in the course of painting. These *pentimenti* can be frequently detected on the surfaces of her paintings.[59] The artist would reposition, add, or subtract flowers almost as if she were arranging an actual bouquet. In *A Vase of Flowers and Two Plums on a Tabletop,* for example, Vallayer-Coster raised the red flower on the left after bringing it near completion, covering her first attempt with the background, while in *Bouquet of Flowers in a Blue Porcelain Vase,* she lowered and reduced the red flowers in the lower right. Sometimes the artist changed even the type of objects she portrayed to find the balance of line she sought as she refined her compositions. In *Bouquet of Flowers in a Terracotta Vase, with Peaches and Grapes,* for example, she converted a Louis XV–style table with a curvilinear-profile leg to a Louis XVI–style, straight-legged table. Perhaps the latter style, with its severe rectilinear form, provided a more satisfying contrast to the rounded form of the terracotta vase.

Bouquet of Flowers in a Terracotta Vase, with Peaches and Grapes displays Vallayer-Coster's work in different genres, because in it we see her combining elements of flower painting, still life, and *bas-reliefs imités,* changing her technique in response to each genre. The basket of grapes and peaches display a soft treatment and muted, chiaroscuro effects associated with Chardin (figs. 18, 19), while the terracotta vase, like a *bas-relief imité,* is treated *alla prima* with opaque paint layers and low impasto. Vallayer-Coster's brightly illuminated flowers with their sharply delineated forms, however, are rendered in layers of full-bodied paint and delicate glazes.

Vallayer-Coster's still lifes, along with her *bas-reliefs imités,* represent the areas where her technique comes closest to Chardin. But her still lifes run the gamut from works that are obviously indebted to the earlier master, such as the early *Still Life with Dead Hare*, to those where she expresses a more individual style. Opaquely painted with areas of low impasto, in a Chardinesque manner, this youthful still life is a study in textural contrasts of different materials. The artist suggests the sheen of the earthenware jug with delicate scumbles, applying thick impasto for the white highlight. Working on top of the white underlayer, Vallayer-Coster modified the rabbit's soft fur with warm glazes. Her treatment of the fur is quite literal, as might be expected in an early work. With painstaking care she describes the fur by painting strands of hair with individual brushstrokes, sometimes using the dry brush technique that is often seen in Chardin's still lifes of dead hares. Vallayer-Coster's most refined dry brushwork can be seen in the head and ear of the rabbit, where she rendered the whiskers and eyelashes with exceptional delicacy. The artist used a variety of techniques in her free treatment of the stone shelf. She painted the vein in the stone wet-in-wet, while she created the upper edges of the shelf with light, dry brushwork. This combined use of wet-in-wet and dry brushwork as well as the differences in handling between the precise treatment of the fur versus the loose treatment of the stone are techniques that can be seen throughout Valayer-Coster's still lifes.

Painted the same year, *Still Life with Seashells and Coral* reflects a refinement of technique that seems extraordinary. Vallayer-Coster drew on her method of combining wet-in-wet and dry brush paint applications in the large central white coral. Working in a sequence of layers, beginning with the granular white ground, the artist used a neutral-toned *imprimatura* followed by two layers of impasto to describe the textured surface of the coral. She rendered the first layer of impasto using a liquid paint, applying the second layer with a dry brush that caused the pigment to break up across the surface, in a crumbly manner that recalls Chardin's technique. Vallayer-Coster frequently delineated the edges of the shells with a dilute brown paint that sometimes covered layers of impasto along the edges. Sometimes the impasto is even mixed wet-in-wet with the brown outlines, suggesting the immediacy with which she worked.

Vallayer-Coster used up to four paint layers of different shades of red for the stringy coral at left. The artist increased the stiffness of her paint in successive layers, with the final surface assuming a crumbly texture similar to that seen in Chardin's still lifes. Whereas Chardin achieved this effect in part by adding chalk to his pigments, it is not known whether Vallayer-Coster employed this method as well. Pigment sampling was not carried out in *Still Life with Seashells and Coral,* but under magnification numerous colorless particles, possibly calcite, could be seen in the surface of the large red shell. Vallayer-Coster, like Chardin, may have sometimes modified the consistency and texture of her paint with additives.[60]

When the surfaces of the shells in *Still Life with Seashells and Coral* are viewed under magnification, Vallayer-Coster's handling appears free and impressionistic, while at a normal viewing distance, the shells appear sharply focused, contributing to the effect of this masterful still life. The artist organized the composition with a careful arrangement of alternating warm and cool elements using shades of blue and red. As seen in her flower paintings, Vallayer-Coster used these colors to enhance the illusion of three-dimensionality, because the red elements seem to advance while the blue forms recede.

Both *The Attributes of Music* and *The Attributes of Painting, Sculpture, and Architecture* exhibit the broad range of paint application that is characteristic of Vallayer-Coster. In her masterful handling of the sheet of music, Vallayer-Coster once again drew on lessons from both the Académie as well as Chardin. For the shadow side of the page, the artist worked in layers, applying brown glazes directly onto the ground. There is only a slight overlap of white and brown paint at the transition from light to shadow. Vallayer-Coster painted the right page of the book *alla prima* with lively, energetic brushwork, applied in numerous directions. The way in which the brushwork seems to dance across the surface almost mirrors the path of the musical notes. The opaque white brushwork is smoother toward the center of the page but becomes increasingly directionless as it reaches the edge of the sheet.

Throughout these two still lifes, Vallayer-Coster used impasto in inventive ways, to suggest highlights and characterize the material of objects. The rich variety of surface texture contributes to the illusion of the scene, imparting an almost physical reality to the objects depicted, similar to the effect of trompe-l'oeil painting. This method of rendering texture also served to make objects appear closer, by giving the viewer a point of focus. Vallayer-Coster used a fine brush and carefully controlled impasto to paint the silver and gold threads in the decorations on the bagpipe in sharp relief. In the lower left foreground, where the bag is closer to the

viewer, she painted the embroidered pattern in even
more exacting detail. In the background where the bag
recedes from the viewer, however, her treatment of
these areas becomes abstract, as she applied the impasto
with greater freedom and economy. For the edge of the
violin, she applied orange impasto, its edges slightly
blurred, to suggest the grain of the wood, while she used
a stiff white paint to suggest the reflection of light from
its polished surface.

Vallayer-Coster created the reflections on the metal
surface of the bell of the horn with a mélange of colors—
including yellow, orange, red, blue, pink, and white—
that mirrors the bagpipe, freely applied in an almost
abstract manner. From a normal viewing distance this
passage reads convincingly as the glint of light on metal,
while on close examination the forms seem to dissolve.

The artist's handling in *The Attributes of Painting, Sculpture, and Architecture* is equally resourceful. Vallayer-
Coster modeled the plaster cast of the Belvedere Torso
wet-in-wet with energetic, loopy brushwork that simu-
lates the appearance of worked clay. The artist applied
broken tints of orange, coral, and pink on top of the
cream-colored impasto in a treatment that recalls
Chardin. Vallayer-Coster's handling of the white portfolio cover and rolled-up paper also evokes the earlier
master. These areas are thickly painted to create dry,
crumbly surfaces. The artist's textural buildup of
impasto in the gold tooling on the book cover relates to
her treatment of the gold fringe in *The Attributes of Music.*

Vallayer-Coster painted the wooden artist's palette
before applying the individual portions of paint, mixed
wet-in-wet, on top. She must have created the palette
before the underlying paint layers had sufficiently dried,
because this area is marked with wide drying cracks.
This type of condition problem is rare in works by
Vallayer-Coster, whose painting technique was generally quite sound, apart from certain irreversible pigment changes, especially compared with Chardin's
works. Technically his paintings have not always survived in good state—many are marked with drying
cracks—especially his figure paintings. Perhaps
Chardin was painting quickly or reworking areas over
medium-rich layers that had not sufficiently dried.
Chardin's legendary slowness relates more to this per-
fectionism than to his handling of a brush, as he is
known to have painted quickly with rapid brushstrokes,
applying multiple, thin layers of paint, and he must not
have allowed sufficient drying time as he worked.[61]

Vallayer-Coster's *Basket of Grapes* (pl. 12), with its
"muted, chiaroscuro effects," is clearly indebted to
Chardin, showing how Vallayer-Coster's style was much
closer to his technique than to the more exact description of Roland Delaporte or even Desportes, whose style
derived from the Flemish still-life style of Frans Snyders
(1579–1657).[62] Vallayer-Coster's still life is a study in
simplicity and shows how the artist was capable of
achieving very different results in the surfaces of her
still lifes and flower paintings. *Basket of Grapes* exhibits
a dry and subtle technique, in contrast to the brilliant
enamel-like surface of *Vase of Flowers;* Vallayer-Coster
altered her grounds and painting method in response
to working in the two different genres.

Still Life with Lobster, signed and dated 1781 (pl. 33),
and its pendant, *Still Life with Game* (pl. 34), display the
finesse of the artist's mature style. *Still Life with Lobster*
is a tour de force in the rendering of differently textured
objects. Working on a light granular ground, the artist
used a brown toning layer, or *imprimatura,* beneath the
footed bowl, glass cruets, and silver soup tureen, scumbling directly on top of this layer with thin layers of
opaque paint to model the glass. Vallayer-Coster applied
the white reflections on the soup tureen with a loaded
brush, painting the highlights wet-in-wet, while she
added pinpoint highlights on the knob.

Vallayer-Coster executed the lobster's shell with
countless dabs of color applied with a loaded brush,
modeling the form through an optical mix of colors rather
than through careful blending. The brushwork exhibits a
joyous freedom, with a dazzling display of red, pink, and
coral tones. The technique almost seems to illustrate
Diderot's famous description in 1763 of Chardin's method
of painting: "Come close and everything becomes blurred,
flattens and disappears; stand back and everything is
created and takes shape again."[63] This painting method,
where the forms come into focus when viewed from a
distance, looks back not only to Chardin but also to
Titian's late work,[64] even while it anticipates nineteenth-
century French impressionist painting.

The delicacy with which Vallayer-Coster depicts the
rabbit's fur in *Still Life with Game* shows her refinement
in the use of the dry brush technique, especially when
compared with her earlier attempt at this subject, *Still
Life with Dead Hare.* The artist painted the feathers of the
bird with a loaded brush on top of dried paint layers, with
some of the highlights displaying the crumbly texture
and broken brushwork reminiscent of Chardin. The

painting exhibits a beautiful color harmony of blues and coral, with the brilliant white belly of the rabbit providing the focal point of the composition. If the dabs of pink and coral in the leather strap recall Vallayer-Coster's treatment of the lobster shell, in both mood and lighting, *Still Life with Game* provides a contrast with its pendant. The midnight blue sky lends a mood of solemnity that differs from the glittering surfaces depicted in *Still Life with Lobster* (pl. 33).

Vallayer-Coster's last exhibited work, the monumental *Still Life with Lobster* (pl. 45), with its compendium of motifs, seems to summarize the achievements of the artist's long and successful career. The soft, diffuse tonality of the still life gives it a timeless, even spiritual quality. The subtlety of Vallayer-Coster's technique can be seen in her selective and controlled use of impasto, from the pinpoint reflections on the surfaces of objects to the economical strokes along the rims of stacked plates. The artist has organized these impasto highlights across the surface in such a way as to keep the eye moving horizontally across the picture plane. The overall impression of her paint layers is less textural, and more optical, than before. Her treatment of the white tablecloth, for example, with its range of cream and gray tints, is quite different from the emphatic treatment of the sheets of music in *The Attributes of Music*, where she used energetic brushwork and thick impasto.

In composition, subject, and even scale, *Still Life with Lobster* seems to allude to Chardin's most famous work, *The Skate* (Musée du Louvre, Paris). Did Vallayer-Coster seek to honor or challenge her distinguished predecessor in this ambitious work? Her masterful use of the dry brush technique and jumble of freely applied brushstrokes in the loaves of bread and delicately scumbled grapes pay open tribute to Chardin's technique. But *Still Life with Lobster* could never be confused as a work by the earlier master. Vallayer-Coster demonstrates her individuality in her finely tuned use of color, where the elements in the composition constitute a study of warm versus cool tonalities, and her painterly skill in rendering a range of textural contrasts with an astute handling of the brush.

Conclusion

Perhaps no other eighteenth-century French artist rivaled Vallayer-Coster's facility in painting in a range of styles, particularly in the decorative genres of still life and flower painting. She elevated the traditional genre of flower painting to create works of exceptional refinement. Her work as a colorist has perhaps not been fully appreciated, given that some pigments in many of her flower paintings have changed as a result of the fading of fugitive glazes. Vallayer-Coster coupled a keen eye for observation with a painterly elegance and developed a distinctive style that stood apart from the highly descriptive works of her contemporary Roland Delaporte as well as the idiosyncratic still lifes of her great predecessor, Chardin. Although Vallayer-Coster was clearly influenced by the techniques of this master, her paintings never fell into slavish imitation. Her technique reflected that of an artist finding her own way, creating a style that drew from the lessons of the French Académie and the art of the past as well as Chardin, while epitomizing the highest expression of rococo elegance.

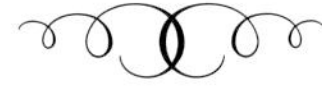

Notes

1. See Paris 1979, 301.

2. Roland Michel 1996, 141.

3. See F. Faré 1999.

4. Eik Kahng, verbal communication. Vallayer-Coster, like Chardin, was also active as a pastelist, in addition to her work in oil, watercolor, and gouache.

5. Christine Benoit examined the paintings under the binocular microscope and prepared photomicrographs; Elisabeth Ravaud provided and interpreted X-radiographs; Patrick Le Chanu studied the paintings under infrared reflectography. Odile Guillon compiled a complete photographic dossier for the two works, and Eric Laval carried out pigment analysis using X-ray fluorescence.

6. Vanderlip de Carbonnel 1981.

7. Benoit and Ravaud 2001. The more loosely woven canvases have approximately 11 threads/cm horizontally and 13 threads/cm vertically, whereas the finer woven canvases have approximately 15 threads/cm vertically and 19 threads/cm horizontally.

8. Benoit and Ravaud 2001.

9. Benoit and Ravaud 2001.

10. Duval 1992. See also Bergeon and Martin 1994; and O'Donoghue, Romero, and Dik 1998. See also Merrill 1981, 123.

11. Wallert 1999, 11.

12. Merrill 1981.

13. Joseph Fronek, "The Materials and Technique of the Los Angeles *Soap Bubbles*," in Los Angeles 1990, 23.

14. Wallert 1999.

15. Examples include *Still Life with Dead Hare, The Attributes of Painting, Sculpture, and Architecture, The Attributes of Music, Vase of Flowers* (Musée des Beaux-Arts, Nancy), *Bouquet of Flowers in a Blue Porcelain Vase, Bouquet of Flowers in a Terracotta Vase, with Peaches and Grapes,* the portrait of Joseph-Charles Roettiers, the portrait of Madame Adélaïde, and *Vase of Flowers.*

16. This is most likely the "Dutch white" used by artists such as Rembrandt. See also Bomford, Brown, and Roy 1988.

17. Benoit and Ravaud 2001, 5.

18. Wallert 1999, 67.

19. Roland Michel 1970, 275.

20. Merrill 1981. See also Los Angeles 1990.

21. Kirsh and Levenson 2000, 82.

22. Verbal communication, Mark Leonard, Conservator of Paintings, The J. Paul Getty Museum. Two of the three David paintings at the Getty Museum are executed on textured grounds.

23. Patrick Le Chanu examined *The Attributes of Music* and *Still Life with Seashells and Coral* under infrared reflectography at the Louvre, while the pendants in the private collection in Dallas, *Female Faun and Putti* and *A Vase of Flowers with Two Plums on a Marble Tabletop,* were examined at the Kimbell Art Museum.

24. Swicklik 1993, 157–158. Oudry also lectured at the Académie on color in 1750.

25. Kirsch and Levenson 2000, 65–78.

26. Bergeon and Martin 1994.

27. Eik Kahng, verbal communication.

28. Wallert 1999, 51.

29. Roland Michel 1970.

30. Roland Michel 1996, 132.

31. De Piles 1766. Corneille 1694, 47–48, also describes the preparation of the three tints for flesh tones on the artist's palette: the lights, the shades, and the half tints.

32. Merrill 1981, 124.

33. Roland Michel 1996, 134.

34. Chardin's practice of adding chalk to his paint is discussed by Merrill 1981; Conisbee and Fronek in Los Angeles 1990; and Roland Michel 1996.

35. Merrill 1981, 125. Analysis was carried out at the time of the 1979 retrospective. The following pigments were identified in works by Chardin: kaolin, white lead, vegetable carbon black, umber, realgar, orpiment, Naples yellow, vermilion, red lakes, yellow lakes, ultramarine blue, ultramarine blue mixed with Prussian blue, Prussian blue, organic brown earth, chalk, iron oxide earth colors, lead-tin yellow.

36. Harley 1970, 47. See also Kühn 1973.

37. Kirby 1993, 62–71.

38. Benoit and Ravaud 2001, 3.

39. Benoit and Ravaud 2001, 4.

40. The following pigments were identified at the Musée du Louvre using X-ray fluorescence: ocher, white lead, calcium carbonate, raw umber, vermilion, Naples yellow, and green earth.

41. This needs to be confirmed, however, through additional analysis.

42. Benoit and Ravaud 2001.

43. Merrill 1981.

44. Examination of the leaves under magnification reveals scattered yellow pigment particles alongside numerous dark blue pits where the yellow particles probably flaked away.

45. Wallert 1999, 84.

46. J.-H. La Fontaine, in his treatise of 1679 (La Fontaine 1679, pt. 2), describes a series of greens mixed in a range of light, medium, and dark tones, while Philippe de La Hyre's treatise on painting materials and methods (La Hyre 1730, 678) also discusses mixed greens. In his *Groot Schilderboek* Gerard de Lairesse (Lairesse 1707, 358) emphasized the importance of using beautiful greens rather than those mixed from black and yellow. See Kirby and Saunders 1998.

47. Wallert 1999, 55.

48. Wallert 1999, 21.

49. O'Donoghue, Romero, and Dik 1998, 188.

50. Quoted in Roland Michel 1996, 131.

51. Roland Michel 1996, 131.

52. Roland Michel 1996, 138.

53. See Chevreul 1967, based on the first English edition of 1854, as translated from the first French edition of 1839, *De la loi du contraste simultané des couleurs.*

54. Eik Kahng, personal communication.

55. Eik Kahng, personal communication.

56. Eik Kahng, personal communication.

57. Wallert 1999, 59.

58. Roland Michel 1996, 137.

59. Because the artist typically painted on lead white grounds, these *pentimenti* are difficult to read in X-radiographs.

60. Many artists, including the Spanish Bartholomé Esteban Murillo (1617/18–1682) and Diego Velázquez (1599–1660), added calcite to increase the transparency and consistency of paint.

61. Merrill 1981; Roland Michel 1996, 134.

62. Conisbee 1981, 163.

63. Quoted in Roland Michel 1996, 137.

64. Roland Michel 1996, 137.

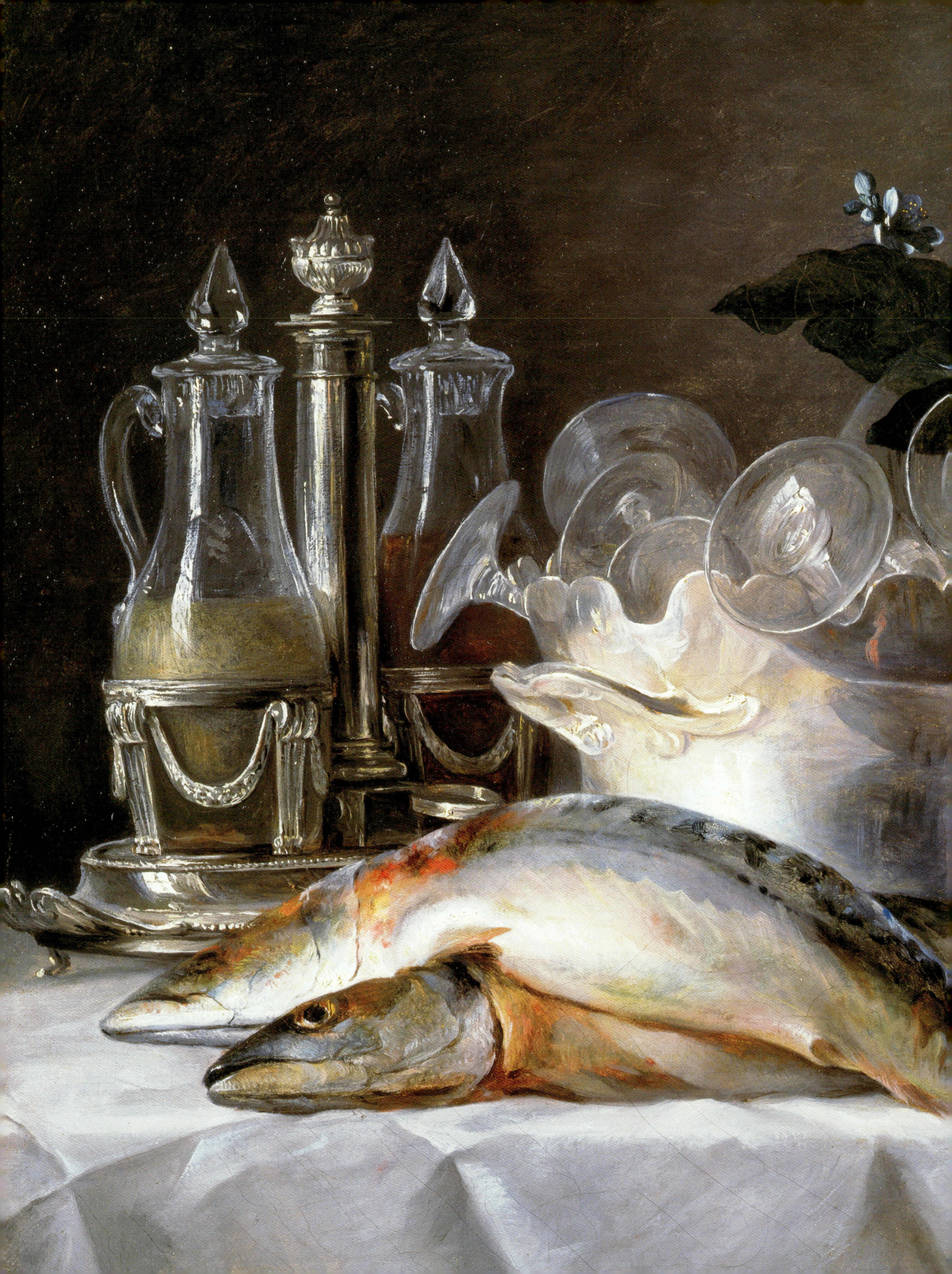

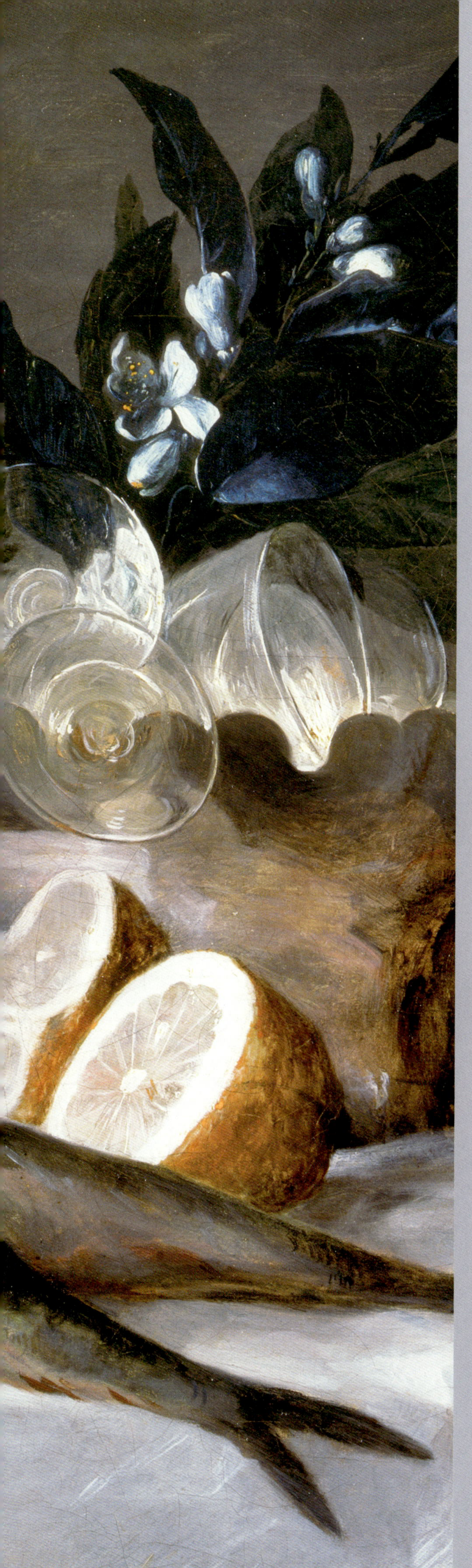

Color Plates of Works Exhibited

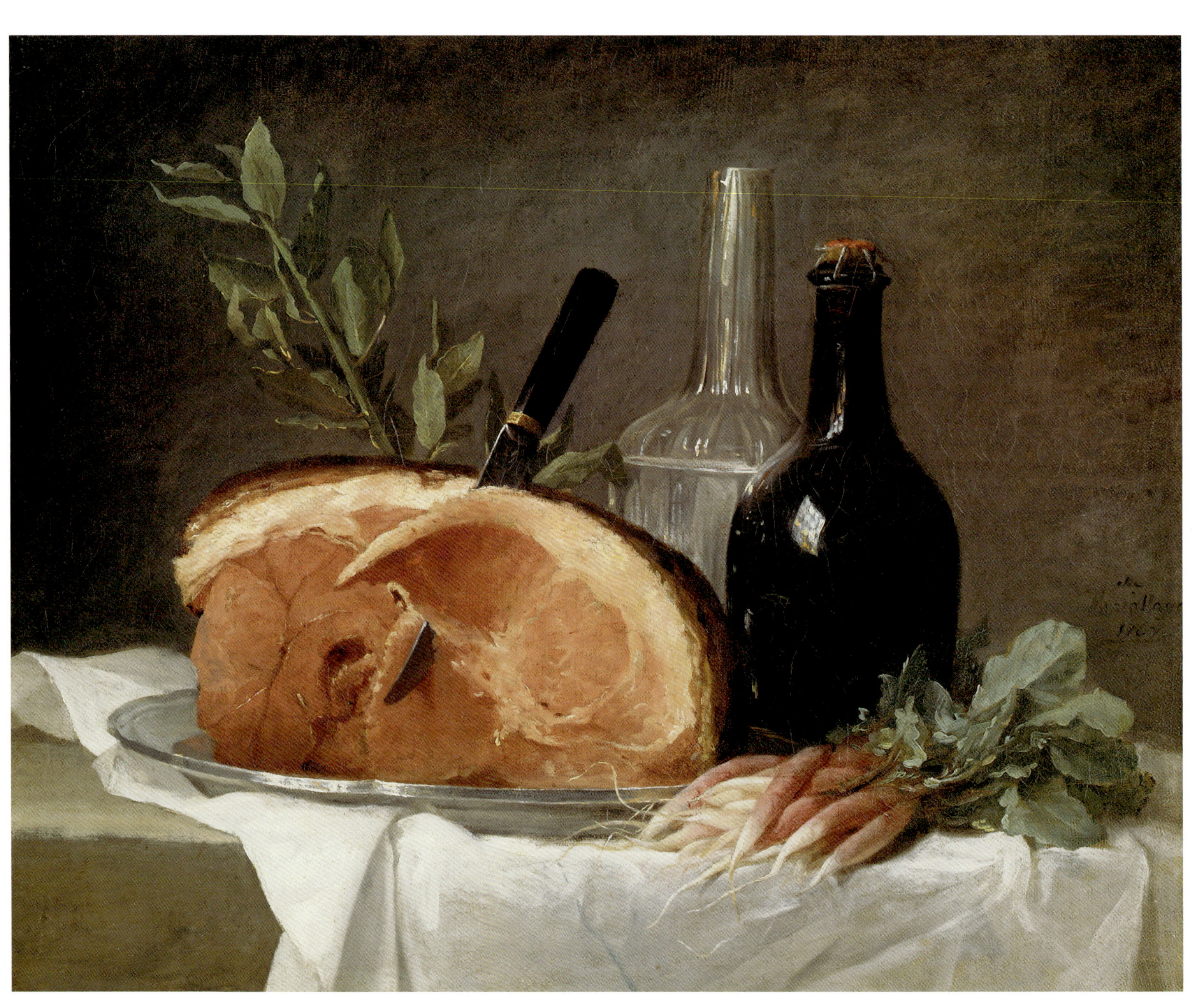

[1]   *Still Life with Ham, Bottles, and Radishes,* 1767

Oil on canvas
17¾ × 21⅝ in.
Staatliche Museen zu Berlin, Gemäldegalerie
(cat. 4)

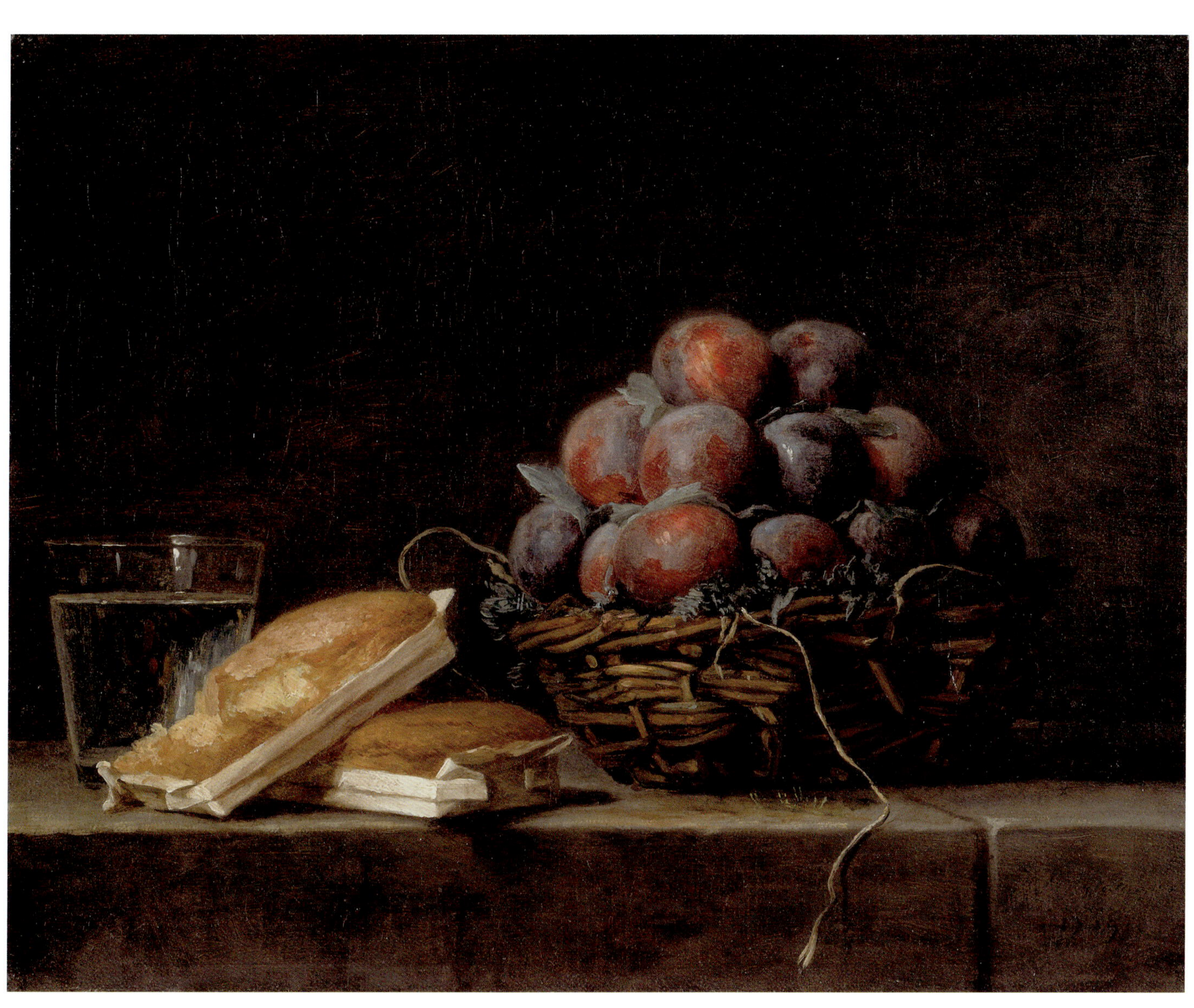

[2] *Basket of Plums*, 1769

Oil on canvas
14.^{15}/$_{16}$ × 18^{3}/$_{16}$ in.
The Cleveland Museum of Art, Mr. and Mrs. William H.
Marlatt Fund, 1971.47
(cat. 7)

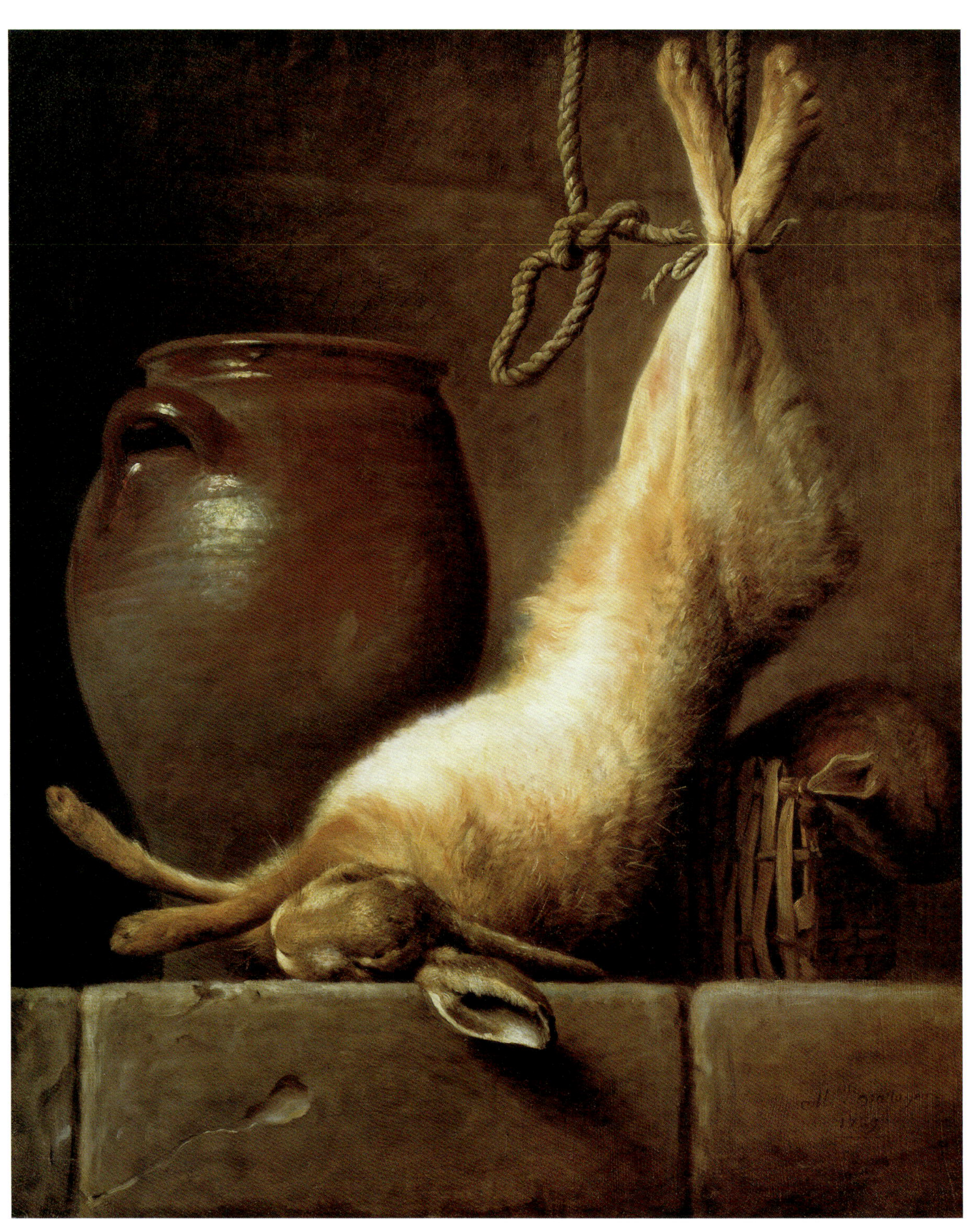

[3] *Still Life with Dead Hare, 1769*

Oil on canvas
29⅜ × 23⅞ in.
Collection of Jeffrey E. Horvitz, Boston
(cat. 10)

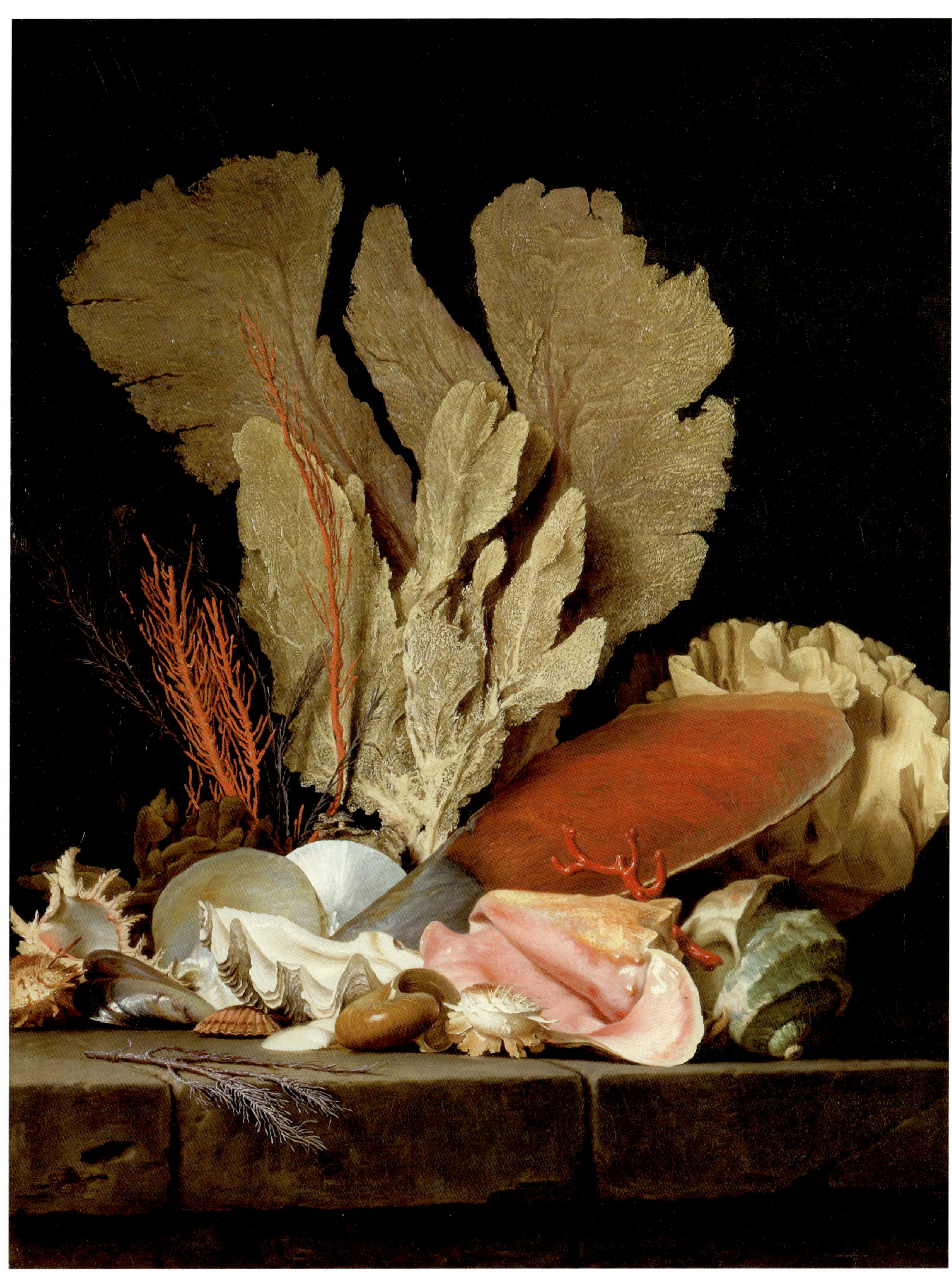

[4]   *Still Life with Seashells and Coral*, 1769

Oil on canvas
51⅛ × 38¼ in.
Musée du Louvre, Paris R.F. 1992-410
(cat. 11)

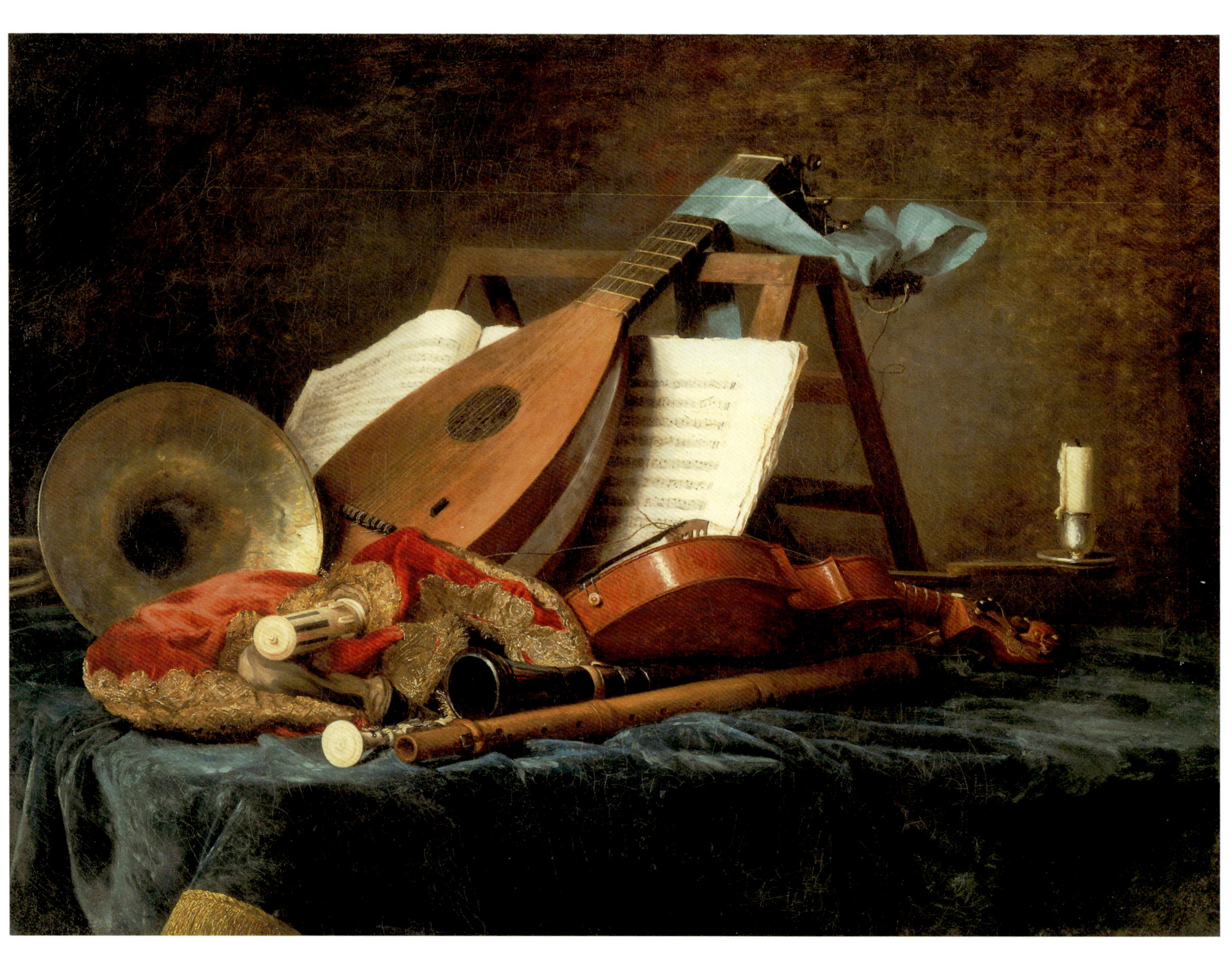

[5]   *The Attributes of Music*, 1770

Oil on canvas
35⅝ × 45⅝ in.
Musée du Louvre, Paris, inv. no. 8260
(cat. 12)

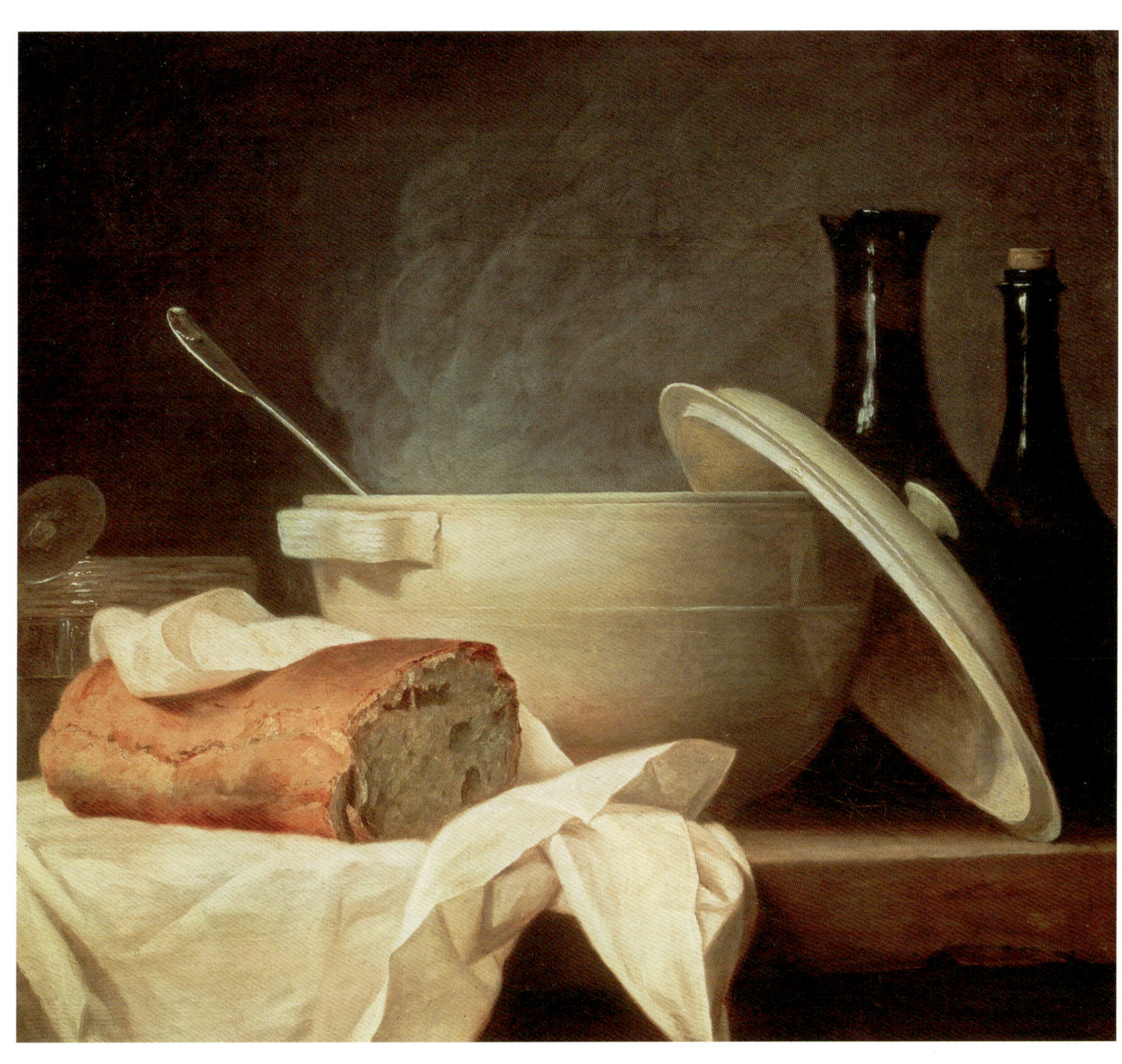

[6]   *The White Soup Tureen*, 1771

Oil on canvas
19⅝ × 24⅜ in.
Private collection, Paris
(cat. 14)

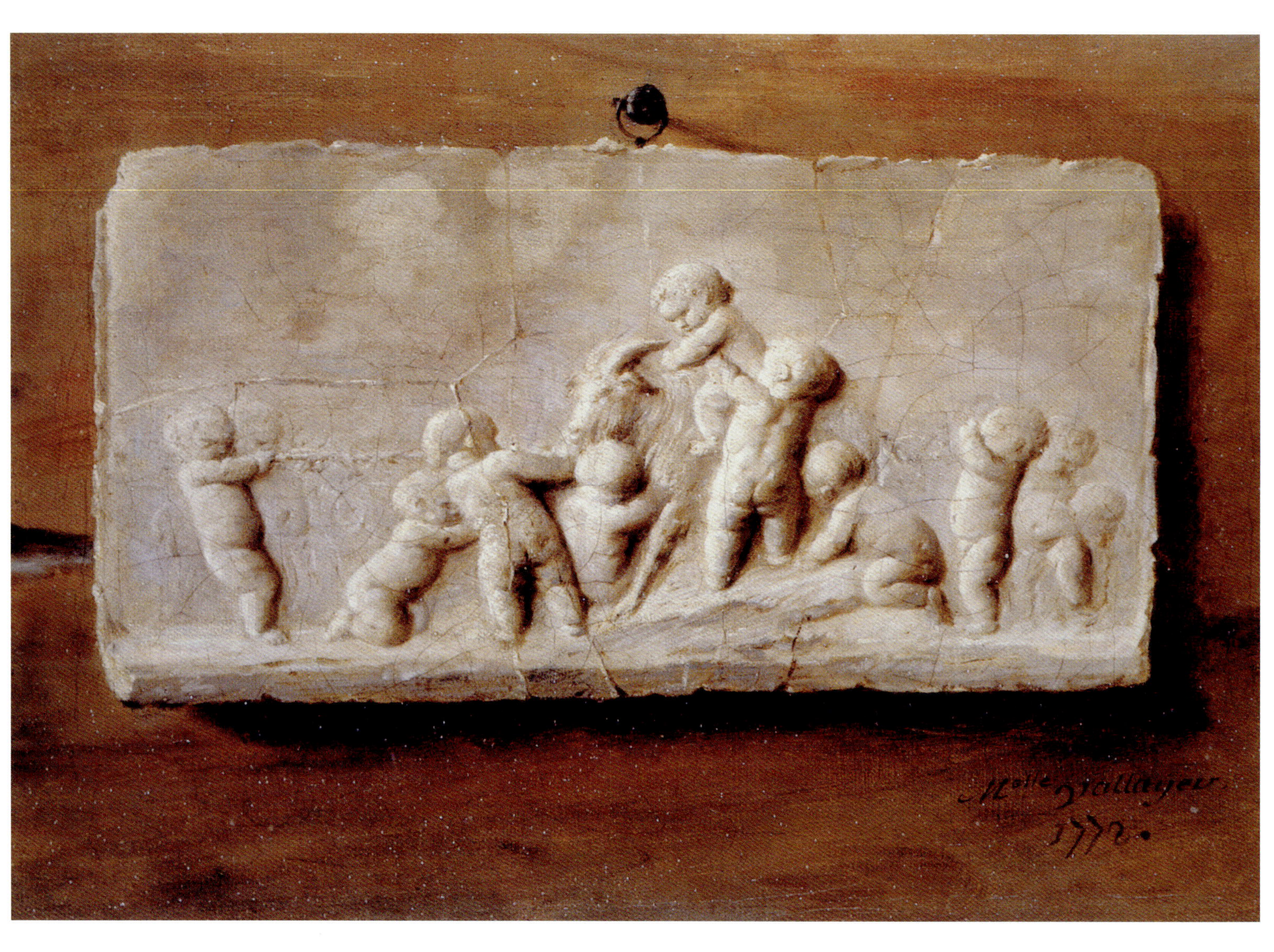

[7]   *Trompe l'Oeil of a Terracotta Bas-Relief (after*
La Rue) Pinned to a Wooden Panel, 1772

Oil on canvas
9⅞ × 14½ in.
Courtesy of Rafael Valls, Ltd, London
(cat. 19)

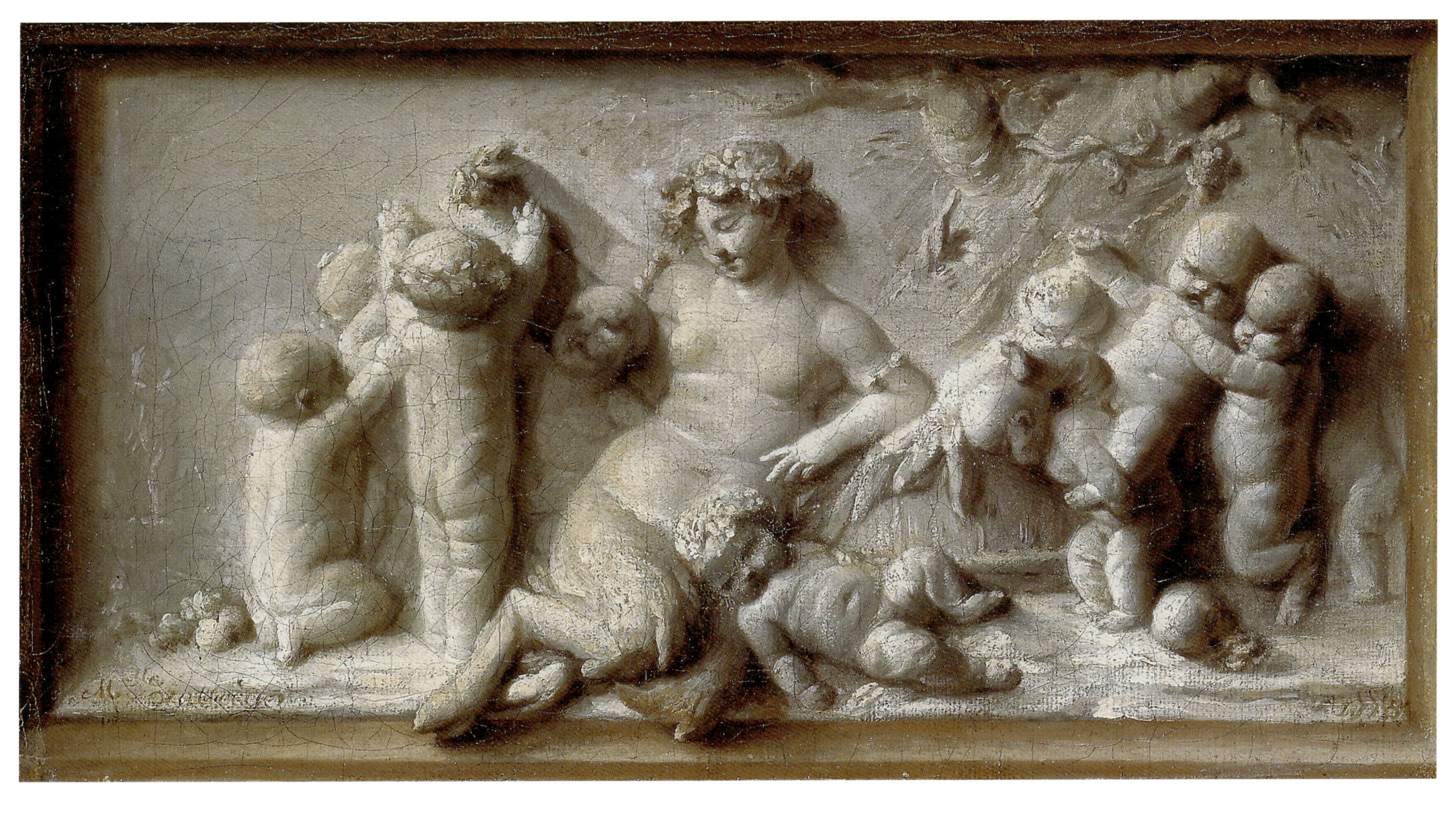

[8]   *Female Faun and Putti*, 1773

Oil on canvas
6³⁄₈ × 11¹⁄₂ in.
Private collection
(cat. 20)

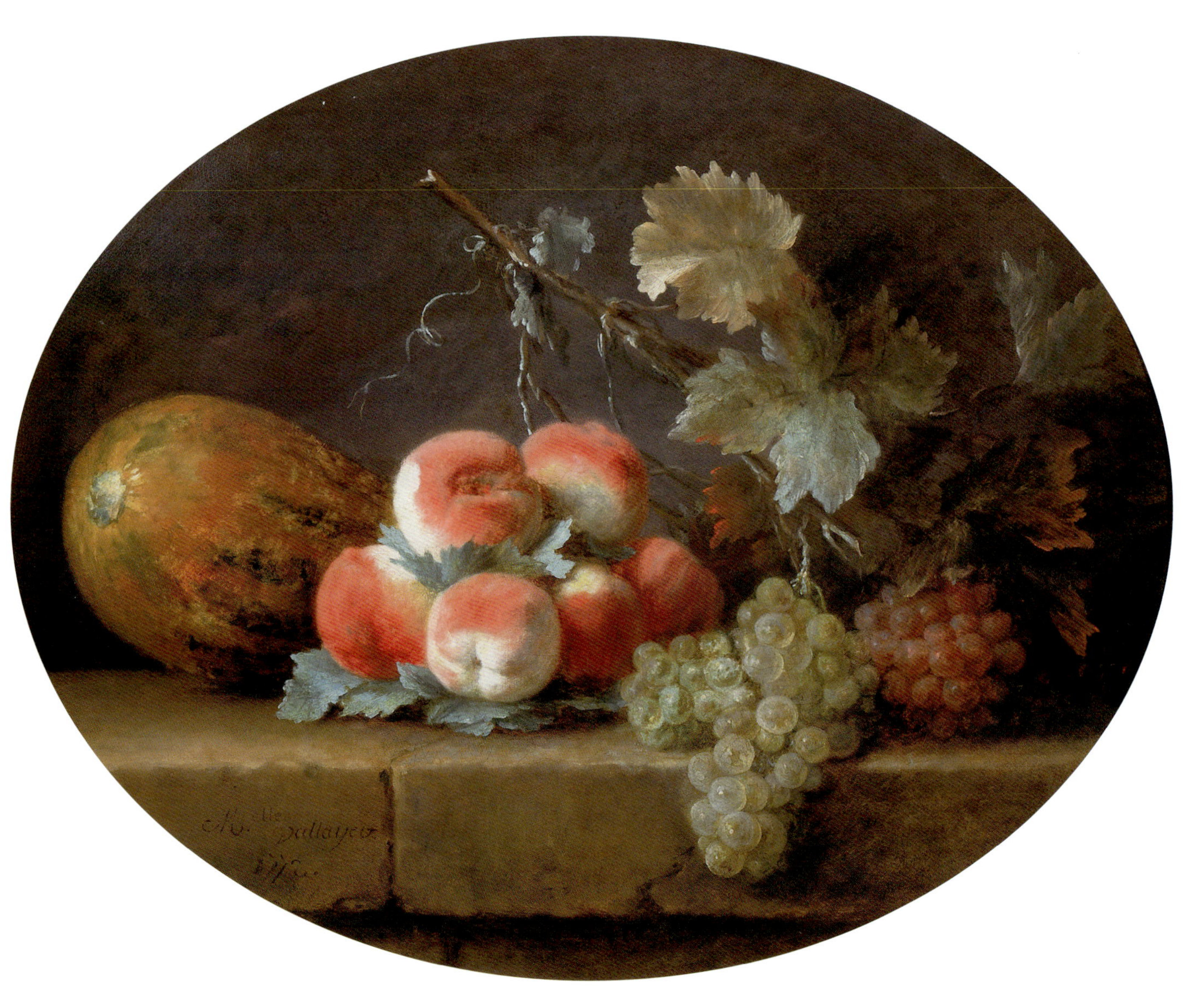

[9] *Basket of Peaches with Melon*, 1772

Oil on canvas, oval
$21\frac{1}{4} \times 25\frac{1}{2}$ in.
Private collection
(cat. 16)

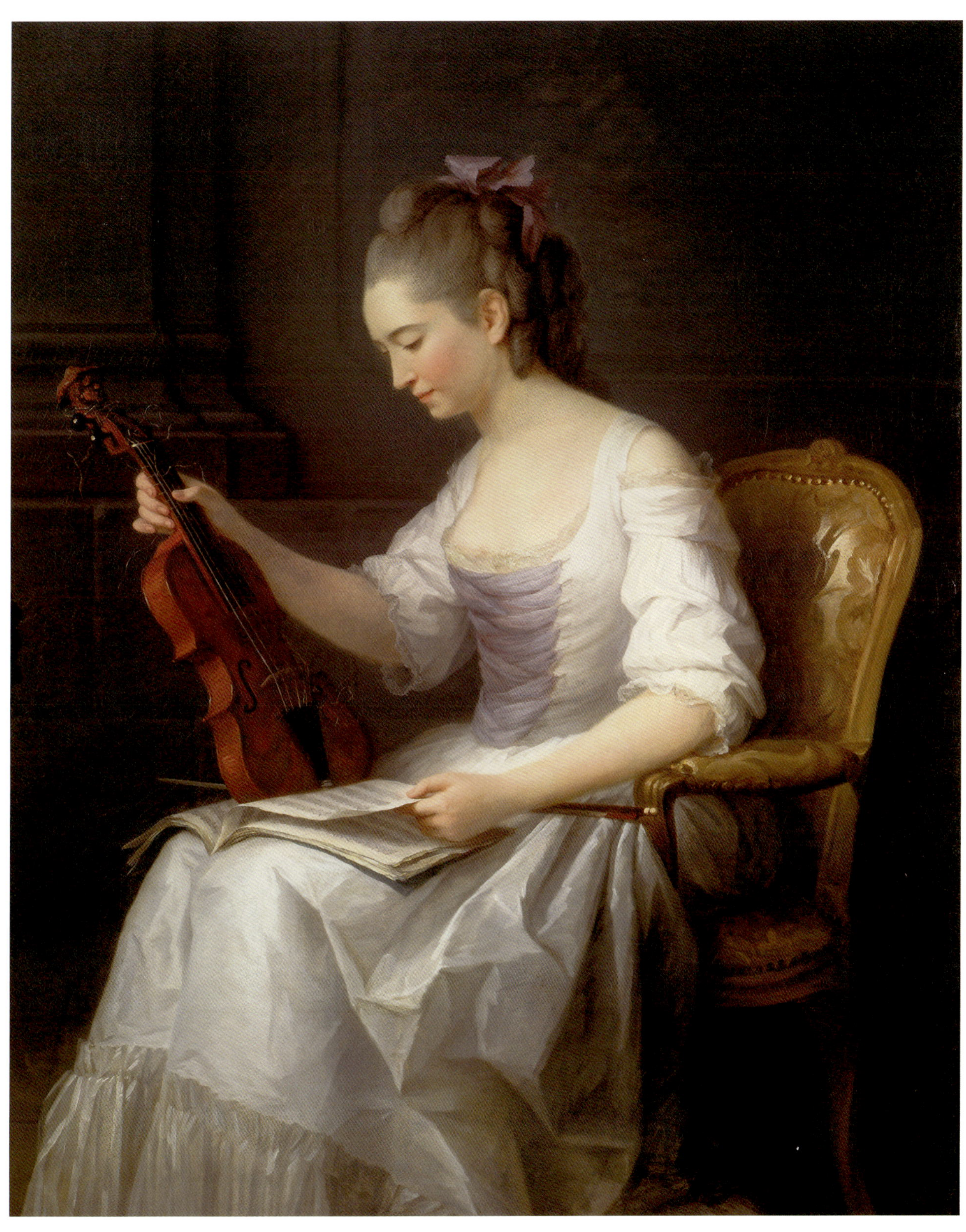

[10]   *Portrait of a Young Violinist*, 1773

Oil on canvas
$47\frac{1}{4} \times 35\frac{3}{8}$ in.
Private collection, Brussels
(cat. 22)

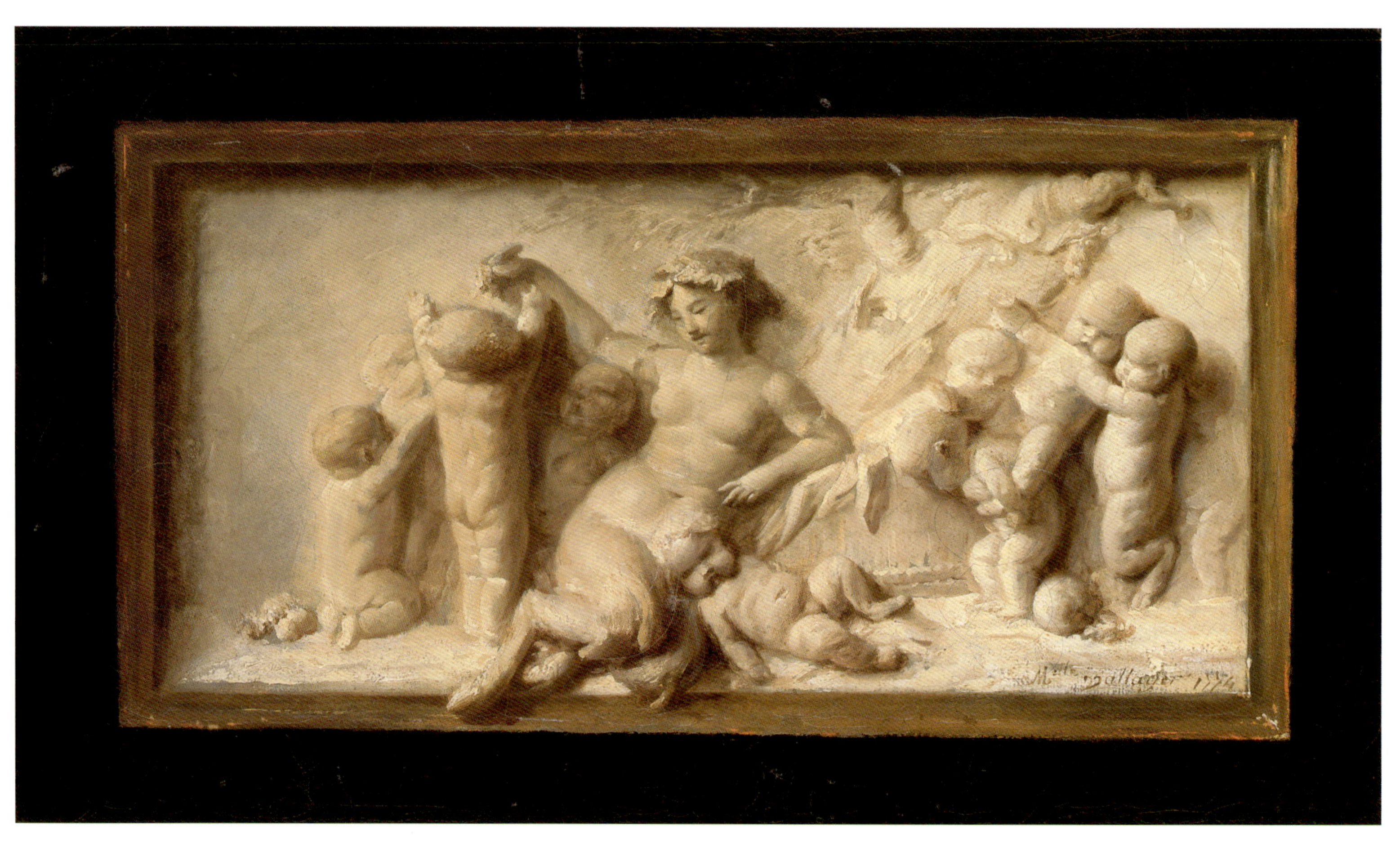

[11]   *Female Faun and Putti*, 1774

Oil on canvas
8⅛ × 13⅞ in.
Private collection
(cat. 27)

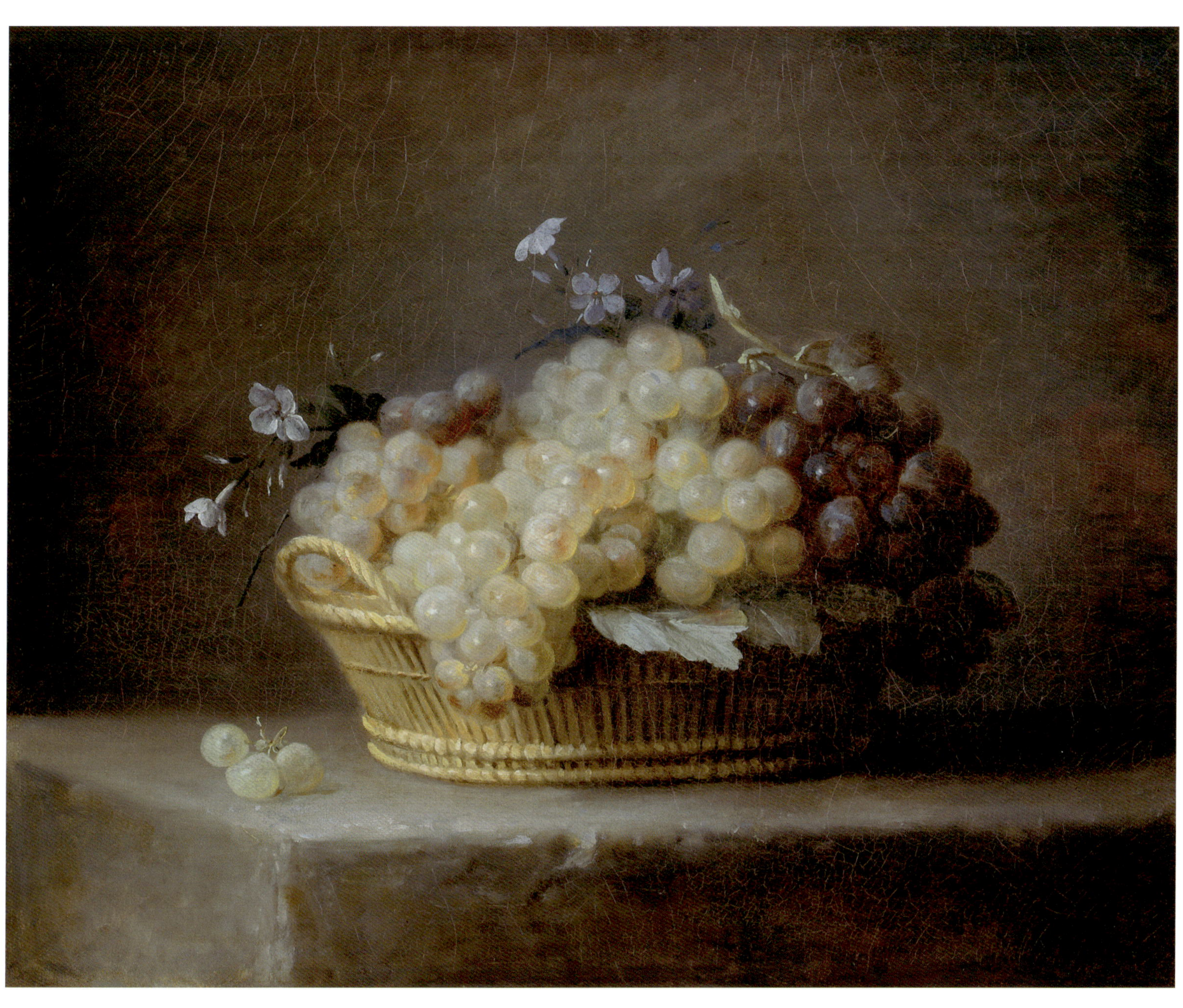

[12]   *Basket of Grapes*, 1774

Oil on canvas
15 × 18⅛ in.
Musée des Beaux-Arts, Nancy
(cat. 25)

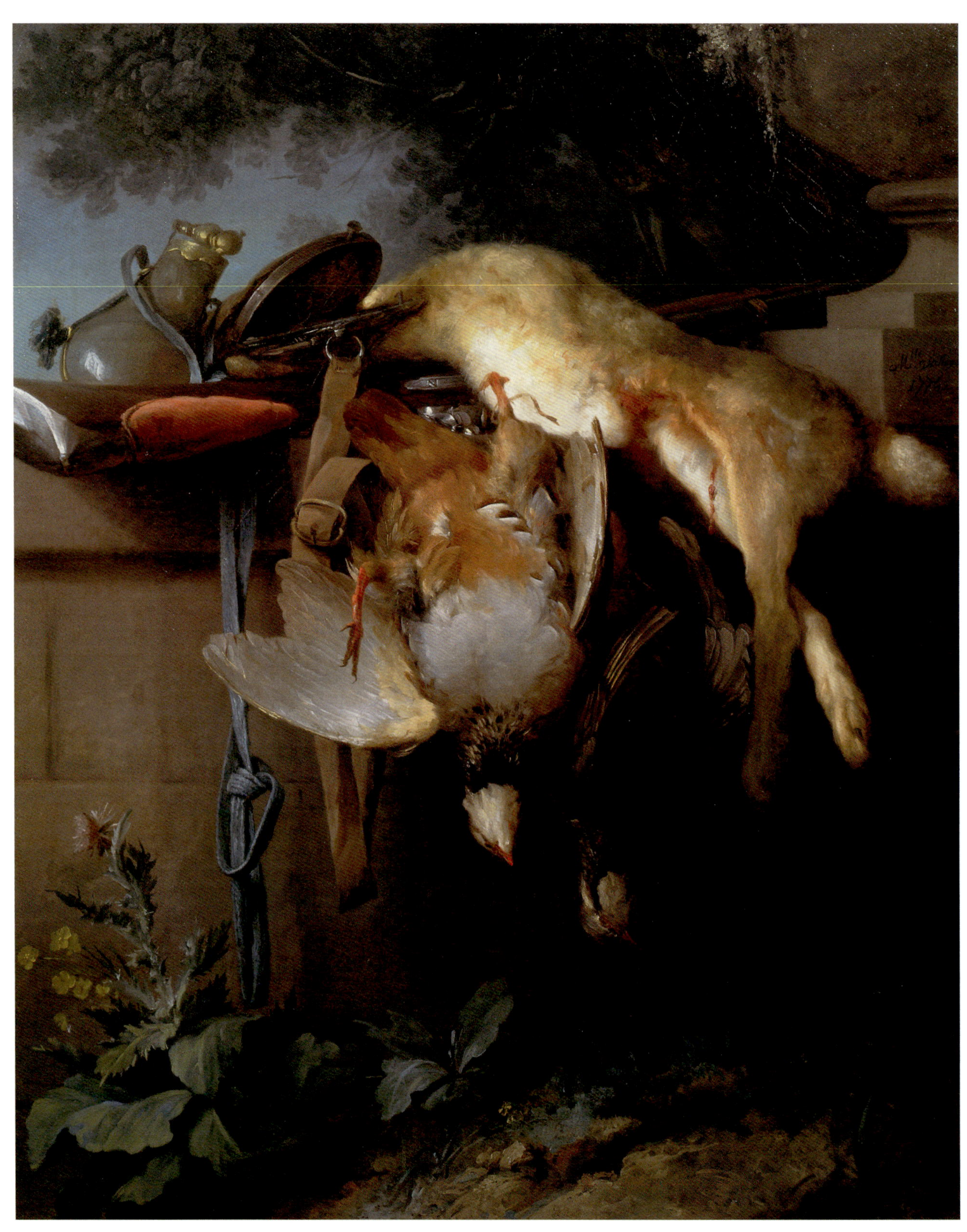

[13]   *Trophies of the Hunt*, 1774

Oil on canvas
35⅞ × 28¾ in.
Galerie Gismondi, Paris
(cat. 28)

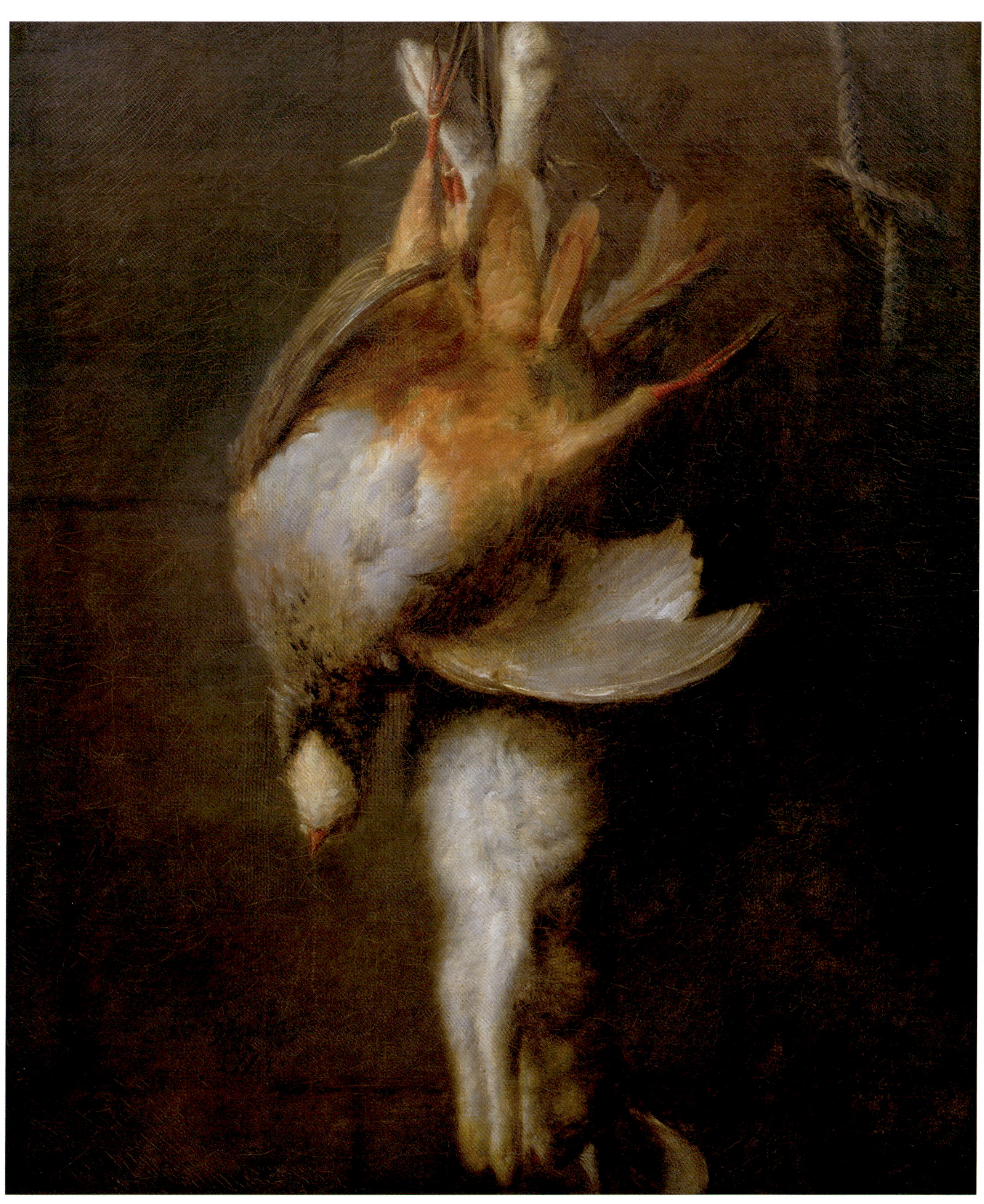

[14] *Trophies of the Hunt*, 1774

Oil on canvas
21¼ × 18½ in.
Private collection
(cat. 29)

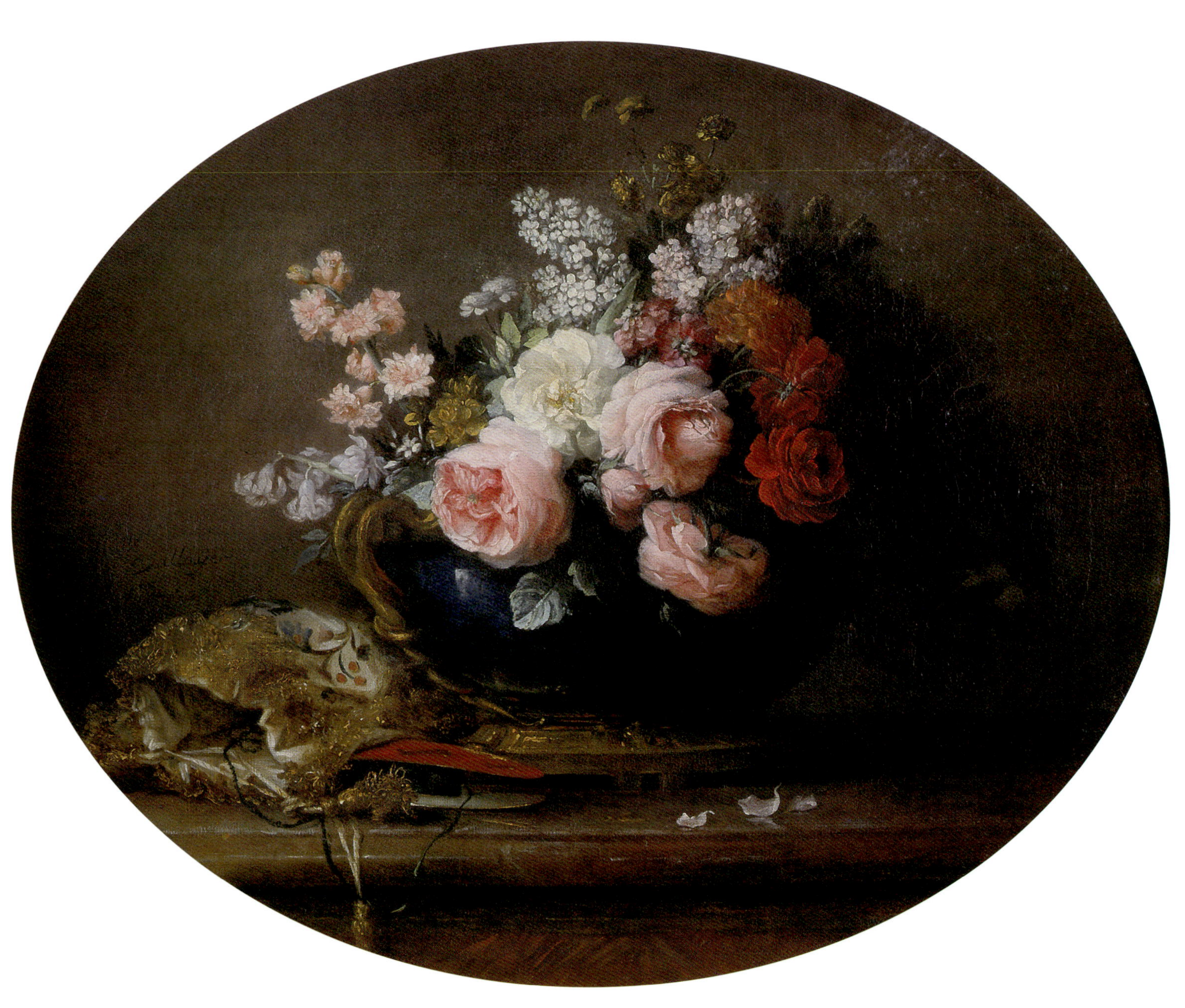

[15]   *Bouquet of Flowers with a Purse,* 1774

Oil on canvas, oval
$20\frac{1}{8} \times 23\frac{7}{8}$ in.
Villa Ephrussi de Rothschild–Institut de France,
Saint-Jean Cap Ferrat
(cat. 26)

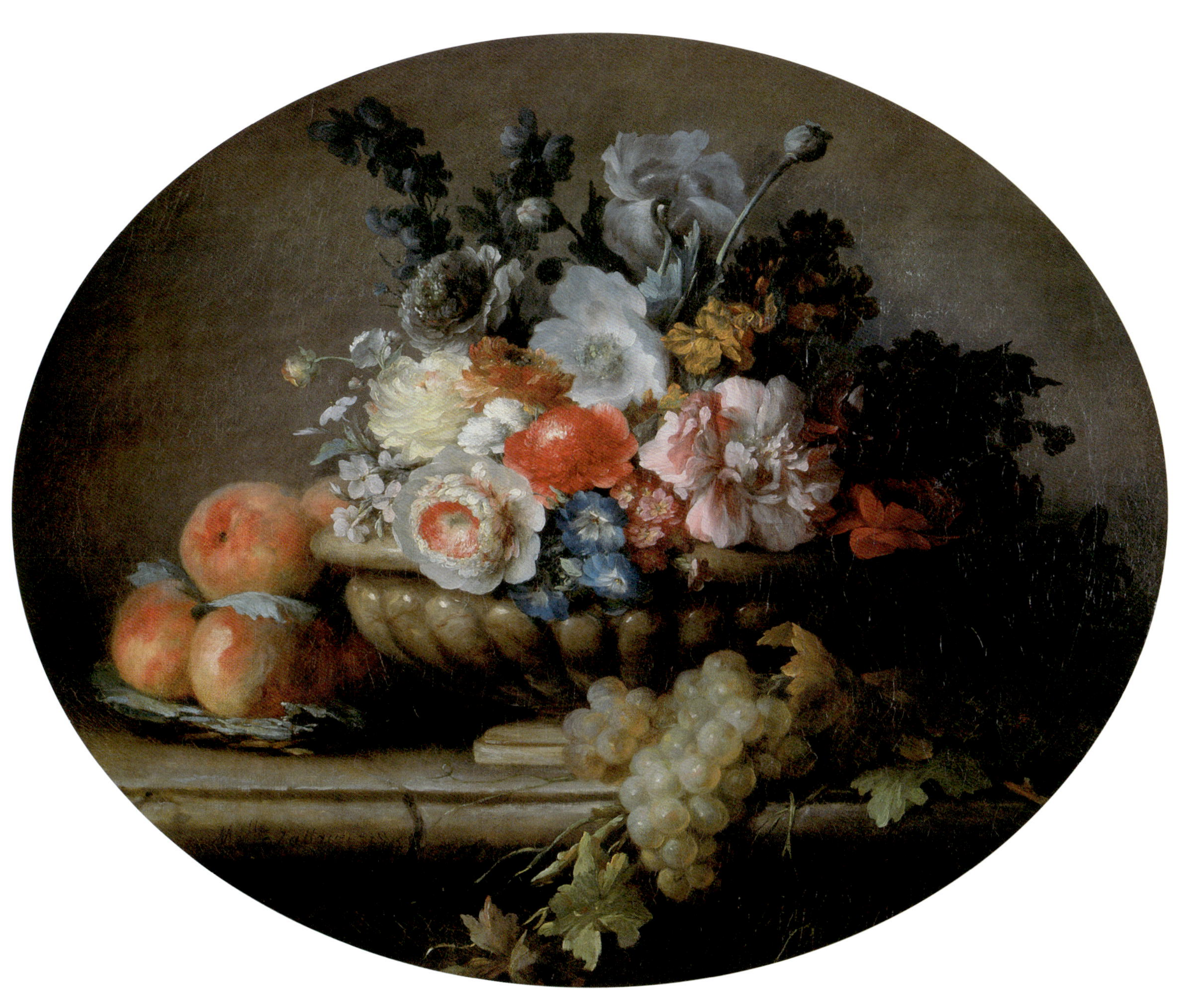

[16]   *Bouquet of Flowers with Grapes and Apples*, 1775

Oil on canvas, oval
20½ × 24¼ in.
Villa Ephrussi de Rothschild–Institut de France,
Saint-Jean Cap Ferrat
(cat. 31)

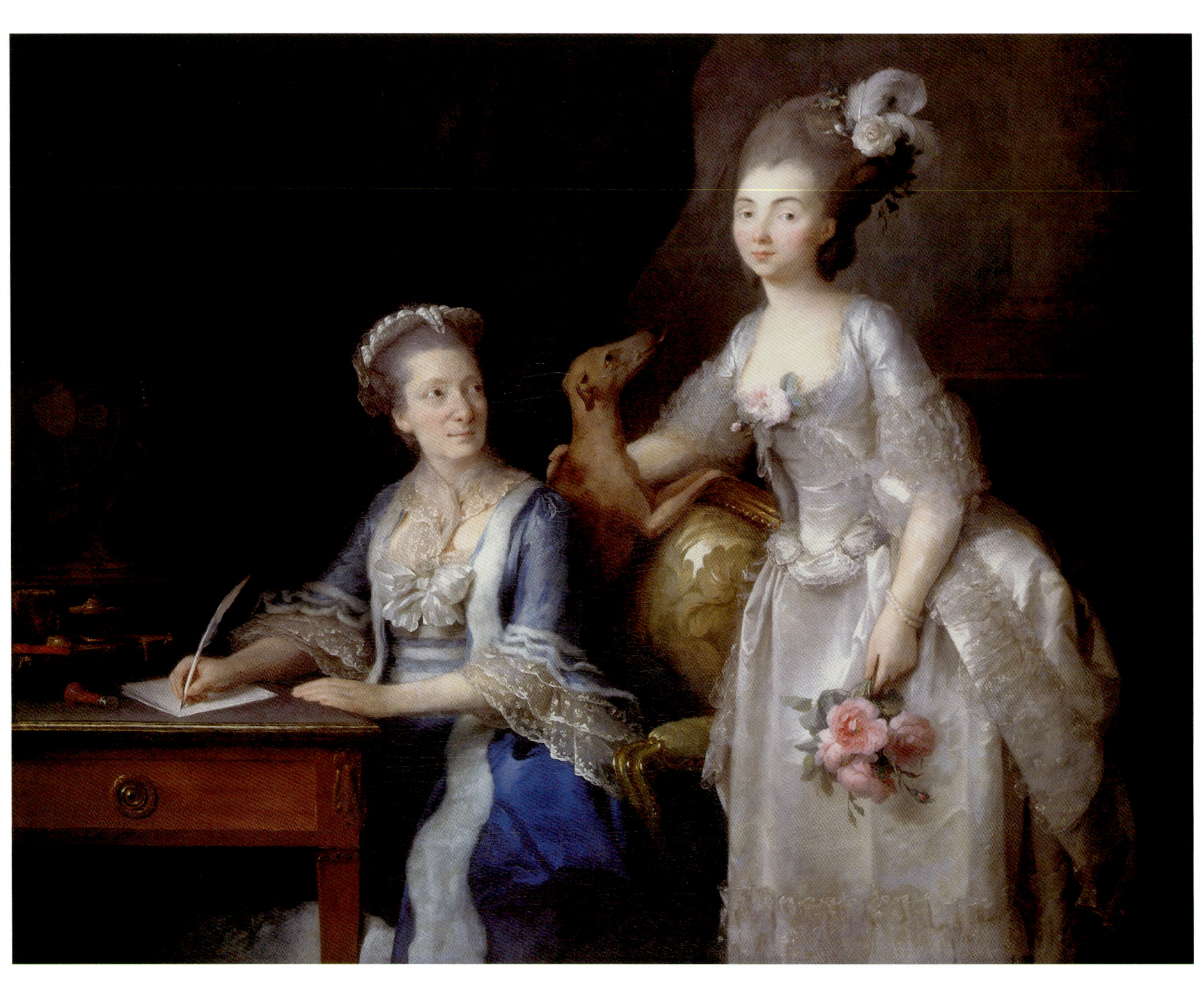

[17]   *Portrait of a Woman Writing and Her Daughter,* 1775

Oil on canvas
24³⁄₈ × 51¹⁄₈ in.
The Bowes Museum, Barnard Castle, Co. Durham,
England
(cat. 33)

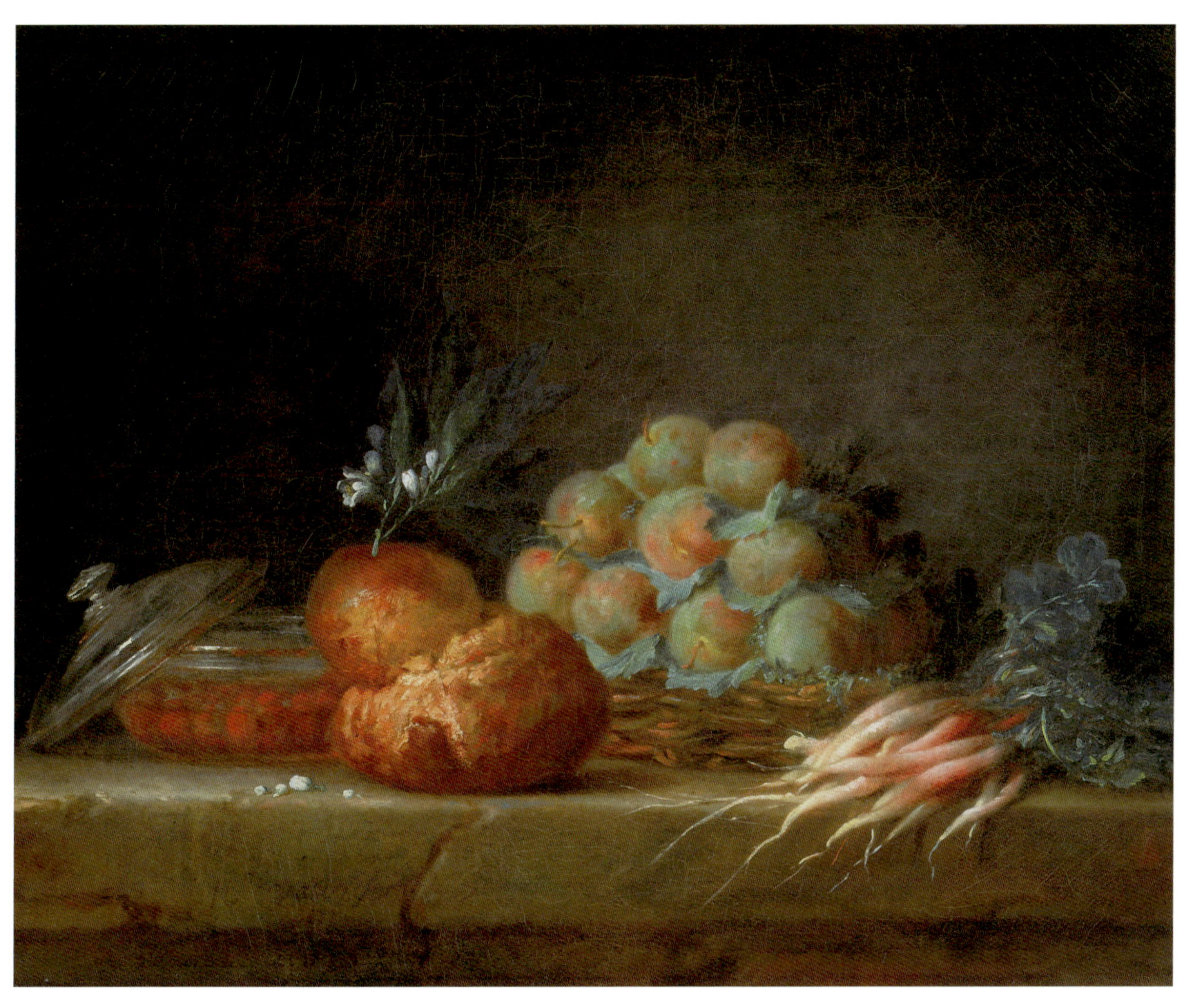

[18]   *Still-Life with Brioche, Fruit, and Vegetables*, 1775

Oil on canvas
17½ × 21¼ in.
Nationalmuseum, Stockholm; Quist Fund, NM 6937
(cat. 34)

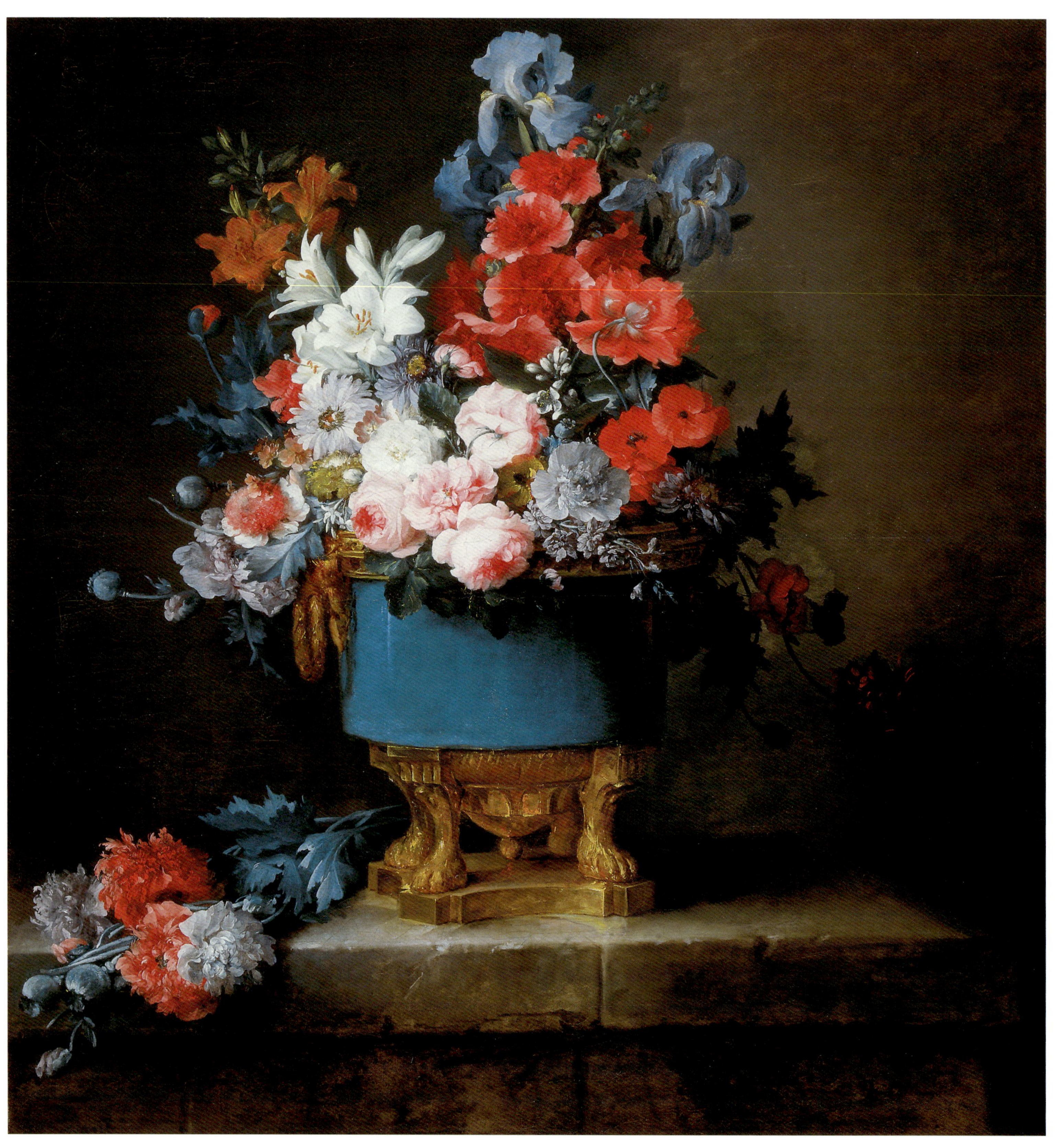

[19] *Bouquet of Flowers in a Blue Porcelain Vase*, 1776

Oil on canvas
48¼ × 44½ in.
Dallas Museum of Art, Dallas, Texas; Dallas Museum
of Art Foundation for the Arts Collection, Mrs. John
O'Hara Fund and gift of Michael L. Rosenberg, 1998.52
(cat. 36)

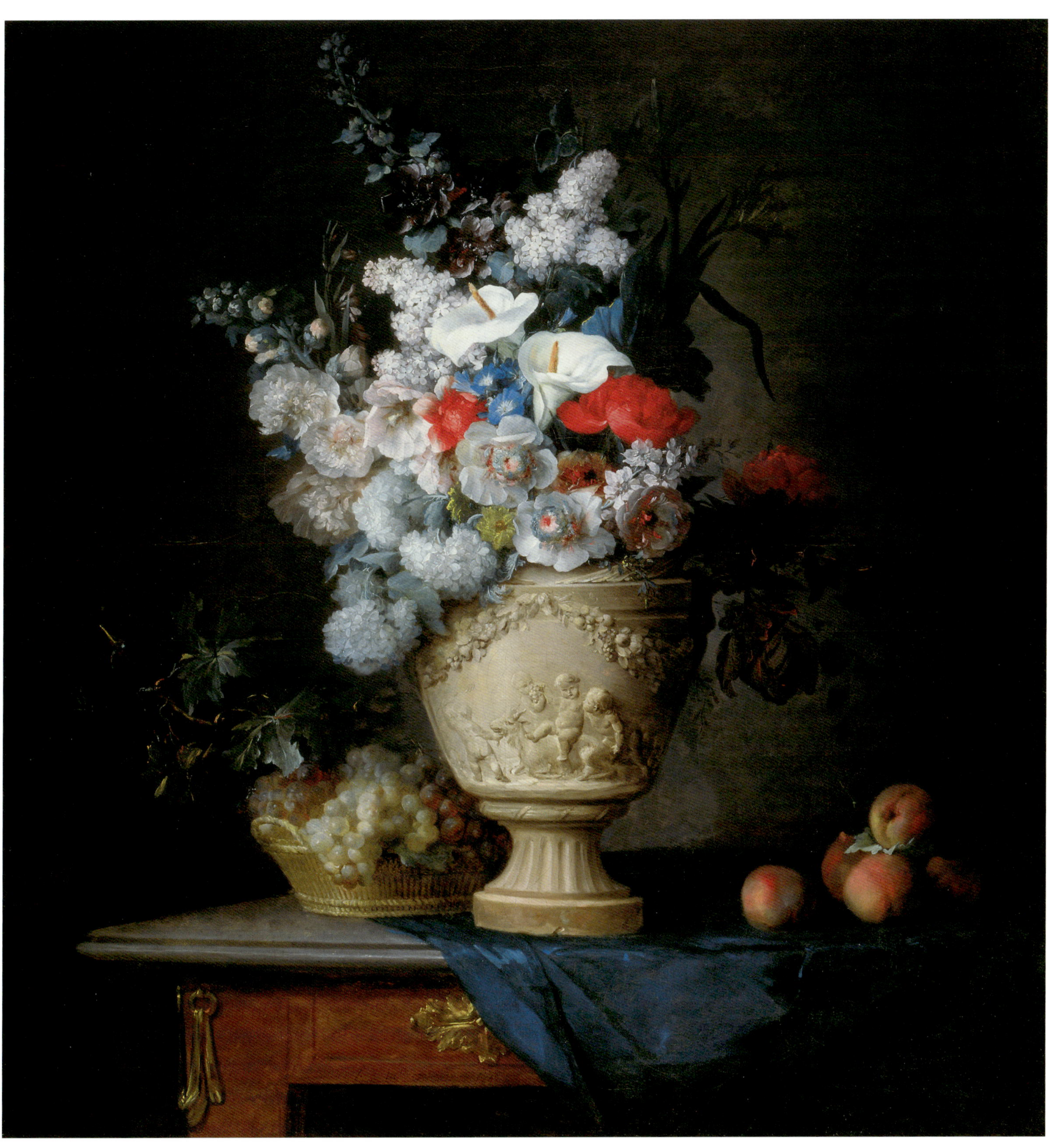

[20]   *Bouquet of Flowers in a Terracotta Vase, with*
          Peaches and Grapes, 1776

Oil on canvas
47⅝ × 44⅝ in.
Dallas Museum of Art, Dallas, Texas; Dallas Museum
of Art Foundation for the Arts Collection, Mrs. John
O'Hara Fund and gift of Michael L. Rosenberg, 1998.51
(cat. 37)

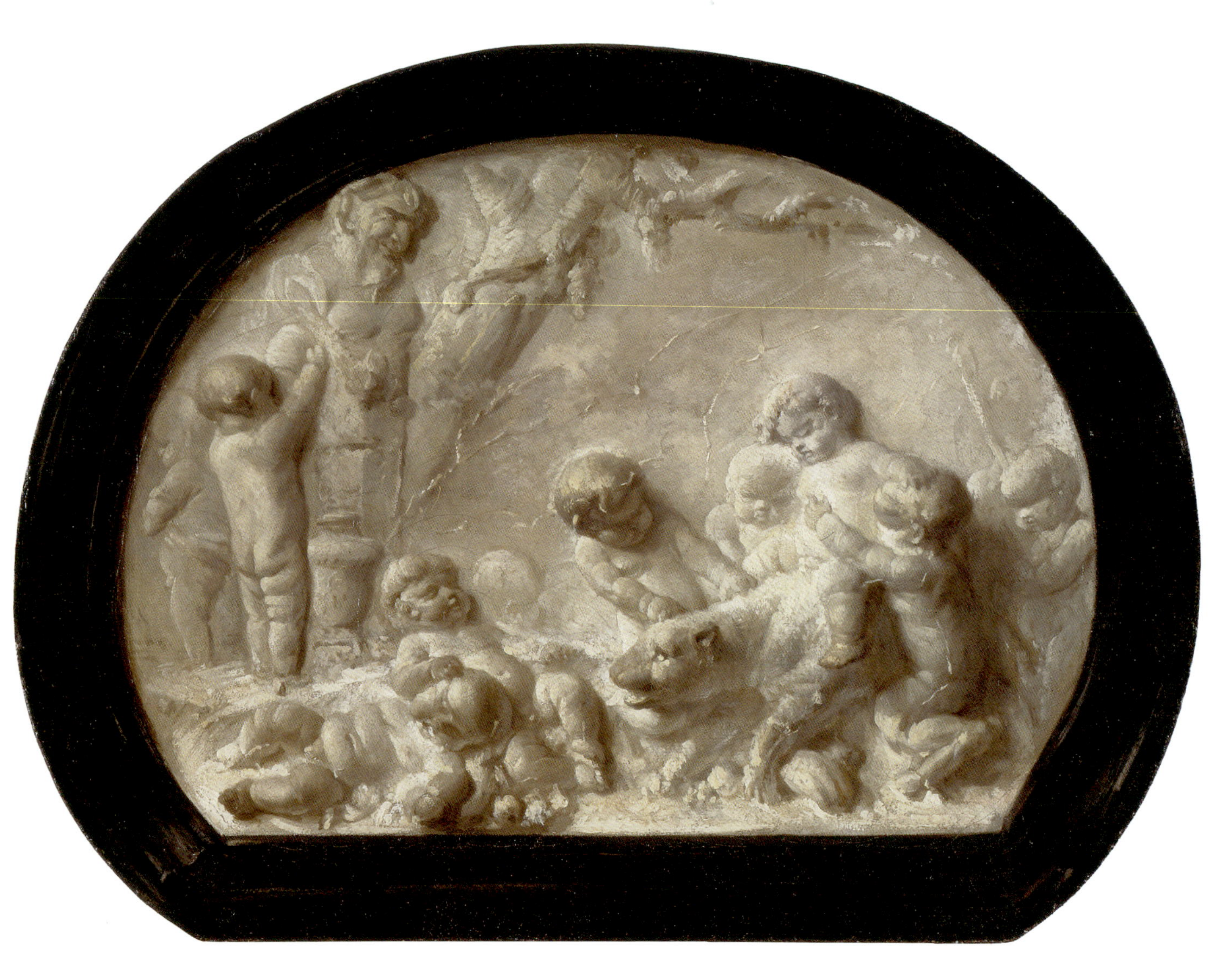

[21] *Satyrs and Putti Playing with a Panther*, 1776

Oil on canvas
11⅜ × 13¾ in.
Private collection
(cat. 40)

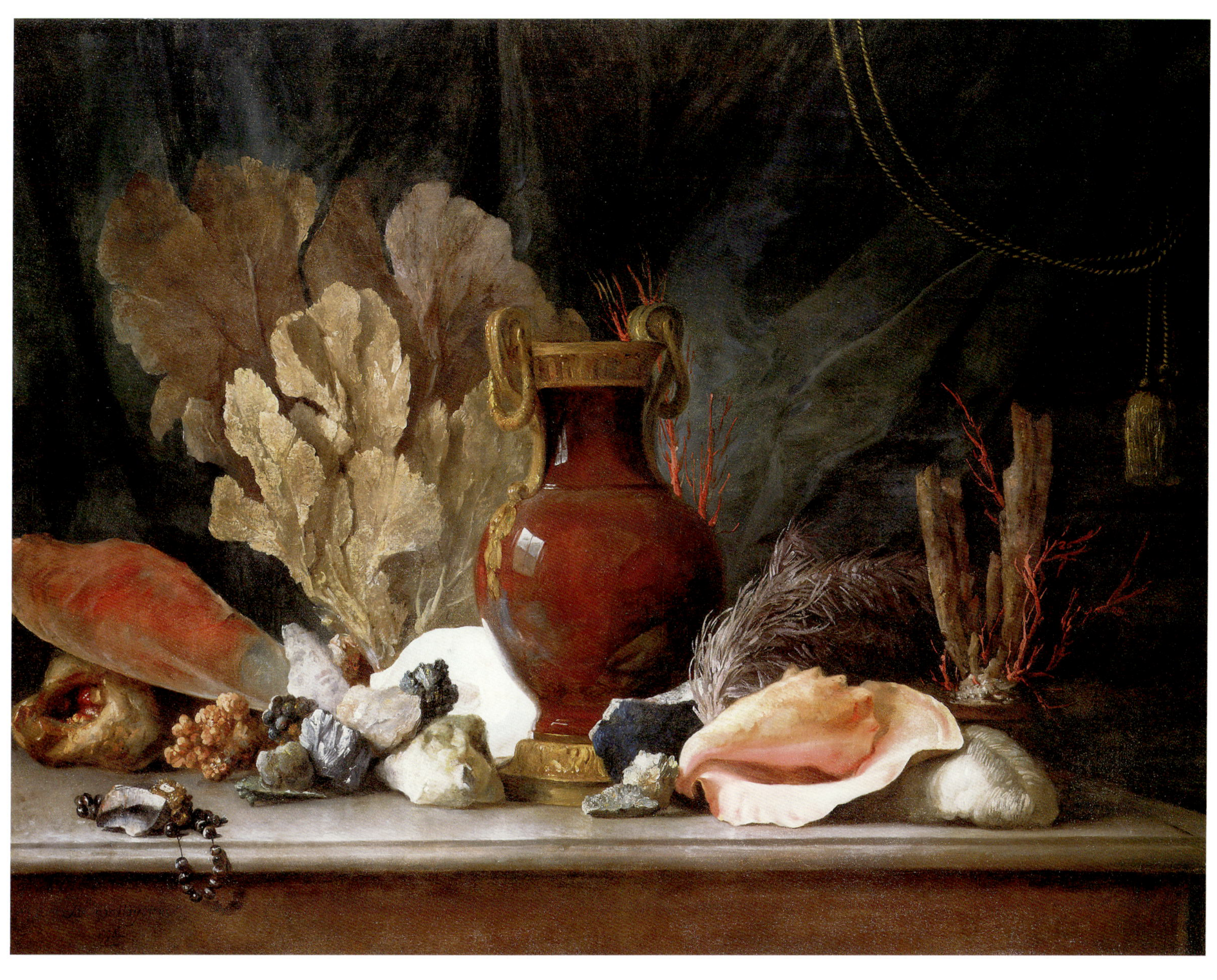

[22]   *Still Life with Porcelain Vase, Marine Plants, Shells,*
and Various Mineralogical Specimens, 1776

Oil on canvas
$42^{5/8} \times 54^{5/8}$ in.
Private collection
(cat. 41)

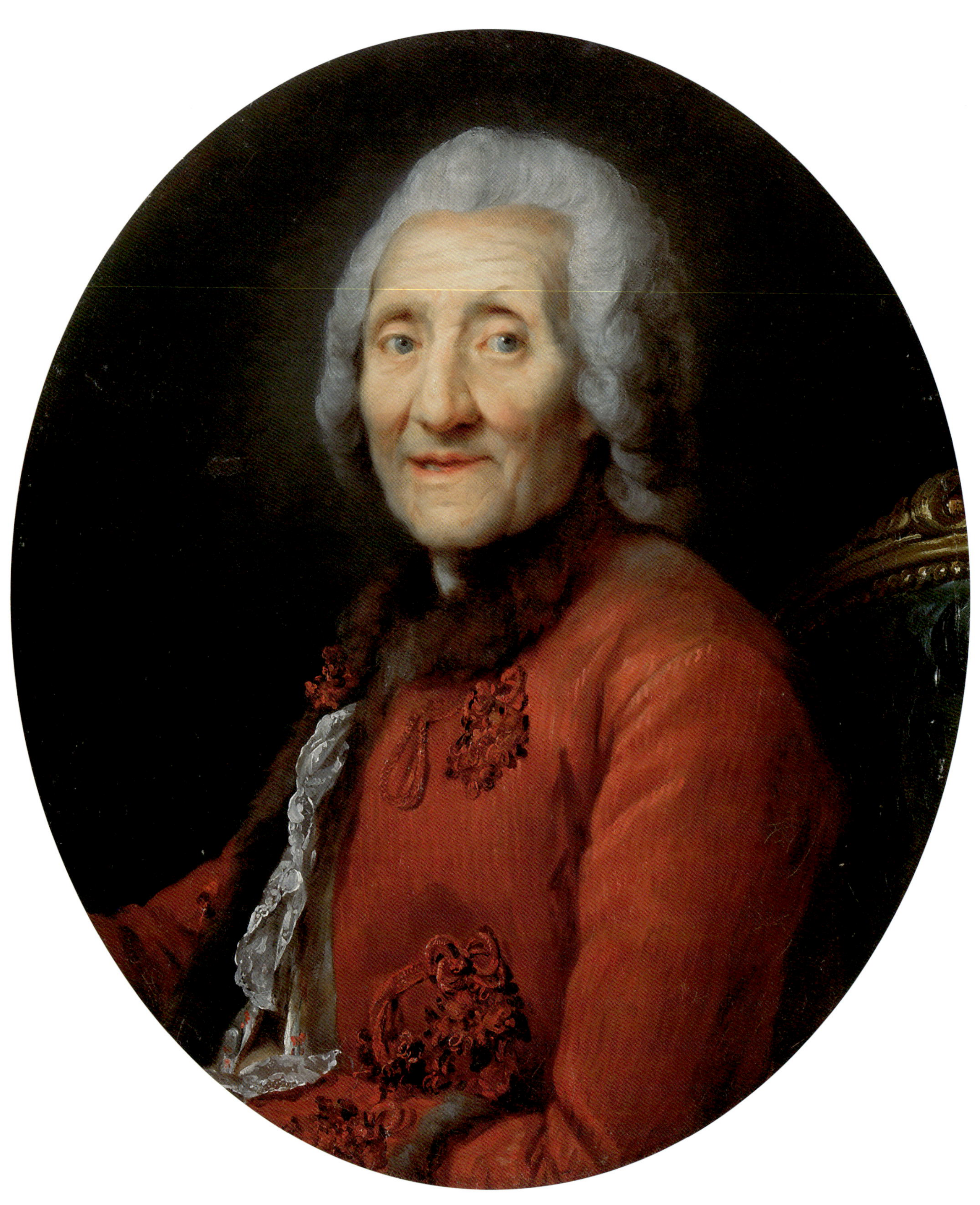

Portrait of Joseph-Charles Roettiers (1692–1779),
1777

Oil on canvas, oval
25⅝ × 21¼ in.
Musée national des Châteaux de Versailles et de
Trianon, MV 5892
(cat. 46)

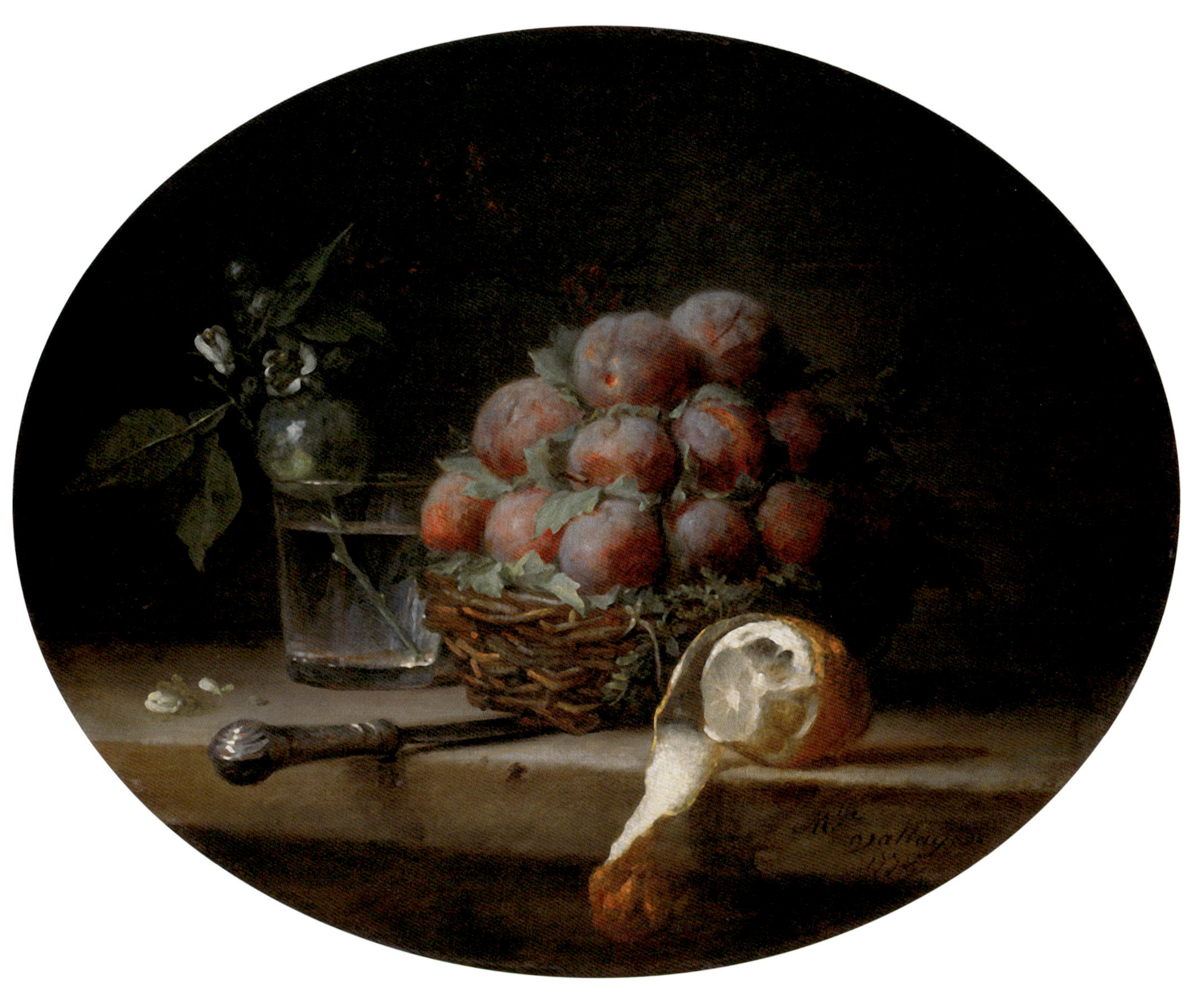

[24] *Still Life with Plums and a Lemon*, 1778

Oil on canvas, oval
16⅜ × 18⅝ in.
Fine Arts Museums of San Francisco, Gift of
Mr. and Mrs. Louis A. Benoist, 1960.30
(cat. 49)

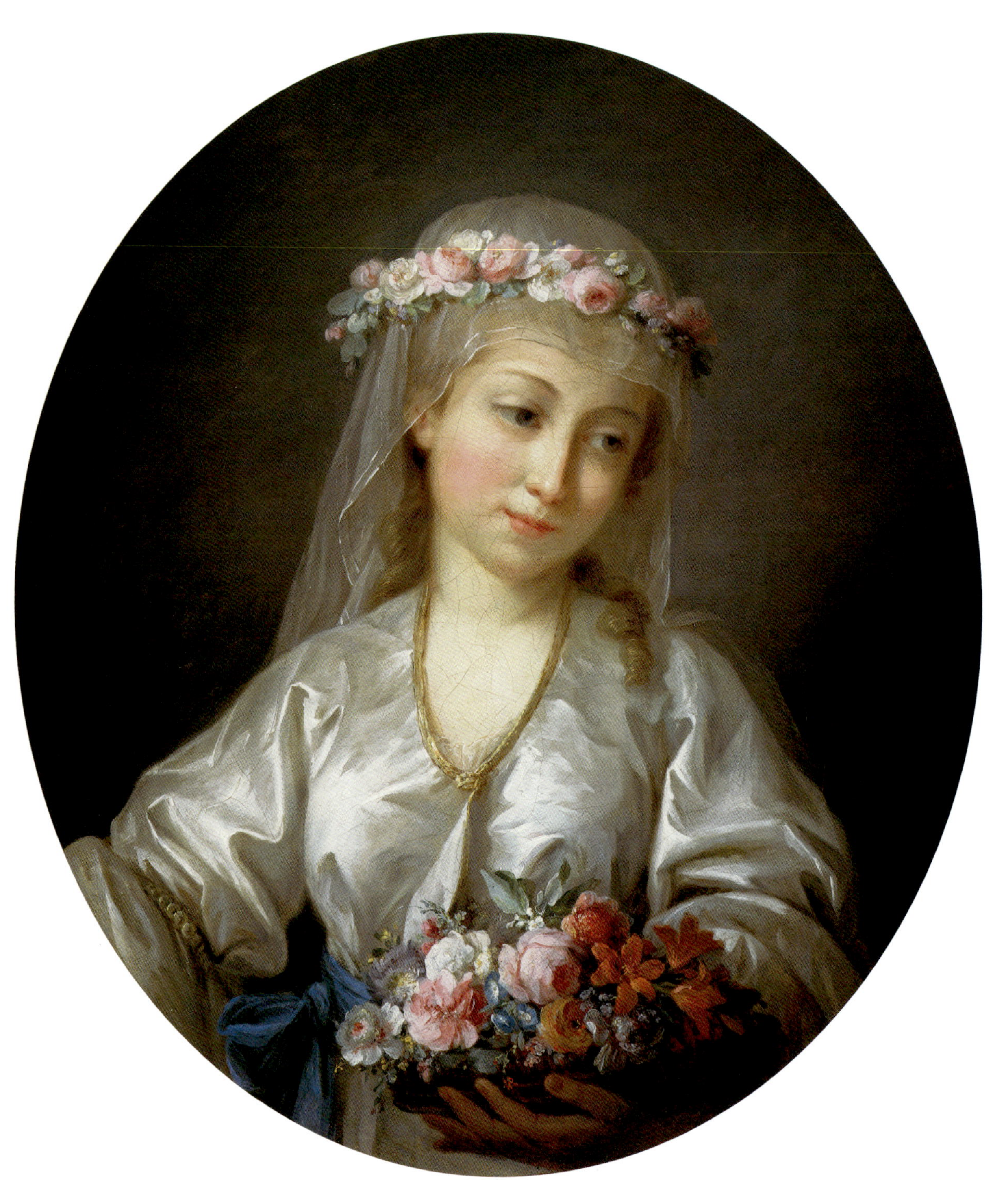

[25] *Bust of a Young Vestal*, 1779

Oil on canvas, oval
18⅛ × 15⅛ in.
Private collection
(cat. 53)

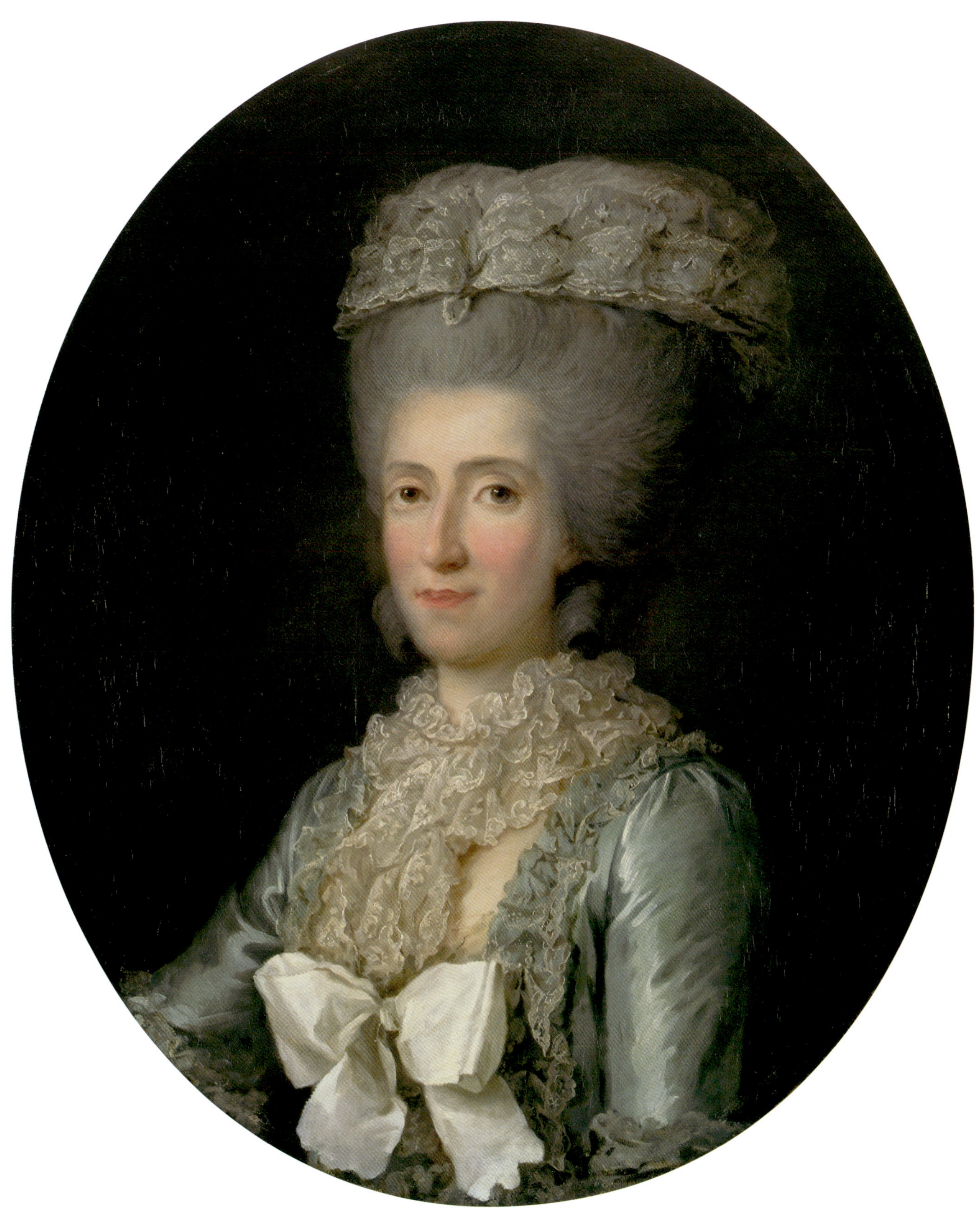

[26] *Portrait of Sophie-Philippe-Elisabeth-Justine de France (1734–1782), called Madame Sophie*, 1779

Oil on canvas, oval
28⅛ × 22⅞ in.
Musée national des Châteaux de Versailles et de
Trianon, MV 3803
(cat. 55)

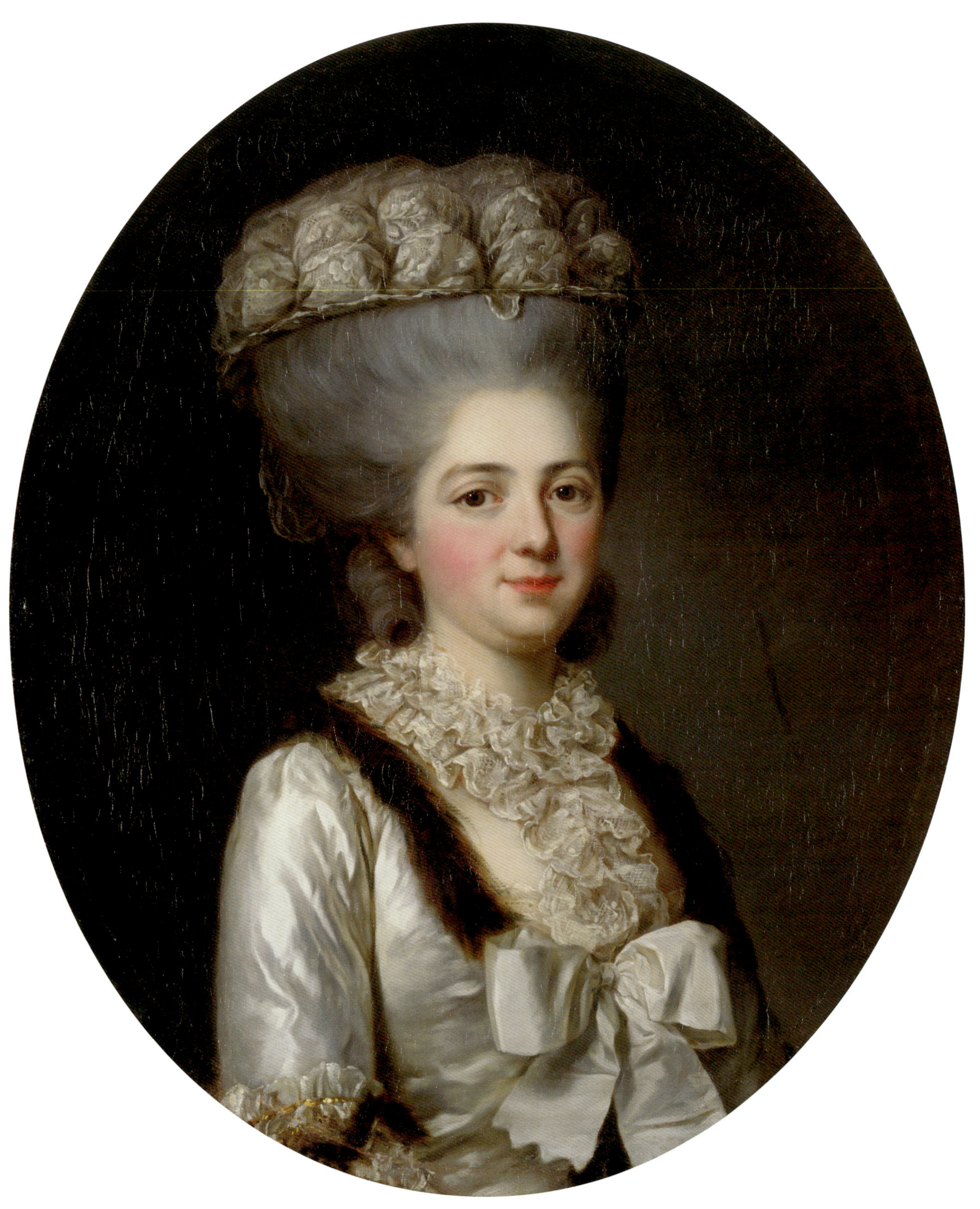

[27]   *Portrait of Marie-Louise-Thérèse-Victoire de France*
         (1733–1799), called Madame Victoire, 1780

Oil on canvas, oval
28⅛ × 22⅞ in.
Musée national des Châteaux de Versailles et de
Trianon, MV 3807
(cat. 60)

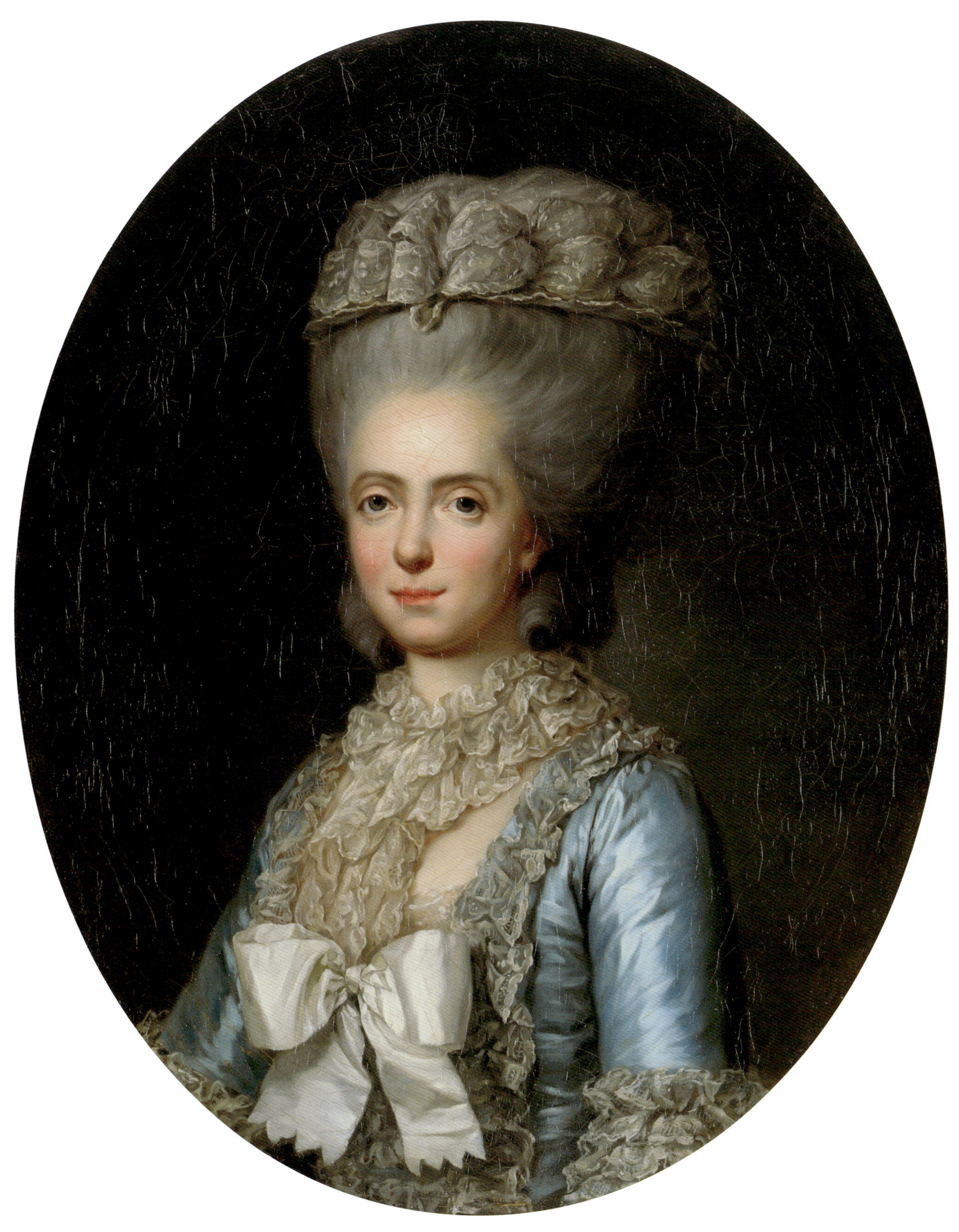

[28] *Portrait of Marie-Adélaïde-Louise de France*
(1732–1800), called Madame Adélaïde, 1780

Oil on canvas, oval
28⅜ × 23¼ in.
Musée national des Châteaux de Versailles et de
Trianon, MV 3812
(cat. 59)

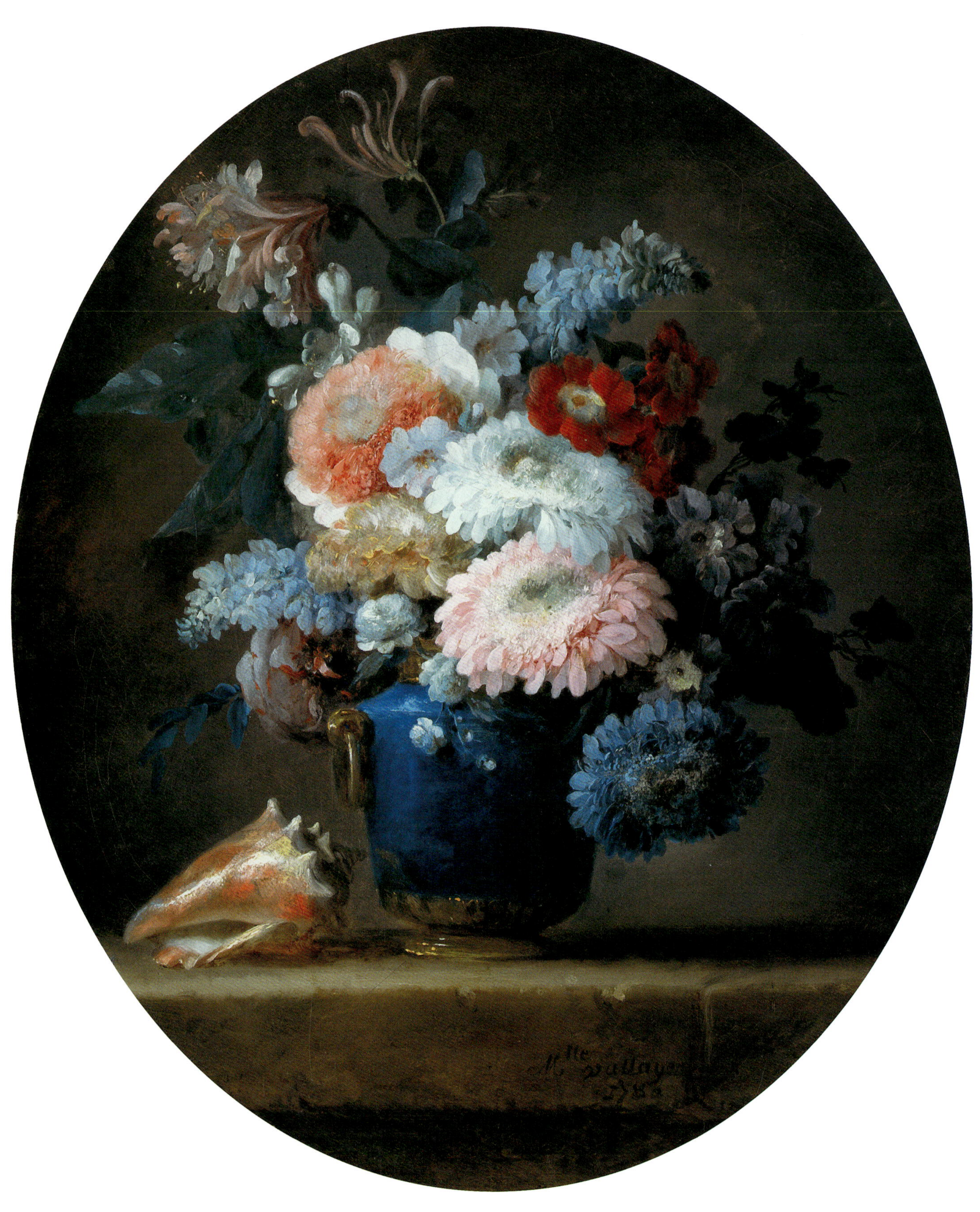

[29]   *Vase of Flowers*, 1780

Oil on canvas, oval
19¾ × 15 in.
The Metropolitan Museum of Art; gift of J. Pierpont
Morgan, 1907, 07.225.504
(cat. 61)

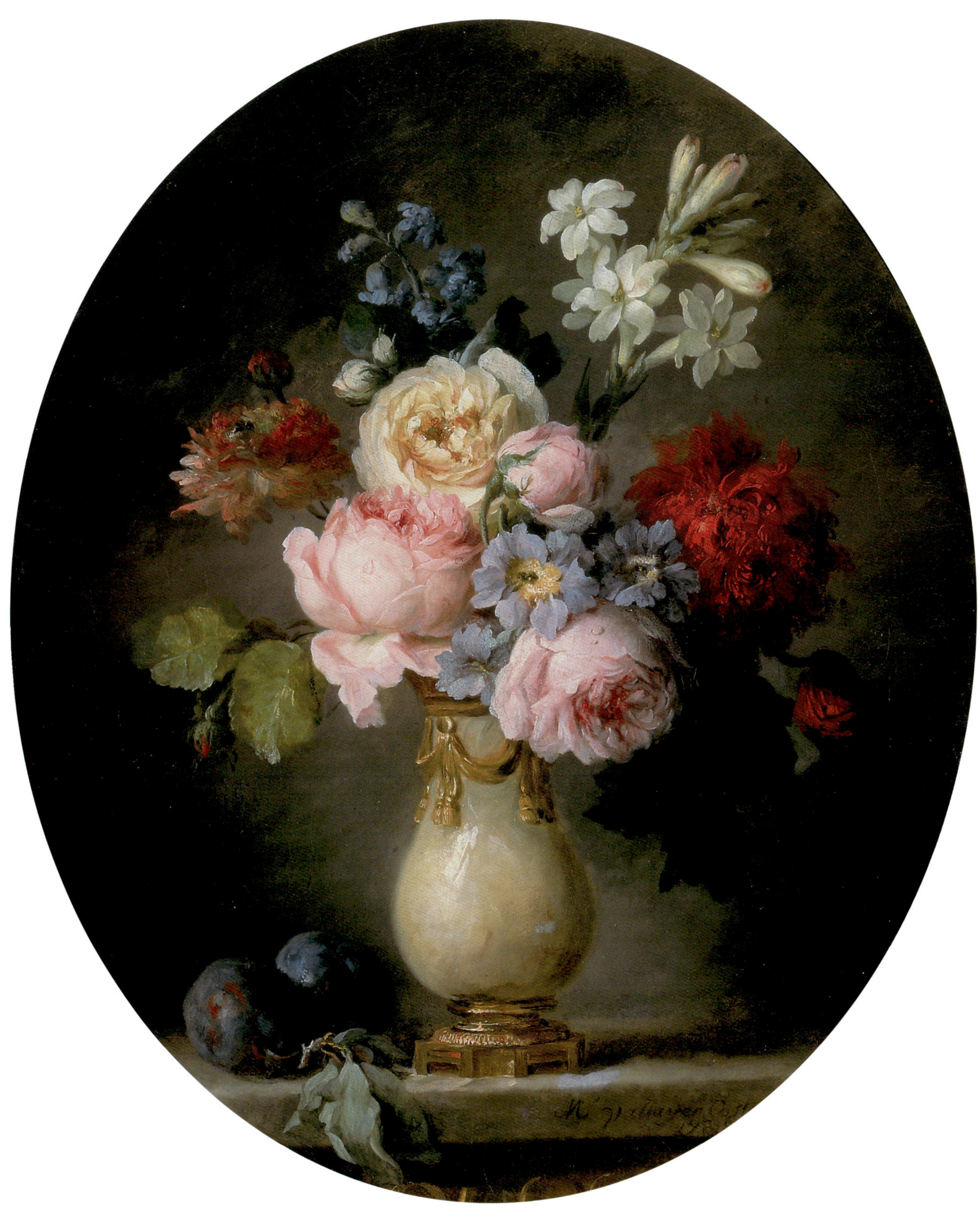

[30]   *A Vase of Flowers and Two Plums on a Marble Tabletop*, 1781

Oil on canvas, oval
18⅞ × 15¾ in.
Michael L. Rosenberg, Dallas
(cat. 67)

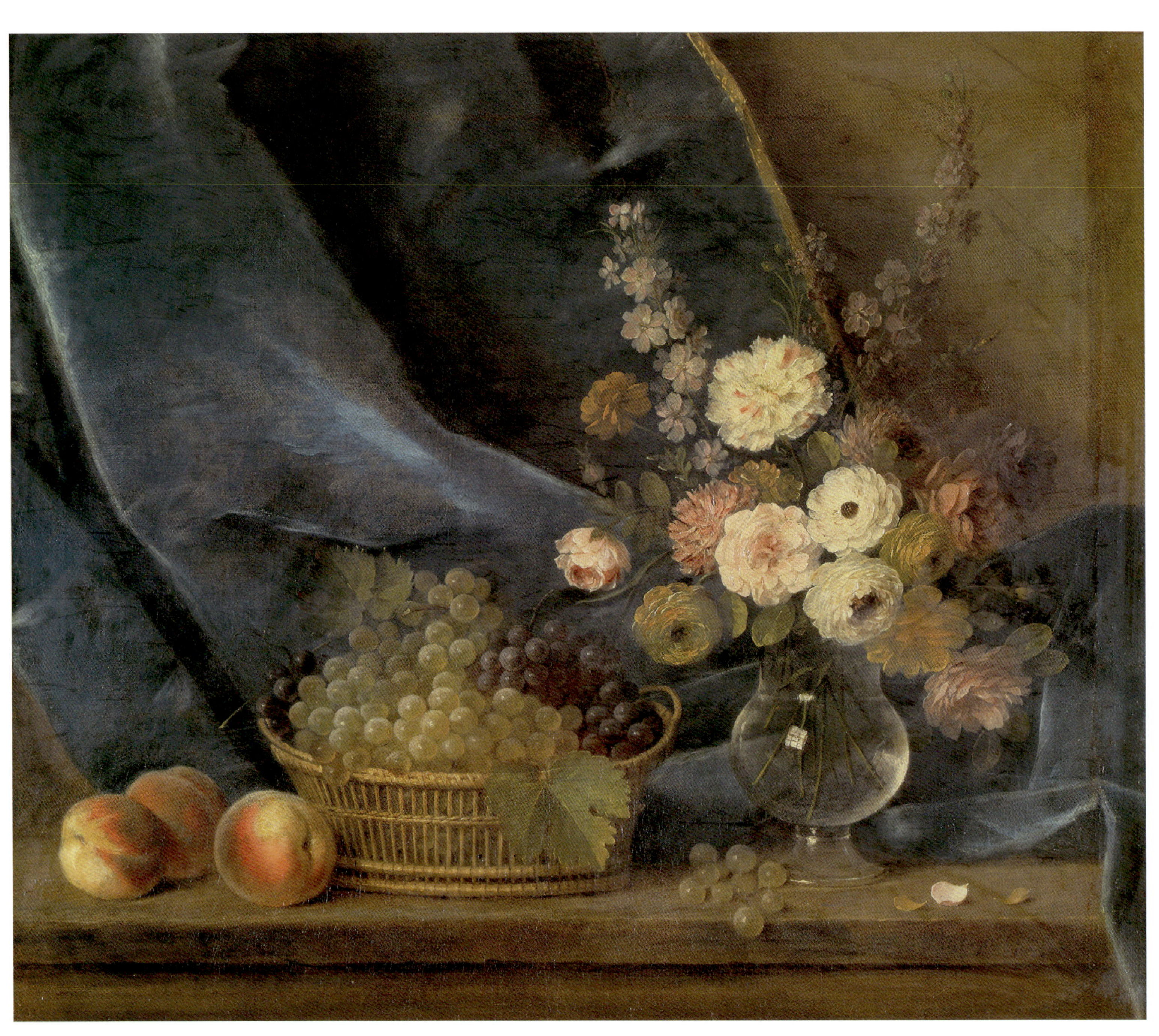

[31]   *Flowers and Fruit with Blue Curtain*, 1781

Oil on canvas
28¾ × 33⅛ in.
Private collection, Paris
(cat. 64)

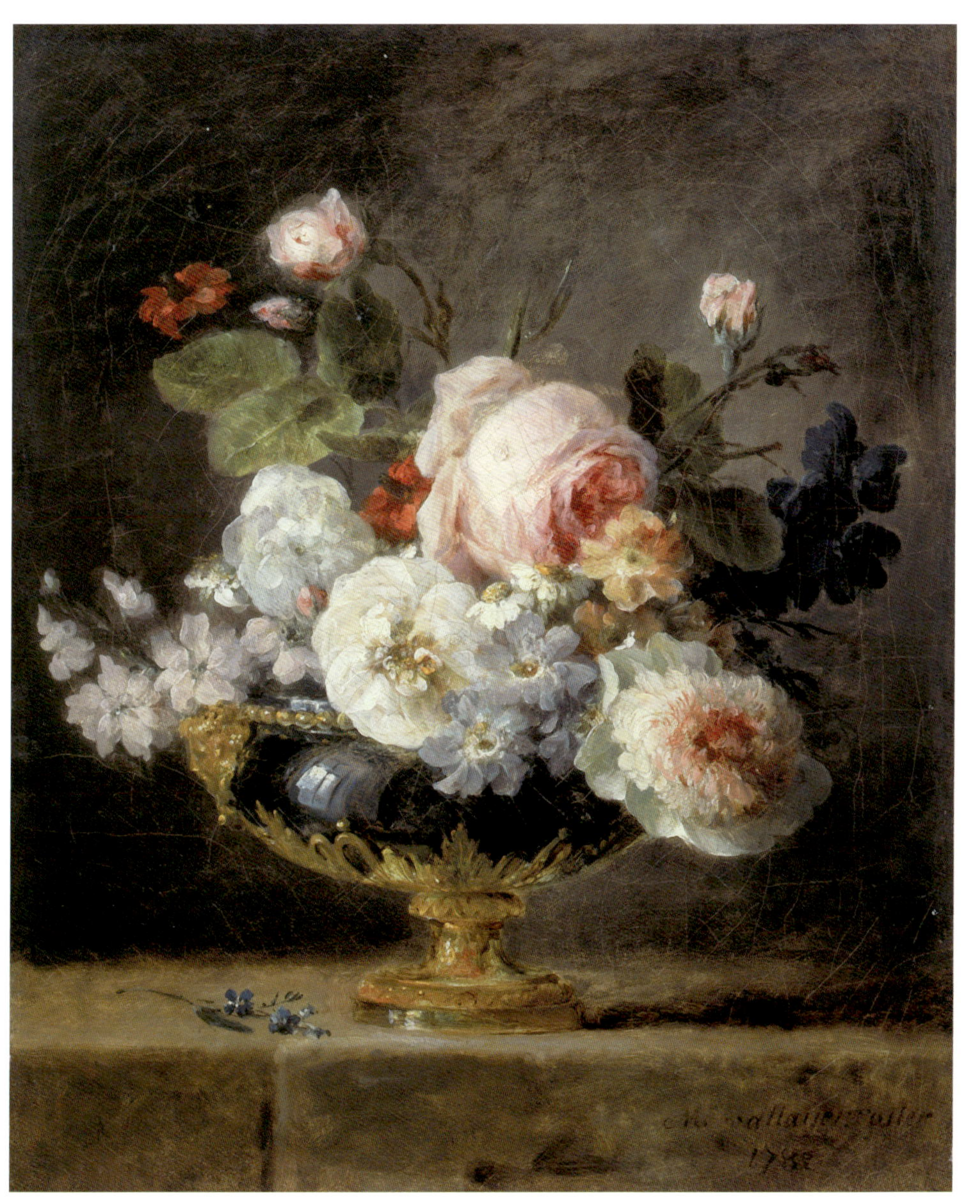

[32]   *Flowers in a Blue Porcelain Vase,* 1782

Oil on canvas
16 × 12¾ in.
Private collection
(cat. 68)

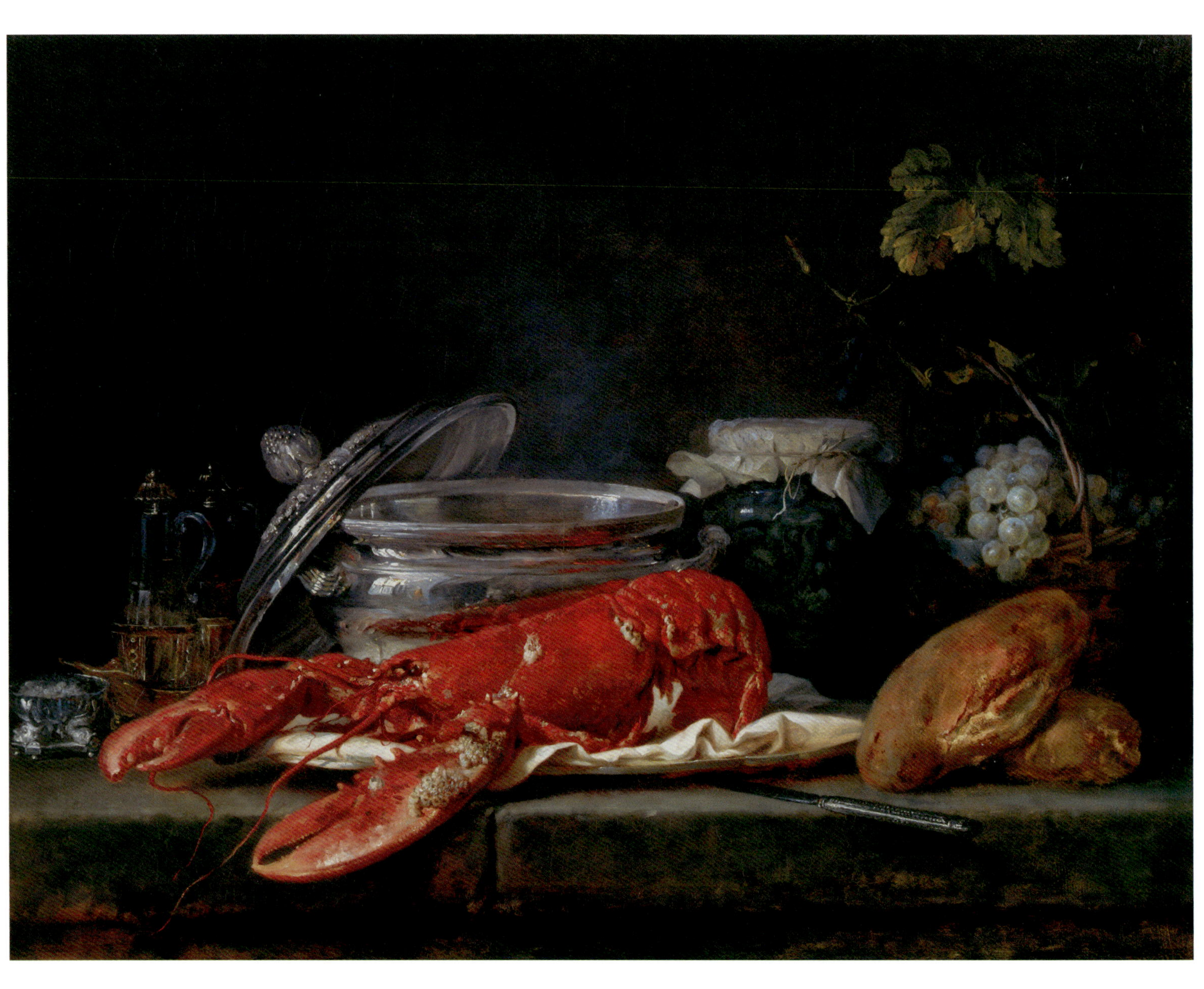

[33] *Still Life with Lobster*, 1781

Oil on canvas
27¾ × 35¼ in.
Toledo Museum of Art, Toledo, Ohio; Purchased with
Funds from the Libbey Endowment, gift of Edward
Drummond Libbey, 1968.1A
(cat. 65)

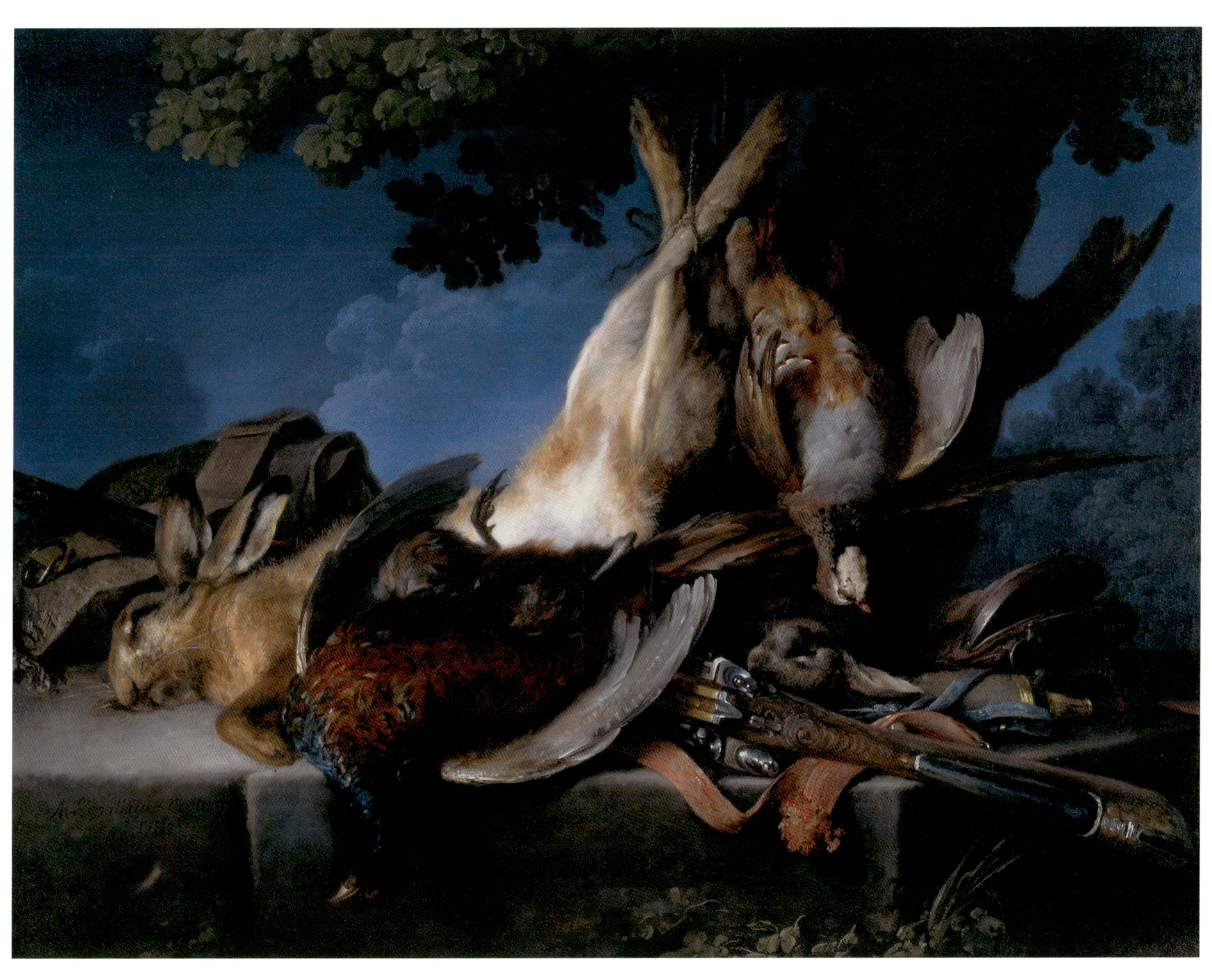

[34]   *Still Life with Game*, 1782

Oil on canvas
28 × 35¼ in.
Toledo Museum of Art, Toledo, Ohio; Purchased with
Funds from the Libbey Endowment, gift of Edward
Drummond Libbey, 1968.1B
(cat. 69)

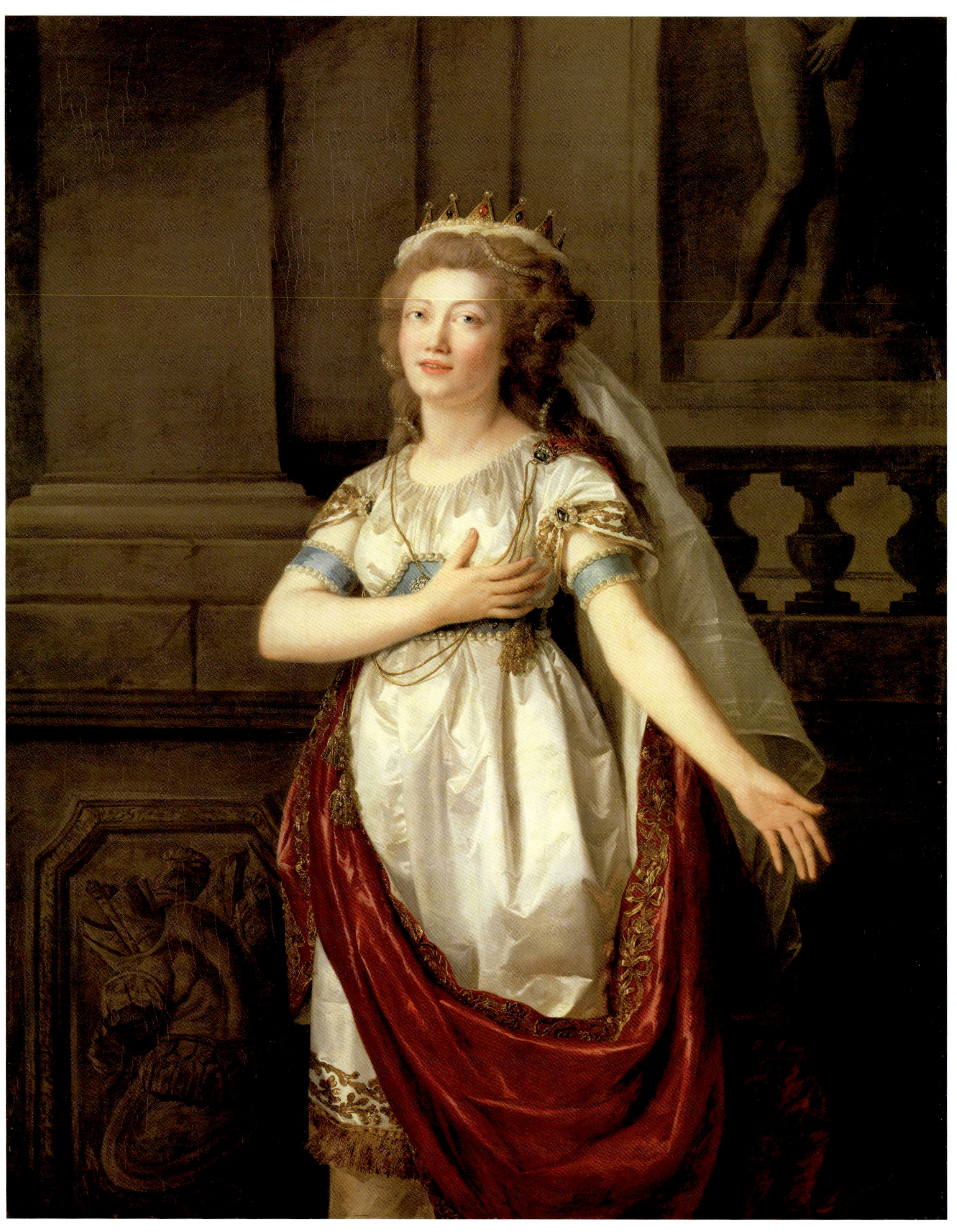

[35]   *Madame de Saint-Huberty in the Rôle of Dido*, 1785

Oil on canvas
57³/₈ × 40 in.
Collection of Wallace and Wilhelmina Holladay
(cat. 72)

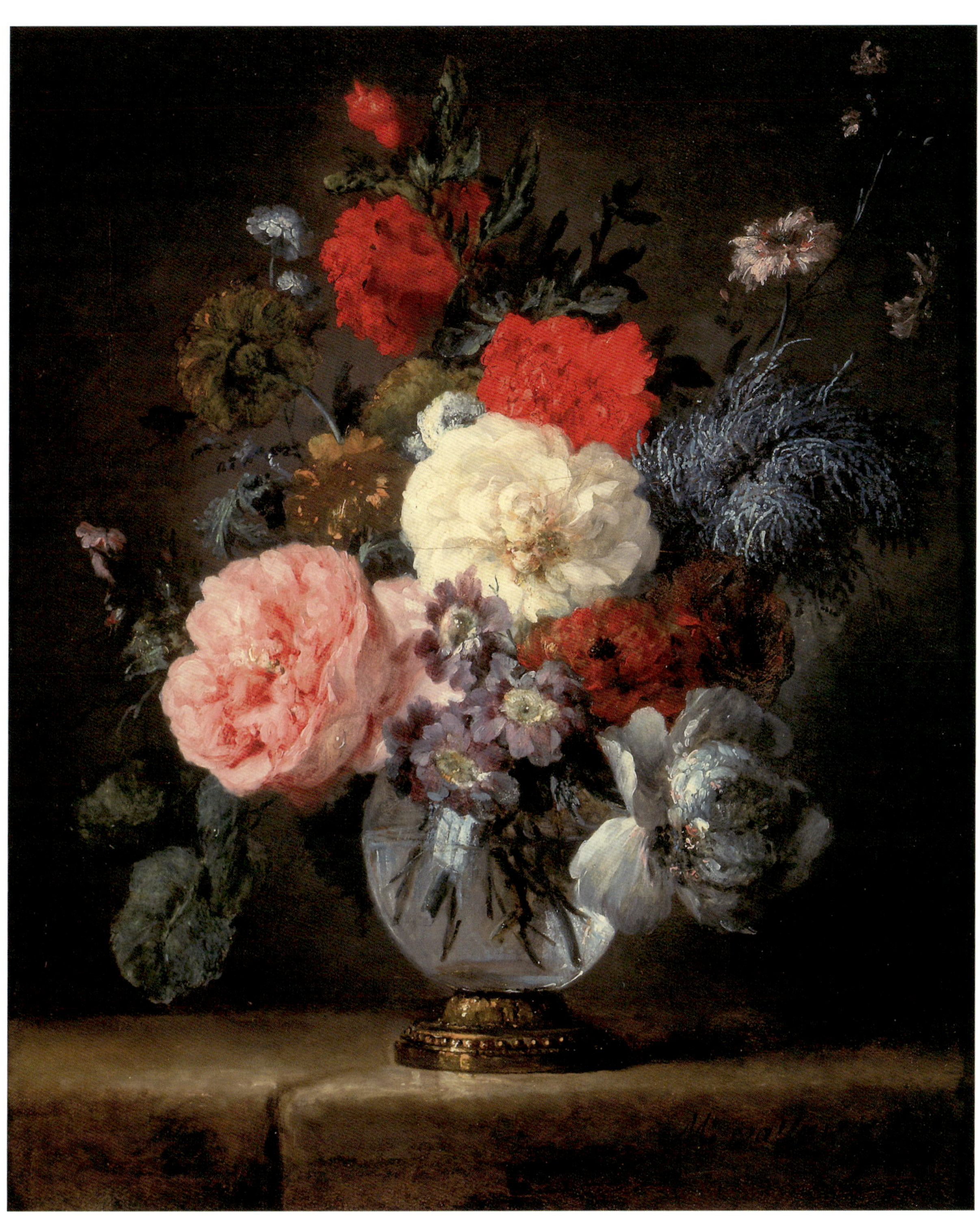

[36] *Flowers in a Crystal Vase*, 1786

Oil on canvas
15 × 12¼ in.
Private collection
(cat. 76)

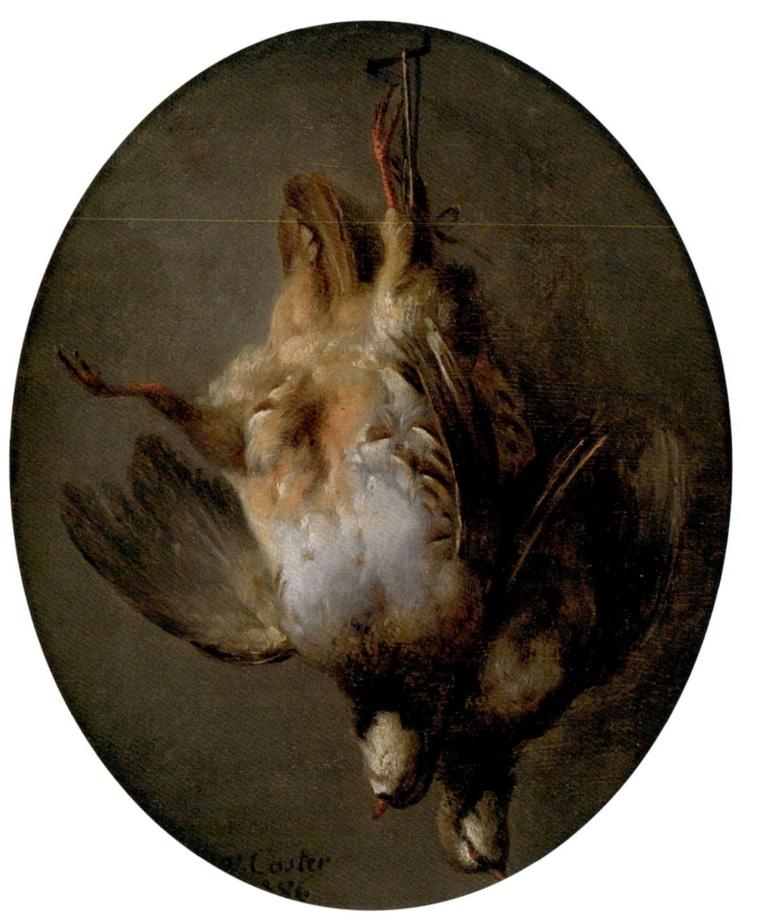

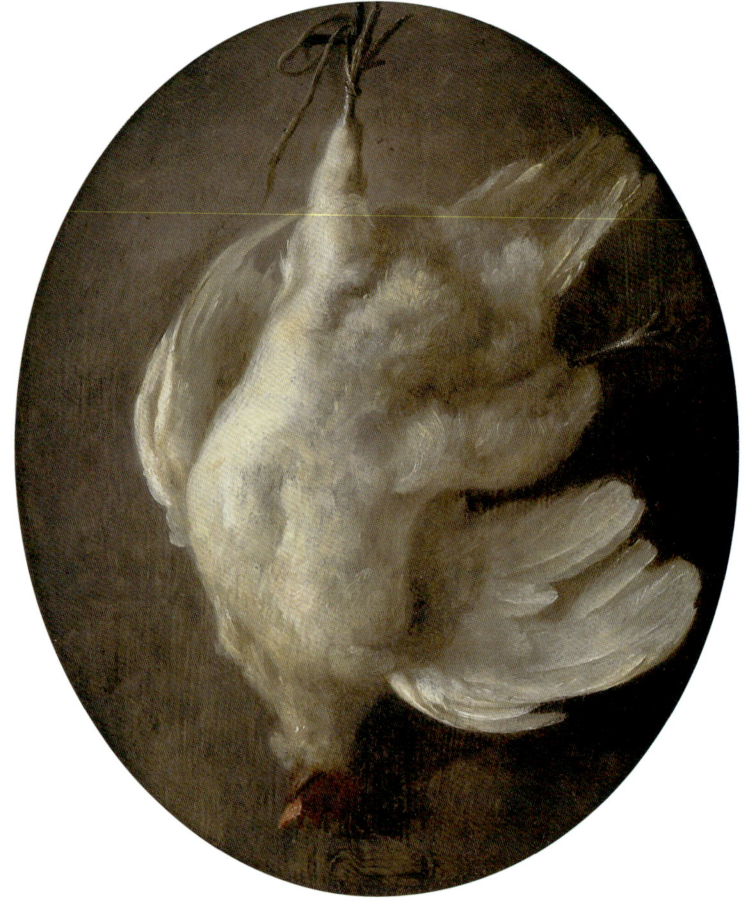

[37] *Partridges*, 1786

Oil on copper, oval
8 × 6½ in.
Marina Rust
(cat. 78)

[38] *A White Hen*, 1786

Oil on copper, oval
8 × 6½ in.
Marina Rust
(cat. 79)

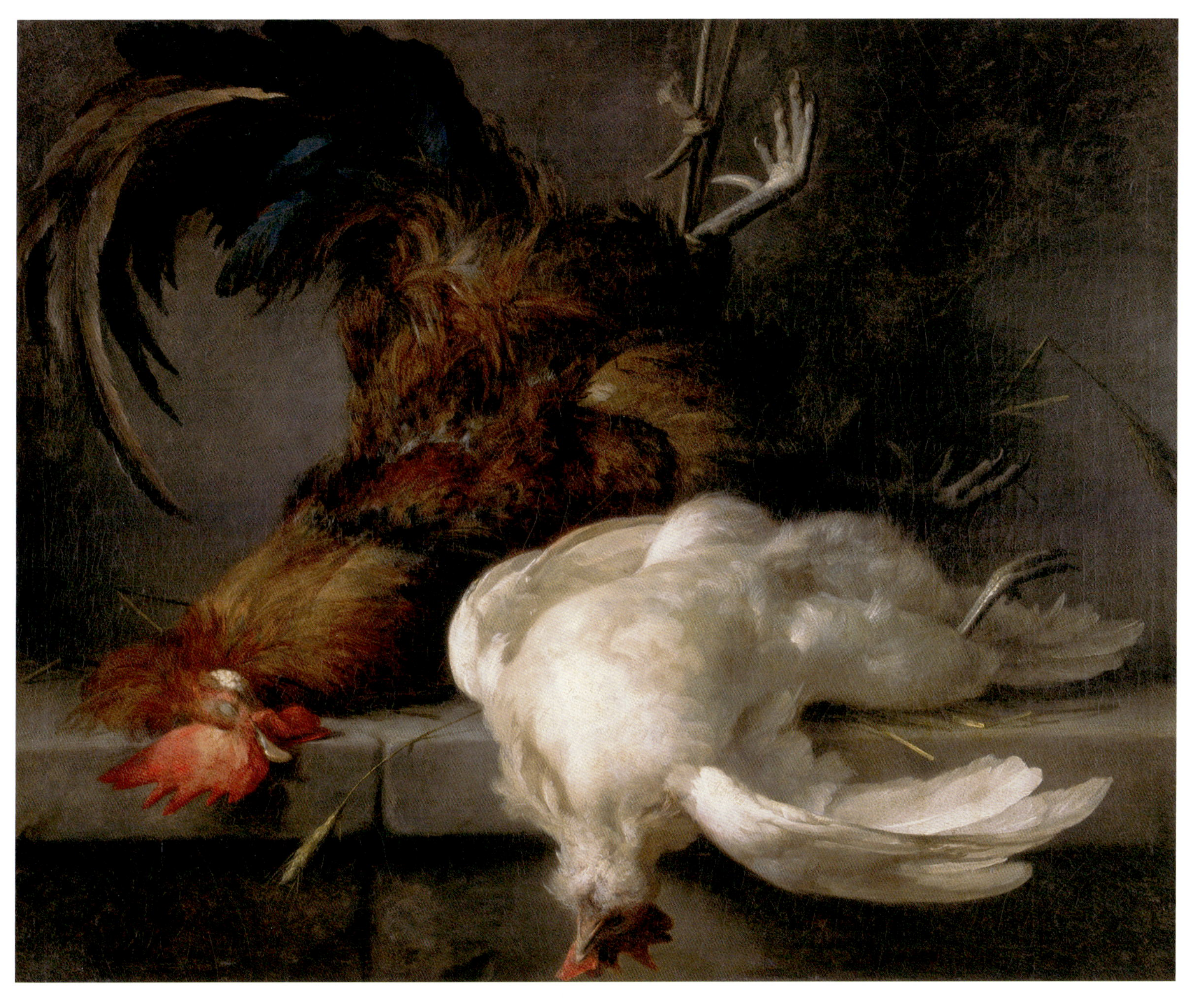

[39] *A Rooster and a White Chicken on a Stone Ledge,*
1787

Oil on canvas
21¼ × 25¼ in.
Musée de Tessé, Le Mans, France, Dépôt de l'Etat 1872
(cat. 80)

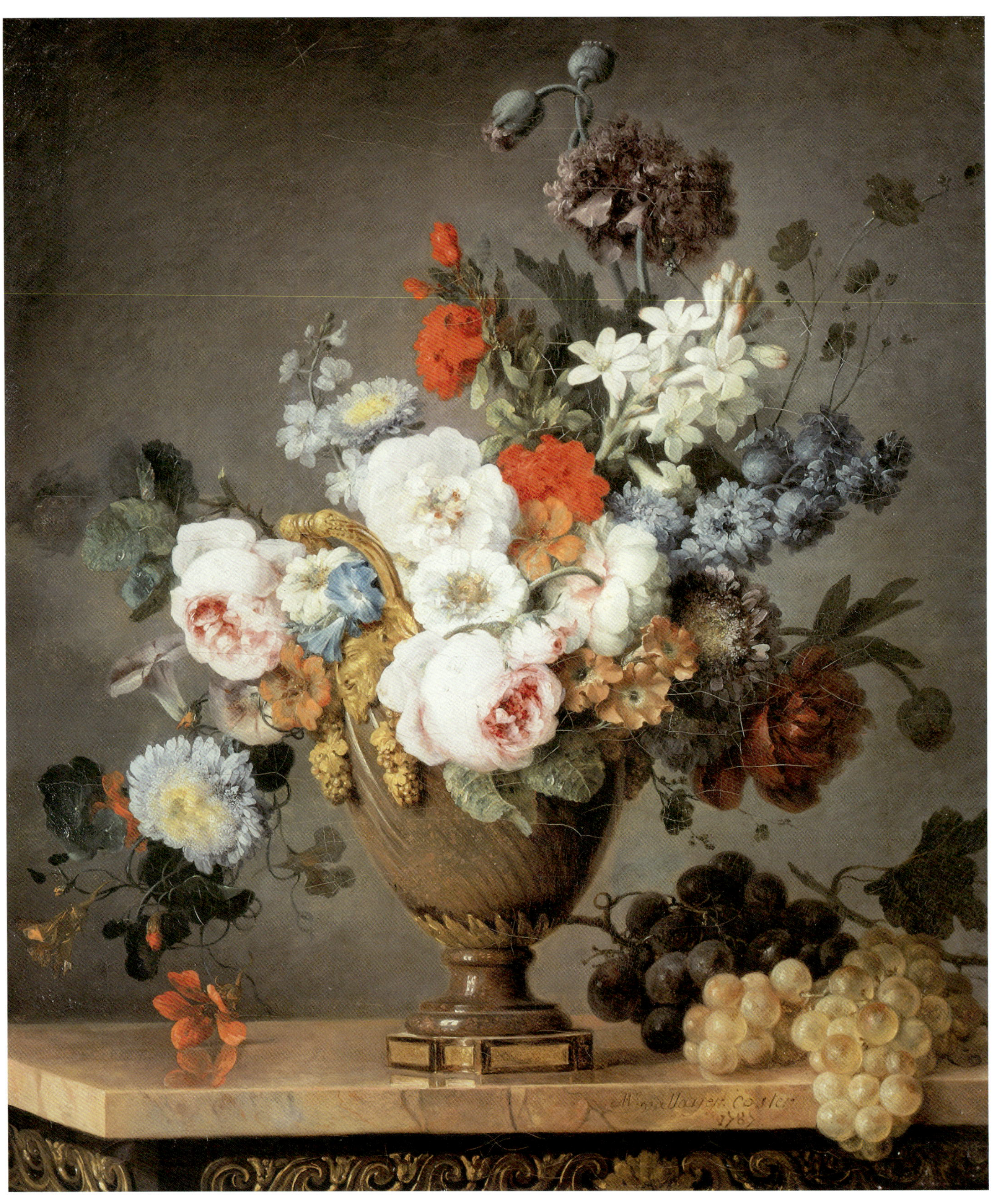

[40]   *Still Life: Flowers and Fruit*, 1787

Oil on canvas
25¼ × 21¼ in.
Collection des Musées d'art et d'histoire,
Ville de Genève, inv. no. CR 207
(cat. 81)

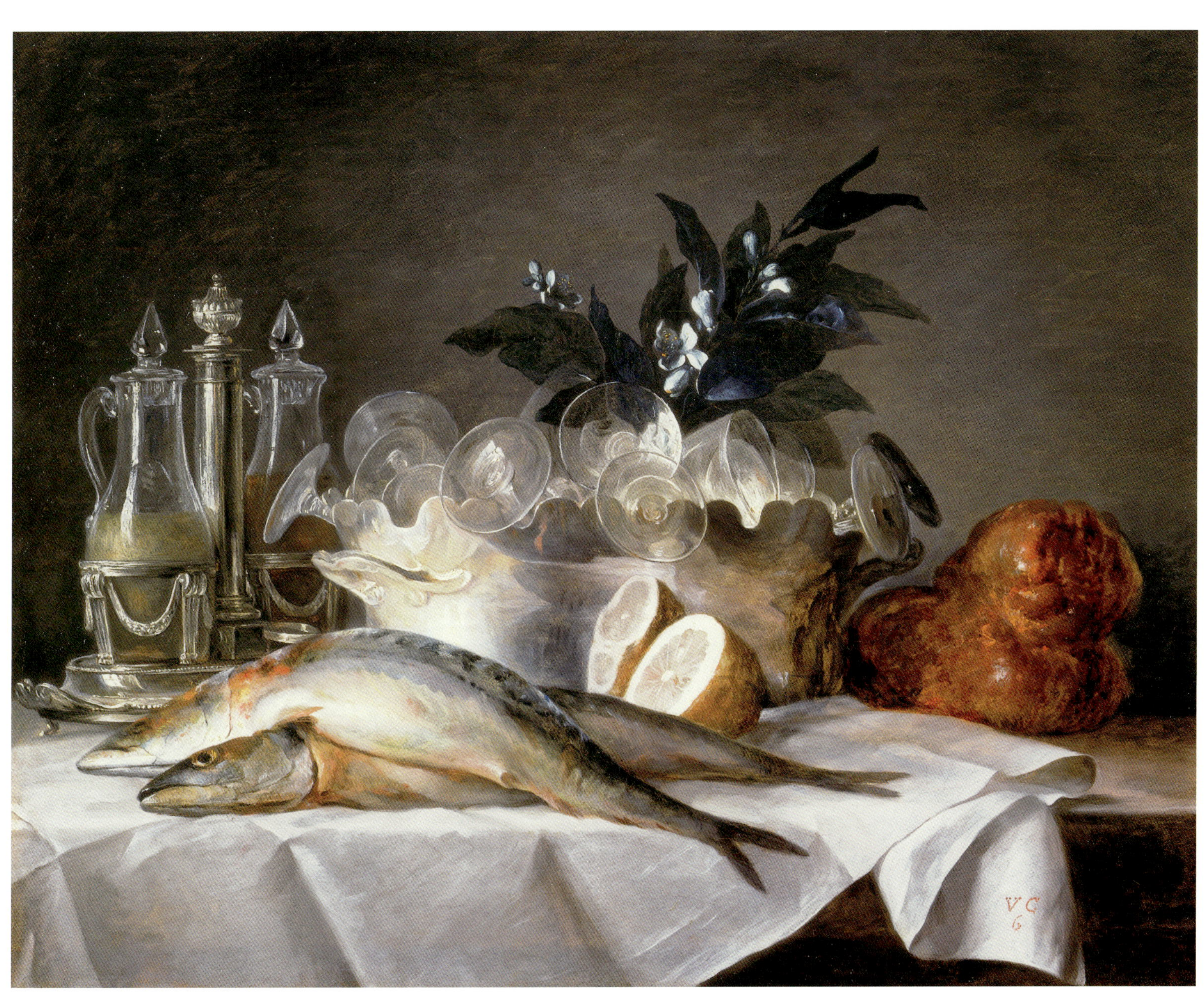

[41]   *Still Life with Glasses and Mackerels*, 1787

Oil on canvas
18¾ × 23½ in.
Mr. and Mrs. Saam Nystad
(cat. 83)

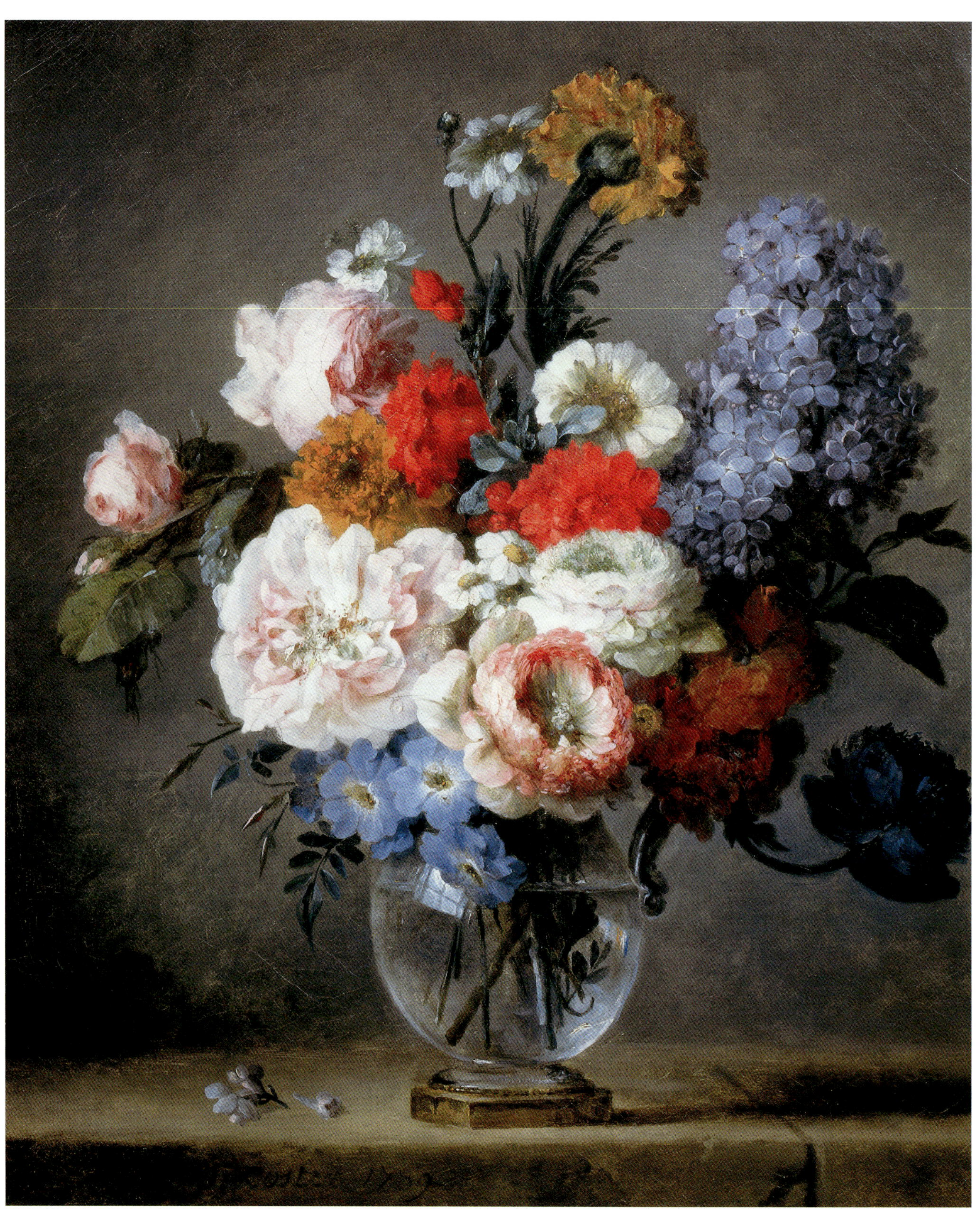

[42] *Flowers in a Crystal Vase*, 1789

Oil on canvas
18⅛ × 15⅜ in.
Private collection, Paris
(cat. 86)

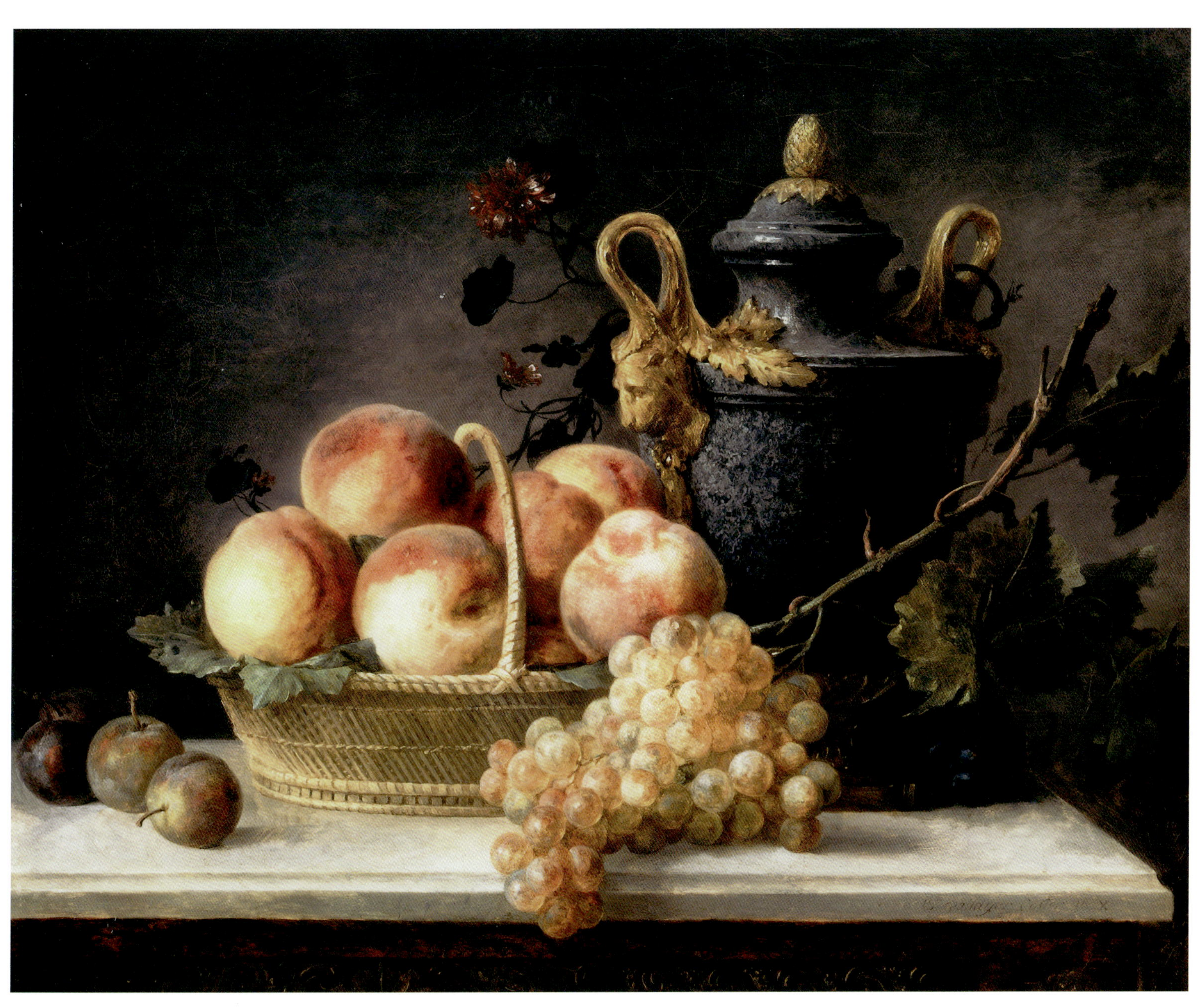

[43]   *Still Life with Porphyry Vase, Basket of Peaches,*
Grapes, and Plums, 1802

Oil on canvas
$18^{1}/_{2} \times 22^{3}/_{8}$ in.
Collection of Abigail Owen-Pontez, Houston
(cat. 95)

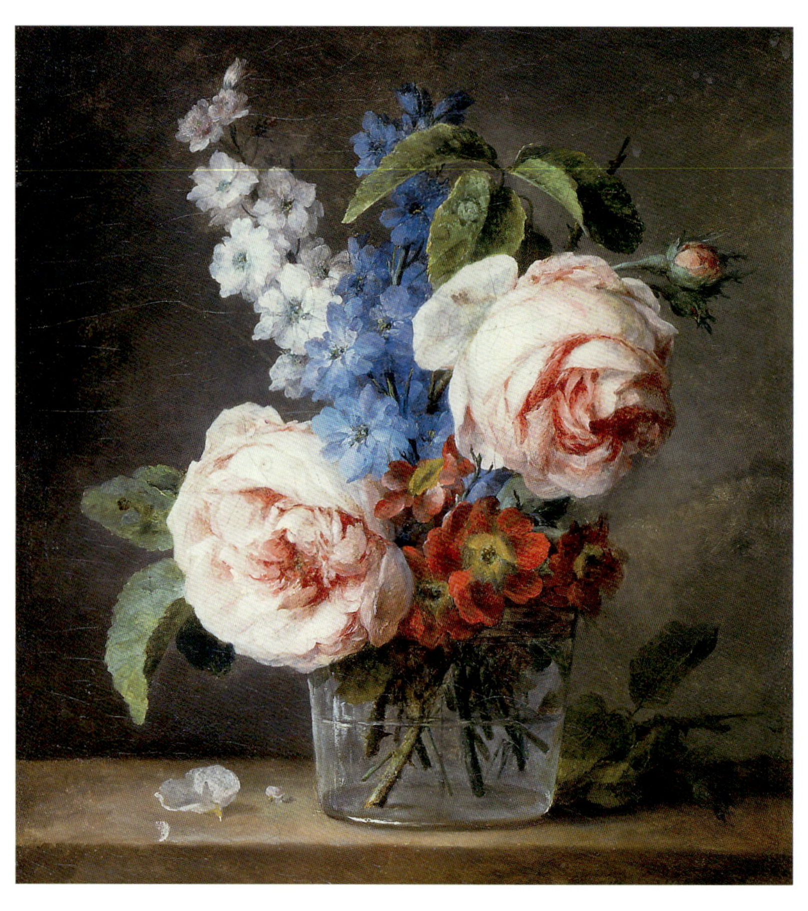

[44]   *Flowers in a Glass Vase,* 1806

Oil on canvas
$12\frac{1}{4} \times 10\frac{5}{8}$ in.
Private collection
(cat. 97)

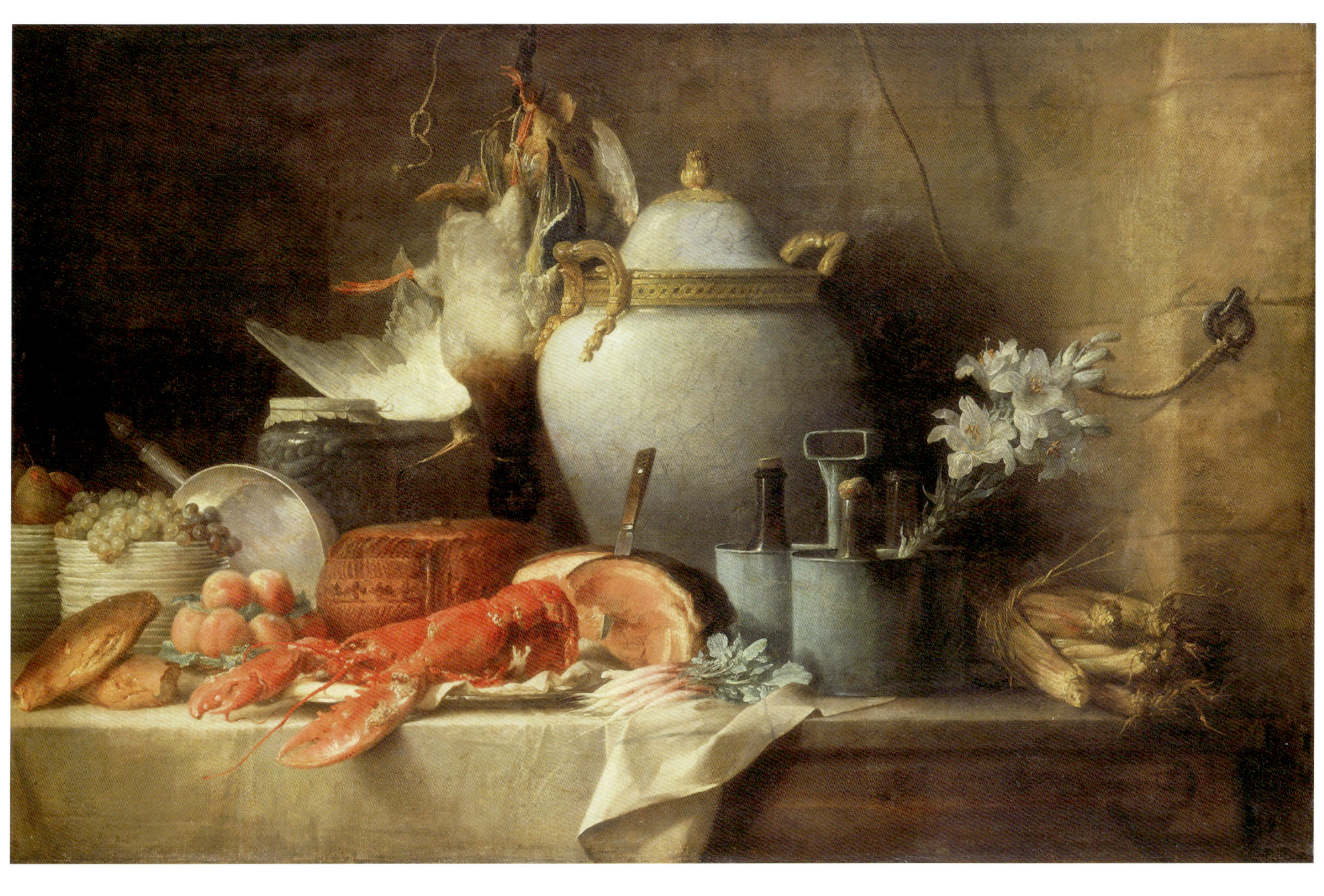

[45]   *Still Life with Lobster*, 1817

Oil on canvas
45¾ × 70⅛ in.
Musée du Louvre, Paris, DL 1977-19
(cat. 99)

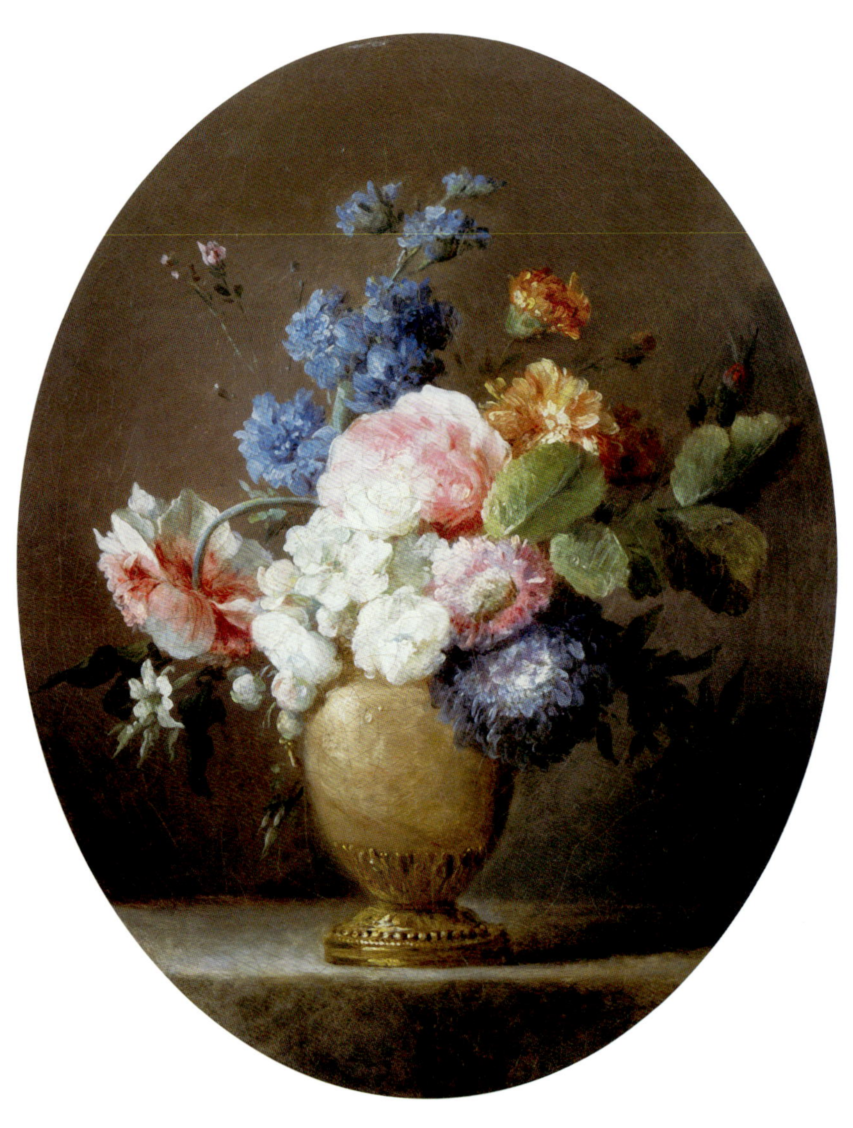

[46]   *Flowers in a Brown Porcelain Vase*, n.d.

Oil on canvas, oval
16⅛ × 12¾ in.
Private collection
(cat. 106)

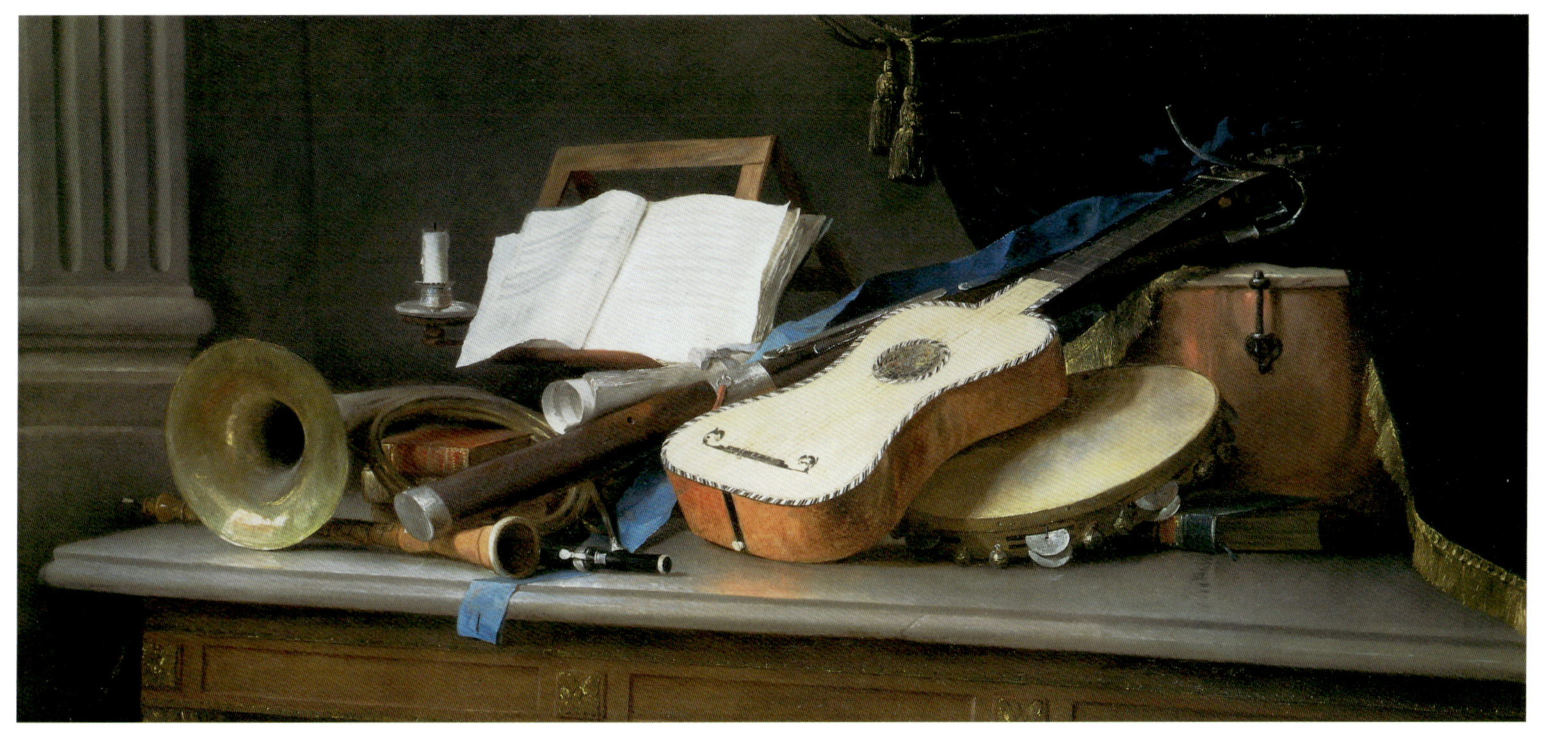

[47]   *Musical Instruments*, n.d.

Oil on canvas
35⅛ × 70½ in.
Private collection, Loan arranged courtesy of
The Matthiesen Gallery, London
(cat. 110)

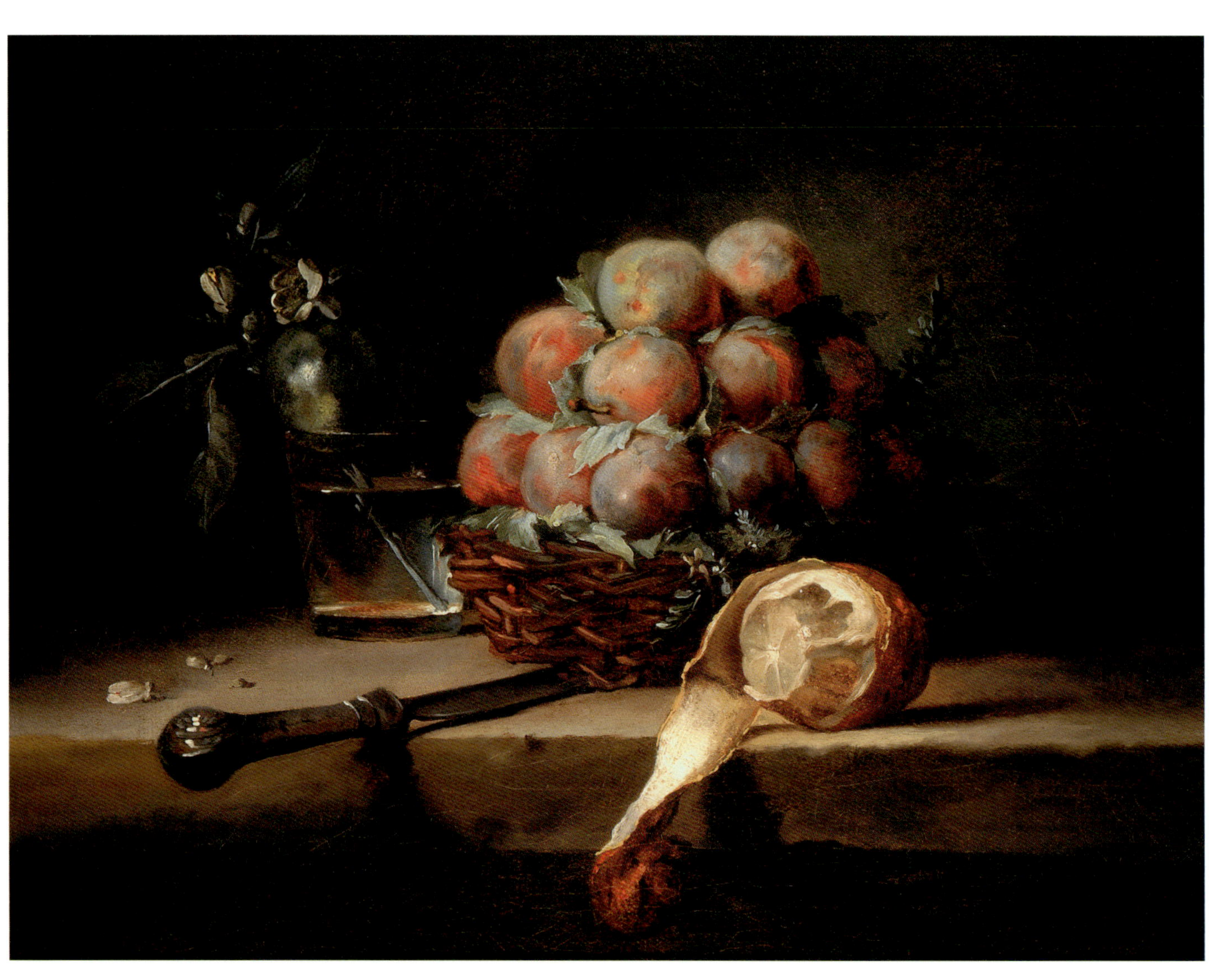

[48] *Plums, a Lemon, and a Knife*, n.d.

Oil on canvas
13¾ × 17¾ in.
Private collection
(cat. 117)

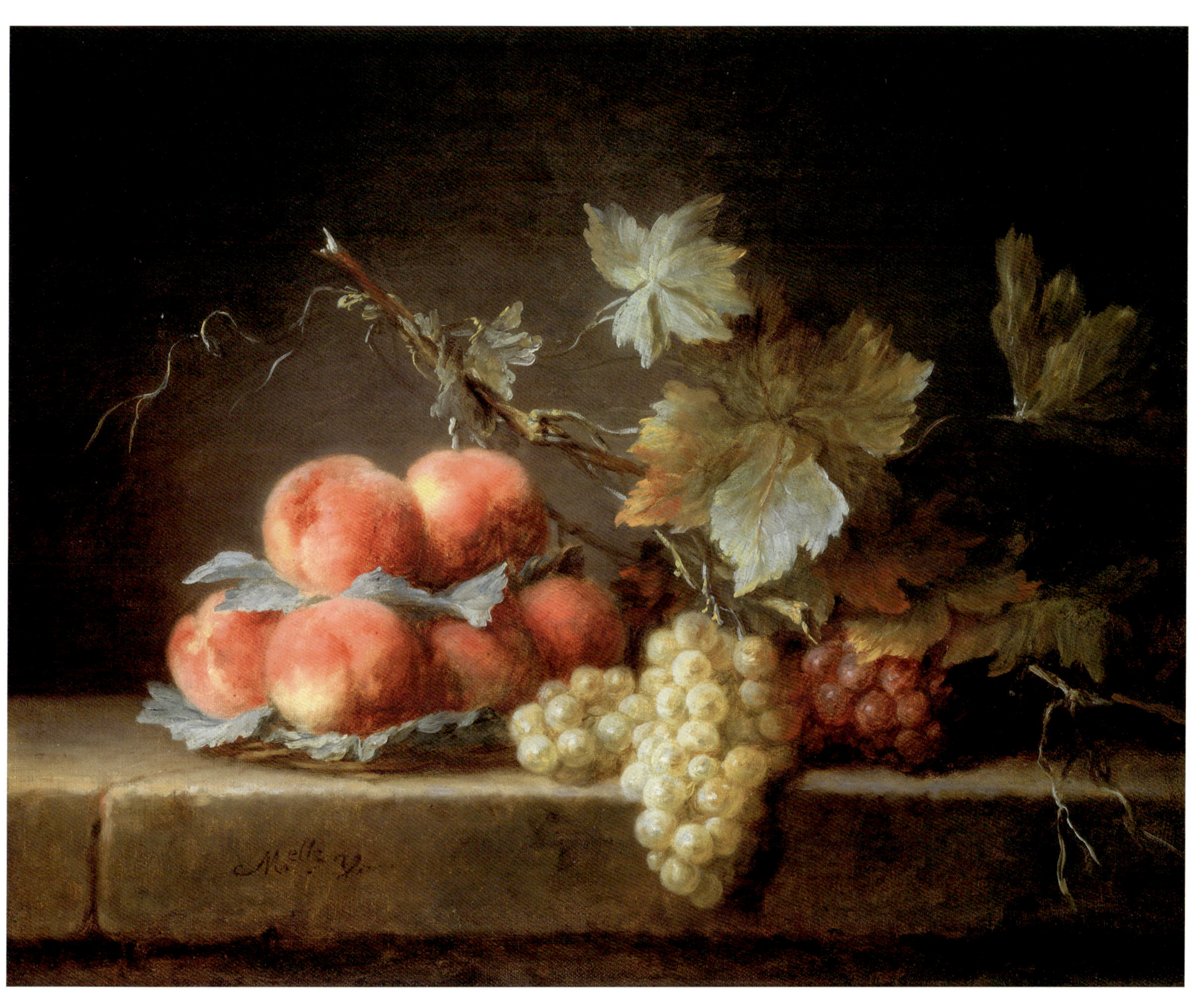

[49] *Still-Life with Peaches and Grapes*, n.d.

Oil on canvas
18⅛ × 21⅝ in.
National Gallery of Canada, Ottawa, Purchased 1965
(cat. 130)

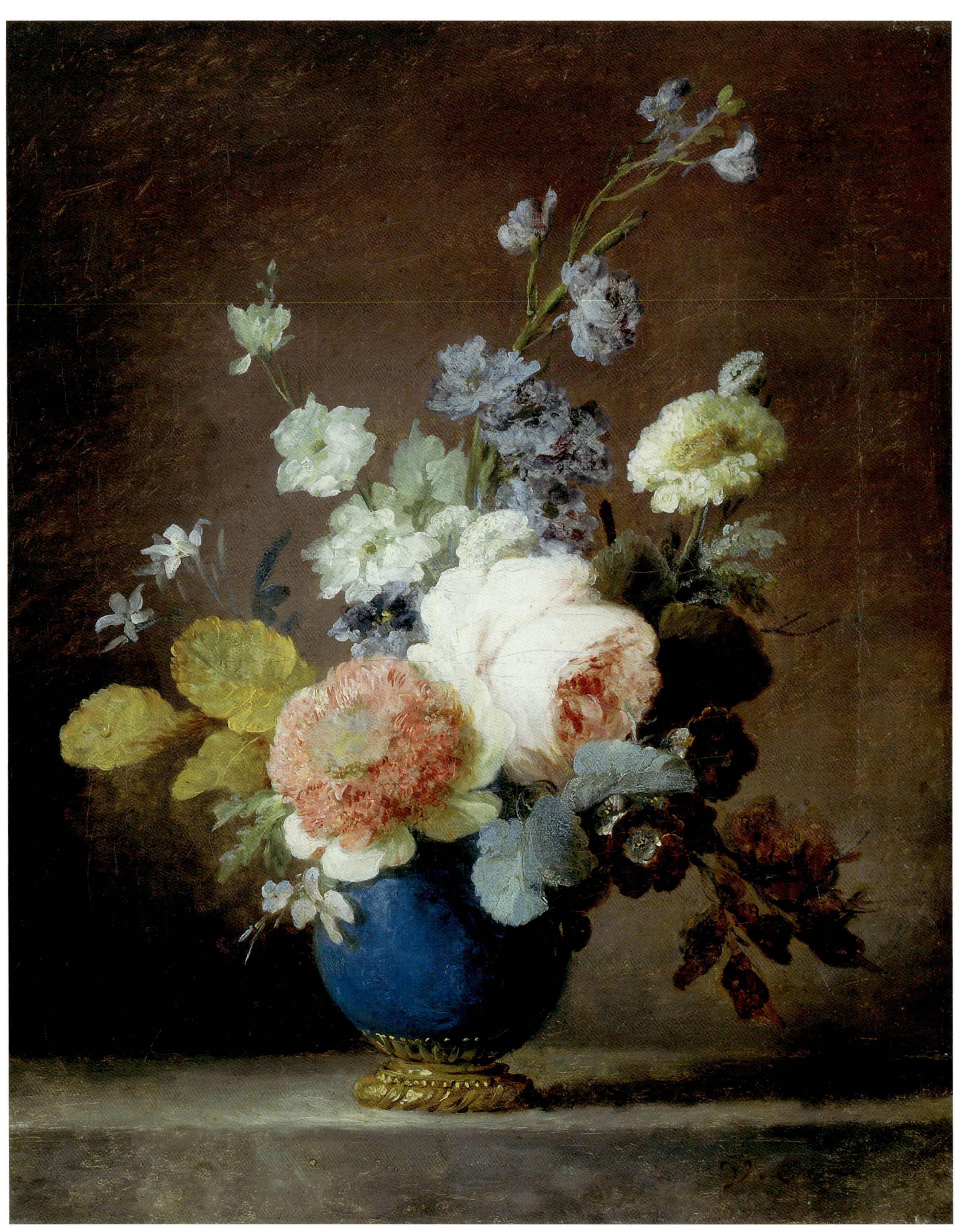

[50]   *Vase of Flowers*, n.d.

Oil on canvas
15¾ × 12¼ in.
Musée des Beaux-Arts, Nancy
(cat. 135)

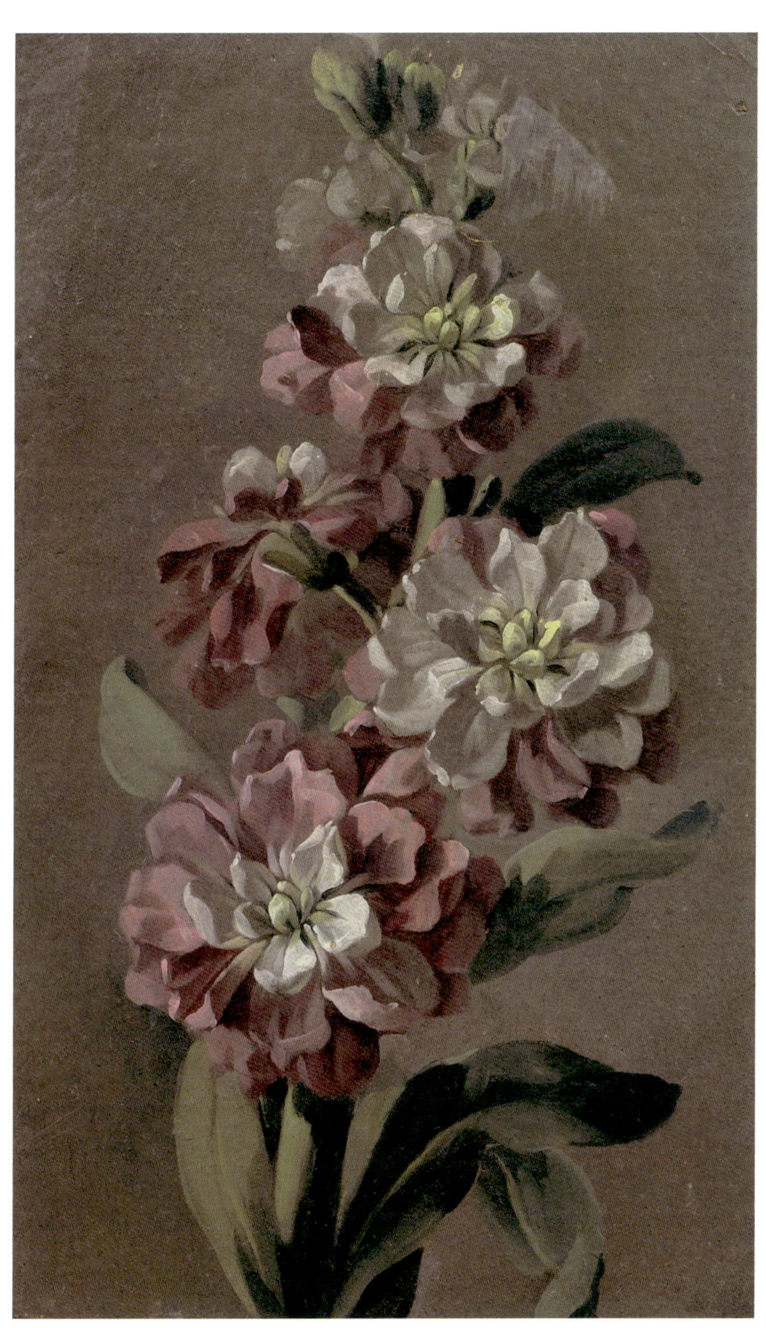

[51]   *Study of a Bouquet of Gillyflowers*, n.d.

Oil on paper affixed to cardboard
8⅞ × 5¼ in.
Private collection
(cat. 131)

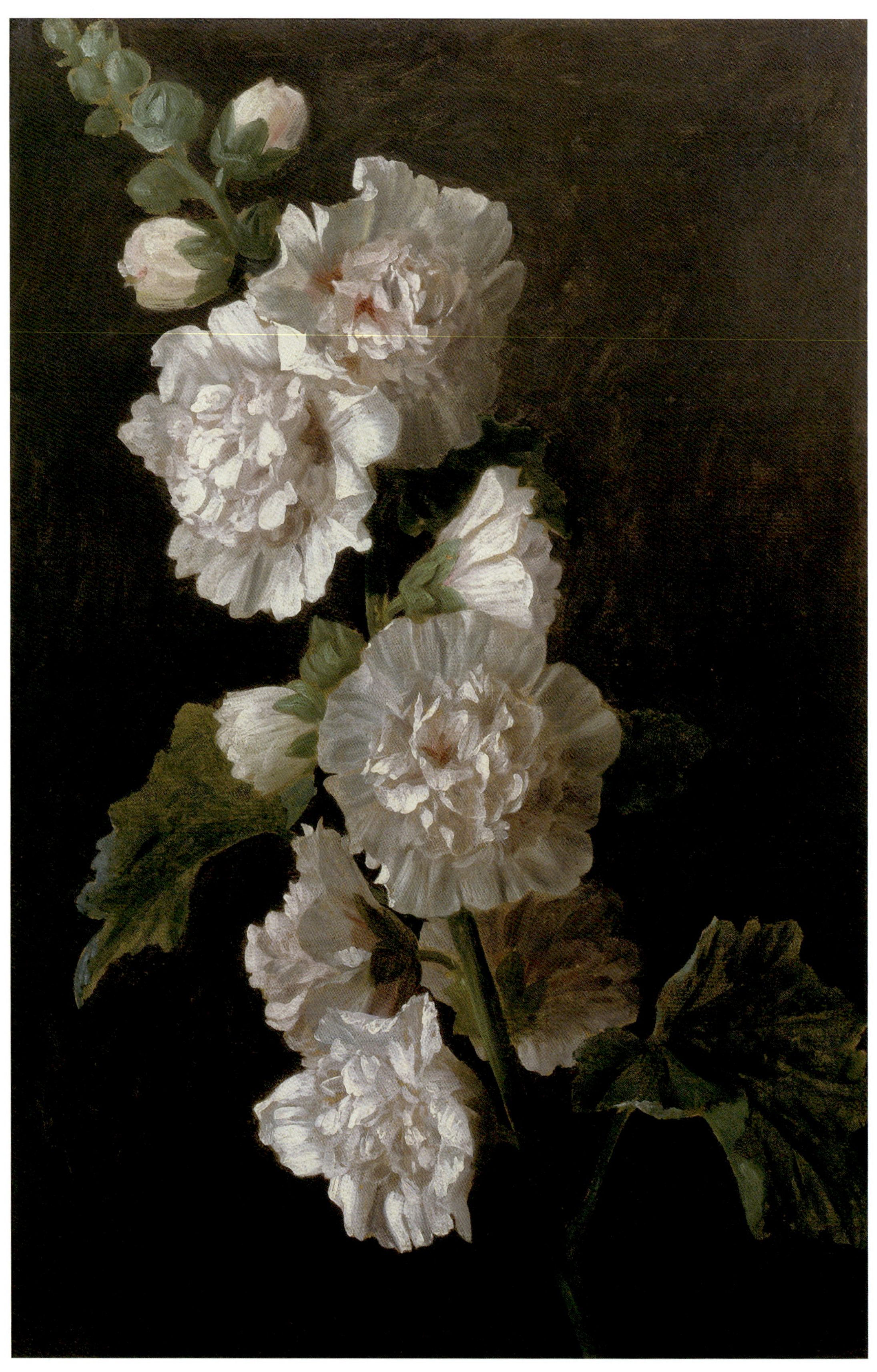

[52] *Study of White Hollyhocks*, n.d.

Oil on paper mounted on board
$25^{5}/_{8} \times 17^{1}/_{8}$ in.
Private collection
(cat. 133)

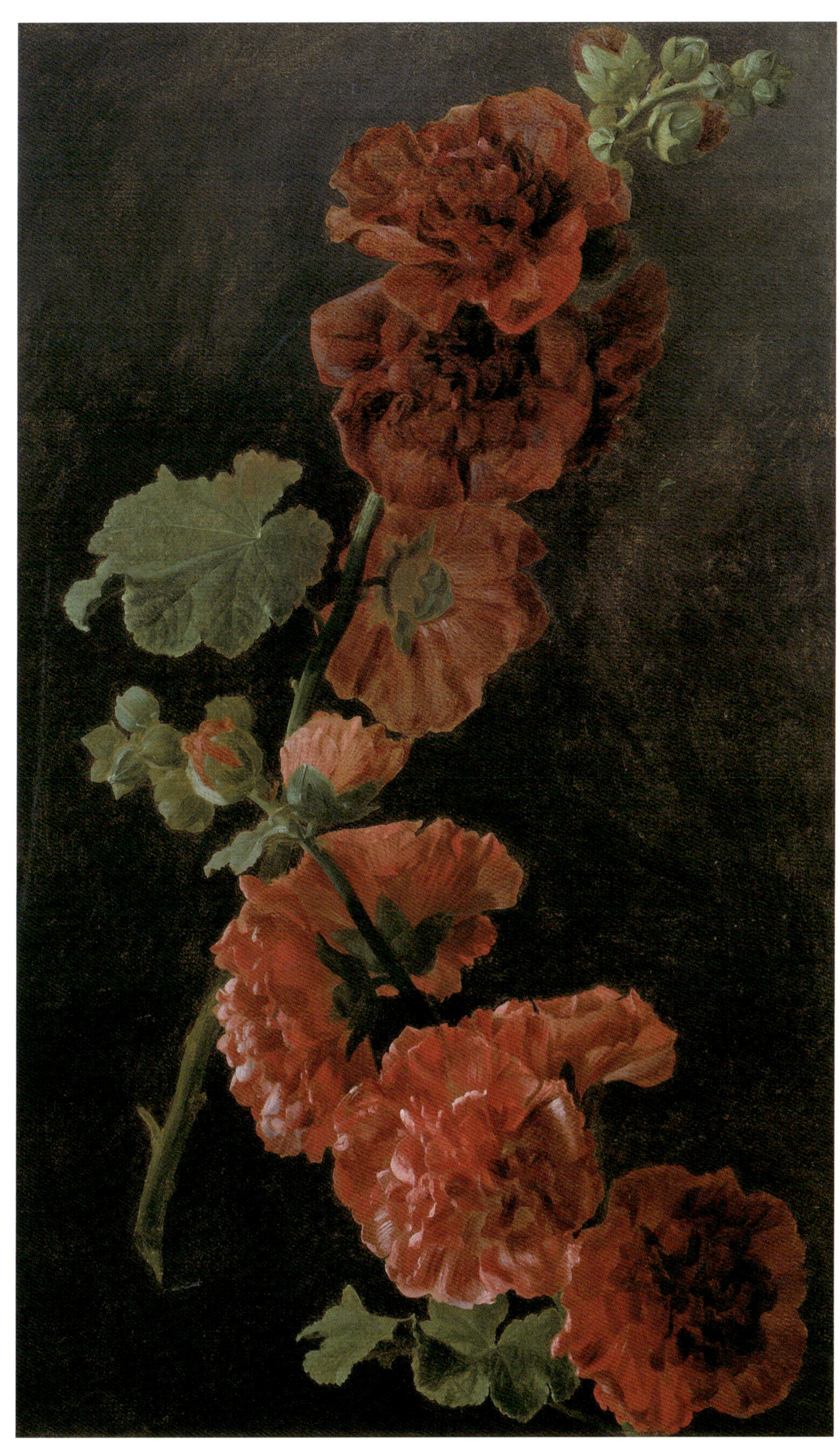

[53]   *Study of Red Hollyhocks*, n.d.

Oil on paper mounted on board
$25^{5}/_{8} \times 17^{1}/_{8}$ in.
Private collection
(cat. 132)

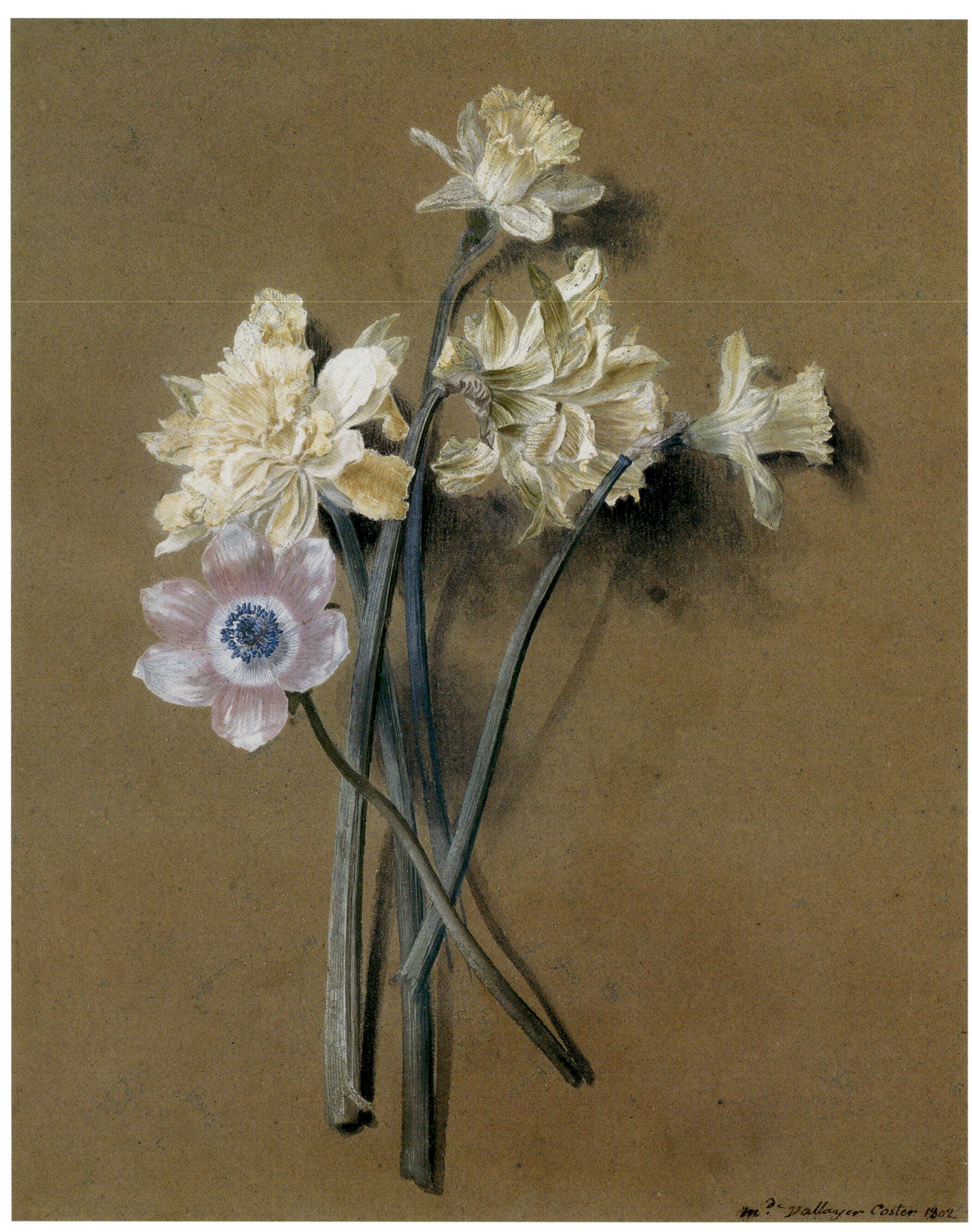

[54] *Study of a Bouquet of Flowers with Daffodils, 1802*

Gouache on paper
12⅛ × 9⅝ in.
Michael L. Rosenberg, Dallas
(cat. 144)

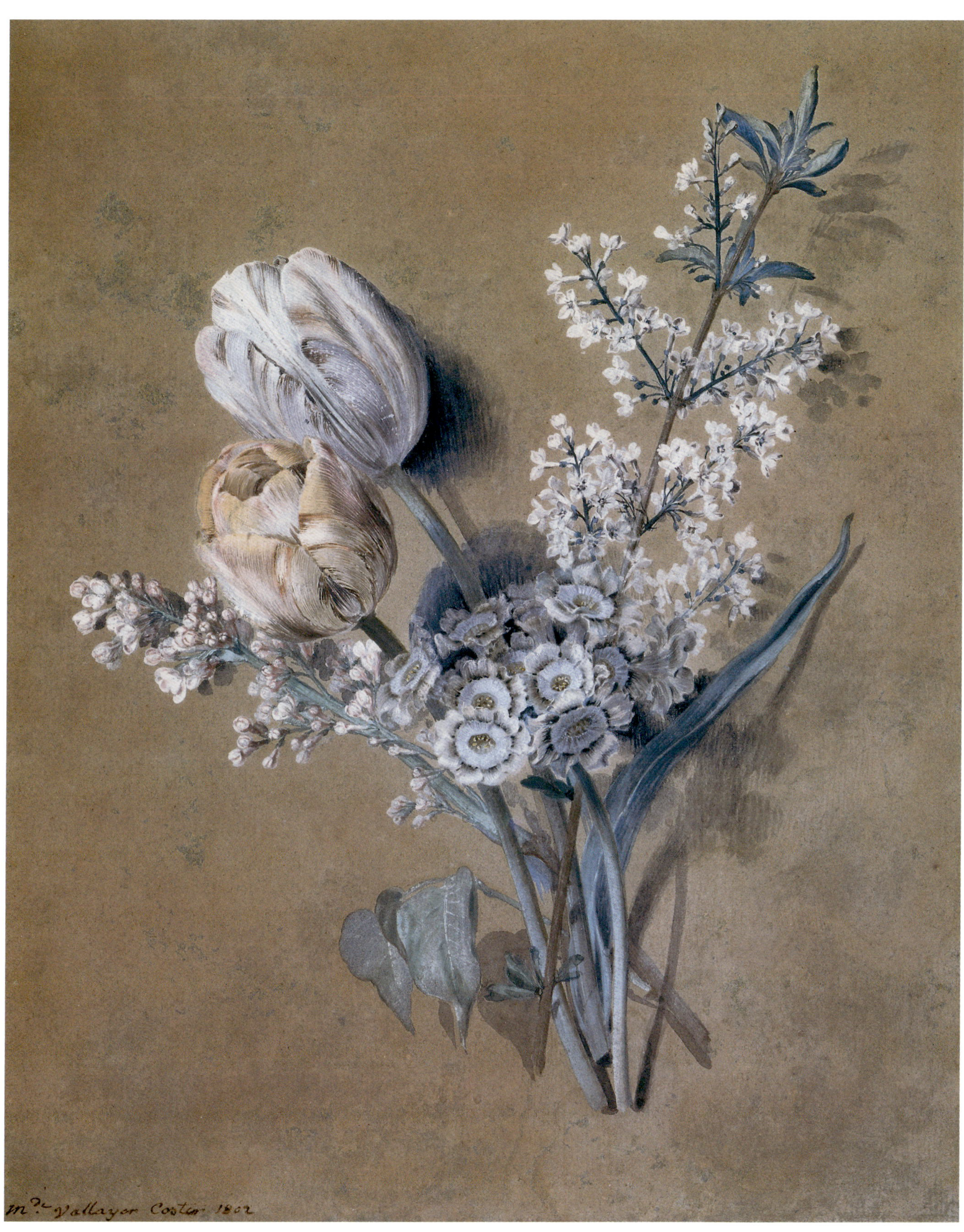

[55] *Study of a Bouquet of Flowers with Tulips,* 1802

Gouache on paper
12⅛ × 9⅝ in.
Michael L. Rosenberg, Dallas
(cat. 145)

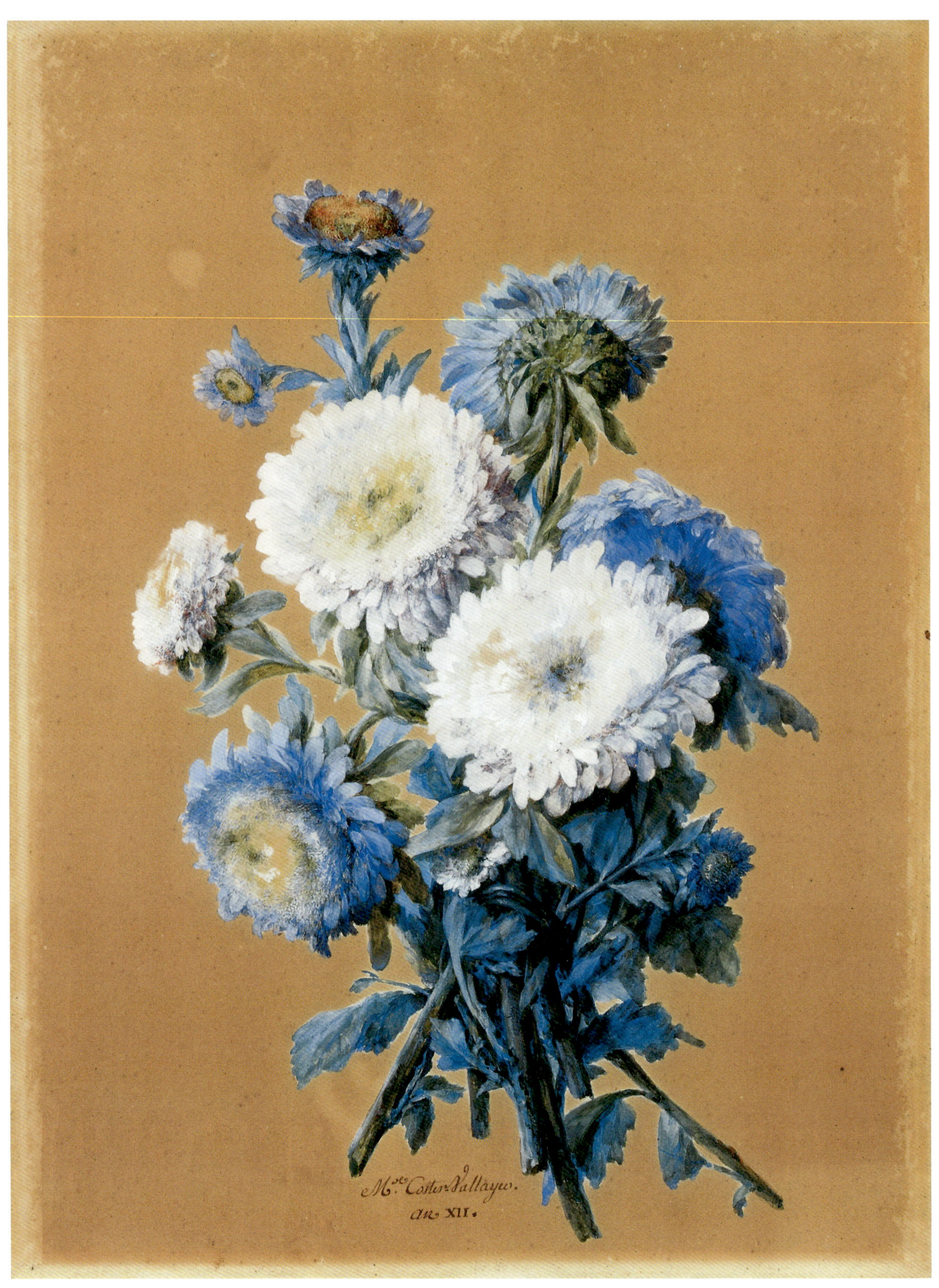

[56] *Bouquet of Dahlias*, 1804

Watercolor on paper
13¾ × 10 in.
Napoleonmuseum Arenenberg, Salenstein,
Switzerland
(cat. 146)

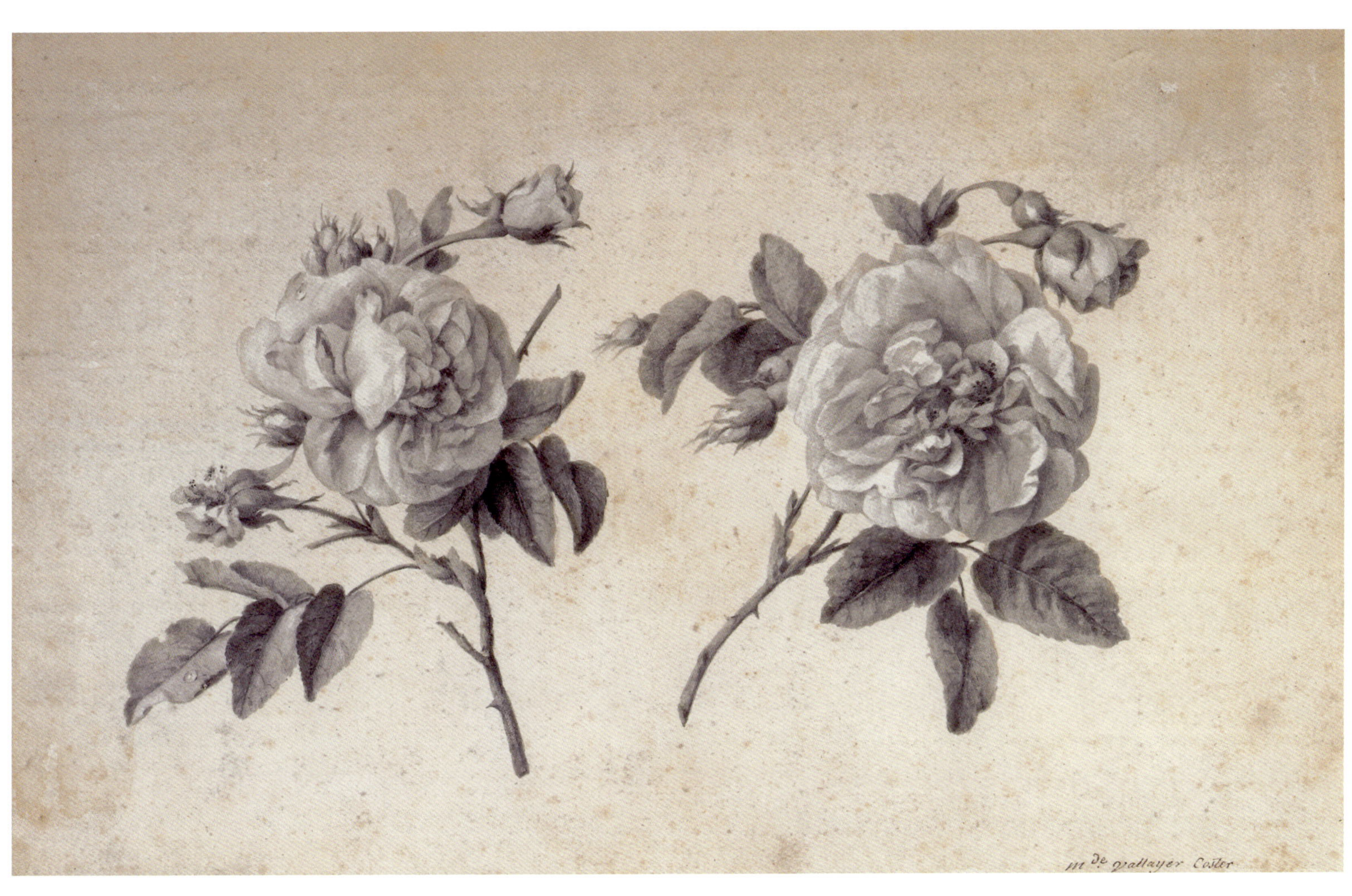

[57]   *Study of Two Roses*, c. 1810

Brush and gray wash on heavy cream laid paper
11 × 14 in.
Cooper-Hewitt, National Design Museum,
Smithsonian Institution, Purchased for the Museum
by the Advisory Council, 1925.1.349
(cat. 149)

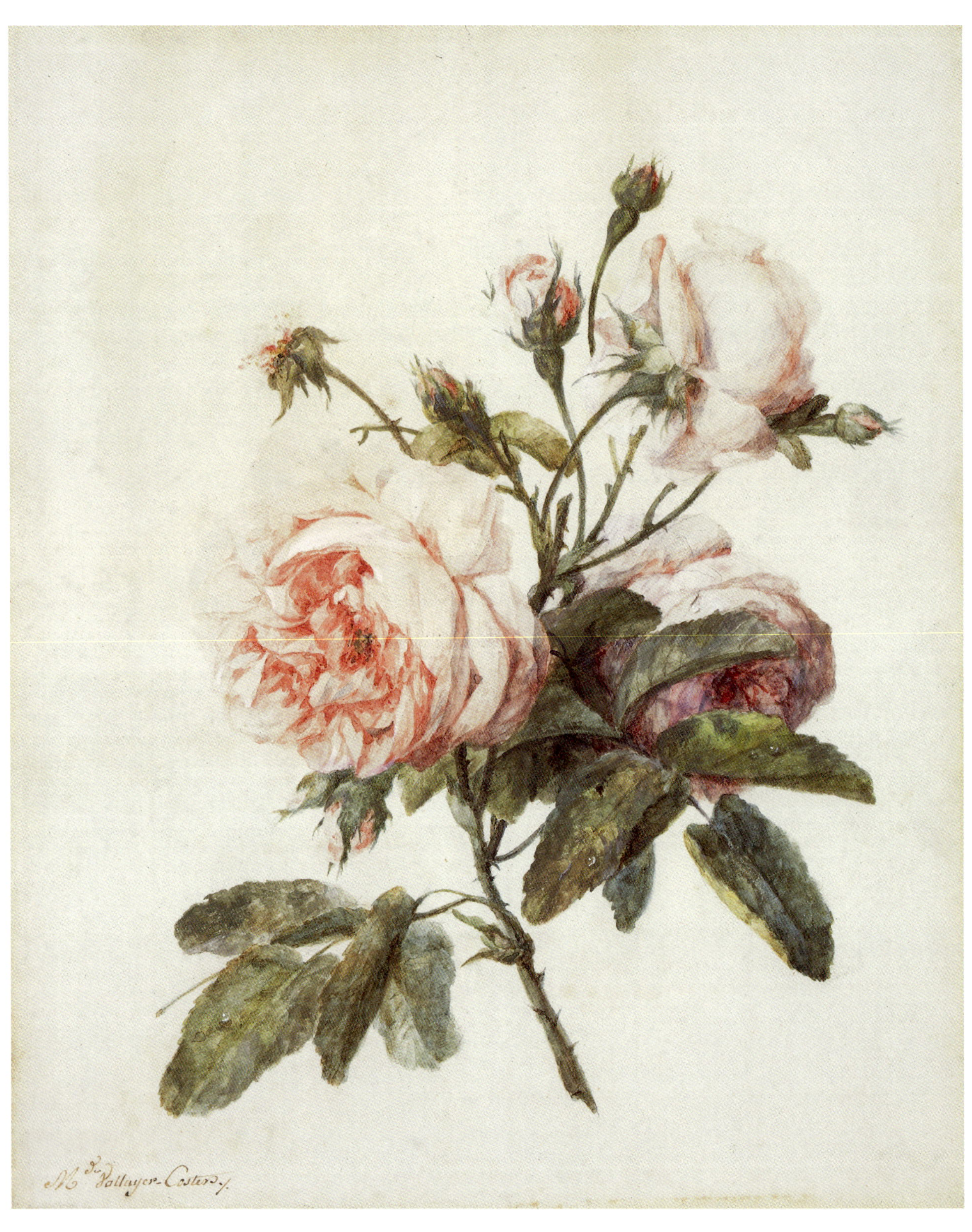

[58] *Roses*, n.d.

Watercolor on laid paper mounted on a small
lightweight panel
10⁷⁄₈ × 8⁷⁄₈ in.
Musée des Beaux-Arts, Nancy
(cat. 147)

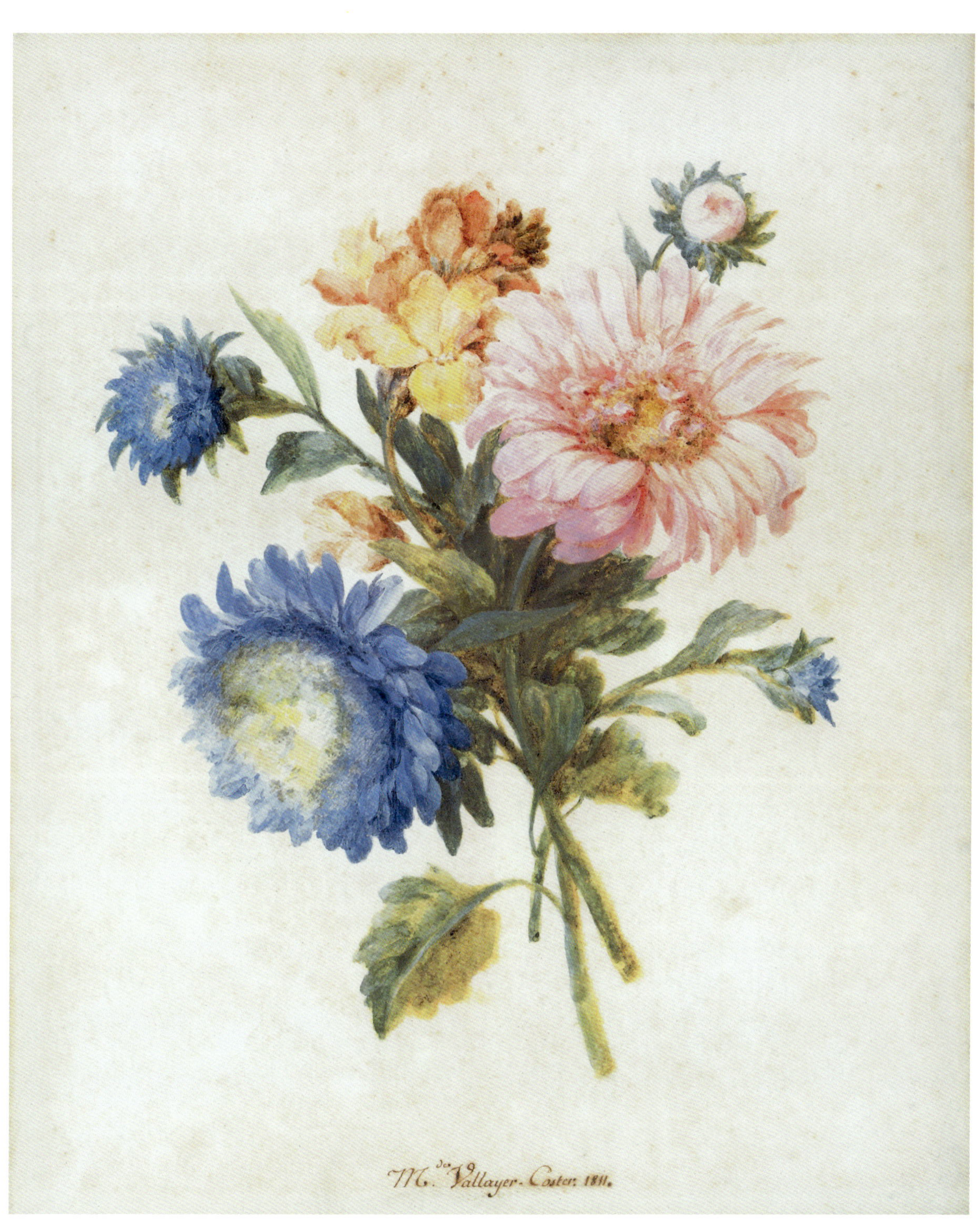

[59] *Autumn Daisies*, 1811

Watercolor on cream-colored paper
10¼ × 8¼ in.
Musée des Beaux-Arts, Nancy
(cat. 148)

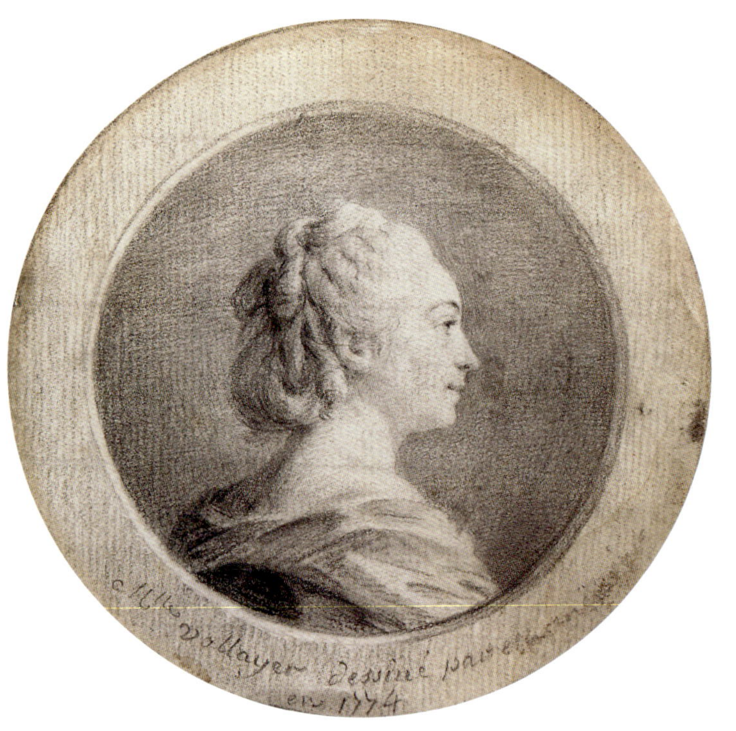 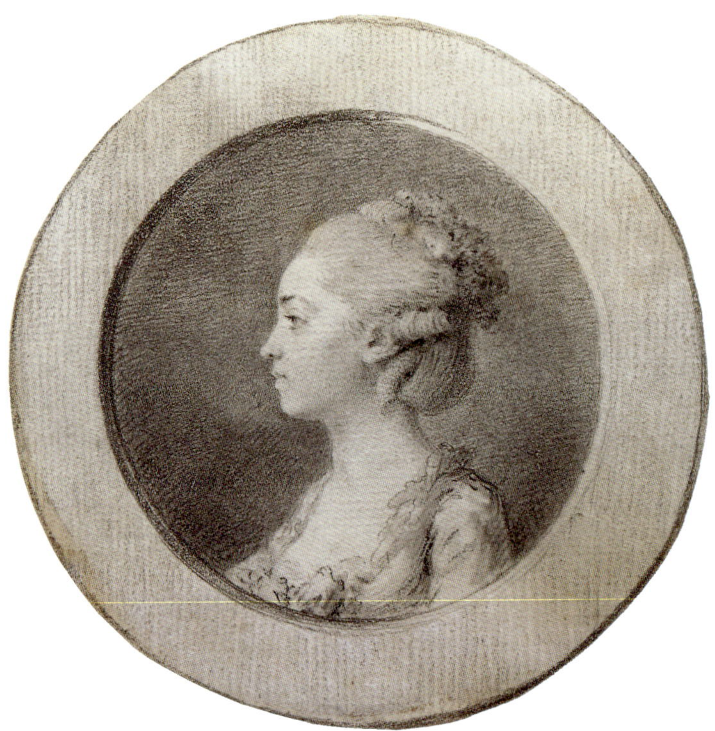

[60]   *Self-Portrait*, 1774

Black chalk on paper
Diam. 4⅜ in.
Musée municipal de Châlons-en-Champagne
(cat. 139)

[61]   *Portrait of the Artist's Sister*, 1774

Black chalk on paper
Diam. 4½ in.
Musée municipal de Châlons-en-Champagne
(cat. 138)

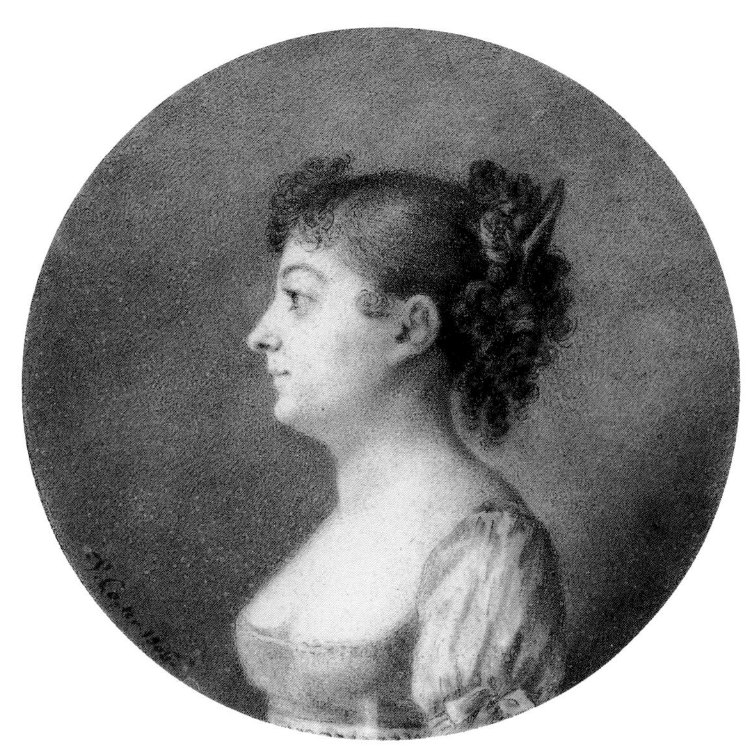

[62] *Medallion Bust Portait of a Woman in Profile*, 1806

Black chalk on paper
Diam. 4 in.
Private collection
(cat. 141)

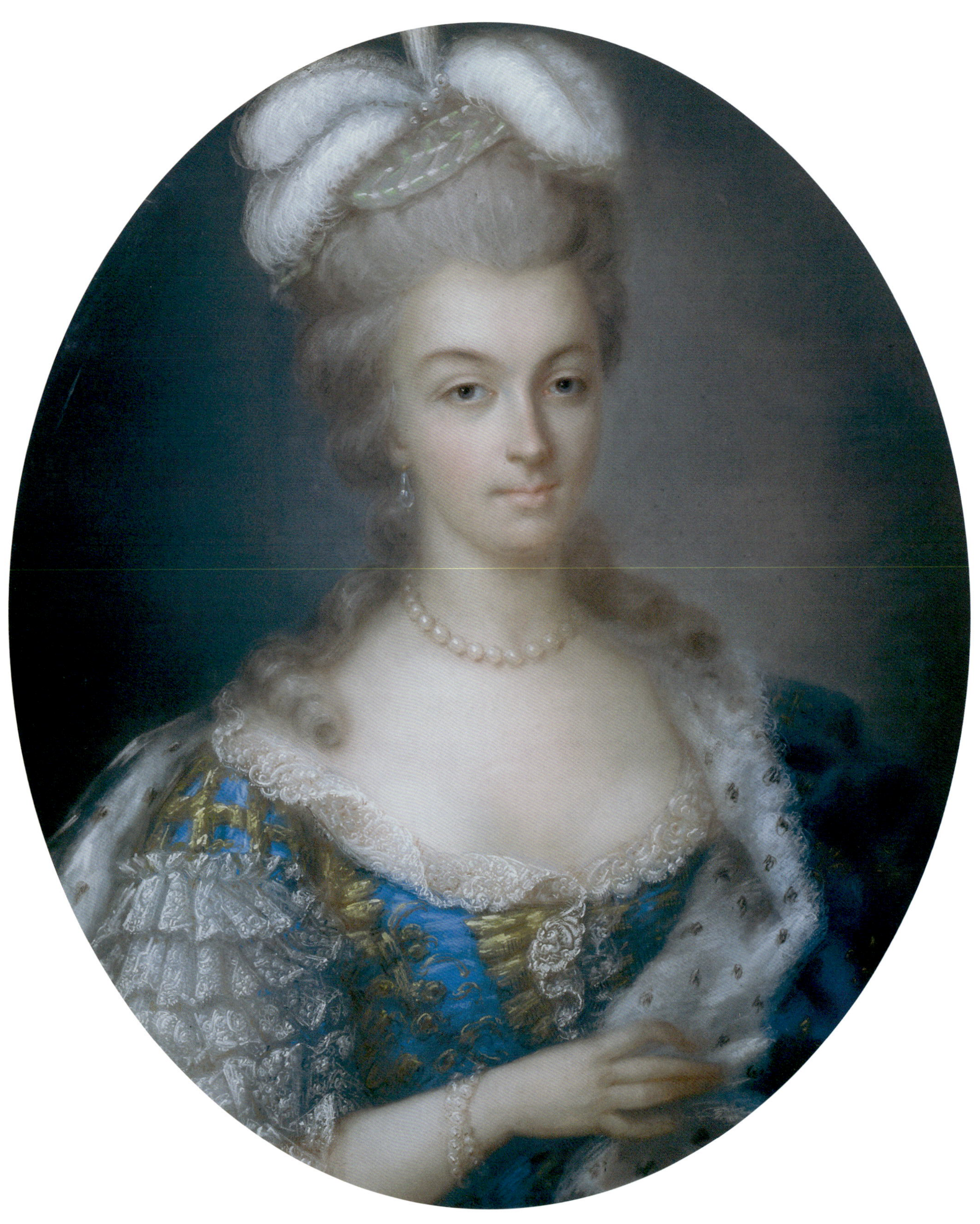

[63] *Portrait of Queen Marie-Antoinette*, 1780

Pastel on paper
28¾ × 24⅜ in.
Florence Bouchy-Picon
(cat. 140)

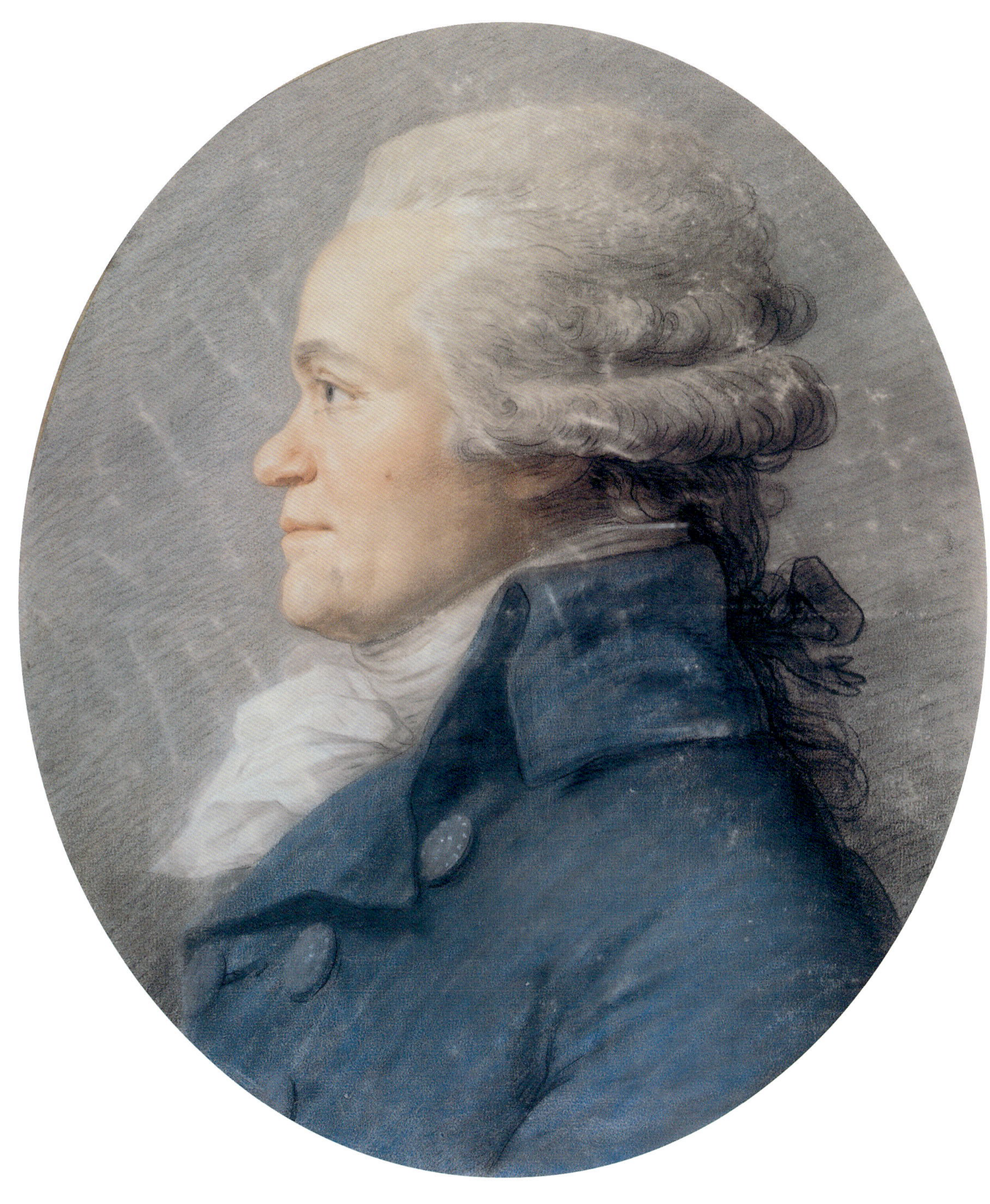

[64] *Portrait of Jean-Pierre-Silvestre Coster, Parliamentary Lawyer*, n.d.

Pastel and colored pencil on paper affixed to cardboard
18⅛ × 15 in.
Musée Carnavalet, Paris, inv. no. 6196
(cat. 142)

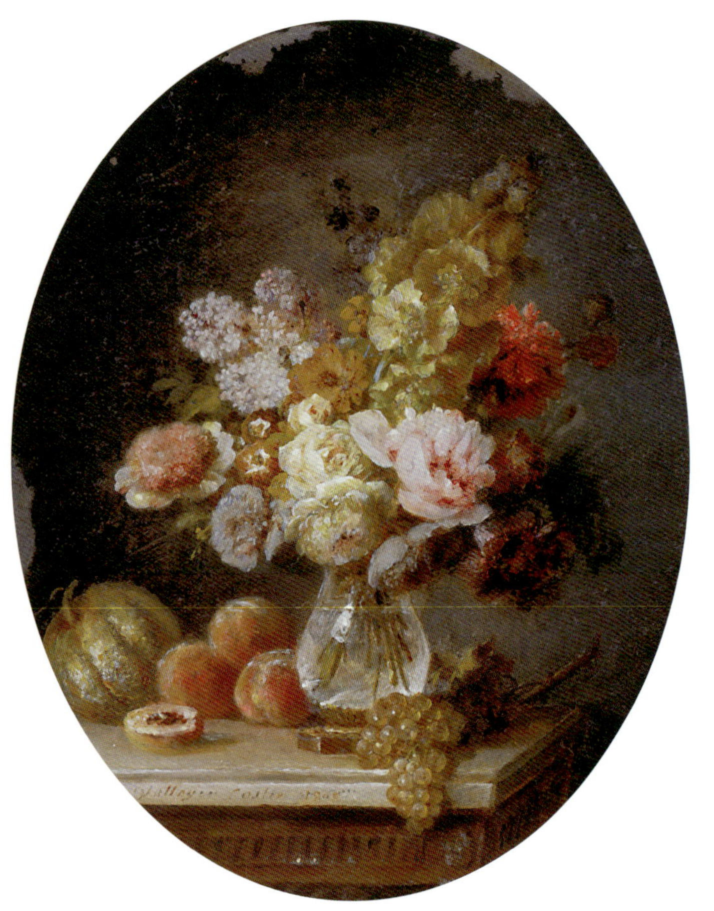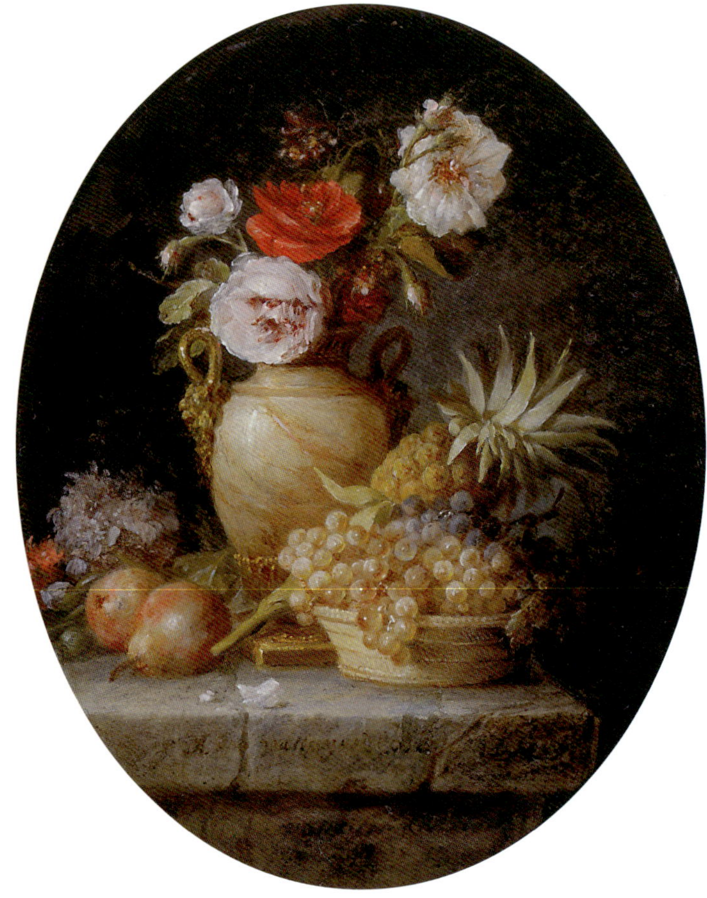

[65] *Bouquet of Flowers and Fruit*, 1808

Oil under glass
5¾ × 4⅝ in.
Musée des Arts décoratifs, Paris, inv. no. 21846A
(cat. 152)

[66] *Bouquet of Flowers and Fruit*, 1808

Oil under glass
5¾ × 4⅝ in.
Musée des Arts décoratifs, Paris, inv. no. 21846B
(cat. 153)

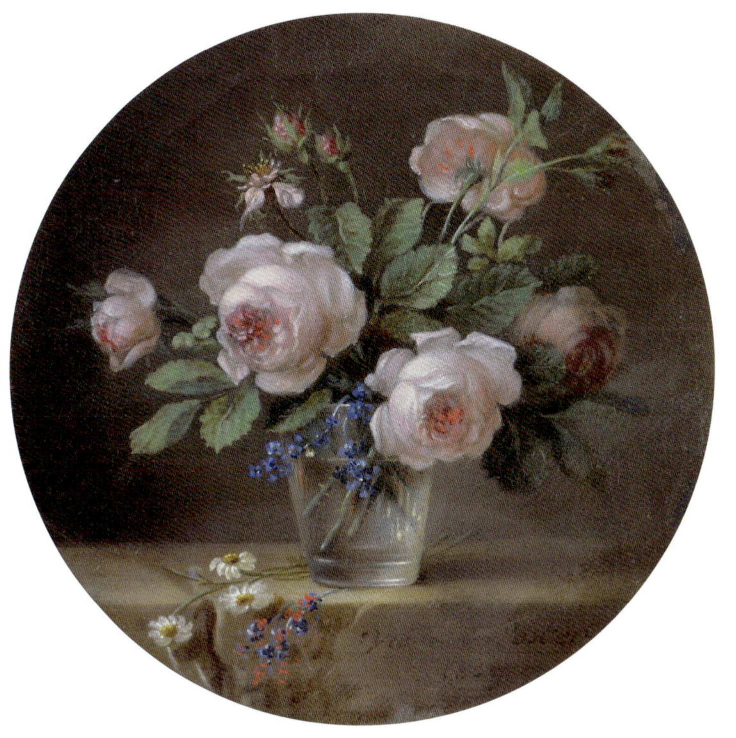

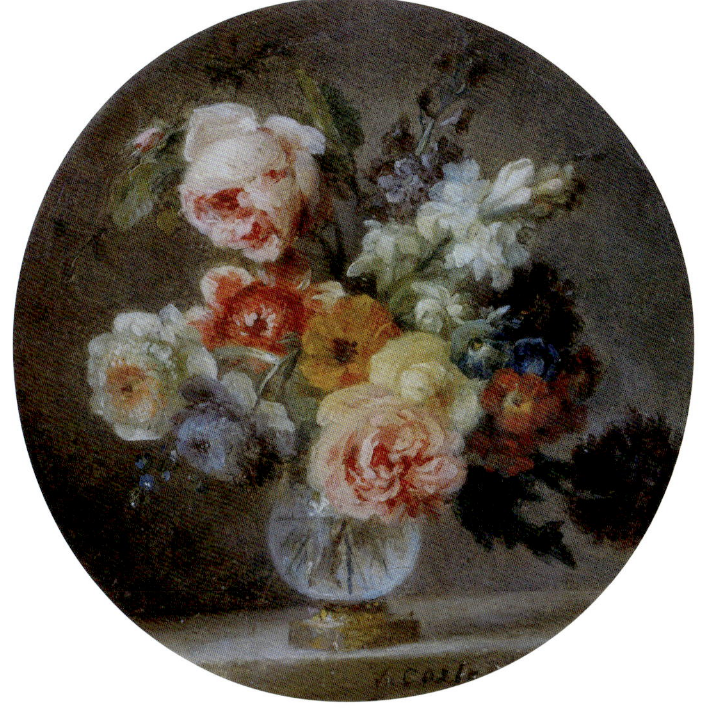

[67]   *Roses in a Glass*, 1809

Bodycolor on cardboard
Diam. 3½ in.
Private collection
(cat. 154)

[68]   *Flowers in a Crystal Vase*, n.d.

Oil under glass
Diam. 3⅛ in.
Anne Lévy-Freitag and Pierre Lévy-Freitag
(cat. 155)

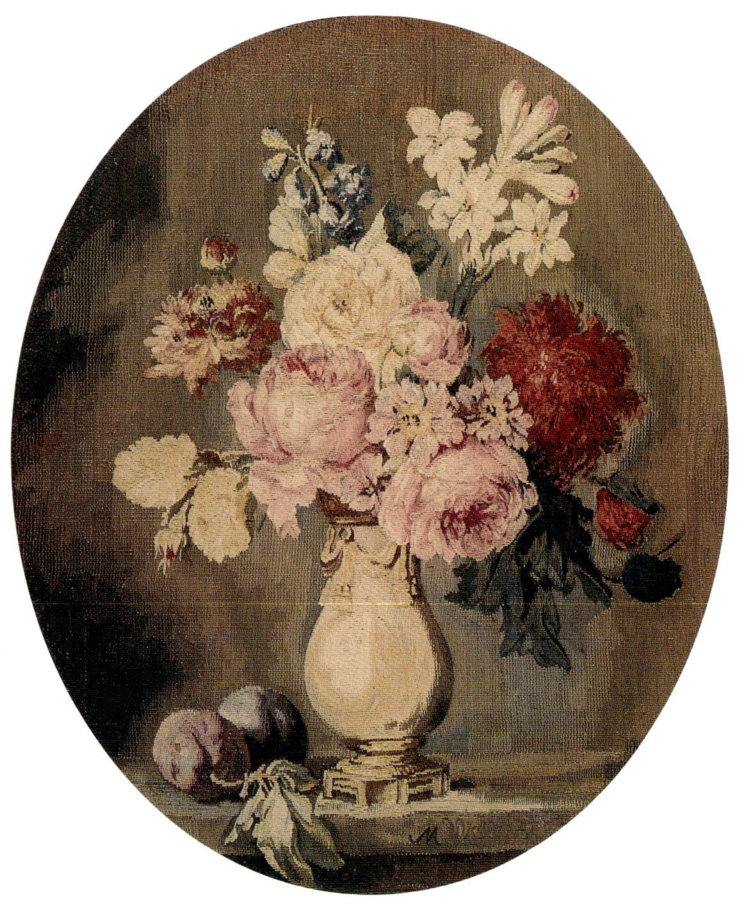 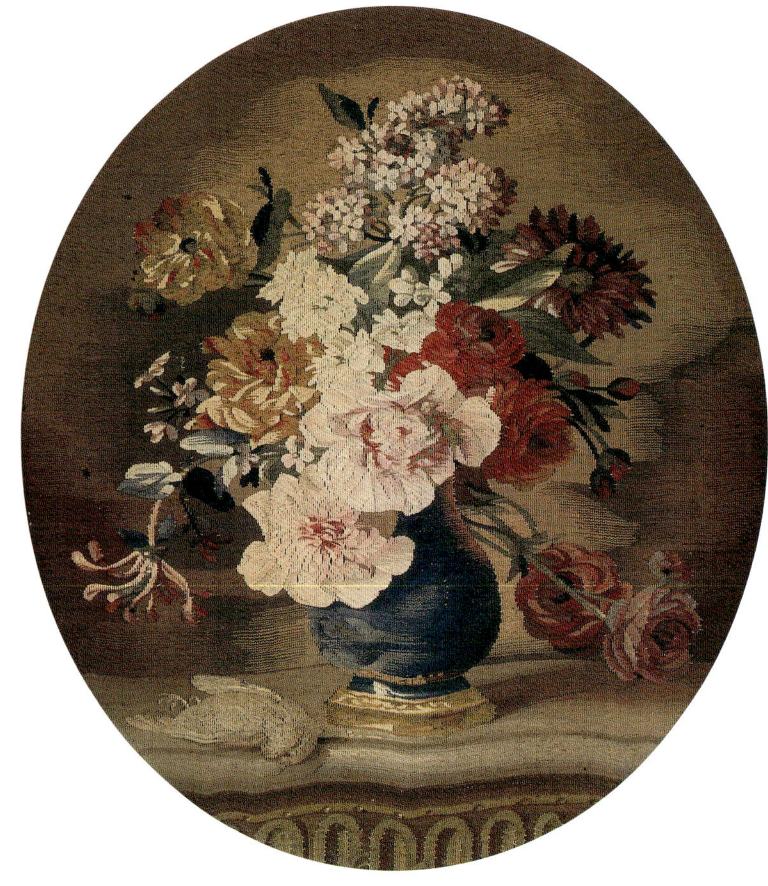

[69]   *Flowers in a Vase and Two Plums*, 1781

Wool and silk tapestry, oval
17⅞ × 14⅝ in.
The Metropolitan Museum of Art; Bequest of
Julie Heidelbach, 1932 (35.116.7)
(cat. 158)

[70]   *Flowers in a Blue Vase with Dead Canary*, n.d.

Wool and silk tapestry, oval
19⅝ × 16¾ in.
Private collection
(cat. 159)

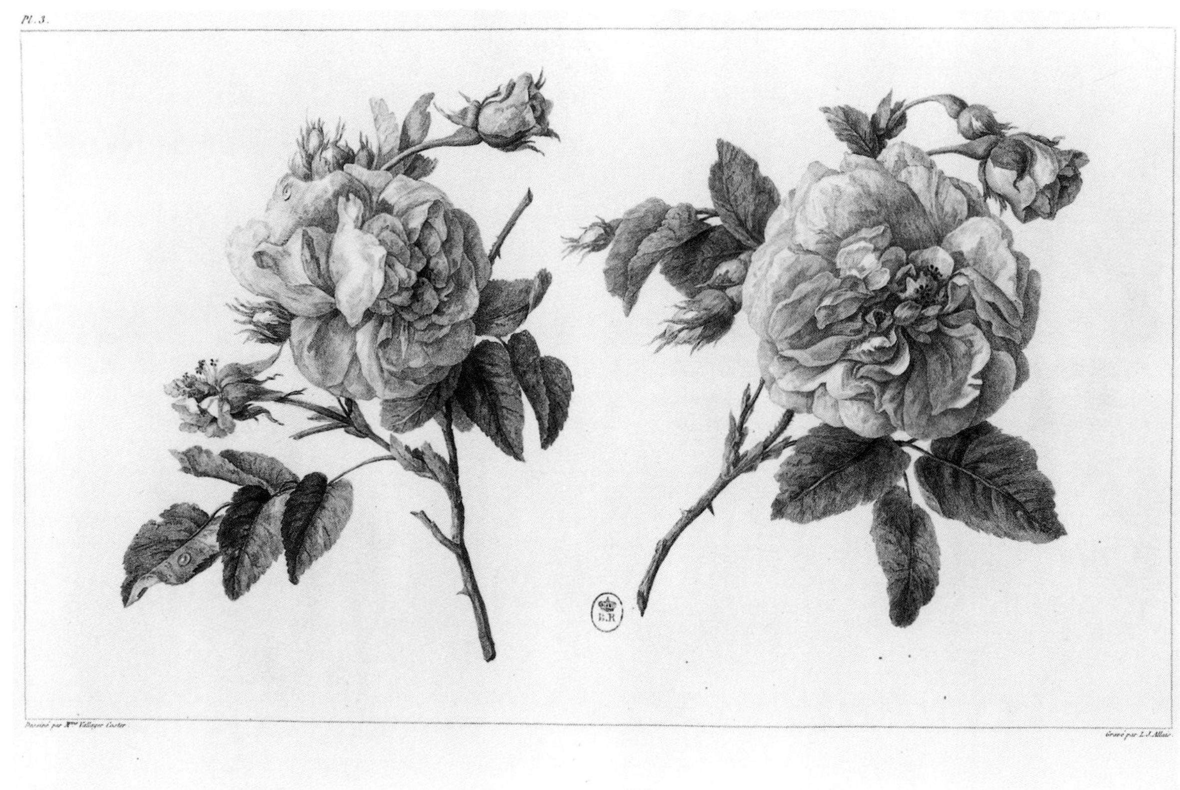

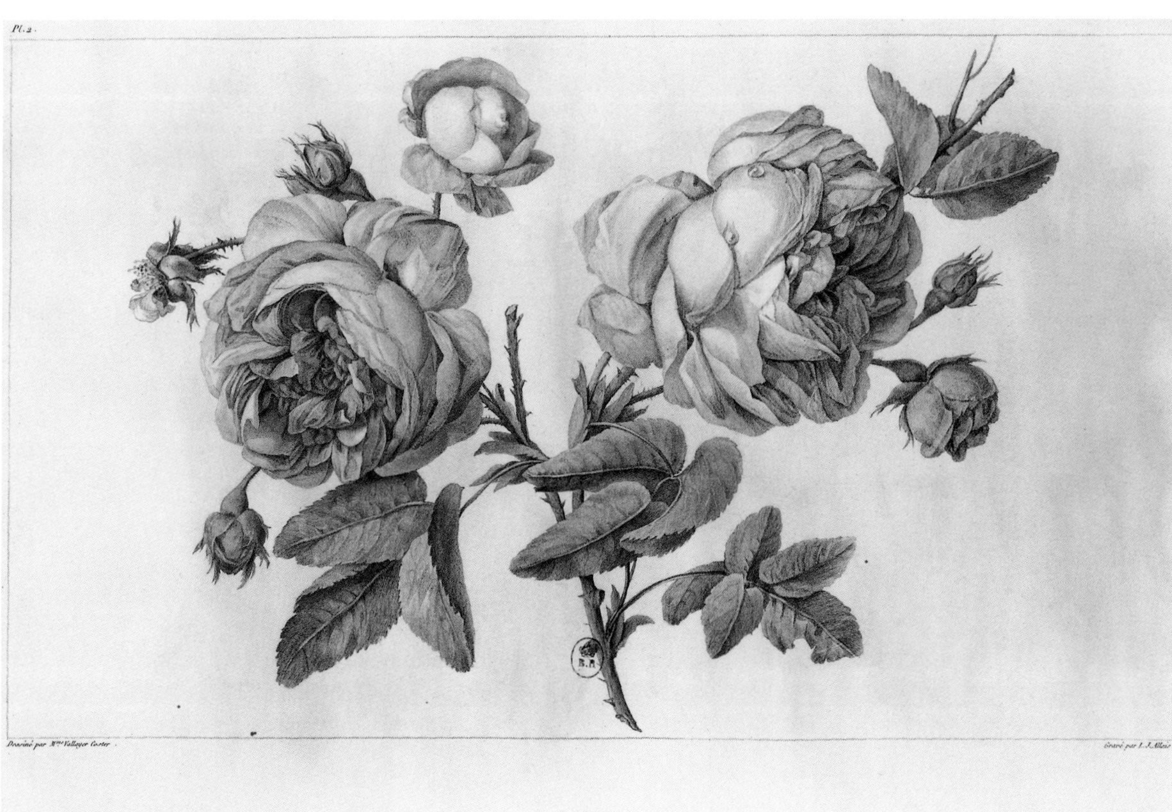

After Anne Vallayer-Coster
Louis-Jean Allais

[71] Untitled (Roses)

Engraving
Bibliothèque nationale de France
(cat. 157)

After Anne Vallayer-Coster
Louis-Jean Allais

[72] Untitled (Roses)

Engraving
Bibliothèque nationale de France
(cat. 157)

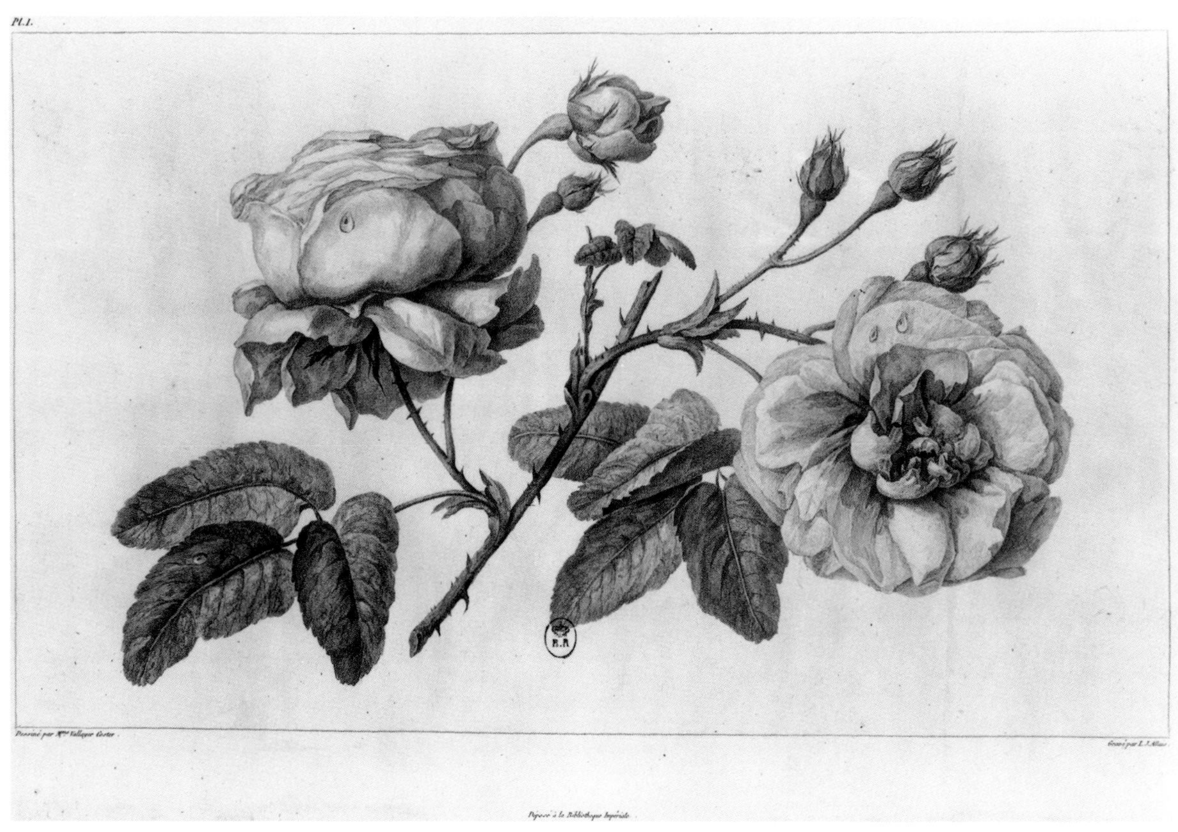

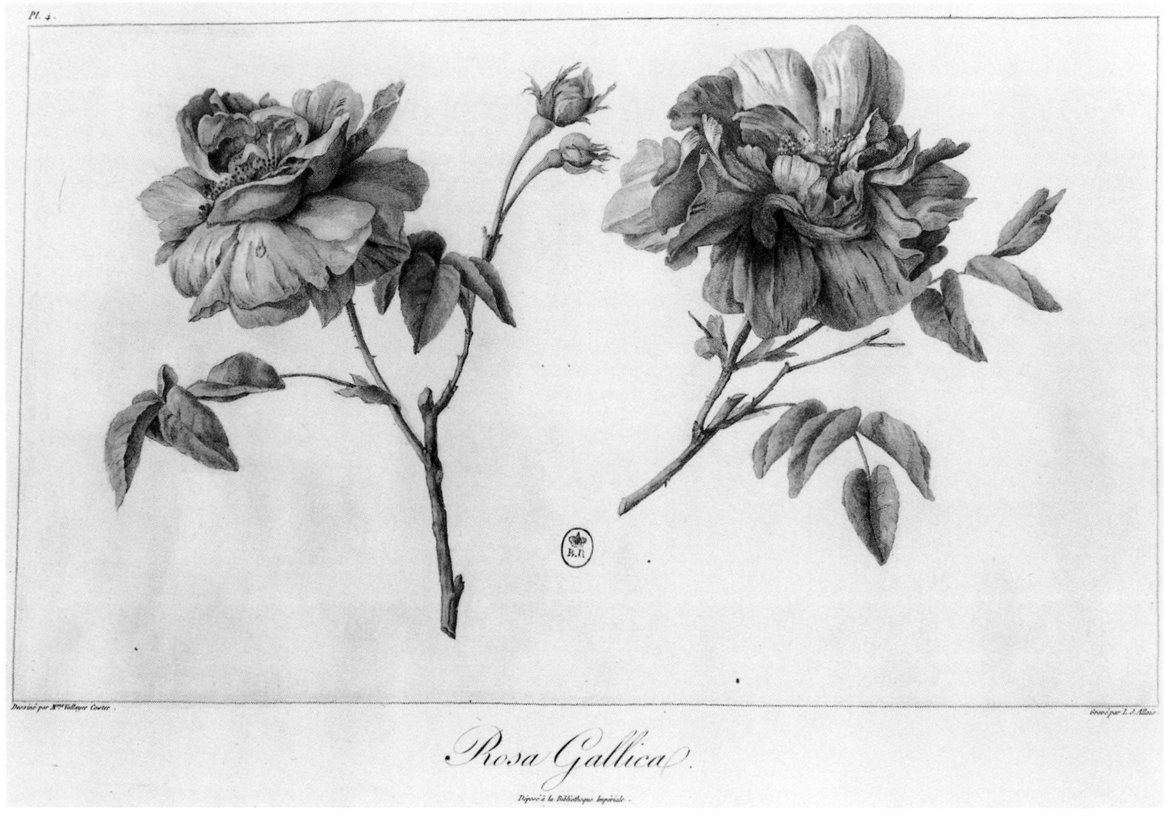

After Anne Vallayer-Coster
Louis-Jean Allais

[73] Untitled (Roses)
Engraving
Bibliothèque nationale de France
(cat. 157)

After Anne Vallayer-Coster
Louis-Jean Allais

[74] *Rosa Gallica*
Engraving
Bibliothèque nationale de France
(cat. 157)

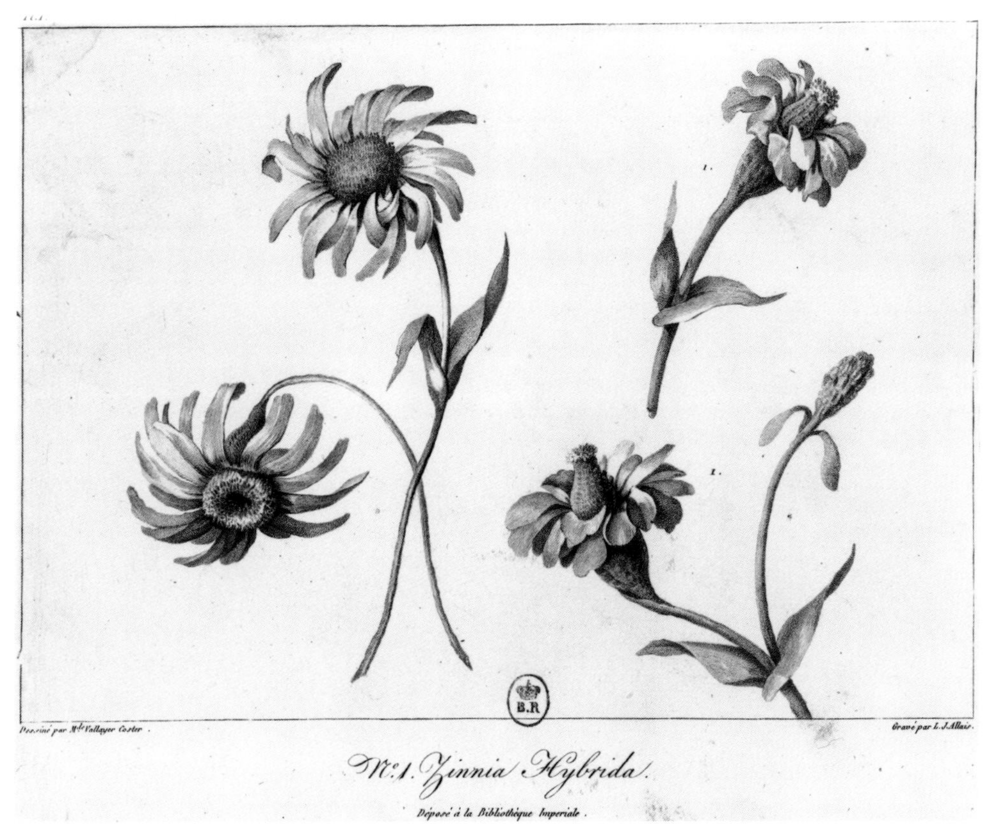

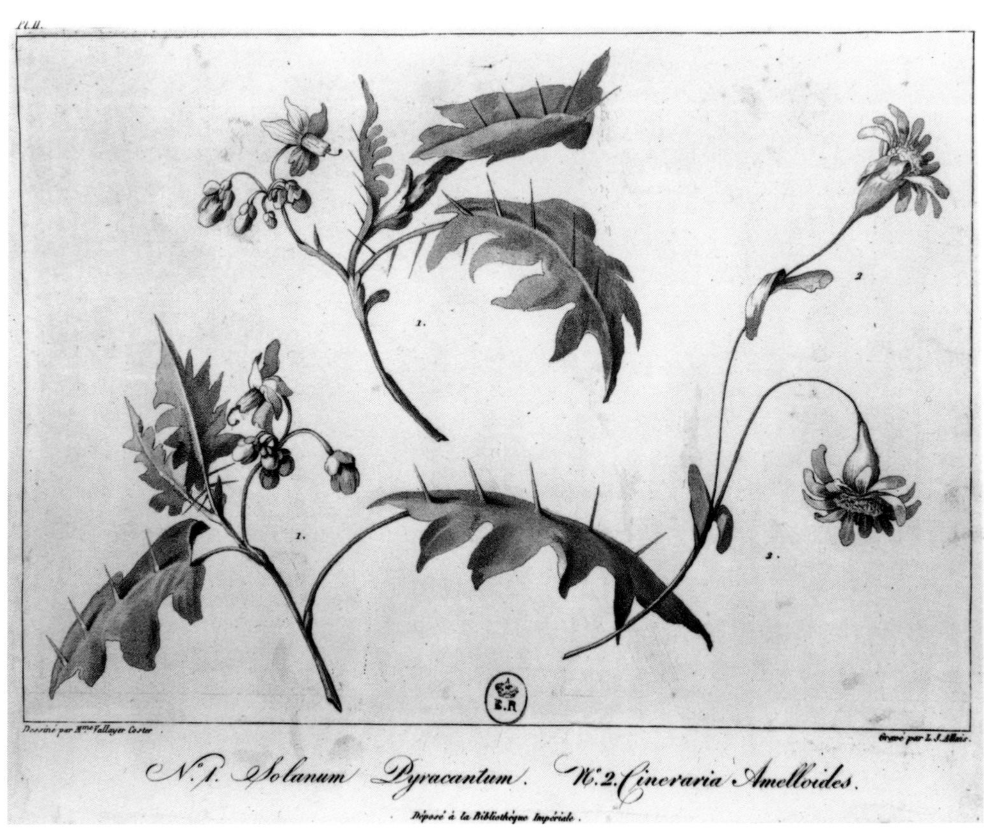

AFTER ANNE VALLAYER-COSTER
LOUIS-JEAN ALLAIS

[75] *No. 1. Zinnia Hybrida*

Engraving
Bibliothèque nationale de France
(cat. 157)

AFTER ANNE VALLAYER-COSTER
LOUIS-JEAN ALLAIS

[76] *No. 1. Solanum Pyracantum. No. 2. Cineraria*
Amelloides

Engraving
Bibliothèque nationale de France
(cat. 157)

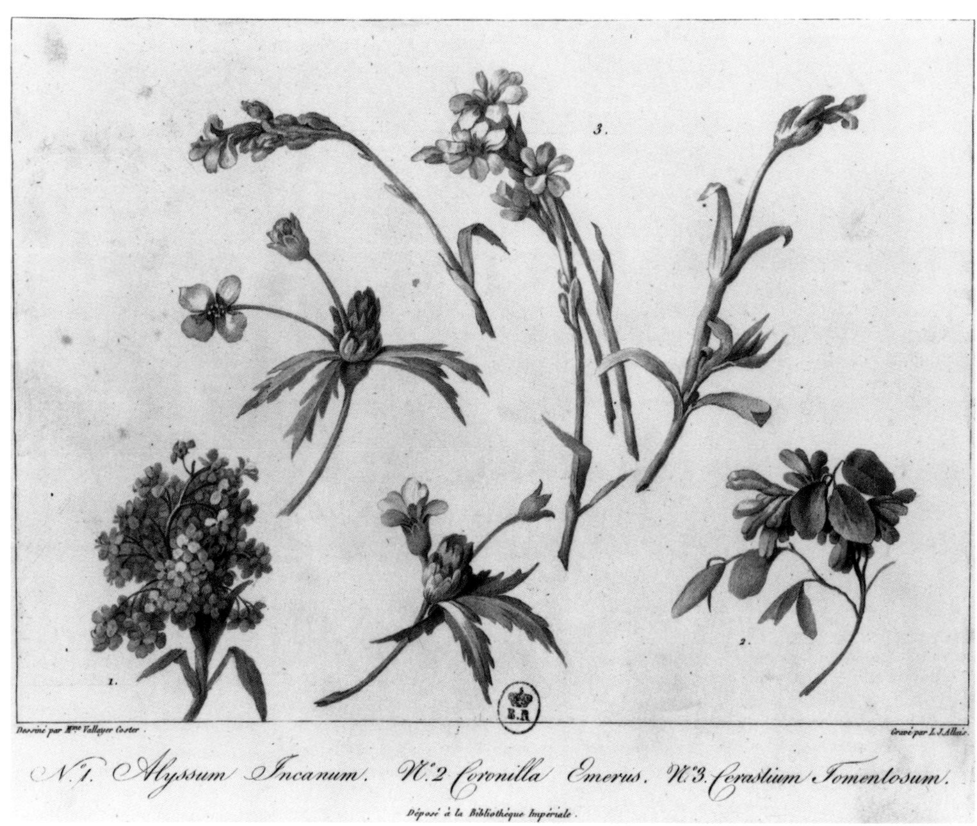

AFTER ANNE VALLAYER-COSTER
LOUIS-JEAN ALLAIS

[77] *No. 1. Alyssum Incanum. No. 2. Coronilla Emerus.*
No. 3. Cerastium Fomentosum

Engraving
Bibliothèque nationale de France
(cat. 157)

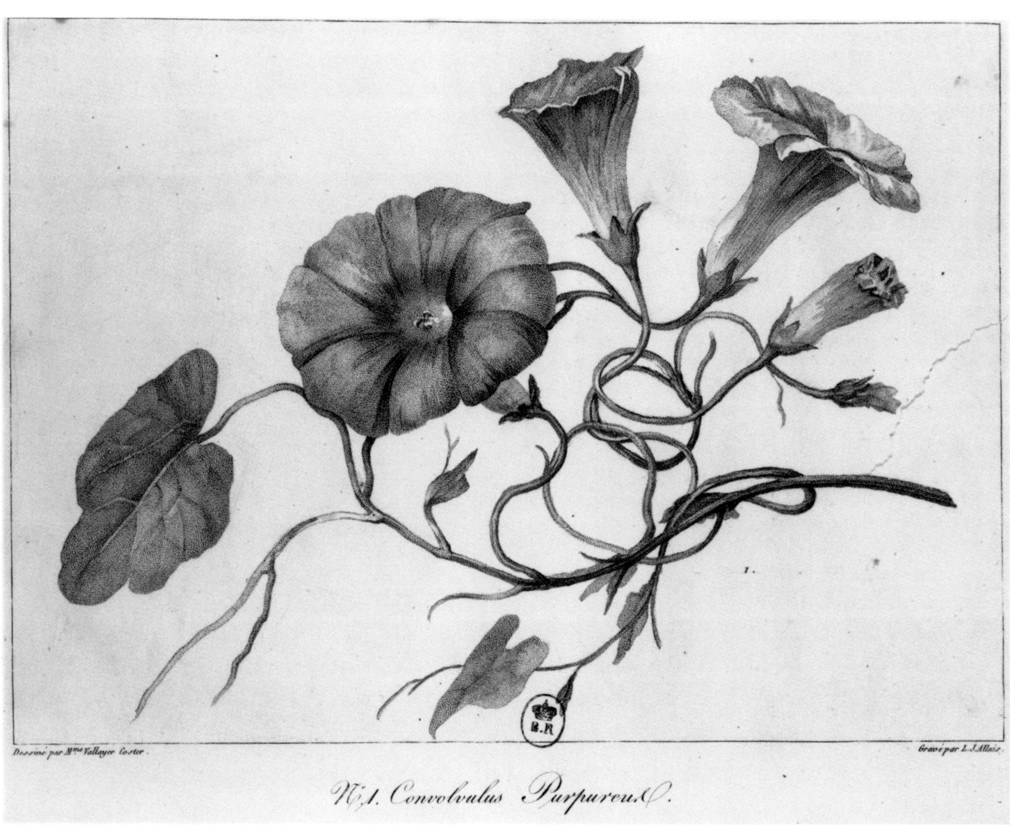

AFTER ANNE VALLAYER-COSTER
LOUIS-JEAN ALLAIS

[78] *No. 1. Convolvulus Purpureus*

Engraving
Bibliothèque nationale de France
(cat. 157)

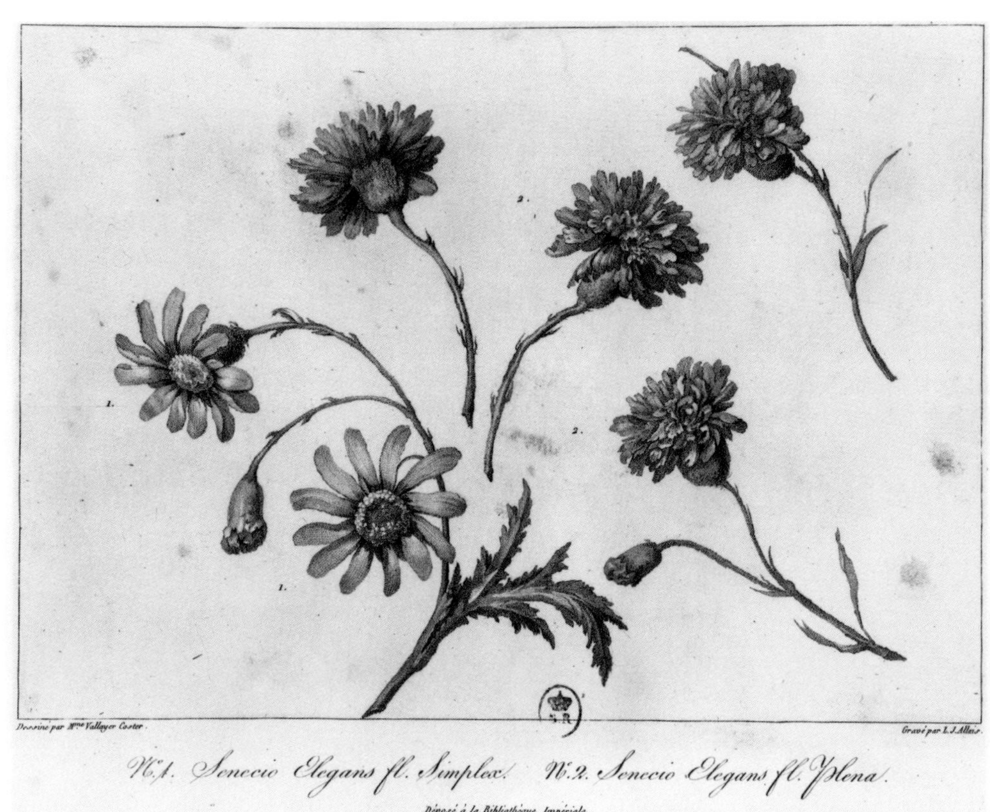

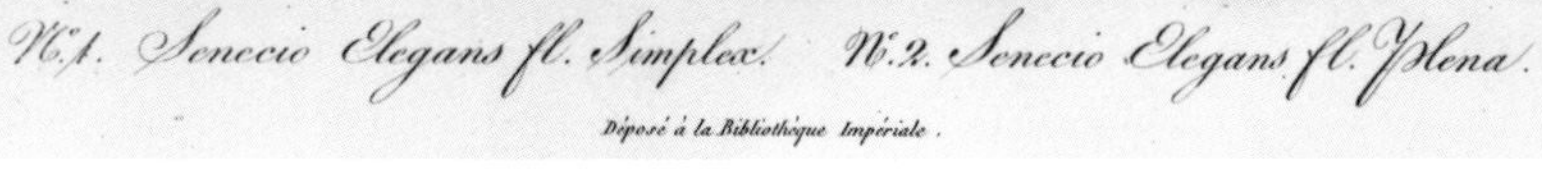

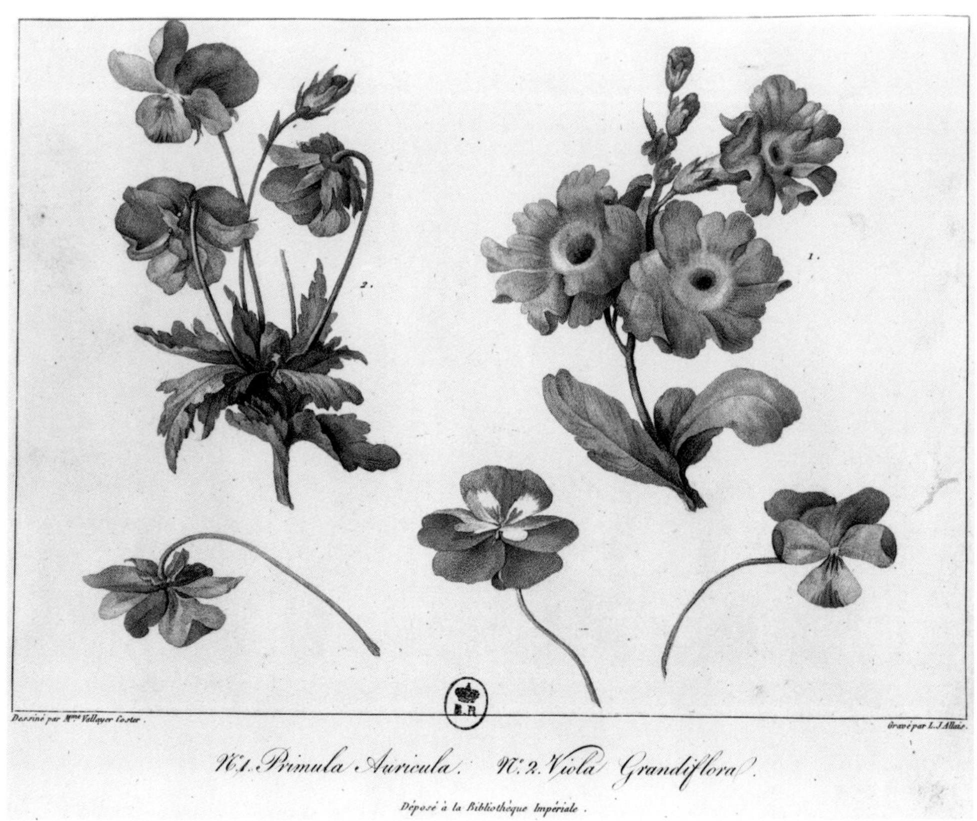

AFTER ANNE VALLAYER-COSTER

LOUIS-JEAN ALLAIS

[79] *No. 1. Senecio Elegans fl. Simplex. No. 2. Senecio Elegans fl. Yslena*

Engraving

Bibliothèque nationale de France

(cat. 157)

AFTER ANNE VALLAYER-COSTER

LOUIS-JEAN ALLAIS

[80] *No. 1. Primula Auricula. No. 2. Viola Grandiflora*

Engraving

Bibliothèque nationale de France

(cat. 157)

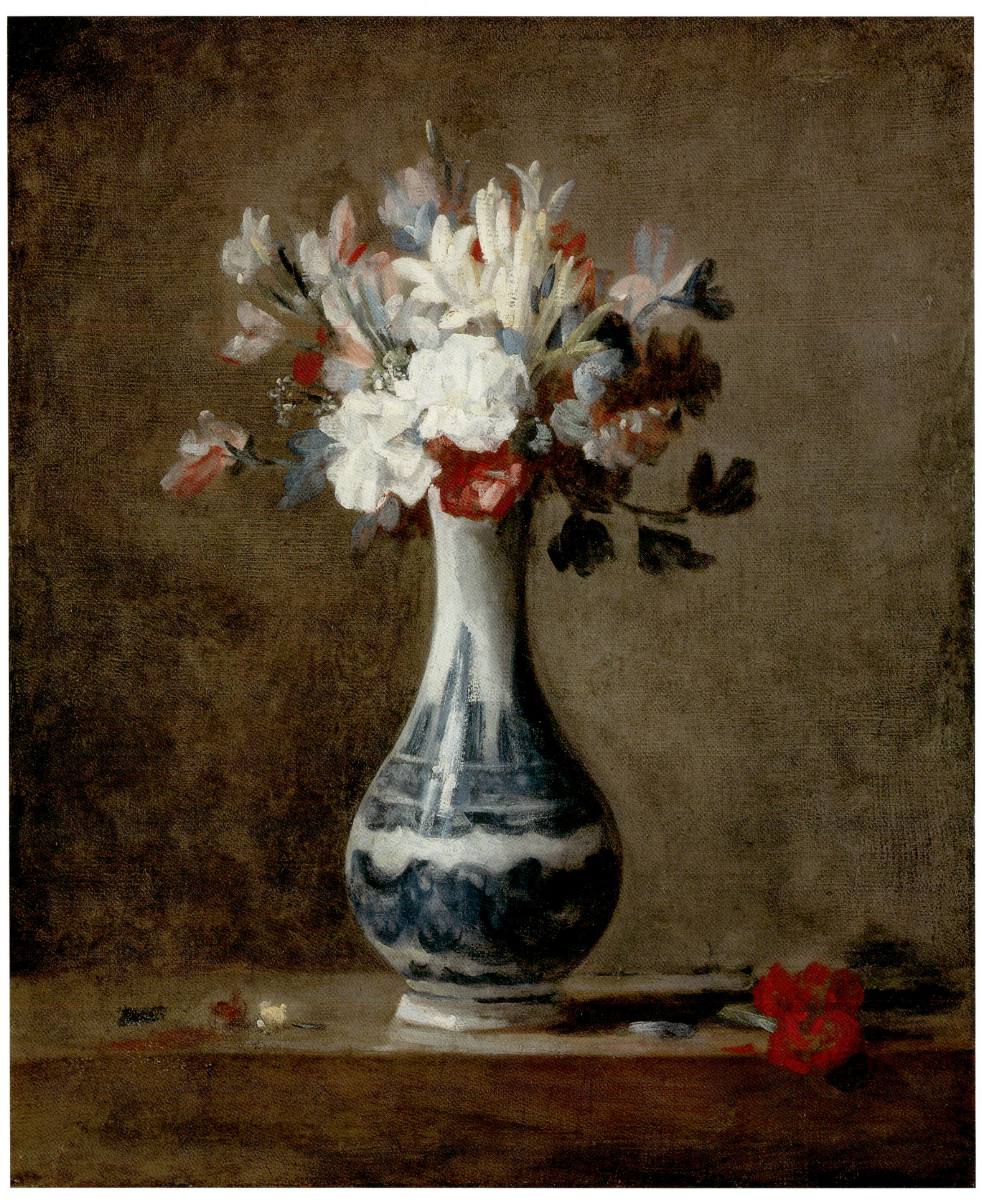

[81]   *Flowers in a White and Blue Porcelain Vase*, n.d.
Oil on canvas
17³⁄₈ × 14¹⁄₈ in.
National Gallery of Scotland, Edinburgh
(cat. A)

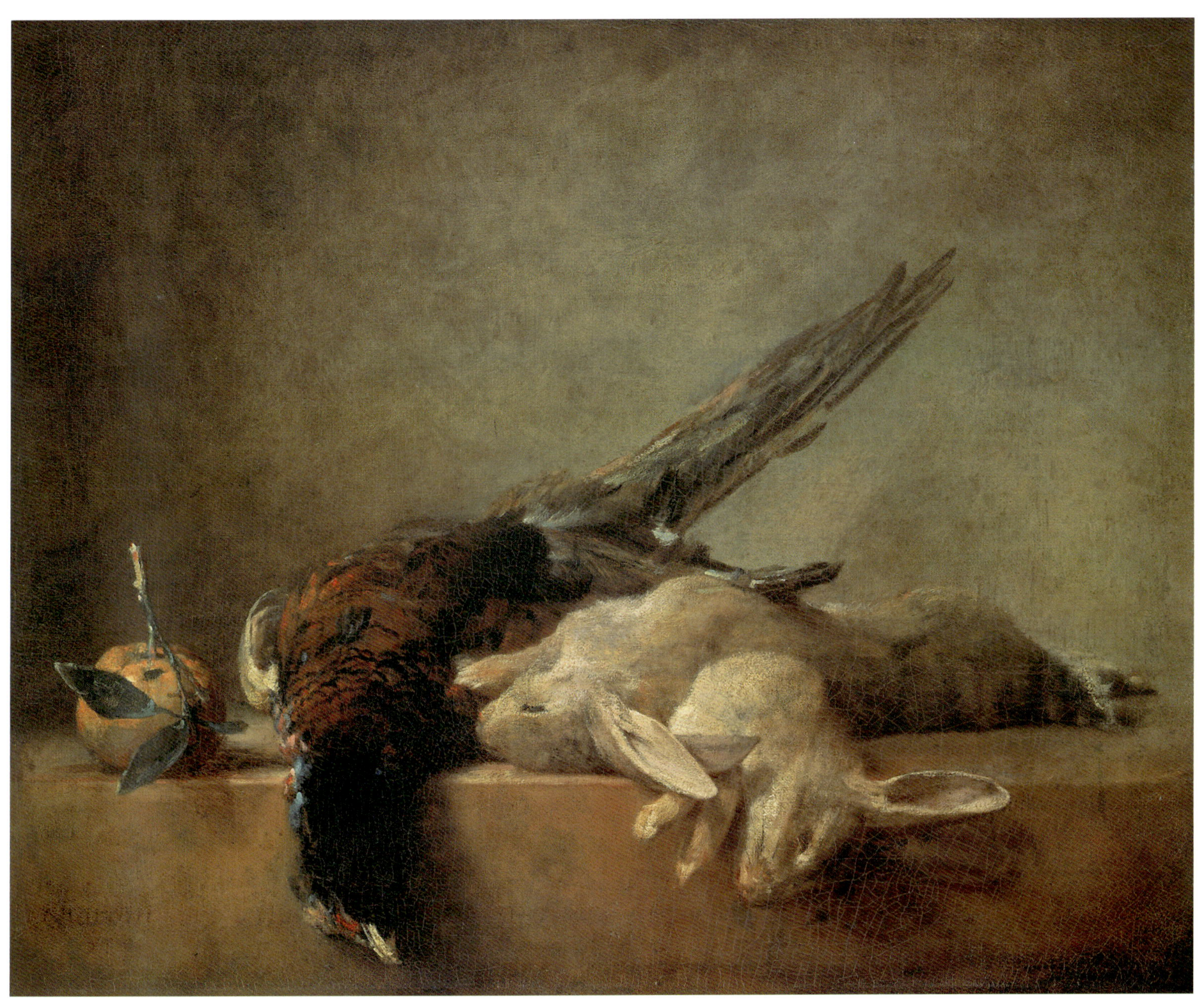

Jean-Siméon Chardin

[82]   *Still Life with Game (Two Rabbits, a Pheasant,*
and a Seville Orange on a Stone Ledge), n.d.

Oil on canvas
19½ × 23⅜ in.
National Gallery of Art, Washington, Samuel H.
Kress Collection, 1952.5.36
(cat. B)

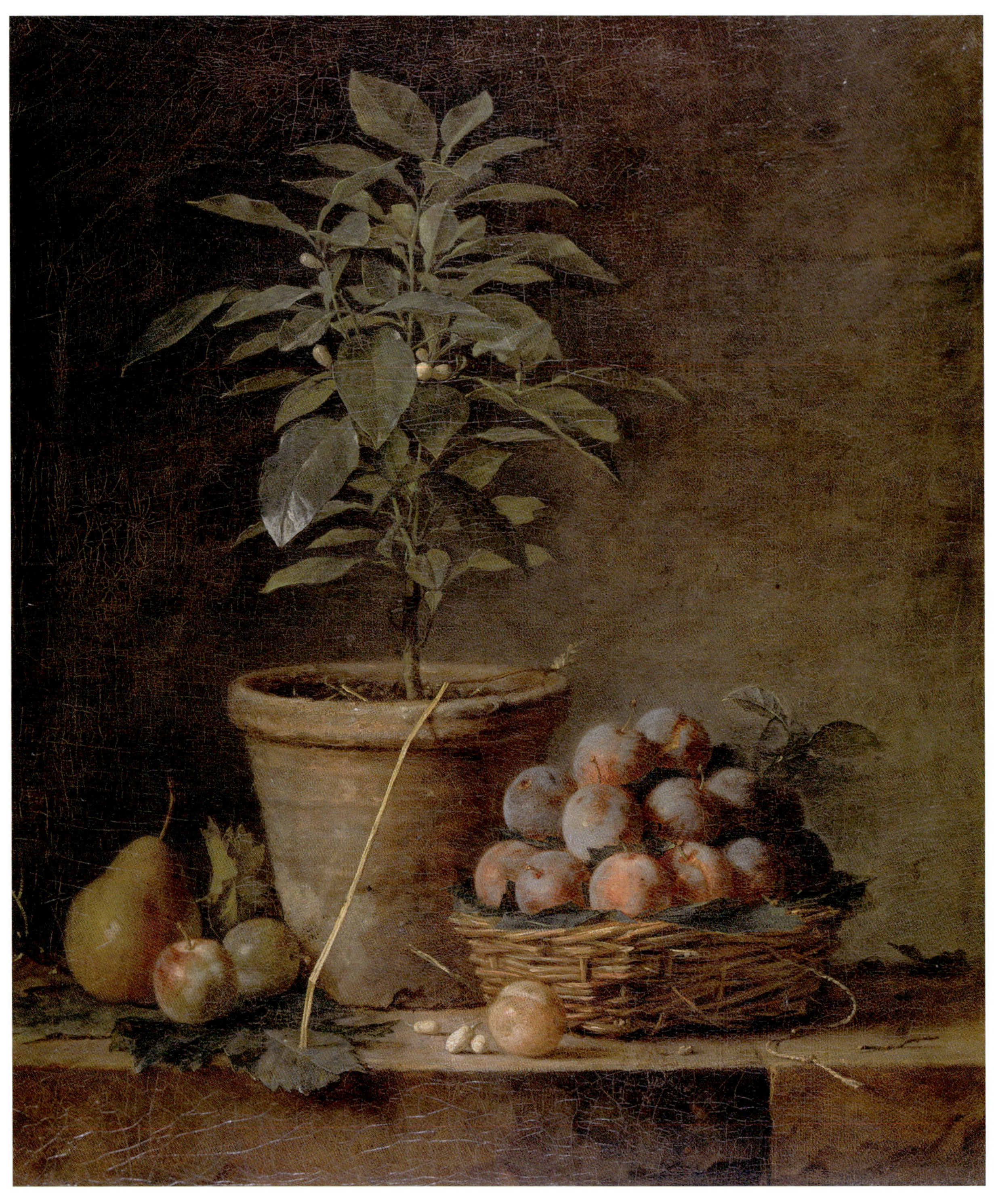

[83] *The Orange Tree*, c. 1765
Oil on canvas
$23^{5}/_{8} \times 19^{1}/_{2}$ in.
Staatliche Kunsthalle Karlsruhe, inv. no. 180
(cat. D)

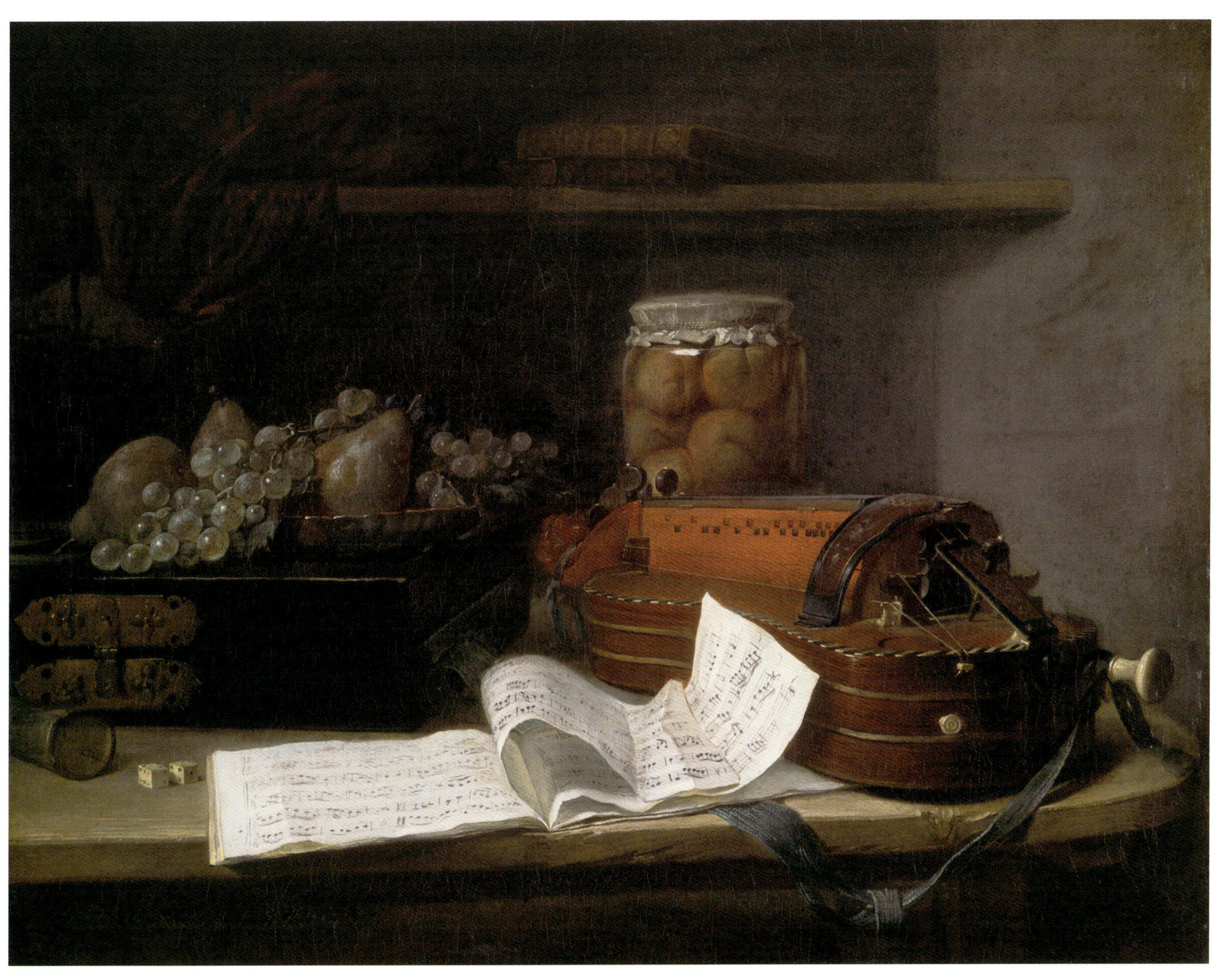

[84] *Still Life with Jar of Apricots and Hurdy-Gurdy,*
c. 1760

Oil on canvas
31½ × 39¾ in.
Musée des Beaux-Arts, Bordeaux
(cat. E)

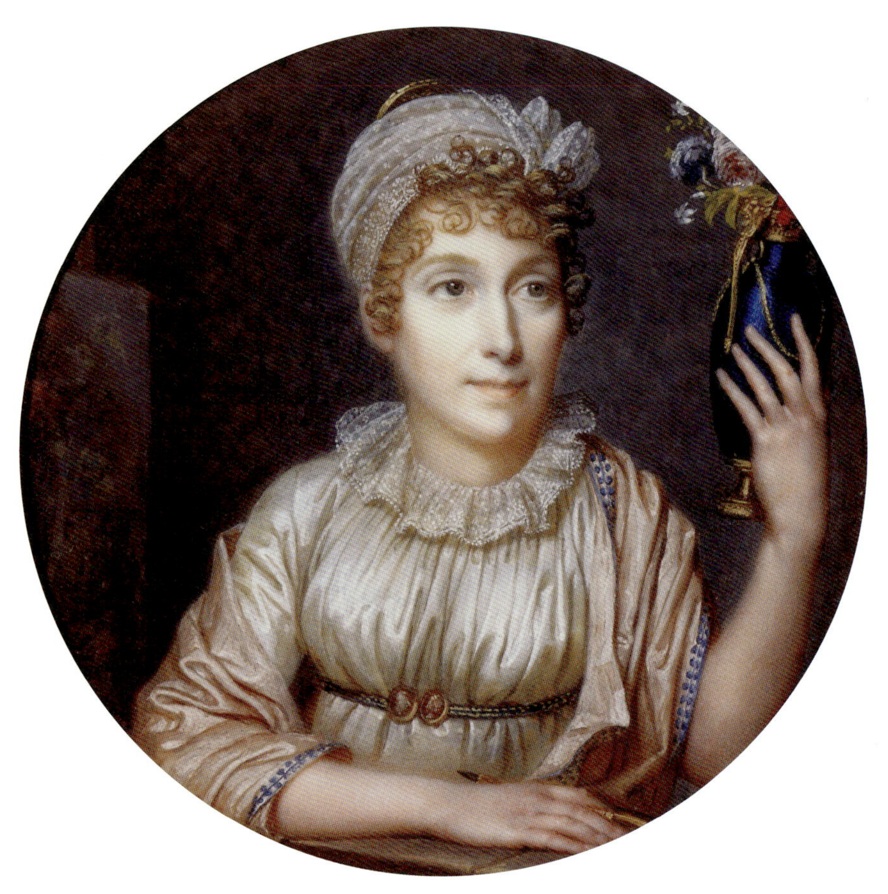

FRANÇOIS DUMONT

[85]   *Anne Vallayer-Coster*, 1804

Gouache on ivory
Diam. 3 in.
The Cleveland Museum of Art, The Edward B. Greene
Collection, 1943.639
(cat. C)

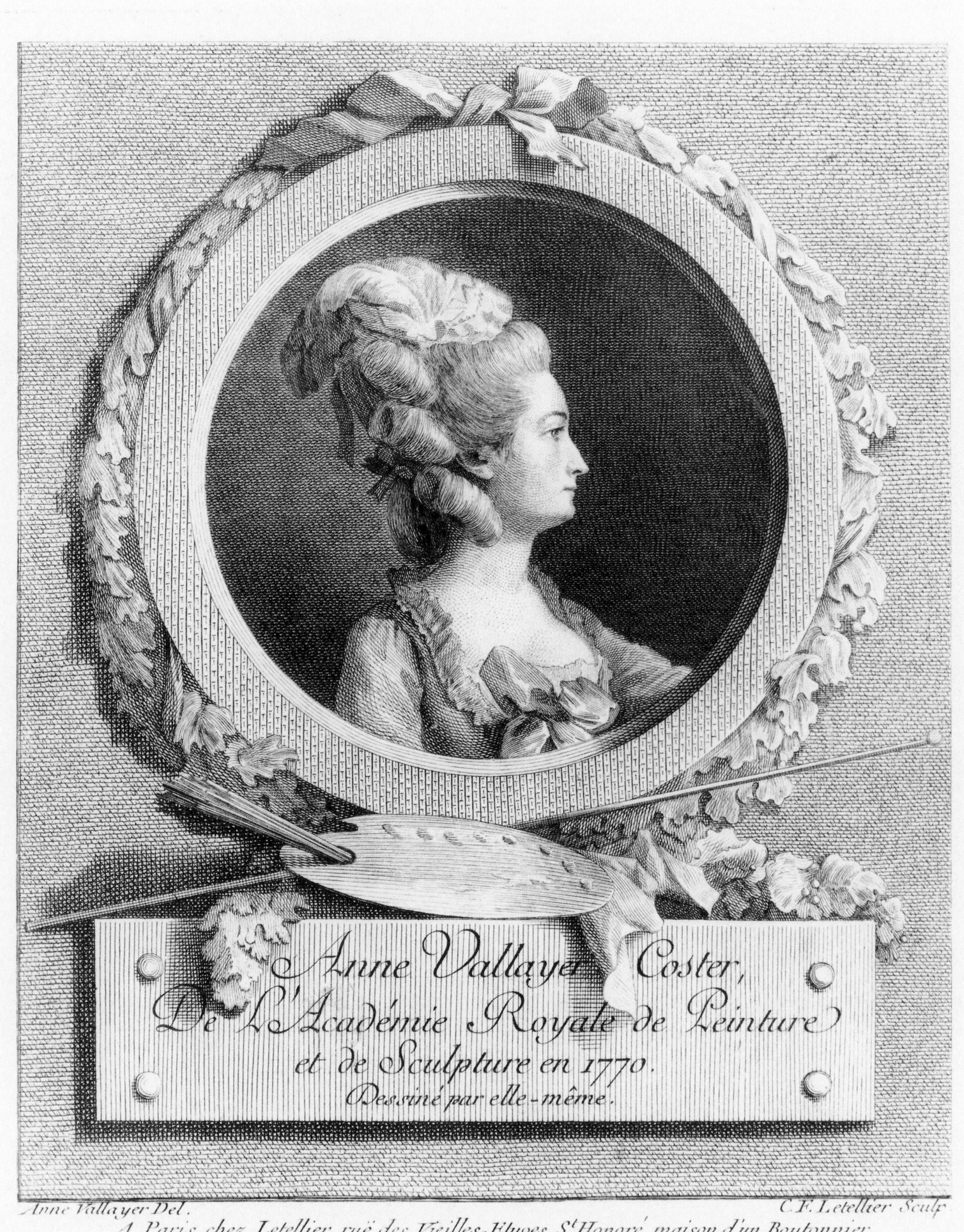

AFTER ANNE VALLAYER-COSTER

CHARLES-FRANÇOIS LETELLIER

[86]   *The Artist's Self-Portrait*, 1781

Engraving
9¼ × 7⅜ in.
Private collection
(cat. 156)

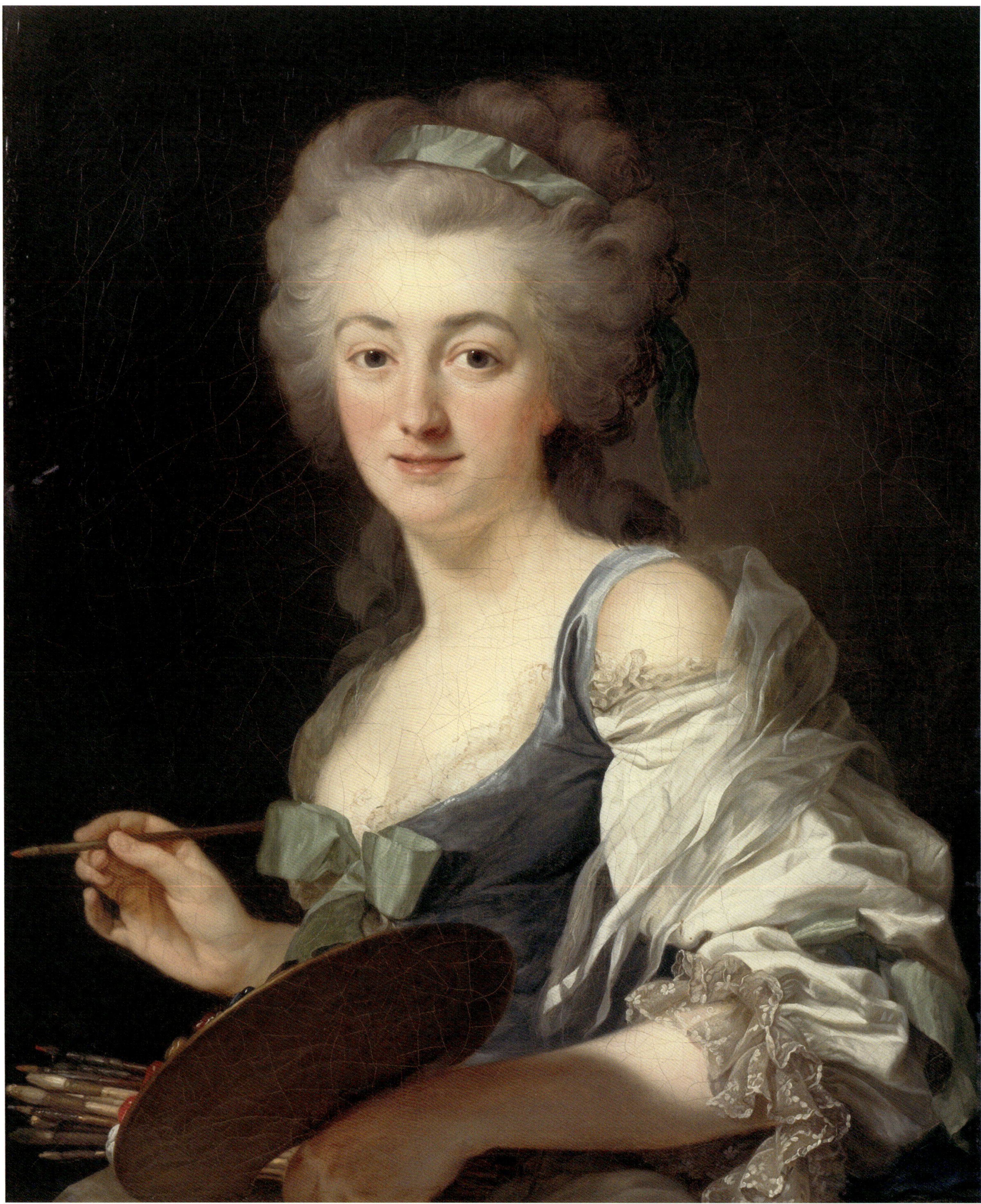

[87]   *Portrait of Anne Vallayer-Coster*, c. 1783

Oil on canvas
29⅛ × 23⅝ in.
Private collection
(cat. F)

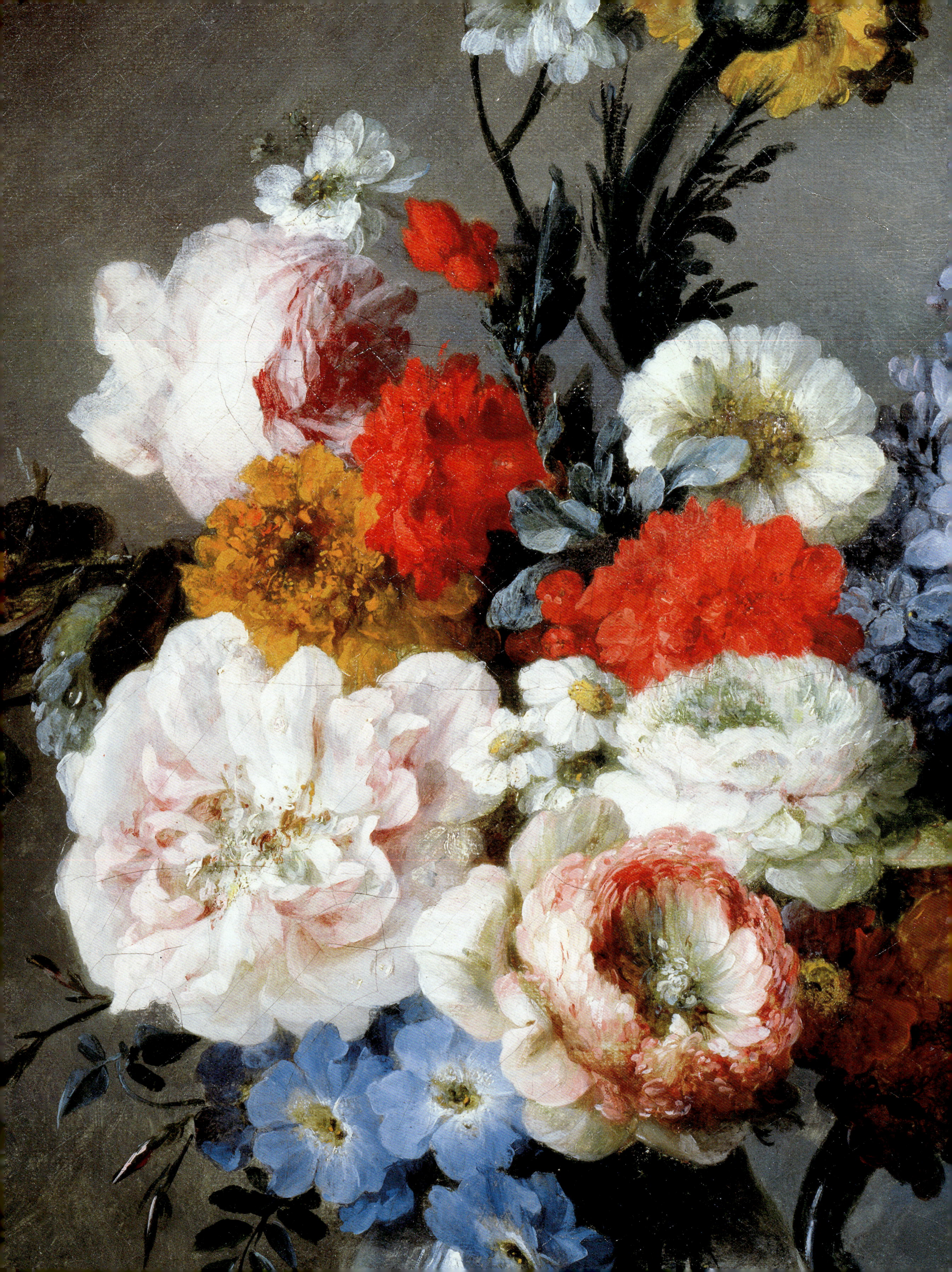

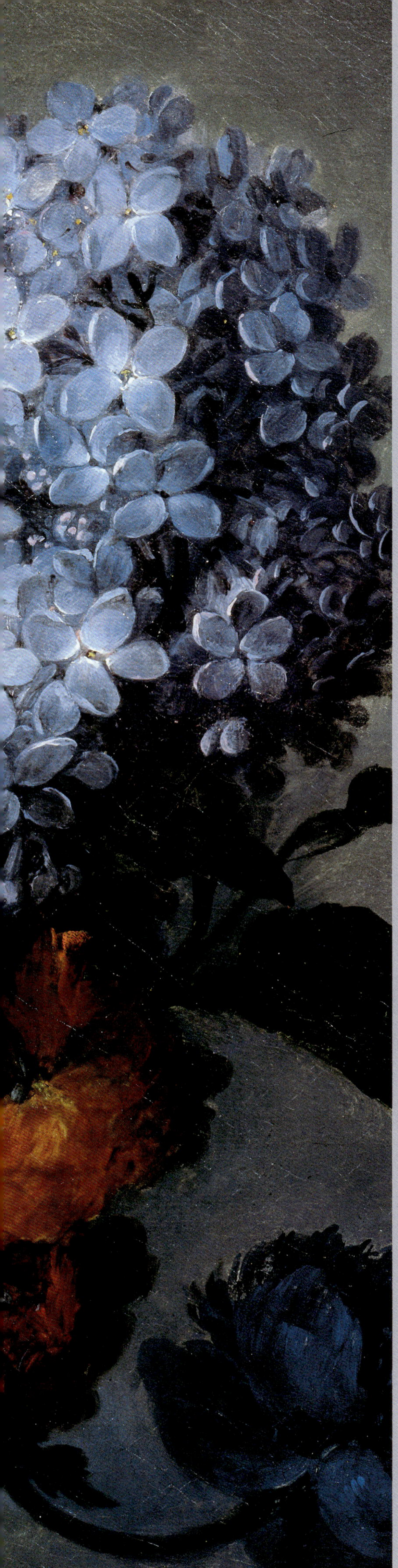

Catalogue

This catalogue is divided into
three parts: Catalogue of Extant
Paintings, including those in the
exhibition; Exhibited Works in Other
Media; and Exhibited Works
by Other Artists.

Works included in this exhibition
are denoted by plate numbers, which
refer to the color plate section
of the book. These works are also
annotated with abbreviations for
the cities where they will appear:
W (National Gallery of Art,
Washington, D.C.), D (Dallas
Museum of Art), and NY (The Frick
Collection, New York). Works are
arranged first chronologically when
dated and then, as far as possible,
alphabetically. Undated works appear
after dated works, alphabetically
by the most usually given title.

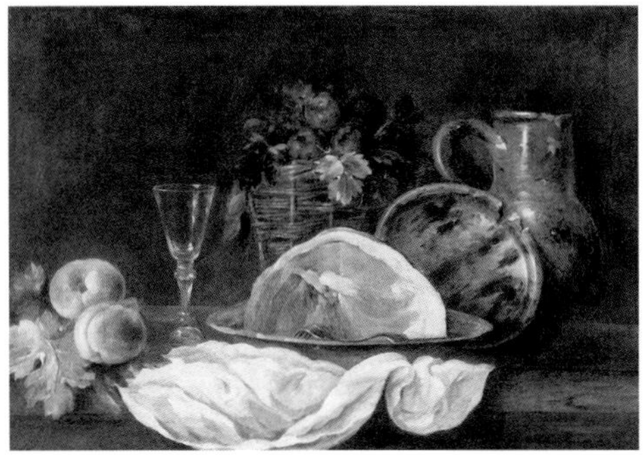

1. *Still Life with Ham*, 1763 or 1765

Oil on canvas, 21½ × 30⅜ in. (54.5 × 77 cm)
Signed and dated lower right: *Melle Vallayer 176[?]*
Private collection, Basel

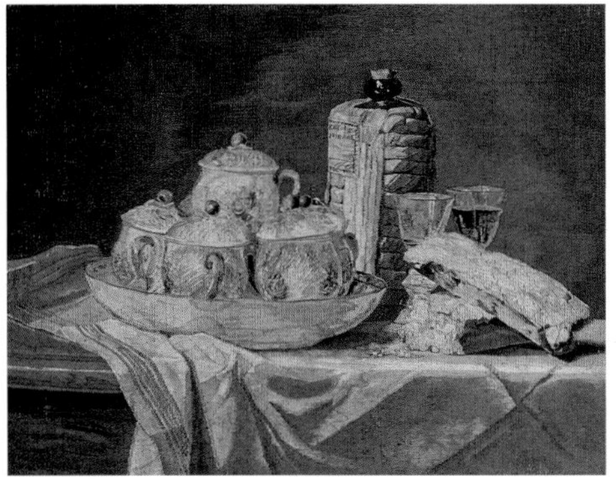

2. *The Dessert*, 1766

Oil on canvas, 14⅝ × 17¾ in. (37 × 45 cm)
Present whereabouts unknown
Provenance: sale, Paris, 12 May 1926, lot 130
(with its pendant, cat. 3); David-Weill
collection.
Selected References: Dimier 1926, 103; Roland
Michel 1965, 189; Roland Michel 1970, no. 219.
Related Works: The painting for which the
tapestry illustrated here is the only known
record, with its pendant, was a model for one of
a pair of Gobelins tapestries first commissioned
in 1809, now at the Musée Nissim de Camondo,
Paris, entitled *Dessert* (or *Le Service à crème*,
illus. here) (Roland Michel 1970, no. 436).

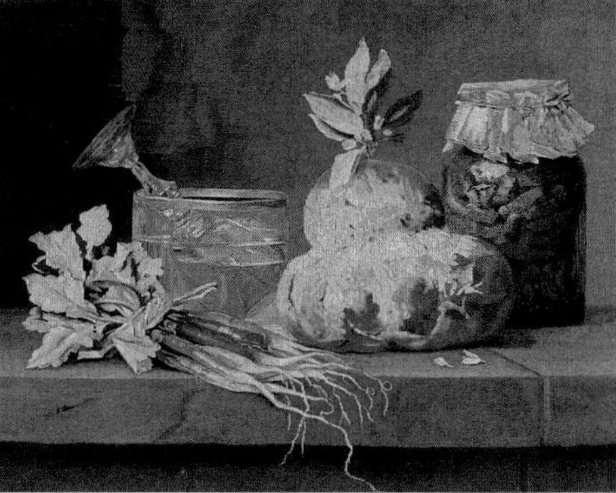

3. *The Lunch*, 1766

Oil on canvas, 14⅝ × 17¾ in. (37 × 45 cm)
Signed and dated: *Melle Vallayer, 1766*
Present whereabouts unknown
Provenance: sale, Paris, 12 May 1926, lot 129
(with its pendant, cat. 2); David-Weill
collection.
Selected References: Dimier 1926, 103; Roland
Michel 1965, 189; Roland Michel 1970, no. 218.
Related Works: The painting for which the
tapestry illustrated here is the only known
record, with its pendant, was a model for one of
a pair of Gobelins tapestries first commissioned
in 1809, now at the Musée Nissim de Camondo,
Paris, entitled *Lunch* (or *La Brioche*, illus. here)
(Roland Michel 1970, no. 435).

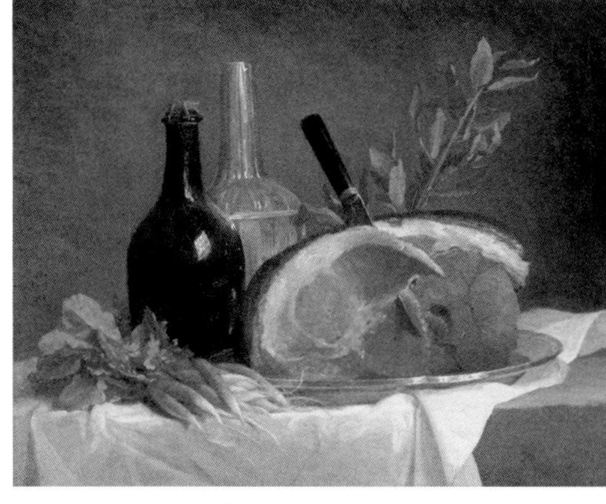

4. *Still Life with Ham, Bottles, and Radishes*, 1767

Oil on canvas, 17¾ × 21⅝ in. (45 × 55 cm)
Signed and dated toward center right: *Melle/
Vallayer/.1767*
Staatliche Museen zu Berlin, Gemäldegalerie
Provenance: bequeathed by Dr. Benedict to the
Kaiser Friedrich Museum, now the Staatliche
Museen zu Berlin, in 1927.
Exhibited: Karlsruhe 1999, no. 160.
Selected References: Kunze 1931, 495,
no. 20.011; M. Faré 1962, 2: fig. 413; Roland
Michel 1965, 189; Roland Michel 1970, no. 221,
illus. 82; M. and F. Faré 1976, 218, with wrong
caption; Bock 1986, 122–123; Bryson 1990,
161–163, illus. 163.
Related Work: According to Roland Michel,
there is a close copy of this work by a Mme Julien
from 1839, which belonged to the descendants
of the artist.
D, NY
Pl. 1

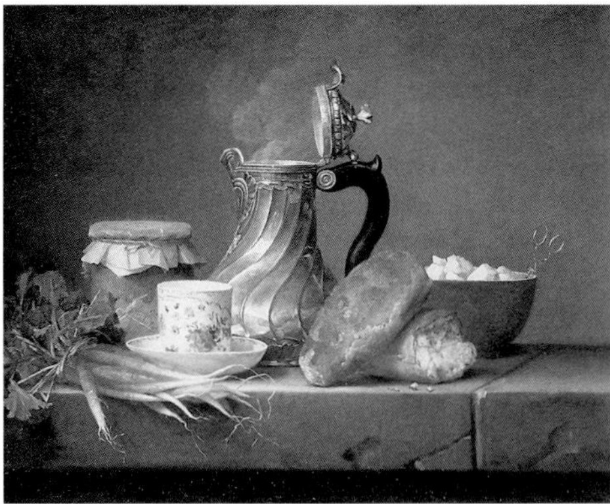

5. *Still Life with Silver Pitcher*, 1767

Oil on canvas, 19½ × 23⅜ in. (49.5 × 59.5 cm)
Signed and dated lower right: *Melle Vallayer/1767*
Private collection, United Kingdom, courtesy
of Thomas and Brenda Brod
Provenance: Belvalette collection; sons of Léon
Helft collection; Maxime Lévy collection; sale,
Paris, Hôtel Drouot, 17 April 1970, pl. 1.
Exhibited: Paris 1908; Paris 1926, no. 90; Paris
1936b, no. 458; Paris 1945, no. 40.
Selected References: M. Faré 1962, 2: fig. 412;
Roland Michel 1965, 189; Roland Michel 1970,
no. 220, illus. 166; M. and F. Faré 1976, fig. 330;
Karlsruhe 1999, fig. 2, 330.
Related Work: A painting of low quality,
inspired by this one, was on the London art
market in 1974.
Commentary: The silver pitcher is almost
identical to the one by the goldsmith Jean-
Guillaume Véalle, dated 1755–1756, in the
Musée des Arts décoratifs, Paris.

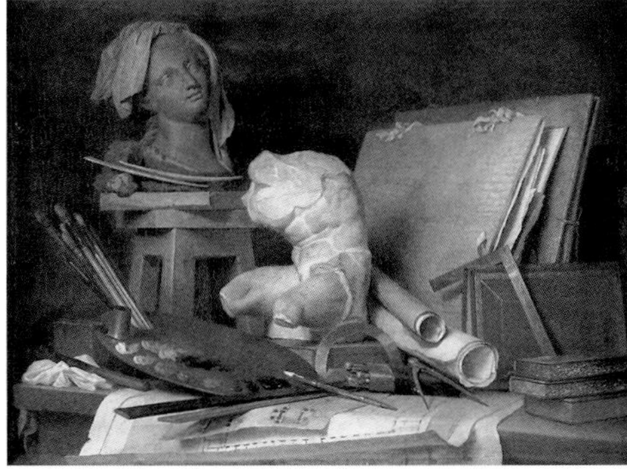

6. *The Attributes of Painting, Sculpture, and
Architecture*, 1769

Oil on canvas, 35⅜ × 47⅝ in. (90 × 121 cm)
Signed and dated lower right: *Melle Vallayer 1769*
Musée du Louvre, Paris, inv. no. 8259
Provenance: collections de l'Académie
(listed in the inventory of the Year II, since
the abolishment of the Académie royale listed
as no. 566-40); documented in 1852 as at the
Ministère de la Justice, from where it entered
the Musée du Louvre on 28 December 1872.
Exhibited: Salon of 1771, no. 149; Musée de
Versailles, 1801; Paris 1926, no. 93.
Selected References: *Mercure de France*,
September 1770, 174, and October 1771, 1:193
(Collection Deloynes, no. 138, 482–483);
Lettres de M. Raphaël le jeune 1771 (Collection
Deloynes, no. 141, 18); *La Muse errante au Sallon*

1771 (Collection Deloynes, no. 145, 33); Legouvé
1801, 14, 43n.; Montaiglon 1875–1892, 8:48–49;
Fontaine 1910a, 202; Suppl. Tauzia 1878, 862;
Brière 1924, no. 893; Oulmont 1928, pl. 45;
Schmid 1948, 50, 51, 60, 62, 70, 71; Seznec
and Adhémar 1957–1967, 4:202; Schmid 1958;
M. Faré 1962, 1:138, 2: fig. 423; Roland Michel
1970, no. 257; Louvre 1972, 379; Rosenberg,
Reynaud, and Compin 1974, 828; M. and F. Faré
1976, fig. 338; Bukdahl 1980, illus. 199; Compin
and Roquebert 1986, 258, no. 8259; Ebert-
Schifferer 1999, 257, pl. 187; F. Faré 1999, 68,
illus.; Fort 1999, 86; Karlsruhe 1999, fig. 1, 330.
Commentary: This is one of Vallayer's two reception pieces for the Académie, 28 July 1770,
together with cat. 12.

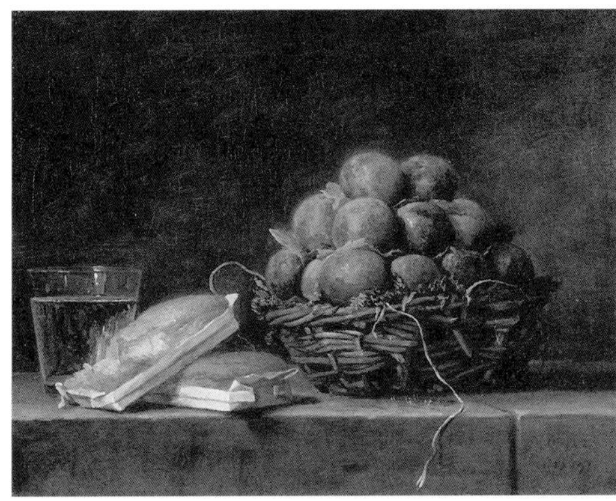

7. *Basket of Plums*, 1769

Oil on canvas, 14¹⁵⁄₁₆ × 18³⁄₁₆ in. (38 × 46.2 cm)
Signed and dated lower right: *Melle Vallayer/
1769*
The Cleveland Museum of Art, Mr. and
Mrs. William H. Marlatt Fund, 1971.47
Provenance: Baron Herzog collection, Buda-
pest; Axel Rydén collection, Stockholm, 1918;
Osborn Kling collection, Stockholm, 1934;
sale, Bukowski, Stockholm, 25–26 Septem-
ber 1934, cat. Bukowski 296, lot 323, pl. 37;
Thorsten Laurin collection, Stockholm, 1938;
Mrs. B. Stijernsward (his daughter), Sakanor,
Sweden; sale, Sotheby's, London, 24 June 1970,
lot 4, illus.; Old Masters Gallery, London;
H. Shickman Gallery, New York, sold in 1971.
Exhibited: perhaps Salon of 1771, no. 147, or
Salon of 1773, no. 143; Stockholm 1918, no. 40;
Göteborg 1938, no. 52; Stockholm 1958, no. 102;
Cleveland 1972, no. 56; Cleveland 1979, no. 7,
illus.
Selected References: Hoppe 1936, no. 399,
pl. 218; Roland Michel 1970, no. 183, illus. 155;
Roland Michel 1973, 52–59, fig. 4; Clark 1974,
309, 313, no. 2, fig. 2; M. and F. Faré 1976,
fig. 332, 217.
W, D, NY
Pl. 2

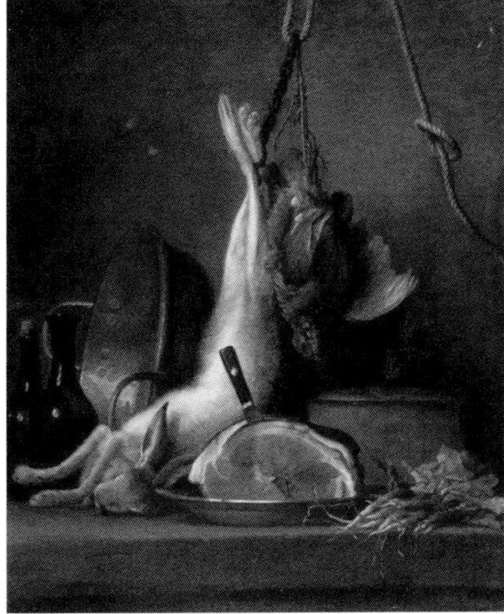

8. *Hare, Partridge, and Ham*, 1769

Oil on canvas, 40⅛ × 31½ in. (101.8 × 80.7 cm)
Signed and dated lower right: *Melle Vallayer
Coster./1769*
Inscribed on the back of the frame in blue
pencil: *NC 505*; in black ink: *(783)*
On deposit at the Musée des Beaux-Arts, Reims
Provenance: purchased for the Städtische
Kunstsammlungen of Düsseldorf, Galerie Alice
Manteau, Paris; transferred to the Musée du
Louvre in 1950; registered in the Musée des
Beaux-Arts, Reims, in 1953.
Exhibited: Paris 1959a, no. 80; Brussels 1975,
no. 95, illus. 136; Moscow and Leningrad 1978,
no. 15.
Selected References: M. Faré 1962, 2: fig. 414;
Vergnet-Ruiz and Laclotte 1962, 84, 354;
Roland Michel 1965, 185; Roland Michel 1970,
no. 281, illus. 202; M. and F. Faré 1976, fig. 333;
Catalogue sommaire 1986, 344.
Commentary: The "Coster" was evidently added
at a later date, which indicates that the painting
was still in the possession of the artist in 1781,
the year of her marriage. This painting was
recovered in Germany after World War II and
entrusted to the care of the Direction des
Musées de France.

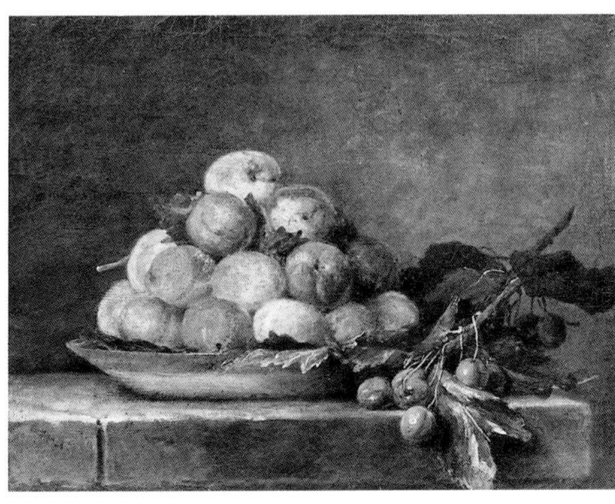

9. *Peaches and Cherries*, 1769

Oil on canvas, 14⅝ × 18⅛ in. (37 × 46 cm)
Signed and dated left: *Melle Vallayer/1769*
Present whereabouts unknown
Provenance: Cournerie collection, sale, Paris,
8–9 December 1891, lot 29; Sedelmeyer collec-
tion, sale, Paris, 16 May 1907, lot 247; sale,
Brussels, Giroux Gallery, 19–20 February 1954;

Pardo Gallery, Paris, in 1958; private collection,
Paris, in 1970.
Exhibited: Paris 1936, no. 49.
Selected Reference: Roland Michel 1970,
no. 127, illus. 146.
Related Work: This composition was also
done in pastel, once attributed to Chardin: see
Roland Michel 1970, no. 388.

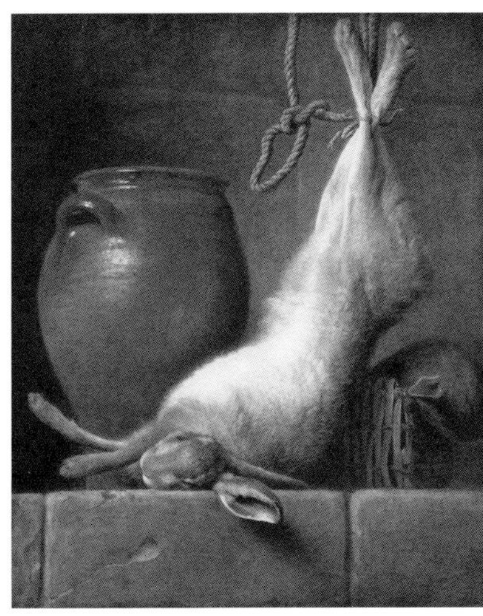

10. *Still Life with Dead Hare*, 1769

Oil on canvas, enlarged on all four sides,
29⅜ × 23⅞ in. (74.5 × 60.5 cm)
Signed and dated lower right: *Melle Vallayer/
1769*
Collection of Jeffrey E. Horvitz, Boston
Provenance: baronne Laurent Atthalin
collection; private collection, Paris; Galerie
Cailleux, Paris; private collection; Maurice
Segoura, Paris, 1995.
Exhibited: Paris 1959b, no. 81.
Selected References: Roland Michel 1965, 189;
Roland Michel 1970, no. 280.
W, D, NY
Pl. 3

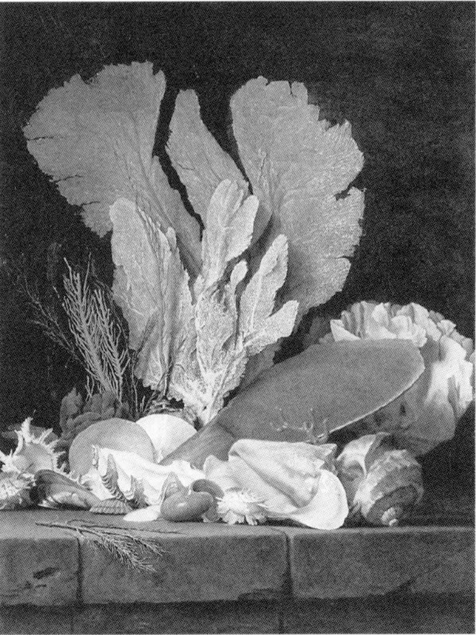

11. *Still Life with Seashells and Coral*, 1769

Oil on canvas, 51⅛ × 38¼ in. (130 × 97 cm)
Signed and dated lower right: *par M.ᵉˡˡᵉ Vallayer/
en 1769*
Musée du Louvre, Paris, R.F. 1992-410

Provenance: this painting and its pendant are described in the aborted [Dubarry] sale, 22 December 1775, lot 35; although they were sold by the artist to Louis-François de Bourbon, prince de Conti, in January 1776; sale, Paris, 8 April–6 June 1777, lot 775; acquired by the dealer Jean-Baptiste Le Brun; Charles Ricketts (1866–1931) collection, as of 1880; Major Price Blackwood sale, Christie's, London, 7 April 1922, lot 62; Cecil Lewis collection, Corfu, as of 1979; Roberto Polo collection, sale, étude Ader-Tajan, Paris, 30 May 1988, lot 2, illus.; sale, Paris, étude Ader-Tajan, 14 December 1992, lot 51, illus.

Exhibited: Salon of 1771, no. 145; L'Isle Adam 2000, 39, illus. 88.

Selected References: *Lettres de M. Raphaël le jeune,* 7 September 1771, 18 (Collection Deloynes, no. 141, 18); *Mercure de France,* October 1771, 1:193; *L'ombre de Raphaël* 1771, 33 (Collection Deloynes, no. 143, 41); "Exposition des peintures, sculptures et gravures," *Journal encyclopédique* 1771 (Collection Deloynes, IL, no. 1318, 482–483); *Exposition au Salon du Louvre des Peintures, Sculptures et Gravures de Messieurs de l'Académie Royale* 1771 (Collection Deloynes, IL, no. 274); Seznec and Adhémar 1957–1967, 4:145, 201–202; Roland Michel 1970, no. 260, illus. 181; Paris 1974–1975, 633; M. and F. Faré 1976, 220, 221, 413 n. 181; Grimm 1995, 226, fig. 123; Rosenberg 1996, 231–234, fig. 190; Sahut in Foucart et al. 1996, 147–150, pl. 10; Pinault Sørensen and Sahut 1998, 57–70; F. Faré 1999, 68, illus. 70; Fort 1999, 86; Temperini 1999, illus. 556.

Commentary: The pendant to this painting, *A Vase, Minerals, Crystals, and Three Vials of Spirit Alcohol on a Table,* was also exhibited at the Salon of 1771. It has been lost since 1777 (see Roland Michel 1970, no. 261).
W, D, NY
Pl. 4

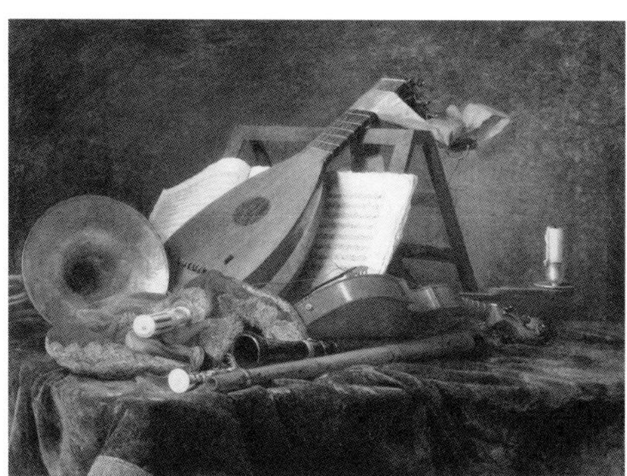

12. *The Attributes of Music,* 1770

Oil on canvas, 35⅝ × 45⅝ in. (88 × 116 cm)
Signed and dated center right: *M.ᶜˡˡᵉ Vallayer/ 1770*
Musée du Louvre, Paris, inv. no. 8260
Provenance: collections de l'Académie (listed in the inventory of 1798, since the abolishment of the Académie royale listed as no. 566-40); documented in 1852 as at the Ministère de la Justice, from where it entered the Musée du Louvre on 28 December 1872; at the palais de

Fontainebleau at the end of the nineteenth century.

Exhibited: Salon of 1771, no. 149; Musée de Versailles 1801; Paris 1926, no. 94; Bordeaux 1969, no. 103; Toledo 1975, no. 105; Peking 1982; Paris 1995; Tokyo 1997, no. 59.

Selected References: *Mercure de France,* September 1770, 174, and October 1771, 1:193 (Collection Deloynes, no. 1318, 482–483); *L'Avant-Coureur,* no. 38 (23 September 1771), 601 (Collection Deloynes, 49, no. 1317, 451); *La Muse errante au Sallon* 1771 (Collection Deloynes, no. 145, 33); *Lettres de M. Raphaël le jeune,* 7 September 1771, 18 (Collection Deloynes, no. 141, 18); Montaiglon 1875–1892, 8:48–49; Chennevières 1881, no. 131; Fontaine 1910b, no. 565-39; Brière 1924, no. 894; Seznec and Adhémar 1957–1967, 4:202; Schlumberger 1958, illus. 68; M. Faré 1962, 2: fig. 424; Mirimonde 1965, 119, illus. 16; Roland Michel 1970, no. 258, illus. 191; Bergamo 1971, mentioned in relation to no. 61; Louvre 1972, 379; Roland Michel 1973, fig. 3; Rosenberg, Reynaud, and Compin 1974, 2: no. 829; M. and F. Faré 1976, 218–219, fig. 334; Bukdahl 1980, illus. 280; Compin and Roquebert 1986, 258, no. 8260; Cantarel-Besson 1992, 249, 257; Levey 1993, 265–267, illus. 266; Goldstein 1996, fig. 24; Lallement 1998, 210, fig. 23; F. Faré 1999, 71; Fort 1999, 86; Temperini 1999, illus. 556; Tours 2000, illus. 275.

Commentary: This is one of Vallayer's two reception paintings for the Académie, 28 July 1770, together with its pendant, cat. 6.
D, NY
Pl. 5

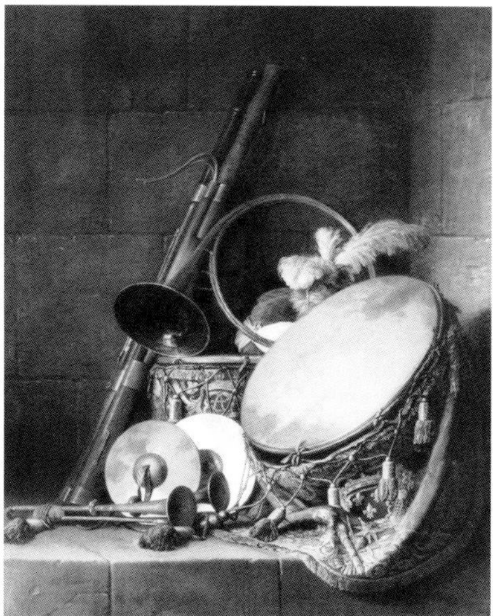

13. *Still Life with Military Musical Instruments,* 1771

Oil on canvas, 63 × 51 in. (160 × 129.5 cm)
Signed and dated lower right: *Melle Vallayer 1771.*
Private collection
Provenance: aborted [Dubarry] sale, 22 December 1775, lot 32 (with its pendant, now lost); remained in the same family in Paris, probably since the eighteenth century; Tajan sale, Paris, 25 June 1996, lot 52.

Exhibited: Salon of 1771, no. 141.

Selected References: *La Muse errante au Sallon* 1771 (Collection Deloynes, no. 145, 33);

Lettres de M. Raphaël le jeune 1771 (Collection Deloynes, no. 141, 18); *L'ombre de Raphaël* 1771 (Collection Deloynes, no. 143, 41); *Plaintes de M. Badigeon* 1771 (Collection Deloynes, no. 144, 11); *Mercure de France,* October 1771, 1:193; Seznec and Adhémar 1957–1967, 4:144–145; Roland Michel 1970, no. 259; Fort 1999, 86.

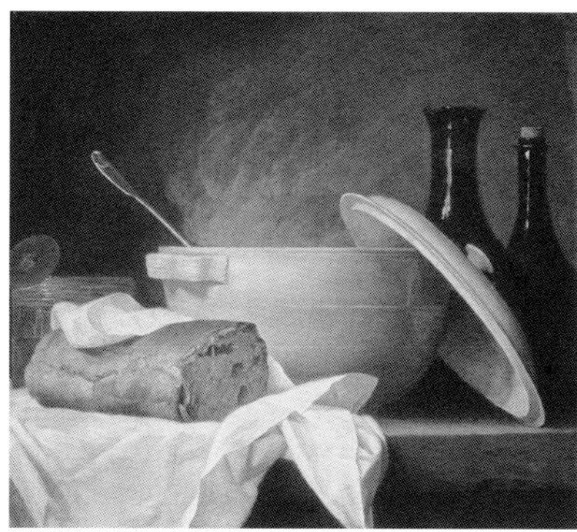

14. *The White Soup Tureen,* 1771

Oil on canvas, 19⅝ × 24⅜ in. (50 × 62 cm)
Private collection, Paris
Provenance: marquis de Marigny collection, sale, Paris, March–April 1782, lot 113; Beaujon collection, sale, Hôtel d'Evreux, Paris, 25 April 1787, lot 209.

Exhibited: Salon of 1771, no. 143; Paris 1956, no. 100; Paris 1959a, no. 82, pl. 37; Los Angeles 1976, no. 52, illus.

Selected References: Seznec and Adhémar 1957–1967, 4:201; M. Faré 1962, 1:178, 2: pl. XII; Roland Michel 1965, 189; Roland Michel 1970, no. 222, illus. 171; M. and F. Faré 1976, fig. 342; F. Faré 1999, 68, illus. 69.
Pl. 6

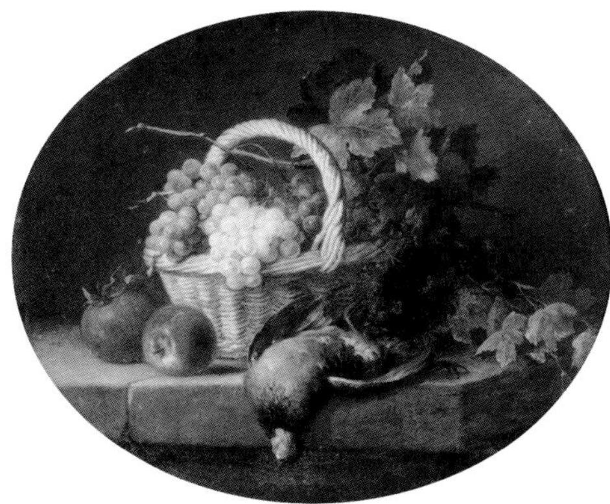

15. *Basket of Grapes, Apples, and Partridge,* 1772

Oil on canvas, oval, 21¼ × 25¼ in. (54 × 64 cm)
Signed and dated at right, on shelf: *Mᵉˡˡᵉ Vallayer/ 1772.*
Musée Nissim de Camondo, Paris
Provenance: Chaix d'Est Ange collection; sale, Paris, 11 December 1934, lot 34.

Exhibited: Salon of 1773, no. 141.

Selected References: *Eloge des tableaux exposés au Louvre* 1773; Schlumberger 1958, illus. 68; Musée Nissim de Camondo 1960, no. 730; Roland Michel 1970, no. 132.

Commentary: Pendant of cat. 16.

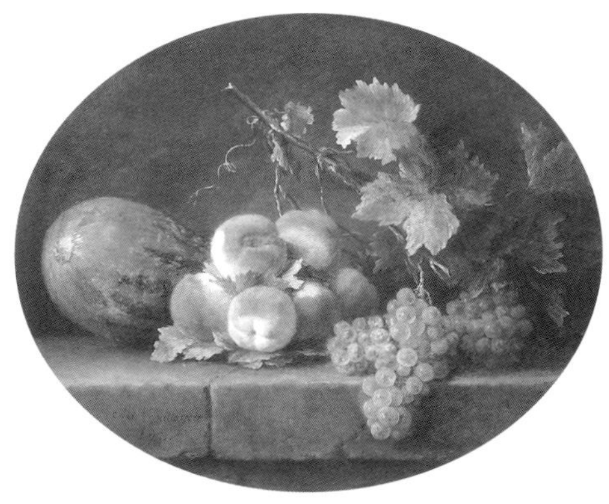

16. *Basket of Peaches with Melon*, 1772

Oil on canvas, oval, 21¼ × 25½ in. (54 × 64.8 cm)
Signed and dated lower left: *Melle Vallayer/1772*
Private collection
Provenance: Cournerie sale, Paris, 8–9 December 1891, lot 24.
Exhibited: Salon of 1773, no. 141.
Selected Reference: Roland Michel 1970, nos. 133, 134.
Commentary: Pendant of cat. 15.
W, D, NY
Pl. 9

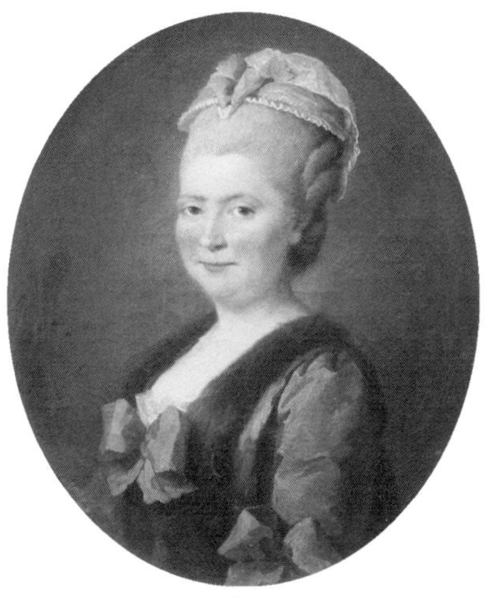

17. *Portrait of Mme de Béricourt*, 1772

Oil on canvas, oval, 23¼ × 19¾ in. (59 × 50 cm)
Signed and dated left: *Mlle Vallayer 1772*
Musée départemental d'Art Ancien et Contemporain des Vosges, Epinal
Provenance: Doctor Paul Oulmont collection (no. 64); given to the museum in 1917.
Selected References: Philippe 1929, 145, no. 64; Roland Michel 1970, no. 308, illus. 220.

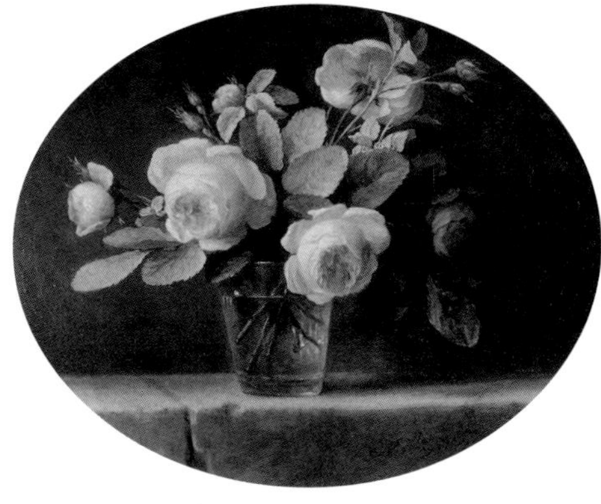

18. *Roses in a Glass*, 1772

Oil on canvas, oval, 15 × 18⅛ in. (38 × 46 cm)
Signed and dated at right: *Melle V. 1772*
Present whereabouts unknown
Provenance: Mme Patrick de Bayser collection, sale, Sotheby's, Monaco, 22 February 1986, lot 228.
Selected Reference: Roland Michel 1970, no. 5; M. and F. Faré 1976, fig. 341.
Commentary: The same motif was used in a miniature from 1809; see cat. 154, pl. 67.

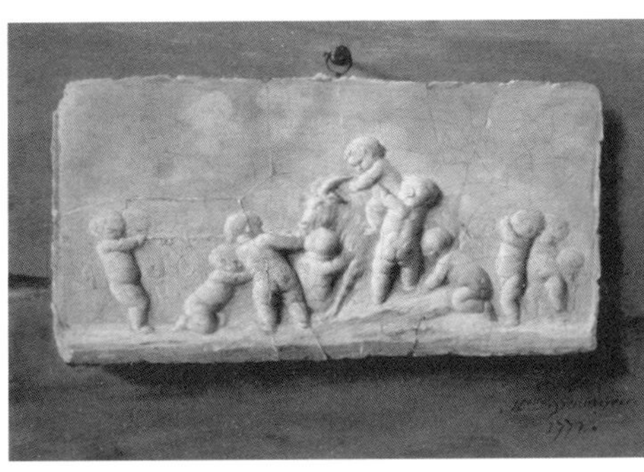

19. *Trompe l'Oeil of a Terracotta Bas-Relief (after La Rue) Pinned to a Wooden Panel*, 1772

Oil on canvas, 9⅞ × 14½ in. (25 × 37 cm)
Signed and dated lower right: *Melle Vallayer/1772.*
Courtesy of Rafael Valls, Ltd, London
Provenance: probably Joseph Vernet collection, bought in November 1776; his sale, 20 April 1790, lot 21; sale, Paris, 17 April 1899, lot 12; sale, Toulouse, 7 November 1998; Rafael Valls.
Exhibited: Salon of 1773, no. 144.
Selected References: Roland Michel 1970, no. 241 (as lost); Roland Michel 1993, 365; Valls 1999, no. 39, illus.
Commentary: In 1970 another version was with the descendants of the artist (Roland Michel 1970, 252, no. 101, cat. 100).
W, D, NY
Pl. 7

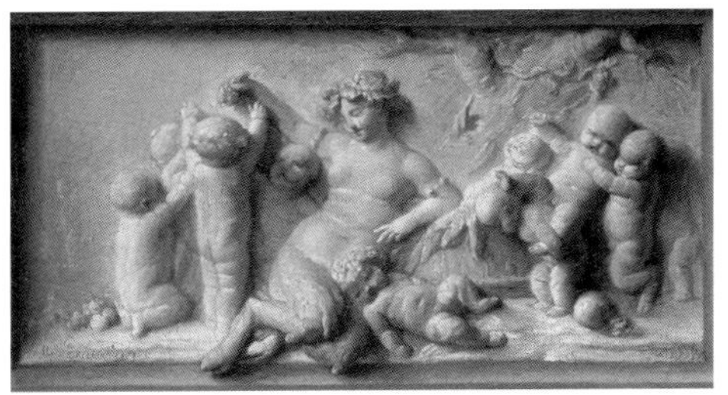

20. *Female Faun and Putti*, 1773

Oil on canvas, 6⅜ × 11½ in. (16.2 × 29.2 cm)
Signed lower left: *Melle Vallayer*; dated lower right: *1773*
Private collection
Provenance: Bécherel collection, sale, Paris, 26–28 November 1883, lot 48; sale, Sotheby's, Monaco, 5–6 December 1991, lot 171A; Lagerfeld collection; Christie's, New York, 23 May 2000, lot 65.
Selected References: Roland Michel 1970, no. 242 (as lost); Roland Michel 1993a, 363 n. 27.
Related Works: According to Roland Michel, this painting, as well as Roland Michel 1970, no. 248 (see cat. 27), was based on a terracotta bas-relief by Clodion, in the collection of the artist (Coster sale 1824, lot 75).
W, D, NY
Pl. 8

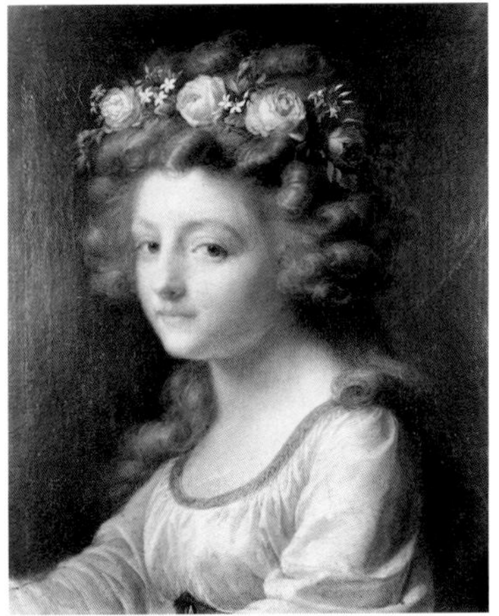

21. *Portrait of Mme de Bouhébent*, 1773

Oil on canvas, 17¾ × 16⅛ in. (45 × 41 cm)
Present whereabouts unknown
Provenance: in the family's possession since 1773; with the baronne de Saint-Palais, great-grandniece of the artist, in 1970.
Exhibited: Salon of 1773, no. 140 (as *Le Portrait de Mme B.*).
Selected Reference: Roland Michel 1970, no. 309, illus. 206.
Commentary: This is a portrait of Elisabeth, second sister of the artist, in 1773, age twenty-six and married for a year to Josué de Bouhébent. In 1992 a copy in pastel was on the art market, Brussels.

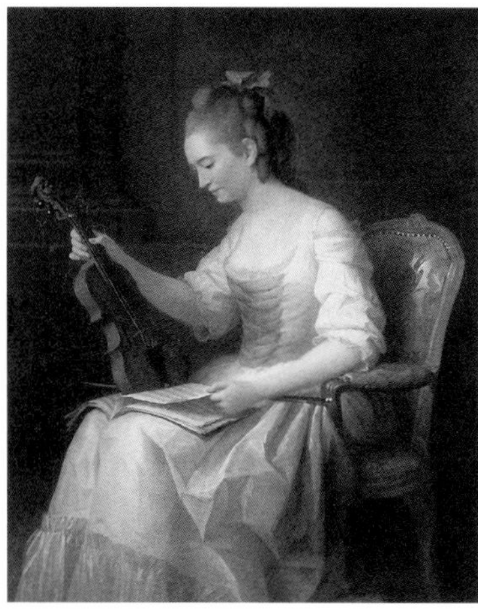

22. *Portrait of a Young Violinist,* 1773

Oil on canvas, 47¼ × 35⅜ in. (120 × 90 cm)
Signed and dated center left: *Melle Vallayer/1773*
Private collection, Brussels
Provenance: sale, 16 May 1783, no. 20; Emile
Barré collection, sale, Paris, 30–31 January
1894, lot 55 (as a self-portrait); F. Doistau
collection, 1st sale, Paris, June 1909, lot 76,
illus. (bought by Féral); Dr. James Simon
collection, Berlin, sale, Amsterdam, Frederick
Müller and Co., 26 September 1927; A. S. Drey
collection, Munich; art market, Paris, c. 1948;
sale, Sotheby's, Monaco, 16 June 1989, lot 378,
illus.; Didier Aaron, Paris.
Selected Reference: Roland Michel 1970,
no. 310 (as lost), 208.
Commentary: According to Roland Michel, this
painting may be a portrait of one of Vallayer-
Coster's sisters.
Pl. 10

23. *A Meal,* c. 1773

Oil on canvas, 17⅜ × 22 in. (44 × 56 cm)
Present whereabouts unknown
Provenance: Floriet collection, Paris (?);
private collection, New York; Lorenzelli,
Bergamo, in 1971.
Exhibited: probably Salon of 1773, no. 142,
"un déjeuner," with its pendant, *A Bowl of Apples*
(see Roland Michel 1970, no. 136); Bergamo
1971, no. 62, illus.
Selected Reference: Roland Michel 1970,
no. 223.

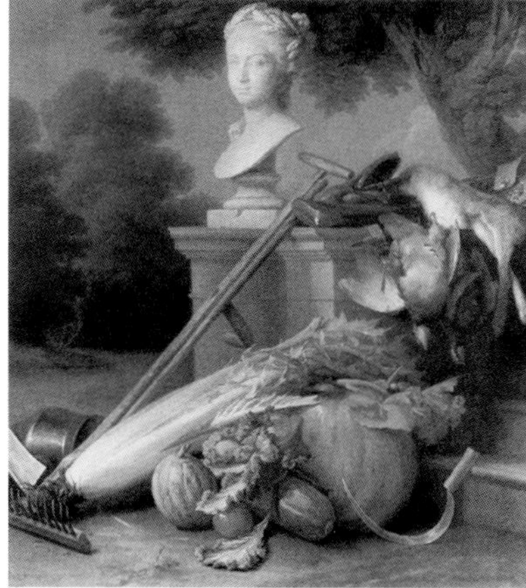

24. *The Attributes of Hunting and Gardening,* 1774

Oil on canvas, 59 × 53 in. (150 × 134.5 cm)
Signed and dated lower right: *Melle Vallayer/
1774*
Present whereabouts unknown
Provenance: abbé Terray collection, sale, Paris,
20 January 1779, lot 13; Cournerie collection,
sale, Paris, 8–9 December 1891, lot 23; F. Doistau
collection, 1st sale, Paris, 9 June 1909, lot 75
(bought by Sortais); sale, Galerie Charpentier, Paris, 3 December 1959, lot 69, illus.;
Sotheby's, London, 29 November 1961, lot 69,
illus.; Mrs. James Hasson; Christie's, London,
20 February 1981, lot 91; Sotheby's, London,
10 December 1986, lot 76.
Exhibited: Salon of 1775, no. 100.
Selected References: *Observations* 1775
(Collection Deloynes, no. 160, 44–45); Seznec
and Adhémar 1957–1967, 4:253; Roland Michel
1970, no. 283 (as lost), illus. 195; M. and F. Faré
1976, fig. 345.
Commentary: Pendant of cat. 30.

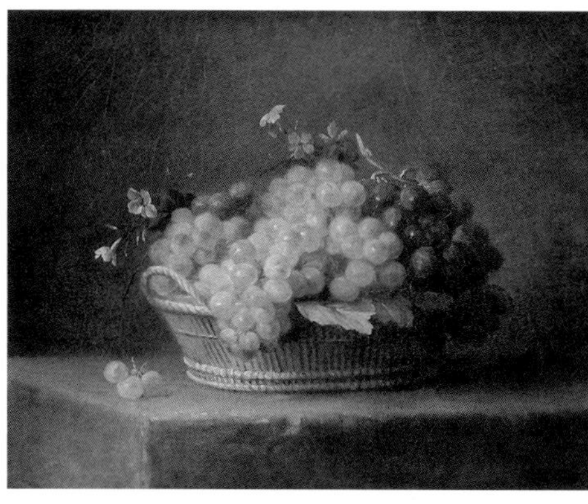

25. *Basket of Grapes,* 1774

Oil on canvas, 15 × 18⅛ in. (38 × 46 cm)
Signed and dated lower right: *Melle Vallayer 1774*
Musée des Beaux-Arts, Nancy, inv. no. 171
Provenance: marquis de Marigny collection,
sale, Paris, March–April 1782, lot 110, sold
to de Courmont; Chamisso collection, Nancy;
seized at the house of the widow of the comte
de Chamisso (1731–1790); inventories of the
Musée de Nancy, 4 December 1793, 30 May
1794, and 1807.
Exhibited: Paris 1959a, no. 83; Paris 1959b,
no. 17; Bordeaux 1999, no. 25, illus. 87; Nancy
2001, no. 67.

Selected References: Guédy 1889, 353; Thieme
and Becker 34:76; Vergnet-Ruiz and Laclotte
1962, 254; Roland Michel 1970, 49, no. 137,
illus. 76; M. and F. Faré 1976, 236, fig. 339;
Rosenblum 1979, 1:295; Bouleau 1993, 87–88;
Gelly-Saldias 1997, no. 10, 17.
W, D, NY
Pl. 12

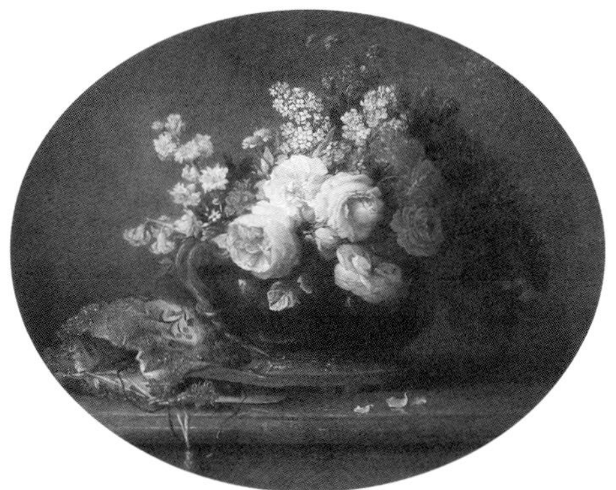

26. *Bouquet of Flowers with a Purse,* 1774

Oil on canvas, oval, 20⅛ × 23⅞ in. (51.2 ×
60.7 cm)
Signed and dated at left: *Mlle Vallayer/1774*
Villa Ephrussi de Rothschild–Institut de
France, Saint-Jean Cap Ferrat
Provenance: comte de La Béraudière collection,
sale, Paris, 18–30 May 1885, lot 80; Ephrussi de
Rothschild collection.
Exhibited: Salon of 1775, no. 102, with its
pendant.
Selected References: Vergnet-Ruiz and
Laclotte 1962, 254; Roland Michel 1970, no. 63;
M. and F. Faré 1976, fig. 343.
Commentary: Pendant of cat. 31.
W, D
Pl. 15

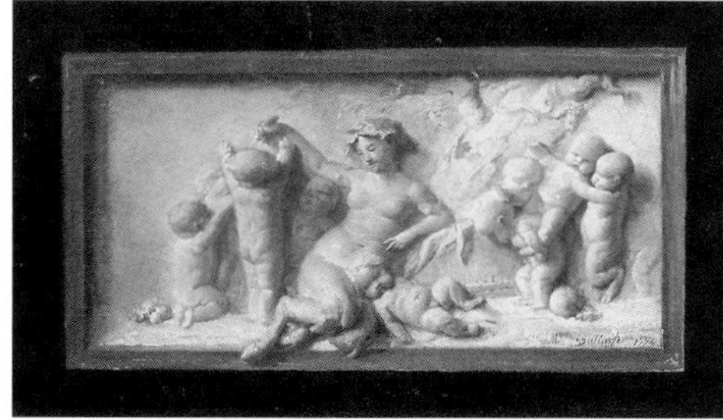

27. *Female Faun and Putti,* 1774

Oil on canvas, 8⅛ × 13⅞ in. (20.8 × 35.4 cm)
Signed and dated lower right: *Melle Vallayer 1774*
Private collection
Provenance: Coster sale 1824, lot 13; sale, Tajan,
Paris, 14 December 1992.
Exhibited: Grasse 1998, 32.
Selected References: Roland Michel 1970,
no. 248 (as lost since 1824); Zanella 2001,
209 illus.
Commentary: Same subject as cat. 20. It is
impossible to tell which version remained
in the artist's collection.
W, D
Pl. 11

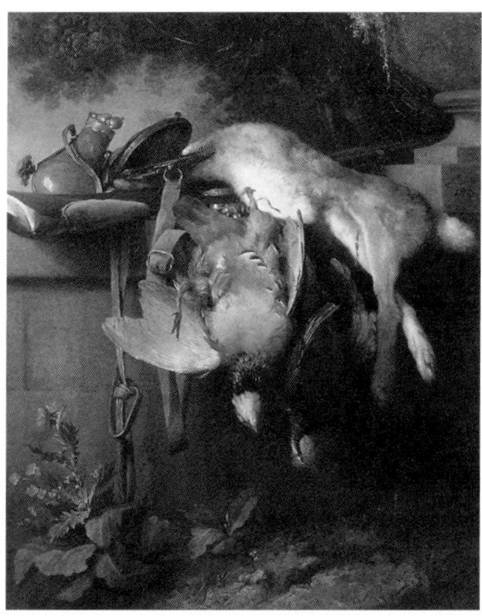

28. *Trophies of the Hunt*, 1774

Oil on canvas, 35⅞ × 28¾ in. (91 × 73 cm)
Signed and dated upper right: *Mlle Vallayer/1774*
Frame stamped: *E. L. Infroit*
Galerie Gismondi, Paris
Provenance: collection of the artist; Coster sale 1824, lot 26; Mme Veuve L. Doucet collection, 1926; sale, Rouen, 10 March 1991, lot 60, illus.
Exhibited: Paris 1926, no. 100bis.
Selected References: Roland Michel 1970, no. 284 (as lost); F. Faré 1999, 68, illus. 69.
W, D
Pl. 13

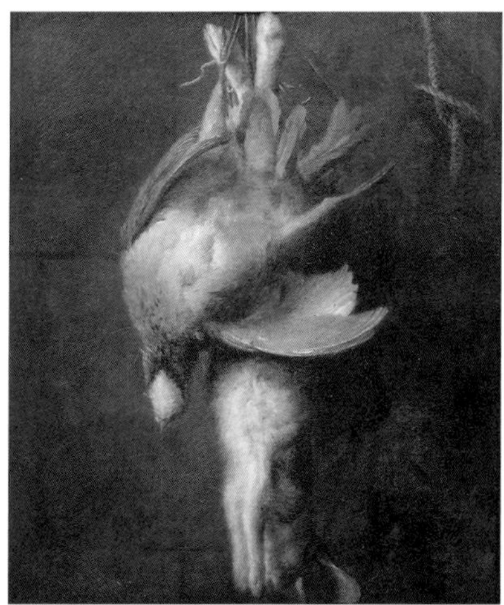

29. *Trophies of the Hunt*, 1774

Oil on canvas, 21¼ × 18½ in. (54 × 47 cm)
Signed and dated lower left: *Mlle Vallayer/1774*
Private collection
Provenance: marquis de Marigny collection, sale, Paris, March–April 1782, lot 112; purchased by the great-grandfather of the present owner.
Selected Reference: Roland Michel 1970, no. 285 (as lost).
D
Pl. 14

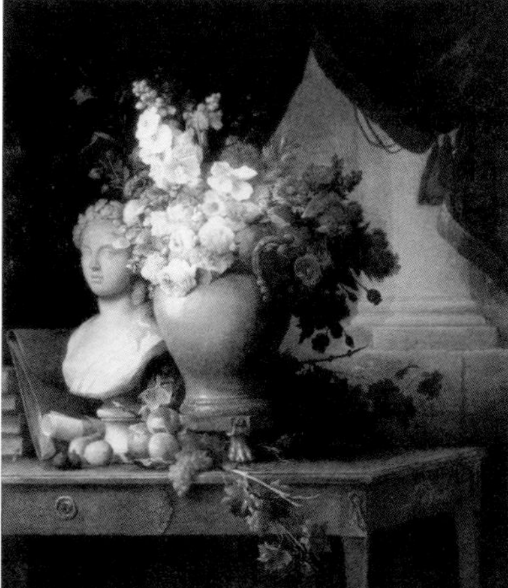

30. *Vase of Flowers with a Bust of Flora*, 1774

Oil on canvas, 60⅝ × 51⅛ in. (154 × 130 cm)
Signed and dated lower left: *Mlle Vallayer./1774*
Private collection
Provenance: abbé Terray collection, sale, Paris, 20 January 1779, lot 92; Le Boeuf collection, sale, 8 April 1783, no. 92; Matthiesen Gallery, London, 1959; Eugene Victor Thaw collection, 1972; Mr. and Mrs. Roberto Polo; sale, Ader Picard Tajan, Paris, 30 May 1988, lot 6; Christie's, New York, 31 January 1997, lot 102.
Exhibited: Salon of 1775, no. 99; Zurich 1958, no. 126; Winston-Salem 1972, no. 9; Los Angeles 1976, no. 53, illus.
Selected References: *Mercure de France*, October 1775, 1:193 (Collection Deloynes, no. 165, 736–737); *Entretiens sur l'exposition des tableaux 1775* (Collection Deloynes, no. 161, 9–10, 17–18); *Observations 1775* (Collection Deloynes, no. 160, 44–45); *La lanterne magique 1775* (Collection Deloynes, no. 163, 20); Seznec and Adhémar 1957–1967, 4:253; M. Faré 1962, 1:178, 229, 2: fig. 408; Roland Michel 1970, no. 1, illus. 103; M. and F. Faré 1976, fig. 345, 226.
Commentary: Pendant of cat. 24.

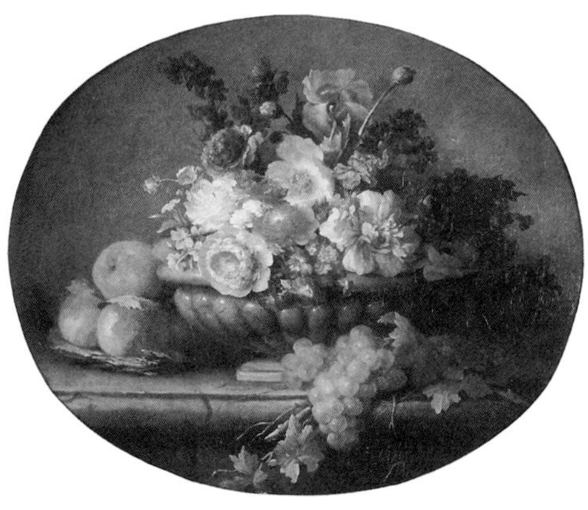

31. *Bouquet of Flowers with Grapes and Apples*, 1775

Oil on canvas, oval, 20½ × 24¼ in. (52 × 61.5 cm)
Signed and dated lower left: *Mlle Vallayer/1775*
Villa Ephrussi de Rothschild–Institut de France, Saint-Jean Cap Ferrat
Provenance: comte de La Béraudière collection, sale, Paris, 18–30 May 1885, lot 81; Ephrussi de Rothschild collection.
Exhibited: Salon of 1775, no. 102.

Selected References: Vergnet-Ruiz and Laclotte 1962, 254; Roland Michel 1970, no. 77; M. and F. Faré 1976, fig. 344.
Commentary: Pendant of cat. 26.
W, D
Pl. 16

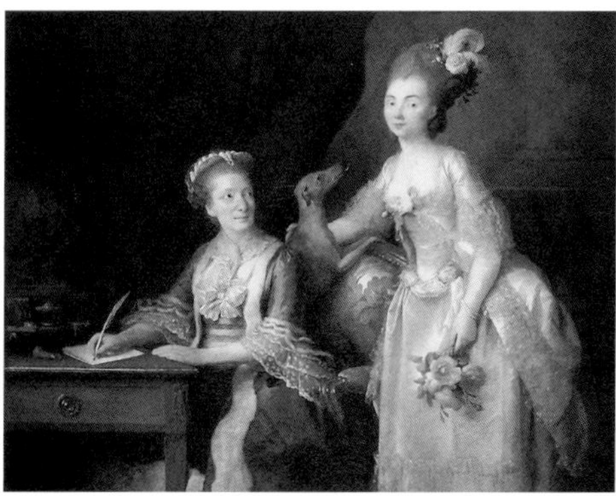

32. *Vase of Flowers*, 1775

Oil on canvas, oval, 12¾ × 10½ in. (32.4 × 26.7 cm)
Signed and dated on the right of the table: *A Vallayer 1775.*
Fitzwilliam Museum, Cambridge, P.D.46-1975
Provenance: Broughton Collection, bequest 1973.
Exhibited: London 1993, no. 20.
Selected References: Grant 1952, no. 128; Roland Michel 1970, no. 5bis.

33. *Portrait of a Woman Writing and Her Daughter*, 1775

Oil on canvas, 24⅜ × 51⅛ in. (61.9 × 130.1 cm)
Signed and dated on drawer of the bureau: *[Me]^lle Vallayer 1775*
The Bowes Museum, Barnard Castle, Co. Durham, England
Provenance: Gogue, 24 March 1863.
Exhibited: London 1968a, no. 691; Nottingham 1982, no. 24.
Selected References: Bowes Museum 1955, no. 329; Bizardel 1957, 435, illus.; Roland Michel 1970, no. 312, illus. 209; Levey 1993, 265–267, illus. 266.
W, D
Pl. 17

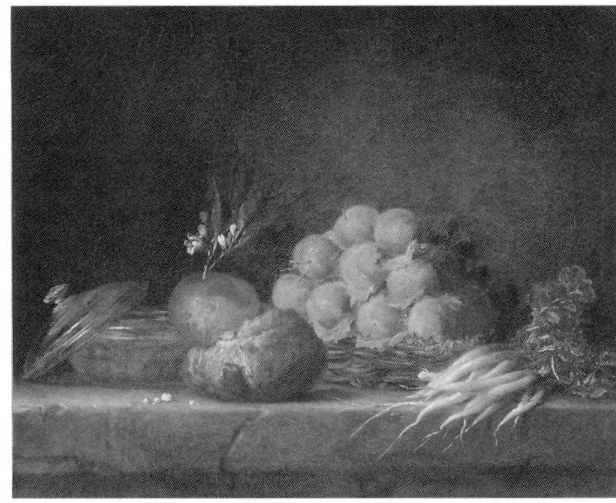

34. *Still-Life with Brioche, Fruit, and Vegetables,* 1775

Oil on canvas, 17½ × 21¼ in. (44.5 × 54 cm)
Signed and dated lower left: *Melle Vallayer/1775*
Nationalmuseum, Stockholm; Quist Fund, NM 6937
Provenance: Floriet collection; Vitale-Bloch collection; Nystad collection, The Hague; Ph. van Ommeren, Rotterdam, by 1965; sale, Drouot Montaigne, Paris, 25 January 1991, lot 66, illus.; Sotheby's, New York, 17 January 1992, lot 91.
Exhibited: Paris 1948, no. 66bis; Paris 1952, no. 82; The Hague 1962; London 1968a, no. 689.
Selected References: Oulmont 1928, pl. 44; Roland Michel 1965, 189; Roland Michel 1970, no. 224, illus. 169; M. and F. Faré 1976, 2:226, fig. 346; Cavalli-Björkmann 1994–1995, 23, illus.; Cavalli-Björkman and Nilsson 1995, 12, 76, 253, illus. 78.
W
Pl. 18

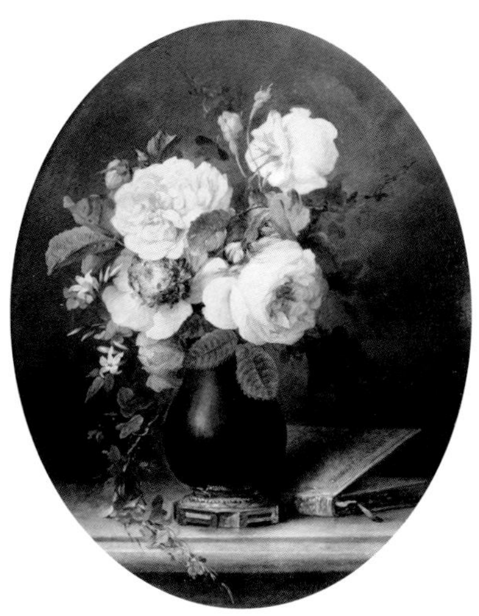

35. *Vase of Flowers and a Book,* 1775

Oil on copper, 18⅛ × 14¾ in. (46 × 37.5 cm)
Signed and dated lower right: *Melle Vallayer/1775*
Present whereabouts unknown
Provenance: Galerie Charpentier, Paris, 15 December 1959, lot 31, illus.; art market, Paris, in 1960.
Selected References: Roland Michel 1970, no. 64, illus. 133.

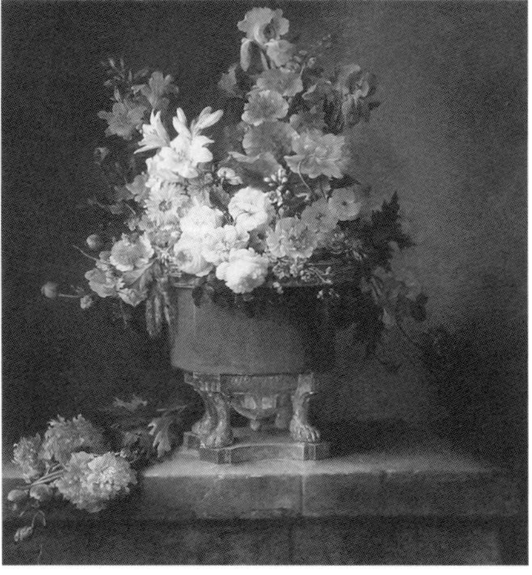

36. *Bouquet of Flowers in a Blue Porcelain Vase,* 1776

Oil on canvas, 48¼ × 44½ in. (122.6 × 113 cm)
Signed and dated lower left: *Melle Vallayer, 1776*
Dallas Museum of Art, Dallas, Texas; Dallas Museum of Art Foundation for the Arts Collection, Mrs. John O'Hara Fund and gift of Michael L. Rosenberg, 1998.52
Provenance: Montullé collection; Cournerie collection, sale, Paris, 8–9 December 1891, lot 21; Henri Lacroix collection, sale, 18 May 1901, lot 69, illus.; sale, Paris, Hôtel Drouot, 7 July 1992; Didier Aaron & Cie, Paris and New York, until 1998.
Exhibited: Salon of 1777, no. 100.
Selected References: *Lettres pittoresques* 1777 (Collection Deloynes, no. 190, 35–36); Roland Michel 1970, no. 3 (as lost); Roland Michel 1993, 365–366 n. 31; Humair 2001, 19, illus.
Commentary: Pendant of cat. 37.
W, D, NY
Pl. 19

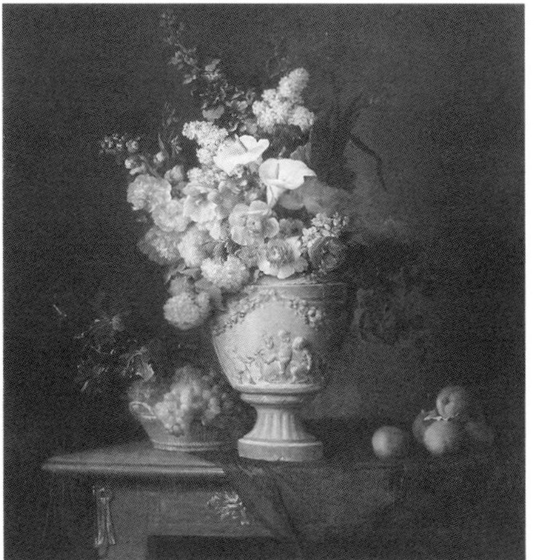

37. *Bouquet of Flowers in a Terracotta Vase, with Peaches and Grapes,* 1776

Oil on canvas, 47⅝ × 44⅝ in. (121 × 113.3 cm)
Signed and dated left of center: *Melle Vallayer 1776*
Dallas Museum of Art, Dallas, Texas; Dallas Museum of Art Foundation for the Arts Collection, Mrs. John O'Hara Fund and gift of Michael L. Rosenberg, 1998.51
Provenance: Montullé collection; Cournerie collection, Paris, sale, 8–9 December 1891, lot 21; Henri Lacroix collection, sale, 18 May 1901, lot 69, illus.; sale, Paris, Hôtel Drouot,

7 July 1992; Didier Aaron & Cie, Paris and New York, until 1998.
Exhibited: Salon of 1777, no. 100.
Selected References: *Lettres pittoresques* 1777, no. 100 (Collection Deloynes, no. 190, 35–36); Roland Michel 1970, no. 2 (as lost), 102, illus.; Roland Michel 1993, 366, fig. 9, n. 31.
Commentary: Pendant of cat. 36.
W, D, NY
Pl. 20

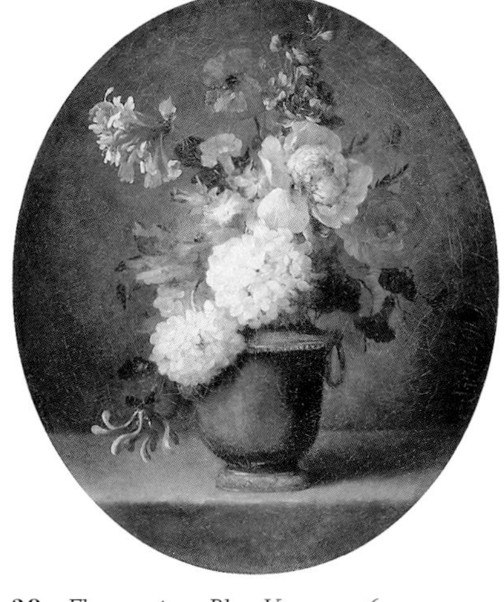

38. *Flowers in a Blue Vase,* 1776

Oil on canvas, oval, 19 × 15¼ in. (48.5 × 39.5 cm)
Signed and dated at right: *Melle Vallayer/1776*
Present whereabouts unknown
Provenance: Etienne Lévy collection; Galerie Cailleux, Paris; Michel Roche; Maurice Segoura, Paris, 1989.
Selected Reference: Roland Michel 1970, no. 25, illus. 145; M. and F. Faré 1976, fig. 348.
Commentary: Pendant of cat. 39.

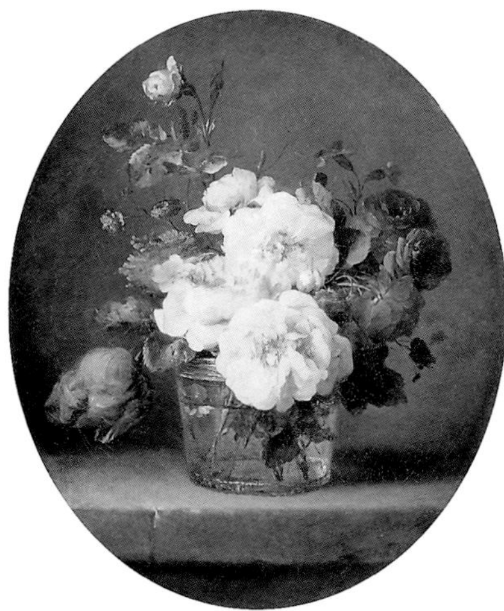

39. *Flowers in a Glass Vase,* 1776

Oil on canvas, 19⅛ × 15½ in. (48.5 × 39.5 cm)
Signed and dated at right, on shelf: *Melle Vallayer/1776*
Present whereabouts unknown
Provenance: Etienne Lévy collection; Galerie Cailleux, Paris; Michel Roche; Maurice Segoura, Paris, 1989.
Selected Reference: Roland Michel 1970, no. 6, illus. 44; M. and F. Faré 1976, fig. 347.

Commentary: This painting, as well as its pendant, cat. 38, is in its original frame, stamped Leverd. The sculptor Leverd was a member of the Académie de Saint-Luc and apparently specialized in oval frames. According to Guiffrey 1915, Leverd was dead in 1776, the year in which these two paintings were executed. It is possible that Leverd made a series of oval frames in this format.

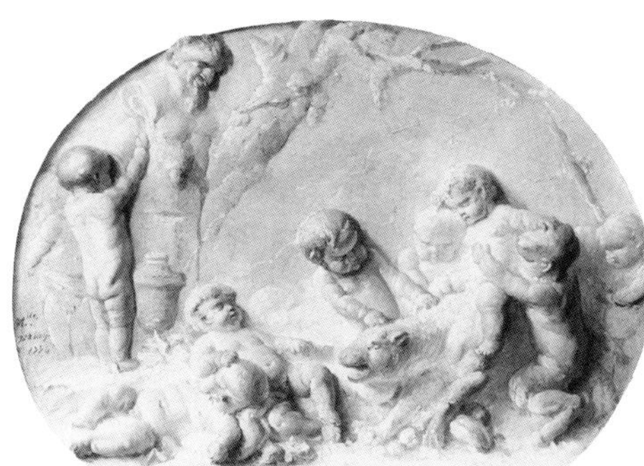

40. *Satyrs and Putti Playing with a Panther*, also known as *Children at Play—Spring*, 1776

Oil on canvas, 11⅜ × 13¾ in. (29 × 35 cm)
Signed and dated on verso: *peint à paris par Mlle Vallayer—août 1776*
Private collection
Provenance: Galerie Cailleux, Paris; sale, Christie's, New York, 23 May 1997, lot 66.
Exhibited: Paris 1985, no. 41, illus.; Paris 1985, no. 33, illus.; Grasse 1998, 34, illus. 35.
Selected References: Roland Michel 1993, 365 n. 30, 368, fig. 10; Faré and Chevé 1996, 222; Zanella 2001, 211 (with an incorrect provenance).
Commentary: Same subject as cat. 42; black frame is painted in trompe-l'oeil.
W, D
Pl. 21

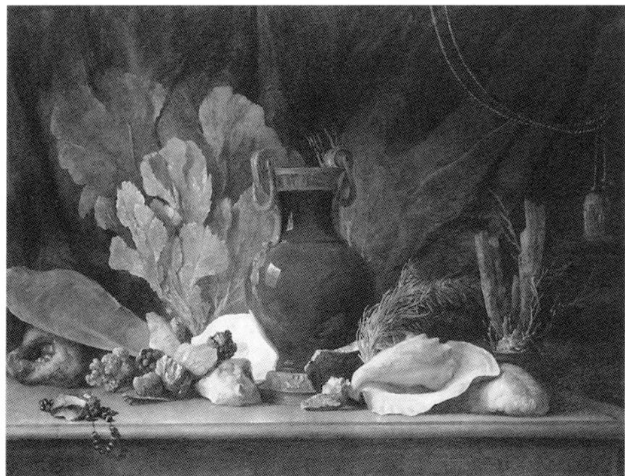

41. *Still Life with Porcelain Vase, Marine Plants, Shells, and Various Mineralogical Specimens*, 1776

Oil on canvas 42⅝ × 54⅝ in. (108.2 × 138.8 cm)
Signed and dated lower left: *Mlle Vallayer./1776*
Private collection
Provenance: Mme Vissitier, as of 1777 (with its pendant, *Bust of Minerva with Military Attributes*, cat. 44*)*; vicomte G. Chabert collection, sale, Galerie Georges Petit, Paris, 5 June 1909, lot 11, illus.; acquired by Georges Sortais, Paris; private collection, until 1923; anonymous sale, Hôtel Drouot, Paris, 9 June 1923, lot 15 (with its

pendant); Mme Potin collection; sale, Galerie Georges Petit, Paris, 22 April 1929, lot 24 (sold separately from its pendant); Stettiner collection; private collection, Paris; Sotheby's, Monaco, 21–22 June 1991, lot 151.
Exhibited: Salon of 1777, no. 101 (with its pendant).
Selected References: "Exposition de peintures" 1777 (Collection Deloynes, no. 1334, 858–861); *Jugement d'une demoiselle* 1777, 19 (Collection Deloynes, no. 178, 19); "IIIe lettre de M. de S** au Vicomte de XX—Le Temple de la Peinture," *Lettres pittoresques* 1777, 35–36 (Collection Deloynes, no. 190, 35–36); Dacier 1909–1921, 4:20–21; Hôtel Drouot, Paris, 7 March 1941, 8, under lot 15; Paris 1959a, under no. 84; M. Faré 1962, 1:179, 229, 339 n. 853; Roland Michel 1970, 188, no. 265 (as 1777); M. and F. Faré 1976, 1:223–224, 413 n. 184, fig. 352; Los Angeles 1976, 183, cited under no. 54 and n. 10; Rosenblum 1979, 1:295; Foucart et al. 1996, 148, illus. 149; Pinault Sørensen and Sahut 1998, 65, 70 n. 58, fig. 13.
Pl. 22

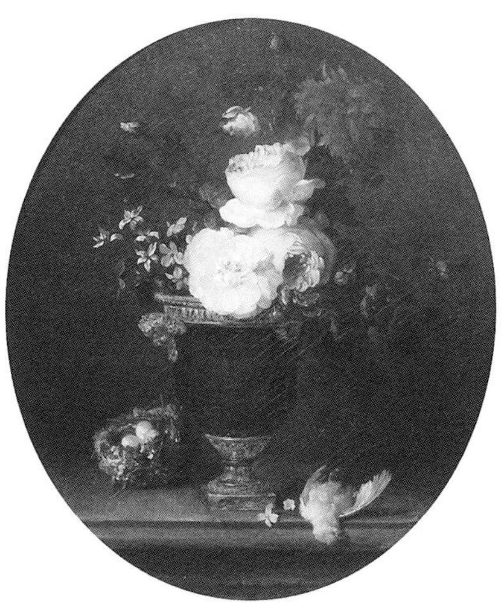

43. *Vase of Flowers, Nest, and Dead Canary*, 1776

Oil on canvas, oval, 21⅝ × 18⅛ in. (55 × 46 cm)
Signed and dated bottom: *Melle Vallayer 1776*
Private collection
Provenance: Cesare Lanza collection, Geneva; Galerie Cailleux, Paris.
Exhibited: Rotterdam 1954, no. 61; Paris 1973, no. 48; Paris 1975, no. 40.
Selected References: Schlumberger 1958, 68, illus.; Roland Michel 1970, no. 65, illus. 125.

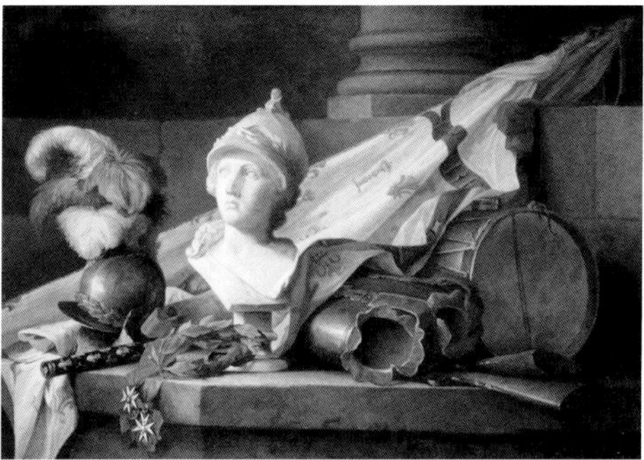

44. *Bust of Minerva with Military Attributes*, 1777

Oil on canvas, 44⅞ × 62½ in. (114 × 158.7 cm)
Signed and dated lower left: *Melle Vallayer/1777*
Present whereabouts unknown
Provenance: Mme Vissitier collection; vicomte G. Chabert collection, sale, Paris, 5 June 1909, lot 12; sale, Paris, 9 June 1923, lot 15, illus.; Mme Potin collection, sale, Paris, 22 April 1929, Galerie Georges Petit, lot 25 (sold separately from its pendant); M. Marcel Midy collection; sale, Paris, Hôtel Drouot, 7 March 1941, lot 15; sale, C. P. Ader, Paris, 15 December 1959, lot 30; Wildenstein, New York and Paris, until 1968; James Ling, Dallas; LTV Steel Corporation, Dallas; Rege Gold, DuBois, Pa.; Christie's, London, 9 July 1993, lot 45.
Exhibited: Salon of 1777, no. 101 (with its pendant); Paris 1959a, no. 84, pl. 38; Los Angeles 1976, no. 54, illus.
Selected References: *Lettres pittoresques* 1777, 7th letter (Collection Deloynes, no. 190, 35–36); Dacier 1909–1921, 4:20–21; Seznec and Adhémar 1957–1967, 4:201; M. Faré 1962, 1:222, 2: fig. 426; Roland Michel 1970, no. 264; M. and F. Faré 1976, 223, 229, fig. 356.
Commentary: Pendant of cat. 41. The two paintings remained together until 1929.

42. *Satyrs and Putti Playing with a Panther* or *Spring*, also known as *Summer*, more probably *Autumn*, 1776

Oil on canvas, 11½ × 13¾ in. (29 × 35 cm)
Signed and dated lower left: *Melle Vallayer/1776*
Private collection
Provenance: Cournerie collection, sale, Paris, 8–9 December 1891, lot 41; comte P. de Jumilhac collection, sale, Paris, 15 June 1929, lot 77 (with its pendant, lot 76); René Fribourg collection, sale, Sotheby's, London, 26 June 1963, lot 130; Clifford Duits collection, London; Schaeffer Galleries, New York; per M. and F. Faré 1976, P. de B. collection, Lisbon; Audap-Solanet, Godeau-Veillet, Paris, 16 June 1995, lot 47 (sold with its pendant, cat. 47).
Exhibited: Salon of 1777, no. 107; Copenhagen 1935, no. 224; London 1968b, no. 29 (as *Spring*), illus.
Selected References: *Mercure de France*, October 1777, 1:183 (Collection Deloynes, no. 191, 108–109); Dacier 1909–1921, 4:20–21; Roland Michel 1970, no. 243, illus. 93; M. and F. Faré 1976, fig. 349.
Commentary: This painting, as well as its pendant, cat. 47, was part of a set of the Seasons, if we believe the sketch by Gabriel de Saint-Aubin in his livret of the 1777 Salon. They were probably intended to be inset into paneling.

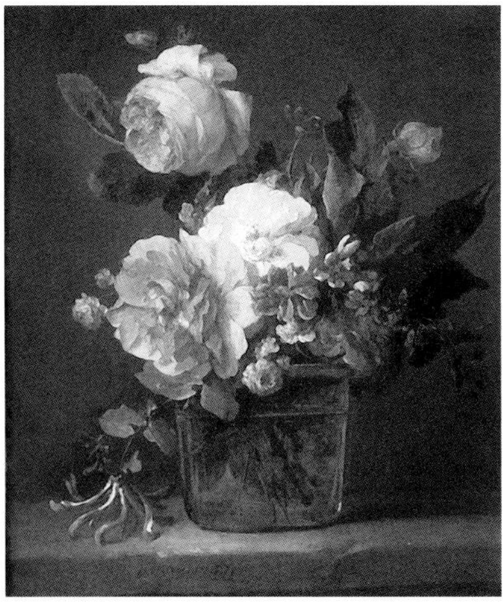

45. *Flowers in a Glass Vase*, 1777

Oil on canvas, originally oval, made rectangular, 16¼ × 13¼ in. (41.5 × 34 cm)
Signed and dated lower left: *Mlle Vallayer 1777*
Segoura Collection
Provenance: Prouvost collection; Palais Galliéra, Paris, 9 March 1961, lot 153, pl. XXXIII.
Selected Reference: Roland Michel 1970, no. 8 (as lost), illus. 113.

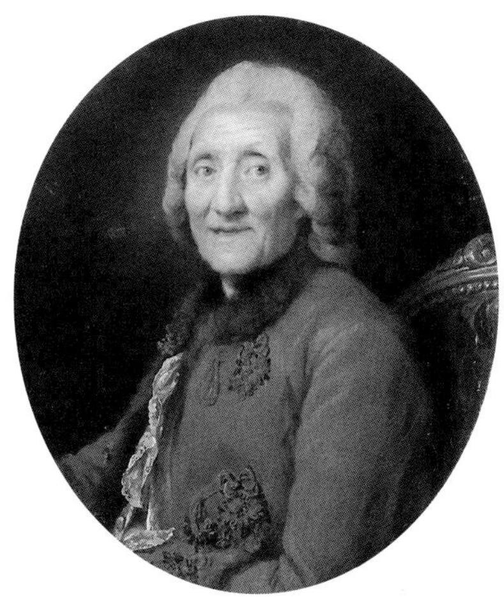

46. *Portrait of Joseph-Charles Roettiers (1692–1779)*, 1777

Oil on canvas, oval, 25⅝ × 21¼ in. (65 × 54 cm)
Signed and dated center left: *Melle Vallayer 1777*
Musée national des Châteaux de Versailles et de Trianon, MV 5892
Provenance: acquired in 1904 by the Musée de Versailles, Inv. R.F.B. 41.
Exhibited: Salon of 1777, no. 104.
Selected References: *Mercure de France*, October 1777, 1:183 (Collection Deloynes, no. 191, 1098); Dacier 1909–1921, 4:20–21; Roland Michel 1970, no. 313, illus. 208; Constans 1980, cat. 4387; Constans 1995, cat. 4946, illus. 4946; Fort 1999, 179.
Commentary: Roettiers, former *ancien graveur général de Monnaies*, a position held by both his father and his son, was very likely a longtime friend of Anne Vallayer's father. He had an apartment at the Louvre, close to Vallayer-Coster's.
W, D, NY
Pl. 23

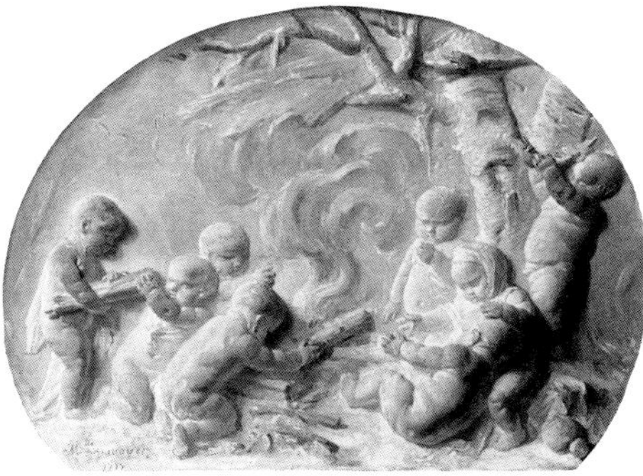

47. *Satyrs and Putti Playing near a Term*, also known as *Winter*, 1777

Oil on canvas, oval, 11½ × 13¾ in. (29 × 35 cm)
Signed and dated lower left: *Melle Vallayer/1777*
Private collection
Provenance: Couernerie collection, sale, Paris, 8–9 December 1891, lot 41; comte P. de Jumilhac collection, sale, Paris, 15 June 1929, lot 76 (with its pendant, lot 77); René Fribourg collection, sale, London, Sotheby's, 26 June 1963, lot 130; Clifford Duits collection, London; Schaeffer Galleries, New York; per M. and F. Faré 1976, P. de B. collection, Lisbon; Audap-Solanet, Godeau-Veillet, Paris, 16 June 1995, lot 47 (with its pendant, cat. 42).
Exhibited: Salon of 1777, no. 107; Copenhagen 1935, no. 224; London 1968b, no. 28, illus.
Selected References: *Mercure de France*, October 1777, 1:183 (Collection Deloynes, no. 191, 1098); Dacier 1909–1921, 4:20–21; Roland Michel 1970, no. 244, illus. 93; M. and F. Faré 1976, fig. 350.
Commentary: Pendant of cat. 42, and also probably part of a set of Seasons.

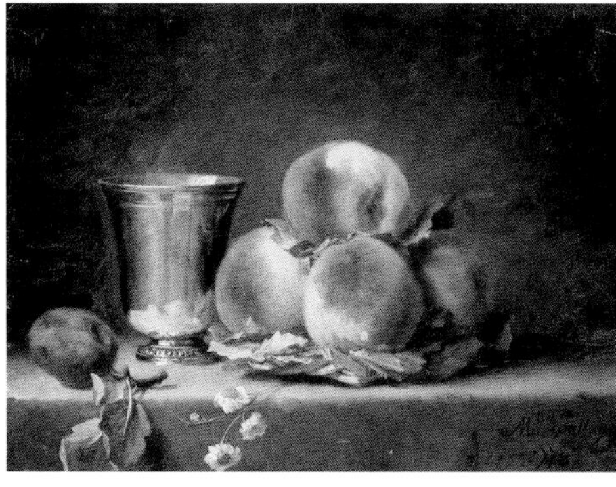

48. *Still Life with a Basket of Peaches and a Silver Goblet*, 1778

Oil on canvas, 12 × 16⅜ in. (30 × 38.5 cm)
Signed and dated bottom right: *Mlle Vallayer/1778*
Present whereabouts unknown
Provenance: Jean Girardot de Marigny collection; Galerie Pardo, Paris; Sotheby's, Monaco, 2–3 December 1988, lot 660.
Exhibited: Salon of 1779, no. 104 (lent by Girardot de Marigny).
Selected References: M. Faré 1962, 2: fig. 416; Roland Michel 1965, 184; Roland Michel 1970, no. 139, illus. 72; M. and F. Faré 1974, 228, fig. 353; Rosenblum 1979, 1:295.
Related Works: There are two versions of this composition (see cat. 89) that are nearly identical. According to Roland Michel, this

painting had a pendant, *Pâté, Liqueur et Raisins* (Roland Michel 1970, no. 140), which has been lost since 1779.

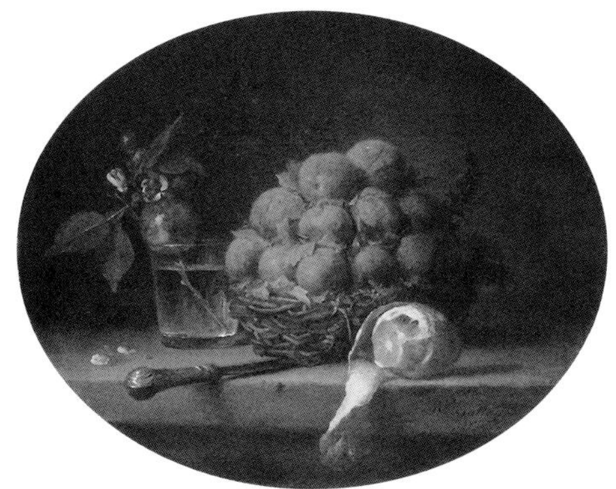

49. *Still Life with Plums and a Lemon*, 1778

Oil on canvas, oval, 16⅜ × 18⅝ in. (41.5 × 47.5 cm)
Signed and dated lower right: *Mlle Vallayer/1778*
Fine Arts Museums of San Francisco, Gift of Mr. and Mrs. Louis A. Benoist, 1960.30
Provenance: A. Weinberger; Harry G. Sperling, October 1958; acquired by the California Palace of the Legion of Honor, 21 July 1960.
Exhibited: perhaps Salon of 1779, no. 105; San Francisco 1975, no cat.; Los Angeles 1976, no. 55, illus.; Denver 1978, no. 38.
Selected References: Roland Michel 1970, no. 138, illus. 144; Roland Michel 1973, 57; Rosenblum 1979, 1:295; Lee 1980, 222, fig. 19; Rosenberg and Stewart 1987, 285–287, 284 illus.; Karlsruhe 1999, fig. 1, 331.
Related Works: There is a rectangular version of this composition. See *Plums, a Lemon, and a Knife*, n.d., cat. 117, pl. 48. A copy of this painting was auctioned in Paris, Hôtel Drouot, 17 December 1883 (as by Chardin), and again at Drouot on 12 June 1981, lot 46 (attributed to Vallayer-Coster).
W, D, NY
Pl. 24

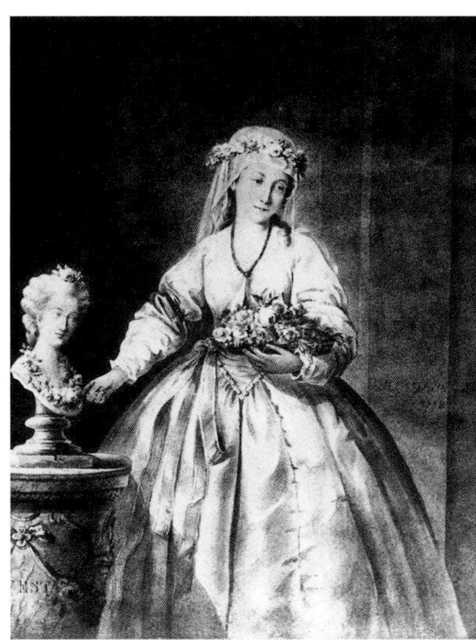

50. *A Young Vestal Showing the Bust of Vesta*, 1778

Dimensions unknown
Present whereabouts unknown

Provenance: Charles Aubry collection, 1928, as a portrait of Marie-Antoinette.
Selected References: Oulmont 1928, pl. 46; Roland Michel 1970, no. 317.
Commentary: Roland Michel (1970) suggested that the bust to the left might be of Marie-Antoinette.

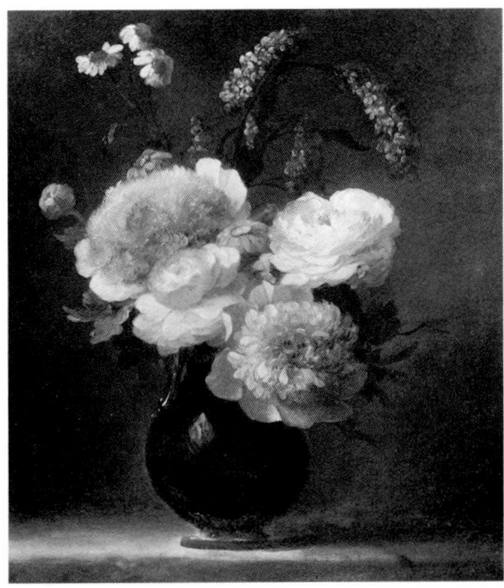

51. *Flowers in a Blue Porcelain Vase*, 1778 or 1780
Oil on canvas, 12⅝ × 10¼ in. (32 × 26 cm)
Present whereabouts unknown
Provenance: Denise Boas collection, sale, Paris, 9 June 1937, lot 58 (with its pendant); Sibilla collection; marquise de Paris, 1970.
Selected Reference: Roland Michel 1970, no. 27.
Commentary: Pendant of cat. 52.

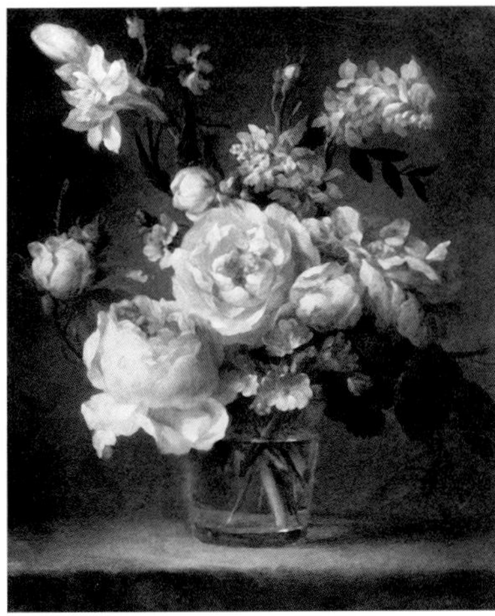

52. *Flowers in a Glass*, 1778 or 1780
Oil on canvas, 12⅝ × 10¼ in. (32 × 26 cm)
Signed and dated lower right: *Melle Vallayer./ 78[?]*
Present whereabouts unknown
Provenance: Denise Boas collection, sale, Paris, 9 June 1937, lot 57 (with its pendant); Sibilla collection; marquise de Paris, 1970.
Selected Reference: Roland Michel 1970, no. 9, illus. 113.
Commentary: Pendant of cat. 51.

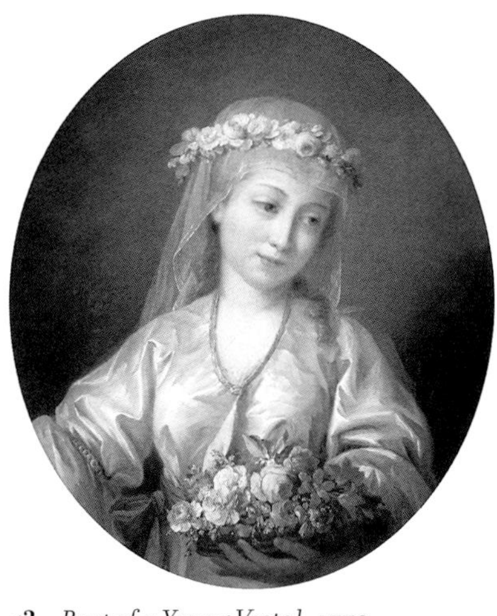

53. *Bust of a Young Vestal*, 1779
Signed and dated left, toward center: *Mlle Vallayer/1779*
Oil on canvas, oval, 18⅛ × 15⅛ in. (46 × 38.4 cm)
Private collection
Inscribed on label on stretcher: in ink, in an old handwriting: *a Mr. Accoyer, chev. de la lég. d'hon. gentilh./serv-hon. près son A. R. Monsieur/ pensionnaire du Roi/rue de la Tour d'Auvergne 14/Peint par Mlle Vallayer en 1779;* more recent label: *M Renier, Paris.*
Provenance: Marie-Antoinette collection (per Roland Michel 1970, no. 318); Accoyer collection; Durand collection, sale, 17 April 1825, lot 91 (with its pendant); Alfred Sussmann collection, sale, Galerie Georges Petit, Paris, 18–19 May 1922, lot 53, illus. (with its pendant, cat. 57, *Melancholy*); bought by Jonas; Galerie Cailleux, Paris.
Exhibited: possibly Salon of 1779, no. 102.
Selected References: possibly *livret* of the Salon de 1779, no. 102; possibly Dupont de Nemours 1908: *Lettre sur le Salon de 1779 . . . ; Le lit de justice du Dieu des Arts, ou le Pied de nez des critiques du Salon 1779* (Collection Deloynes, no. 214, 485); Roland Michel 1970, no. 319 (as lost), illus. 213.
Related Works: See Roland Michel 1970, nos. 318, 320, and 321 (as lost).
Commentary: This painting, which the artist most probably gave to the queen, is the first in a series of Vestals, a very fashionable subject in the eighteenth century, for reasons both moral and political. See also cats. 56, 137.
W, D
Pl. 25

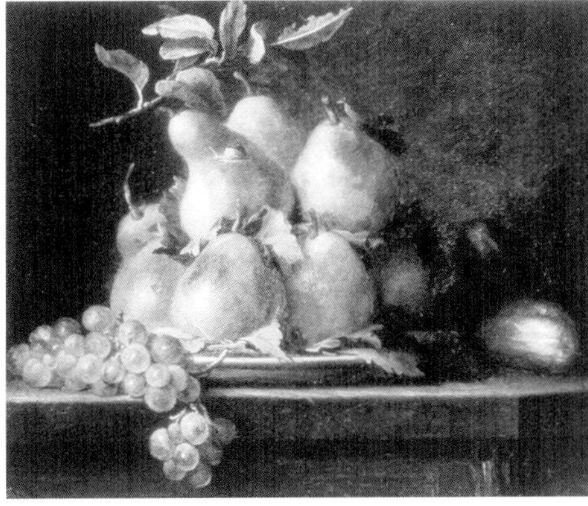

54. *Pears, Grapes, and Eggplants*, 1779
Oil on canvas, 15 × 18 in. (38 × 46 cm)
Signed and dated bottom right: *Melle Vallayer/ 1779*
Private collection
Provenance: Cournerie collection, sale, Paris, 8–9 December 1891, lot 35 (with a false signature and date); F. Doistau collection, 1st sale, Paris, 9 June 1909, lot 79 (to M. Desachée); Van Dieman collection, Amsterdam; Goudstikker collection, The Hague and Amsterdam, by 1927; Harry G. Sperling collection, New York, by 1962; Mrs. Jules Fribourg collection, New York, by 1970; Dr. Edward Binney III, given to the San Diego Museum of Art, 1985; Sotheby's, New York, 10 January 1991, lot 71; Galerie Koller, Zurich, 24 March 1995, lot 63; Patrick Weiller, Paris, 1997.
Exhibited: Amsterdam 1927, no. 128; Amsterdam 1933, no. 319; Grasse 1998, 46, illus. 47.
Selected References: M. Faré 1962, 2: fig. 417; Roland Michel 1970, no. 142, illus. 140; M. and F. Faré 1976, 228, fig. 354; Zanella 2001, 214.

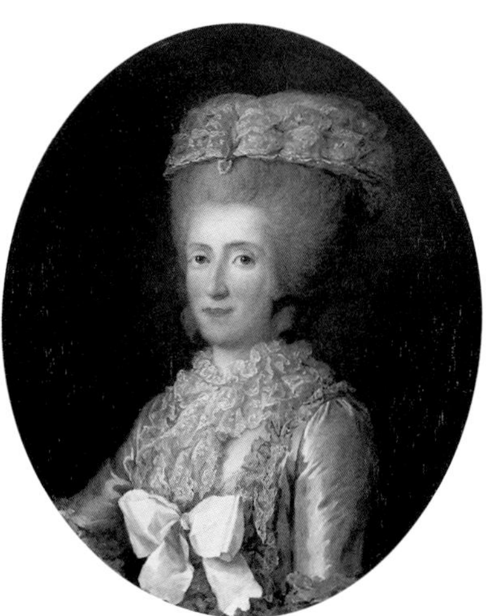

55. *Portrait of Sophie-Philippe-Elisabeth-Justine de France (1734–1782), called Madame Sophie*, 1779
Oil on canvas, oval, 28⅛ × 22⅞ in. (71.4 × 58 cm)
Musée national des Châteaux de Versailles et de Trianon, MV 3803
Provenance: Private collection; entered Versailles under Louis-Philippe, 1837.
Selected References: Roland Michel 1970, no. 327; Constans 1980, cat. 5659; Constans 1995, cat. 6059, illus. 1073 (as Madame Adélaïde).

Commentary: Painted as a study for a lost full-length portrait of Madame Sophie. See Roland Michel 1970, no. 328, and Hugues's appendix in the present volume.
D
Pl. 26

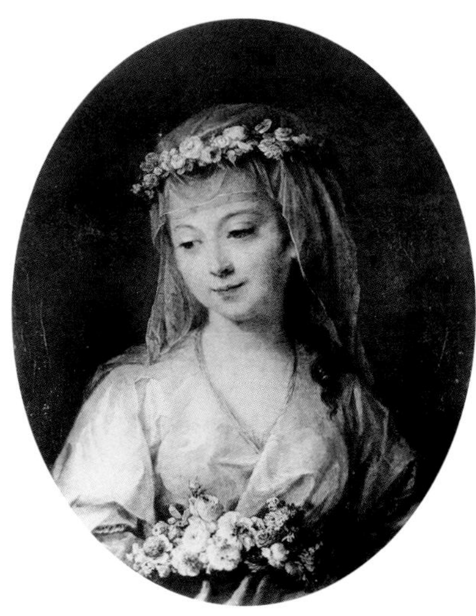

56. *A Vestal Crowned with Roses and Holding a Basket of Flowers*, 1779

Oil on canvas, oval, 15¾ × 12⅜ in. (40 × 31.4 cm)
Signed and dated center right: *Melle Vallayer 1779*
Present whereabouts unknown
Provenance: Victor Bessereau collection, in 1926; Galerie Georges Petit, Paris, 21 April 1921, lot 22, illus. (as a portrait of Mme Elisabeth, sister of Louis XVI, said to have been exhibited at the Salon of 1779); Hôtel Drouot, Ader, Picard, Tajan, Paris, 16 June 1987, lot 69, illus.
Exhibited: Paris 1926, no. 95.
Selected Reference: Roland Michel 1970, no. 320 (as lost), illus. 212.

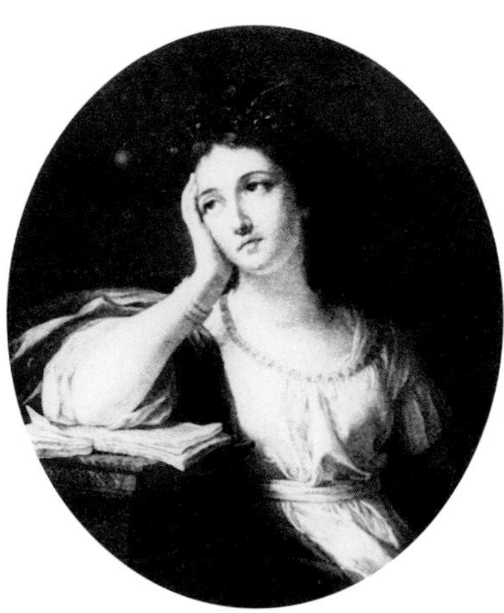

57. *Melancholy*, c. 1779

Oil on canvas, oval, 17¾ × 15 in. (45 × 38 cm)
Present whereabouts unknown
Provenance: Durand collection, sale, 17 April 1825, lot 91, with a *Vestal* as a pendant (cat. 53); Alfred Sussmann collection, sale, Galerie Georges Petit, Paris, 18–19 May 1922, lot 54 (as pendant to cat. 53).
Selected Reference: Roland Michel 1970, no. 324.

Commentary: It is not clear when or for whom *Melancholy* was painted, but it was clearly made as a pendant to *Bust of a Young Vestal*.

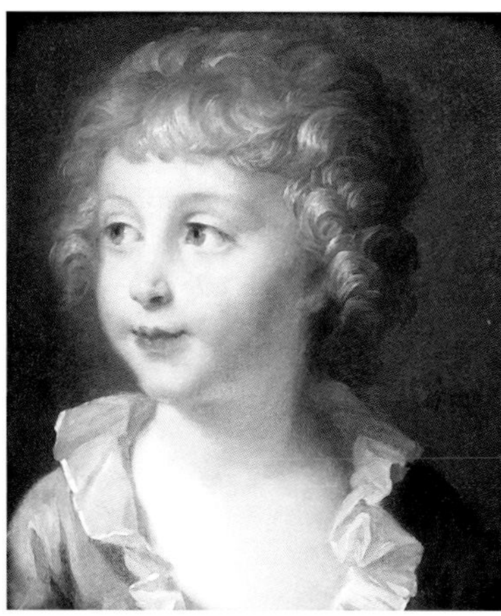

58. *Portrait of a Boy*, 1779[?]

Oil on canvas, 16 × 12¾ in. (40.5 × 32.5 cm)
Signed and dated middle right: *Mlle Vallayer/ 177[9?]*
Inscribed on label on verso: *donné par le comte d'Holstein en 1895*
Private collection
Provenance: duchesse de Tourzel, governess of the Enfants de France, who was the great-grandmother of the owner's mother.

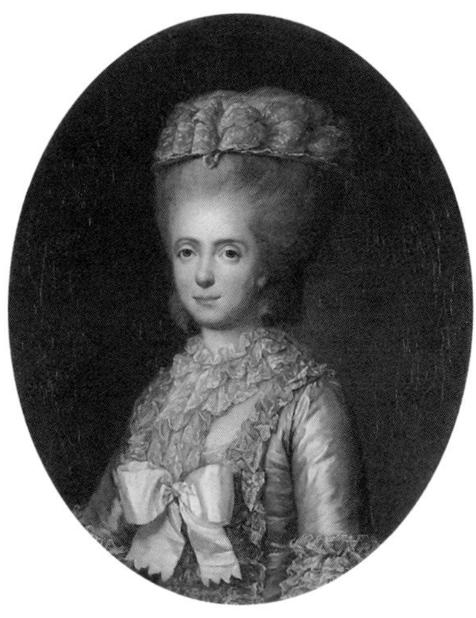

59. *Portrait of Marie-Adélaïde-Louise de France (1732–1800), called Madame Adélaïde*, 1780

Oil on canvas, oval, 28⅜ × 23¼ in. (72 × 59 cm)
Musée national des Châteaux de Versailles et de Trianon, MV 3812
Provenance: private collection; entered Versailles under Louis-Philippe, 1837.
Selected References: Constans 1980, cat. 5657; Constans 1995, cat. 6061, illus. 1073 (as Madame Sophie).
D
Pl. 28

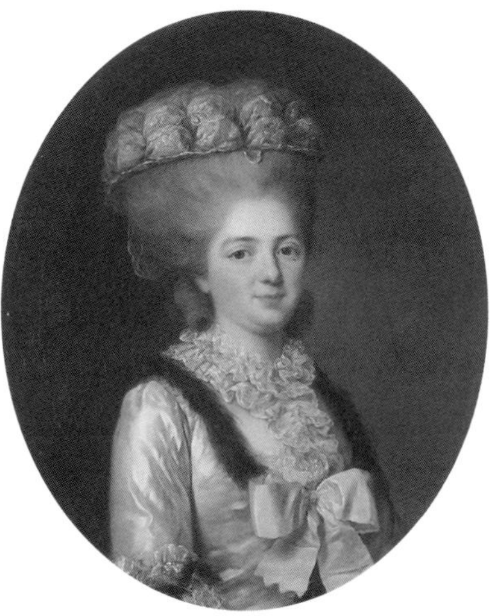

60. *Portrait of Marie-Louise-Thérèse-Victoire de France (1733–1799), called Madame Victoire*, 1780

Oil on canvas, oval, 28⅛ × 22⅞ in. (71.4 × 58 cm)
Musée national des Châteaux de Versailles et de Trianon, MV 3807
Provenance: private collection; entered Versailles under Louis-Philippe, 1837.
Selected References: Constans 1980, cat. 5658; Constans 1995, cat. 6060, illus. 1073.
Related Work: There is a rectangular version of the same subject, in pastel, known only through an old photograph in the Bibliothèque nationale. For the two portraits of Mesdames, see cats. 122, 124, and the appendix in this volume by Hugues.
D
Pl. 27

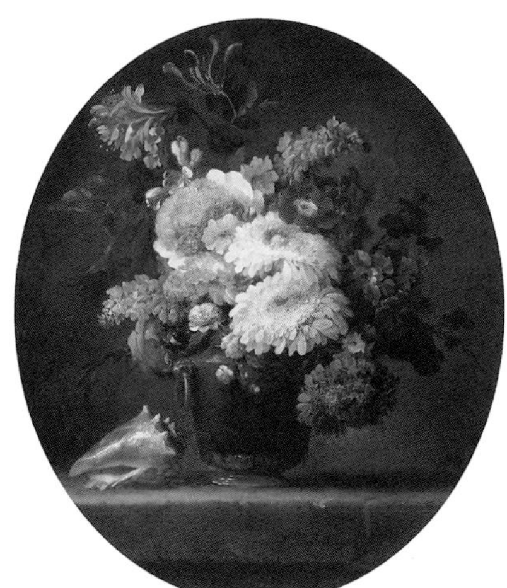

61. *Vase of Flowers*, 1780

Oil on canvas, oval, 19¾ × 15 in. (50.2 × 38.1 cm)
Signed and dated lower right: *Mlle Vallayer/1780*
The Metropolitan Museum of Art; gift of J. Pierpont Morgan, 1907, 07.225.504
Provenance: Cournerie collection, sale, Paris, 8–9 December 1891, lot 23; Georges Hoentschel collection, Paris, until 1906; acquired by J. P. Morgan, who bequeathed the painting to the Metropolitan Museum of Art in 1906.
Exhibited: most probably one of the three ovals with flowers and fruit exhibited at the Salon of 1781, no. 105 (see cat. 67); North Salem 1974; New York 1976, 35–36, illus. 35.

Selected References: Pératé and Brière 1908, 3:
pl. 136; Sterling and Salinger 1955, 1:179, illus.
179; Seznec and Adhémar 1957–1967, 4:324,
365, fig. 150; Roland Michel 1970, no. 67, illus.
121; M. and F. Faré 1976, fig. 358, 230; Baetjer
1995, 385.
Commentary: Sterling (Sterling and Salinger
1955) and Seznec (Seznec and Adhémar 1957–
1967, 4:365, no. 106 [*sic*, for 105]) identify this
painting as one of the three Vallayer-Coster
exhibited at the Salon of 1781 under no. 105,
together with cat. 67.
W, D, NY
Pl. 29

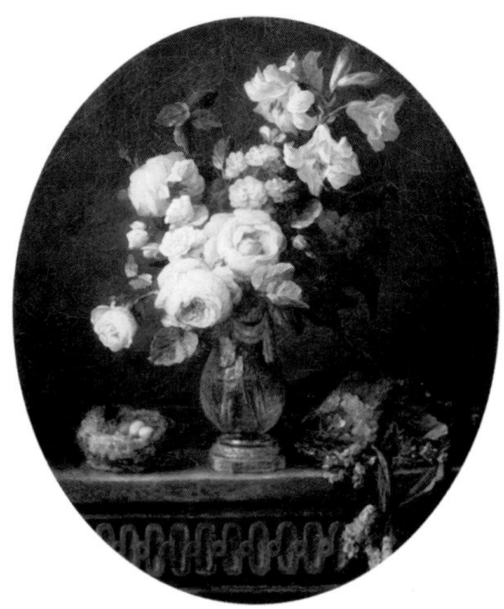

62. *Vase of Flowers, Bird's Nest, and Purse,* c. 1780

Oil on canvas, oval, perhaps enlarged, 24¾ ×
20¼ in. (63 × 51.5 cm)
Private collection
Provenance: vicomtesse de Courval collection;
Mme Wyrouboff, in 1970.
Selected Reference: Roland Michel 1970,
no. 71.

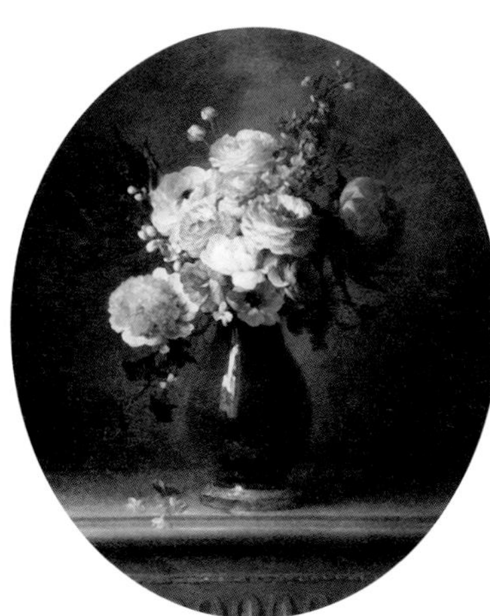

63. *Flowers in a Lapis Blue Vase,* before 1781

Oil on canvas, oval, 25⅝ × 21⅝ in. (65.1 ×
54.9 cm)
Signed lower right: *Mlle Vallayer*
Present whereabouts unknown
Provenance: sale [Groult], Paris, 20 November
1941, lot 34, pl. XVIII; Galerie Cailleux, Paris;
Cesare Lanza collection; Galerie Cailleux;

private collection; Sotheby's, New York, 16 May
1996, lot 122; private collection; Sotheby's, New
York, 24 January 2002, lot 59.
Exhibited: Paris 1945, no. 36; Paris 1952, no. 81;
Rennes 1953, no. 22; Rotterdam 1954, no. 62,
pl. 34; London 1954, no. 226; Zurich 1955,
no. 343; Paris 1975, no. 41; Paris 1979b, no. 54.
Selected References: M. Faré 1962, 2: fig. 407;
Roland Michel 1970, no. 28, illus. 126; M. and
F. Faré 1976, 233, fig. 364.

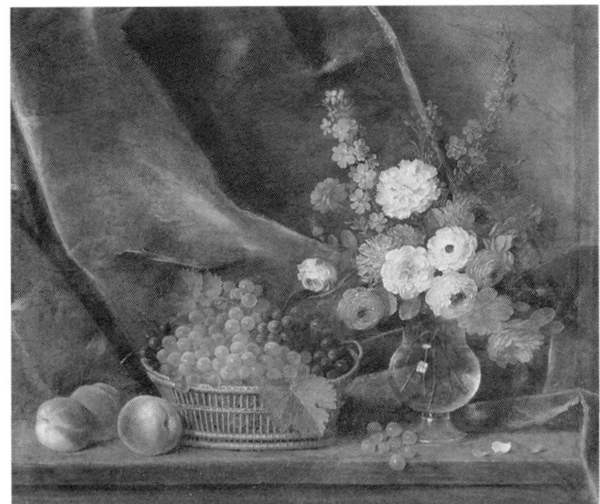

64. *Flowers and Fruit with Blue Curtain,* 1781

Oil on canvas, 28¾ × 33⅛ in. (73 × 84 cm)
Signed and dated lower right: *Coster/1781*
Private collection, Paris
Provenance: Sibilla collection; Galerie Pardo,
Paris.
Selected Reference: Roland Michel 1970, no. 78,
illus. 111 (as 1778).
NY
Pl. 31

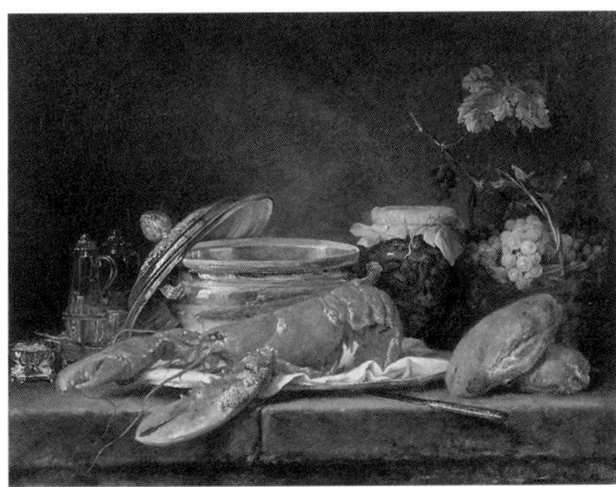

65. *Still Life with Lobster,* 1781

Oil on canvas, 27¾ × 35¼ in. (70.5 × 89.5 cm)
Signed and dated lower left: *Mme Vallayer-
Coster/1781*
Frame stamped: *E. L. Infroit*
Toledo Museum of Art, Toledo, Ohio; Purchased
with Funds from the Libbey Endowment, gift
of Edward Drummond Libbey, 1968.1A
Provenance: Jean Girardot de Marigny collec-
tion; Achille Fould collection; Vente X, Paris,
Hôtel Drouot, 22 May 1967, lot 20, with its
pendant; Galerie Cailleux, Paris.
Exhibited: Salon of 1783; Atlanta 1983, no. 61,
135–136, illus. 127.
Selected References: Roland Michel 1965, 186;
Gazette des Beaux-Arts 1969, no. 296, 71; *Museum
News* 1969, illus. 114; Roland Michel 1970,

no. 226; M. and F. Faré 1976, fig. 366, 233;
Toledo Museum of Art 1976, pl. 206, 161–162;
Rosenblum 1979, 1:295; Baillio 1984, 23,
fig. 13; Chadwick 1990, 49, 75 (as 1767); Sayre
1994, 149, fig. 201; Kansas City 1996, illus. 15
(not in exh.).
Commentary: Pendant of cat. 69.
W, D, NY
Pl. 33

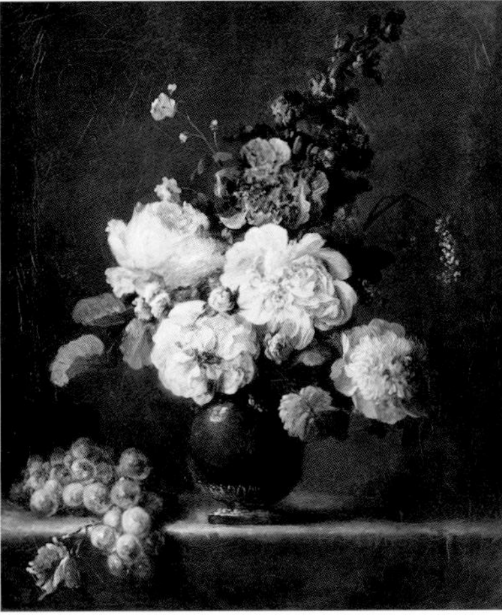

66. *Vase of Flowers and Grapes,* 1781

Oil on canvas, 16⅝ × 14¾ in. (42 × 37.5 cm)
Signed and dated lower right: *Mme V^{er} Coster/1781*
Present whereabouts unknown
Provenance: Fernand Houget collection,
Verviers.
Exhibited: London 1954, no. 187.
Selected References: M. Faré 1962, 2: fig. 410;
Roland Michel 1970, no. 80, illus. 14; M. and
F. Faré 1976, fig. 361.

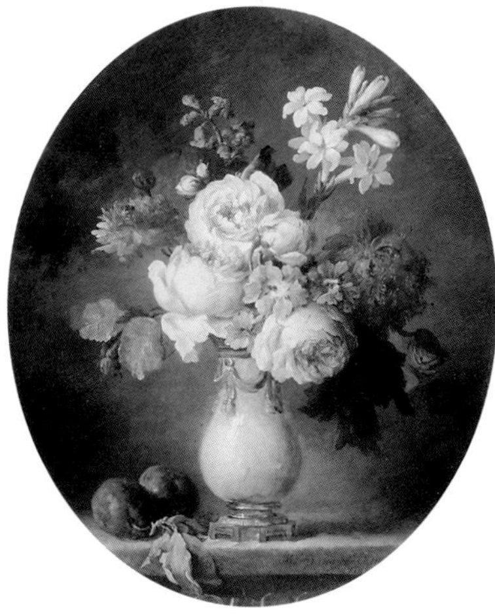

67. *A Vase of Flowers and Two Plums on a Marble
Tabletop,* 1781

Oil on canvas, oval, 18⅞ × 15¾ in. (48 ×
39.8 cm)
Signed and dated bottom right: *Me Vallayer
Coster/1781*
Michael L. Rosenberg, Dallas
Provenance: private collection, France; with
Didier Aaron; Christie's, New York, 29 January
1999, lot 43.

Exhibited: most probably one of the three ovals with flowers and fruit exhibited at the Salon of 1781, no. 105 (see cat. 61).
Commentary: This painting was used as the model for a Gobelins tapestry (see Roland Michel 1970, nos. 429, 430, 431, illus. 114, illus. 248) and cat. 158.
W, D, NY
Pl. 30

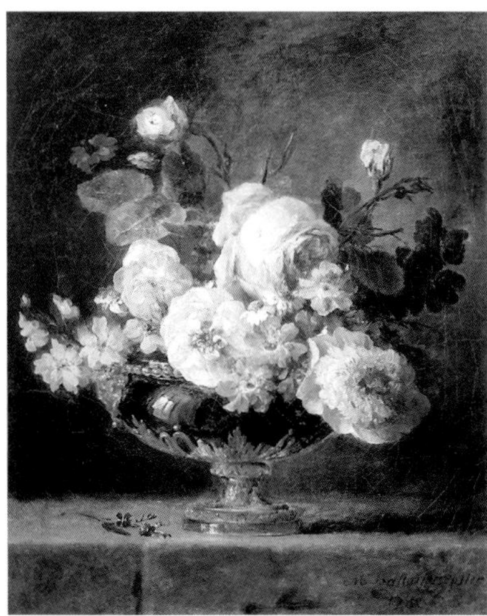

68. *Flowers in a Blue Porcelain Vase*, 1782

Oil on canvas, 16 × 12¾ in. (40.5 × 32.3 cm)
Signed and dated lower right: *Me Vallayer Coster/1782*
Private collection
Exhibited: Munich 1958, no. 213, pl. 56; Paris 1959a, no. 86, pl. 39; Paris 1968, no. 23; Bordeaux 1978, no. 148; Paris 1979b, no. 55.
Selected References: Roland Michel 1970, no. 29, illus. 127; Mitchell 1973, illus. 237; M. and F. Faré 1976, fig. 360, 231; F. Faré 1999, 68, illus. 70.
Related Work: A copy of the work was on the art market, Paris, in 1985.
W, D
Pl. 32

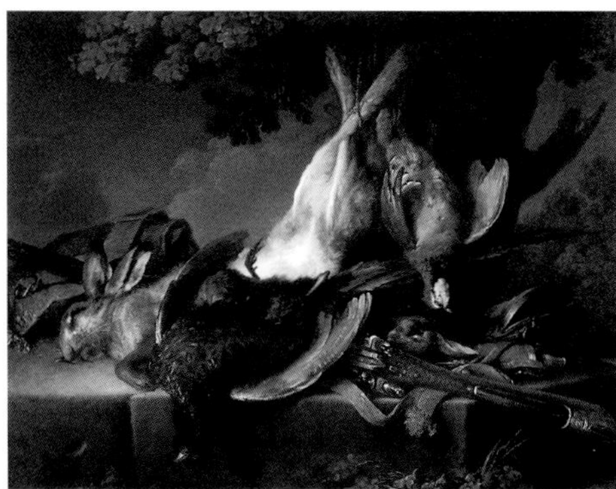

69. *Still Life with Game*, 1782

Oil on canvas, 28 × 35¼ in. (71.1 × 89.5 cm)
Signed and dated lower left: *Mme Vallayer-Coster/1782.*
Frame stamped: *E. L. Infroit*
Toledo Museum of Art, Toledo, Ohio; Purchased with Funds from the Libbey Endowment, gift of Edward Drummond Libbey, 1968.1B

Provenance: Jean Girardot de Marigny collection; Archille Fould collection; Monsieur X sale, Hôtel Drouot, Paris, 22 May 1967, lot 20, with its pendant; Galerie Cailleux, Paris.
Exhibited: Salon of 1783, no. 76 (as *Un Tableau de gibier avec des attributs de chasse*, lent by Girardot de Marigny).
Selected References: Archives nationales, Paris, estate inventory of Jean Girardot de Marigny (Minutier Central, L/802, 23 Germinal an IV); *Apelle au Sallon* 1783 (Collection Deloynes, no. 288, 24); *La critique est aisée* 1783 (Collection Deloynes, no. 287, 219–220); *Journal de Paris*, no. 263, 20 September 1783 (Collection Deloynes, no. 312, 989); *Le Salon à l'encan* 1783 (Collection Deloynes, no. 285, 25–27); M. Faré 1963, 1:180; *Gazette des Beaux-Arts* 1969, no. 297; *Museum News* 1969, illus. 114; Roland Michel 1970, no. 286, illus. 200; M. and F. Faré 1976, fig. 370; Petersen and Wilson 1976, 59, illus.; Toledo Museum of Art 1976, 161–162, pl. 207; Cleveland 1979, fig. 33; Rosenblum 1979, 1:195; Atlanta 1983, fig. v.2, 136; Petit 1988, 16, illus.
Commentary: Pendant of cat. 65.
W, D, NY
Pl. 34

70. *Decoration for a Salon (Seasons and Arts)*, 1783

Oil on canvas affixed to panels: upper panels 23⅝ × 51¼ in. (60 × 130.2 cm), lower panels 61⅛ × 35½ in. (155.3 × 90.2 cm)
Villa Moricet, Versailles, owned by the Moulonguet family
Selected References: Jarry 1931, pls. 17, 18, 19; Roland Michel 1970, no. 239.
Commentary: The house in Versailles, where these paintings are located, belonged to the comtesse d'Estrades, later acquired by Forquenot de la Fortelle, *grand porte-manteau du roi*, in 1766. The attribution to Anne Vallayer-Coster is possible, although there is no proof. Forquenot enlarged the house in 1783 by adding three rooms that were adorned with stuccos, paintings, and bas-reliefs.

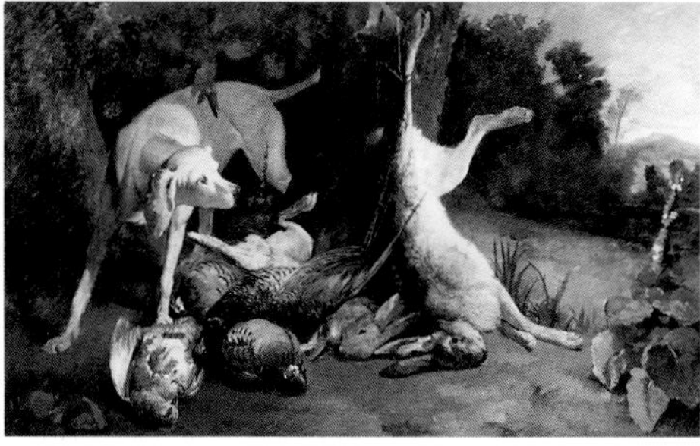

71. *A Hound with Dead Game in a Landscape*, 1785

Oil on canvas, 34¼ × 55¼ in. (87 × 140.3 cm)
Signed lower left: *Mme Vallayer Coster*; inscribed on label on verso: *Coll. J. P. Coster*
Present whereabouts unknown
Provenance: collection of the artist; Coster sale 1824, lot 32; sale, Galliéra, Paris, June 1961, lot 13; Giorgini collection, until 1965; Leeb collection, 1971; sale, Christie's, London, 17 July 1981, lot 28, as Vallayer-Coster after Desportes.

Exhibited: perhaps Salon of 1785, no. 60.
Selected References: *Journal général de la France*, no. 111, 15 September 1785 (Collection Deloynes, no. 363, 930–931); *Jugement d'un musicien* 1785 (Collection Deloynes, no. 341, 16); *Observations critiques* 1785 (Collection Deloynes, no. 326, 19); *Observations sur le Salon* 1785 (Collection Deloynes, no. 339, 35); *Promenade de Critès* 1785 (Collection Deloynes, no. 334, 34–39) (all related to its possible exhibition in the Salon of 1785); Roland Michel 1970, no. 288 (as lost since 1824).
Commentary: If this is the painting that was exhibited in the Salon of 1785 as no. 60, it has since been cut down in height.

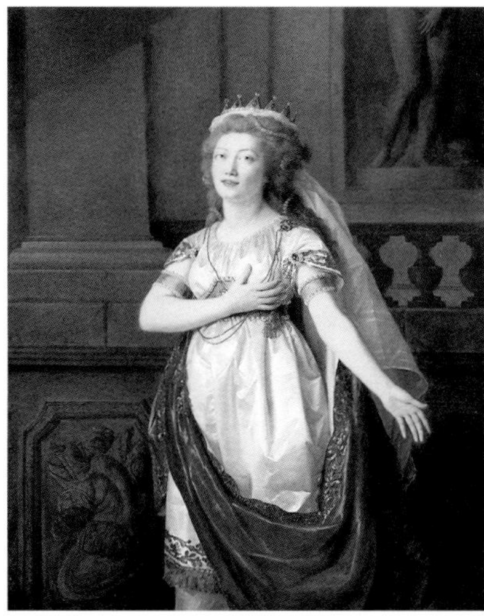

72. *Madame de Saint-Huberty in the Rôle of Dido*, 1785

Oil on canvas, 57⅜ × 40 in. (145.8 × 101.7 cm)
Signed and dated center left: *Mde Vallayer Coster/1785*
Collection of Wallace and Wilhelmina Holladay
Provenance: Coster sale 1824, lot 2; marquis de Méry; baron de Ponsort collection, château de Champguyon, near Esternay; Mme de Cuny collection; Wildenstein collection, in 1970; Christie's, Geneva, 17 November 1992, lot 482; E. Coatalem, Paris; Wildenstein, New York.
Exhibited: Salon of 1785, no. 58; Copenhagen 1935, no. 226; London 1936, no. 21; Versailles 1937, no. 298, 113; New York 1948, no. 47, illus.; Versailles 1955, no. 362; Los Angeles 1976, 180; London 1983, 63, illus. 35; New York 1989, no. 27, illus. 36; Roslyn 1997, 103, unnumbered entry, fig. 8 (image flopped).
Selected References: *L'aristarque moderne* 1785 (Collection Deloynes, no. 340, 12, no. 58); *Figaro au Salon* 1785 (Collection Deloynes, no. 330, 20); *Journal de Paris*, no. 258, 15 September 1785 (Collection Deloynes, no. 351, 826); *Jugement d'un musicien* 1785 (Collection Deloynes, no. 341, 61); *Mélanges et doutes* 1785 (Collection Deloynes, no. 336, 13, no. 58); *Minos au Sallon*, October 1785, 28 (Collection Deloynes, no. 345, 16–17); *Observations critiques* 1785 (Collection Deloynes, no. 326, 19); Charnois 1787; Goncourt 1882, 9, 253 (as lost); *Illustrated London News*, 14 May 1938, illus. 871; Bizardel 1957, 439, illus.; Schlumberger 1958, no. 73, 67, illus.; Roland Michel

1970, no. 345, 50, 57, 87, illus. 226, 273, 274;
Whiteley 1983, 506, fig. 73; Fort 1999, 300.
Commentary: As noted by Roland Michel,
comparison with the drawing by Dutertre in
Costumes et annales des grands théâtres de Paris
(1787) provides visual evidence that in this
portrait the actress is singing the famous verse:
"Ah que je fus bien inspirée / Quand je vous
reçus dans ma Cour!" (Oh, how inspired I was /
when I received you at my court!)

Anne-Antoinette Clavel, known as Saint-
Huberty (1756–1812), debuted in Paris in 1777.
On 1 December 1783, she performed the title
role of Niccolò Piccinni's opera *Didon*, a role that
brought her great success. She had her costume
designed following a drawing commissioned
from Moreau le jeune. It represented an important innovation, given the elaborate wigs,
dresses, and flounces that typically weighed
down actresses at the time. In comparison, Saint-
Huberty's simple linen tunic, with sandals laced
onto bare feet, caused a sensation. Mme Vigée-
Le Brun wrote of the performer, "Mme Saint-
Huberti n'était pas jolie, mais son visage était
ravissant de physionomie et d'expression"
(Madame Saint-Huberty was not pretty, but
her face was of a ravishing physiognomy and
expression) (Vigée-Lebrun 1986, 1:105).
D
Pl. 35

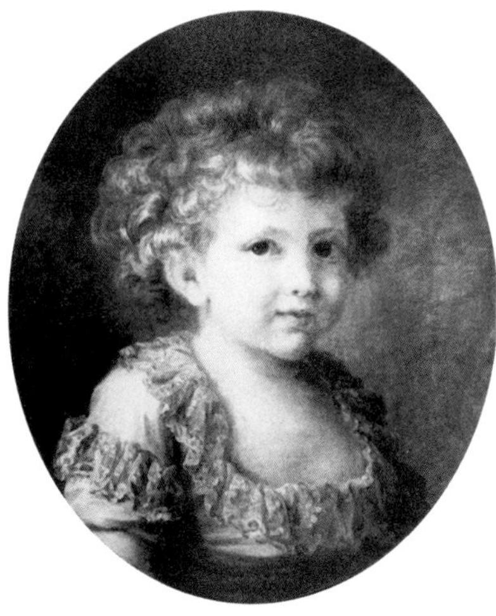

73. *Presumed Portrait of Little Mario Coster*, 1785

Oil on canvas, oval, dimensions unknown
Signed and dated at left, toward center:
[illegible] *Coster, 1785*
Present whereabouts unknown
Provenance: with the baronne of Saint-Palais,
great-grandniece of the artist, in 1970.
Selected References: Schlumberger 1958, illus.
68; Roland Michel 1970, no. 346, illus. 224.
Commentary: This portrait was said to represent the dauphin of France, who died in 1789.
However, comparison with another portrait
by Vallayer-Coster of her nephew (see cat. 85)
confirms the likely identity of the sitter as the
same little boy.

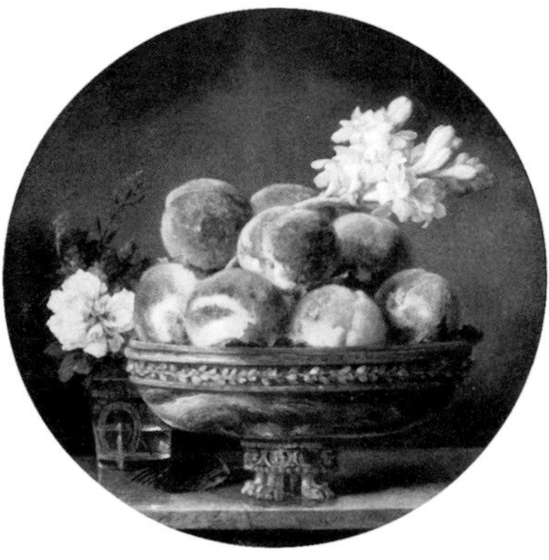

74. *An Alabaster Bowl Trimmed in Bronze with Peaches*, 1786

Oil on canvas, diam. 17 in. (43.2 cm)
Signed lower right: *Vallayer Coster*
Private collection
Provenance: Coster sale 1824, lot 25; with Peter
Mitchell, London, in 1994, for this and cat. 75.
Exhibited: Salon of 1787, no. 70.
Selected References: *L'ami des artistes au Sallon*
1787 (Collection Deloynes, no. 379, 30–31);
Lanlaire 1787 (Collection Deloynes, no. 375, 21);
Lettre d'un amateur 1787 (Collection Deloynes,
no. 381, 20); Roland Michel 1970, no. 148 (as
lost since 1824).
Commentary: Pendant of cat. 75.

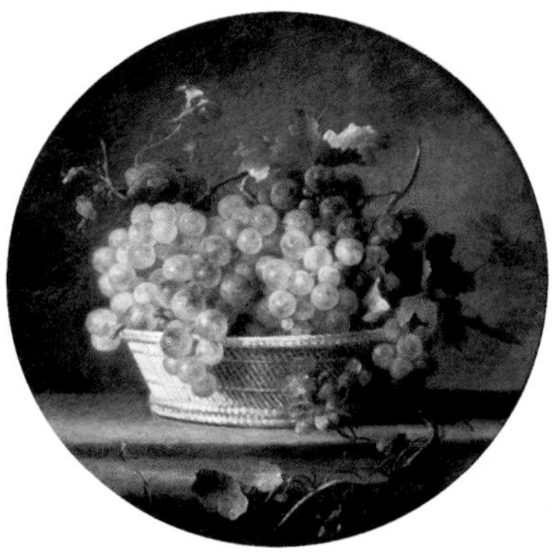

75. *A Basket of Grapes*, 1786

Oil on canvas, diam. 17 in. (43.2 cm).
Signed and dated lower left: *Vallayer Coster 1786*
Private collection
Exhibited: Salon of 1787, no. 70.
Provenance: Coster sale 1824, lot 25.
Selected References: *Lettre d'un amateur* 1787
(Collection Deloynes, no. 381, 20); *Lanlaire* 1787
(Collection Deloynes, no. 375, 21); *L'ami des
artistes au Sallon* 1787 (Collection Deloynes,
no. 379, 30–31); Roland Michel 1970, no. 147
(as lost since 1824).
Commentary: Pendant of cat. 74.

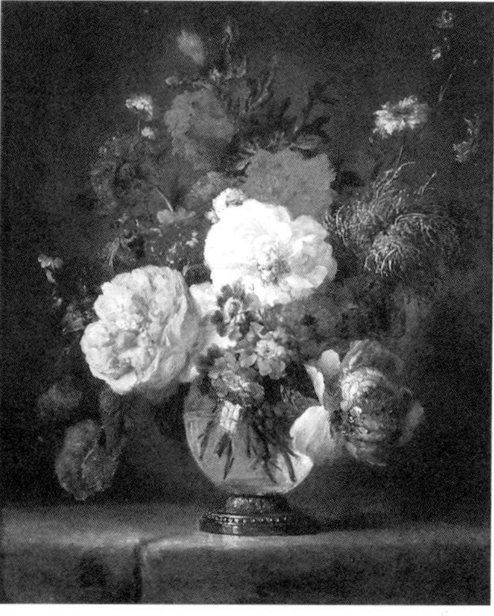

76. *Flowers in a Crystal Vase*, 1786

Oil on canvas, 15 × 12¼ in. (38 × 31 cm)
Signed and dated lower right: *M. Vallayer-
Coster/1786*
Private collection
Provenance: Galerie Cailleux, Paris; private
collection, Paris.
Exhibited: Paris 1930, no. 97; Paris 1936a,
no. 48; Göteborg 1938; Paris 1945, no. 38;
Munich 1958, no. 214; Paris 1968, no. 24;
Paris 1979b, no. 56; Grasse 1998, 40, illus. 41.
Selected References: Florisoone 1948, pl. 76;
Schlumberger 1958, 65; Schönberger and
Soenher 1959, 264; M. Faré 1962, 2: fig. 411;
Roland Michel 1970, no. 11, illus. 106 and
cover; M. and F. Faré 1976, fig. 362, 232;
Zanella 2001, 216, illus. 217.
W, D, NY
Pl. 36

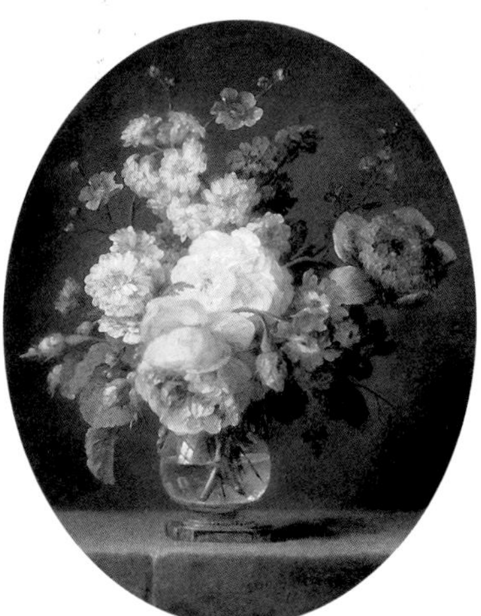

77. *Flowers in a Crystal Vase*, 1786

Oil on canvas, oval, 15¾ × 12⅜ in. (40 × 31.5 cm)
Signed and dated lower right: *Vallayer Coster/
1786*
Private collection, Europe
Provenance: Private collection, France, until
1988; Ader, Picard, Tajan, Paris, 14 April 1988,
lot 76; Richard Green Gallery, London.

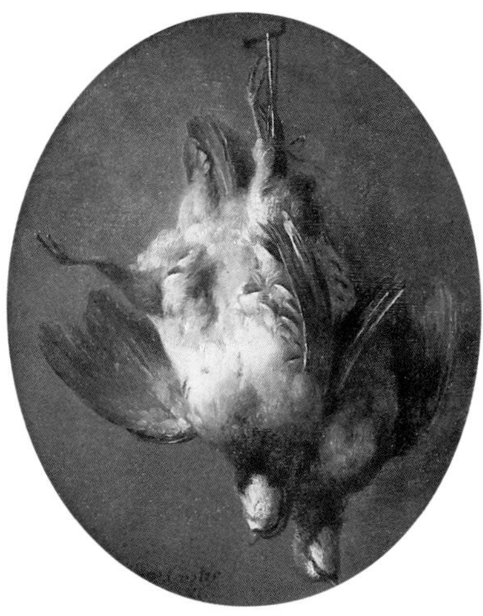

78. *Partridges,* 1786

Oil on copper, oval, 8 × 6½ in. (20.3 × 16.5 cm)
Signed and dated lower left: [illegible] *V. Coster/ 178*[6 illegible]
Marina Rust
Provenance: Victor Spark.
Exhibited: Salon of 1787, no. 75 (with its pendant); New York 1963, no. 37 (with its pendant).
Selected References: Roland Michel 1970, no. 301; M. and F. Faré 1976, fig. 368, 234.
Commentary: Pendant of cat. 79.
W, D, NY
Pl. 37

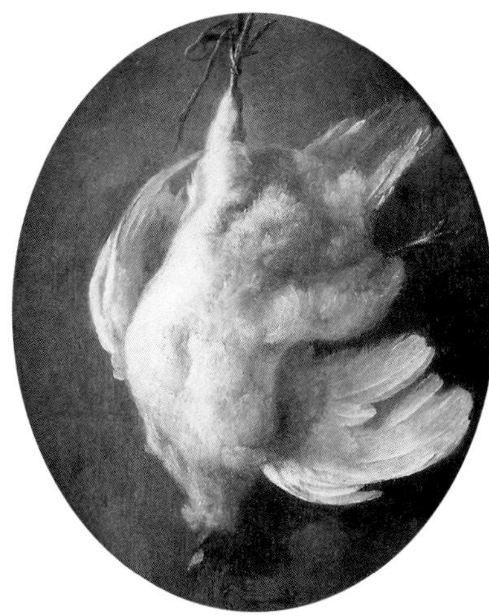

79. *A White Hen,* 1786

Oil on copper, oval, 8 × 6½ in. (20.3 × 16.5 cm)
Marina Rust
Provenance: Victor Spark.
Exhibited: Salon of 1787, no. 75 (with its pendant); New York 1963, no. 36 (with its pendant).
Selected References: Roland Michel 1970, no. 300; M. and F. Faré 1976, fig. 367, 234.
Commentary: Pendant of cat. 78.
W, D, NY
Pl. 38

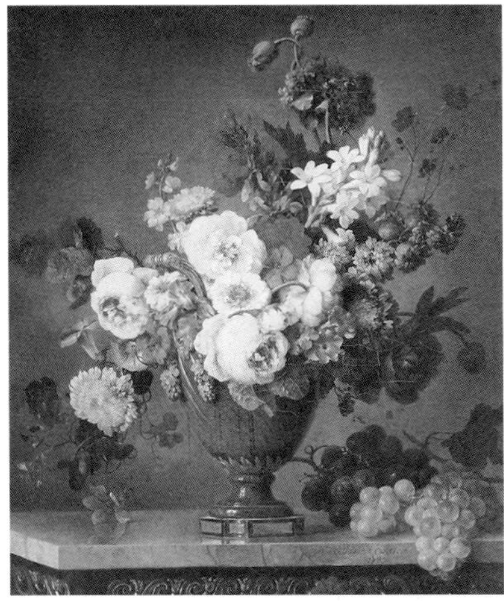

80. *A Rooster and a White Chicken on a Stone Ledge,* 1787

Oil on canvas, 21¼ × 25¼ in. (54 × 64 cm)
Signed and dated lower left: *M^de Coster 1787*
Musée de Tessé, Le Mans, France, Dépôt de l'Etat 1872
Provenance: comte d'Angiviller collection, seized during the Revolution; in the trust of the Musée de Tessé in 1872, this painting had the Musées impériaux inventory number 10028.
Exhibited: Salon of 1787, no. 71; Bordeaux 1958; Biron 1989, no. 75.
Selected References: *L'ami des artistes au Sallon* 1787 (Collection Deloynes, no. 379, 30–31); *La bourgeoise au Sallon* 1787 (Collection Deloynes, no. 384, 13–14); *Lanlaire* 1787 (Collection Deloynes, no. 375, 21); *Lettre d'un amateur* 1787 (Collection Deloynes, no. 381, 20); *Promenades d'un observateur* 1787 (Collection Deloynes, no. 372, 24); Le Mans 1892, 60 n. 365; Lefeuvre 1932, no. 381b is (as by Hondecoeter); Vergnet-Ruiz and Laclotte 1962, 84, 254; Roland Michel 1970, no. 294, illus. 199; M. and F. Faré 1976, fig. 369; Denon 1999, 154.
Commentary: Pendant of cat. 84. See Roland Michel's discussion of the painting's shipment to Paris and then to Versailles, according to correspondence from Vivant Denon in 1804, in this volume, 18, 33 n. 62.
W, D
Pl. 39

81. *Still Life: Flowers and Fruit,* 1787

Oil on canvas, 25¼ × 21¼ in. (64 × 54 cm)
Signed and dated lower right: *Me Vallayer-Coster/1787*

Collection des Musées d'art et d'histoire, Ville de Genève, inv. no. CR 207
Provenance: Clavière collection, Paris, 1789; Nicolas Reber collection, Basel; sale, Paris, 12 May 1823; James Audeoud collection, Geneva; Gustave Revilliod collection, Geneva; bequeathed in 1890 to the Musées d'art et d'histoire de la Ville de Genève.
Exhibited: Salon of 1787, no. 69
Selected References: *Le bouquet du Sallon* 1787; *Lanlaire* 1787, 21; *Mercure de France,* September 1787, 174; *Catalogue d'une riche collection . . . de . . . Reber* 1809, no. 399; *Catalogue des tableaux . . . Audeoud* 1848, 54–55, no. 95; Musée Ariana 1895, no. 246; Sidler 1901, no. 140; Sidler 1905, no. 240; Gielly 1937, 21; Deonna 1938, no. 207; Thieme and Becker 34:76; Hautecoeur 1948, 74; Roland Michel 1970, nos. 38, 82, illus. 42; Paris 1974, 631; Loche 1996, no. 68.
Related Work: The painting was copied in enamel by Mme George-Juillard (see *Catalogue de l'exposition* 1852, no. 185).
D
Pl. 40

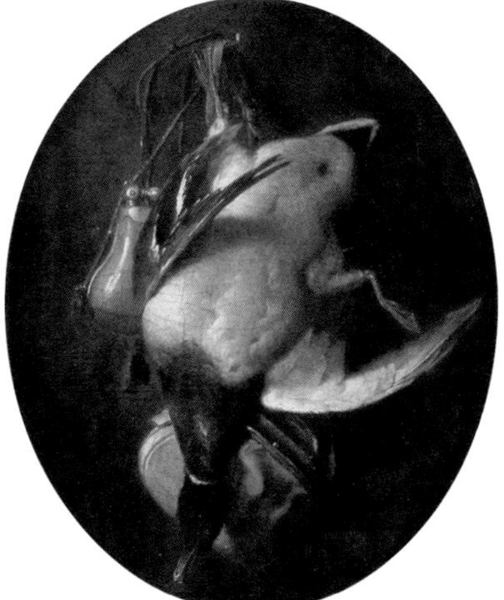

82. *Still Life with Duck,* 1787

Oil on canvas, oval, 12¾ × 10⅜ in. (32.5 × 26.5 cm)
Signed and dated lower right: *M. V.* [illegible] *Coster 1787* (a signature appears underneath this one, partially covered by the artist when, according to Roland Michel, the artist changed the background of the painting)
Musée des Beaux-Arts de Strasbourg, inv. 1286
Provenance: purchased in 1931, in Paris, by the Musée des Beaux-Arts de Strasbourg.
Exhibited: Salon of 1787, no. 75 (with its pendant, *Two Red Partridges;* see Roland Michel 1970, no. 291, as lost since 1787); Strasbourg 1954, no. 59.
Selected References: Haug 1938, no. 347; M. Faré 1962, 2: fig. 415; Vergnet-Ruiz and Laclotte 1962, 254; Roland Michel 1970, no. 290, illus. 197; M. and F. Faré 1976, fig. 372.

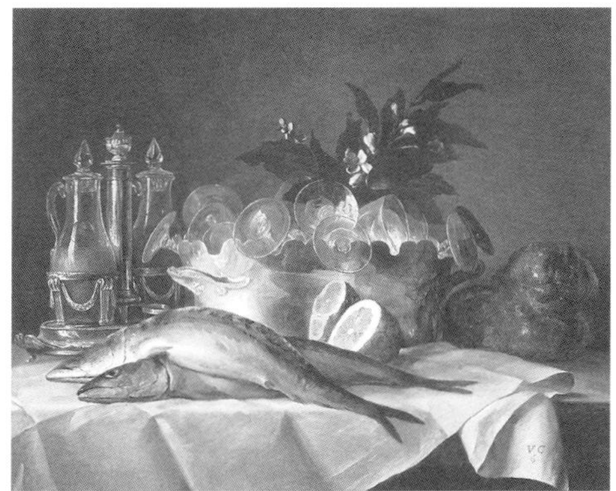

83. *Still Life with Glasses and Mackerels*, 1787

Oil on canvas, 18¾ × 23½ in. (47.6 × 59.7 cm)
Signed and dated at right, toward lower center:
Mme V. Coster 1787; monogrammed on a corner of
the napkin: *VC/6*
Mr. and Mrs. Saam Nystad
Provenance: Coster sale 1824, lot 31; Coursherie
collection, sale, Paris, 8–9 December 1891, lot 36;
L. Coblentz collection; F. Doistau collection,
1st sale, Paris, 9 June 1909, lot 77; G. B. Lasquin
collection, sale, Paris, 21–23 November 1932,
lot 424, illus.; Doistau collection, sale, Paris,
5–6 March 1937, lot 31; art market, Paris;
Saam Nystad; M. Ph. van Ommeren collection,
Rotterdam, in 1970.
Exhibited: Salon of 1787, no. 72; Paris 1926,
no. 91; London 1968a, no. 690, fig. 201.
Selected References: *Journal de Paris*, no. 262,
19 September 1787 (Collection Deloynes,
no. 394, 759); *Lanlaire* 1787 (Collection
Deloynes, no. 375, 21); Roland Michel 1970,
no. 227; M. and F. Faré 1976, fig. 371; Polak
1999, illus. 73.
Related Work: The monogrammed signature
is almost identical to the one found in the
miniature *Fruit and Flowers*, 1810 (Roland
Michel 1970, no. 378, as lost).
W, D, NY
Pl. 41

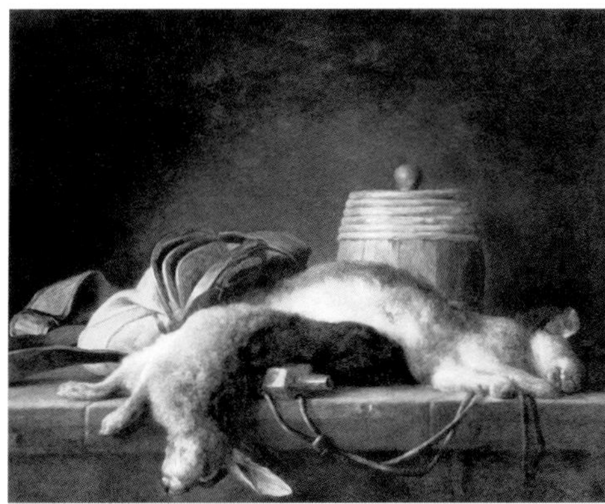

84. *Trophies of the Hunt*, 1787

Oil on canvas, 21¼ × 25⅜ in. (54 × 64.5 cm)
Signed lower right: *[Mme?] Vallayer-Coster*
Present whereabouts unknown
Provenance: Lefèvre-Bougon collection,
Amiens, sale, Paris, 1 April 1895, lot 59;
Mme Rambourg collection; Mme Ruby
collection; Galerie Cailleux, Paris; private
collection, Switzerland.
Exhibited: Salon of 1787, no. 71 (with its
pendant).

Selected References: *L'ami des artistes au
Sallon* 1787 (Collection Deloynes, no. 379,
30–31); *La bourgeoise au Sallon* 1787 (Collec-
tion Deloynes, no. 384, 13–14); *Lanlaire* 1787
(Collection Deloynes, no. 375, 21); *Lettre d'un
amateur* 1787 (Collection Deloynes, no. 381, 20);
Promenades d'un observateur 1787 (Collection
Deloynes, no. 372, 24); Roland Michel 1970,
no. 293, illus. 203; M. and F. Faré 1976, fig. 374.
Commentary: Pendant of cat. 80.

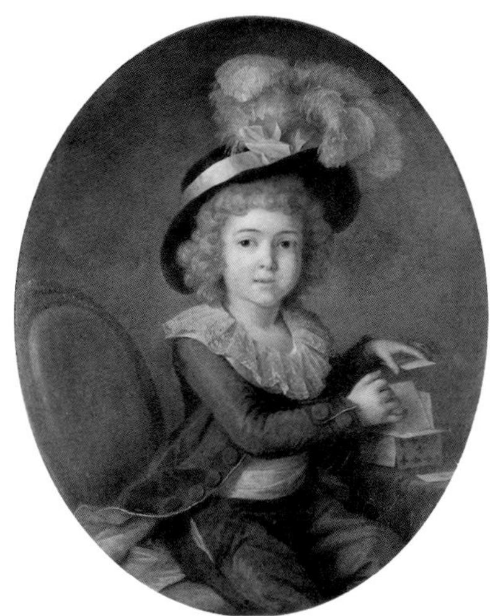

85. *Mario Coster Building a House of Cards*, 1789

Oil on canvas, oval, 30⅜ × 24 in. (77 × 61 cm)
Signed and dated at right, toward center:
M^{de} Coster/1789
Present whereabouts unknown
Provenance: with a great-grandnephew of the
artist, in 1970.
Exhibited: Salon of 1789, no. 49.
Selected References: Roland Michel 1970,
no. 348, illus. 210; Heim, Béraud, and Heim
1989, no. 49, illus.; Karlsruhe 1999, fig. 8.
Commentary: This nephew of the artist,
then six years old, is the same child as the one
portrayed in cat. 73. Both pictures were kept
by the artist's descendants.

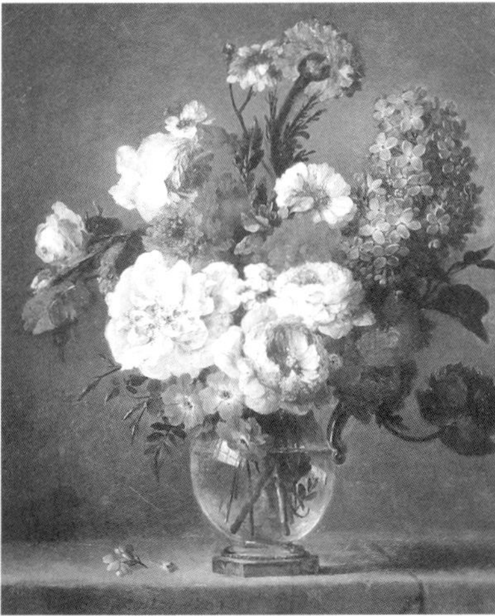

86. *Flowers in a Crystal Vase*, 1789

Oil on canvas, 18⅛ × 15⅜ in. (46 × 39 cm)
Signed and dated lower left: *Mme V. Coster, 1789*.
Private collection, Paris

Provenance: Lady Kent, others sale, Galerie
Charpentier, Paris, 18 March 1959, lot 92, illus.
Selected Reference: Roland Michel 1970,
no. 12, illus. 107.
W, D, NY
Pl. 42

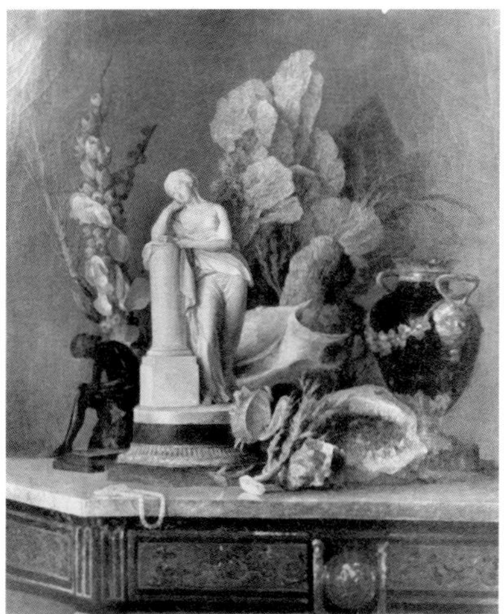

87. *Still Life with Minerals*, c. 1789

Oil on canvas, 29⅛ × 23⅝ in. (74 × 60 cm)
Traces of a signature
Present whereabouts unknown
Provenance: with the baronne de Saint-Palais,
great-grandniece of the artist, in 1970.
Exhibited: Salon of 1789, no. 48, although
the dimensions given in the Salon *livret* do not
correspond, the description fits this work;
Paris 1974, no. 180, pl. 49.
Selected Reference: Roland Michel 1970,
no. 266 or 267, illus. 179; Heim, Béraud, and
Heim 1989, illus.

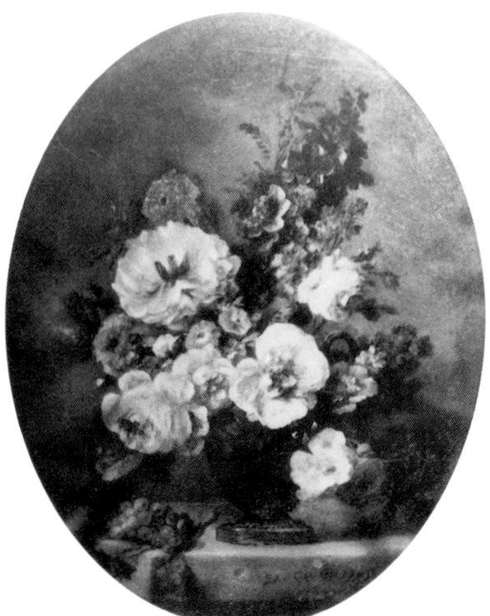

88. *Vase of Flowers and Grapes*, 1793

Oil on canvas, oval, dimensions unknown
Signed and dated toward right, on marble:
V. Coster 1793
Present whereabouts unknown
Provenance: remained in the artist's family;
private collection, La Rochelle, in 1970.
Selected Reference: Roland Michel 1970,
no. 83.

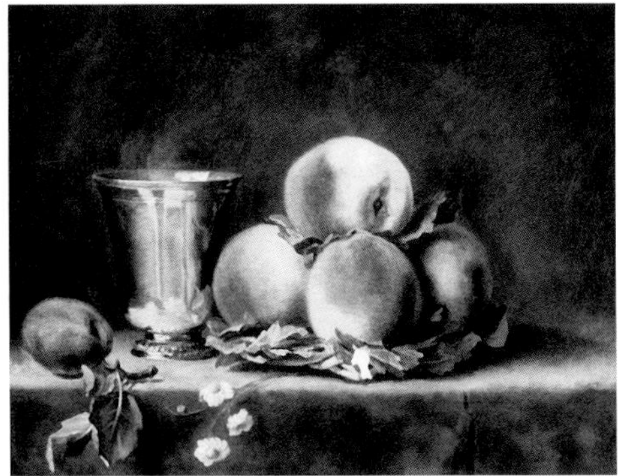

89. *Peaches and Silver Goblet*, 1797

Oil on canvas, 12¾ × 16 in. (32.5 × 40.5 cm)
Signed and dated lower right: *M.* [illegible]/
1797
Private collection
Provenance: sale, Hôtel Drouot, Paris, 8 December 1961; art market, Paris, in 1970.
Exhibited: Karlsruhe 1999, no. 161.
Selected References: Roland Michel 1965, 189; Roland Michel 1970, no. 149.
Related Work: This is an exact replica of cat. 48, which was executed in 1778.

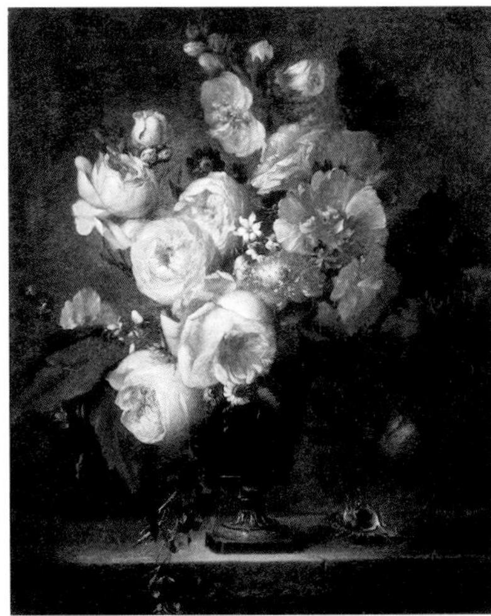

90. *Flowers in a Vase with Shell*, 1799

Oil on canvas, 19½ × 15½ in. (49.5 × 39.4 cm)
Signed and dated lower right: *A. Coster 1799*
Private collection, New York

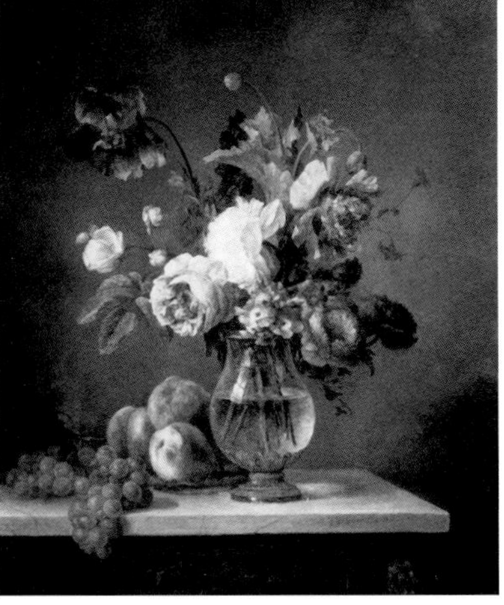

91. *Still Life with a Vase of Flowers with Peaches and Grapes*, 1800

Oil on canvas, 25¼ × 21 in. (64.1 × 53.3 cm)
Signed and dated lower right: *Vallayer Coster an 8ᵉ*
Collection of Lynda and Stewart Resnick, Beverly Hills, California
Provenance: d'Oustrac collection; Sotheby's, Monaco, 22 February 1986, lot 227; Edward Speelman, Ltd, London.

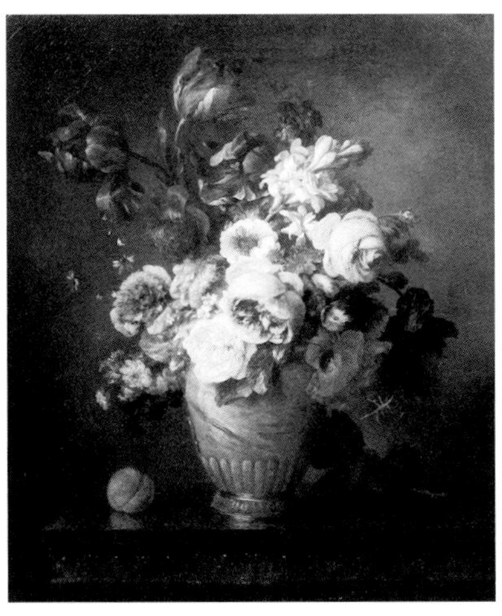

92. *Some Flowers in an Alabaster Vase*, 1800

Oil on canvas, 25⅝ × 21¼ in. (65 × 54 cm)
Signed and dated lower right: *Vallayer-Coster an 8è.*
Private collection
Exhibited: Salon of the Year IX (1801), no. 339.
Provenance: Coster sale 1824, lot 3; Laveissière collection; de Lesseps collection.
Selected Reference: Roland Michel 1970, no. 39 (as lost since 1824).

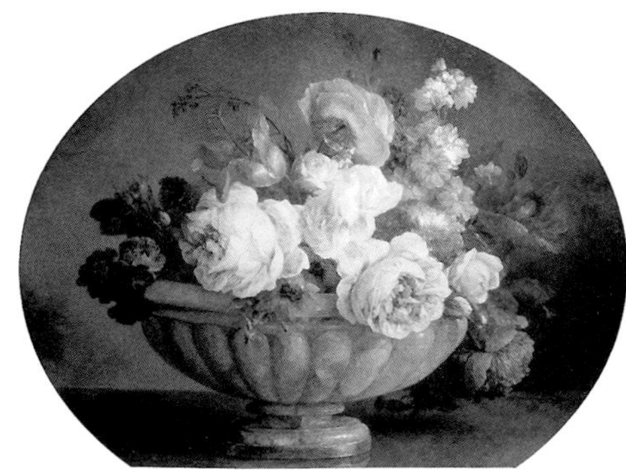

93. *Bouquet of Flowers in an Alabaster Vase*, 1801

Oil on canvas, oval, 14¾ × 17¾ in. (37.5 × 45 cm)
Signed and dated lower left: *Mde Vallayer-Coster an 9*
Private collection, North America
Provenance: sale, Mercier et Cie, Lille, 24 March 1997; Richard Green Gallery, London, until 1999.
Commentary: Pendant of cat. 94.

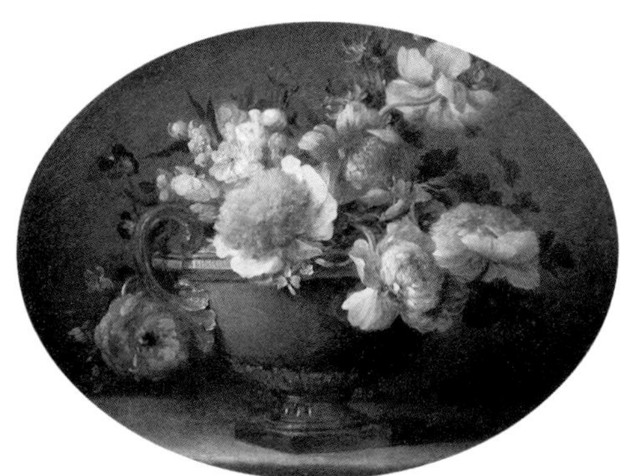

94. *Flowers in a Blue Vase*, 1801

Oil on canvas, oval, 15 × 16⅝ in. (38 × 42 cm)
Private collection
Provenance: vicomtesse de Courval collection; princesse de Poix collection; mme la duchesse de Mouchy Douairière collection, in 1970.
Selected Reference: Roland Michel 1970, no. 34, illus. 117.
Commentary: Pendant of cat. 93.

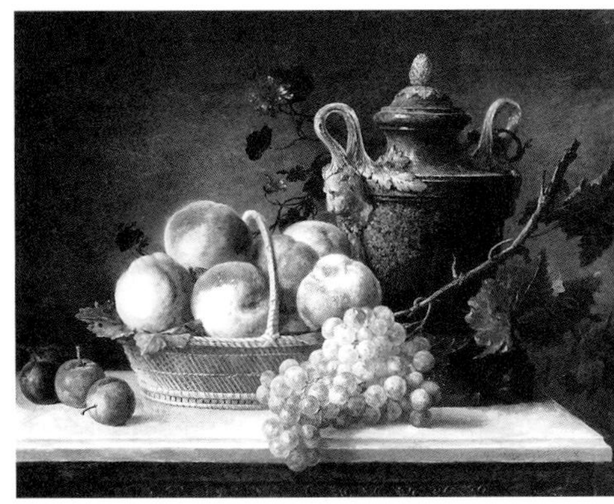

95. *Still Life with Porphyry Vase, Basket of Peaches, Grapes, and Plums*, 1802

Oil on canvas, 18½ × 22⅜ in. (47 × 56.8 cm)
Signed and dated lower right: *Mᵐᵉ Vallayer-Coster an X*
Collection of Abigail Owen-Pontez, Houston

Provenance: Coster sale 1824, lot 29; château de Balleroy; Etienne Lévy collection, Paris; sold in 1992 by Galerie Cailleux, Paris, to present owner.
Exhibited: Salon of the Year X (1802), no. 283; Paris 1959b, no. 87.
Selected References: Roland Michel 1970, no. 151, illus. 131; M. and F. Faré 1976, fig. 376, 238.
D, NY
Pl. 43

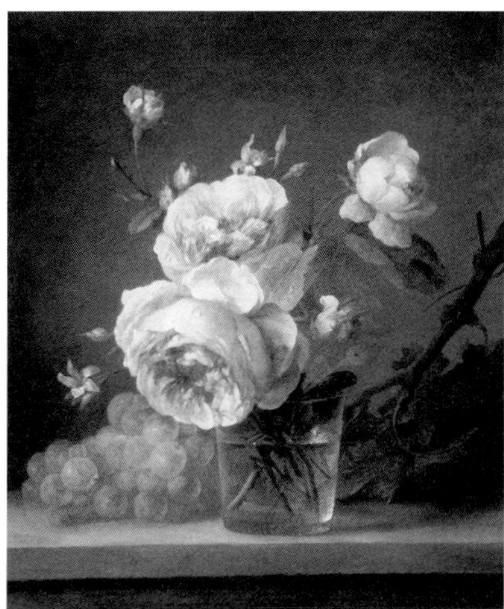

96. *Roses in a Glass and Grapes*, 1804

Oil on canvas, 12¾ × 10½ in. (32.5 × 26.5 cm)
Signed and dated lower right: *Vallayer-Coster/ an XII.* [1804; *I* partially effaced]
Private collection, North America
Provenance: Cournerie collection, sale, Paris, 8–9 December 1891, lot 40; Eugène Féral collection, sale, Paris, 22–24 April 1901, lot 65; de Chaudenay collection, Paris; Galerie Cailleux, Paris; Sotheby's, Monaco, 29 November 1986, lot 365; Roberto Polo collection; Sotheby's, New York, 11 January 1990, lot 96; Richard Green Gallery, London, until 2000.
Exhibited: probably Salon of the Year XII (1804), no. 480.
Selected References: Roland Michel 1970, no. 84 and 86 (as lost since 1804); Hardouin-Fugier and Grafe 1989, 377.

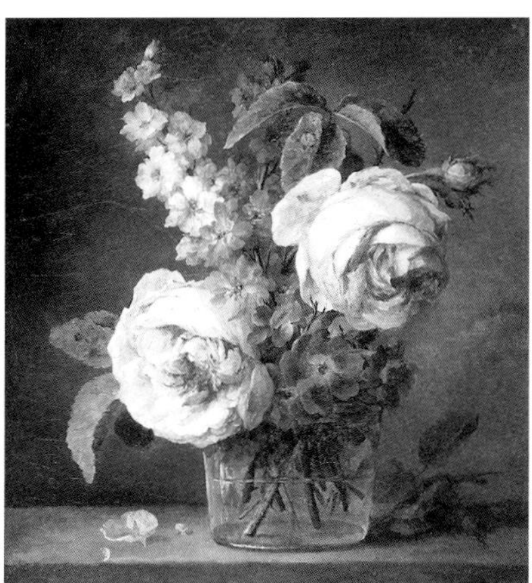

97. *Flowers in a Glass Vase*, 1806

Oil on canvas, 12¼ × 10⅝ in. (31 × 27 cm)
Signed and dated lower right: *Mme V. Coster 1806.*
Private collection

Provenance: Cailleux collection.
Exhibited: Paris 1930, no. 98; Amsterdam 1933, no. 323; Paris 1936a, no. 47; Paris 1938, no. 22; Liège 1939; Rotterdam 1954, no. 59, pl. 33; Paris 1968, no. 25; Grasse 1998, 42, illus. 43.
Selected References: Faniel et al. 1956, 21; Schlumberger 1958, illus. 69; Roland Michel 1970, no. 14; Zanella 2001, 219.
W, D, NY
Pl. 44

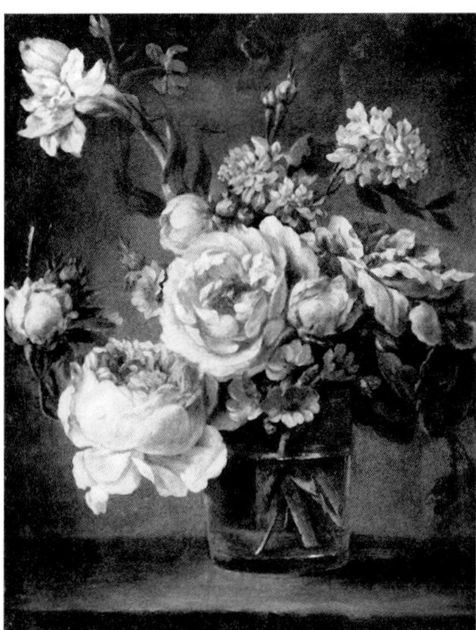

98. *Flowers in a Glass Vase*

Oil on metal, 12⅝ × 9⅜ in. (32 × 23.9 cm)
Private collection, Bordeaux, in 1970
Selected Reference: Roland Michel 1970, no. 16, illus. 116.
Commentary: According to Roland Michel, this painting was initialed and dated 1812; initials and date did not survive cleaning. Facture is very dry. The authenticity of this painting, known only from a black-and-white photograph, is questionable.

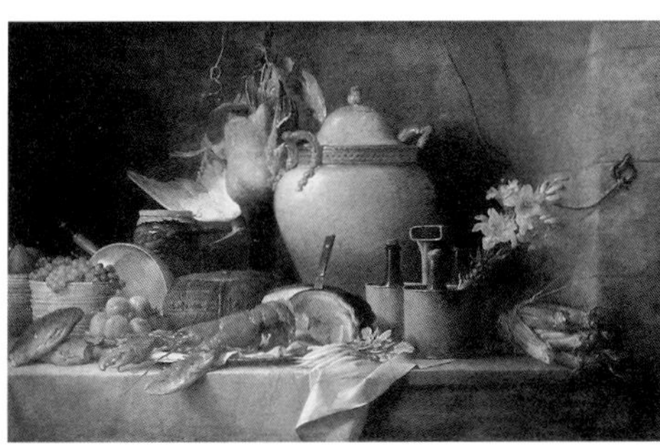

99. *Still Life with Lobster*, 1817

Oil on canvas, 45¾ × 70⅛ in. (116 × 178 cm)
Signed at right: *Mme Vallayer-Coster*
Musée du Louvre, Paris, DL 1977-19
Provenance: Louis XVIII collection, most probably given by the artist; château de La Motte-Beuvron, after 1850; entered the Mobilier National in 1884 (inv. L. B. 553); in 1977 deposited at the Musée du Louvre.
Exhibited: Salon of 1817, no. 747; Melbourne 1980, no. 116; Lille 1985, 115.

Selected References: Roland Michel 1965, 185–190, illus.; Roland Michel 1970, no. 228, illus. 8–9; Rosenberg, Reynaud, and Compin 1974, 5: annexe I, 10; M. and F. Faré 1976, fig. 375, 237; *Guide* 1993, 113, salle 52; Hardouin-Fugier 1998, 53–55, illus.; Berlin 1999, illus. 199.
W, D, NY
Pl. 45

100. *Bas-Relief*, n.d.

Oil on canvas, 10⅜ × 15⅛ in. (26.4 × 38.4 cm)
Signed lower right: *Vallayer-Coster*
Present whereabouts unknown
Provenance: with a great-grandnephew of the artist, in 1970.
Selected Reference: Roland Michel 1970, no. 252.
Commentary: The signature was probably added later. This painting is an autograph replica of cat. 19.

101. *A Bouquet of Flowers*, n.d.

Oil on canvas, oval, 15¾ × 12⅝ in. (40 × 32 cm)
Initialed at lower right: *VC.*
Inscribed on stretcher: Vallayer-Coster
Present whereabouts unknown
Provenance: with a great-grandnephew of the artist, in 1970.
Selected Reference: Roland Michel 1970, no. 120.

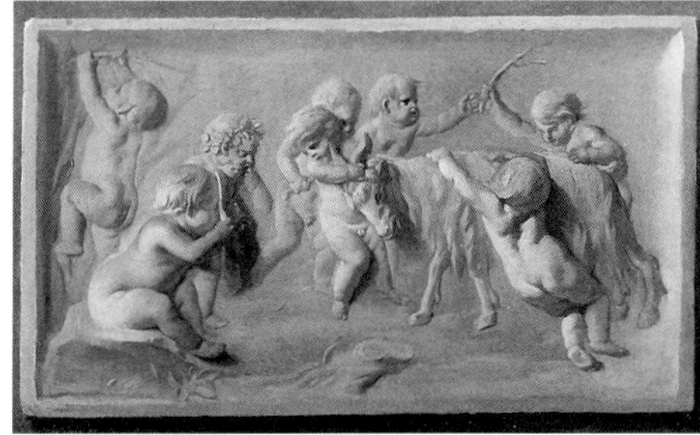

102. *Children with a Goat*, n.d.

Oil on canvas, 10⅝ × 16½ in. (27 × 42 cm)
Private collection, Paris
Provenance: Aubert collection, jeweler to the crown; sale, 2 March 1786, lot 78; sale, Galliéra, Paris, 7 March 1970, lot 6 (as by Sauvage).
Commentary: The sculpted model for this painting was very successful. Several versions existed in bronze or in plaster in Parisian collections in the eighteenth century that were also copied by Desportes or Chardin, as well as by lesser-known artists. The monogram *V. Cer* was visible on the verso, before relining.

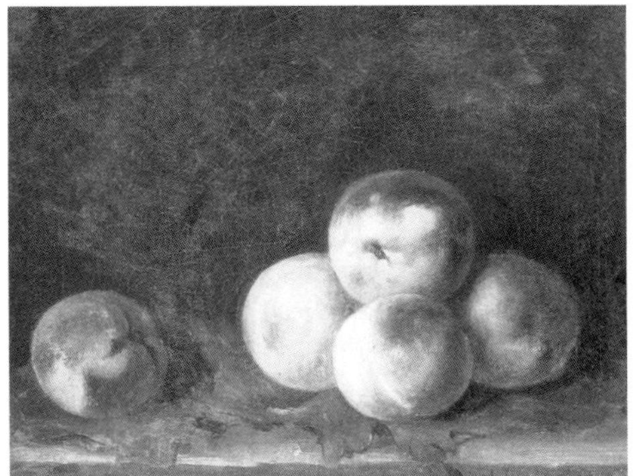

103. *Five Peaches*, n.d.

Oil on canvas, 12⅞ × 16 in. (32.8 × 40.5 cm)
Signed lower right: *Vall*[illegible]*ter*
Museo Nacional de San Carlos, INBA
Provenance: possibly Marcille collection,
sale, 12 January 1857, lot 134, 14 January 1857,
lot 304 or 305, or 4 March 1857, lot 302; un-
known private collection, Mexico.
Exhibited: Mexico City 1996, no. 51.
Selected References: Roland Michel 1970,
possibly no. 152, 153, 154, or 155.
We wish to thank Marie-Paule Vial for her help
in finding this work.

104. *Flowers in a Basket*, n.d.

Oil on canvas, originally oval, enlarged to
a rectangle, 18⅛ × 15 in. (46 × 38 cm)
Present whereabouts unknown
Provenance: Haviland collection, 5th sale,
Paris, 14–15 December 1922, lot 60; Coincy
collection; sale, Galliéra, Paris, 15 June 1962,
lot 64; private collection, Bordeaux, 1970.
Selected Reference: Roland Michel 1970,
no. 59.

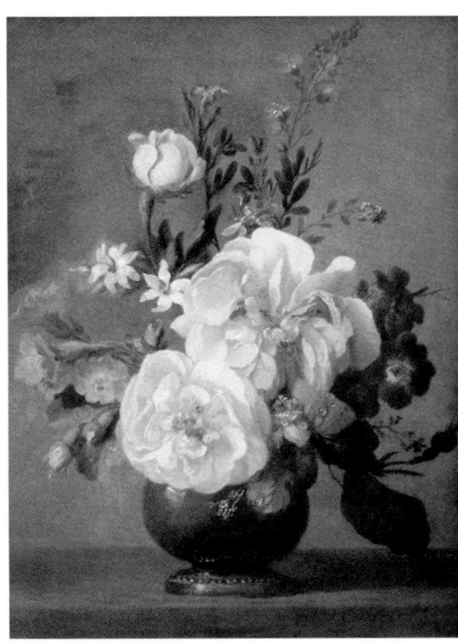

105. *Flowers in a Blue Vase*, n.d.

Oil on canvas, 12⅞ × 9½ in. (32.6 × 24 cm)
Signed lower right: *V. Coster* (signature repeats
first name initial; possibly reinforced)
Private collection, England
Provenance: private collection, Paris; Sotheby's,
London, 9 July 1998, lot 217; Adam Williams
Fine Art, Limited, New York, until 2000.
Selected Reference: Roland Michel 1970,
no. 33, illus. 123; M. and F. Faré 1976, fig. 365.

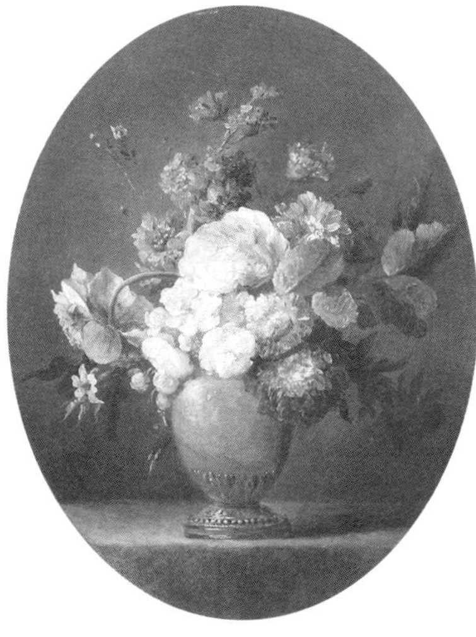

106. *Flowers in a Brown Porcelain Vase*, n.d.

Oil on canvas, oval, 16⅛ × 12¾ in. (41 × 32.5 cm)
Signed lower right: *V. C.*
Private collection
Provenance: Galerie Charpentier, Paris,
10 June 1954, lot 56, pl. xv; Etienne Lévy col-
lection, in 1970; Galerie Cailleux, Paris; art
market, Paris.
Exhibited: Paris 1959a, no. 85; Grasse 1998, 44.
Selected References: Roland Michel 1970,
no. 40, illus. 105; M. and F. Faré 1976, fig. 357,
230; Zanella 2001, 220.
W, D, NY
Pl. 46

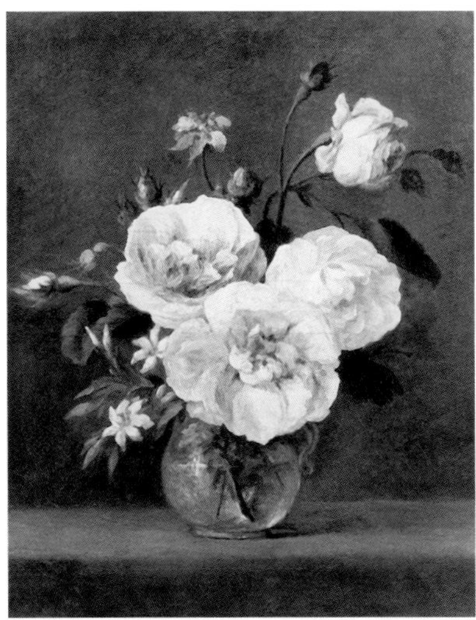

107. *Flowers in a Crystal Vase*, n.d.

Oil on canvas, 12¾ × 10⅝ in. (32.5 × 27 cm)
Present whereabouts unknown
Provenance: perhaps Sauvage sale, 6 December
1808, lot 29; Seligmann collection, before 1939;
private collection, Paris, in 1970.
Selected Reference: Roland Michel 1970,
no. 18, illus. 108.

108. *Flowers in a Crystal Vase*, n.d.

Oil on canvas, 12¾ × 10⅞ in. (32.5 × 27.7 cm)
Signed at right, on shelf: *a. v.*
Present whereabouts unknown
Provenance: perhaps Sauvage sale, 6 Decem-
ber 1808, lot 29 (see cat. 107); Broughton
collection, England, in 1970.
Selected References: Grant 1952, no. 127, pl. 43;
Pavière 1963, 66, pl. 62; Roland Michel 1970,
no. 24ter.
Commentary: Based on a photograph, the
attribution seems correct, but the signature
is doubtful.

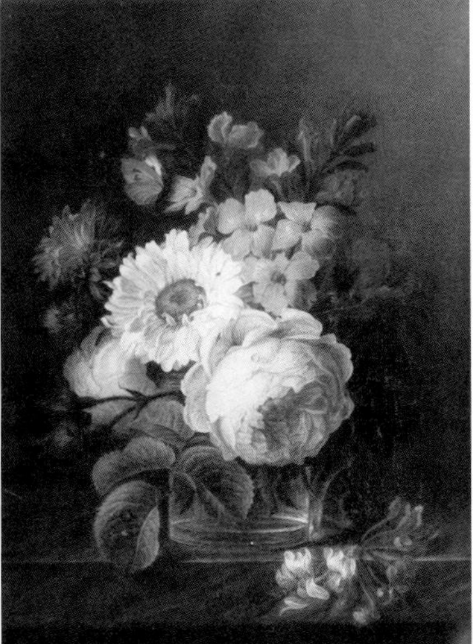

109. *Flowers in a Glass*, n.d.

Oil on canvas, 13 × 9½ in. (33 × 24 cm)
Musée des Beaux-Arts de Carcassonne
Provenance: this painting is included in the
earliest inventory of the Musée de Carcassonne
in 1830.
Exhibited: Carcassonne 1938, no. 208; Biron
1989, no. 76.
Selected References: catalogues of the Musée
de Carcassonne 1845, no. 85; 1846, no. 96; 1847,
no. 98; 1864, no. 147; 1878, no. 173; 1894,
no. 173; Roland Michel 1970, no. 20.

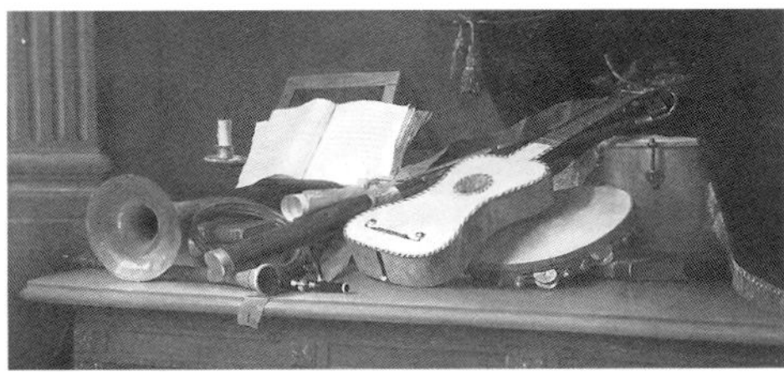

110. *Musical Instruments*, n.d.

Oil on canvas, 35⅛ × 70½ in. (89.2 × 179.1 cm)
Private collection, Loan arranged courtesy of
The Matthiesen Gallery, London
Provenance: Jacques Doucet collection,
sale, Paris, 16 May 1906, lot 88; Companini-
Bonomi collection, Milan; Baron-Stumm-
Holzhausen collection; Julius Böhler collection,
in 1970; Matthiesen Gallery, London, in 1987.
Selected References: M. Faré 1962, 2: fig. 425;
Roland Michel 1970, no. 269, illus. 175; M. and
F. Faré 1976, fig. 337.

Related Work: This composition in pastel, "signed" and dated 1779, was sold at Drouot, Paris, 29 November 1995, lot 12, illus.
W, D
Pl. 47

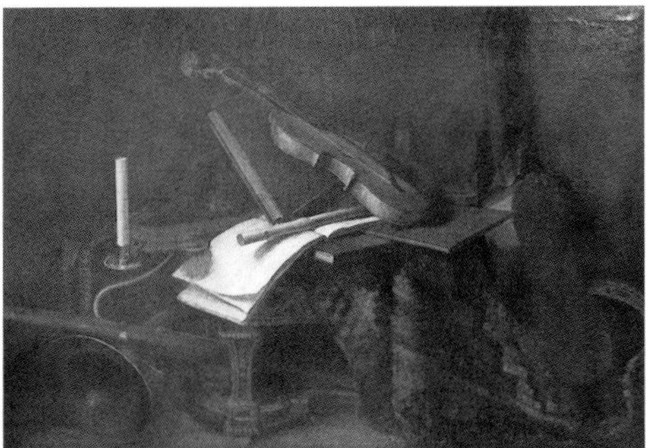

111. *Musical Instruments Firescreen*, n.d.

Oil on canvas, 37⅜ × 55⅛ in. (94.9 × 140 cm)
Signed lower left: *Vallayer-Coster*
Present whereabouts unknown
Provenance: Rothan collection, in 1879; King Edward VII collection; given by him in France to his violin teacher, M. Falcon, who sold it to M. Larramendy; Pierre Larramendy collection, Chantaco, in 1970.
Exhibited: Bordeaux 1969, no. 104.
Selected References: Gonse 1879, illus.; Roland Michel 1970, no. 268, illus. 186; M. and F. Faré 1976, 221, fig. 336.

112. *Peaches*, n.d.

Oil on canvas, oval, 12⅝ × 16 in. (32 × 40.5 cm)
Present whereabouts unknown
Provenance: possibly Marcille collection, sale, 12 January 1857, lot 134, 14 January 1857, lot 304 or 305, 4 March 1857, lot 302, or 6–8 March 1857, lot 48; Galliéra, Paris, 4 December 1963, lot 120, illus.; Benito Pardo collection, in 1970.
Selected Reference: Roland Michel, 1970, nos. 152–158.

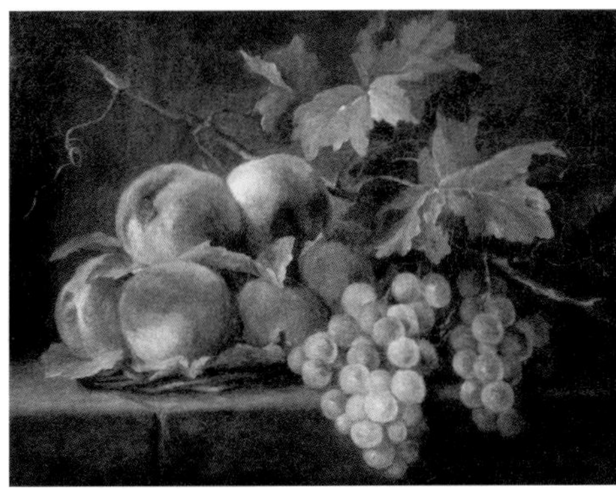

113. *Peaches and Grapes*, n.d.

Oil on canvas, 12⅜ × 16⅛ in. (31.5 × 41 cm)
Present whereabouts unknown
Provenance: Galerie Cailleux, Paris, in 1970; private collection, Switzerland.
Exhibited: Paris 1968, no. 27.
Selected Reference: Roland Michel 1970, no. 168, illus. 130.

Related Works: This composition is very similar to that of *Still Life with Peaches and Grapes*, in the National Gallery of Canada, Ottawa (cat. 130), and identical to that of the tapestry *Peaches and Grapes*, 1779 (Roland Michel 1970, no. 426).

114. *Peaches and Various Objects*, n.d.

Oil on canvas, 14¾ × 18⅛ in. (37.5 × 46 cm)
Present whereabouts unknown
Provenance: P. de Boer collection, Amsterdam; Brod collection, London; Sidney J. van den Bergh collection, in 1970; Nystad collection, The Hague.
Exhibited: London 1965, no. 33, with the dimensions reversed.
Selected Reference: Roland Michel 1970, no. 161, illus. 149.

115. *Peaches, Bread, and Wine*, n.d.

Oil on canvas, 13⅛ × 16⅛ in. (33.5 × 41 cm)
Present whereabouts unknown
Provenance: private collection, Paris, in 1970.
Exhibited: Paris 1959b, no. 19.
Selected Reference: Roland Michel 1970, no. 164.

116. *Peaches, Grapes, and Bread*, n.d.

Oil on canvas, oval, 17½ × 21¼ in. (44.5 × 54 cm)
Signed at right: *A. Vallayer-Coster*.
Present whereabouts unknown
Provenance: private collection (great-grandnephew of Anne Vallayer-Coster), in 1970.
Selected Reference: Roland Michel 1970, no. 172, where she doubts the authenticity of the signature.

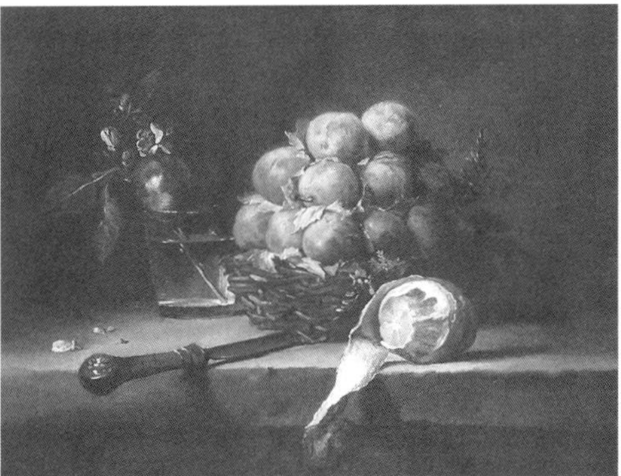

117. *Plums, a Lemon, and a Knife*, n.d.

Oil on canvas, 13¾ × 17¾ in. (35 × 45 cm)
Private collection
Provenance: Galerie Cailleux, Paris; Consuela Vanderbilt Balsan collection, Paris and New York; Marlborough collection, New York; Newhouse Galleries, New York; John Lowenthal collection, New York; art market, Paris.
Exhibited: Salon of 1771; Copenhagen 1935, no. 222, pl. 27; Paris 1936a, no. 46; Grasse 1998, 39.
Selected References: Sterling 1952, pl. 78; M. Faré 1962, 2: fig. 419; Roland Michel 1970, no. 182, illus. 154 (as lost); Roland Michel 1973, 57–58; M. and F. Faré 1976, fig. 355, 228; Rosenberg and Stewart 1987, 285; Zanella 2001, 213.
Related Work: This composition also exists in an oval format, *Still Life with Plums and a Lemon*, 1778, at the Fine Arts Museums of San Francisco (cat. 49).
W, D
Pl. 48

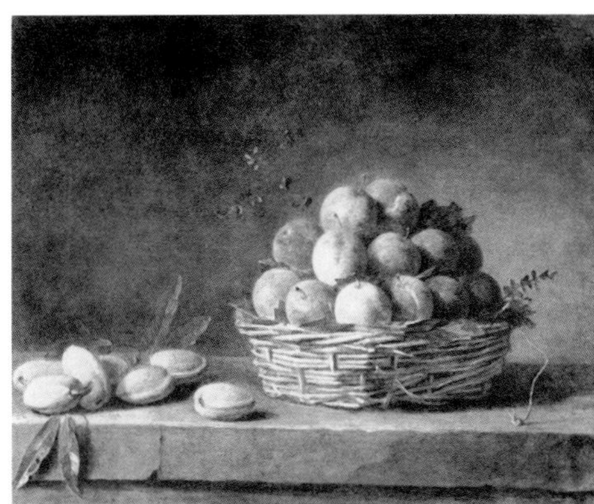

118. *Plums and Almonds*, n.d.

Oil on canvas, 14⅝ × 17¾ in. (37 × 45 cm)
Present whereabouts unknown
Provenance: sale comtesse X . . . , Galliéra, Paris, 26 March 1963, lot 34, illus.; Heim-Gairac, Paris; Newhouse Galleries, New York, in 1970.
Selected Reference: Roland Michel 1970, no. 184, illus. 157.
Related Works: There is another version of this composition (see Roland Michel 1970, no. 185). It was used as the model for a Savonnerie tapestry (before 1780) that was part of the collection of the marquis de Marigny (Roland Michel 1970, no. 428). In the nineteenth century, it was copied by Mme Reys-Allais, daughter of the engraver Louis-Jean Allais, who produced a series of engravings after flower studies by Vallayer-Coster (see cat. 157).

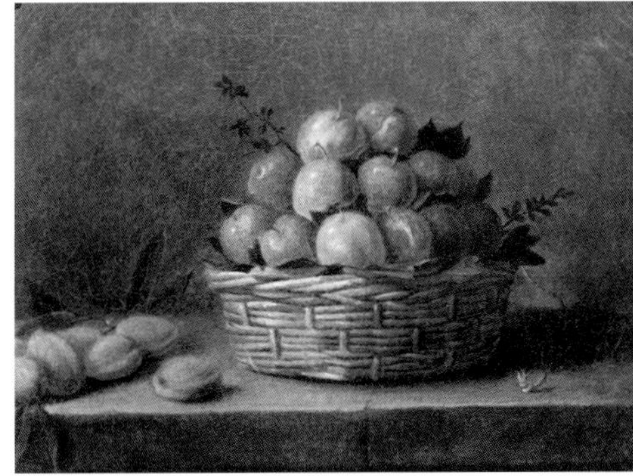

119. *Plums and Almonds*, n.d.

Oil on canvas, 13⅛ × 16⅛ in. (33.5 × 41 cm)
Signed lower right: *V* [the rest of the signature is illegible]
Present whereabouts unknown
Provenance: Lemonnier collection, Paris.
Selected Reference: Roland Michel 1970, no. 185.
Related Work: see cat. 120.

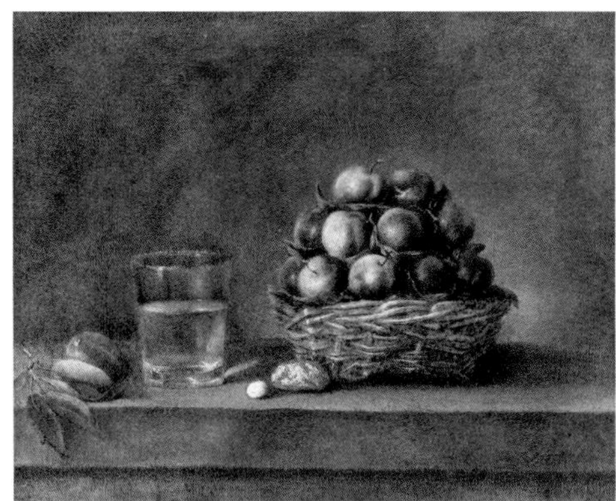

120. *Plums, Glass, and Almonds*, n.d.

Oil on canvas, 13 × 16⅛ in. (33 × 41 cm)
Present whereabouts unknown
Selected Reference: Roland Michel 1970,
no. 186.
Commentary: The authenticity of this painting,
known only from a black-and-white photograph, is questionable.

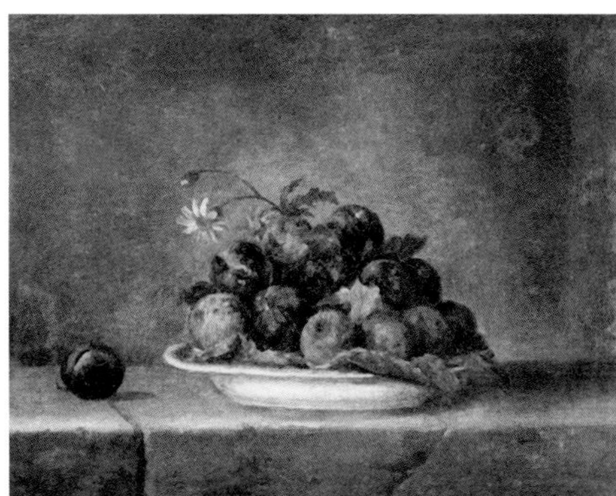

121. *Plums on a Ledge*, n.d.

Oil on canvas, 12⅝ × 16⅛ in. (32 × 41 cm)
Present whereabouts unknown
Provenance: sale, Paris, 10 November 1928,
as attributed; Dr. A. Scharf collection, London;
Paul Drey Gallery, New York, in 1978.
Selected Reference: Roland Michel 1970,
no. 181.

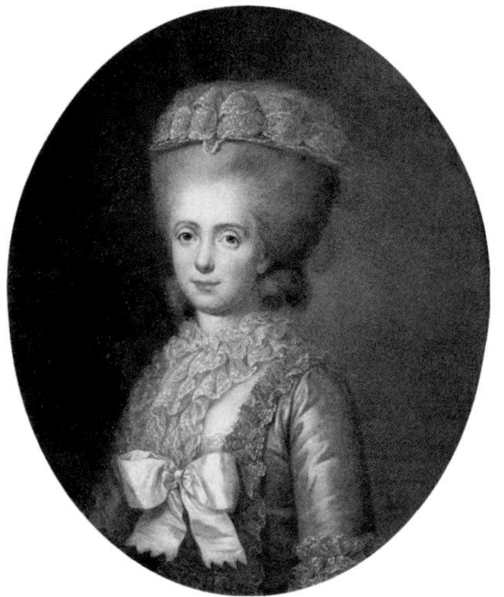

122. *Portrait of Madame Adélaïde*, n.d.

Oil on canvas, oval, 28⅛ × 22⅞ in. (71.4 ×
58 cm)
Etablissement Thermal de Vichy

Provenance: duchesse d'Angoulême, daughter
of Louis XVI, in 1821.
Exhibited: Grand salons, Vichy.
Selected Reference: Castanié 1865, 79.
Commentary: This is an autograph replica of
cat. 59.

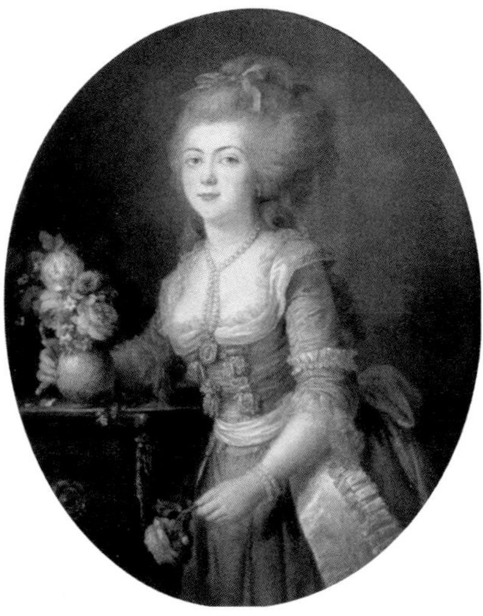

123. *Portrait of Madame Auguié*, n.d.

Oil on canvas, oval, 38⅛ × 29⅞ in. (97 × 76 cm)
Signed on upper drawer of dresser:
Mme Vallayer Coster
Private collection, Monaco
Provenance: comte André de Ganay collection;
Wildenstein; E. L. Illife, sale, Sotheby's,
London, 10 June 1959, lot 86; Hallsborough,
London; G. and R. Schubert, until 1973.
Exhibited: perhaps Salon of 1781 (see Com-
mentary); London 1938; Rome 1962, no. 194,
pl. 61.
Selected References: Oulmont 1928, pl. 43;
Bazin 1962, pl. 144; Roland Michel 1970,
no. 333.
Related Works: A rectangular copy in pastel
by Kucharsky was with the descendants of
Mme Auguié. An oval replica (100 × 81 cm)
was for sale at Hôtel Drouot, Paris, 15 November 1976, lot 22, as French School, *Portrait of
Adélaïde Genet Holding a Vase of Flowers.*
Commentary: At the Salon of 1781 Vallayer-
Coster exhibited a portrait entitled *A Woman
Arranging Flowers,* which brought her great
success (see Roland Michel 1970, no. 332). A
handwritten note by Diderot in the manuscript
for the Salon of 1781 tells us that the sitter was
a lady-in-waiting *(femme de chambre)* to the
queen. Mme Auguié occupied this post, which
explains why it has been thought that the
present painting was the one exhibited at the
Salon. However, the dimensions indicated in
the *livret* (126 × 189 cm) are not compatible
with this identification. Even if the painting
was greatly cut down to the dimensions listed
above, it is difficult to explain why its copies or
replicas would have retained the same dimensions as this reduced version. The artist may
have executed two paintings of Mme Auguié,
or perhaps the now-lost painting that was exhibited at the Salon of 1781 was a portrait of her
sister, Mme Campan, who was also a lady-in-
waiting to Marie-Antoinette.

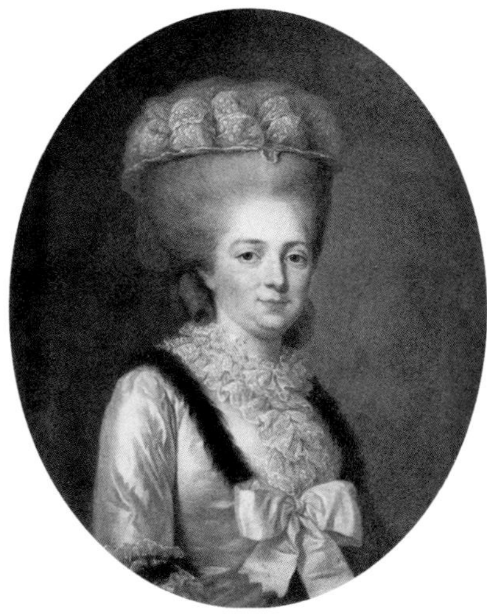

124. *Portrait of Madame Victoire*, n.d.

Oil on canvas, oval, 28⅛ × 22⅞ in. (71.4 ×
58 cm)
Etablissement Thermal de Vichy
Provenance: duchesse d'Angoulême, daughter
of Louis XVI, in 1821.
Exhibited: Grand salons, Vichy.
Selected Reference: Castanié 1865, 79.
Commentary: This is an autograph replica of
cat. 60.

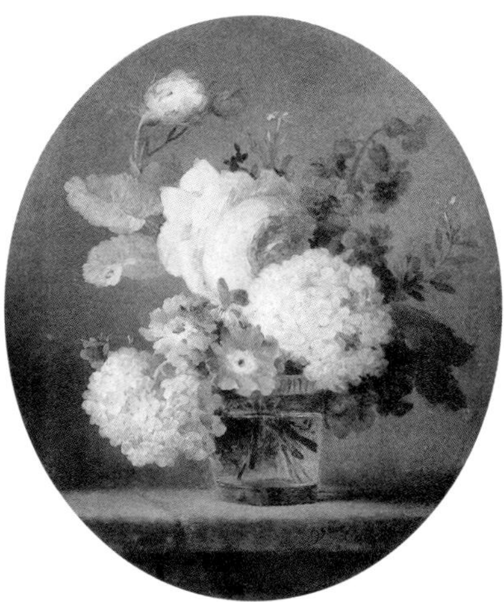

125. *Roses, Snowballs, Peonies, and Hyacinths in
a Glass*, n.d.

Oil on canvas, oval, 12⅝ × 10⅝ in. (32 × 27 cm)
Signed lower right, on edge of table: *V^er Coster.*
Present whereabouts unknown
Provenance: Cournerie collection, sale, Paris,
8–9 December 1891, lot 34; perhaps Doistau
collection, sale, Paris, 5–6 March 1937, lot 32;
private collection, Paris, 1970; Drouot Montaigne, Paris, 12 December 1988, lot 67.
Exhibited: Paris 1945, no. 37; Paris 1968,
no. 26; Paris 1975, no. 42, illus.
Selected Reference: Roland Michel 1970,
no. 17, illus. 109 (possibly also no. 21 as lost).

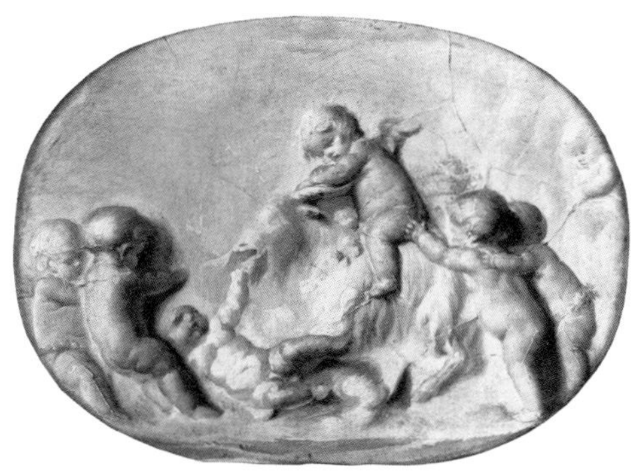

126. *Spring* or *Children's Game*, n.d.

Oil on canvas, oval, 9⅞ × 13⅜ in. (25 × 34 cm)
Private collection
Provenance: Hôtel Drouot (Audap-Solanet),
Paris, 25 June 1993, lot 96, illus.

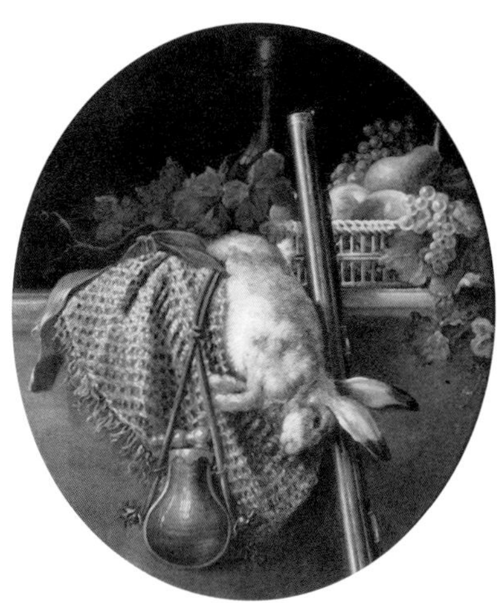

127. *Still Life with a Basket of Fruit, Rifles, and
Hare on a Table*, n.d.

Oil on canvas, oval, 26 × 21½ in. (66 × 54.5 cm)
Signed at center right: *vallayer Coster*
Private collection
Provenance: baron de Beurnonville collection,
sale, Paris, Hôtel Drouot (Maître Pillet), 9 May
1881, lot 179; sale, Etude Tajan, Paris, 12 December 1995, lot 112, illus.
Selected Reference: Roland Michel 1970,
no. 296 (as lost).

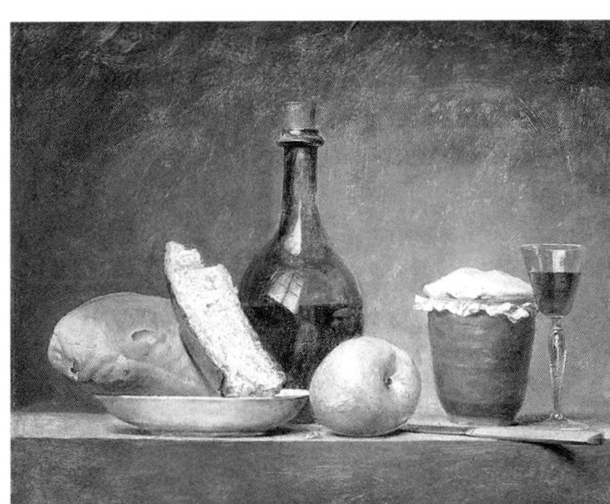

128. *Still Life with a Frugal Repast*, n.d.

Oil on panel, 10⅞ × 12¾ in. (27.5 × 32.5 cm)
Staatliche Museen zu Berlin, Gemäldegalerie
Provenance: Julius Böhler collection; be-
queathed by Böhler to the Kaiser Friedrich
Museum, now the Staatliche Museen zu Berlin,
in 1915.

Selected References: Bode 1916, 64, pl. 29
(as Chardin); Kunze 1931, no. 1731; M. Faré
1962, 2: no. 406, illus.; Roland Michel 1970,
no. 229, illus. 165; M. and F. Faré 1976, fig. 340;
Bryson 1990, 161–163, illus. 163.

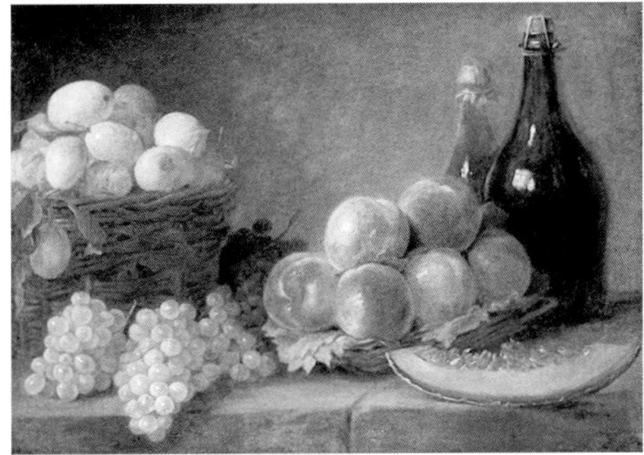

129. *Still Life with Fruit and Bottles*, n.d.

Oil on canvas, 16⅝ × 21¾ in. (42 × 55 cm)
Frame stamped: *Cᵗ PEPIN* (Claude Pépin was
a Parisian frame maker)
Private collection
Provenance: Grange collection, London; Galerie
Cailleux, Paris; private collection, France; sale,
Tajan, Paris, 28 June 1993, lot 61; Christie's,
New York, 23 October 1998, lot 54.
Selected References: Schlumberger 1958, 66,
illus.; Roland Michel 1970, no. 188 (as lost),
illus. 40.

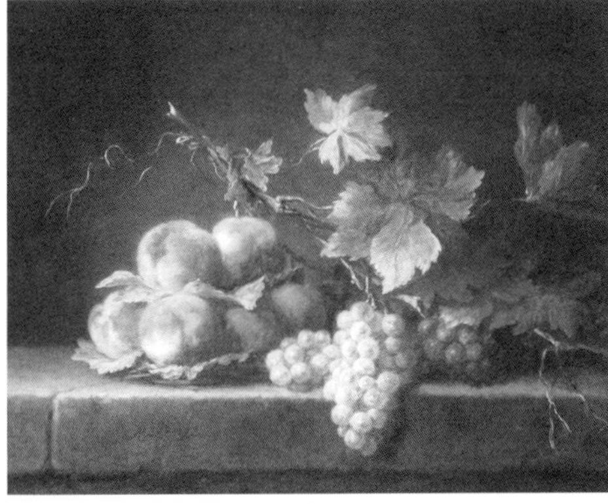

130. *Still-Life with Peaches and Grapes*, n.d.

Oil on canvas, 18⅛ × 21⅝ in. (46 × 55 cm)
Signed lower left: *Melle V.*
National Gallery of Canada, Ottawa, Purchased
1965
Provenance: A. Beurdeley collection, 1st sale,
Paris, 6–7 May 1920, lot 199; Hector Brame,
Paris; Galerie Cailleux, Paris; National Gallery
of Canada, purchased in 1965.
Exhibited: Paris 1945, no. 39; Paris 1946,
no. 66bis; Paris 1951, no. 184; Rotterdam 1954,
no. 60, pl. 35; Saint-Etienne 1954, no. 5;
London 1954, no. 188; Bourg-en-Bresse 1955,
no. vi.
Selected References: Roland Michel 1960,
fig. 1; M. Faré 1962, 2: fig. 418; Roland Michel
1965, 189; Roland Michel 1970, no. 143, illus.
147; M. and F. Faré 1976, 2: fig. 351; Laskin and
Pantazzi 1987, 285–286, illus. 285.
Related Works: There is a Gobelins Savonnerie
tapestry dated 1779 that is very close to this

composition (Roland Michel 1970, no. 426),
sold at auction (Tajan, Paris, George V, 3 April
1996, lot 216). There is also another undated
version of this painting (Roland Michel 1970,
no. 168; cat. 113).
W, D
Pl. 49

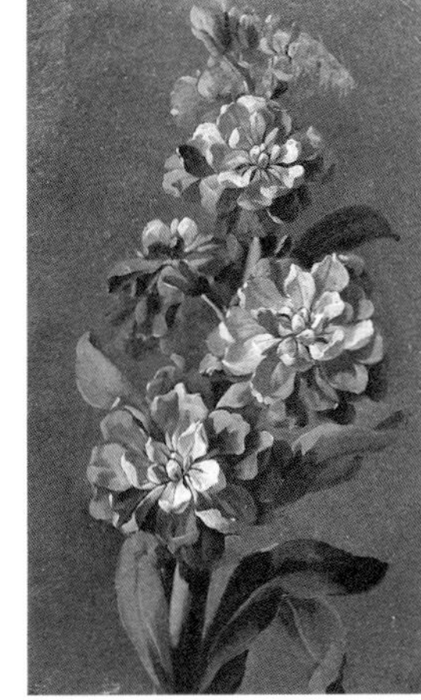

131. *Study of a Bouquet of Gillyflowers*, n.d.

Oil on paper affixed to cardboard, 8⅞ × 5¼ in.
(22.6 × 13.2 cm)
Private collection
Provenance: Coster sale 1824, no. 12, together
with a *Study of Hyacinths*, both framed.
Selected Reference: Roland Michel 1970,
no. 103.
W, D, NY
Pl. 51

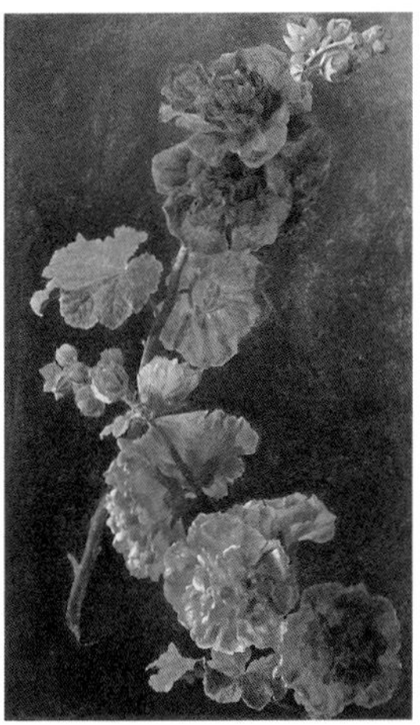

132. *Study of Red Hollyhocks*, n.d.

Oil on paper mounted on board, 25⅝ × 17⅛ in.
(65.1 × 43.5 cm)
Private collection
Provenance: probably Coster sale 1824, lot 37;
comte de Lastic, in 1970.
Selected Reference: Roland Michel 1970,
no. 118.
Commentary: See cat. 133.
W, D, NY
Pl. 53

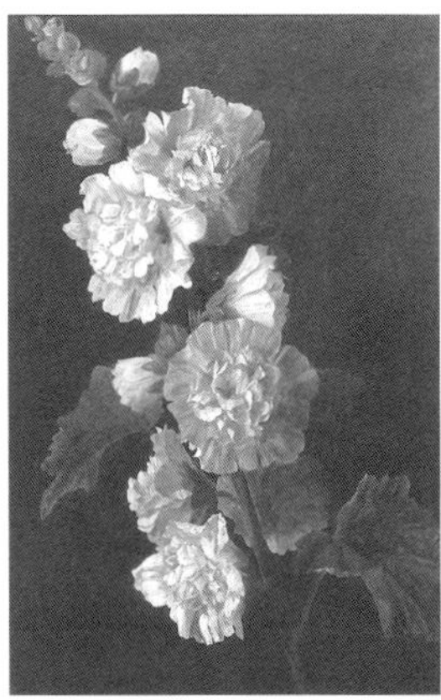

133. *Study of White Hollyhocks*, n.d.

Oil on paper mounted on board, 25⅝ × 17⅛ in.
(65.1 × 43.5 cm)
Private collection
Provenance: probably Coster sale 1824, lot 37;
comte de Lastic, in 1970.
Selected Reference: Roland Michel 1970,
no. 117.
Commentary: This study has always been with
its "pendant," cat. 132; the two together help
explain how the artist worked.
W, D, NY
Pl. 52

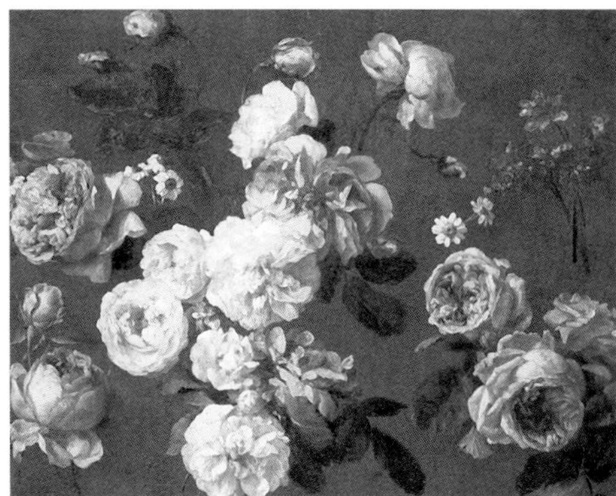

134. *Study of Roses*, n.d.

Oil on paper mounted on card, 14 × 17¼ in.
(35.6 × 43.8 cm)
Private collection
Provenance: Eliot Hodgkin collection.
Exhibited: London 1990, no. 98.

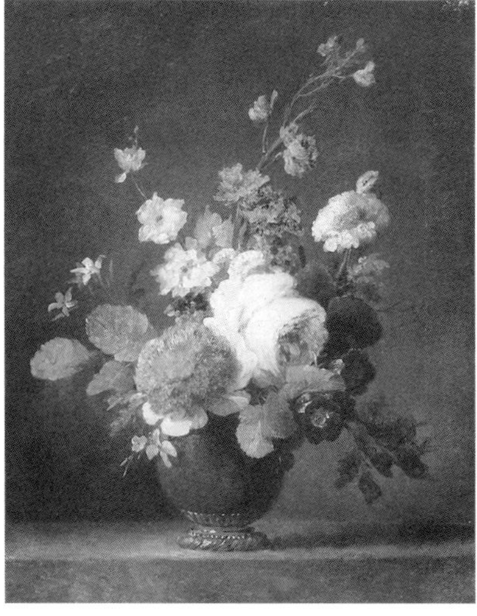

135. *Vase of Flowers*, n.d.

Oil on canvas, 15¾ × 12¼ in. (40 × 31 cm)
Signed lower right: *V. C.*
Musée des Beaux-Arts, Nancy
Provenance: Beaulieu bequest, between 1827
and 1840.
Exhibited: Paris 1959b, no. 18.
Selected References: Guédy 1889, 353; Thieme
and Becker 34:76; M. Faré 1962, 2: fig. 409;
Vergnet-Ruiz and Laclotte 1962, 254; Roland
Michel 1970, 84–85, no. 30, illus. 22; M. and
F. Faré 1976, 232, fig. 363; Rosenblum 1979,
1:295; Bouleau 1993, no. 92, 88–89; Gelly-
Saldias 1997, 17–18; Bouleau 1999, 138–139.
D, NY
Pl. 50

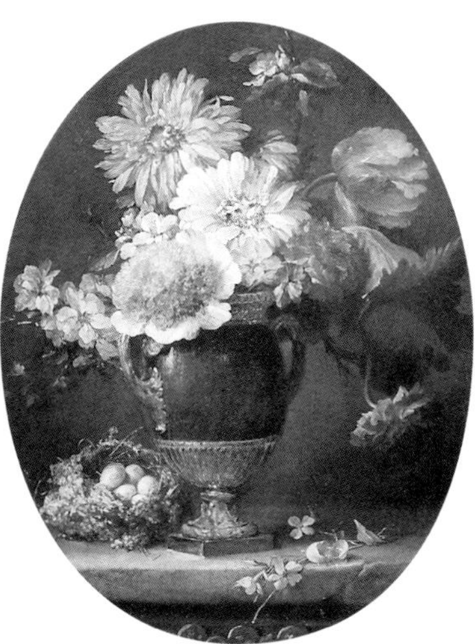

136. *Vase of Flowers and Bird's Nest*, n.d.

Oil on canvas, oval, 18¼ × 14⅝ in. (46.5 ×
37 cm)
Private collection
Provenance: Guillaumont collection, sale,
15 January 1808, lot 21; probably Cournerie
collection, sale, 8–9 December 1891, lot 21;
vicomtesse L. de Courval collection; comtesse
de Ganay, in 1970.
Selected Reference: Roland Michel 1970,
no. 69 and/or no. 70, illus. 112.

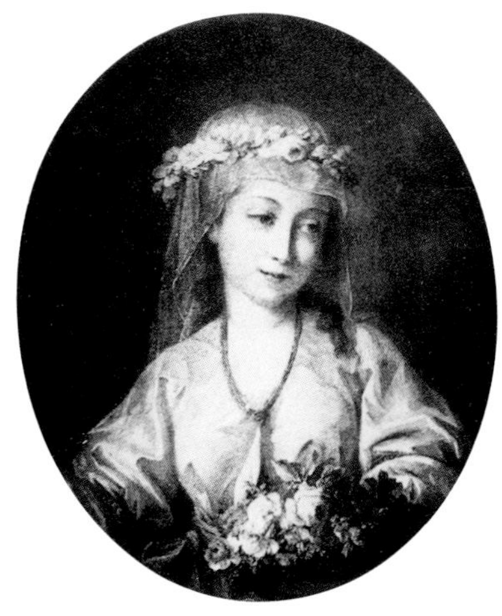

137. *A Vestal*, n.d.

Oil on wood, 6⅛ × 5⅛ in. (15.5 × 13 cm)
Present whereabouts unknown
Provenance: Octave Homberg collection;
sale, Paris, 3–5 June 1931, lot 37, illus.; sale,
Couturier Nicolay, Paris, 7 December 1990,
lot 143.
Selected Reference: Roland Michel 1970,
no. 321.
Related Works: See cats. 53, 56.

Works in Other Media

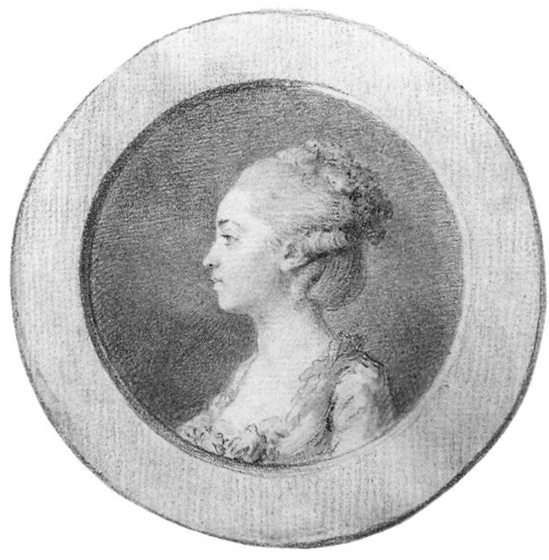

138. *Portrait of the Artist's Sister*, 1774

Black chalk on paper, diam. 4½ in. (11.2 cm)
Musée municipal de Châlons-en-Champagne
Provenance: M. Bertrand bequest,
Courlandon, Marne, 1885.
Selected Reference: Châlons-sur-Marne 1891,
no. 653bis.
D
Pl. 61

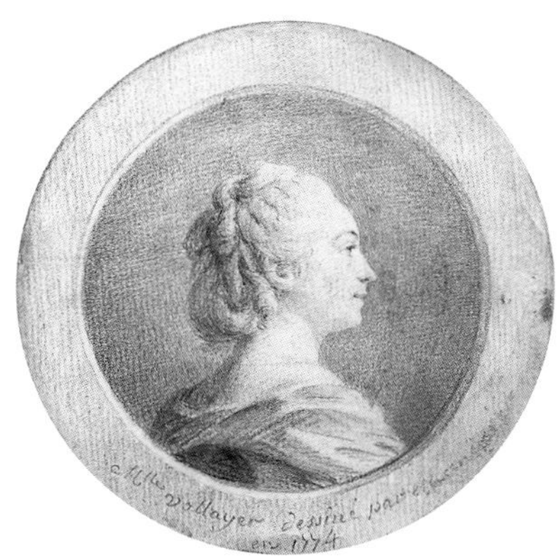

139. *Self-Portrait*, 1774

Black chalk on paper, diam. 4⅜ in. (11.3 cm)
Signed and dated on the mount: *Mlle Vallayer dessiné par elle/en 1774*
Musée municipal de Châlons-en-Champagne
Provenance: M. Bertrand bequest, Courlandon, Marne, 1885.
Selected Reference: Châlons-sur-Marne 1891, no. 653bis; M. and F. Faré 1976, fig. 335.
D
Pl. 60

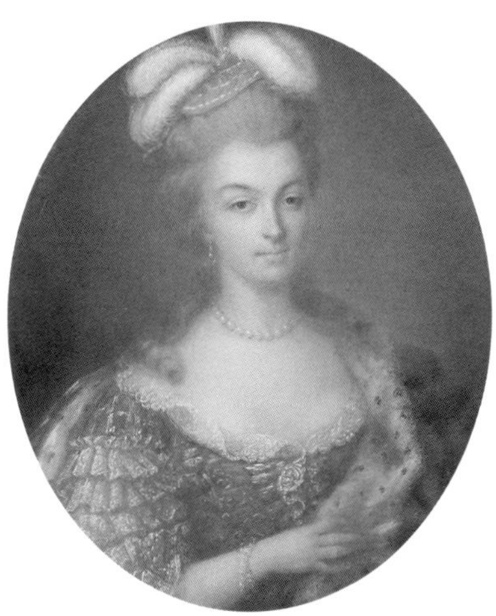

140. *Portrait of Queen Marie-Antoinette*, 1780

Pastel on paper, 28¾ × 24⅜ in. (73 × 62 cm)
Signed and dated center left: *Vallayer/1780*
Florence Bouchy-Picon
Selected References: Engerand 1901, 470; Roland Michel 1970, no. 329 (as lost since 1780).
Commentary: A letter from Anne Vallayer to the comte d'Angivillier, dated 17 July 1780 (AN, O¹ 1912) states: "Je n'ai pas encore remis la lettre que vous avez eu la bonté de me donner pour la princesse de Chimay, parce qu'elle n'étoit pas à Versailles lorsque j'y ai été pour travailler au portrait de la Reine et que l'on m'a conseillé d'attendre que son portrait soit entièrement terminé pour réclamer ses bontés; j'espère que dans les premiers jours de la semaine prochaine je pourrai en faire usage" (I have not yet delivered the letter that you had the goodness to give me for the princesse de Chimay because she was not at Versailles when I was there to work on the portrait of the queen, and they advised me to wait until her portrait

would be entirely finished to beseech her indulgence; I hope that in the early part of next week I will be able to make use of it). Concerning this portrait, see Roland Michel in this volume, 19.
D
Pl. 63

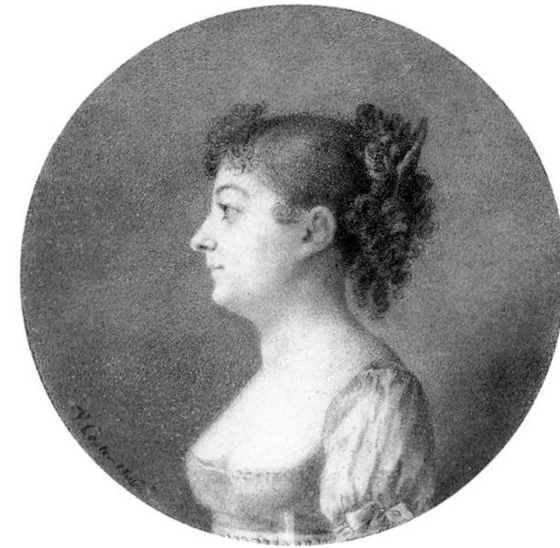

141. *Medallion Bust Portrait of a Woman in Profile*, 1806

Black chalk on paper, diam. 4 in. (10.2 cm)
Signed and dated lower left, in ink: *V. Coster 1806*
Inscribed on verso: *Esprit, grâce, vertu; Tout se plaît à l[orner] / Et cependant, Elle est modeste autant qu[e belle] / La plume, ou le pinceau ne peut que se b[orner] / A nous donner l'Esquisse du Modèle*
Private collection
Provenance: Christie's, London, 6 December 1988, lot 160; Galerie Cailleux, Paris.
Exhibited: Paris 1991, no. 76, illus.
D
Pl. 62

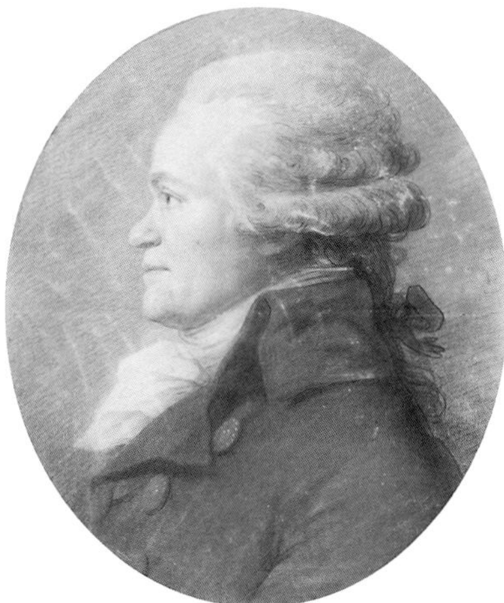

142. *Portrait of Jean-Pierre-Silvestre Coster, Parliamentary Lawyer*, n.d.

Pastel and colored pencil on paper affixed to cardboard, 18⅛ × 15 in. (46 × 38 cm)
Inscribed on verso: *Jean-Pierre Silvestre Coster, avocat au Parlement, secrétaire intime du Prince de Beauvau; Receveur général des Fermes à Paris; chevalier de l'ordre royal de la Legion d'Honneur. Né à Nancy, le 30 décembre 1745; marié le 25 avril 1782 à Anne Vallayer; ces époux furent honorés*

de la confiance et des faveurs de la Reine Marie-Antoinette. Mort à Paris le 28 avril 1824 (Jean-Pierre Silvestre Coster, lawyer in the Parlement, personal secretary to the prince de Beauveau; *receveur général des fermes* in Paris; knight of the royal order of the Legion of Honor. Born in Nancy, 30 December 1745; married on 25 April 1782, to Anne Vallayer; this couple was honored by the trust and favor of Queen Marie-Antoinette. Died in Paris on 28 April 1824).
Musée Carnavalet, Paris, inv. no. 6196
Provenance: Marcel Guérin; bequeathed to museum, 1940.
Selected Reference: Musée Carnavalet 1982, 33.
Commentary: This portrait has a pendant (illustrated below), now in the collection of the château de Versailles. The pendants are of the same format and medium and are nearly identical in dimensions. They both come from the collection of Marcel Guérin. In 1970 Roland Michel identified the Versailles drawing as a self-portrait (see Roland Michel 1970, no. 411). However, Xavier Salmon (Rouen 2001, no. 76) has recently correctly questioned the identity of the sitter, and even its attribution to Vallayer-Coster, this last wrongly, in our opinion. Considering the hairstyle of the woman and the probable age of Coster, the two pastels should be dated c. 1790–1792. In this case, the woman—certainly a member of the family—might be one of Vallayer-Coster's nieces born c. 1772.
Pl. 64

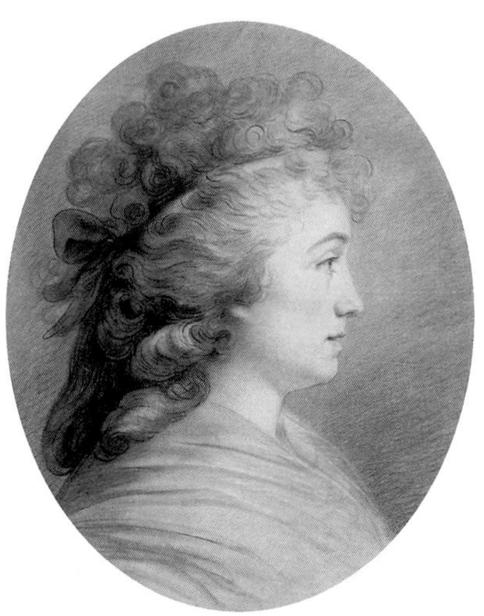

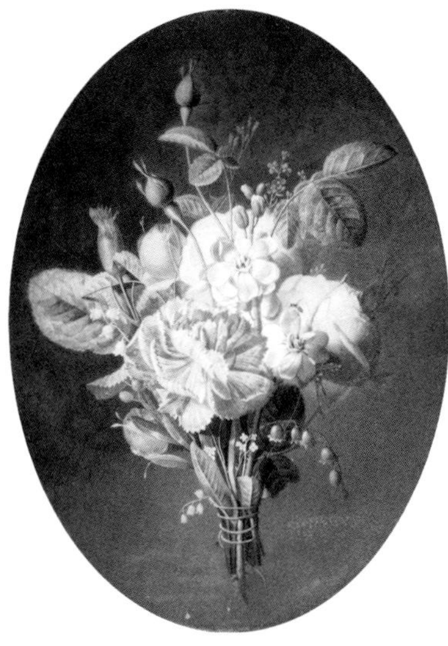

143. *Bouquet of Flowers*, 1780

Gouache on paper, oval, 15¾ × 11½ in. (40 × 29 cm)
Inscribed on verso: *Peint par Mme Vallayer-Coster en 1780*
Musée des Beaux-Arts de Narbonne
Provenance: the work was given in the nineteenth century to the museum by Mathieu Barathier (1764–1867), painter, lithographer, and collector, former student of David.
Selected References: Berthommieu 1923, no. 815; Schlumberger 1958, 69; Roland Michel 1970, no. 390, illus. 239.

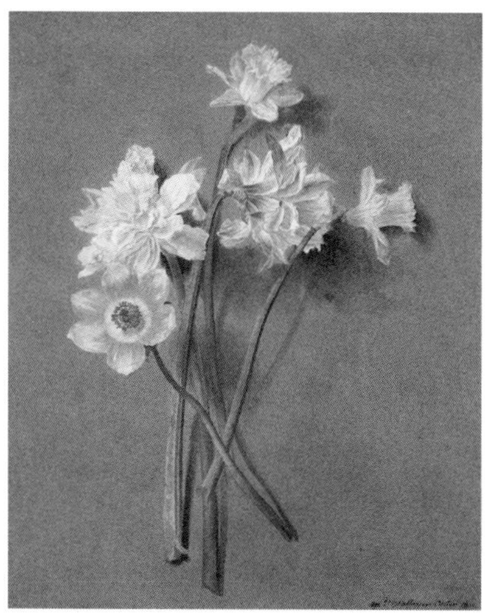

144. *Study of a Bouquet of Flowers with Daffodils*, 1802

Gouache on paper, 12⅛ × 9⅝ in. (30.8 × 24.5 cm)
Signed and dated lower left: *M. ᵈᵉ Vallayer-Coster 1802*
Michael L. Rosenberg, Dallas
Provenance: sale, Sotheby's, New York, 27 January 1999, lot 176.
D
Pl. 54

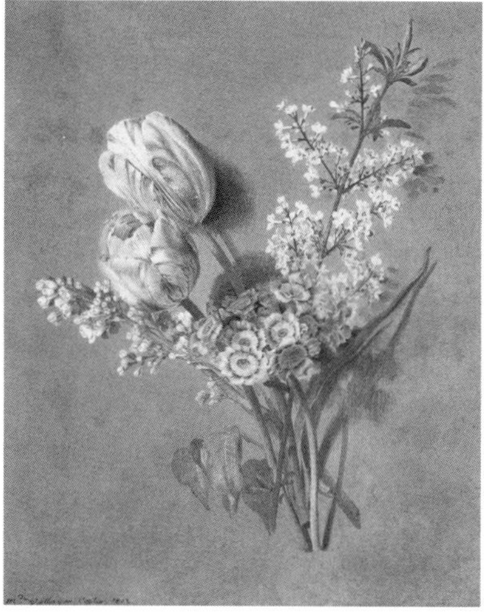

145. *Study of a Bouquet of Flowers with Tulips*, 1802

Gouache on paper, 12⅛ × 9⅝ in. (30.8 × 24.5 cm)
Signed and dated lower right: *M. ᵈᵉ Vallayer-Coster 1802*
Michael L. Rosenberg, Dallas
Provenance: sale, Sotheby's, New York, 27 January 1999, lot 177.
D
Pl. 55

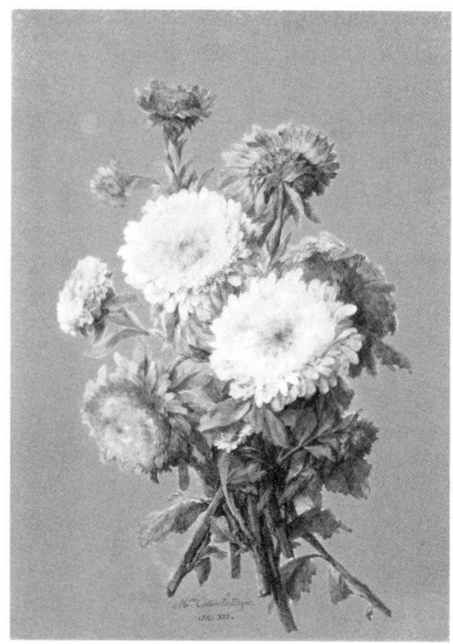

146. *Bouquet of Dahlias*, 1804

Watercolor on paper, 13¾ × 10 in. (34.9 × 25.4 cm)
Signed and dated lower center: *Mᵐᵉ Coster-Vallayer/an XII*; on the stretcher: *8 à droite en entrant. No. 242*
Napoleonmuseum Arenenberg, Salenstein, Switzerland
Provenance: Her Majesty Empress Josephine collection, until 1814; Queen Hortense and Empress Eugénie; Napoleonmuseum, since 1906.
Exhibited: Salon of the Year XII (1804), no. 482.
Selected References: Roland Michel 1970, no. 393 (with an incorrect provenance); Denon 1999, 1:195 (letter 1450, 27 fructidor XII [14 September 1804]).
D
Pl. 56

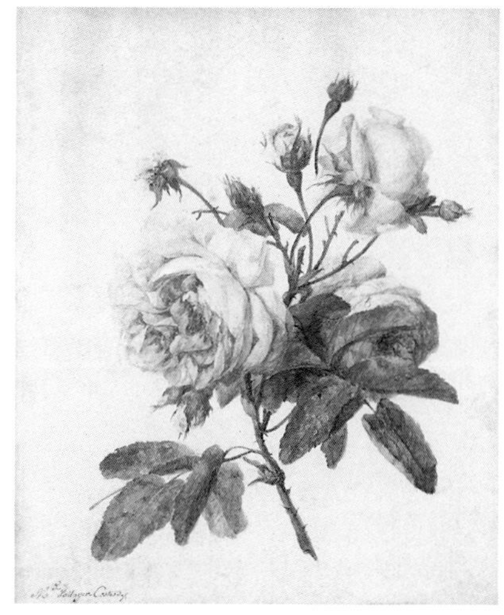

147. *Roses*, n.d.

Watercolor on laid paper mounted on a small lightweight panel, 10⅞ × 8⅞ in. (27.6 × 22.5 cm)
Signed at lower left: *M. ᵈᵉ Vallayer-Coster*
Musée des Beaux-Arts, Nancy
Provenance: possibly Coster sale 1824, lot 43 (with its pendant); possibly Cournerie collection, sale, Paris, 8–9 December 1891, lot 150; Duplessis bequest to the Musée des Beaux-Arts, Nancy, in 1898.
Selected References: *Bulletin des sociétés artistiques* 1899, 45.
Commentary: Pendant of cat. 148. It should be noted that Vallayer-Coster often paired roses with dahlias (or autumn daisies). Such is the case with the two watercolors of 1804, which belonged to Josephine (see cat. 146) and of the framed studies sold at the Coster sale in 1824, lot 7.
Pl. 58

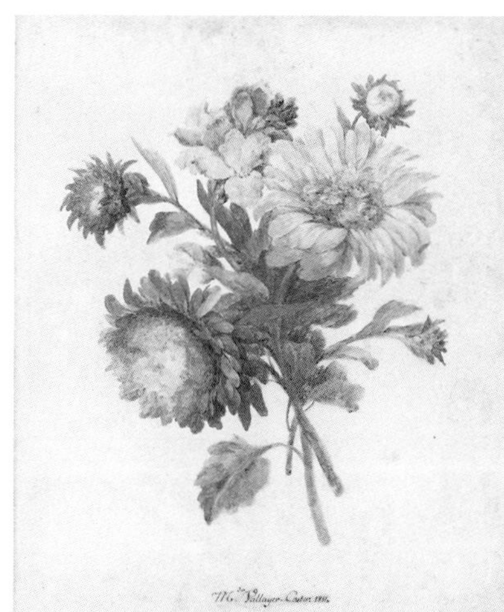

148. *Autumn Daisies*, 1811

Watercolor on cream-colored paper mounted on a small lightweight panel, 10⅝ × 8⅝ in. (27 × 22 cm)
Signed and dated lower center: *M. ᵈᵉ Vallayer-Coster. 1811.*
Musée des Beaux-Arts, Nancy
Provenance: same as cat. 147.
Selected References: *Bulletin des Sociétés . . .* 1899, 45; Roland Michel 1970, no. 393.
Commentary: Pendant of cat. 147.
Pl. 59

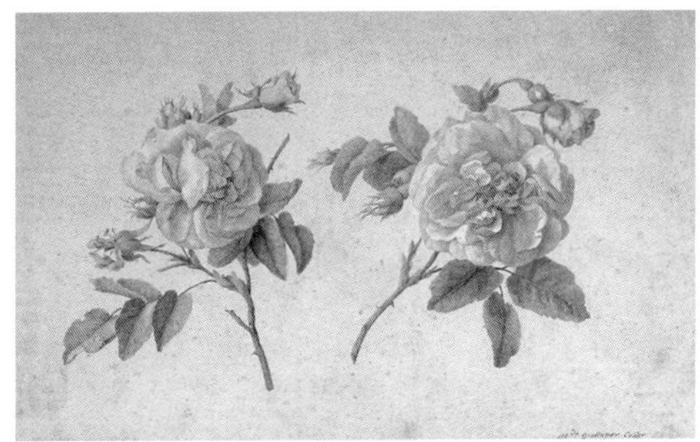

149. *Study of Two Roses,* c. 1810

Brush and gray wash on heavy cream laid paper,
9 × 14 in. (22.8 × 35.6 cm)
Signed lower right in pen and black ink:
M^{de} Vallayer Coster
Cooper-Hewitt, National Design Museum,
Smithsonian Institution, Purchased for the
Museum by the Advisory Council, 1925.1.349
Provenance: Coster sale 1824, lot 38 or 41.
Exhibited: New York 1999.
Selected References: Roland Michel 1970,
no. 397; Roland Michel 1987, 163, pl. 191.
Commentary: Engraved in the same direction
by Louis-Jean Allais (see cat. 157).
D
Pl. 57

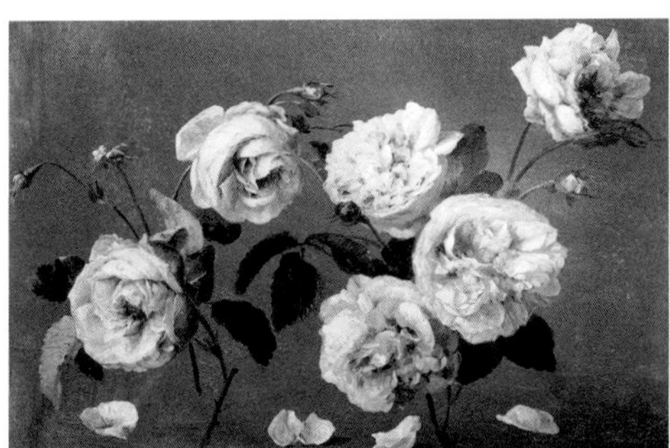

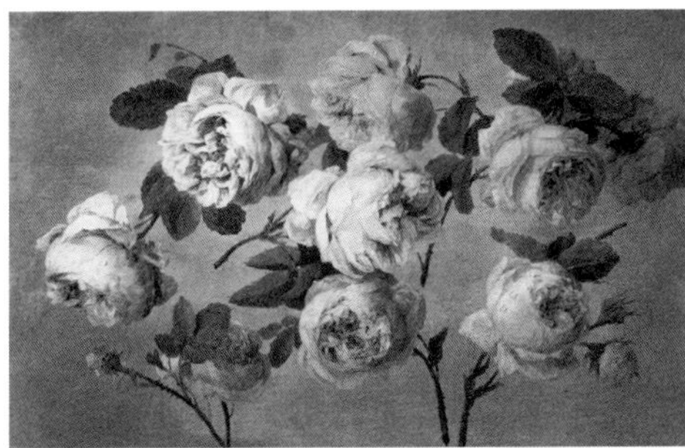

150. *Two Studies for Roses,* n.d.

Oil on paper affixed to canvas, 11³⁄₈ × 17³⁄₈ in.
(29 × 44 cm)
Provenance: Coster sale 1824, lots 16 and 17;
art market, Paris, in 1966.
Selected References: Roland Michel 1970,
nos. 106 and 107, 136–137, illus.

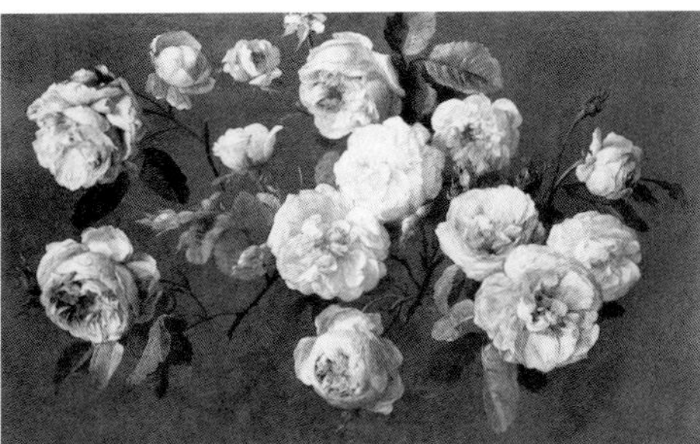

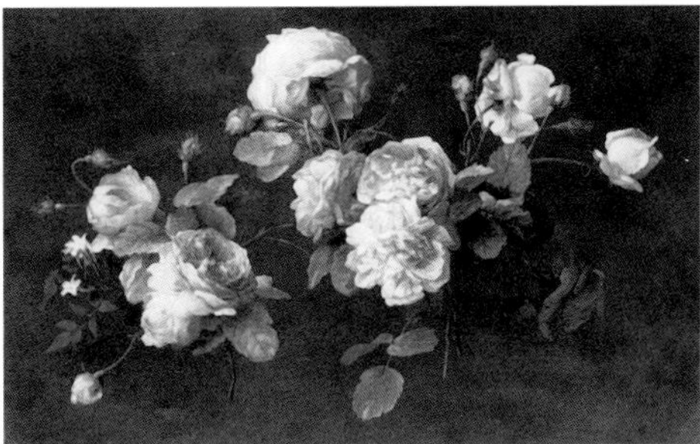

151. *Two Studies for Roses on a Brown Background,*
n.d.

Oil on paper affixed to canvas, 16⁷⁄₈ × 20¹⁄₂ in.
(43 × 52 cm)
Present whereabouts unknown
Provenance: Coster sale, 22 June 1824, lot 20;
art market, Paris, in 1966; art market, London,
in 1967; private collection, New York.
Selected Reference: Roland Michel 1970,
no. 108 and 109.

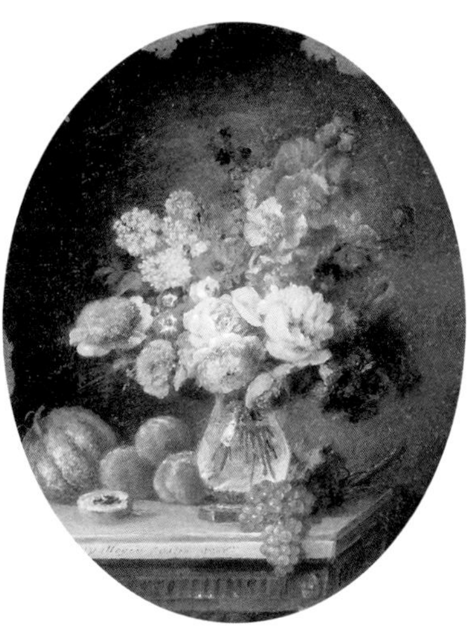

152. *Bouquet of Flowers and Fruit,* 1808

Oil under glass, 5³⁄₄ × 4⁵⁄₈ in. (14.5 × 11.8 cm)
Signed lower left: *A. Vallayer-Coster.*
Musée des Arts décoratifs, Paris, inv. no. 21846A
Provenance: Coster sale 1824, lot 19; Président
de Viefville collection, bequeathed to the
Musée des Arts décoratifs, 14 May 1920.
Exhibited: Paris 1926, no. 30.
Selected Reference: Roland Michel 1970,
no. 377.
Commentary: Pendant of cat. 153.
D, NY
Pl. 65

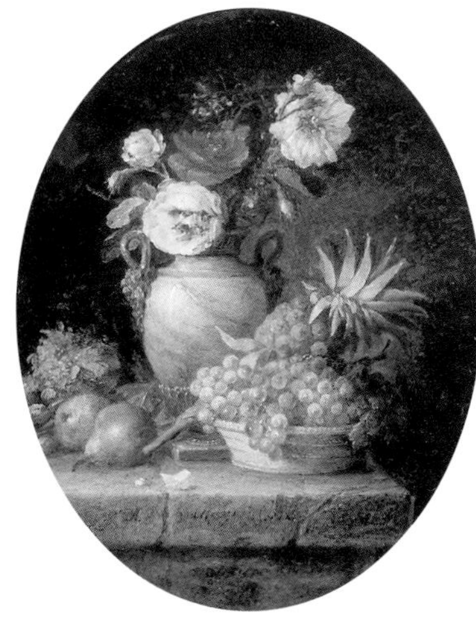

153. *Bouquet of Flowers and Fruit,* 1808

Oil under glass, 5³⁄₄ × 4⁵⁄₈ in. (14.5 × 11.8 cm)
Signed and dated on edge of table: *Vallayer-
Coster, 1808*
Musée des Arts décoratifs, Paris, inv. no. 21846B
Provenance: same as cat. 152.
Exhibited: Paris 1926, no. 31.
Selected Reference: Roland Michel 1970,
no. 376, illus. 110.
Commentary: Pendant of cat. 152.
D, NY
Pl. 66

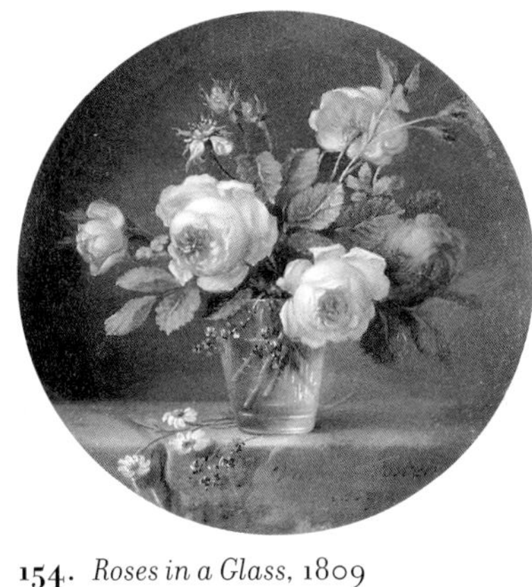

154. *Roses in a Glass,* 1809

Bodycolor on cardboard, diam. 3¹⁄₂ in. (8.9 cm)
Signed and dated lower right: *Va[llayer]
[C]oster/1809*
Private collection
Related Work: This miniature repeats the motif
of a painting from 1772 (cat. 18).
Commentary: Used to cover a tortoiseshell box
W, D, NY
Pl. 67

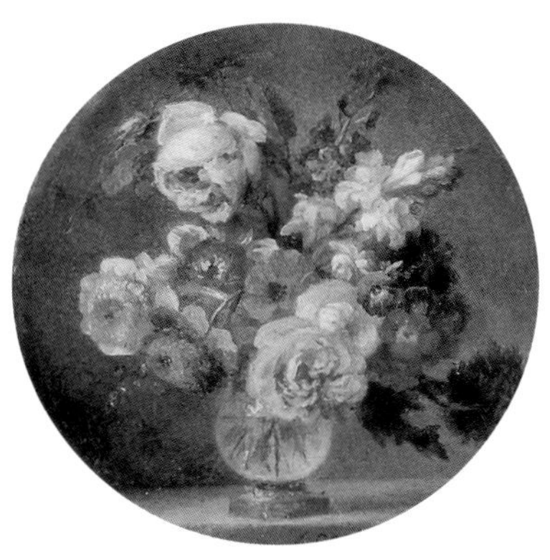

155. *Flowers in a Crystal Vase*, n.d.

Oil under glass, diam. 3⅛ in. (8 cm)
Signed lower right: *V. Coster.*
Anne Lévy-Freitag and Pierre Lévy-Freitag
Provenance: Etienne Lévy collection.
Selected Reference: Roland Michel 1970,
no. 379.
Commentary: The vase also appears in cat. 76,
dated 1786.
W, D, NY
Pl. 68

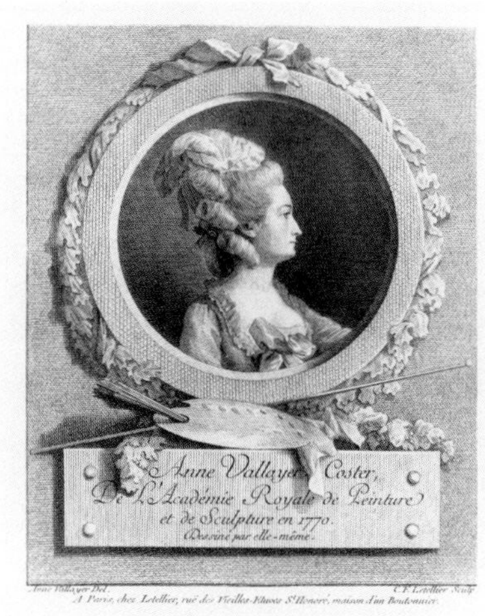

156. Charles-François Letellier (1743–1800),
after Anne Vallayer-Coster

The Artist's Self-Portrait, 1781
Engraving, 9¼ × 7⅜ in. (23.4 × 18.6 cm)
Inscribed in cartouche: *Anne Vallayer Coster,/
De L'Académie Royale de Peinture/et de Sculpture
en 1770/Dessiné par elle-même*
Private collection
Selected References: *Journal de Paris*, no. 203
(July 1781); *Mercure de France*, August 1781;
Roland Michel 1970, no. 334, illus. 58.
Related Works: According to Roland Michel,
the drawing on which the engraving was prob-
ably based dates to about 1777–1778, as indi-
cated by the hairstyle.
D
Pl. 86

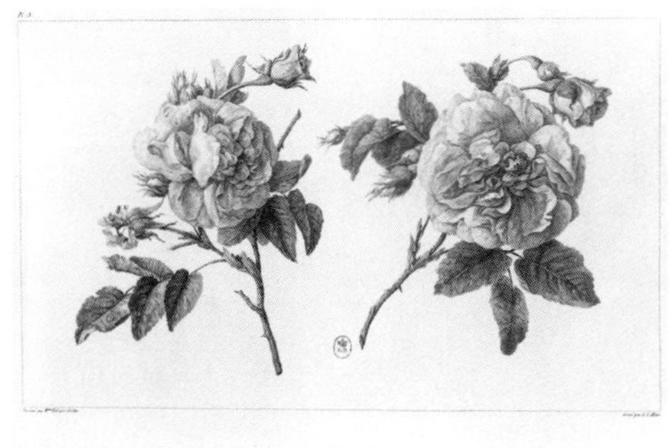

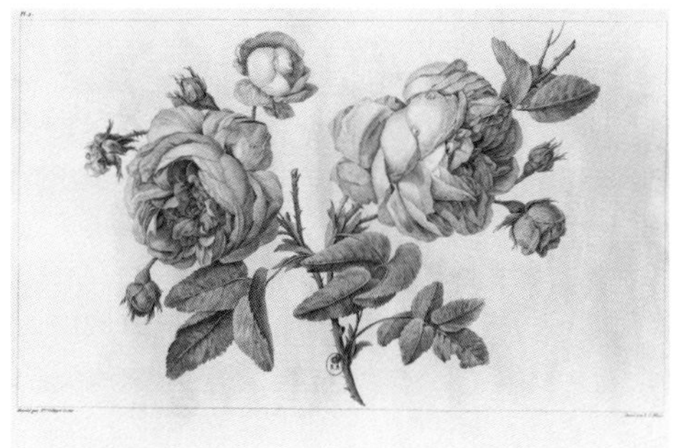

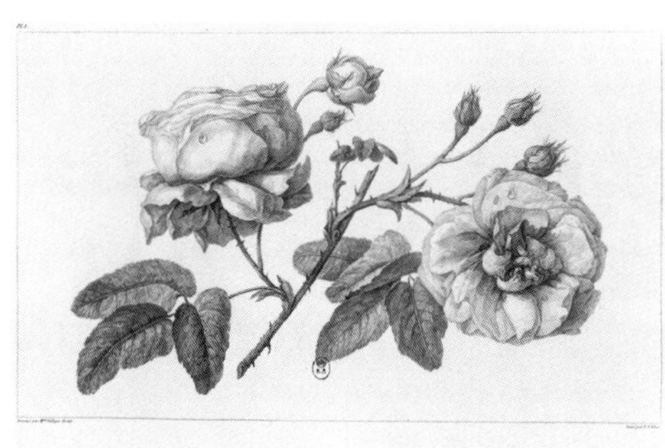

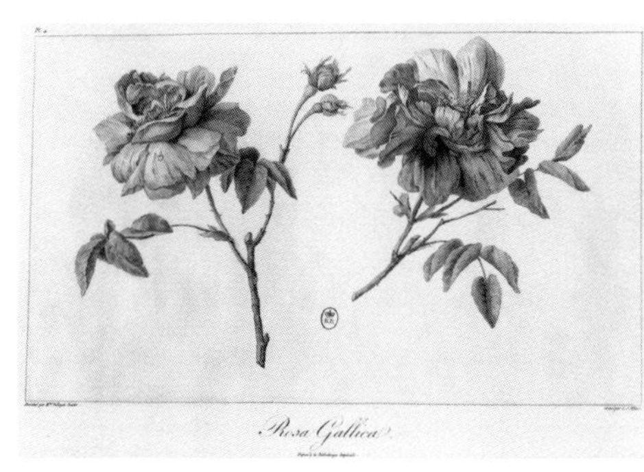

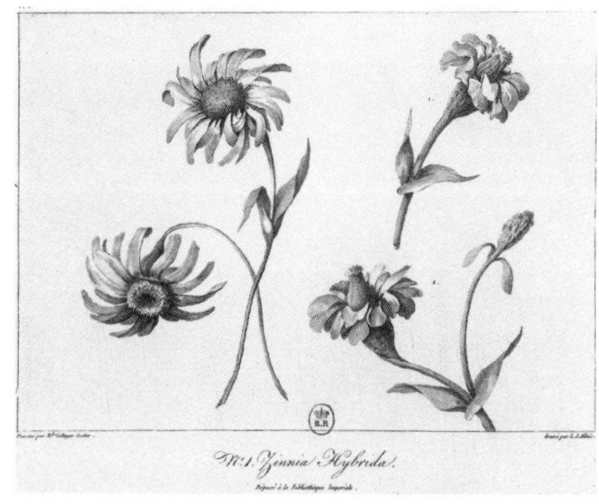

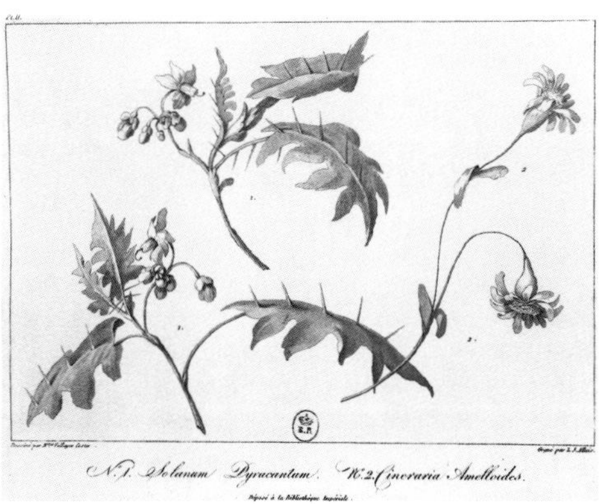

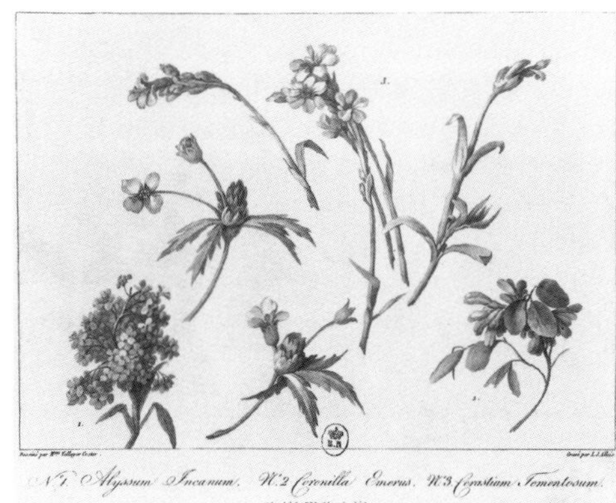

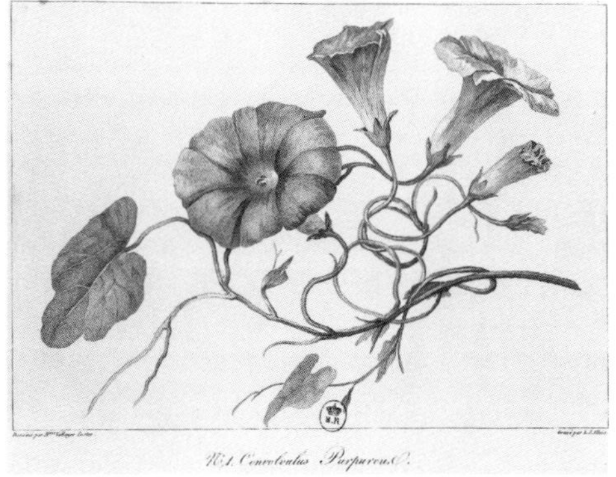

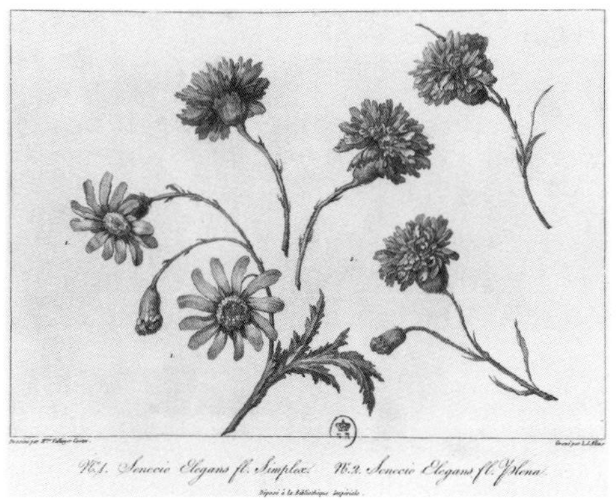

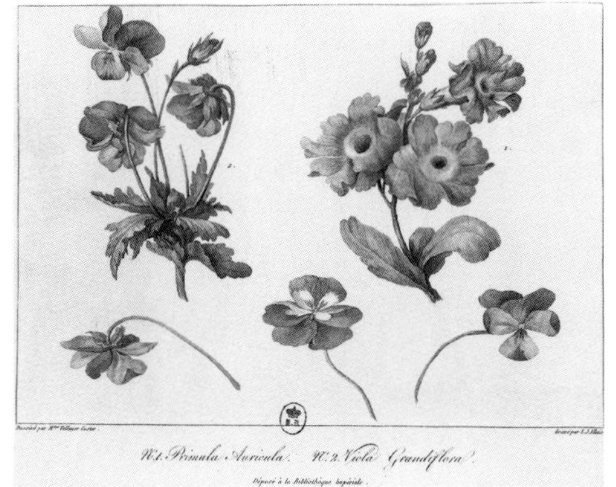

157. Louis-Jean Allais (1762–1833)

Ten Engravings of Flower Studies after Vallayer-Coster, c. 1810

Bibliothèque nationale de France, département des Estampes, Ef 140 f°

All signed: *Dessiné par Mme Vallayer Coster—gravé par L. J. Allais*

Four plates, two to a page, numbered 1–4, are studies of roses; the fourth is entitled *Rosa Gallica*. The next six, on the same page, are numbered I–VI and bear titles. They are all engraved after wash drawings, of which only one is known (cat. 149).

Plate I: 1/Zinnia Hybrida

Plate II: 1/Solanum Pyracantum 2/Cineraria Amelloides

Plate III: 1/Alyssum Incanum 2/Coronilla Emerus 3/Cerastium Fomentosum

Plate IV: 1/Convolvulus Purpureus

Plate V: 1/Senecio Elegans fl. Simplex 2/Senecio Elegans fl. Yslena

Plate VI: 1/Primula Auricula 2/Viola Grandiflora

Provenance: These ten engravings were deposited in the Bibliothèque impériale on 12 January 1811. At the Coster sale in 1824, six copperplates were listed under lot 64 and four under lot 65. The original drawings were sold together with the plates, as well as the very few prints that had been pulled.

Selected References: *Inventaire du Fonds français après 1800*, vol. 1, Allais; Roland Michel 1966, pl. VI, fig. 4; Roland Michel 1970, nos. 416–425, illus. 244, 251.

Untitled (Roses): Pl. 71

Untitled (Roses): D, Pls. 72, 73

Rosa Gallica: D, Pl. 74

Plate I: D, Pl. 75

Plate II: D, Pl. 76

Plate III: Pl. 77

Plate IV: Pl. 78

Plate V: Pl. 79

Plate VI: D, Pl. 80

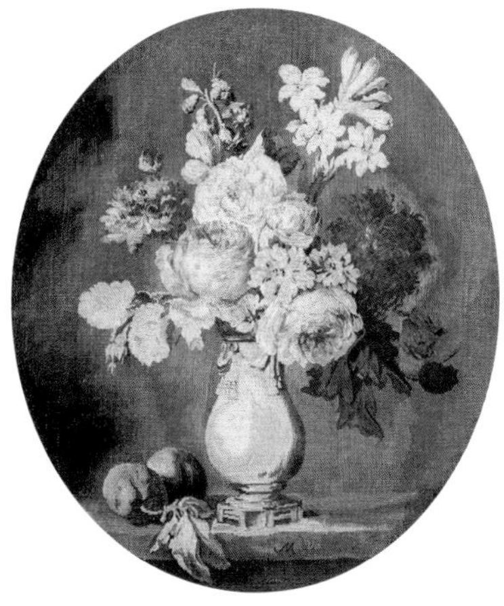

158. After Anne Vallayer-Coster; woven by Deyrolle, at the Gobelins Manufactory

Flowers in a Vase and Two Plums, 1781

Wool and silk tapestry, 17⅞ × 14⅝ in. (45 × 37 cm)

Signed and dated: *M. Vallayer-Coster 1781*

The Metropolitan Museum of Art, Bequest of Julie Heidelbach, 1932 (35.116.7)

Exhibited: Paris 1926, no. 99; Paris 1930.

Selected References: Fenaille 1903–1923, 5:351; Phillips 1936, 29 (signature and date noted); Roland Michel 1970, no. 430; Standen 1985, 1:417.

Related Works: The present work is based on a painting dated 1781 by Vallayer-Coster, now in a private collection (see cat. 67). At least one other version, also dated 1781, was in a private collection (Roland Michel 1970, no. 429). A third version, in the Musée Nissim de Camondo, Paris, was probably woven at the Gobelins Manufactory between 1800 and 1804 (Roland Michel 1970, no. 431). It had a pendant, also woven at the Gobelins, also based on a lost painting exhibited at the Salon of 1781. See cat. 159.

D

Pl. 69

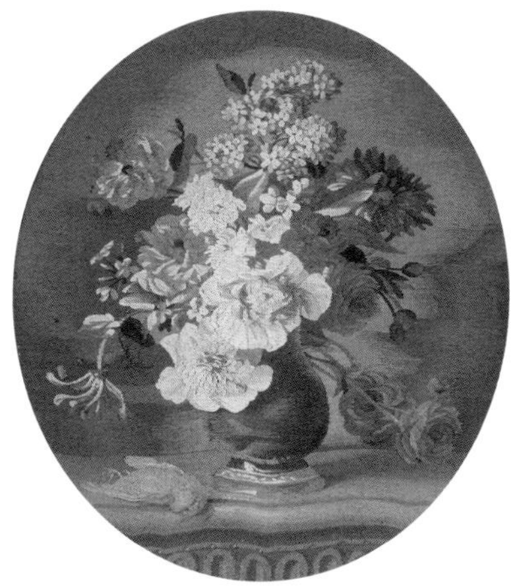

159. After Anne Vallayer-Coster; woven probably by Deyrolle, at the Gobelins Manufactory

Flowers in a Blue Vase with Dead Canary, n.d.

Wool and silk tapestry, oval, 19⅝ × 16¾ in. (50 × 42.5 cm)

Private collection

Provenance: vicomtesse de Courval collection.

Selected Reference: Roland Michel 1970, no 432.

Related Works: This tapestry was woven, probably c. 1781, as a pendant to *Flowers in a Vase and Two Plums* (cat. 158). It might be based on a lost painting exhibited in 1781 (see cat. 158). A rectangular version was woven at the Gobelins at the beginning of the nineteenth century (Musée Nissim de Camondo, Paris; Roland Michel 1970, no. 433).

D

Pl. 70

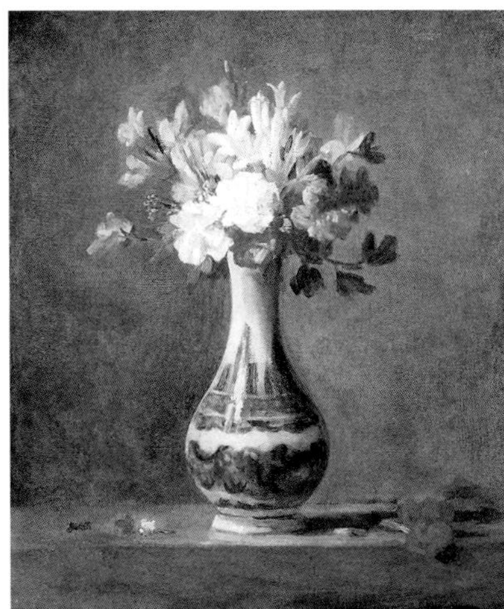

A. Jean-Siméon Chardin (1699–1779)

Flowers in a White and Blue Porcelain Vase, n.d.
Oil on canvas, 17³⁄₈ × 14¹⁄₈ in. (44 × 36 cm)
National Gallery of Scotland, Edinburgh
Provenance: Aved collection, sale, 24 November 1766, lot 136; Marcille collection, in the nineteenth century.
Exhibited: Paris 1979, no. 100, illus. 302; Paris 1999, no. 72, illus. 273.
Selected References: Rosenberg 1983, 23, fig. 7; Conisbee 1986, 184, 188, pl. 179; Démoris 1991, 144; Roland Michel 1994, 138, 171, 173, 187, pl. on 166; Rosenberg and Temperini 1999, no. 140; Rochebrune in Paris 1999, 40, 41, fig. 4.
W, D
Pl. 81

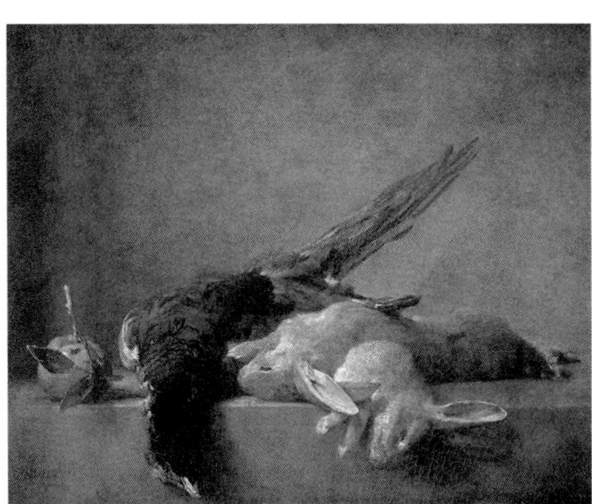

B. Jean-Siméon Chardin (1699–1779)

Still Life with Game (Two Rabbits, a Pheasant, and a Seville Orange on a Stone Ledge), c. 1760/1765
Oil on canvas, 19¹⁄₂ × 23³⁄₈ in. (49.6 × 59.4 cm)
Signed lower left: *Chardin*
National Gallery of Art, Washington, Samuel H. Kress Collection, 1952.5.36
Provenance: Wildenstein and Co., Paris; sold by 1926 to David David-Weill, Neuilly-sur-Seine, on consignment by 1937 with Wildenstein & Co., New York; sold 1946 to the Samuel H. Kress Foundation, New York.

Exhibited: New York 1937, no. 5; New York 1939, no. 18, as *The Pheasant*; Washington 1965; Paris 1979, no. 99; Paris 1999, no. 99, 27 colorpl.
Selected References: Eisler 1977, 314–315, fig. 277; Rosenberg 1983, no. 138, illus.; Walker 1984, 323, no. 428, illus.; National Gallery of Art 1985, 86, illus.; Conisbee 1986, 189, pl. 185, detail pl. 184; Held and Schneider 1993, 37 illus.; Roland Michel 1996, 134–137, 143, no. 18, 187 n. 19, 136 illus.; Rosenberg and Temperini 1999, no. 139.
W, D
Pl. 82

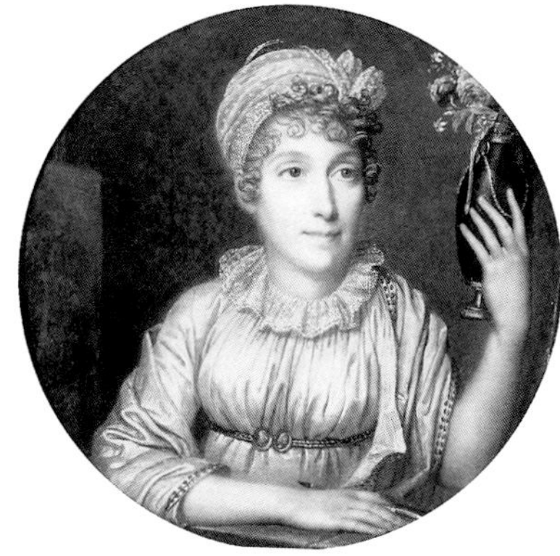

C. François Dumont (1751–1831)

Anne Vallayer-Coster, 1804
Gouache on ivory, diam. 3 in. (7.6 cm)
Signed and dated left: *Dumont/F. 1804*
The Cleveland Museum of Art; The Edward B. Green collection, 1943.639
Provenance: Edward B. Greene collection, Cleveland.
Selected Reference: *Greene Collection* 1951, no. 62, 34, pl. XXXVII.
W, D, NY
Pl. 85

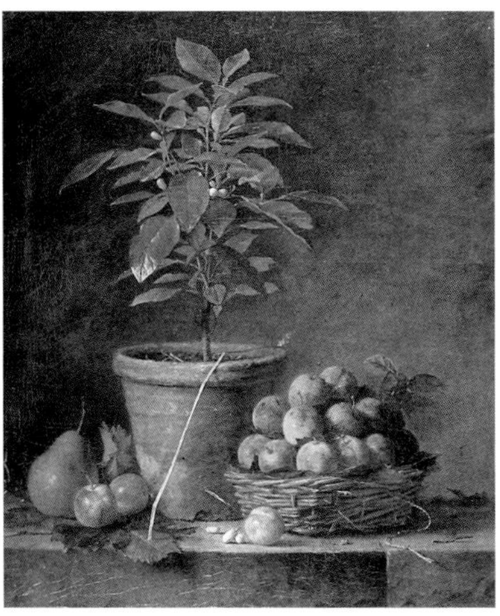

D. Henri-Horace Roland Delaporte (1724–1793)

The Orange Tree, c. 1765
Oil on canvas, 23⁵⁄₈ × 19¹⁄₂ in. (60 × 49.5 cm)
Staatliche Kunsthalle Karlsruhe, inv. no. 180
Provenance: Margravine Karoline Luise.
Exhibited: Salon of 1763, no. 147; Karlsruhe 1999, no. 154, illus.

Selected References: Kircher 1928, 95 (as Roland Delaporte); Ridder 1932, 69 (as Roland Delaporte); Kircher 1933, no. 75 (as Roland Delaporte); Wildenstein 1933, no. 788 (as Delaporte); Thieme and Becker 28:532 (as Delaporte); Pinder 1938, 25 (as Chardin); Seznec and Adhémar 1957–1967, 1:184, 185 (as Roland Delaporte); Lauts 1957, no. 70, illus. 75 (as Delaporte); M. Faré 1962, 1:166, 2: illus. 377; Lauts 1966, no. 32, illus.; Lüdke in Karlsruhe 1999, 321, 322.
Commentary: This work was shown in the Salon of 1763 and was later incorrectly cited as a work by Chardin in the 1784 inventory of the estate of the margravine Karoline Luise, until 1928, when Kircher, on the grounds of the correspondence and a receipt from Eberts, corrected the attribution.
W, D
Pl. 83

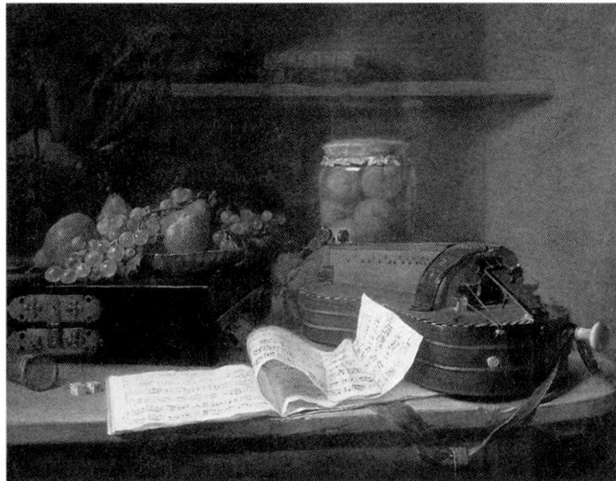

E. Henri-Horace Roland Delaporte (1724–1793)

Still Life with Jar of Apricots and Hurdy-Gurdy, c. 1760
Oil on canvas, 31¹⁄₂ × 39³⁄₄ in. (80.5 × 101 cm)
Musée des Beaux-Arts, Bordeaux
Provenance: Belay sale, Bordeaux, 14 May 1872, lot 6; Théodore Gardere collection, Bordeaux.
Exhibited: Bordeaux 1947, no. 93 (as Chardin); Geneva 1949 (as Chardin); Bristol 1950, no. 6 (as Chardin); Bordeaux 1952, no. 128 (as Chardin); Paris 1959a, no. 69 (as Delaporte); Tel Aviv 1964, no. 64; Bordeaux 1969, no. 38; Paris 1969, no. 37; Ghent 1970, no. 40; Nagoya 1971, no. 34; Brussels 1975, no. 94; Bordeaux 1978, no. 138; Moscow 1978, no. 88; Paris 1980, no. 204; Amiens 1983, no. 75; Tours 1986, no. 9; Lourdes 1991, no. 76; Karlsruhe 1999, no. 155.
Selected References: M. Faré 1962, 2: pl. 381 (as Delaporte); Vergnet-Ruiz and Laclotte 1962, 84, 250; Rosenberg 1968, 137 (as Delaporte?); M. and F. Faré 1976, illus. 187, pl. 279; Mirimonde 1975–1977, 2:17; Boysson 1980, no. 13, illus.; Walter 1980, 169, fig. 9; Rapetti 1987, 38.
W, D
Pl. 84

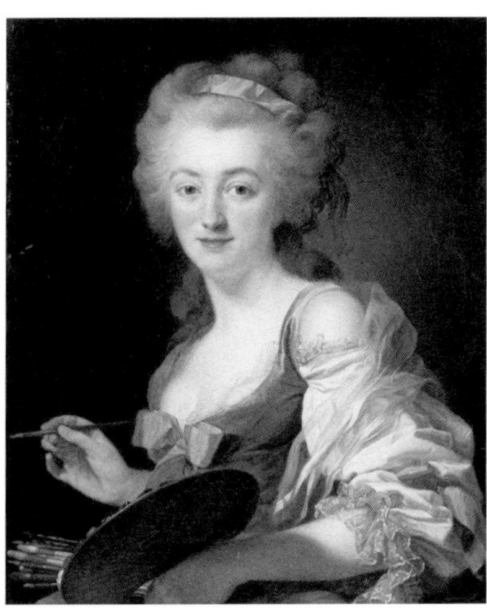

F. Alexandre Roslin (1718–1793)

Portrait of Anne Vallayer-Coster. c. 1783
Oil on canvas, 29⅛ × 23⅝ in. (74 × 60 cm)
Private collection
Provenance: Madame Jules Porgès collection;
Carl Trugger collection; Galerie Cailleux, Paris.
Exhibited: Salon of 1783, no. 39; Paris 1926,
no. 92, as a self-portrait; Versailles 1937,
no. 302.
Selected References: Roslin 1913; Lundberg
1938; Lundberg 1957, 1:125, 219, 237, 310, 2:164,
no. 552; Roland Michel 1970, 25.
W, D, NY
Pl. 87

Appendix: The Portraits of Mesdames de France, the Aunts of Louis XVI, by Anne Vallayer-Coster

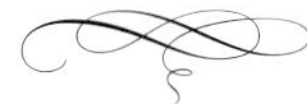

MANY ARTISTS MADE PORTRAITS of the daughters of Louis XV (known as Mesdames). During their father's lifetime, Mesdames were dependents, for fiscal purposes, of the Maison du roi (Household of the King), and their portraits were commissioned and paid for either by the Surintendance des Bâtiments (Department of Royal Works) or by the Menus-Plaisirs du roi (the agency responsible for royal entertainments, ephemeral decorations, and the like). The many portraits, copies as well as originals, executed at their request prompted some cutting remarks from the administrators at the Bâtiments. In the margins of an invoice submitted by Jean-Marc Nattier in 1752, for instance, one of them wrote: "These portraits not having been ordered from Sr Nattier by MM the Directors General, they cannot be invoiced until it has been determined whether this matter properly concerns the Bâtiments or whether these portraits are to be paid for out of the purse of the royal family."[1]

Louis XVI bestowed on his aunts a household of their own, but its surviving archives are full of gaps. Accounting records, notably as regards commissions for portraits and other works of art, are virtually nonexistent. One certain commission is that of the bust and full-length portraits by Anne Vallayer-Coster of Madame Sophie (pl. 26).[2] This extremely timid princess, who led a withdrawn existence in the very heart of the court, had been educated at the royal abbey of Fontevrault; she remained attached to the place and was interested in the education of young daughters of the nobility. She wanted to lend her support to the renovation of the priory of L'Argentière in the diocese of Lyon.[3] Under threat of closure since 1762, reduced to five nuns, the priory again became

viable thanks to the efforts of Marie-Madeleine de Gayardon de Fenoyl, named prioress on 21 May 1776.[4] In June 1777 Louis XVI raised the status of the priory to that of a chapter of noble canonesses. Young women were eligible for admission from age ten, became provisional canonesses at fourteen, and continued their education until they were twenty-five. Then, without being obliged to take religious orders, they could reside in a house close to the abbey. The chapter began with six canonesses in 1777; by 1790, when it was suppressed, there were eighty-three, including Lucile de Chateaubriand, sister of the future writer.

Madame de Fenoyl entrusted the reconstruction of the abbey to the Lyonnais architect Joseph-François Désarnod (act. from 1772), and the cornerstone was laid on 13 October 1777. An *Elevation perspective du chapitre noble de l'Argentière*, engraved at Désarnod's instigation, records the original appearance of the complex.[5] Dedicated to Monsieur, the king's brother (better known as the comte d'Artois), this engraving testifies to his financial support of the institution.[6] The lack of archival documents pertaining to Madame Sophie's participation makes it impossible to specify its nature and extent, but she surely contributed funds to help cover the construction costs, for she chose to have herself painted holding the plans for the abbey.

In a letter dated 3 July 1779, the comte d'Angiviller, *directeur* of the Bâtiments du roi, chose an artist for this portrait who was highly regarded as a still-life painter but whose portraiture was little known: Anne Vallayer-Coster.[7]

It being the intention of Madame Sophie, mademoiselle, to have herself painted, I thought I could do no better than to recommend you to the princess for the execution of this work, being persuaded on the one hand, by the knowledge I possess of your talent, that you will fulfill her wishes to her greatest satisfaction, and on the other hand that you will be pleased to see arise this occasion to make yourself known finally to this princess and to the royal family. In question is a full-length portrait 7 pieds 5–6 pouces high by 5 pieds 9 pouces. But as Madame Sophie [crossed out: has indicated she cannot] can pose only a very few times, it will first be necessary for you to arrange your picture and to see at least a portrait of this princess that is now in the cabinet of the king's pictures, if you cannot begin also to arrange the head such that you will need only a few sittings to capture the likeness. When you come to Versailles, I will discuss this matter with you at greater length.

I have the honor of being, mademoiselle, your etc.[8]

This letter is crucial to a proper understanding of the work by Anne Vallayer-Coster and of the critical response it received at the Salon of 1781.

Madame Sophie wanted to avoid long posing sessions for an artist whom she did not know. This concern was one she shared with many members of the nobility, beginning with Louis XVI and Marie-Antoinette, who, when requesting a portrait from her cousin Charlotte von Hesse-Darmstadt, specified: "So as not to impose unduly on you, I send you [Vittoriano] Campana, who requires only five minutes per session."[9]

It was common practice at the time to begin such works before having obtained posing sessions for the face, as the princess wished; full-length portraits were begun in the atelier using mannequins and accessories. Conversely, the use of an existing portrait for the face itself, which is what d'Angiviller proposed, was limited to the execution of copies or of variants in which elements from several extant pictures were recombined. The only possible explanation for this way of proceeding is that Madame Sophie wanted to avoid posing, a thesis confirmed by the initial, unrevised wording of d'Angiviller's letter: "Madame Sophie has indicated she [cannot] can pose only a very few times."

Can we identify the portrait of the princess that d'Angiviller said was "in the cabinet of the king's pictures," and that was made available to Vallayer-Coster? The last portraits of Madame Sophie to have been commissioned and paid for by the Bâtiments du roi

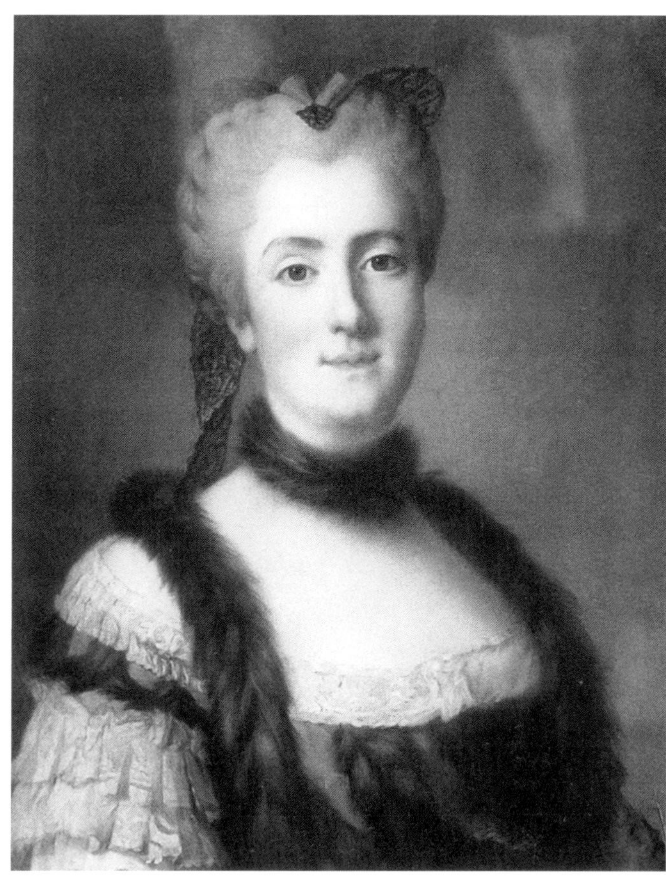

Fig. 1. Franz-Bernhard Frey, *Madame Sophie*, 1766. Pastel, 22½ × 17⅜ in. (57 × 44 cm). Present whereabouts unknown.

are those painted by François-Hubert Drouais in 1762 and 1763,[10] and a pastel portrait by Franz-Bernhard Frey (1716–1806) delivered in 1766 (fig. 1). The second of the portraits by Drouais, in which the princess holds a musical score, is perhaps the one that was lent; it shows her in three-quarter profile facing right, whereas the figure in the Vallayer-Coster portrait faces three-quarters left. The work by Frey, long considered lost, is in my view to be identified with a pastel portrait of an unknown lady sold in Stockholm on 25–26 October 1988 (lot 313), when it was attributed to Léon Glain (act. 1749–1774).[11] The face is quite close to that in the Vallayer-Coster portrait and likewise turns toward the right. Only Joseph Ducreux had painted the princess between 1763 and 1779: to be precise, in 1775, on the occasion of the marriage of Madame Clotilde, the sister of Louis XVI, to the prince of Piedmont. This portrait, now lost, would not have been in the charge of the *surintendance*, having been paid for directly by Madame Sophie.

The orientation of the heads in the portraits by Drouais and Frey is not consistent with the iconographic program given to Vallayer-Coster, which proves that her bust-format likeness was a study for the full-length portrait. This bust-length portrait is not mentioned in d'Angiviller's letter, but it was paid for at the same time as Vallayer-Coster's full-length portrait, their completion and delivery having been certified on 17 November 1781 as part of the budgeted expenses for 1780.[12] The bust length was sent to Versailles in 1837 from the Mobilier de la couronne (Royal Furniture), along with the portraits of Mesdames Adélaïde and Victoire discussed below, and a portrait of Madame Louise dressed as a Carmelite nun that in 1926 was sent to the Musée du Carmel de Saint-Denis.[13] The circumstances under which these four portraits entered the collection of the Mobilier royal remain unknown, and I have been unable to determine the original destination of the portrait of Madame Sophie.

An attribution of the bust length to Vallayer on the basis of stylistic considerations is confirmed by an inscription in ink on the original stretcher: *Mlle Vallayer toille* (Mlle Vallayer canvas). The work is not signed, but this precious indication—the result of a consistent practice of the Bâtiments du roi, which had the name of the artist-recipient inscribed on the stretchers intended for paintings commissioned by the agency—proves that it is autograph.

A note accompanying d'Angiviller's letter of 3 July 1779 indicates that the portrait was "given by Madame Sophie to Madame the comtesse de Fenoyle abbess of the chapter of lady countesses of Largentière in the year 1779."[14] The large portrait exhibited at the Salon of 1781, according to the notice in the *livret* (catalogue booklet), was "destined for Mme the comtesse de Perroyse, abbess of the noble chapter of lady countesses of Largentière." Without dwelling on the misspelling of the recipient's name in the Salon *livret* or on the vagueness of the indication there of the placename, which has hitherto misled scholars, it will be useful at this point to review the evidence proving that the bust portrait was given to Madame de Fenoyl.

Etienne Jeaurat (1699–1789), who was in charge of the king's pictures, made the following entry in his account books for 1781: "On 23 March for having sent four men to Paris to carry on a stretcher a large picture with its frame representing [sic] a full-length portrait of Madame Sophie addressed to Mme la Comtesse de Fenoys [sic] abbess of L'Argentière, paid for the trip . . . 24 l[ivres]."[15] This transport to Paris must have been connected with the work's exhibition at the Louvre, for it could not have been sent to its intended recipient before closure of the Salon in the fall of 1781. The abbé Pierre Duret, who was close to Madame de Fenoyl, noted in his diary immediately after the date 6 June 1780: "The prioress of l'Argentière[16] arrived with the portraits of Mesdames, of Madame Adélaïde, Victoire and Sophie, is going to place the first stone of her church, Monsieur and Madame Victoire will be godfather and godmother."[17] This crucial document proves that Madame de Fenoyl, in the course of her visits to Versailles to solicit princely donations, had succeeded in winning to her cause, in addition to Monsieur and Madame Sophie, Mesdames Adélaïde and Victoire, the last of whom had agreed to be godmother to the church. This is why she brought back portraits of the aunts of the king: bust portraits, certainly, so as not to encumber her baggage.

There is nothing surprising in the fact that Mesdames Adélaïde and Victoire, who were accustomed to giving portraits of themselves to their intimates and to those beholden to them, should have wanted to honor Madame de Fenoyl in the same way as their sister. It is just as natural that they should have turned to Vallayer-Coster. The unrevised wording of d'Angiviller's letter to the artist ("you will be pleased to see arise this occasion to make yourself known finally to this princess and to the royal family") suggests that Vallayer had previously met one of the king's aunts. By a rare stroke of luck, historical serendipity delivered all three portraits to us together: in 1837, at the request of Louis-Philippe, all of them were transferred to the Mobilier de la couronne at the Musée de Versailles (pls. 26, 27, 28).

Like the portrait of Madame Sophie, those of her sisters are unsigned. The old stretchers are not inscribed *Mlle Vallayer*, for they were not provided by the Bâtiments, having been paid for by Mesdames Adélaïde and Victoire. These two portraits, then, are finished works in bust format, while that of Madame Sophie is a study for the full-length portrait.

In the portraits of Mesdames Sophie and Adélaïde, the poses are identical, as are the blue silk gowns and lace collarettes. Madame Victoire is similarly posed and attired, but her torso is oriented in the opposite direction (toward the right), while her dress is made of white silk with sable trim. Bonnets of bunched lawn lace atop high powdered coiffures and lace guipures culminating in "noeuds du parfait contentement" (bows of perfect contentment) figure in all three portraits, and the handling of these elements is consistent throughout

the set. But the handling of the faces varies: the modeling and drawing are more confident in the portraits of
Mesdames Adélaïde and Victoire, while the rendering
of Madame Sophie's features is hesitant, even uncertain.
This vibrating touch is not altogether foreign to the artist's work, and it makes for an unfinished quality that is
perhaps not surprising in a portrait study. Then again,
the paucity of sittings accorded the artist by Madame
Sophie may explain some of her difficulty in producing an authoritative likeness. If we make the plausible
assumption that the features in the full-length portrait
were based on this oil study, then Diderot's dismissive
judgment, that "the head is not a good likeness and
so much the better" (a view shared by the critic in the
Mémoires secrets, who wrote of a "lack of resemblance"),
becomes readily understandable.[18]

The portraits of the two elder princesses, by contrast,
are very close to those executed in 1768 and 1776 by
Joseph Ducreux (figs. 2, 3).[19] His graphic and rather dry
handling differs from that of Vallayer, which softens
the features and makes the sitters seem younger.

Two other portraits of Mesdames Adélaïde and Victoire
(cats. 122, 124), likewise heretofore considered anonymous works, are now in the Etablissement Thermal
de Vichy, to which they were donated by the duchesse
d'Angoulême, daughter of Louis XVI, in 1821, a gesture
intended to recall the sojourn of her great-aunts in the
thermal resort in 1785 from 1 June to 2 August.[20] These
canvases, unquestionably of high quality, must be considered autograph replicas.[21] Finally, mention must be
made of a rectangular version in pastel of the portrait
of Madame Victoire, known only through an old photograph in the Bibliothèque nationale.[22] The poor quality
of the image precludes final judgment of the quality of
the work itself, which seems respectable enough.

The archives document Monsieur's generosity toward
the noble chapter of L'Argentière, but they are silent
when it comes to dispositions of Madame Sophie. Of the
three princesses, she must have been the one most com-
mitted to the institution, for she, like Monsieur, donated
to it a full-length portrait of herself that, according to
the *livret* of the 1781 Salon, represented her "in her cabinet, in front of a bust of Louis XV, holding in her hands
a plan of the abbey of Largentière."

The work was delivered to Madame de Fenoyl, who
had it installed in the salon of her apartment in the
new buildings of the abbey, as is indicated by this invoice from the architect Désarnod dated 23 June 1787:

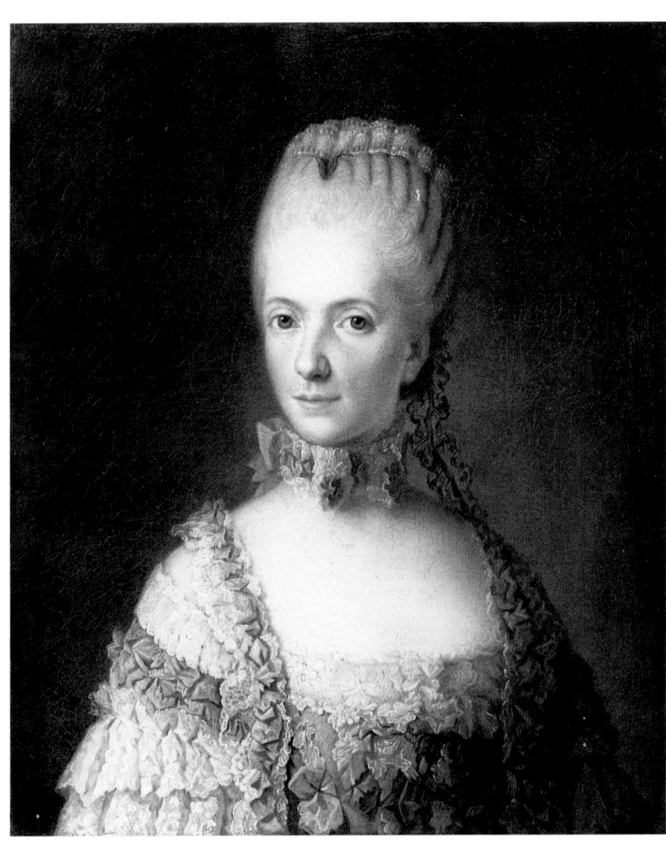

Fig. 2. Joseph Ducreux, *Madame Adélaïde*, 1768. Oil on canvas,
28⅛ × 22⅞ in. (71.4 × 58.1 cm). Private collection.

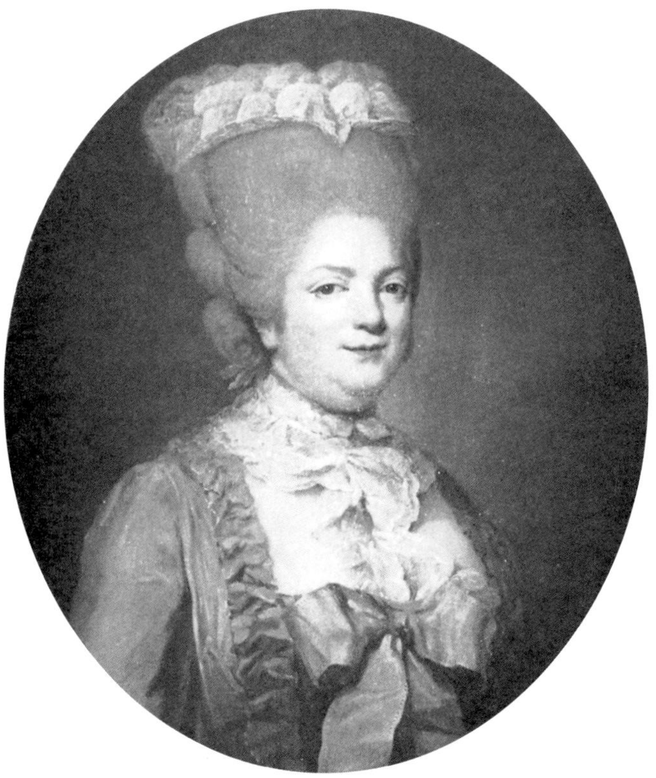

Fig. 3. Joseph Ducreux, *Madame Victoire*, 1776. Oil on canvas,
28 × 23 in. (71.1 × 58.4 cm). Private collection.

"Woodwork and varnishing of the Salon . . . article 5.
The four sides of the Salon of Mme the abbess will be
decorated with full panels within which a place is to
be left empty for the portrait[s] of Monsieur and of
Madame Sophie."[23]

Scarcely had the church been consecrated when the
Constituent Assembly's decree dissolving such religious
congregations dispersed the canonesses. Madame de
Fenoyl immigrated to Switzerland and her effects were
confiscated. A summary record indicates that "she left
behind some furnishings in the house of the former
abbey of Largentière . . . these effects of middling value
are inside the archives building which is secure, the
municipality has the keys to it," and an annotation in
the margin refers to the impending sale of these effects.[24]
Would the presence of a large, full-length portrait of
Madame Sophie have gone unmentioned? This seems
unlikely. Although speculative, I think it worthwhile to
sketch the probable fate of the painting. The full-length
portraits of Monsieur and of Madame Sophie were set into
paneling of the abbess's salon in 1787. In 1792 the few
remaining canonesses were forced to leave their abbey,
abandoning the building to the peasants of Aveize and
to bands of pillagers who set fire to the buildings and
tried to demolish part of them.[25] It seems very likely that
the two royal portraits, whose "monarchical" character
would have been conspicuous because of their placement
and their armorial frames, were destroyed at this time.

Family tradition has retained no anecdotes about
such a sad fate, and it would seem that the former abbess
never evoked this disaster during her exile. But the marquis de Fenoyl still has in his possession an object that
lends support to the thesis that the work was destroyed.[26]
It is an oval cartouche surrounded by mutilated oak
leaves that bears the inscription: DONNE / PAR MADAME
SOPHIE DE FRANCE / A ME DE FENOYL / ABBESSE DU CHAPITRE
DE LARGENTIERE / EN 1780 (Given / by Madame Sophie
de France / To Me de Fenoyl / Abbess of the Chapter of
Largentiere / in 1780).[27] Traditionally thought to be the
crossbar of a chair back, it is in fact the cartouche that
decorated the bottom of the frame carved by Buteux.
Burn marks and mutilations of the foliage leave little
room for doubt as to the destruction of the masterpiece
by Anne Vallayer-Coster, who shares this sad privilege
with Adélaïde Labille-Guiard, whose large painting
representing the induction of a knight by Monsieur into
the Order of Saint-Lazare was destroyed on orders of the
Convention.

No one knows how this souvenir of the princely gift
came to be salvaged from the flames. The bust portraits,
which bore no royal insignia, were doubtless confiscated
and sold under circumstances whose specifics will never
be known. We think that they are the portraits that, after
being reacquired by the crown for the Garde-Meuble,
were returned to Versailles in 1837, making possible their
restoration to their proper place in the iconography of
the royal family, and to the apartments where Mesdames
spent their days in tranquility before the Revolution.

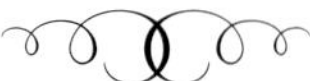

NOTES

1. "Ces portraits n'ayant point été ordonnés au Sr Nattier
par MM les Directeurs Généraux, on ne peut en dresser
de mémoires qu'il n'ait été décidé si cela doit regarder les
Bâtiments ou si ces portraits seront payés sur la cassette
de la famille royale." [N.B.: The plural "MM. les Directeurs
Générales" was used here because the occupant of this post
had recently changed: on the death of Charles-François-
Paul Lenorment de Tournehem (1684–1751), it was awarded
to Abel-François Poisson de Vandières (1727–1781), later
named marquis de Ménars and de Marigny—trans.] Archives
nationals, Paris (hereafter AN), O¹ 1965, 7: "Mémoire des
ouvrages dûs, inventaire des papiers . . . qui se sont trouvés
sous les scellés de M. Coypel . . . 1752."

2. Sophie-Philippe-Elisabeth-Justine de France (1734–1782),
sixth daughter of Louis XV and Marie Leszczyńska.

3. On the history of this priory, see Baudrillart 1930, 40–41;
Leistenschneider 1905.

4. Marie-Madeleine de Gayardon de Gresolles de Fenoyl
(1743–1803), prioress, 1770–1780, abbess, 1784–1790.

5. Leistenschneider 1905, pl. 7. Situated in the commune
d'Aveize, l'Argentière was a small seminary between 1804
and 1905; it is now a medical clinic.

6. AN, R 5 140, "Fondation par Monsieur, frère du Roy au
chapitre de Largentière," the prince, desiring "contribuer
au bien de ce chapitre et notamment à la reconstruction de
son église a . . . fondé et établi . . . six places de chanoinesses,"
made a donation of 40,000 livres; act of 21 April 1781.

7. See Roland Michel 1970, 214–215.

8. "Madame Sophie ayant le dessein, mademoiselle, de se
faire peindre, j'ai pensé ne pouvoir mieux faire que de vous
indiquer à cette princesse pour l'exécution de cet ouvrage,
persuadé d'un côté par la connaissance que j'ai de votre
talent, que vous remplirez ses vûes à sa plus grande satisfaction, et de l'autre, que vous verrez naître avec plaisir cette
occasion de vous faire connaître [crossed out: définitivement

à cette princesse et] à la famille royale. Il s'agit d'un portrait en pied dont le champ est de 7 p[ieds] 5 à 6 pouces de hauteur sur 5 p[ieds] 9 pouces. mais comme Madame Sophie [crossed out: a annoncé ne] ne peut donner qu'un petit nombre de séances, il faudrait d'abord que vous disposassiez votre tableau et que vous vissiez au moyen d'un portrait de cette princesse qui existe au cabinet des tableaux du Roi, si vous ne pourriez pas commencer à disposer aussi la tête de manière à ne plus avoir besoin que de peu de séances pour saisir la ressemblance. Lorsque vous viendrez à Versailles, je m'entretiendrai plus au long avec vous sur ce sujet / J'ai l'honneur d'être, mademoiselle votre etc." AN, O¹ 1915, 122. This is a working draft of the letter, which explains the indicated editorial revisions, the first of which suggests that Vallayer-Coster had previously met Mme Sophie.

9. "Pour fatiguer le moins possible votre complaisance, je vous envoie Campana qui n'exige que cinq minutes par séance." As cited by Vuaflart and Bourin 1909–1910, 2:134.

10. Now, respectively, The Metropolitan Museum of Art, New York; Musée national des Châteaux de Versailles et de Trianon, Versailles.

11. Pastel, 57 × 44 cm; I would like to thank Jean-Jacques Petit for bringing this work to my attention.

12. AN, O¹ 1922 B 1.

13. Archives du Musée du Louvre, 2DD4.

14. "Donné à Mme la Comtesse de Perroyse, abbesse du noble chapitre des dames comtesses de Largentière." AN, O¹ 1915, 120.

15. "Du 23 mars pour avoir envoyé quatre hommes à Paris porter sur un brancard un grand tableau avec sa bordure représentant le portrait de madame Sophie en pied adressé à Mde la Comtesse de Fenoys [sic] abbesse de L'Argentière, payé pour le voyage . . . 24 l[ivres]." AN, O¹ 1934 B 2.

16. The title of abbesse, which was conferred on her by the royal administration, seems to have become effective only in 1784.

17. "La prieure de l'Argentière arrivée avec les portraits de Mesdames, de Madame Adélaïde, Victoire et Sophie, va poser la 1è pierre de son église, Monsieur et Madame de Victoire seront parrain et marraine." Lyon, Bibliothèque Municipale, Ms 104, fol. 13r and v; I would like to thank Paul Feuga and Gérard Bruyère for having sent me this document. The certification of the benediction of the church, which took place on 20 February 1790, confirms the date, specifying that "la première pierre fut bénite le 7 juin 1780." Archives Communales d'Aveize, E. suppl. 76 (GG3).

18. "La tête ne ressemble pas et tant mieux"; "un défaut de ressemblance." Quoted in Roland Michel 1970, 214.

19. *Portrait of Madame Adélaïde*, private collection; *Portrait of Madame Victoire*, sold at Christie's, New York, 10 November 1962, lot 194.

20. See Décoret 1899, 149–153.

21. They are oval canvases of dimensions identical to those at Versailles. In the nineteenth century, these portraits were exhibited in the grands salons at Vichy. See Castanié 1865, 79. My thanks to Pascal Chambriard, archivist of the Compagnie Fermière de Vichy, for these references.

22. Bibliothèque Nationale, Cabinet des Estampes, N2 Fol, portraits, France, vol. 594.

23. "Boiseries et vernis du Salon . . . article 5è. Les quatre côtés du Salon de Mad. L'abbesse seront revetus d'une boiserie pleine dans laquelle sera réservé la place du portrait de Monsieur et de Madame Sophie." Archives Départementales du Rhône (hereafter ADR), 1 Q 1055. I would like to thank my colleague Elisabeth Antoine for having carried out this research.

24. "Elle a laissé quelques meubles dans la maison de la cydevant abbaye de Largentière . . . ces effets d'une modique valeur sont renfermés dans le bâtiment des archives qui est sûr, la municipalité en a les clefs." ADR, 1 Q 546, biens de seconde origine, 1793–1795.

25. Baudrillart 1930, 41.

26. I would like to express my warm gratitude to the marquis and marquise de Fenoyl for having corresponded with me about this matter.

27. Carved and gilded wood, 34 × 55 cm. Note that the inscription records the date of the decision to make the donation, not that of its delivery to the intended recipient.

Abbreviated References

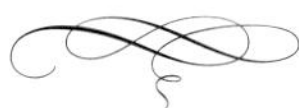

Books and Articles

L'ami des artistes au Sallon 1787
L'ami des artistes au Sallon, par M. l'A. R. à Paris. Paris, 1787.

Antonetti 1963
Antonetti, G. *Une maison de banque à Paris au XVIIIe siècle, Greffulhe, Montz et Cie (1789–1793).* Toulouse, 1963.

Apelle au Sallon 1783
Apelle au Sallon. Paris, 1783.

L'aristarque moderne 1785
L'aristarque moderne au Salon. Paris, 1785.

Aulanier 1958
Aulanier, Christiane. *Le pavillon du roi, les appartements de la Reine.* Vol. 7 of *Histoire du palais et du musée du Louvre.* Paris, 1958.

Auricchio 2000
Auricchio, Laura. "Portraits of Impropriety: Adélaïde Labille-Guiard and the Careers of Professional Women Artists in Late Eighteenth-Century Paris." Ph.D. diss. Columbia University, 2000.

Badinter 1983
Badinter, Elisabeth. *Emilie, Emilie: l'ambition féminine au XVIIIe siècle.* Paris, 1983.

Baer 1999
Baer, W. "Zur Entwicklung des botanischen Malerei beim Porzellan." In *Das Flora-Danica Service, 1790–1802: Höhepunkt des botanischen Porzellanmalerei.* Berlin, Schloss Charlottenburg, 1999.

Baetjer 1995
Baetjer, Katherine. *European Paintings in the Metropolitan Museum of Art by Artists Born before 1865.* New York, 1995.

Bailey 1985
Bailey, Colin B. "Le marquis de Véri collectionneur." *Bulletin de la société de l'histoire de l'art français 1983* (1985): 67–83.

Bailey 1988
Bailey, Colin B., ed. *Ange-Laurent de La Live de Jully: A Facsimile Reprint of the Catalogue Historique (1764) and the Catalogue Raisonné des Tableaux (5 March 1770).* New York, 1988.

Bailey 1989
Bailey, Colin B. "*Quel dommage qu'une telle dispersion*: Collectors of French Painting and the French Revolution." In *1789: French Art during the Revolution*, ed. A. P. Wintermute, 10–26. New York, 1989.

Bailey 1993
Bailey, Colin B. "The Abbé Terray: An Enlightened Patron of Modern Sculpture." *Burlington Magazine* 135 (March 1993): 121–132.

Bailey 2002
Bailey, Colin B. *"Patriotic Taste": Collecting Modern Art in Pre-Revolutionary Paris.* New Haven and London, in press [2002].

Baillio 1984
Baillio, Joseph. "French Rococo Paintings: A Notable Exhibition in Atlanta." *Apollo* 119, no. 263 (January 1984): 16–23.

Baillio 1988
Baillio, Joseph. "Une artiste méconnue: Rose Adélaïde Ducreux." *L'Oeil* 399 (1988): 20–27.

Baillio 1996
Baillio, Joseph. "Vie et oeuvre de Marie-Victoire Lemoine." *Gazette des Beaux-Arts* 127 (April 1996): 125–164.

Baudrillart 1930
Baudrillart, Alfred. *Dictionnaire d'histoire et de géographie écclésiastiques.* Vol. 4. Paris, 1930.

Baxandall 1985
Baxandall, Michael. *Patterns of Intention: On the Historical Explanation of Pictures.* New Haven and London, 1985.

Bazin 1962
Bazin, Germain. *A Gallery of Flowers.* London, 1962.

Bénézit 1999
Bénézit, E. *Dictionnaire critique et documentaire des peintres, sculpteurs, dessinateurs et graveurs de tous les temps et de tous les pays par un groupe d'écrivains spécialistes français et étrangers.* 14 vols. Paris, 1999.

Benoit and Ravaud 2001
Benoit, Christine, and Elisabeth Ravaud. "Filière matière picturale et arts graphiques." Rapport 4605, 13 July 2001. Paris, Musée du Louvre.

Bergeon and Martin 1994
Bergeon, Ségolène, and Elisabeth Martin. "La Technique de la peinture française des XVII et XVIIIe siècles." *Techne*, no. 1 (1994): 65–78.

Berthommieu 1923
Berthommieu, Louis. *Catalogue du Musée de Narbonne.* Toulouse, 1923.

Beuchot 1829–1834
Beuchot, Adrian-Jean-Quentin, ed. *Oeuvres de Voltaire.* 70 vols. Paris, 1829–1834.

Bizardel 1957
Bizardel, Yvon. "Les académiciennes au XVIIIe siècle." *Jardin des Arts,* no. 31 (March 1957): 435–442.

Bjürstrom 1987
Bjürstrom, Per. "Marie-Jeanne Boucher." *Konsthistorisk Tidskrift* 56 (1987): 38–41.

Bocher 1875/1882
Bocher, E. *Les gravures françaises du 18ème siècle.* Paris, 1875–1882.

Bock 1986
Bock, Henning, ed. *Gemäldegalerie Berlin. Gesamtverzeichnis der Gemälde.* Berlin, 1986.

Bode 1916
Bode, Wilhelm. "Amtliche Berichte aus den Königl." *Kunst Sammlungen* 37, no. 14 (January 1916): 60–76.

Bomford, Brown, and Roy 1988
Bomford, David, Christopher Brown, and Ashok Roy. *Art in the Making: Rembrandt.* The National Gallery. London, 1988.

Bouchary 1939–1942
Bouchary, Jean. *Les manieurs d'argent à la fin du XVIIIe siècle.* 3 vols. Paris, 1939–1942.

Bouleau 1993
Bouleau, Cécile. "Musée des beaux-arts de Nancy. Inventaire des tableaux de l'école française, seconde moitié du XVIIIe siècle." Mémoire de D.E.A., Université de Paris IV. Paris, 1993.

Bouleau 1999
Bouleau, Cécile. Section on eighteenth-century paintings. In *Collection du Musée des Beaux-Arts de Nancy: Regards,* ed. Béatrice Salmon, 112–146. Paris, 1999.

Le bouquet du Sallon 1787
Le bouquet du Sallon. Paris, 1787.

La bourgeoise au Sallon 1787
La bourgeoise au Sallon. London and Paris, 1787.

Bowes Museum 1955
Bowes Museum. *Illustrated Handbook. Catalogue of the Bowes Museum.* Barnard Castle. Durham, 1955.

Boysson 1980
Boysson, B. de. "Catalogue des peintures de l'école française du XVIIIè siècle. Musée des Beaux-Arts de Bordeaux." Mémoire de maîtrise, Université de Bordeaux III, 1980.

Brière 1924
Brière, Gaston. *Musée national du Louvre. Catalogue des peintures exposées dans les galeries.* Paris, 1924.

Bryson 1990
Bryson, Norman. *Looking at the Overlooked: Four Essays on Still Life Painting.* Cambridge, 1990.

Bukdahl 1980
Bukdahl, Else Marie. *Diderot, Critique d'Art.* 2 vols. Vol. 1, *Théorie et pratique dans les Salons de Diderot.* Vol. 2, *Diderot, les salonniers et les esthéticiens de son temps.* Copenhagen, 1980.

Bukdahl and Lorenceau 1984
Bukdahl, Else Marie, and Annette Lorenceau, eds. *Diderot sur l'art.* Paris, 1984.

Bukdahl et al. 1995
Bukdahl, Else Marie, et al., eds. *Diderot, héros et martyrs: Salons de 1769, 1771, 1775, 1781.* Paris, 1995.

Bulletin des sociétés artistiques 1899
Bulletin des sociétés artistiques de l'EOL, no. 6 (April 1899).

Cailleux 1969a
Cailleux, Jean. "Portrait of Madame Adélaïde of France. Daughter of Louis XV." *Burlington Magazine* 111, no. 22 (March 1969): "L'art du XVIIIè siècle," supplement, i–iv.

Cailleux 1969b
Cailleux, Jean. "Themes and Survivals in Connection with Two Still Life Paintings by François Desportes." *Burlington Magazine* 111, no. 24 (November 1969): "L'art du XVIIIe siècle," supplement, i–viii.

Cameron 1984
Cameron, Vivian. "Woman as Image and Image-Maker in Paris during the French Revolution." Ph.D. diss., Yale University, 1984.

Campan 1988
Campan, Jeanne-Louise-Henriette. *Mémoires de Madame Campan, première femme de chambre de Marie-Antoinette.* Introduction by Jean Chalon, notes by Carlos de Augulo. Paris, 1988.

Cantarel-Besson 1992
Cantarel-Besson, Yveline. *Musée du Louvre (janvier 1797–juin 1798): procès-verbaux du Conseil d'administration du Musée central des Arts.* No. 2. Paris, 1992.

Castanié 1865
Castanié, P. de. *Nouveau guide complet aux bains de Vichy.* Paris, 1865.

Catalogue de l'exposition 1852
Catalogue de l'exposition de peinture, sculpture, gravure, dessins et émaux. Geneva, 1852.

Catalogue des tableaux . . . Audeoud 1848
Catalogue des tableaux composant la collection de M. James Audeoud de Genève. Geneva, 1848.

Catalogue des Tableaux . . . Merle 1784
Catalogue des Tableaux qui composent le cabinet de M. le Comte de Merle. Paris, 1 March 1784.

Catalogue de Tableaux Précieux 1775
Catalogue de Tableaux Précieux, de Figures de Marbre antique, de Bronze . . . d'un Cabinet distingué. Paris, 20 December 1775.

Catalogue d'une riche collection . . . de . . . Reber 1809
Catalogue d'une riche collection de tableaux, dessins, estampes et différents objets de curiosités qui composaient le Cabinet de Monsieur Nicolas Reber, négociant à Basle. Basel, 1809.

Catalogue d'une très-belle collection . . . de feu M. l'Abbé Terray 1779
Catalogue d'une très-belle collection de Tableaux, Sculptures en Marbre, Bronze . . . provenans de la succession de feu M. l'Abbé Terray. Paris, 20 January 1779.

Catalogue raisonné . . . de Tableaux . . . de . . .
[Le Boeuf] 1783
Catalogue raisonné d'une très-belle collection
de Tableaux . . . provenans du Cabinet de
*M.*** [Le Boeuf]. Paris, 8 April 1783.*

Catalogue sommaire 1986
Catalogue sommaire illustré des peintures
du musée du Louvre et du musée d'Orsay, 5,
Ecole française, Tableaux déposés par le
Louvre. Paris, 1986.

Cavalli-Björkmann 1994–1995
Cavalli-Björkmann, Görel. "A Still Life
by Anne Vallayer-Coster." *Art Bulletin*
of the Nationalmuseum, Stockholm 1–2
(1994–1995): 23.

Cavalli-Björkman and Nilsson 1995
Cavalli-Björkman, Görel, and Bo Nilsson.
Still Leben. Stockholm, 1995.

Caviglia 1997
Caviglia, S. "Le artiste all'Academie
royale di Parigi nel secolo dei lumi:
ostacoli e conquiste." Thesis, Academy
"La Sapienza," Rome, 1997.

Chadwick 1990
Chadwick, Whitney. *Women, Art, and*
Society. London, 1990.

Chadwick 1996
Chadwick, Whitney. *Women, Art and*
Society. London, 1996.

Châlons-sur-Marne 1891
Châlons-sur-Marne. *Ville de Châlons-sur-*
Marne, Catalogue du Musée. N.p., 1891.

Charnois 1787
Charnois, M. de. *Costumes et annales de*
grands théâtres de Paris. Paris, 1787.

Chatelus 1991
Chatelus, Jean. *Peindre à Paris au XVIIIe*
siècle. Paris, 1991.

Chaudonneret 1999
Chaudonneret, Marie-Claude. *L'Etat et les*
artistes: de la Restauration à la Monarchie de
Juillet. Paris, 1999.

Chennevières 1881
Chennevières, Henry de. *Notice des*
tableaux appartenant à la collection du
Louvre exposés dans les salles du musée
de Fontainebleau. Paris, 1881.

Chennevières 1903
Chennevières, Henry de. "François
Dumont. Miniaturiste de Marie-
Antoinette." *Gazette des Beaux Arts* 29
(March 1903): 177–192.

Chevreul 1967
Chevreul, M. E. *The Principles of Harmony*
and Contrast of Colors and Their Applications
to the Arts. New York, 1967.

Clark 1974
Clark, Carol C. "Jean-Baptiste Siméon
Chardin: Still Life with Herring." *Cleve-*
land Museum of Art Bulletin 61, no. 9 (1974):
309–314.

Cleray 1910
Cleray, Edmond. "Mad. Filleul, Peintre
de Portraits." *L'Art et les Artistes* 12
(November 1910): 62–68.

Cleveland 1972
Year in Review for 1971. Cleveland, 1972.

Collection Deloynes
Pièces sur les beaux-arts, imprimées et
manuscrites, recueillies par Pierre-Jean
Mariette, Charles-Nicolas Cochin, et
M. Deloynes. Bibliothèque nationale
de France, Cabinet des estampes. 63 vols.
517 microfiches. Paris, 1980.

Compin and Roquebert 1986
Compin, Isabelle, and Anne Roquebert.
Catalogue sommaire illustré des peintures du
musée du Louvre et du musée d'Orsay. Vol, 4,
Ecole française, L–Z. Paris, 1986.

Conisbee 1981
Conisbee, Philip. *Painting in Eighteenth-*
Century France. Ithaca, N.Y., 1981.

Conisbee 1986
Conisbee, Philip. *Chardin.* Oxford, 1986.

Constans 1980
Constans, Claire. *Musée national du château*
de Versailles, catalogue des peintures. Paris,
1980.

Constans 1995
Constans, Claire. *Musée national du château*
de Versailles, Les Peintures. Vol. 2. Paris,
1995.

Coster sale 1824
Notice des tableaux de fleurs peints par
Mme Vallayer Coster, Ancien membre de
l'Académie royale de Peinture. Paris, 1824.

La critique est aisée 1783
La critique est aisée, mais l'art est difficile.
Paris, 1783.

Crow 1985
Crow, Thomas. *Painters and Public Life in*
Eighteenth-Century Paris. New Haven and
London, 1985.

Dacier 1909–1921
Dacier, Emile. *Catalogues de ventes et livrets*
de Salons illustrés par Gabriel de Saint-
Aubin. 11 vols. in 6. Paris, 1909–1921.

Dacier, Hérold, and Vuaflart 1921–1929
Dacier, Emile, Jacques Hérold, and Albert
Vuaflart. *Jean de Jullienne et les graveurs*
de Watteau au XVIII siècle. 4 vols. Paris,
1921–1929.

Décoret 1899
Décoret, G. *Une page sur Vichy et ses environs.*
Vichy, 1899.

Démoris 1991
Démoris, René. *Chardin, la chair et l'objet.*
Paris, 1991.

Denon 1999
Vivant Denon, directeur des musées sous le
Consulat et l'Empire: Correspondance, 1802–
1815. Introduction by Jean Tulard, edited
by Marie-Anne Dupuy, Isabelle Le Masne
de Chermont, and Elaine Williamson.
2 vols. Paris, 1999.

Denton 1998
Denton, Margaret Field. "The Gendering
of Genres in Post-Revolutionary French
Painting." *Art History* 21 (1998): 219–246.

Deonna 1938
Deonna, Waldemar. *Catalogue du Musée*
Ariana. Geneva, 1938.

Dézallier d'Argenville 1762
Dézallier d'Argenville, A.-J. *Abrégé de la vie*
des plus fameux peintres. 5 vols. Paris, 1762.

Diderot 1984
Diderot, Denis. *Essai sur la peinture; Salons*
de 1759, 1761, 1763. Paris, 1984.

Dimier 1926
Dimier, Louis. "Tableaux qui passent."
Gazette des Beaux-Arts, sér. 5, 13 (1926):
119–122.

Discours sur l'origine 1785
Discours sur l'origine, les progrès et l'état
actuel de la peinture en France. Paris, 1785.

Doria 1928
Doria, Arnauld, comte. "Tocqué et les
commandes royales." *Gazette des Beaux-*
Arts, 5 pér., t. 18 (September–October
1928): 149–166.

[Ducrest] 1829
[Ducrest, Georgette.] *Mémoires sur*
l'Impératrice Joséphine, ses contemporains,
la cour de Navarre et de Malmaison. 3 vols.
Paris, 1829.

Duplessis 1857
Duplessis, G., ed. *Mémoires et journal de J.-G. Wille, graveur du roi.* 2 vols. Paris, 1857.

Dupont de Nemours 1908
Dupont de Nemours, Pierre-Samuel. "Lettres sur les Salons de 1773, 1777 et 1779 adressées par Du Pont de Nemours à la Margravine Caroline-Louise de Bade." Edited by Karl Obser. *Archives de l'art français,* nouv. pér., 2 (1908): 1–122.

Duval 1992
Duval, Alain R. "Les préparations colorées des tableaux de l'école française des dix-septième et dix-huitième siècles." *Studies in Conservation* 37 (1992): 239–258.

Ebert-Schifferer 1999
Ebert-Schifferer, Sybille. *Still-life: A History.* New York, 1999.

Edwards 1998
Edwards, JoLynn. *Alexandre Paillet. Expert et marchand de tableaux à la fin du XVIII siècle.* Paris, 1998.

Eisler 1977
Eisler, Colin. *Paintings from the Samuel H. Kress Collection: European Schools Excluding Italian.* Oxford, 1977.

Engerand 1901
Engerand, Fernand. *Inventaire des tableaux commandés et achetés par la direction de Bâtiments du roi, de 1709 à 1792.* Paris, 1901.

Entretiens sur l'exposition de tableaux 1775
Entretiens sur l'exposition de tableaux de l'année 1775. Paris, 1775.

Explication 1775
Explication des Peintures, Sculptures, et Gravures de Messieurs de l'Académie royale. Paris, 1775.

"Exposition de peintures" 1777
"Exposition de peintures, sculptures, et gravures." *Journal encyclopédique.* Paris, 1777.

Faniel et al. 1956
Faniel, Stéphane, with the collaboration of Jean Cailleux et al. *Le XVIIIe siècle français.* Paris, 1956.

F. Faré 1999
Faré, Fabrice. "Elèves et émules de Chardin." *Dossier de l'art,* no. 60 (September 1999): 58–71.

Faré and Chevé 1996
Faré, Fabrice, and D. Chevé. "Les tableaux de trompe-l'oeil ou la jouissance de l'illusion." In *Le Trompe-l'Oeil: de l'antiquité au XXe siècle,* by Patrick Mauriès, 169–251. Paris, 1996.

M. Faré 1962
Faré, Michel. *La nature morte en France: son histoire et son évolution du XVIIe au XXe siècle.* 2 vols. Geneva, 1962.

M. and F. Faré 1976
Faré, Michel, and Fabrice Faré. *La vie silencieuse en France: La nature morte au XVIIIe siècle.* Paris and Fribourg, 1976.

Fenaille 1903–1923
Fenaille, Maurice. *Etat général des tapisseries de la Manufacture des Gobelins.* 5 vols. Paris, 1903–1923.

Fidière 1885
Fidière, Octave. *Les femmes artistes à l'Académie royale de peinture et de sculpture.* Paris, 1885.

Figaro au Salon 1785
Figaro au Salon de peinture. Rome, 1785.

Florisoone 1948
Florisoone, Michel. *La peinture française: le 18e siècle.* Paris, 1948.

Fontaine 1909
Fontaine, André. *Les doctrines d'art en France, peintres, amateurs, critiques, de Poussin à Diderot.* Paris, 1909.

Fontaine 1910a
Fontaine, André. *Les collections de l'Académie royale de peinture et sculpture.* Paris, 1910.

Fontaine 1910b
Fontaine, André. *Vie d'artistes du XVIIIe siècle. Discours sur la peintures et la sculpture du comte de Caylus.* Paris, 1910.

Fort 1999
Bachaumont, Louis Petit de. *Les Salons des "Mémoires secrets," 1767–1787.* Edited by Bernadette Fort. Paris, 1999.

Foucart et al. 1996
Foucart, Jacques, et al. *Musée du Louvre: Nouvelles acquisitions du département des peintures, 1991–1995.* Paris, 1996.

Fraser 2001
Fraser, Antonia. *Marie-Antoinette.* London, 2001.

Furcy-Raynaud 1903–1904
Furcy-Raynaud, Marc, ed. "Correspondance de Marigny avec Lépicié." *Nouvelles archives de l'art français,* 3e sér., 19–20 (1903–1904).

Furcy-Raynaud 1905–1906
Furcy-Raynaud, Marc, ed. "Correspondance de M. d'Angiviller avec Jean-Baptiste-Marie Pierre." *Nouvelles archives de l'art français,* 3e sér., 21–22 (1905–1906).

Gaehtgens and Lugan 1988
Gaehtgens, Thomas, and Jacques Lugan. *Joseph-Marie Vien. Peintre du roi.* Paris, 1988.

Garnier-Pelle 1995
Garnier-Pelle, Nicole. *Chantilly Musée Condé. Peintures du XVIII siècle.* Paris, 1995.

Gaskell 1990
Gaskell, Ivan. *The Thyssen-Bornemisza Collection, Seventeenth-Century Dutch and Flemish Painting.* London, 1990.

Gault de Saint-Germain 1805
Gault de Saint-Germain, Pierre-Marie. *Collection de fleurs et de fruits peint d'après nature par Jean Louis Prévost.* Paris, 1805.

Gazette des Beaux-Arts 1969
"La Chronique des arts." *Gazette des Beaux-Arts* 73, no. 1201 (February 1969).

Gelly-Saldias 1997
Gelly-Saldias, Clara. "Natures mortes françaises du musée des beaux-arts de Nancy." *Peristyles,* no. 10 (July 1997): 11–18, 33–38.

Gielly 1937
Gielly, Louis. "La réorganisation de la section des peintures au Musée Ariana." *Genava* 15 (1937): 17–21.

Goldstein 1996
Goldstein, Carl. *Teaching Art: Academies and Schools from Vasari to Albers.* Cambridge and New York, 1996.

Goncourt 1882
Goncourt, Edmond de. *La Saint-Huberty.* Paris, 1882.

Goncourt 1854
Goncourt, Jules de, and Edmond de Goncourt. *La revolution dans les moeurs: La famille, le monde, la vielle femme, les jeunes gens, le mariage, les demoiselles à marier, les gens riches, les lettres et les arts, la pudeur sociale, le catholicisme.* Paris, 1854.

Goncourt 1880/1884
Goncourt, Jules de, and Edmond de Goncourt. *L'art du dix-huitième siècle.* 2 vols. Paris, 1880, 1884.

Gonse 1879
Gonse, L. "Bibliographie: *Les instruments à archet* par Antoine Vidal." *Gazette des Beaux-Arts* (May 1879): 502–504.

Goodman 1994
Goodman, Dena. *The Republic of Letters: A Cultural History of the French Enlightenment.* Ithaca, N.Y., 1994.

Goodman 1995
Diderot on Art. Translated by John Goodman. 2 vols. Vol. 1: *"The Salon of 1765"* and *"Notes on Painting."* Vol. 2: *"The Salon of 1767."* New Haven and London, 1995.

Gordon 1996
Gordon, Alden R. "Maison du Roi," 20:131–139. In *The Dictionary of Art.* Edited by Jane Turner. 34 vols. London, 1996.

Grandjean 1981
Grandjean, Serge. *Catalogue des tabatières, boîtes et étuis des XVIIIè et XIXè siècles du musée du Louvre.* Paris, 1981.

Grant 1952
Grant, M. H. *Flower Paintings through Four Centuries: The Broughton Collection.* Leigh-on-Sea, 1952.

Greene Collection 1951
The Cleveland Museum of Art. *Portrait Miniatures: The Edward B. Greene Collection.* Cleveland, 1951.

Greer 1979
Greer, Germaine. *The Obstacle Race.* New York, 1979.

Grimm 1995
Grimm, Claus. *Stilleben: die italienischen, spanischen und französischen Meister.* Stuttgart, 1995.

Guédy 1889
Guédy, T. *Musées de France et collections particulières.* Paris, 1889.

Guide 1993
Guide du visiteur, la peinture française au musée du Louvre. Paris, 1993.

Guiffrey 1873
Guiffrey, Jules. "Logements d'artistes au Louvre." *Nouvelles archives de l'art français* 1e sér., 2 (1873): 1–221.

Guiffrey 1874–1875
Guiffrey, Jules. "Ecoles de demoiselles dans les ateliers de David et de Suvée." *Nouvelles archives de l'art français* 3 (1874–1875): 394–398.

Guiffrey 1893
Guiffrey, Jules. "Correspondance de Joseph Vernet." *Nouvelles archives de l'art français* 9 (1893): 1–99.

Guiffrey 1915
Guiffrey, Jules. *Histoire de l'Académie de Saint-Luc. Archives de l'art français,* nouv. pér., sér. 3, 9 (1915).

Gutwirth 1992
Gutwirth, Madelyn. *Twilight of the Goddesses: Women and Representation in the French Revolutionary Era.* Brunswick, N.J., 1992.

Habermas 1989
Habermas, Jürgen. *The Structural Transformation of the Public Sphere: An Inquiry into a Category of Bourgeois Society.* Cambridge, 1989.

Hardouin-Fugier 1998
Hardouin-Fugier, Elisabeth. *Les peintres de natures mortes en France au XIXe siècle.* Paris, 1998.

Hardouin-Fugier and Grafe 1989
Hardouin-Fugier, Elisabeth, and Etienne Grafe. *French Flower Painters of the 19th Century.* London and New York, 1989.

Hardouin-Fugier and Grafe 1996
Hardouin-Fugier, Elisabeth, and Etienne Grafe. "Mille et un bouquets: Les tableaux de fleurs au XIXe siècle en France." In *L'Empire de flore: Histoire et représentation des fleurs en Europe du XVIe au XIXe siècle,* ed. S. van Sprong, 289–306. Brussels, 1996.

Harley 1970
Harley, R. D. *Artist's Pigments, c. 1600–1835.* New York, 1970.

Haskell 2000
Haskell, Francis. *The Ephemeral Museum: Old Master Paintings and the Rise of the Art Exhibition.* New Haven and London, 2000.

Haug 1938
Haug, Hans. *Musée des beaux-arts de la ville de Strasbourg. Catalogue des peintures anciennes.* Strasbourg, 1938.

Hautecoeur 1948
Hautecoeur, Louis. *Catalogue de la Galerie des beaux-arts.* Geneva, 1948.

Heim, Béraud, and Heim 1989
Heim, Jean-François, Claire Béraud, and Philippe Heim. *Les Salons de Peinture de la Révolution Française, 1789–1799.* Paris, 1989.

Held and Schneider 1993
Held, Jutta, and Norbert Schneider. *Sozialgeschichte der Malerei vom Spätmittelalter bis ins 20. Jahrhundert.* Cologne, 1993.

Hofstetter 1994
Hofstetter, Bodo. "Le miniaturiste François Dumont, 1751–1831." 4 vols. Thesis, Université de Paris IV, 1994.

Hofstetter 1995
Hofstetter, Bodo. "Aperçu historique de l'art du portrait en miniature." In *L'Age d'or du petit portrait,* 13–24. Paris, 1995.

Hoppe 1936
Hoppe, Ragnar. *Katalog över Thorsten Laurins Samling av mälereu och Skulptur.* Stockholm, 1936.

Humair 2001
Humair, Sylviane. "Fleurs de France." *La Gazette de l'Hôtel Drouot,* no. 33 (14 September 2001): 18–20.

Hunt 1984
Hunt, Lynn Avery. *Politics, Culture, and Class in the French Revolution.* Berkeley, 1984.

Hunt 1992
Hunt, Lynn Avery. *The Family Romance of the French Revolution.* Berkeley, 1992.

Hyde forthcoming
Hyde, Melissa. "Adélaïde Labille-Guiard Paints Madame Adélaïde." In *Women, Art, and the Politics of Identity in Eighteenth Century Europe,* edited by Melissa Hyde and Jennifer Milam. Aldershot, Eng., and Brookfield, Vt., forthcoming.

Hyde and Milam forthcoming
Hyde, Melissa, and Jennifer Milam. *Women, Art, and the Politics of Identity in Eighteenth Century Europe.* Aldershot, Eng., and Brookfield, Vt., forthcoming.

Inventaire du Fonds français
*Inventaire du Fonds français du cabinet
des estampes: graveurs du XVIIIe siècle.*
Bibliothèque nationale. 14 vols. Paris,
1931–1977.

Inventaire du Fonds français après 1800
Inventaire du Fonds français après 1800.
Bibliothèque nationale, Cabinet des
estampes. 15 vols. Paris, 1930–1985.

Jallut 1955
Jallut, Marguerite. *Marie-Antoinette et ses
peintres.* Paris, 1955.

James-Sarazin 2001
James-Sarazin, Ariane. "Le miroir de
la reine: Marie-Antoinette et ses por-
traitistes." In *Les autours de la reine*, 15–16.
Archives nationales. Paris, 2001.

Jarry 1931
Jarry, Paul. *La guirlande de Paris, ou Maisons
de plaisance des environs aux XVIIe et XVIIIe
siècles.* 2 vols. Paris, 1931.

Jeannerat 1923
Jeannerat, Carlo. "Vittoriano Campana."
*Bolletino della Societa Piemontese di Archeolo-
gia e Belle Arte* (1923): 77–89.

Jean-Richard 1994
Jean-Richard, Pierrette. *Miniatures sur
ivoire du Louvre et du musée d'Orsay.* Paris,
1994.

Jeffares 1999
Jeffares, Neil. "Jacques-Antoine-Marie
Lemoine." *Gazette des Beaux-Arts*, sér. 6,
133 (February 1999): 61–136.

Jouin 1883
Jouin, Henri. *Conférences de l'Académie
royale de peinture et de sculpture.* Paris,
1883.

Jugement d'une demoiselle 1777
*Jugement d'une demoiselle de quatorze ans
sur le Salon de 1777.* Paris, 1777.

Jugement d'un musicien 1785
*Jugement d'un musicien sur le Salon de pein-
ture de 1785.* Paris, 1785.

Kauffmann 1972
Kauffman, C. M. "Victoriana and Rococo."
Apollo 95 (March 1972): 176–185.

Kirby 1993
Kirby, Jo. "Fading and Colour Change of
Prussian Blue: Occurrences and Early
Reports." *National Gallery Technical Bulle-
tin* 14 (1993): 62–94.

Kircher 1928
Kircher, Gerda. "Chardin Doppelgänger
Roland de la Porte." *Der Cicerone* 20 (1928):
95–101.

Kircher 1933
Kircher, G. *Karoline Luise als Kunstsam-
mlerin.* Karlsruhe, 1933.

Kirsh and Levenson 2000
Kirsh, Andrea, and Rustin S. Levenson.
*Seeing through Paintings: Materials and
Meanings in the Fine Arts.* Vol. 1. New Haven
and London, 2000.

Kühn 1973
Kühn, Hermann. "Terminal Dates for
Paintings Derived from Pigment Analysis." In *Application of Science in Examination of Works of Art*, ed. William J. Young,
199–205. Boston, 1973.

Kunze 1931
Kunze, Irene, ed. *Beschreibendes Verzeichnis
der Gemälde im Kaiser Friedrich-Museum
und Deutschen Museum. Staatliche Museen
zu Berlin.* Berlin, 1931.

La Font de Saint-Yenne 1970
La Font de Saint-Yenne. *Réflexions sur quelques causes de l'état présent de la peinture
en France: avec un examen des principaux
ouvrages exposés au Louvre le mois d'août
1746.* The Hague, 1747. Reprint. Geneva,
1970.

Lagrange 1864
Lagrange, Léon. *Joseph Vernet et la peinture
au XVIIIe siècle.* Paris, 1864.

Lairesse 1778
Lairesse, Gérard de. *The Act of Painting, in
All Its Branches, Methodically Demonstrated
by Discourses and Plates, and Exemplified by
Remarks on the Paintings of the Best Masters;
and Their Perfections and Oversights Laid
Open.* Translated by John Frederick
Fritsch. London, 1778.

Lallement 1998
Lallement, N. "Inventaire des tableaux à
sujets musicaux du Louvre: II. La peinture
française des XVIIè et XVIIIè siècles."
In *Nouveaux timbres, nouvelles sensibilités
au XVIIIè siècle* (1ère partie). Paris, 1998.

Landes 1988
Landes, Joan. *Women and the Public Sphere
in the Age of the French Revolution.* Ithaca,
N.Y., 1988.

Lanlaire 1787
*Lanlaire au Salon académique de peinture
par M. L. B. . . . de plusieurs académies.*
Gattières and Paris, 1787.

La lanterne magique 1775
*La lanterne magique aux Champs-Elysées,
ou Entretiens des Grands Peintres sur le
Sallon de 1775.* Paris, 1775.

Larcher 1909
Larcher, Jules. *Catalogue du Musée de Nancy.*
Nancy, 1909.

Laskin and Pantazzi 1987
Laskin, Myron, Jr., and Michael Pantazzi.
*Catalogue of the National Gallery of Canada,
Ottawa: European and American Painting,
Sculpture, and Decorative Arts, 1300–1800.*
Vol. 1. Ottawa, 1987.

Launay 1991
Launay, Elisabeth. *Les frères Goncourt
collectionneurs de dessins.* Paris, 1991.

Lauts 1957
Lauts, Jan. *Meisterwerke.* Karlsruhe, 1957.

Lauts 1963
Lauts, Jan. *Französische Meister aus der
Staatlichen Kunsthalle Karlsruhe.* Karlsruhe,
1963.

Lauts 1966
Lauts, Jan. *Katalog: alte Meister bis 1800.*
Karlsruhe, 1966.

Lawrence 1997
Lawrence, Cynthia, ed. *Women and Art in
Early Modern Europe: Patrons, Collectors, and
Connoisseurs.* University Park, Pa., 1997.

Lebrun 1776
Lebrun, Jean-Baptiste-Pierre. *Almanach
historique et raisonné des architectes, peintres,
sculpteurs, graveurs et cizeleurs.* Paris, 1776.

Lee 1980
Lee, Thomas P. "Recently Acquired
French Paintings: Reflections on the
Past." *Apollo* 111, no. 217 (March 1980):
217–225.

Lefeuvre 1932
Lefeuvre, Arsène. *Catalogue du Musée
des arts, Musée du Mans, Hôtel de Tessé.*
Le Mans, 1932.

Léger 1945
Léger, Ch. *Redouté et son temps.* Paris,
1945.

Legouvé 1801
Legouvé, Gabriel. *Le mérite des femmes, poème.* Paris, 1801.

Leistenschneider 1905
Leistenschneider, A. *L'argentière.* Lyon, 1905.

Le Mans 1892
Catalogue du Musée de peinture et d'histoire naturelle du Mans. Le Mans, 1892.

Lespinasse 1929
Lespinasse, Pierre. *La miniature en France au XVIIIe siècle.* Brussels, 1929.

Lettres de M. Raphaël le jeune 1771
Lettres de M. Raphaël le jeune, à un de ses amis, architecte à Rome. Paris, 1771.

Lettre d'un amateur 1787
Lettre d'un amateur de Paris à un amateur de province sur le Sallon de peinture de l'année 1787. Paris, 1787.

"Lettres inédites" 1907
"Lettres inédites d'artistes du XVIIIe siècle." *Archives de l'art français,* nouv. pér., 1 (1907): 105–106.

Lettres pittoresques 1777
Lettres pittoresques à l'occasion des tableaux exposés au Sallon en 1777. Paris, 1777.

Levey 1993
Levey, Michael. *Painting and Sculpture in France, 1700–1789.* New Haven and London, 1993.

Loche 1996
Loche, Renée. *Catalogue raisonné des peintures et pastels de l'école française XVIe, XVIIe and XVIIIe siècles, Musée d'Art et d'Histoire.* Geneva, 1996.

Locquin 1978
Locquin, Jean. *La peinture d'histoire en France de 1747 à 1785.* Paris, 1912. Reprint. Paris, 1978.

Longyear 1993
Longyear, Teresa. "Giambattista Tiepolo: The Energetic and Fluent Brush." In *Giambattista Tiepolo, Master of the Oil Sketch,* ed. Beverly Louise Brown, 64–78. New York, 1993.

Louvre 1972
Musée national du Louvre, Catalogue des peintures, 1, *Ecole français.* Paris, 1972.

Lundberg 1938
Lundberg, Gunnar W. "Nytt Roslin porträt uppäckt i Paris," *Svenske Dagbladet,* 5 June 1938.

Lundberg 1957
Lundberg, Gunnar W. *Roslin: liv och verk.* With a summary in French and a catalogue of works. 3 vols. Malmö, 1957.

Luxenburg 1997
Luxenburg, Alisa. "Figaros and Free Agents: Some Perspectives on French Painters in Eighteenth-Century Spain." In *Painting in Spain in the Age of Enlightenment: Goya and His Contemporaries,* 39–64. Exh. cat., Indianapolis Museum of Art, 1997.

Lyon 1958
Lyon, Georgette. *Joseph Ducreux: Premier peintre de Marie-Antoinette.* Paris, 1958.

Mabille 1984
Mabille, Gérard. *Orfèvrerie française des XVIe, XVIIe et XVIIIe siècles: catalogue raisonné des collections du Musée des Arts décoratifs et du Musée Nissim de Camondo.* Paris, 1984.

Malouet 1868
Malouet, P.-V. de. *Mémoires de Malouet.* 2 vols. Paris, 1868.

Mariette 1966
Mariette, Pierre-Jean. *Abecedario.* Edited by Philippe de Chennevières and André de Montaiglon. Paris, 1851–1860. Reprint. Paris, 1966.

Mélanges et doutes 1785
Mélanges et doutes et d'opinions sur les tableaux exposés au Louvre en 1785. Paris, 1785.

Mémoires secrets
Mémoires secrets pour servir à l'histoire de république des lettres en France, depuis MDCCLXII jusqu'à nos jour. Edited by L. Petit de Bachaumont, M.-F. Pidansat de Mairobert, Mouffle d'Angerville, et al. 36 vols. London, 1777–1789.

Merrill 1981
Merrill, Ross. "A Step toward Revising Our Perception of Chardin." In *Preprints of Papers Presented at the Ninth Annual Meeting, Philadelphia, Pennsylvania,* The American Institute for Conservation of Historic and Artistic Works, 27–31 May 1981, 123–128. Philadelphia, 1981.

Michaud 1854–1865
Michaud, Joseph-François, and Louis-Gabriel Michaud. *Biographie universelle ancienne et moderne.* 45 vols. Paris, 1854–1865.

Michel 1987
Michel, Christian. *Charles Nicolas Cochin et le livre illustré au XVIIIe siècle.* Geneva, 1987.

Michel 1993
Michel, Christian. *Charles-Nicolas Cochin et l'art des lumières.* Paris, 1993.

Minos au Sallon 1785
Minos au Sallon, ou la Gazette infernale, par M.L.D.B., à Gattières et se trouve à Paris. Paris, 1785.

Mirimonde 1965
Mirimonde, A. P. de. "Les oeuvres françaises à sujet de musique au Musée du Louvre—II. Natures mortes des XVIIIe et XIXe siècles." *Revue du Louvre et des Musées de France,* no. 3 (1965): 111–124.

Mirimonde 1975–1977
Mirimonde, A. P. de. *L'iconographie musicale sous les rois Bourbons. La musique dans les arts plastiques (XVIIè–XVIIIè siècles).* 2 vols. Paris, 1975–1977.

Mitchell 1973
Mitchell, Peter. *Great Flower Painters.* Woodstock, N.Y., 1973.

Moissy 1947
Moissy, Pierre. "A Pupil of Greuze: Geneviève Brossard de Beaulieu." *Gazette des Beaux-Arts* 32 (1947): 177–184.

Montaiglon 1875–1892
Montaiglon, Anatole de, ed. *Procès-verbaux de l'Académie royale de peinture et de sculpture, 1648–1793.* 10 vols. Paris, 1875–1892.

Montesquieu 1964
Montesquieu, Charles de Secondat, baron de. *Lettres persanes.* Paris, 1721. Reprint. Paris, 1964.

Musée Ariana 1895
Musée Ariana. *Catalogue sommaire du Musée Ariana.* Geneva, 1895.

Musée de Carcassone
Catalogues of the musée de Carcassonne: 1845, 1846, 1847, 1864, 1878, 1894.

Musée Carnavalet 1982
"Pastels du Musée Carnavalet." *Bulletin du Musée,* nos. 1–2 (1982).

Musée Nissim de Camondo 1960
Musée Nissim de Camondo. *Catalogue du Musée Nissim de Camondo.* Rev. ed. Paris, 1960.

La Muse errante au Sallon 1771
La Muse errante au Sallon, apologie-critique en vers libres, suivant l'ordre des numéros, des Peintures, Sculptures, et Gravures exposés au Louvre en l'année 1771. Paris, 1771.

Museum News 1969
(The Toledo Museum of Art) *Museum News* 12, no. 14 (winter 1969).

National Gallery of Art 1985
National Gallery of Art. *European Paintings: An Illustrated Catalogue.* Washington, D.C., 1985.

"Nécrologe des artistes et des curieux"
"Nécrologe des artistes et des curieux." Entry on Basseporte by Poincenet. Reprint. *Revue universelle des Arts* 13 (May 1861): 139–147.

Nochlin 1988
Nochlin, Linda. "Why Have There Been No Great Women Artists?" In *Women, Art, and Power and Other Essays,* 145–178. New York, 1988.

Nocq 1926–1931
Nocq, Henri. *Le poinçon de Paris.* 5 vols. Paris, 1926–1931.

Observations 1775
Observations sur les Ouvrages exposés au Sallon du Louvre, ou Lettre à M. le Comte de. . . . Paris, 1775.

Observations critiques 1785
Observations critiques sur les tableaux du Sallon de 1785 pour servir de suite au discours sur la peinture. Paris, 1785.

Observations sur le Sallon 1785
Observations sur le Sallon de 1785 . . . extraits du "Journal général de la France." Paris, 1785.

O'Donoghue, Romero, and Dik 1998
O'Donoghue, Elma, Rafael Romero, and Joris Dik. "French Eighteenth-Century Painting Techniques." In *Painting Techniques: History, Materials, and Studio Practice.* International Institute for Conservation of Historic and Artistic Works, Contributions to the Dublin Congress, 7–11 September 1998, ed. Ashok Roy and Perry Smith, 185–189. London, 1998.

L'ombre de Raphaël 1771
L'ombre de Raphaël, ci-devant peintre de l'Académie de St. Luc, à son neveu Raphaël, élève des écoles gratuites de dessins, en réponse à sa lettre sur les peintures, gravures et sculptures, exposées cette année au Louvre. Paris, 1771.

Oppenheimer 1995
Oppenheimer, Margaret. "Women Artists in Paris, 1791–1814." Ph.D. diss., New York University, 1995.

Oulmont 1928
Oulmont, Charles. *Les femmes peintres du XVIIIe siècle.* Paris, 1928.

Outram 1989
Outram, Dorinda. *The Body and the French Revolution: Sex, Class, and Political Culture.* New Haven and London, 1989.

Pahin de la Blancherie 1783
Pahin de la Blancherie, Mammès-Claude. *Essai d'un tableau historique des peintres de l'Ecole françoise depuis Jean Cousin.* Paris, 1783.

Pascal and Gaucheron 1931
Pascal, André, and Roger Gaucheron. *Documents sur la vie et l'oeuvre de Chardin.* Paris, 1931.

Passez 1973
Passez, Anne-Marie. *Adélaide Labille-Guiard, 1749–1803.* Paris, 1973.

Passez 1989
Passez, Anne-Marie. *Antoine Vestier, 1740–1824.* Paris, 1989.

Pavière 1963
Pavière, Sydney. *A Dictionary of Flower, Fruit and Still-Life Painters.* Vol. 2, *Eighteenth Century.* Amsterdam, 1963.

Peloux 1930
Peloux, Charles du, vicomte. *Répertoire biographique et bibliographique des artistes du XVIIIe siècle français.* 2 vols. Paris, 1930, 1941.

Pératé and Brière 1908
Pératé, A., and G. Brière. *Collections Georges Hoentschel.* 4 vols. Paris, 1908.

Petersen and Wilson 1976
Petersen, Karen, and J. J. Wilson. *Women Artists: Recognition and Reappraisal from the Early Middle Ages to the Twentieth Century.* New York, 1976.

Petit 1988
Petit, David A. "A Historical Overview of Dutch and French Still-life Painting: A Guide for the Classroom." *Art Education* 41, no. 5 (September 1998).

Philippe 1929
Philippe, André. *Musée Départementale des Vosges. Catalogue de la section des Beaux-Arts: Peintures, dessins, sculptures.* Epinal, 1929.

Phillips 1936
Phillips, John Goldsmith. "A Bequest of Gobelins, Beauvais, and Savonnerie Panels." *Metropolitan Museum of Art Bulletin* 31 (1936): 29–30.

Pinault Sørensen and Sahut 1998
Pinault Sørensen, Madeleine, and Marie-Catherine Sahut. "Panaches de mer, lithophytes et coquilles (1769), un tableau d'histoire naturelle par Anne Vallayer-Coster." *Revue du Louvre* 48, no. 1 (February 1998): 57–70.

Pinder 1938
Pinder, W. "J.B.S. Chardin." In *Gesammelte Aufsätze.* Leipzig, 1938.

Pinon 1989
Pinon, Pierre, et al. *Des Menus Plaisirs aux Droits de l'Homme.* Versailles, 1989.

Polak 1999
Polak, Ada. *Glass: Its Makers and Its Public.* London, 1999.

Préaud 1990
Préaud, Tamara. "Recherches sur les sources iconographiques utilisées par les décorateurs des porcelaine de Vincennes (1740–1756)." *Bulletin de la société d'histoire de l'art français,* année 1989 (1990): 105–115.

Promenade de Critès 1785
Promenade de Critès au Salon de l'année 1785. Paris, 1785.

Promenades d'un observateur 1787
Promenades d'un observateur au Salon de l'année 1787. London and Paris, 1787.

Rapetti 1987
Rapetti, Rodolphe. *Le Musée des Beaux-Arts de Bordeaux. Guide des collections.* Bordeaux, 1987.

Réau 1960
Réau, Louis. "La Diane et l'Apollon de Houdon à la Fondation Calouste Gulbenkian." *Colóquio* (June 1960): 2–9, 169–176.

Ridder 1932
Ridder, A. de. *J.B.S. Chardin.* Paris, 1932.

Roche 1978
Roche, Daniel. *Le siècle des lumières en province: Académies et académiciens provinciaux, 1680–1789.* 2 vols. Paris, 1978.

Roche 1921
Roche, Denis. "Jean-Laurent Mosnier et ses portraits à l'huile." *Renaissance de l'art français et des industries de luxe* 4 (April 1921): 169–176.

Roland Michel 1960
Roland Michel, Marianne. "Tapestries on Designs by Anne Vallayer-Coster." *Burlington Magazine.* "L'Art du XVIIIe Siècle." 102, no. 5 (November 1960): supplement, 509.

Roland Michel 1965
Roland Michel, Marianne. "A propos d'un tableau retrouvé de Vallayer-Coster." *Bulletin de la société de l'histoire de l'art français* (1965): 185–190.

Roland Michel 1966
Roland Michel, Marianne. "Sur quelques représentations de fleurs dans la seconde moitié du XVIIIe siècle." *Bulletin de la société d'histoire de l'art français* (1966): 169–176.

Roland Michel 1970
Roland Michel, Marianne. *Anne Vallayer-Coster: 1744–1818.* Paris, 1970.

Roland Michel 1973
Roland Michel, Marianne. "A Basket of Plums." *The Cleveland Museum of Art Bulletin* 60, no. 2 (February 1973): 52–59.

Roland Michel 1987
Roland Michel, Marianne. *Le dessin français au XVIIIe siècle.* Fribourg and Paris, 1987.

Roland Michel 1993
Roland Michel, Marianne. "Mode ou imitation: sculpture et peinture en trompe-l'oeil au XVIIIe siècle," 353–371. In *Actes du colloque Clodion et la Sculpture française de la fin du XVIIIe siècle.* Paris, 1993.

Roland Michel 1996
Roland Michel, Marianne. *Chardin.* New York, 1996.

Rosenberg 1968
Rosenberg, Pierre. "Notes sur l'exposition 'La Peinture en Suède,' Bordeaux, 1967." *Revue de l'art* 1–2 (1968): 137.

Rosenberg 1972
Rosenberg, Pierre. *Master Drawings of the 17th and 18th Centuries in North American Collections.* London, 1972.

Rosenberg 1983
Rosenberg, Pierre. *L'opera completa di Chardin.* Milan, 1983.

Rosenberg 1996
Rosenberg, Pierre. "Jacques Linard, 'peintre de coquilles,'" 231–234. In *Napoli, l'Europa: ricerche di storia dell'arte in onore di Ferdinando Bologna.* Catanzaro, 1996.

Rosenberg and Stewart 1987
Rosenberg, Pierre, and Marion C. Stewart. *French Painting, 1500–1825, The Fine Arts Museums of San Francisco.* San Francisco, 1987.

Rosenberg and Temperini 1999
Rosenberg, Pierre, and Renaud Temperini. *Chardin: suivi du catalogue des oeuvres.* Paris, 1999.

Rosenberg, Reynaud, and Compin 1974
Rosenberg, Pierre, Nicole Reynaud, and Isabelle Compin. *Musée du Louvre. Catalogue illustré des peintures. Ecole française, XVIIe et XVIIIe siècle.* 2 vols. Paris, 1974.

Rosenblum 1979
Rosenblum, Robert, ed. Emile Bellier de la Chavignerie and Louis Auvray: *Dictionnaire général des artistes de l'école française depuis l'origine des arts du dessin jusqu'à nos jours.* 1882–1887. Reprint. 5 vols. New York, 1979.

Rosenthal 1997
Rosenthal, Angela. "She's Got the Look! Eighteenth-Century Female Portrait Painters and the Psychology of a Potentially 'Dangerous Employment.'" In *Portraiture: Facing the Subject,* ed. Joanna Woodall, 147–166. Manchester, 1997.

Roslin 1913
Roslin, C. "Alexandre Roslin." *Revue de l'Histoire de Versailles,* 1913, 106.

Rousseau 1989
Rousseau, Jean-Jacques. *Politics and the Arts: Letter to M. d'Alembert on the Theater.* Translated by Allan Bloom. Ithaca, N.Y., 1989.

Salmon 1997
Salmon, Xavier. *Les pastels du Musée national du Château de Versailles.* Paris, 1997.

Salmon 1999
Salmon, Xavier. "Le Cabinet du Roi." *Dossier de l'Art. Nattier. Peintre de la Beauté* 62 (November 1999): 18–19.

Le Salon à l'encan 1783
Le Salon à l'encan: rêve pittoresque, mêlé de vaudeville. Paris, 1783.

Salvi 1999
Salvi, Claudia. *Pierre-Joseph Redouté, le Prince des Fleurs.* Tournai, 1999.

Salvi 2000
Salvi, Claudia. *D'après nature: La nature morte en France au XVIIe siècle.* Tournai, 2000.

Sandoz 1979
Sandoz, Marc. *Nicolas-Guy Brenet, 1728–1792.* Paris, 1979.

Sani 1985
Sani, Bernadetta. *Rosalba Carriera: lettere, diari, frammenti.* 2 vols. Florence, 1985.

Sani 1988
Sani, Bernadetta. *Rosalba Carriera.* Turin and Milan, 1988.

Sayre 1994
Sayre, Henry M. *A World of Art.* Englewood Cliffs, N.J., 1994.

Schabol 1770
Schabol, R., abbé. *La pratique du jardinage, ouvrage redigé après sa mort sur ses Mémoires par M. D.* 2 vols. Paris, 1770.

Scherf 1991
Scherf, Guilhem. "Autour de Clodion: variations, répétitions, imitations." *La Revue de l'art* 91 (1991): 47–59.

Schlumberger 1958
Schlumberger, E. "Anne Vallayer-Coster." *Connaissance des Arts* (March 1958): 64–69.

Schmid 1948
Schmid, Frédéric. *The Practice of Painting.* London, 1948.

Schmid 1958
Schmid, Frédéric. "Some Observations on Artist's Palettes." *Art Bulletin* 40 (December 1958): 334–336.

Schönberger and Soenher 1959
Schönberger, Arno, and Halldor Soenher.
Die Welt des Rokoko. Munich, 1959.

Scott 1989
Scott, Katie. "Hierarchy, Liberty, and
Order: Languages of Art and Institutional
Conflict in Paris, 1766–1776." *Oxford Art
Journal* 12 (1989): 59–70.

Seznec and Adhémar 1957–1967
Seznec, Jean, and Jean Adhémar, eds.
Denis Diderot. Les Salons. 4 vols. Paris,
1957–1967. Vol. 1 (1957), Salons of 1759,
1761, 1763; vol. 2 (1960), Salon of 1765;
vol. 3 (1963), Salon of 1767; vol. 4 (1967),
Salons of 1769, 1771, 1775, 1781.

Seznec and Adhémar 1983
Seznec, Jean, and Jean Adhémar, eds.
Denis Diderot: Salons. 3 vols. 2d ed. Oxford,
1983.

Sheriff 1996
Sheriff, Mary. *The Exceptional Woman.
Elisabeth Vigée-Lebrun and the Cultural
Politics of Art.* Chicago, 1996.

Sheriff and Roworth 1994
Sheriff, Mary, and Wendy Roworth.
"Anatomy Is Destiny: Regarding the Body
in the Work of Angelica Kauffman." In
*Femininity and Masculinity in Eighteenth-
Century Art and Culture,* ed. Gill Perry and
Michael Rossington, 41–62. Manchester,
1994.

Sidler 1901
Sidler, Godefroy. *Catalogue officiel du
Musée Ariana.* Geneva, 1901.

Sidler 1905
Sidler, Godefroy. *Catalogue officiel du
Musée Ariana.* Geneva, 1905.

Silverman 1989
Silverman, Deborah. *Art Nouveau in
Fin-de-Siècle France.* Berkeley, 1989.

Snoep-Reitsma 1973
Snoep-Reitsma, Ella. "Chardin and the
Bourgeois Ideals of His Time." *Nederlands
Kunsthistorich Jaarboek* 24 (1973): 147–243.

Soubeyran and Vilain 1975
Soubeyran, Françoise, and Jacques
Vilain. "Gabriel Bouquier, critique du
Salon de 1775." *La Revue du Louvre* 25,
no. 2 (1975): 96–104.

Standen 1985
Standen, Edith A. *European Post-Medieval
Tapestries and Related Hangings in the
Metropolitan Museum of Art.* 2 vols. New
York, 1985.

Starobinski 1987
Starobinski, Jean. *L'invention de la liberté,
1700–1789.* Geneva, 1964. Reprint.
Geneva, 1987.

Sterling 1952
Sterling, Charles. *La nature morte de
l'antiquité à nos jours.* Paris, 1952.

Sterling and Salinger 1955
Sterling, Charles, and Margaretta M.
Salinger. *French Paintings: A Catalogue of
the Collection of the Metropolitan Museum
of New York.* 3 vols. New York, 1955.

Suppl. Tanzia 1878
Tanzia, Both de. *Notice supplémentaire des
tableaux exposés dans les galeries du Musée
national du Louvre et non décrits dans les
trois catalogues des diverses écoles de
peinture.* Paris, 1878.

Swicklik 1993
Swicklik, Michael. "French Painting
and the Use of Varnish, 1750–1900." In
Conservation Research, 157–174. Studies in
the History of Art, 41. Washington, D.C.,
1993.

Temperini 1999
Temperini, Renaud. "Gli ultimi fasti
dell'Ancien régime." In *La pittura francese.*
Milan, 1999.

Tessier 1926
Tessier, André. "Louis Boquet. Dessinateur et inspecteur des Menus-Plaisirs."
Revue de l'art ancien et modern 49 (1926):
15–26.

Thieme and Becker
Thieme, Ulrich, and Felix Becker.
*Allgemeines Lexikon der bildenden Künstler
von Antike bis zur Gegenwart.* 37 vols.
Leipzig, 1907–1950.

Thierry 1787–1788
Thierry. *Guide des amateurs et des étrangers
voyageant à Paris, ou Description raisonnée
de cette ville et de tout ce qu'elle contient de
remarquable.* 2 vols. Paris, 1787–1788.

Timken Art Gallery 1983
*Timken Art Gallery: European and American
Works of Art in the Putnam Foundation
Collection.* San Diego, 1983.

Toledo Museum of Art 1976
The Toledo Museum of Art. *European
Paintings.* Toledo, 1976.

Tuetey 1902
Tuetey, Louis. *Procès-verbaux de la Commission temporaire des arts, publiés et
annotés par M. Louis Tuetey.* 2 vols. Paris,
1902.

Valls 1999
Rafael Valls Limited. *Old Master Paintings
Catalogue: 1999 Recent Acquisitions.*
London, 1999.

Vanderlip de Carbonnel 1981
Vanderlip de Carbonnel, Katrina.
"A Study of French Painting Canvases."
*Journal of the American Institute for
Conservation* 20 (1981): 3–20.

Vergnet-Ruiz and Laclotte 1962
Vergnet-Ruiz, Jean, and Michel Laclotte.
*Petits et grands Musées de France: La peinture
française des primitifs à nos jours.* Paris,
1962.

La Verité Critique 1781
*La Verité Critique des Tableaux exposés au
Sallon du Louvre.* Paris, 1781.

Versini 1994–1997
Denis Diderot, Oeuvres. Edited by Laurent
Versini. 5 vols. Paris, 1994–1997.

Vigée-Le Brun 1835–1837
Vigée-Le Brun, Louise-Elisabeth.
Souvenirs de Madame Vigée-Le Brun. 3 vols.
Paris, 1835–1837.

Vigée-Lebrun 1986
Vigée-Lebrun, Louise-Elisabeth.
Souvenirs. Edited by Claudine Hermann.
2 vols. Paris, 1986.

Vuaflart and Bourin 1909–1910
Vuaflart, Albert, and Henri Bourin.
"Les portraits de Marie-Antoinette: étude
d'iconographie critique." 2 vols. Biblio-
thèque d'art et d'archéologie Jacques
Doucet, Ms 380.

Walker 1984
Walker, John. *National Gallery of Art,
Washington.* Rev. ed. New York, 1984.

Wallert 1999
Wallert, Arie. *Still Lifes: Techniques and
Styles.* Zwolle, 1999.

Walter 1980
Walter, Elisabeth. "A propos de la petite
collation de Roland Delaporte." *La Revue
du Louvre et des musées de France* 3 (1980):
157–165.

Watelet and Lévêque 1972
Watelet, Claude-Henri, and Pierre-
Charles Lévêque. *Encyclopédie méthodique—
Beaux-Arts.* Reprint. Geneva, 1972.

Weigert 1959
Weigert, Roger-Armand. "Femme peintres
du XVIIIe siècle. Les deux Marie Silvestre."
Archives de l'art français, nouv. pér., 22
(1959): 129–135.

Wells-Robertson 1978
Wells-Robertson, Sally. "Marguerite
Gérard, 1761–1837." Ph.D. diss., New York
University, 1978.

West 1999
West, Shearer. *Italian Culture in Northern
Europe in the Eighteenth Century.* New York,
1999.

Whiteley 1983
Whiteley, Jon J.L. "London: French Art,
1750–1850." *Burlington Magazine* 125,
no. 965 (August 1983): 506–509.

G. Wildenstein 1933
Wildenstein, Georges. *J.B.S. Chardin.*
Paris, 1933.

G. Wildenstein 1963
Wildenstein, Georges. *Chardin.* Zurich,
1963.

D. and G. Wildenstein 1969
Wildenstein, Georges. *Chardin.* English
ed. revised and expanded by Daniel
Wildenstein. Greenwich, Conn., 1969.

Wrigley 1993
Wrigley, Richard. *The Origins of French Art
Criticism.* Oxford, 1993.

Wrigley 1995
Wrigley, Richard. *The Origins of French Art
Criticism: From the Ancien Régime to the
Restoration.* Oxford, 1995.

Zanella 2001
Zanella, Andrea. *Les collections de peinture
d'un amateur de Provence.* Vence, 2001.

EXHIBITIONS

Listed in Chronological Order

Paris 1908
Exposition rétrospective d'art féminin.
Lyceum Club.

Stockholm 1918
*English, French, Italian, Netherlandish,
Spanish, and German Art.* National-
museum.

Paris 1926
*Exposition des femmes peintres du XVIIIe
siècle.* L'Hôtel des négociants en objets
d'art, tableaux, et curiosités. Rue de la
Ville l'Evêque.

Amsterdam 1927
*Nouvelles acquistions de la galerie Goudstik-
ker.* Galerie Goudstikker.

Paris 1930
La fleur. Galerie Charpentier.

Amsterdam 1933
*Het Stilleven, Ten Bate de Vereeniging
"Rembrandt."* Goudstikker Gallery.

Copenhagen 1935
L'art français au XVIIIe siècle. Charlotten-
borg Palace.

Paris 1936a
Des fleurs et des fruits. Galerie Guy Stein.

Paris 1936b
*Orfèverie française civile de province du XVIe
au XVIIIe siècles.* Musée des Arts Décoratifs.

New York 1937
Paintings from the David-Weill Collection.
Wildenstein & Company.

Versailles 1937
Deux siècles de l'histoire de France. Château
de Versailles.

Carcassonne 1938
Chefs d'oeuvre du musée de Carcassonne.
Musée de Carcassonne.

Göteborg 1938
Three Centuries of Still Life. Göteborg
Konstmuseum.

London 1938
Fair Women of France in the XVIIIth Century.
Wildenstein Gallery.

Paris 1938
La Rose. Bagatelle.

Liège 1939
*Exposition internationale de la technique de
l'eau. Grande saison international de l'eau.*
Congrès international des ingénieurs
navals.

New York 1939
The Great Tradition of French Painting,
Wildenstein & Company.

Paris 1945
Peintures de la réalité au XVIIIe siècle.
Galerie Cailleux.

Paris 1946
Tableaux de la vie silencieuse. Galerie
Charpentier.

Bordeaux 1947
La vie du musée de 1939 à 1947. Musée des
Beaux-Arts.

New York 1948
French XVIIIth Century Paintings. Wildenstein Gallery.

Paris 1948
La vie silencieuse. Galerie Charpentier.

Geneva 1949
Trois siècles de peinture française. Musée
Rath.

Bristol 1950
Bristol–Bordeaux: French Week. City Art
Gallery.

Paris 1951
Plaisir de France. Galerie Charpentier.

Bordeaux 1952
Les chefs-d'oeuvres des musées de Bordeaux.
Galerie des Beaux-Arts.

Paris 1952
La nature morte de l'antiquité à nos jours.
Musée de l'Orangerie.

Rennes 1953
Natures mortes anciennes et modernes.
Musée de Rennes.

London 1954
European Masters of the 18th Century. Royal
Academy of Arts.

Rotterdam 1954
Vier Eeuwen Stilleven in Frankrijk. Boymans
Museum.

Saint-Etienne 1954
Natures mortes de l'antiquité au XVIIIe siècle.
Musée d'Art et d'Industrie.

Strasbourg 1954
*Natures mortes du Musée des Beaux-Arts
de Strasbourg.* Musée des Beaux-Arts
de Strasbourg.

Bourg-en-Bresse 1955
*Art et gastronomie. Bicentennaire de Brillat-
Savarin.* Musée de Bourg-en-Bresse.

Versailles 1955
*Marie-Antoinette. archiduchesse, dauphine
et reine.* Château de Versailles.

Zurich 1955
Schönheit des 18. Jahrhunderts. Kunsthaus.

Paris 1956
Le cabinet d'un amateur. Musée de
l'Orangerie.

Bordeaux 1958
Paris et les ateliers provinciaux au XVIIIe.
Galeries des Beaux-Arts.

Munich 1958
Die Europäische Rokoko. Residenzmuseum.

Stockholm 1958
Five Centuries of French Art. Nationalmuseum.

Zurich 1958
Die Frau als Künstlerin. Kunsthaus.

Paris 1959a
Hommage à Chardin. Galerie Heim.

Paris 1959b
*Natures mortes françaises du XVIIIe siècle
à nos jours.* Galerie Daber.

The Hague 1962
*Vier generaties Nystad, 1862–1962: Jubileum-
uitgave.* Nystad Antiquairs.

Rome 1962
Il ritratto francese da Clouet à Degas. Palazzo
Venezia.

New York 1963
French Masters of the 18th Century. Finch
College Museum of Art.

Paris 1964
Dessins de l'école de Parme. Musée du
Louvre.

Tel Aviv 1964
The Treasures of the Bordeaux Museums.
Museum of Fine Arts.

London 1965
Peaches and Various Objects. Alfred Brod
Gallery.

Washington 1965
The Chester Dale Bequest. National Gallery
of Art.

London 1968a
France in the 18th Century. Royal Academy
of Arts.

London 1968b
*French Paintings and Sculptures of the
18th Century.* Heim Gallery.

Paris 1968
*Fleurs et fruits, présentation de peintures des
XVIIe et XVIIIe siècles.* Galerie Cailleux.

Bordeaux 1969
L'art et la musique. Musée de Bordeaux.

Paris 1969
*Peintures du dix-huitième siècle du Musée
des Beaux-Arts de Bordeaux.* Galerie
Cailleux.

Ghent 1970
*Chefs-d'oeuvres du Musée des Beaux-Arts
de Bordeaux.* Musée des Beaux-Arts.

Bergamo 1971
*La natura in posa. Aspetti dell'antica natura
morta straniera nelle collezioni private Berga-
masche.* Galleria Lorenzelli.

Nagoya 1971
*Exposition des chefs-d'oeuvres du Musée des
Beaux-Arts de Bordeaux.* Musées et Centres
Culturels.

Winston-Salem 1972
Women. The Salem Fine Art Center; North
Carolina Museum of Art.

Paris 1973
Autour du néoclassicisme. Galerie Cailleux.

North Salem 1974
Women and Art. Hammond Museum,
North Salem, N.Y.

Paris 1974
*De David à Delacroix: la peinture française
de 1774 à 1830.* Grand Palais.

Brussels 1975
De Watteau à David. Musée des Beaux-Arts.

Paris 1975
Eloge de l'ovale. Galerie Cailleux.

San Francisco 1975
Women Artists: Review and Recognition.
Fine Arts Museums of San Francisco.

Toledo 1975
*The Age of Louis XV: French Painting,
1710–1774.* The Toledo Museum of Art.

London 1976
Claude-Joseph Vernet, 1714–1789. Kenwood
House.

Los Angeles 1976
Women Artists, 1550–1950. Los Angeles
County Museum of Art.

New York 1976
Circa 1776. Grey Art Gallery and Study
Center, New York University.

Bordeaux 1978
La nature morte de Brueghel à Soutine.
Galerie des Beaux-Arts.

Denver 1978
*Masterpieces of French Art: The Fine Arts
Museums of San Francisco.* Denver Art
Museum.

Moscow and Leningrad 1978
Peinture française du XVIIIe siècle en U.R.S.S.
Pushkin Museum; The State Hermitage
Museum.

Cleveland 1979
*Chardin and the Still-Life Tradition in
France.* The Cleveland Museum of Art.

Paris 1979a
Chardin, 1699–1779. Grand Palais.

Paris 1979b
*Peintres de fleurs en France du XVIe au XIXe
siècles.* Musée du Petit Palais.

Melbourne 1980
The Revolutionary Decade.

Paris 1980
L'instrument de musique populaire. Musée
National des Arts et Traditions populaires.

Fort Worth 1982
Elisabeth Vigée-Le Brun, 1755–1842. Kimbell
Art Museum.

Nottingham 1982
Women's Art Show, 1550–1970. Castle
Museum.

Peking 1982
250 ans de peinture de Poussin à Courbet.

Amiens 1983
*La vie musicale en Picardie au temps des
Puys.* Musée de Picardie.

Atlanta 1983
*The Rococo Age: French Masterpieces of the
Eighteenth Century.* High Museum of Art.

London 1983
La douceur de vivre: Art, Style and Decoration in XVIIIth Century France. Wildenstein Gallery.

Lille 1985
Au temps de Watteau, Fragonard et Chardin: Les Pays-Bas et les peintres français du XVIIIè siècle. Musée des Beaux-Arts.

Paris 1985
Oeuvres de jeunesse de Watteau à Ingres. Galerie Cailleux.

Paris 1985
Trompe-l'oeil, anciens et modernes, Paris. Mairie du 10e arrondissement; Mairie du 16e arrondissement.

Tours 1986
Musique de cours. Musée des Beaux-Arts.

Paris 1988
Fragonard. Galeries nationales du Grand Palais.

Biron 1989
La vie en France autour de 1789: images et representation 1785–1789. Château de Biron.

New York 1989
The Winds of Revolution. Wildenstein Gallery.

London 1990
Eliot Hodgkin, 1905–1987: Painter and Collector. Hazlitt, Gooden and Fox.

Los Angeles 1990
Masterpiece in Focus: "Soap Bubbles" by Jean-Siméon Chardin. Los Angeles County Museum of Art.

Lourdes 1991
L'art français au XVIIIème siècle. Palais des Congrès.

Paris 1991
Le rouge et le noir. Galerie Cailleux.

London 1993
Pick of the Bunch. John Mitchell.

Paris 1995
Les violons: Lutherie vénitienne. Hôtel de Ville.

Kansas City 1996
Objects of Personal Significance. The Nelson-Atkins Museum of Art.

Mexico City 1996
Naturaleza y verdad siglos XVII al XX. Museo Nacional de San Carlos.

Washington 1996
In the Light of Italy: Corot and Early Open-Air Painting. National Gallery of Art.

Roslyn 1997
Faces and Figures. Nassau County Museum of Art, Roslyn, N.Y.

Tokyo 1997
Les peintures françaises du XVIIIè siècle de la collection du musée du Louvre.

Grasse 1998
Trois femmes peintres dans le siècle de Fragonard. Musée de la Parfumerie Fragonard.

Berlin 1999
1789–1989. Zweihundert Jahre französische Revolution. Staatliche Kunsthalle.

Bordeaux 1999
Les raisins du silence. Musée des Beaux-Arts.

Karlsruhe 1999
Jean Siméon Chardin: Werk Herkunft Wirkung. Staatlichen Kunsthalle Karlsruhe.

New York 1999
Eighteenth-Century French Drawings in New York. The Metropolitan Museum of Art.

Paris 1999
Chardin. Galeries nationales du Grand Palais.

Versailles 1999
Jean-Marc Nattier. Château de Versailles.

L'Isle-Adam 2000
Les trésors des princes de Bourbon Conti. Musée d'Art et d'Histoire Louis-Senlecq.

Tours 2000
Les peintres du roi, 1648–1793. Musée des Beaux-Arts.

Nancy 2001
De l'an II au sacre de Napoléon: Le premier musée de Nancy. Musée des Beaux-Arts.

Rouen 2001
Trésors cachés: chefs-d'oeuvre du cabinet d'art graphique du château de Versailles. Musée des Beaux-Arts.

Index

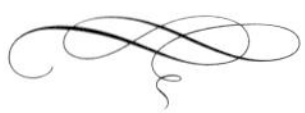

Photograph Credits

Mr. and Mrs. William H. Marlatt Fund, 1971.47; cat. 8: Musée des Beaux-Arts, Reims; cat. 9: Courtesy of Dr. Marianne Roland Michel; cat. 10 (pl. 3): © The Horvitz Collection. Photo: David Mathews; cats. 11 (pl. 4), 12 (pl. 5): Musée du Louvre, Paris, © Photo RMN–R. G. Ojeda; cat. 13: Maître Tajan; cat. 14 (pl. 6): Private collection; cat. 15: All rights reserved. Musée Nissim de Camondo, Paris, Photograph by Laurent-Sully Jaulmes; cat. 16 (pl. 9): Jean-Michel Routhier; cat. 17: Musée départemental des Vosges, Epinal; cat. 18: Courtesy of Dr. Marianne Roland Michel; cat. 19 (pl. 7): Courtesy of Rafael Valls, Ltd, London; cat. 20 (pl. 8): © Christie's Images New York 2002; cat. 21: Courtesy of Dr. Marianne Roland Michel, Photograph by Millet; cat. 22 (pl. 10): Courtesy of Didier Aaron & Cie; cat. 24: Courtesy of Sotheby's; cat. 25 (pl. 12): Cliché C. Philippot; cat. 26 (pl. 15): Villa Ephrussi de Rothschild–Institut de France; cat. 27 (pl. 11): Private collection; cats. 28 (pl. 14), 29 (pl. 13): Jean-Michel Routhier; cat. 30: © Christie's Images New York 2002; cat. 31 (pl. 16): Villa Ephrussi de Rothschild–Institut de France; cat. 32: Copyright of the Fitzwilliam Museum, University of Cambridge; cat. 33 (pl. 17): The Josephine and John Bowes Museum, Barnard Castle, UK; cat. 34 (pl. 18): © Fotograf Erik Cornelius, Nationalmuseum; cat. 35: Courtesy of Dr. Marianne Roland Michel; cats. 36 (pl. 19), 37 (pl. 20): © 2002 Dallas Museum of Art, Photo: Tom Jenkins; cats. 38, 39: Courtesy of Dr. Marianne Roland Michel; cat. 40 (pl. 21): Private collection; cat. 41 (pl. 22): Courtesy of Wildenstein and Co., Inc.; cat. 42: Courtesy of Eric Turquin; cat. 43: Courtesy of Dr. Marianne Roland Michel; cat. 44: © Christie's Images New York 2002; cat. 45: Th. Hennocque; cat. 46 (pl. 23): Musée national des Châteaux de Versailles et de Trianon, © Photo RMN–Gérard Blot; cat. 47: Courtesy of Eric Turquin; cat. 48: Courtesy of Dr. Marianne Roland Michel; cat. 49 (pl. 24): Fine Arts Museums of San Francisco; cats. 50, 51, 52, 53 (pl. 25): Courtesy of Dr. Marianne Roland Michel; cat. 54: Private collection; cat. 55 (pl. 26): Musée national des Châteaux de Versailles et de Trianon, © Photo RMN–Gérard Blot; cats. 56, 57, 58: Courtesy of Dr. Marianne Roland Michel; cats. 59 (pl. 28), 60 (pl. 27): Musée national des Châteaux de Versailles

et de Trianon, © Photo RMN–Gérard Blot; cat. 61 (pl. 29): © 2001 The Metropolitan Museum of Art; cat. 62: Photograph: Jean-Michel Routhier; cat. 63: Courtesy of Sotheby's; cat. 64 (pl. 31): Jean-Michel Routhier; cat. 65 (pl. 33): Image Source; cat. 66: Courtesy of Dr. Marianne Roland Michel; cat. 67 (pl. 30): © 2002 Dallas Museum of Art, Photo: Brad Flowers; cat. 68 (pl. 32): Private collection; cat. 69 (pl. 34): Image Source; cat. 71: Courtesy of Dr. Marianne Roland Michel; cat. 72 (pl. 35): Courtesy of Wildenstein and Co., Inc.; cat. 73: Courtesy of Dr. Marianne Roland Michel; cats. 74, 75: Courtesy of John Mitchell and Son, Photograph by P. J. Gates (Photography) Ltd; cat. 76 (pl. 36): Private collection; cat. 77: © Richard Green Gallery, London; cats. 78 (pl. 37), 79 (pl. 38): Kevin Noble; cat. 80 (pl. 39): Direction des Musées de France, Cliché musée de Tessé; cat. 82: Musée des Beaux-Arts de Strasbourg; cat. 81 (pl. 40): © Musées d'art et d'histoire, Ville de Genève; cat. 83 (pl. 41): Mr. and Mrs. Saam Nystad; cat. 84: Courtesy of Galerie Cailleux; cat. 85: Courtesy of Dr. Marianne Roland Michel; cat. 86 (pl. 42): Jean-Michel Routhier; cat. 87: Courtesy of Dr. Marianne Roland Michel, Photograph by Millet; cat. 88: Courtesy of Dr. Marianne Roland Michel; cat. 89: Courtesy of Dr. Marianne Roland Michel, Photograph by Pierre Golendorf; cat. 90: Kevin Noble; cat. 91: Lynda and Stewart Resnick, Beverly Hills, California; cat. 92: Jean-Michel Routhier; cat. 93: © Richard Green Gallery, London; cat. 94: Jean-Michel Routhier; cat. 95 (pl. 43): Private collection; cat. 96: © Richard Green Gallery, London; cat. 97 (pl. 44): Private collection; cat. 98: Courtesy of Dr. Marianne Roland Michel; cat. 99 (pl. 45): Musée du Louvre, Paris, © Photo RMN–R. G. Ojeda; cat. 102: Courtesy of Dr. Marianne Roland Michel, Photograph by Jean-Michel Routhier; cat. 103: Arturo Piera; cat. 105: Courtesy Adam Williams Fine Arts Limited; cat. 106 (pl. 46): Private collection; cat. 107: Courtesy of Dr. Marianne Roland Michel, Photograph by Jean-Michel Routhier; cat. 109: Cliché Patrice Cartier; cats. 110 (pl. 47), 111, 113: Courtesy of Dr. Marianne Roland Michel; cat. 117 (pl. 48): Private collection; cats. 118, 119, 120, 121: Courtesy of Dr. Marianne Roland Michel;

cat. 122: Courtesy of Laurent Hugues; cat. 123: Courtesy of Dr. Marianne Roland Michel; cat. 124: Cliché Laurent Hugues; cat. 125: Courtesy of Dr. Marianne Roland Michel; cat. 126: Courtesy of Audap Solanet; cat. 127: Maître Tajan; cat. 128: © Bildarchiv Preussischer Kulturbesitz, Berlin, 2002, Staatliche Museen zu Berlin, Gemäldegalerie, Photo: Jörg P. Anders; cat. 129: © Edimedia; cat. 130 (pl. 49): National Gallery of Canada, Ottawa; cats. 131 (pl. 51), 132 (pl. 52), 133 (pl. 53): cat. 134: © Hazlitt, Gooden & Fox; cat. 135 (pl. 50): Cliché C. Philippot; cat. 136: Jean-Michel Routhier; cat. 137: Courtesy of Dr. Marianne Roland Michel; cats. 138 (pl. 61), 139 (pl. 62): Musées de Châlons-en-Champagne, Photograph by Hervé Maillot; cat. 140 (pl. 63): Jean-Michel Routhier; cat. 141 (pl. 62): Courtesy of Dr. Marianne Roland Michel; cat. 142 (pl. 64): © Photothèque des Musées de la Ville de Paris, cliché Ph. Joffre; cat. 142: Musée national des Châteaux de Versailles et de Trianon, © Photo RMN–Franck Raux; cat. 143: Musée des Beaux-Arts de Narbonne; cats. 144 (pl. 54), 145 (pl. 55): © 2002 Dallas Museum of Art, Photo: Tom Jenkins; cat. 146 (pl. 56): Napoleon-museum Arenenberg, Salenstein, Switzerland; cats. 147 (pl. 58), 148 (pl. 59): Cliché Nancy, Musée des Beaux-Arts; cat. 149 (pl. 57): Cooper-Hewitt, National Design Museum, Smithsonian Institution/Art Resource, NY, Photograph by Matt Flynn; cats. 150, 151: Courtesy of Dr. Marianne Roland Michel; cats. 152 (pl. 65), 153 (pl. 66): Musée des Arts décoratifs, Paris, Photograph by Laurent-Sully Jaulmes. All rights reserved; cats. 154 (pl. 67), 155 (pl. 68), 156 (pl. 86): Jean-Michel Routhier; cat. 157 (pls. 71–80): Cliché Bibliothèque nationale de France, Paris; cat. 158 (pl. 69): © 2001 The Metropolitan Museum of Art; cat. 159 (pl. 70): Jean-Michel Routhier; cat. A (pl. 81): National Gallery of Scotland, Edinburgh; cat. B (pl. 82): © Board of Trustees, National Gallery of Art, Washington; cat. C (pl. 85): © The Cleveland Museum of Art, 2001, The Edward B. Greene Collection; cat. D (pl. 83): Staatliche Kunsthalle Karlsruhe; cat. E (pl. 84): Musée des Beaux-Arts, Bordeaux; cat. F (pl. 87): Philip Håkanson.